DUMBARTON OAKS
MEDIEVAL LIBRARY

Jan M. Ziolkowski, General Editor

THE HISTORIES

VOLUME I

LAONIKOS CHALKOKONDYLES

DOML 33

The Histories

Laonikos Chalkokondyles

VOLUME I

Translated by

ANTHONY KALDELLIS

DUMBARTON OAKS
MEDIEVAL LIBRARY

Harvard University Press
CAMBRIDGE, MASSACHUSETTS
LONDON, ENGLAND
2014

Printed in the United States of America

Library of Congress Cataloging-in-Publication Data
Chalkokondyles, Laonikos, approximately 1430–approximately 1490.
[De rebus Turcicis.]
The histories / Laonikos Chalkokondyles ; translated by Anthony Kaldellis.
volumes cm.—(Dumbarton Oaks medieval library ; doml 33) (Dumbarton Oaks medieval library ; doml 34)
In Greek with English translation on the recto.
Includes bibliographical references and index.
ISBN 978-0-674-59918-5 (volume 1 : alkaline paper)—ISBN 978-0-674-59919-2 (volume 2 : alkaline paper) 1. Byzantine Empire—History—1081–1453—Early works to 1800. 2. Turkey—History—1288–1453—Early works to 1800. 3. Istanbul (Turkey)—History—Siege, 1453—Early works to 1800. 4. Greece—History—323–1453—Early works to 1800. I. Kaldellis, Anthony. II. Title.
DF600.C47 2014
949.5′04—dc23 2014004768

Contents

Introduction

The Life of Laonikos Chalkokondyles

Nikolaos Chalkokondyles, the real name of our author "Laonikos," was born around 1430 into one of the leading Greek families of Athens, a city that was then ruled by the Acciaiuoli of Florence; his father's name was Georgios.[1] When the duke Antonio I died in early 1435, his widow tried to secure power for herself and Georgios Chalkokondyles, but Antonio's nephews Nerio II and Antonio II prevailed in the ensuing struggle and expelled the Chalkokondyles family from Athens.[2] They are attested in the summer of 1447 at Mistra, the court of the despot Konstantinos Palaiologos (subsequently the last emperor of Byzantium, 1449–1453). The traveler and antiquarian Kyriacus of Ancona met "the youth" Nikolaos there in the company of the despot and the greatest philosopher of the age, Georgios Gemistos "Plethon." Kyriacus says that Nikolaos was fluent in both Greek and Latin and that he gave him a tour of the antiquities of nearby Sparta.[3] In the years before this encounter, the despot had been building up his power in southern Greece at the expense of the Ottoman sultan Murad II (1421–1451) and the Acciaiuoli, and having the leading Greek family of Athens by his side would have been advantageous. Those ambitions,

however, were shattered in 1446, when Murad smashed through the Isthmia wall and subjected the despotate of the Morea to vassal status. The young Nikolaos may have been present at that battle, which he vividly described later as the historian Laonikos; his father had been used by Konstantinos as an envoy to Murad.[4]

We have no more definite information about the life of Nikolaos-Laonikos, except for the fact that he stopped work on his monumental *Histories* sometime between 1464 and 1468.[5] The work cannot be said to be finished, as it peters out in the midst of discussing the opening phases of the first great Venetian-Ottoman war in 1464, but we do not know why the author stopped working on it.

The influence of the neopagan Plethon on Laonikos's thought is pervasive, including the idea that the Byzantines were really Greeks and not Romans, an indifference to Christian belief and ritual, an acceptance of the World Soul, and the ability to break from Byzantine tradition and view Islam not as a theological error but, in Herodotean terms, as a legitimate set of cultural norms given by the *nomothetes* (lawgiver) Muhammad to his people.[6] Laonikos also obtained from Plethon his personal copy of Herodotos, Laur. Plut. 70.6 (Florence), a manuscript created in 1318, corrected in Plethon's own hand, and used by Bessarion in 1436 to make another copy. Laonikos added his own subscription to the end (340v):

> [Belonging to] Laonikos the Athenian. It seems to me that the Greeks displayed a virtue greater than what is merely human, and that they made a demonstration of deeds such as to amaze us when we learn about

> them in our inquiries. They [the Greeks] were also fortunate to have a herald who himself did not fall far short in worth of the deeds themselves, I mean Herodotos of Halikarnassos, who recounted these events in the way in which each happened, in a manner akin to a divine procession [i.e., of events].[7]

Laonikos's astonishment at the valor displayed by the Greeks against their oriental assailants in Herodotos could have stemmed only from his personal experience of their dismal failure to repel the Ottoman Turks in his own day. In his *Histories,* which begins with the same classical naming formula, he asserts that the Greeks have historically enjoyed a better fortune than their virtue would warrant.[8]

It was probably in the 1450s that Laonikos conceived the project of writing an imitation of Herodotos replete with ethnographic digressions, but one in which the barbarians of Asia prevail, especially under Mehmed II (1451–1481). Unfortunately, we have no information about Laonikos's movements after 1447. Scholars have wanted to situate him against a Western humanist context and place him (on no evidence whatsoever) either in Venice or in Venetian Crete. This bias is partly due to the attraction exerted by the career of his famous cousin (?) Demetrios Chalkokondyles, who relocated to Italy, took up the chair of Greek established at Padua by the Venetian senate in 1463, and was a major player in the dissemination of Greek learning.[9] We should resist this reading. Laonikos was not writing in the 1490s, as used to be believed, but in the 1460s, when there were few Italians who could read his level of Greek. Attempts to identify him with individuals mentioned in other

sources fail.[10] Laonikos was writing for a Greek audience, most likely in postconquest Constantinople. That was where the first extant manuscript of the *Histories* was copied,[11] only a few years after the work acquired its final form. Moreover, he reveals no bias against the Turks or Islam and does not overtly support a Crusade, which his cousin was calling for at the same time. In his reporting and some of his sources, Laonikos is rooted in the transitional world of the postconquest Balkans; for example, he had access to Mehmed II's accountants and may have attended the circumcision of the sultan's sons at Adrianople in 1457.[12] His knowledge of the West, by contrast, is spotty and often garbled. The *Histories* is a post-Byzantine work, not a protohumanist one.

The *Histories:* Structure, Models, Sources, and Style

Laonikos is one of the four Greek historians of the Fall of Constantinople: the other three are the anti-Turkish and pro-Union Doukas, writing at the same time but independently; Kritoboulos, who wrote a panegyrical account of the early years of the reign of Mehmed II, studiously avoiding the question of religion throughout, and who may have known Laonikos's *Histories;* and the anti-Turkish and anti-Union Sphrantzes, whose scattered notes about his own career are not exactly a work of history. These works are dramatically different from each other in terms of structure, style, and outlook, and Laonikos is the least studied among them.

The *Histories* is basically an attempt to write a new He-

rodotos for the fifteenth century. The backbone of the narrative is the sequence and conquests of the Ottoman sultans, exactly the role played in Herodotos by the Persian kings. Greek history is again related in pieces and interludes, against the backdrop of barbarian history. Laonikos does write as a Greek—praising the Greek language and hoping for the restoration of a national Greek kingdom in the future—but his narrative focus is Turkish. He presents the conquest of Constantinople, for example, through Ottoman eyes, just as Herodotos's narrative follows Xerxes's expedition from Asia into Europe. Moreover, Laonikos criticizes no one in his work as harshly as he does the Greek kings and rulers, for the incompetence that cost them their freedom. He praises many Ottoman conquerors, especially the early sultans, and seems to be neutral toward the Turks and Muslims in general, though he criticizes the cruelty of Mehmed II, especially in Books 9–10.

The *Histories* begins by tracing the prehistory of both Greeks and Turks (starting with the god Dionysos and the Oğuz, respectively), their stories slowly coalescing at some point in the early fourteenth century. The narrative becomes increasingly more detailed and focused. Book 1 ends with the first battle of Kosovo in 1389, after which a steadier sequence of historical events follows the succession of the sultans, except for Book 3, which focuses on the reign of Timur. The narrative becomes more detailed as it reaches the time of composition (ca. 1464); the final three books are devoted to the first twelve years of Mehmed II.

There is not a single date in the *Histories,* probably the result of a zealous attempt to imitate Herodotos, which results in many chronological errors. Book 1 is especially gar-

bled: Laonikos has no framework (other than the sequence of the sultans) by which to coordinate events, and so he was often unable to integrate Ottoman and non-Ottoman history when his sources did not do it for him. He seems to have relied primarily on oral sources in any case. There is no evidence, for instance, that he had access to the works of the last Byzantine historians, Nikephoros Gregoras and Ioannes Kantakouzenos, whose narratives end in the 1360s, so he was just as much on his own before that decade as after.[13] His coverage of early Ottoman history bears the imprint of Turkish oral (or at least poetic) tradition, as shown by a comparison between his account and the earliest Ottoman sources.[14] Laonikos was essentially an Ottoman historian, albeit one writing in Greek and enmeshed in the classical tradition. In his coverage of the early phase of Turkish expansion, many of his episodes are clearly modeled on passages in Herodotos, which he has adapted. But this feature rarely appears after Book 1 (e.g., in Book 3, Timur's war against the Golden Horde is modeled on Darius's campaign against the Skythians). And as he comes closer to the present, his narrative becomes less garbled chronologically and more detailed. It is especially valuable as a primary source for events after 1421 (the accession of Murad II).

Another Herodotean feature of the *Histories,* which also sets it apart from the middle Byzantine tradition, is its ethnographic and geographic digressions. Laonikos pauses to comment on the location and customs of many people, from Britain to Arabia and Central Asia. He characterizes most nations positively and reveals no religious bias. These digressions are fascinating for being the products of a Byzantine, but they are not always reliable or informative. Laoni-

kos tends to make generic comments about abstract cultural categories: e.g., the French are arrogant and have a more luxurious way of life than the Italians; the Russians follow the Greeks in religion, the Germans the pope. His coverage of the recent history of Italy is the fullest (though an Italian might cringe at some of the errors), followed by that of Spain and France (and the Hundred Years' War). Book 3 contains most of his information on Muslim peoples and Asia, including an excursus on the tenets and practices of Islam. There are some mistakes (e.g., Muhammad's tomb is not at Mecca, and the *hajj* does not involve a pilgrimage to it), but he also attempts to counter Christian slanders against Islam (e.g., the accusation that the tomb was believed to float in the air). Laonikos can also be shown to have used the Western *roman* tradition for his information about Charlemagne and possibly also about battles in Spain and the Hundred Years' War.[15] This complements his use of oral Turkish tradition, making him a valuable source for oral history in the fifteenth century. It seems that he preferred this type of material over histories and chronicles, resulting in an episodic and romantic coverage of foreign history, all transposed onto a high Thucydidean register of Greek prose.

Laonikos's foreign information peters out for all regions in the mid-1450s, which suggests that he had by then collected most of that material, possibly with the aim of writing nine books that would begin, like Herodotos's *Histories,* with ethnography linked to barbarian expansion, and end with the final conquest of Constantinople, the Peloponnese, and Trebizond.

The *Histories* tacitly breaks from Byzantine tradition. Laonikos does not mention any previous Greek or Byzantine

historian. He was not at all interested in the Roman and Christian dimensions of Byzantine civilization, preferring, like his master Plethon, to view the Byzantines exclusively as Greeks. For example, he calls their former capital Byzantion and not Constantinople, and he tries to avoid mentioning Constantine. He has no interest in the details of Christian disputes, as he probably stood with Plethon outside the Christian tradition. While he does not mention Herodotos and Thucydides, his prose style imitates and combines theirs in curious ways.[16] He emulates the syntactical complexity and obscurity of Thucydides, making his text sometimes difficult or impossible to understand. The prose is repetitive, minimalist, and dry. There are hardly any poetic allusions, metaphors, or images. More generally, Laonikos exhibits a kind of Thucydidean austerity that moderates potential Herodotean flights of fancy. There are no tall tales in the *Histories,* or strange creatures at the ends of the earth, no dreams, visions, miracles, or gods; there are few anecdotes and almost no humor. Motivation of his protagonists is restricted to the ambition to conquer and the fear of being conquered. It is in such terms that the ancient drama of East versus West, or of Asia versus Europe, plays out in the *Histories.*

Note on the Translation

In the sixteenth century Laonikos's *Histories* was translated loosely into Latin and French. In the twentieth century it was translated fully only into Romanian and partially into English, Turkish, and Modern Greek (see the Bibliography). This is the first complete English translation.

Laonikos's style presents many challenges, in part because the *Histories* was left unrevised and probably uncorrected.[17] There are numerous grammatical errors, and these may be attributable more to the author than to the few copyists who transmitted the text between him and our (very early) first witness, Par. gr. 1780. Case endings often have to be changed so that sentences make sense; the subject of genitive absolute clauses is sometimes also the subject of the main clause of a sentence, violating the rules of Greek grammar; there are abrupt and unannounced changes of subject even within individual sentences, and subjects are not always identified, so that translation requires an uncomfortable degree of guesswork. There are often two "kings" or "rulers" interacting in some passages, and it is sometimes hard to know who is meant each time, and other passages are syntactically garbled or corrupted in the transmission.

As a result, there are many parts of the text whose meaning remains opaque despite the best efforts of expert philologists to decipher them. I have tried to give what we take to be the intended sense, but there is room for more guesswork. Still, most of the *Histories* is not in such a bad state. The prose, as mentioned above, is repetitive, minimalist, and dry, and so the translation will sometimes have those qualities too. Punctuation is one area where a new edition of the Greek text can be dramatically improved. As it stands, the punctuation feels almost as if it was randomly placed, but in English I have tried to break the text into coherent sentences and clauses. I have introduced the term "sultan" to clarify passages full of generic "kings" (see below), and I often name subjects where they are not specified by Laonikos and are unclear from the context.

The text is divided into ten books (the first five of which appear in this volume, and the remaining five in volume 2, DOML 34), but the section divisions beyond that (between 60 and 110 per book) are introduced here for the first time. The corresponding volume numbers and page numbers of the latest critical edition of the Greek text, that by E. Darkó, which is reproduced here (see the Note on the Text), are given in square brackets within the facing Greek text. The notes also posed a challenge. The policy of the Dumbarton Oaks Medieval Library is to limit notes to what is absolutely necessary, but the *Histories* range over the entire known world from Portugal to Central Asia, and readers cannot be presumed to know all the people, places, and events mentioned in the narrative. In these days of extreme specialization, there is no guarantee that even Byzantinists will know the basics of Ottoman history, or vice versa, to say nothing of material that ranges farther afield. Therefore, to make the two volumes accessible to the broadest possible audience, the notes clarify most references in the text and correct some of the major errors. I have stopped short, however, of giving a detailed commentary, because there is no space and that is not the goal of the series. A separate note must now be made on how I have rendered names, places, titles, and some technical terms.

Note on Names, Terms, and Titles

Laonikos uses classical ethnonyms for contemporary peoples (e.g., he calls the French *Celts,* the Hungarians *Paionians,* the Wallachians *Dacians*). In most cases, I have used the modern names in the translation; the reader can in any case

easily glance over at the Greek version. The exceptions are a few names that cannot easily be deciphered (e.g., the Assyrians in 2.9, 3.36) and the Skythians, by whom Laonikos means the Mongols, but not only them: like many Byzantine writers, he seems to have believed in a Skythian type that remained in existence from antiquity to the present. So I have left that term as is, because "Skythian" was a charged ethnonym in the Byzantine worldview, designating the nomadic alternative to settled agricultural and urban life.

I have also used the geographical names that correspond to the modern ethnonyms, except where Laonikos uses well-known classical toponyms. In a few cases, I have converted his classical place names to Byzantine ones, e.g., Sparta to Mistra and Epidauros (Limera) to Monembasia. Some of his place-names cannot easily be deciphered and so they have been left as they are, e.g., what he calls "Hungarian Wallachia" *(Paionodakia),* which must roughly correspond to Transylvania, except that he also uses the name Ardeal, which means roughly the same. I have used the term Byzantion for the city ("Byzantium" is a modern term, which refers to the empire as a whole). The Appendix lists the "classical" forms of place-names and ethnonyms that Laonikos used.

As for personal names, I have generally used the forms that correspond to their current "native" spellings, though in this matter there is much variation in scholarly conventions,[18] and culturally sensitive spellings that are established today were not always the forms used in the fifteenth century. In any case, there is no justification for the Latinization or Anglicization of Byzantine names, which I have spelled as they are in the Greek (e.g., Ioannes, Theodoros). The ex-

ceptions are Manuel and Michael, which Laonikos, going against Byzantine convention, renders as Emmanouelos and Michaelos, possibly in order to formalize or further Hellenize them. I use their more familiar forms.

Laonikos's political vocabulary is minimalist, again because of his imitation of Herodotos. He has "kings" *(basileus),* autonomous or subordinate "rulers" *(hegemon),* and "lords" or "governors" under them *(archon).* He does not use the plethora of distinctive titles that we encounter in modern histories, e.g., sultan, emir, emperor, tsar, voivode, etc. The only exception to this pattern is what we call "the emperor of the Romans," but this title he reserves only for the Western emperors. He marks the difference between a king *(basileus)* and an emperor by using for the latter the Byzantine title *basileus kai autokrator.* What we call the "emperor of Byzantium" was for him only a national king, and the "king of the Greeks" at that (or "the king of Byzantion," meaning the city). Laonikos was among the first theorists to argue that the Byzantines were not Romans as they claimed to be, but Greeks (1.5), a thesis that has been very influential in the modern field of Byzantine Studies from Edward Gibbon to Konstantinos Paparrigopoulos and Speros Vryonis. He was emphatic that the ruler of these Greeks was not an "emperor," so it would be a distortion of both his practice and that of the Byzantines to use the term "emperor of the Greeks." There has never been such a thing.

Laonikos's minimalism is deliberate and we should not lightly override it, imposing a host of terms on his text that are foreign to its outlook. However, so many kings are difficult to tell apart, especially when they appear in the same sentence without their personal names. What I have done

to clarify the narrative is to supply their names more often than Laonikos does, and I call the protagonists of the *Histories,* namely the Ottoman rulers, sultans rather than kings, again for the purpose of clarity. It is important for the reader to know that Laonikos does not distinguish them in this way.

Finally, Laonikos uses ancient units of measurement for distance, weight, and volume. There is no way to know whether he understood their values to be the same as those that we assign to them today based on the ancient sources and archaeological evidence. Some he uses only once, and they are explained in the notes to those passages. These two he uses often: a "stade" is a unit of length roughly equal to 183 meters (600 feet), and a "talent" is a unit of weight roughly equal to 26 kilograms (57 pounds). Turkish terms from the Ottoman administration and army that Laonikos occasionally uses are explained in the notes the first time they occur: readers can find those passages by looking up the terms in the Index.

I have incurred many debts while working on this project. Ian Mladjov drew up about a quarter of the notes, and, if the series allowed for a "busier" title page, his contribution might have been acknowledged there too; he also helped me resolve problems of dating and spelling and made the excellent maps that accompany the volume. I have not always followed his recommendations, which may have been a mistake. The first draft of my translation benefited from a thorough scouring by the most intimidating team of philologists a Byzantinist can ask for: Alice-Mary Talbot, the mov-

ing force behind the Greek subseries; Richard Greenfield; Niels Gaul; and John Duffy. I thank all the members of this "dream team" for their detailed comments that corrected errors in the translation and improved the flow of my English. Their many hours of work are appreciated, and Laonikos cannot have been an easy assignment. Further help with difficult passages was provided at all stages by Charis Messis and Stephanos Efthymiades. Jane Hathaway, my colleague at OSU, deserves special mention for reading the entire translation and providing detailed information on matters Ottoman and Islamic, much of which I have included in the notes. A reliable and enthusiastic source of information on all matters relating to the fifteenth century has been Marios Philippides, whom I have consulted frequently; he has often set me straight.[19] Finally, I thank also all those whom I have pestered over the years with questions about Laonikos and his age and who have given me both information and insight: Aslıhan Akışık, Alexander Alexakis, Patrick Baker, Daniele Bianconi, Bruce Fudge, Thierry Ganchou, Tim Greenwood, Walter Hanak, Scott Kennedy, Han Lamers, Scott Levi, Tim Miller, David Niremberg, Inmaculada Pérez Martín, Parvaneh Pourshariati, Steve Rapp, Dean Sakel, Stefan Stantchev, Rudolf Stefec, Niketas Siniossoglou, Vasileios Syros, Julia Verkholantsev, and Diana Wright.

Notes

1 We infer Laonikos's date of birth from the territories remaining to Byzantium that he lists at *Histories* 1.8. His father's name is given by Kyriacus: see below. The family name was probably Chalkokondyles, which "Laonikos" classicized to Chalkokandyles.

2 *Histories* 6.50–52.

3 *Cyriac of Ancona: Later Travels,* tr. E. D. Bodnar (with C. Foss) (Cambridge, Mass., 2003), 298–301.

4 *Histories* 7.19–25.

5 Kaldellis, "The Date."

6 For these aspects of Plethon's influence on Laonikos, see Kaldellis, *A New Herodotos.*

7 For the text, see A. Turyn, *The Byzantine Manuscript Tradition of the Tragedies of Euripides* (Urbana, Ill., 1957), 230 n. 212a. The translation is my own. The history of the manuscript is discussed in detail in Kaldellis, *A New Herodotos,* Appendix 4.

8 *Histories* 1.3.

9 D. J. Geanakoplos, *Interaction of the "Sibling" Byzantine and Western Cultures in the Middle Ages and Italian Renaissance (330–1600)* (New Haven, Conn., 1976), 241–64.

10 Kaldellis, *A New Herodotos,* Appendix 1.

11 See the Note on the Text below.

12 *Histories* 8.78 and 8.69–71, respectively.

13 Kaldellis, "The Greek Sources."

14 Kaldellis, *A New Herodotos,* ch. 4.

15 E.g., M. Morfakidis and E. Motos Guirao, "Un pasaje de Laonicos Calcocondylas relativo a la batalla de la Higueruela y a sus consecuencias inmediatas," in *Relaciones exteriores del Reino de Granada: IV Coloquio de Historia medieval Andaluza,* ed. C. Segura Graiño (Almeria, 1988), 71–82.

16 For specific borrowings from Herodotos, see the list in Kaldellis, *A New Herodotos,* Appendix 3; and from Thucydides, see F. Rödel, "Zur Sprache des Laonikos Chalkondyles und des Kritobulos aus Imbros," *Programm des königlichen humanistischen Gymnasiums Ingolstadt 1904–1905* (Munich, 1905), 12–34.

17 See the Note on the Text below.

18 I have followed the scholarly conventions for late Seljuk studies for the rendering of Turkish proper names, although they differ from those used by Ottomanists; thus 'Ala' al-Din for the Seljuk sultan, versus Alaeddin for an Ottoman Turk of the same name.

19 In fact, many decades ago Marios had himself hammered out a draft translation of the *Histories* on a typewriter, but he did not have enough confidence in its reliability to publish it. It was subsequently lost,

but Marios remembered that he had sent a copy to Stephen Reinert (now at Rutgers). I contacted Stephen who graciously tracked it down, scanned it, and sent it to me. Marios warned me not to rely on his translation, and I did not, but in the treacherous prose of Laonikos all help is welcome.

THE HISTORIES

Α'

[1.1] Λαονίκῳ Ἀθηναίῳ τῶν κατὰ τὸν βίον οἱ ἐς ἐπὶ θέαν τε καὶ ἀκοὴν ἀφιγμένων ἐς ἱστορίαν ξυγγέγραπται τάδε, ὥστε δὴ χρέος τοῦτο ἐκτινύναι τῇ φύσει ἅμα οἰόμενος καὶ μηδὲν αὐτῶν ἀκλεῶς ἔχειν ἐς τοὺς ἐπιγιγνομένους ξυνενεχθέντων, ὡς ἐμοὶ δοκεῖ, οὐδαμῇ ἐλασσόνων τῶν κατὰ τὴν οἰκουμένην ποτὲ γενομένων μνήμης ἀξίων. Τῆς τε Ἑλλήνων φημὶ τελευτῆς τὰ ἐς [1.2] τὴν ἀρχὴν αὐτῶν ἐπισυμβεβηκότα, καὶ Τούρκων ἐπὶ μέγα δυνάμεως καὶ ἐπὶ μέγιστον τῶν πώποτε ἤδη ἀφικομένων. Ἀφ' ὧν δὴ τὴν τοῦδε τοῦ βίου εὐδαιμονίαν ἐπὶ τἀναντία φερομένην ἐπιλεγόμενος ἴσχειν αὐτῇ καὶ ἄλλοτε ἄλλως, θέμις ἡγοῦμαι εἶναι περὶ ἀμφοῖν τούτοιν μνήμην ποιεῖσθαι οὐκ ἀεικῆ. Ξυγγραφὴν δὲ τήνδε ἀποδεικνύμενοι ἐπιμνησόμεθα καὶ περὶ ἄλλων τῶν κατὰ τὴν οἰκουμένην γενομένων, οὐκ ἀμφὶ τόνδε τὸν ἐπ' ἐμοῦ χρόνον, οἷς τε αὐτὸς παρεγενόμην θεασάμενος, καὶ τἆλλα ἀπό τε τοῦ εἰκότος, μάλιστα δὲ συμβαλλόμενος, καὶ ὡς ἔτι παρὰ τῶν τὰ ἀμείνω φρονούντων ἐδόκουν πυθέσθαι περὶ αὐτῶν, ἀλλ' ᾗ ἂν εἰς μάλιστα ἔχοι ὡς ἀσφαλέστατα ἐπὶ τὸ ἄμεινον ἀληθείας εἰρῆσθαι.

2 Μὴ δὲ ἐκεῖνό γε πάνυ ἐκφαύλως ἔχον ἡμῖν, ὡς Ἑλληνικῇ φωνῇ ταῦτα διέξιμεν, ἐπεὶ ἥ γε τῶν Ἑλλήνων φωνὴ

Book 1

Laonikos the Athenian has written here, in the form of a history, the events that came to his attention during his lifetime, both those that he witnessed and those he heard about. He thought in this way to pay back the debt that he owed to Nature, believing also that none of the events he included should be forgotten by future generations. In my opinion, those events are in no way less worthy of being remembered than any that have ever taken place anywhere in the world. I am referring to the fall of the Greeks and the events surrounding the end of their realm, and to the rise of the Turks to great power, greater than that of any other powerful people to date. Realizing that the happiness of this life tends to reverse itself, being sometimes in one state and at others in its opposite, I believe it is proper to leave a fitting record of these two peoples. In writing this history we will recount also other events that happened throughout the world, not all of which occurred during my own time; some I was able to witness personally, others I describe based on the most reasonable conjecture that I have been able to form about them. Moreover, it has seemed to me appropriate to consult those who know better about these things, but only insofar as that might enable me to speak as accurately as possible and with the highest degree of veracity.

Let no one disparage us for recounting these matters in 2
the Greek language, for the language of the Greeks has

πολλαχῇ ἀνὰ τὴν οἰκουμένην διέσπαρται καὶ συχναῖς ἐγκαταμέμικται. Καὶ κλέος μὲν αὐτῇ μέγα τὸ παραυτίκα, μεῖζον δὲ καὶ ἐς αὖθις, ὁπότε δὴ ἀνὰ βασιλείαν οὐ φαύλην Ἕλλην τε αὐτὸς βασιλεὺς καὶ ἐξ αὐτοῦ ἐσόμενοι βασιλεῖς, οἳ δὴ καὶ οἱ τῶν Ἑλλήνων παῖδες ξυλλεγόμενοι κατὰ τὰ σφῶν αὐτῶν ἔθιμα ὡς ἥδιστα μὲν σφίσιν αὐτοῖς, τοῖς δὲ ἄλλοις ὡς κράτιστα πολιτεύοιντο.

3 Ἕλληνες μὲν οὖν ὅσα ἀποδεικνύμενοι ἔργα μεγάλα τε καὶ [1.3] περιφανῆ ἐπὶ μέγα ἀφίκοντο κλέος κατά τε ἄλλα καὶ Εὐρώπην καὶ δὴ καὶ Λιβύην, ἐπὶ Γάγγην τε καὶ Ὠκεανὸν καὶ ἐπὶ Καύκασον ἔτι ἐλαύνοντες, ἐπὶ ταῦτα δὲ προεληλυθότων ἄλλων τε πολλῶν καὶ δὴ καὶ Ἡρακλέους καὶ ἔτι πρότερον Διονύσου τοῦ Σεμέλης υἱέος, καὶ πρός γε ἔτι Λακεδαιμονίων καὶ Ἀθηναίων, μετὰ δὲ ταῦτα Μακεδόνων τοῦ βασιλέως καὶ τὴν τούτου ὕστερον ἡγεμονίαν ἐχόντων, πολλοὶ πολλαχῇ ἕκαστα, ὡς ἐγένοντο, ἄλλοι ἐπιμνησάμενοι καὶ συνεγράψαντο. Ἕλληνες μὲν οὖν ταῦτα διεπράττοντο ἐπὶ πολὺ ὡς μάλιστα τοῦ χρόνου διαγενόμενοι καὶ ἐπὶ συχνὰς γενεὰς τύχην ἀρετῆς ἐνδεᾶ σχόντες ἁπανταχοῦ, ξύμμετρον δὲ οὐδαμοῦ.

4 Ἐπὶ τούτων τε γὰρ πολλαχῇ ἀνὰ τὴν οἰκουμένην εὐδαιμονούντων Ἀσσυρίους μὲν τὸ παλαιότατον ἐπυθόμεθα ἀκοῇ ἐπὶ τὸ μνήμης μακρότατον ἀφικόμενοι ἐπὶ τὴν τῆς Ἀσίας ἀρχὴν προεληλυθέναι, μετὰ δὲ ταῦτα Μήδους ἐς τοῦτο καθισταμένους ἡγησαμένου Ἀρβάκεω τοῦ Σαρδαναπάλου Ἀσσυρίων βασιλέως τὴν ἡγεμονίαν ἀφελομένου, ὕστερον ὑπὸ Περσῶν τὴν βασιλείαν ἀποβαλεῖν ἡγουμένου

spread to many places throughout the world and has mixed with many other languages. It is already exceedingly prestigious and will be even more so in the future, when a king who is Greek himself, along with the kings that follow after him, will rule over a substantial kingdom. There the sons of the Greeks may finally be gathered together and govern themselves according to their own customs, in a manner that is most favorable for themselves and from a position of strength with regard to other peoples.

Many others have, at various times, made records and 3
written the history of each of the deeds of the Greeks as they occurred: their great and glorious achievements by which they attained such great fame in so many places, including Europe and Africa, and then when they marched even as far as the Ganges, the surrounding Ocean, and the Caucasus.[1] Among many others, Herakles especially had reached such places and, even earlier, Dionysos, the son of Semele; then again, the Lakedaimonians and the Athenians, and after them the king of the Macedonians[2] and those who succeeded to his throne later on. The Greeks accomplished these things over a long period of time and in the course of many generations, but their virtue was everywhere lacking in comparison to the fortune they enjoyed, and nowhere commensurate to it.

While they were enjoying this good fortune in many 4
places throughout the world, it was the Assyrians who first attained dominion over Asia. We have heard this by extending our inquiries into the most remote depths of human memory. After that, the Medes took their place under the leadership of Arbakes,[3] who seized control from Sardanapalos, the Assyrian king.[4] Later they too lost this hegemony

Κύρου τοῦ Καμβύσεω, καὶ Πέρσας τὸ ἀπὸ τοῦδε ἐπὶ μέγα χωρῆσαι δυνάμεως τά τε ἄλλα καὶ δὴ καὶ ἐς Εὐρώπην διαβάντες. Μετὰ δὲ ταῦτα ὕστερον οὐ πολλαῖς γενεαῖς Ἀλέξανδρον τὸν Φιλίππου, [1.4] Μακεδόνων βασιλέα Πέρσας ἀφελόμενον τὴν ἡγεμονίαν καὶ Ἰνδοὺς καταστρεψάμενον καὶ Λιβύης μοῖραν οὐκ ὀλίγην, πρὸς δὲ καὶ Εὐρώπης, τοῖς μεθ' ἑαυτὸν τὴν βασιλείαν καταλιπεῖν.

5 Ἐς ὃ δὴ Ῥωμαίους ἐπὶ τὴν τῆς οἰκουμένης μεγίστην ἀρχὴν ἀφικομένους, ἰσοτάλαντον ἔχοντας τύχην τῇ ἀρετῇ, ἐπιτρέψαντας Ῥώμην τῷ μεγίστῳ αὐτῶν ἀρχιερεῖ καὶ διαβάντας ἐς Θρᾴκην, ὑφηγουμένου ἐπὶ τάδε τοῦ βασιλέως, καὶ Θρᾴκης ἐπὶ χώραν, ἥτις ἐς τὴν Ἀσίαν ἐγγυτάτω ᾤκηται, Βυζάντιον Ἑλληνίδα πόλιν μητρόπολιν σφῶν ἀποδεικνύντας, πρὸς Πέρσας, ὑφ' ὧν ἀνήκεστα ἐπεπόνθεισαν, τὸν ἀγῶνα ποιεῖσθαι, Ἕλληνάς τε τὸ ἀπὸ τοῦδε Ῥωμαίοις αὐτοῦ ἐπιμιγνύντας, γλῶτταν μὲν καὶ ἤθη διὰ τὸ πολλῷ πλέονας Ῥωμαίων Ἕλληνας αὐτοῦ ἐπικρατεῖν διὰ τέλους φυλάξαι, τοὔνομα μέντοι μηκέτι κατὰ τὸ πάτριον καλουμένους ἀλλάξασθαι, καὶ τούς γε βασιλεῖς Βυζαντίου ἐπὶ τῷ σφᾶς αὐτοὺς Ῥωμαίων βασιλεῖς τε καὶ αὐτοκράτορας σεμνύνεσθαι ἀποκαλεῖν, Ἑλλήνων δὲ βασιλεῖς οὐκέτι οὐδαμῇ ἀξιοῦν.

6 Τοὺς μέντοι Ῥωμαίους ἐπυθόμεθα καὶ αὐτῶν ἀρχιερέα τὸν μέγιστον οὐκ ὀλίγα ἄττα κατὰ τὴν θρησκείαν ἀπὸ πολλῶν ἐτῶν διενεχθέντας διακεκρίσθαι τά τε ἄλλα ἀφ' Ἑλλήνων, καὶ δὴ καὶ βασιλέα Ῥωμαίων ἐπιψηφιζομένους, ὁτὲ μὲν ἀπὸ Γαλατῶν, ὁτὲ δὲ [1.5] ἀπὸ Γερμανῶν, ἐς τόνδε ἀεὶ τὸν χρόνον ἀποδεικνύναι. Διαπρεσβεύεσθαι δὲ αἰεὶ

to the Persians, who were led by Cyrus, the son of Cambyses. From this point on, the power of the Persians became great as is seen in many ways, but especially by their crossing over into Europe. Not many generations after that, Alexander, the son of Philip and king of the Macedonians, seized control from the Persians and conquered the Indians as well as a large portion of Africa, in addition to Europe. He left this kingdom to his successors.

At that point the Romans attained the greatest realm in 5
the world, because their virtue was in proportion to their fortune. They entrusted Rome to their great pontiff and crossed over into Thrace under the command of their king.[5] In the land of Thrace, which is the closest to Asia, they made the Greek city of Byzantion their capital for carrying on the struggle against the Persians, at whose hands they had suffered such terrible things. From this point on, the Greeks mixed with the Romans in this place, and because many more Greeks ruled there than Romans, their language and customs ultimately prevailed, but they changed their name and no longer called themselves by their hereditary one. They saw fit to call the kings of Byzantion by a title that dignified them, "emperors of the Romans," but never again "kings of the Greeks."[6]

We have learned that, after the Romans and their great 6
pontiff had diverged for many years and in many ways from the Greeks with respect to religion, they also set themselves apart in other matters, especially in electing for themselves a king of the Romans, sometimes from among the French and sometimes among the Germans, and they have continued to appoint one down to the present time. Yet they are

πρὸς τοὺς Ἕλληνας, οὐκ ἔστιν ὅτε διαλείποντας, ὥστε τὰ ἐς θρησκείαν σφίσι ξύμφωνά τε καὶ ξυνῳδὰ καταστῆσαι ἀλλήλοις, κατὰ ταὐτὸ ξυνιόντας. Καὶ μέντοι Ἕλληνας μὴ ἐθελῆσαι Ῥωμαίοις διὰ χρόνου συμφερομένοις[1] τὰ πάτρια σφίσι καθεστῶτα συγχέαι. Καὶ ἀπὸ ταύτης δὴ τῆς διαφορᾶς συχνούς τε τῶν ἑσπερίων καὶ δὴ καὶ Ἑνετούς, ἐνάγοντος ἐπὶ τάδε τοῦ Ῥωμαίων ἀρχιερέως, στόλῳ στρατεύεσθαι μεγάλῳ ἐπὶ τοὺς Ἕλληνας καὶ ἐπιόντας ἐς τὸ Βυζάντιον ἀφικέσθαι καὶ Βυζαντίου τὴν πόλιν κατὰ κράτος ἑλεῖν. Βασιλέα τε Βυζαντίου καὶ Ἑλλήνων τοὺς ἀρίστους οἴχεσθαι διαβάντες ἐς τὴν Ἀσίαν, ἀφικομένους δὲ ἀποδεικνύναι σφίσι Νίκαιαν τὴν Ἑλληνίδα πόλιν, τὰ βασίλεια ἐν αὐτῇ ποιουμένους. Μετὰ δὲ ταῦτα οὐ πολλοῖς ἔτεσιν ὕστερον ἀπολαβεῖν τε αὖθις Βυζάντιον, κρύφα εἰσεληλυθότας ἐς τὴν πόλιν, καὶ ἐς τὴν Εὐρώπην αὖ διαβάντας διαγενέσθαι ἐν αὐτῇ βασιλεύοντας.

7 Βασιλέα δὲ Ἑλλήνων μετὰ ταῦτα Ἰωάννην ἐπὶ ξυροῦ ἀκμῆς ἤδη αἰσθόμενον τὰ Ἑλλήνων πράγματα, λαβόντα τε τοὺς Βυζαντίου ἀρχιερεῖς καὶ Ἑλλήνων τοὺς ἐλλογίμους, διαπλεῦσαι ἀπιόντα ἐς Ἰταλίαν, ἔς γε τὸν ἀπὸ Τούρκων ἐπηρτημένον οἱ κίνδυνον ἐπικουρίαν οἰόμενος οἴσεσθαι, [1.6] ἢν ἐκείνοις τὰ κατὰ τὴν θρησκείαν ξυμβῇ. Γενόμενον δὲ ἐν Ἰταλίᾳ καὶ κοινωσάμενον τῷ Ῥωμαίων ἀρχιερεῖ τὴν περὶ τὴν θρησκείαν διαφοράν, εἰς διάλεξιν μέντοι καταστῆναι πολυπραγμονοῦντας, τελευτῶντα δὲ ξυμβῆναι αὐτῷ ἅμα τοῖς Ἕλλησι τὰ κατὰ τὴν διαφορὰν σφίσι ξυνῳδὰ ἀποδεικνυμένους καὶ τὴν διαφορὰν σφίσι διαλυομένους, ἐπικουρίας δὲ τυχόντα ἐν μέρει ἀποκομίζεσθαι αὖθις ἐπὶ

always sending embassies to the Greeks—indeed, there has been no time when they let up in this effort—in order to establish religious concord with them and an accord between the two sides, and thus create unity concerning this. But after they had thus treated with the Romans for some time, the Greeks were unwilling to mix up their own established ancestral customs with theirs. Because of this disagreement and at the instigation of the pontiff of the Romans, many westerners and especially the Venetians mustered a great expedition against the Greeks.[7] They set out, came to Byzantion, and seized the city of Byzantion by force. The king of Byzantion and the leading Greeks departed and crossed over into Asia. When they arrived, they chose the Greek city of Nikaia for themselves, and established their royal court there. A few years later they recovered Byzantion again by secretly entering the city,[8] and, crossing back into Europe, they once more ruled from there.

After this Ioannes was the king of the Greeks and he real- 7
ized that the affairs of the Greeks stood already upon the razor's edge.[9] He thus took the senior clergy from Byzantion and the most learned Greeks and set sail for Italy, hoping that he would receive assistance against the impending Turkish threat, provided that he reached an agreement with them on religious matters. He arrived in Italy and consulted with the pontiff of the Romans regarding their religious differences. This led to long and detailed discussions of many matters, but, finally, he reached an agreement with him and at the same time with the Greeks, and they made an accord regarding the differences between them. Having resolved their differences, the king secured partial assistance and

Βυζαντίου. Τοὺς μέντοι Ἕλληνας ἐπ' οἴκου γενομένους μὴ ἐμμεῖναι τοῖς ἐν Ἰταλίᾳ καὶ ἐν συνόδοις πεπραγμένοις, ἀξιοῦντας σφίσι μηδαμῇ εὐαγὲς εἶναι Ῥωμαίοις, ὡς δὴ μὴ αἴσια διϊσχυριζομένοις, συντίθεσθαι τὸ παράπαν, καὶ οὕτω δὲ διάφορα διὰ τέλους γενέσθαι Ἕλλησι τὰ πρὸς Ῥωμαίους. Ταῦτα μὲν ἐς τοσοῦτόν μοι ἀποχρώντως ἔχοντα ἐπιδεδείχθω περί τε τῆς Ἑλλήνων βασιλείας καὶ τῆς ἐς Ῥωμαίους ἐχούσης αὐτῶν διαφορᾶς, ὡς δὴ οὐκ ὀρθῶς τά γε ἐς βασιλείαν καὶ ἐς τοὔνομα αὐτὸ προσηγορεύετο τούτοις.

8 Παραγενόμενος μὲν οὖν αὐτὸς ἔγωγε ἐπὶ τόνδε τὸν βίον κατέλαβον Ἕλληνάς τε καὶ Ἑλλήνων βασιλέα ὑπό τε τῶν ἐν Θρᾴκῃ γενῶν πρῶτα, μετὰ δὲ ταῦτα καὶ ὑπ' αὐτῶν γε δὴ τῶν βαρβάρων τῆς ἄλλης ἀρχῆς ἀπεληλαμένους, ἀρχὴν τήνδε βραχεῖάν τινα περιέπειν, Βυζάντιον καὶ Βυζαντίου τὴν κάτω παραλίαν ἄχρις Ἡρακλείας πόλεως, [1.7] κατὰ δὲ Εὔξεινον πόντον τὴν ἄνω παραλίαν ἄχρι Μεσημβρίας πόλεως, Πελοπόννησόν τε αὖ ξύμπασαν πλὴν ἢ τριῶν ἢ τεττάρων πόλεων τῶν Ἑνετῶν, ὡσαύτως Λῆμνον, Ἴμβρον καὶ νήσους τὰς αὐτοῦ ταύτῃ ἐν τῷ Αἰγαίῳ ᾠκημένας. Ὡς οὖν ἕκαστα τούτων ξυνέβη γενέσθαι, ὡς τὰ τῶν Ἑλλήνων πράγματα κατὰ βραχὺ ἀπώλετο, φθειρόμενα ὑπὸ Τούρκων, καὶ ὡς τὰ ἐκείνων μεγάλα ἐγένετο, ἐς μέγα ἀεὶ ἐς τόνδε τὸν χρόνον ἰόντα εὐδαιμονίας, ἐπιμνησόμεθα ἐπεξιόντες, ἐφ' ὅσον δὴ ἐς τὸ ἀκριβέστερον ἐπυθόμεθα.

9 Τούρκους δὴ οὖν ἔγωγε οὐκ οἶδ' ὅ τι ἂν καλέσαιμι κατὰ τὸ παλαιόν, ὥστε τἀληθοῦς μὴ διαμαρτεῖν. Οἱ μὲν γὰρ Σκυθῶν ἀπογόνους τοὺς Τούρκους οἴονται εἶναι, ὀρθότερον δὴ συμβαλλόμενοι περὶ αὐτῶν, διὰ τὸ ἐς ἤθη οὐ πολὺ

returned to Byzantion. But when the Greeks got home they did not abide by what had been worked out in Italy and at the councils, holding that it would not be right at all for them to be fully united with the Romans, who did not make a proper affirmation of the faith. Thus the Greeks remained at odds with the Romans to the end. As far as I am concerned, I trust this is a sufficient account, for my part at least, regarding both the kingdom of the Greeks and their differences with the Romans, and why they[10] do not call the kingdom by its proper name.

When I myself was born, I found the Greeks and the king of the Greeks reduced, first by the peoples who live in Thrace[11] and after that by the barbarians[12] who drove them out of the rest of their territory, to a small realm, namely Byzantion and the coast below Byzantion as far as the city of Herakleia; the coast above by the Black Sea as far as the city of Mesembria; the entire Peloponnese except only for three or four cities of the Venetians; and Lemnos, Imbros, and other inhabited islands of the Aegean in that area.[13] I am thus going to provide a detailed account, as accurately as I have been able to ascertain it, of how these things happened, each in its turn; that is, how the affairs of the Greeks were quickly ruined, destroyed by the Turks, and how the latter rose to greatness, continuously reaching new peaks of prosperity during this period. 8

I do not know by what ancient name to call the Turks that would not fall short of the truth about the matter. Some believe that the Turks are descendants of the Skythians,[14] which is quite a reasonable conjecture about them, given 9

διεστηκότα καθισταμένους γλώττῃ σύνεγγυς μάλα διαχρῆσθαι ἔτι καὶ νῦν τῇ αὐτῇ. Σκύθας τε γάρ φασι τὸ ἕβδομον ἤδη ἀπὸ Τανάϊδος ὡρμημένους καταστρέφεσθαι τὴν ἄνω Ἀσίαν, Πάρθων τὴν ἡγεμονίαν ἐχόντων, τήν τε Περσῶν χώραν καὶ Μήδων καὶ Ἀσσυρίων, μετὰ δὲ ταῦτα ἐπικαταβάντας ἐς τὴν κάτω Ἀσίαν, ἐπὶ Φρυγίαν, Λυδίαν τε καὶ Καππαδοκίαν, τὰ ἐς τήνδε τὴν χώραν ὑποχείρια σφίσι ποιήσασθαι. Καὶ νῦν ἔστιν ἰδεῖν, ᾗ λέγουσι, πολλὰ τοῦ γένους τούτου πολλαχῇ τῆς Ἀσίας ἐπινεμόμενα, πρὸς Σκυθῶν [1.8] τῶν νομάδων ἤθη τε καὶ δίαιταν τετραμμένα οὐδαμῇ τῆς Ἀσίας ἔσχον καταφανῆ τὴν διατριβήν. Κἀκείνῃ δὲ ἔτι συμβάλλονται, ὡς Ἀσίας τὴν κάτω χώραν ἐνοικοῦντα βάρβαρα ἔθνη Τούρκων, Λυδίαν, Καρίαν, Φρυγίαν τε καὶ Καππαδοκίαν, Σκύθαις τὴν ἀπὸ Τανάϊδος ἐπὶ Σαρματίαν χώραν ἐπινεμομένοις ὁμόγλωττά τε ἐστι καὶ ὁμόσκευα.

10 Ἔνιοι δὲ Πάρθων ἀπογόνους Τούρκους φασὶν εἶναι. Τούτους γὰρ ὑπὸ Σκυθῶν τῶν νομάδων διωκομένους ἐς τὴν κάτω Ἀσίαν ἐπικαταβῆναι, καὶ ἐς τὸ νομαδικώτερον ἀποκλίναντας σκεδασθῆναι ταύτῃ ἀνὰ τὰς πόλεις, καὶ ἀπὸ τούτου ὡς δὴ νομάδας Τούρκους τὸ γένος τοῦτο καλεῖσθαι. Ἄλλοι δέ φασιν ἀπὸ Τούρκης τῶν Περσῶν πόλεως μεγάλης τε καὶ εὐδαίμονος, προελθεῖν τε τὸ γένος τοῦτο διϊσχυρίζονται, καὶ εἰς τὴν κάτω χώραν τῆς Ἀσίας ἀπαλλαττομένους σκεδασθῆναι ταύτῃ ἀνὰ τὴν Ἀσίαν ἐπικατασχόντας τὴν χώραν. Εἰσὶ δὲ οἳ βούλονται Τούρκους ἀπὸ Συρίας μᾶλλον τῆς κοίλης καὶ Ἀραβίας ἢ ἀπὸ Σκυθῶν ἐπὶ τήνδε τὴν χώραν ἀφικομένους μετὰ Ὀμάρεω τοῦ τὴν

that their customs are not all that different and that their languages are even now closely related. They say that the Skythians burst out of the Don region for the seventh time[15] and subjugated Greater Asia when the Parthians[16] held sway there, and then the land of the Persians, Medes, and Assyrians. After this they attacked Asia Minor, specifically Phrygia, Lydia, and Kappadokia, and made these lands subject to themselves. Even today, so they say, it is possible to see numerous offshoots of this people roaming about in many parts of Asia, who tend to follow the ways and customs of the nomadic Skythians and have clearly not settled down in any particular part of Asia. And they also add that the barbarian nations of the Turks who live in Asia Minor, I mean in Lydia, Karia, Phrygia, and Kappadokia, speak the same language and have the same dress as the Skythians who roam the lands from the Don into Russia.

10 Others say that the Turks are the descendants of the Parthians. They were pursued by the nomadic Skythians and moved down into Asia Minor. Turning to a more nomadic way of life, they became dispersed among the cities there, and since then these people have been known as the nomadic Turks. Others again say that this people had its origin in Tourke, a large and prosperous city of the Persians.[17] They affirm that they left it for Asia Minor and became scattered there, maintaining control over Asia. There are some, however, who would have it that the Turks came to this land from Koile Syria and Arabia, rather than from the Skythians, and that they did so in the company of ʻUmar, who

νομοθεσίαν διαδεξαμένου ἐπὶ τὴν τῆς Ἀσίας ἀρχὴν προεληλυθέναι, καὶ ταύτῃ αὐτοῦ καταλειφθέντας ἐς τὸ νομαδικώτερον ἀποκλῖναι. Ὡς μὲν οὖν τούτων ἕκαστα ἔχει ἀληθείας, καὶ ἐφ' ἃ [1.9] δέῃ τούτων χωροῦντας πείθεσθαι ἄμεινον, οὐκ ἔχω ξυμβαλέσθαι ὡς ἀσφαλέστατα. Τοσόνδε μέντοι εἰρήσεται, ὡς τοῖς ἀπὸ Σκυθῶν γενέσθαι τὴν ἀρχὴν τούτοις διϊσχυριζομένοις ἔχοι ἂν τις συμφέρεσθαι ἄμεινον, διὰ τὸ Σκύθας τοὺς ἐν τῇ Εὐρώπῃ πρὸς ἕω ἔτι καὶ νῦν διαγενομένους κατὰ τὴν ἀγορὰν καλουμένην τῶν ἐν τῇ Ἀσίᾳ Τούρκων ἐπαΐειν οὐ χαλεπῶς, διαίτῃ τε καὶ σκευῇ ἔτι καὶ νῦν τῇ αὐτῇ ἄμφω τὼ γένεε διαχρωμένους, διὰ τὸ Σκύθας ἐπικρατῆσαι ἁπανταχῇ τῆς Ἀσίας. Δηλοῖ δὲ καὶ τοὔνομα αὐτὸ τὸν[2] τὴν νομαδικὴν δίαιταν προῃρημένον καὶ τὸν ταύτῃ τοῦ βίου πλέον αὐτῷ ποιούμενον.

11 Τὸ δὴ γένος τοῦτο, τοὺς Τούρκους μέγα τε ὂν καὶ ἐπὶ πολὺ διῆκον ἐς μοίρας ἐπίσταμαι διακεκρίσθαι τινάς, ἄλλας τε δὴ καὶ Ὀγουζίων τὴν μοῖραν, γένος οὐ φαῦλον, οὐδὲ ἀγεννές. Ἀπὸ τούτων δὲ τῶν Ὀγουζίων γενέσθαι Ἰονδουζάλπην, ἄνδρα ἐπιεικῆ τε καὶ τῆς τῶν Ὀγουζίων μοίρας ἡγησάμενον. Τοῦτον δὲ ἐπ' ἀρετῇ εὐφημούμενον ἀπομνημονεύουσι δικαιότατόν τε ἅμα γεγονέναι καὶ τοῖς Ὀγουζίοις διαιτητὴν καταστάντα ἑλομένοις δικάσαι σφίσιν αὐτοῖς δίκην ἡντινοῦν, ὁπότε ἐπιδικάσαιτο τοῖς προσιοῦσιν [1.10] αὐτῷ, ἀπαλλάττεσθαι ἀγαπῶντας ἑκατέρους, οἷς ἂν ἐπιδικάσαιτο. Καὶ τοῦτό φασιν ἐνιδόντας αὐτῷ τοὺς Ὀγουζίους, διαπραξαμένους πρὸς τὸν τῆς χώρας βασιλεύοντα, ἐπιστῆσαι σφίσιν αὐτοῖς τὸν Ἰονδουζάλπην δικαστήν, μετὰ δὲ ταῦτα ἐπιτρέψαι σφᾶς αὐτῷ διαθεῖναι, ᾗ

succeeded as lawgiver,[18] and so established their realm in Asia; when they had been left behind there by him, however, they turned to a more nomadic way of life. I am not able to say with certainty how much truth each of these views contains or to what degree one should trust in each. But this much, at least, can be said, that it would be better to side with those who ascribe a Skythian origin to these people, because the Skythians who even now remain in the eastern parts of Europe in the so-called Horde[19] have no difficulty in understanding the Turks of Asia. Both nations have one and the same way of life and use the same dress even now, because the Skythians prevailed throughout Asia. Anyway, the name Skythian itself obviously designates anyone who follows a nomadic way of life and spends most of his time doing this.

I do know that this people, the Turks, being large and 11
having spread far and wide, is divided into separate tribal groups, including, among others, that of the Oğuz, a noble people not to be despised.[20] The Oğuz produced Gündüz-Alp, a decent man who became the leader of the Oğuz tribe. It is recorded that this man was praised for his virtue, was most just, and was chosen by the Oğuz to be their arbiter and to adjudicate all manner of legal cases for them. Whenever he adjudicated a dispute for those who came to his court, he would reconcile them to each other before they departed, even concerning those matters about which they were in dispute. And they say that because the Oğuz discerned the man's quality, they managed to get the ruler of that land to appoint Gündüz-Alp over them as their judge and, after that, they permitted themselves to be ruled by

ἂν αὐτῷ δοκοίη ἐπὶ τὸ ἄμεινον. Μετὰ δὲ ταῦτα τὸν τούτου παῖδα Ὀγουζάλπην διαδεξάμενον τὴν ἀρχὴν τῆς Ὀγουζίων μοίρας ἐπὶ τὸ τυραννικώτερον ἐξηγήσασθαι, πρός τε τοὺς Ἕλληνας πολεμοῦντα κατὰ τὴν Ἀσίαν μέγα εὐδοκιμῆσαι.

12 Ὀρθογρούλην δὲ Ὀγουζάλπεω παῖδα δραστήριόν τε ἐς τὰ πάντα γενόμενον καὶ ἐπὶ πολέμους ἡγησάμενον ἄλλῃ τε πολλαχῇ εὐδοκιμῆσαι, καὶ δὴ καὶ πλοῖα ναυπηγησάμενον ἐπιληστεύειν νήσους ἐπιπλέοντα τὰς ἐν τῷ Αἰγαίῳ τῇ τε Ἀσίᾳ καὶ Εὐρώπῃ ἐπικειμένας, καὶ τήν τε Εὐρώπην πορθοῦντα, τά τε ἄλλα καὶ ἐς Τέαρον ἐμβάντα ποταμὸν τὸν κατὰ τὴν Αἶνον ἐπὶ πολὺ τοῦ ποταμοῦ σὺν ταῖς ναυσὶ προελθεῖν. Λέγεται δὲ αὐτὸν καὶ ἄλλῃ τε πολλαχῇ τῆς Εὐρώπης ἀποβάσεις ποιήσασθαι, καὶ ἐπὶ Πελοπόννησον ἀφικόμενον καὶ ἐπὶ Εὔβοιαν καὶ Ἀττικήν, τήν τε χώραν δῃῶσαι, καὶ ἀνδράποδα ὡς πλεῖστα ἀπενεγκάμενον μεγάλα κερδᾶναι. Ὀρθογρούλην δὲ τοῦτον μετὰ ταῦτα ἐν τῇ Ἀσίᾳ τραπόμενόν φασιν ἐπὶ διαρπαγῇ τῆς περιοικίδος χώρας ἐπεξιέναι τε καὶ ἀπὸ τούτου ὁρμώμενον ξυναγεῖραι τε στράτευμα καὶ ἐπιόντα καταστρέφεσθαι τούς τε ὁμόρους Ἕλληνας καὶ τοὺς [1.11] ταύτῃ σφίσιν αὐτῶν περιοίκους, καὶ τὸ ἀπὸ τοῦδε ληϊζόμενον τοὺς δὲ ἑπισπομένους αὐτῷ ἐν βραχεῖ δὴ ὀλβίους ἀποδεικνύναι καὶ οὕτω δὴ συχνοὺς τῶν νομάδων ἐπιγενομένους αὐτῷ συμπολεμῆσαί τε αὐτῷ ἅμα καὶ συνδιενέγκαι τὸν πόλεμον ἐπὶ τοὺς ὁμόρους, καὶ ταχὺ δὲ οὕτως ἐπὶ ἀρχὴν παρεληλυθέναι οὐ φαύλην, διὰ δὴ ταῦτα καὶ παρὰ Ἀλαδίνῃ μέγα εὐδοκιμῆσαι. Ἔνιοι δέ φασιν Ὀγουζίων τὴν μοῖραν ἡγουμένου Ὀρθογρούλεω χωρία ἐρυμνὰ περὶ τὸν Ταῦρον καταλαβόντα ἐπὶ

him in whatever way he deemed best.[21] After that his son Oğuz-Alp succeeded him as ruler of the Oğuz tribe. Although he ruled in a more tyrannical way, he still enjoyed great success in fighting against the Greeks in Asia.

Ertoğrul,[22] the son of Oğuz-Alp, was dynamic in every- 12
thing that he did. He enjoyed success while fighting wars in many places and he even built ships in order to sail to the islands of the Aegean, both those near Asia and those near Europe, and pillage them. He ravaged Europe: among other exploits, he even entered the river Tearos, the one by Ainos, and sailed his ships up a long stretch of it. He is also said to have made landings at many other places in Europe, reaching the Peloponnese, Euboia, and Attica, where he plundered the land and made huge profits by carrying off as many captives as possible as slaves.[23] After that, they say, this Ertoğrul turned his attention to ravaging the lands that lay next to his own in Asia. He hurriedly assembled an army, marched out from there, and attacked both the neighboring Greeks and the people who lived in their vicinity. From then on, because he soon made his followers rich by plundering, nomads flocked to him in great numbers to fight alongside him and keep up the war against his neighbors. He thus quickly acquired a substantial realm, and because of this he was also held in high esteem by 'Ala' al-Din.[24] Some say that under the leadership of Ertoğrul the Oğuz tribe captured some fortified places by the Tauros Mountains and

τῆς ταύτῃ ὁμόρου χώρας καταστροφῇ ἐντεῦθεν ὡρμῆσθαι, καὶ τούς γε Ἑλλήνων περιοίκους ἄγειν, καὶ ἐπὶ μέγα χωρῆσαι δυνάμεως. Ὡς μὲν οὖν ἀρχὴν ἔσχε τούτοις τὰ πράγματα, καὶ ὡς ταύτῃ ἢ ἄλλῃ ἐγένετο, οὐκ ἂν οὕτω ῥᾳδίως εἰπεῖν ἔχοιμι, ὑπὸ πολλῶν μέντοι λεγόμενα ταῦτα δὲ ἐς τοσοῦτον ἐπιμνησάμενος παρίημι.

13 Ὡς δὲ Ὀτουμανίδαι τῆς Ὀγουζίων μοίρας ἐπὶ τήνδε ἀφίκοντο τὴν ἀρχήν, ὧδε γενέσθαι ἐπυθόμην. Ἔστι Σογούτη παρὰ Μυσίαν κώμη οὕτω καλουμένη εὐδαίμων, καὶ ποταμὸς παρ' αὐτῇ οὕτω καλούμενος. Διέχει δὲ ἀπὸ θαλάττης τῆς τοῦ Εὐξείνου πόντου σταδίους ὡσεὶ πεντήκοντα καὶ διακοσίους· καλοῖτο δ' ἂν αὕτη Ἰταίας κώμη. Ἐς ταύτην δὲ τὴν χώραν ἀφικομένους τοὺς Ὀγουζίους ἐνοικῆσαι ἐπί τινα χρόνον. Ὀτουμάνον δὲ τὸν Ὀρθογρούλεω παῖδα, οὐ πάνυ τι εὖ πράττοντα τὴν ἀρχήν, [1.12] γενέσθαι τήν τε ψυχὴν ἐλευθεριώτατον, καὶ τοὺς ἐν τῇ κώμῃ φιλοφρονούμενον ἐκ τῶν προσόντων, ὡς οἷόν τ' ἦν μάλιστα αὐτῷ, τούς τε ἐν τῇ κώμῃ ἀνακτήσασθαι, ὥστε διαφορᾶς σφίσι πρὸς τοὺς Ἕλληνας αὐτῶν περιοίκους γενομένης ἡγεῖσθαι κελεύειν τοὺς ἐν τῇ κώμῃ Ὀτουμάνον τὸν Ὀρθογρούλεω· καὶ μαχεσάμενον τρέψασθαί τε τοὺς ταύτῃ Ἕλληνας, καὶ ἀπὸ τούτου ὁρμώμενον ἐπὶ πολὺ ἐπεξελθεῖν τε τοὺς Ἕλληνας, καὶ παρὰ Ἀλαδίνῃ εὖ μάλα εὐφημούμενον μέγα εὐδοκιμῆσαι, ἐπὶ στρατηγίας τε καθιστάμενον καὶ ἔργα ἀποδεικνύμενον ἄξια λόγου. Τελευτήσαντος δὲ Ἀλαδίνεω βασιλέως, καὶ τῶν ἀρίστων αὐτοῦ ἐς διαφορὰν σφίσιν ἀφικνουμένων, λέγεται ἀφικέσθαι τε ἐς λόγους αὐτοῖς, καὶ ἐκείνους ἀλλήλοις, ξυμμαχίαν τε καὶ ὁμαιχμίαν

used them as bases for subduing neighboring lands, driving out the neighbors of the Greeks and greatly increasing their own strength. But how their history began, and whether it was in this or in some other way, I could not easily say. I will only go so far as to say that these things are reported by many others.

As for the Ottomans of the Oğuz tribe, I have ascer- 13
tained that they rose to their current position of power in the following way. There is a prosperous little town in Mysia called Söğüt, next to a river with the same name. It is situated about two hundred and fifty stades away from the Black Sea; this town would be called Itaia [in Greek].[25] When the Oğuz arrived, they lived in this area for some time. Osman, Ertoğrul's son,[26] was not terribly successful as a leader but he had a most liberal disposition and, making indulgent use of the local resources, he made every possible effort to win over the townspeople. As a result, when a dispute arose between them and their Greek neighbors, the townspeople asked Osman, the son of Ertoğrul, to assume command. He fought a battle and routed the local Greeks. After this he started going after the Greeks much more aggressively and was held in high esteem by 'Ala' al-Din, who praised him greatly. He was appointed to a military command and performed notable deeds. When Sultan 'Ala' al-Din died[27] and his leading men started disputing among themselves, Osman is said to have entered into negotiations with them, and they among themselves. He managed to

ἐκείνοις συνθέμενον ξυμβῆναι αὐτοῖς, ὅρκια ποιησάμενον, ἐφ' ᾧ ὁμοῦ πάντας κοινῇ συνδιαφέρειν τὸν πόλεμον καὶ καταστρέφεσθαι τὴν χώραν, ὅσην ἂν δύνωνται, ὅσην δ' ἂν ὑπάγωνται, ἐπιδιελέσθαι σφίσι κατὰ τὰ κοινῇ σφίσιν αὐτοῖς δεδογμένα· καὶ οὕτω δὴ ἅμα ἐκείνοις ἐλαύνοντα καταστρέψασθαι χώραν οὐκ ὀλίγην, καὶ ἔργα ἀποδεικνύμενον μεγάλα καὶ χρήματα συχνὰ ἐπικτώμενον, ὥστε ἐν βραχεῖ ἐπὶ ἀρχὴν παρεληλυθέναι οὐ φαύλην.

14 Τούτους δὲ ἡγεμόνας ἑπτὰ γενομένους, ὅσην ὑπηγάγοντο ἀρχήν, διανεμεῖσθαι μετὰ ταῦτα σφίσιν αὐτοῖς. Λαχεῖν δὴ [1.13] Καραμάνον τὴν μεσόγαιαν τῆς Φρυγίας ἄχρι Κιλικίας καὶ Φιλαδελφείας, Σαρχάνην δὲ ἐντεῦθεν τὴν παράλιον τῆς Ἰωνίας χώραν ἔστε ἐπὶ Σμύρνην ἐλθεῖν, τὰ δὲ Λυδίας ἔστε ἐπὶ Μυσίαν Καλάμην σὺν τῷ παιδὶ αὐτοῦ Καρασῇ τὰ πρὸς Ὄλυμπόν τε καὶ Βιθυνίαν Ὀτουμάνον λαχεῖν μετὰ Τεκίεω· τὰ δὲ πρὸς τὸν Εὔξεινον πόντον καὶ Παφλαγονίαν λαχεῖν τοὺς Ὀμούρεω παῖδας. Τὸν δὲ Κερμιανὸν οὐ τῶν ἑπτὰ τούτων γεγονέναι φασίν, ἀλλὰ βασιλέα πρόσθεν γενόμενον Ἰκονίου τῆς Καρίας πόλεως, ἐν ᾗ τὰ βασίλεια ἐπὶ συχνόν τινα χρόνον διεγένετο τούτοις, ἀπεληλαμένον ἐντεῦθεν ἐπὶ Ἰωνίαν ἀπᾶραι, κἀκεῖ ἰδιωτεύοντα ἡσυχίαν ἄγειν. Οἱ μέντοι ἑπτὰ ἐτύγχανον ὄντες οἱ σύμπασαν τήνδε κοινῇ ὑπαγόμενοι σφίσι τὴν χώραν· ᾗ χωρὶς ὃς ἕκαστος, καὶ ᾗ ἄλλῳ ἄλλη ξυνέβαινεν, ἐπὶ τὴν αὐτοῦ ἀρχὴν παρεγένετο ἕκαστος, οὐκ ἂν δὴ οὕτως ἐν δέοντι πολυπραγμονοίην.

15 Σογούτην μέντοι ἐπίσταμαι κώμην ὡς οἱ ἀπ' ἐκείνης γενόμενοι Ὀτουμανίδων βασιλεῖς ἐτίμων τε ἐπὶ πλεῖστον

forge a mutual military alliance with them and took an oath that he would wage war in common with them all. They would subjugate as much territory as they possibly could, and however much land they conquered they would divide among themselves in accordance with their common agreements. And so he marched out with them and subjugated a large area, performing great deeds and amassing much money, so that in a short time he acquired a considerable realm.

There were seven leaders and, after this, they divided 14
among themselves whatever territory had come into their power. Karaman was allotted the interior of Phrygia all the way to Kilikia and Philadelpheia,[28] and Saruhan the coast of the Ionian region as far as Smyrna.[29] Kalamshah and his son Karası were allotted Lydia as far as Mysia,[30] while Mount Olympos and Bithynia were given to Osman and Teke.[31] The sons of Umur were allotted the lands toward the Black Sea and Paphlagonia.[32] They say that Germiyan was not among the original seven but had already become the king of Ikonion, a city of Karia, where they used to have their court for a long time.[33] But when he was driven out from there, he went to Ionia, where he lived a peaceful private life. So these seven were the ones who together subjected this whole land to themselves. However, there is no point in concerning oneself with whether each acted on his own or in agreement with someone else in some other way, when each obtained his realm.

I do know that the Ottoman sultans used to honor the 15
town of Söğüt, for it was where they came from, and would

ἐπιφοιτῶντες ταύτῃ τῇ κώμῃ, καὶ τοῖς ἐνοικοῦσιν αὐτὴν ἀποδιδόασι γέρα τὰ νομιζόμενα. Ἀπὸ ταύτης δὲ ἐπίσταμαι ἀκοῇ γενέσθαι Ὀτουμάνον τὸν Ὀρθογρούλεω παῖδα, πρῶτον δὴ τοῦ γένους τούτου ἄλλας τέ οἱ πόλεις ὑπαγόμενον ἐν τῇ Ἀσίᾳ, ἐν δὲ δὴ καὶ Προῦσαν τὴν ἐν Μυσίᾳ πόλιν καὶ τότε εὐδαίμονα παραστησάμενον, ὑπὸ λιμοῦ ἐκπολιορκῆσαι ἑλόντα τὴν πόλιν, καὶ ἐν αὐτῇ τὰ βασίλεια [1.14] ποιησάμενον, καὶ ἀπὸ ταύτης ὁρμώμενον ἔργα μεγάλα τε καὶ περιφανῆ ἀποδειξάμενον, παῖδάς τε καὶ ἀρχὴν οὐ φαύλην καταλιπόντα τελευτῆσαι ἐν Προύσῃ. Τοῦτον δὲ ἴσμεν ἡμεῖς τοῦ γένους τοῦδε τά τε ἄλλα ὡς οἷόν τε ἄριστα καθιστάντα, καὶ τὴν ἀρχὴν ἐς τὸ ἐπιτηδειότατον αὐτῷ καταστησάμενον, τάξιν τε ἀρίστην ἀποδείξασθαι ἀμφ᾽ αὐτόν, ἣν θύρας βασιλέως καλοῦσι, καὶ ταύτῃ γε τῇ δυνάμει τὸ ἀπὸ τοῦδε δεδιττόμενον δέει τῷ ἀμφ᾽ αὐτὸν κατέχειν τοὺς ὑπὸ τὴν ἀρχὴν αὐτοῦ ξύμπαντας, ἐν τάχει παραγενομένους, ὅπῃ ἂν αὐτῷ δοκοίη, καὶ ἐπιτελοῦντας, ἅττ᾽ ἂν ἐπιτάττοι ὁ βασιλεύς, καὶ ἐπὶ τὰ παραγγελλόμενα ὑπὸ τῶν βασιλέως θυρῶν κατὰ τάχος ἰόντας. Τοῦτον δὴ οὖν ἐπυθόμεθα γενναιότατόν τε ἐς τὰ πάντα γενόμενον, ταύτῃ τε ὡς ἐπὶ πλεῖστον νομισθῆναι δαιμόνιον, καταλιπεῖν τε ἀπὸ τούτου τὴν ἐπωνυμίαν τοῖς ἀπ᾽ ἐκείνου γενομένοις, Ὀτουμάνου παῖδας ἔτι καὶ νῦν καλεῖσθαι.

16 Ἐπὶ τούτου βασιλεύοντος ὀκτακισχίλιοι Τούρκων ἐς τὴν Εὐρώπην διαβάντες περὶ Ἑλλήσποντον, καὶ ἐν Χερρονήσῳ κατασχόντες φρούριον Ἑλληνικόν, καὶ ἀπὸ τούτου ὁρμώμενοι, τήν τε Θρᾴκην ἐς Ἴστρον ἐλαύνοντες ἐληΐζοντο τὴν χώραν ἐπιδραμόντες, τά τε πολλὰ διήρπαζον,

often visit it; and they gave its inhabitants appropriate privileges. I have heard that Osman, the son of Ertoğrul and founder of this people, was from there. But he subjected other cities in Asia to himself, among them Prousa, the then prosperous city in Mysia. He took this city by starving it in a siege and set up his court there.[34] Using it as his base, he accomplished great and glorious deeds. He also died at Prousa,[35] leaving behind children and a substantial realm. I know that he arranged matters as excellently as possible for his people and set up its government in the most suitable way. He instituted a superb administration around himself which they call the "king's Porte."[36] And from then on, with this power, the intimidation produced by the awe that surrounded him kept everyone in his realm under control. In short, they presented themselves to him wherever he saw fit, carried out whatever the sultan decreed, and swiftly went about the orders from the sultan's Porte. We have discovered that he was extremely courageous in all circumstances, and because of this he was generally believed to have supernatural powers. He passed his name on to his descendants, who are even now called "the sons of Osman."[37]

During his reign, eight thousand Turks crossed over into Europe at the Hellespont and seized a Greek fort in the Chersonese. They made it their base and advanced through Thrace all the way to the Danube, devastating the land as they overran it. They looted most of it and, taking as many 16

καὶ ἀνδράποδα ὡς πλεῖστα ἑλόμενοι ἐς τὴν Ἀσίαν διεβίβαζον, τούς τε Ἕλληνας καὶ Τριβαλλοὺς ἦγον καὶ ἔφερον. Ἐν τούτῳ δὴ Σκυθῶν μοῖρα οὐκ ὀλίγη ἀπὸ Σαρματίας ἐπὶ τὸν Ἴστρον ἐλάσαντες καὶ τόν γε Ἴστρον διαβάντες, τούς τε Τούρκους ἐν τῇ Θρᾴκῃ κατέλαβον καὶ μαχεσάμενοι ἐτρέψαντο, καὶ πλὴν ὀλίγων τινῶν διεχρήσαντο [1.15] σύμπαντας ἀφειδέστατα. Ὅσοι δὲ οὐκ ἐφθάρησαν, διασωθέντες ἐς τὴν Χερρόνησον, ἐς τὴν Ἀσίαν αὖθις διαβάντες οὐκέτι πάλιν ἀφίκοντο.

17 Τότε οὖν τὰ Ἑλλήνων πράγματα ἐταλαντεύετο ἐπ᾽ ἀμφότερα, διαφερομένων σφίσι κατὰ τὴν Βυζαντίου βασιλείαν ἀμφοῖν βασιλέοιν τοῖν Ἀνδρονίκοιν, τοῦ τε πάππου καὶ υἱϊδοῦ, τῶν Παλαιολόγων. Ἐφ᾽ ὧν δὲ ἐς διαφορὰν σφίσιν ἀφικομένων οἵ τε Ἕλληνες πρὸς ἑκατέρους διέστησαν, καὶ αὐτοῖς τὰ πράγματα ἤδη πάμπαν ἐφθείρετο. Τῷ γὰρ πρώτῳ Ἀνδρονίκῳ ἐγεγόνει παῖς Μιχαῆλος, ὃς ἐτελεύτησε, πρὶν ἢ ἐς τὴν βασιλείαν ἐλθεῖν. Μετὰ δὲ τὴν ἐκείνου τελευτὴν Ἀνδρόνικος ὁ παῖς αὐτοῦ γεγηρακότι ἤδη τῷ πάππῳ, ἀξιῶν αὐτὸς ἔχειν τὴν βασιλείαν, καθίσταντο ἐς διαφοράν, αὐθαδέστερος ὢν ἢ ὥστε πείθεσθαι, καὶ πράγματα παρεῖχεν ἀνήνυτα, τούς τε Τριβαλλοὺς ἐπαγόμενος καὶ Ἑλλήνων τοὺς ἀρίστους οἱ προσεταιριζόμενος ἐς τὴν βασιλείαν, ὡς διὰ ταῦτα μηδὲ ἐξεῖναι αὐτοῖς τὸ παράπαν τοὺς Τούρκους ἐς τὴν Εὐρώπην διαβάντας ἀμύνεσθαι. Καθ᾽ ὃν δὴ χρόνον ἥ τε Προῦσα ἐξεπολιορκήθη λιμῷ ἁλοῦσα ὑπὸ Ὀτουμάνου, καὶ ἄλλαι κατὰ τὴν Ἀσίαν πόλεις ἑάλωσαν.

18 Ὅθεν οἵ τε Τοῦρκοι ἐπὶ μέγα ἐχώρουν δυνάμεως κατὰ

prisoners as they could enslave, transported them over to Asia; and so they despoiled the Greeks and Serbs. At this point, however, a large contingent of Skythians advanced from Russia to the Danube. They crossed the Danube and met the Turks in Thrace where they routed them in battle. Except for a few, they mercilessly slaughtered them all. Those who were not killed sought refuge in the Chersonese, and then they crossed over into Asia and never returned.[38]

At that time the affairs of the Greeks hung in the bal- 17
ance, as there was a dispute between two kings, both named Andronikos, regarding the throne in Byzantion; they were grandfather and grandson, of the Palaiologos family.[39] When the dispute arose between the two of them, the rest of the Greeks also took sides, and their affairs were greatly harmed. The elder Andronikos had a son, Michael [IX], who died before he could come to the throne. After his death, his son Andronikos decided that he should hold the throne himself, as his grandfather had already grown old, and so they fell out with each other. He was too stubborn to submit and caused endless trouble. He brought in the Serbs[40] and allied himself with the leading Greeks in his struggle for the throne. As a result they could do nothing to prevent the Turks from crossing over into Europe. It was at this time that Prousa was besieged, starved out, and taken by Osman,[41] and other cities in Asia were captured.

Thus the Turks acquired great power in Asia and crossed 18

τὴν Ἀσίαν, καὶ ἐς τὴν Εὐρώπην διαβάντες κακῶς ἐποίουν τὴν Θρᾴκην, ἄλλοι τε οὐκ ὀλίγοι καὶ δὴ καὶ Χαλίλης, ὃς δὴ ἐς τὸ κατὰ τὴν Χερρόνησον φρούριον ὑπὸ Ἑλλήνων συνελαθεὶς μετεπέμπετο Τούρκους ἀπὸ τῆς Ἀσίας, καὶ τόν τε βασιλέα ἐπιόντα ἠμύνατο, καὶ ἐπὶ πολὺ ἐξελαύνων τῆς Θρᾴκης ἐληΐζετο, ὁπότε δὴ ἐπαγόμενος τόν τε Τριβαλλῶν [1.16] ἡγεμόνα καὶ τοὺς ἀπὸ Ἰταλίας τό τε φρούριον ἐξεπολιόρκησε κατ' ἤπειρον καὶ κατὰ θάλατταν. Οἱ μὲν οὖν Τοῦρκοι ἔλαθον δρασμῷ ἐπιχειρήσαντες ἐς τὴν Ἀσίαν νυκτὸς διαβάντες. Ἀνωμάλως μὲν ἔς τε τὰ ἄλλα σφίσιν ἔχοντες οὗτοι οἱ βασιλεῖς, καὶ αὐτομόλοις Τούρκων ἡγεμόσι, τῷ τε Ἀζατίνῃ καὶ ἄλλοις, οὐ καλῶς ἐχρήσαντο, ὥστε ἐπιτηδείως ἔχειν σφίσιν τούς τε ἀπὸ Ταρακῶνος καὶ Ἰταλίας, οὓς δὴ μετεπέμπετο ἐπὶ τὸν Τούρκων βασιλέα Ὀρχάνην, ὃς Φιλαδέλφειαν ἐπολιόρκει, καὶ ἐς τὴν ἐπὶ τῇ Χερρονήσῳ φυλακὴν τῆς Καλλιουπόλεως.

19 Οὗτοι μὲν οὖν οἱ Ταρακῶνες καὶ οἱ ἀπὸ Ἰταλίας ἐς τὴν Καλλιουπόλεως φυλακὴν τεταγμένοι, τοῖς μετὰ Ἀζατίνεω αὐτομόλοις χρησάμενοι Τούρκοις, συνεστήσαντο ἀλλήλοις ὡς τῇ πόλει ἐπιθησόμενοι, καὶ ἐπειδὴ ἔγνωσαν κατάδηλοι ὄντες, ἐμηνύθη γὰρ ὑπ' αὐτῶν τινὸς τοῖς Ἕλλησι, διὰ τῆς Θρᾴκης ἴεντο, καὶ τὴν Ῥοδόπην διαβάντες ἀφίκοντο ἐς Κασσάνδρειαν, Πύδναν[3] τὸ πάλαι καλουμένην. Ἐντεῦθεν δὲ τῶν μὲν μετὰ Ἀζατίνεω Τούρκων, ὅσοι παρῆσαν, ἀφίκοντο ἐς τὸν Τριβαλλῶν βασιλέα, οἱ δὲ ἀπὸ τῆς Ἀσίας τὰ ἔμπαλιν γενόμενοι ἴεντο πεζοὶ ἐπὶ τὴν Χερρόνησον, αὖθις ἐν νῷ ἔχοντες, ὅτῳ ἂν δύναιντο τρόπῳ, ἐς τὴν Ἀσίαν διαβῆναι. Καί πη καὶ σπονδὰς τοῖς Ἕλλησι

over into Europe, where they caused trouble in Thrace. There were many of them, including Halil, who was blockaded by the Greeks in a fort of the Chersonese and summoned Turks over from Asia. He defended himself against the attacks of the king, and then marched out and heavily plundered Thrace.[42] At that point the king of the Greeks brought in the ruler of the Serbs and the men from Italy and besieged the fort by both land and sea.[43] But the Turks escaped without being detected and crossed over to Asia at night.[44] As these kings had bad relations with each other over other matters, they did not make good use of the Turkish leaders who had defected to their side, such as 'Izz al-Din and the others.[45] Thus they had to make an alliance with the men from Aragon and Italy,[46] whom the king of the Greeks sent against Orhan,[47] the sultan of the Turks, who was besieging Philadelpheia,[48] and use them to garrison Gallipoli in the Chersonese.

These Aragonese and Italians who had been stationed to 19
garrison Gallipoli cut a deal with the Turks who had defected with 'Izz al-Din, and arranged to attack the city together. But when they learned that they had been exposed—for they were betrayed by one of their own people to the Greeks—they went through Thrace, crossed Rodope, and arrived at Kassandreia,[49] which was formerly called Pydna.[50] But then the Turks with 'Izz al-Din, however many there were, went over to the king of the Serbs, while those from Asia turned around and went back on foot to the Chersonese with the intention of crossing straight over to Asia, in whatever way they could.[51] But even though they had made a treaty with the Greeks, the Greeks were apparently

ποιησάμενοι, ὡς ἐπεβούλευον αὐτοὺς οἱ Ἕλληνες ἑλεῖν βουλόμενοι, ἔς τι φρούριον τὸ κατὰ τὴν Χερρόνησον διεσώζοντο. Καὶ οὗτοι αὖθις κακῶς ἐποίουν τοὺς Ἕλληνας.

20 Οἱ μέντοι ἀπὸ ἑσπέρας τε καὶ Ἰταλίας ἄνδρες, [1.17] διὰ Μακεδονίας τε καὶ Θετταλίας ἐς Βοιωτίαν ἀφικόμενοι, κατέσχον αὐτὴν καὶ τὰς Θήβας ἠνδραποδίσαντο ἀφροσύνῃ τοῦ ἡγεμόνος, ὃς δεδιότας αὐτοὺς ὑπολογιζόμενος ἐπῄει ὡς ἀναρπασόμενος. Οὗτοι μὲν οὖν ταφρεύσαντες τὸ χωρίον, καὶ ὕδωρ ἐς αὐτὸ ἐμβαλόντες, ἐπὶ πολὺ ἄβατον τοῖς ἱππεῦσιν ἐποίησαν τὸ χωρίον. Οἱ μὲν οὖν ἱππεῖς οἱ μετὰ τοῦ ἡγεμόνος ἔθεον δρόμῳ ἐπὶ τοὺς ἑσπερίους ὡς ἀναρπασόμενοι, ἐμβάντες δὲ ἐς τὸ χωρίον χαλεπῶς ἐχρήσαντο σφίσιν αὐτοῖς· οἱ δὲ Ταρακῶνες καταπέλταις τε καὶ τόξοις βάλλοντες καὶ ἀκοντίοις τοὺς πολλοὺς τῶν Βοιωτῶν αὐτοῦ ταύτῃ διεχρήσαντο, ὕστερον δὲ ἐπὶ τὴν πόλιν ἐλθόντες αὐτοβοεί τε τὴν πόλιν εἷλον καὶ ἠνδραποδίσαντο. Οὗτος μὲν οὖν ὕστερον ἐς Ἰταλίαν περαιούμενος ἐπ' οἴκου ἐτράποντο ἕκαστος.

21 Ἕλληνες δὲ μετὰ Ἀνδρονίκου τοῦ βασιλέως, καὶ τοῖς ἀπὸ Τούρκων ἐπὶ σφᾶς αὐτομόλοις καὶ τοῖς ἀπὸ Ἰταλίας κακῶς χρησάμενοι, οὐχ ὅπως οὐδὲν εὕραντο ἐπιτήδειον, ἀλλὰ καὶ πολεμίους σφίσιν ἔχοντες τούτους, ἐπὶ τὸ τοὺς σφῶν εὐγενεῖς θεραπεύειν μόνον τραπόμενοι τῆς τε ἀρχῆς εἰσόδους κατανήλισκον, καὶ οὔτε στράτευμα συνέλεγον, οὔτε ξένους μισθωσάμενοι, καὶ τοὺς πολεμίους ἐπιόντας σφίσι τιμωρεῖν ἠβούλοντο.

22 Ἐπάνειμι δὲ ἐπ' ἐκεῖνο τοῦ λόγου, ὅθεν μοι ἐξέλιπε. Ὀτουμάνος μὲν οὖν Ὀρθογρούλεω, τὰ πλέω τῆς ἐς τὴν

plotting against them, as they wanted to catch them, and so the Turks protected themselves in some fort in the Chersonese. And thus they caused trouble for the Greeks again.[52]

As for the men from the far west and from Italy, they 20
passed through Macedonia and Thessaly and arrived in Boiotia, which they occupied. They also enslaved Thebes through the ineptitude of its ruler, who thought they would be afraid and marched out to overpower them. However, they dug a ditch at the place and filled it with water, thereby making the place mostly impassable for cavalry. The commander's knights charged in to overpower the westerners, but they found that the terrain which they had entered was working against them. The men of Aragon shot at them with catapults, bows, and spears and killed the majority of the Boiotians right there.[53] Then they came to the city, captured it without a blow, and enslaved it. Later each of them crossed over to Italy and returned home.[54]

Thus the Greeks and King Andronikos made bad use 21
both of the Turks who defected to their side and of the men from Italy. Not only did they fail to obtain any benefit from them, they even had to face them as enemies. They squandered the revenues of their realm by using them solely to gratify their own nobility, and neither enlisted an army nor hired foreign mercenaries. They showed no will to avenge themselves on the enemies who were attacking them.

I return now to that point of my narrative from where 22
I had digressed. Osman, the son of Ertoğrul, having con-

Ἀσίαν Ἑλλήνων χώρας καταστρεψάμενος, ἐς Νίκαιάν τε ἐσέβαλε καὶ ἐς Φιλαδέλφειαν, οὐ μέντοι γε εἷλε τὸ ἄστυ· καὶ πρὸς Τούρκους τοὺς μετὰ Ὀμούρεω διενεχθεὶς ἐπολέμησεν· ἄρξας δὲ ἐν Προύσῃ, [1.18] ἐν ᾗ τὰ βασίλεια ἐπεποίητό οἱ, ἐτελεύτησε, καταλιπὼν παῖδας καὶ χώραν οὐ φαύλην καὶ στρατὸν οὐκ ἀγεννῆ. Τελευτήσαντος δὲ Ὀτουμάνου ὁ νεώτερος τῶν παίδων αὐτοῦ γενόμενος τοὺς ὅτι ἐγγύτατα παρὰ τῷ πατρὶ διαιτωμένους, ὡς οἷόν τ᾽ ἦν αὐτῷ, ἀνακτώμενος ἐπιτηδείους τε αὐτῷ εἶχε καὶ ἐς τὰ μάλιστα συνήθεις. Ἀπὸ τούτων δὴ ἐπεί τε τάχιστα ἐπύθετο τελευτῆσαι Ὀτουμάνον, ὄντα ἤδη, ᾗ φασιν, ἐπὶ γήραος οὐδῷ, ἀποφυγεῖν μὲν αὐτίκα τοὺς ἀδελφοὺς ἐκποδὼν γενόμενον[4] ἐπὶ Ὄλυμπον τῆς Μυσίας ὄρος, διαπορευόμενον δὲ κατὰ τὴν ὁδὸν περιτυχεῖν ἵππων φορβῇ ταύτῃ που τῆς χώρας ἐπινεμομένῃ, καὶ διανεῖμαι ταύτην ἀνδράσι τοῖς ἀπὸ τοῦ ὄρους ἐπ᾽ αὐτὸν συλλεγομένοις, καὶ ἐπικαταβαίνοντα ἐς τὸ πεδίον ἐπιτρέπειν αὐτοῖς διαρπάζειν, ὅσα γ᾽ ἂν τούτοις προχωροίη, ὁρμώμενον δὲ ταύτῃ ἀπὸ τοῦ ὄρους ἄγειν καὶ φέρειν τὴν πόλιν.

23 Τῶν δὲ ἀδελφῶν αὐτοῦ σφίσιν ἀλλήλοις διαπολεμούντων τε καὶ ἀμφὶ τοὺς οἰκείους ἐχόντων πολέμους, ἐς ὃ δὴ καὶ οὐκ ὀλίγων τῶν ἀπὸ τῆς πόλεως καὶ ἀμφὶ τὼ ἀδελφὼ ἐπιγενομένων αὐτῷ, ἐπικαταβῆναί τε ἐς τὸ πεδίον, καὶ ἐς πόλεμον καθιστάμενον τοῖς ἀδελφοῖς οὖσι διῃρημένοις καὶ ἀνὰ μέρος ἑκατέρῳ στρατοπεδευομένῳ μαχέσασθαι, καὶ περιγενόμενον ἀνελεῖν ἄμφω τὼ ἀδελφώ, καὶ οὕτω τὴν βασιλείαν παραλαβεῖν. Τοῦτο δὲ ἔγωγε ἀναπυνθανόμενος εὗρον οὐ γνώμην [1.19] ταύτην περὶ τῶν

quered most of the Greek lands in Asia, attacked Nikaia and Philadelpheia but did not capture them.[55] And he fell out with the Turks of Umur,[56] and fought against them too. He ruled from Prousa, where he established his court, and died leaving behind him sons, a substantial territory, and a formidable army.[57] When Osman died, the youngest of his sons [i.e., Orhan] had done everything he could to gain the favor of his father's innermost circle and especially to make them his own supporters. It was from them that he was instantly informed of Osman's death—the latter was already, as they say, on the threshold of old age[58]—and he escaped at once from his brothers, taking himself off to Mount Olympos in Mysia. As he was traveling along the road, he happened upon a herd of horses grazing in that area and distributed them among the men who were coming from the mountain to join him. Going down onto the plain, he allowed them to plunder whatever they came across. Using the mountain as his base, he despoiled the city.[59]

Now, Orhan's brothers were fighting against each other 23
and were preoccupied with their own wars, to the point where many people joined up with him from the city and from the followers of both his brothers. So he went down onto the plain and made war against his brothers, who were divided into two sides and encamped across from each other about to join battle. He overcame and then killed both his brothers, and thus assumed the throne. Although I have made a thorough inquiry, I have been unable to confirm this

ἀδελφῶν, χρῆσθαι σφίσιν αὐτοὺς ὡς πολεμίους, ἀποφηναμένοις νομίζεσθαι παρ' αὐτοῖς ἔτι καὶ ἐς τόνδε τὸν χρόνον· ἀλλ' ὑπὸ τῶν τοῖς Ὀγουζίοις ἡγεμόνων καθιστάμενον[5] καὶ πρόσθεν γενόμενον διεπυθόμην.

24 Ὀρχάνης μὲν οὖν ἐπεί τε εἰς τὴν βασιλείαν παρήει, σύμπασάν τε τὴν Λυδίαν κατεστρέφετο, καὶ τοῖς ἐν τῇ Ἀσίᾳ Ἕλλησι καθίστατο ἐς πόλεμον, καὶ συχνὰς τῶν ταύτῃ Ἑλληνίδων πόλεων πολιορκίᾳ παραστησάμενος ὑπηγάγετό οἱ, τῶν γε Βυζαντίου βασιλέων πρὸς τοὺς ἐν τῇ Θρᾴκῃ Τριβαλλούς τε ἅμα καὶ Μυσοὺς κατὰ τοῦτο τοῦ χρόνου ἐπικειμένους σφίσιν ἐς τὰ μάλιστα τὸν πόλεμον διαφερόντων. Μετὰ δὲ ταῦτα ἐπὶ Καππαδοκίαν ἐλαύνων, ἔστιν ἃ τῶν πολισμάτων ὑφ' αὑτῷ ποιησάμενος, ἐπὶ Νίκαιαν τὴν ἐν Βιθυνίᾳ πόλιν ἐστρατεύετο. Ἐπολιόρκει μὲν οὖν τὴν πόλιν. Ἐνταῦθα ὡς ἡ ἀγγελία ἦλθεν ἐς τὸν Ἑλλήνων βασιλέα, τήν τε Νίκαιαν πολιορκεῖσθαι καὶ τοὺς ἐν τῇ πόλει, εἰ μή τις ἐπαμύνοι σφίσι, προσχωρήσειν τῷ βαρβάρῳ, στράτευμά τε συνελέγετο ἐς τὴν βασιλείαν ἤδη παριών, οὐ περιοψόμενος τὴν Νίκαιαν, ὡς τιμωρήσειν παρεσκευάζετο διαμαχούμενος οὐδὲν ἧττον πρὸς Ὀρχάνην τὸν Ὀτουμάνεω ἢ ἀναστησόμενος ἀπὸ τῆς Νικαίας.

25 Οὗτος μὲν δὴ ὡς τῶν ἄλλων πολλαχῶς ἐπιχειρησάντων οὐ προεχώρησεν ἐπὶ τὴν βασιλείαν, τούς τε Ἕλληνας συνιστῶν ἐπὶ τὸν πάππον καὶ νεώτερα πράσσων πράγματα, Μιχαῆλον τὸν [1.20] Μυσῶν ἡγεμόνα ἐπηγάγετό οἱ ἐς συμμαχίαν, ἐπιγαμίαν ποιησάμενος, τὴν ἀδελφὴν αὐτῷ ἐς γάμον ἐκδοὺς γήμαντι πρόσθεν τὴν τοῦ βασιλέως Τριβαλλῶν ἀδελφήν. Ὅθεν ὁ Τριβαλλῶν ἡγεμὼν ἐπ' αὐτὸν

view of the brothers, namely that they were treating each other as enemies, but this is the usual story that is told about them even now.[60] What I did find out was that Orhan had been established in power by the rulers of the Oğuz in advance.[61]

When Orhan had gained the throne, he conquered all of 24
Lydia[62] and made war against the Greeks in Asia. He took many of the Greek cities there by siege and subjected them to himself, for the kings of Byzantion were at odds with the Serbs in Thrace and with the Bulgarians, and they were waging a bitter war against each other at that time. After that, he advanced on Kappadokia, occupied some of its towns, and then marched against Nikaia, the city in Bithynia.[63] Orhan laid siege to the city, but the news reached Andronikos [III], the king of the Greeks, that Nikaia was being besieged and that the people in the city would go over to the barbarian if no one came to their aid. As he had just come to the throne, he raised an army, for it was not his intention to neglect Nikaia. He was prepared to fight back so that he could demand nothing less from Orhan, the son of Osman, than his departure from Nikaia.

Andronikos had not previously advanced to the throne 25
because the others had contrived all sorts of things.[64] But he turned the Greeks against his grandfather [Andronikos II] and overturned the established order. He made an alliance with Mihail, the ruler of the Bulgarians, establishing a marriage connection by giving him his sister in marriage, although Mihail had previously married the sister of the king of the Serbs.[65] For this reason the king of the Serbs marched

τε ὥρμητο στρατεύεσθαι, ἔχων μεθ' ἑαυτοῦ τὸν Μιχαήλου ἀδελφιδοῦν Ἀλέξανδρον· τόν τε Μιχαῆλον μάχῃ ἐκράτησε, καὶ Ἀλέξανδρον τὸν ἀδελφιδοῦν αὐτοῦ ἐς τὴν βασιλείαν καταστησάμενος. Τῆς ἐς αὐτὸν ὕβρεως αἰτιασάμενος οὖν τοὺς Ἕλληνας ἐστρατεύετο ἐπ' αὐτούς, καὶ πολίσματα ἄττα ἐξελὼν ἀπεχώρησεν ἐπ' οἴκου. Ὕστερον μέντοι σπονδὰς ἐποιήσαντο, ἐφ' ᾧ ξένοι καὶ φίλοι εἶναι ἀλλήλοις.

26 Ἐνταῦθα ἐπυνθάνετο Ὀρχάνην ἐπιδραμόντα τὰ κατὰ τὴν Βιθυνίαν χωρία καὶ ἀνδραποδισάμενον πολιορκεῖν τε τὴν Νίκαιαν καὶ οὐκ ἀνιέναι προσβάλλοντα τῷ τείχει. Στράτευμά τε ξυναγείρας καὶ ἐς τὴν Ἀσίαν διαβὰς ἤλαυνεν ἐπὶ Νίκαιαν, ἀμύνειν βουλόμενος τοῖς ἐν τῇ πόλει. Ὀρχάνης μέν, ἐπειδὴ ἠγγέλθη ἐπιέναι ἐπ' αὐτὸν στράτευμα Ἑλληνικόν, συνταξάμενος ἀντεπῄει, τό τε στράτευμα ἔχων ἐν τάξει ὡς μαχούμενος τὸν στρατὸν ἀντεπήγαγε καὶ ἐν Φιλοκρήνῃ γενόμενος εὗρε στρατοπεδευόμενον τὸν Βυζαντίου βασιλέα. Οὐ πολὺ δὲ ὕστερον μάχης ἰσορρόπου γενομένης αὐτός τε ὁ βασιλεὺς ἐτρώθη εἰς τὸν πόδα, καὶ Ἑλλήνων οὐκ ὀλίγοι τραυματίαι γενόμενοι ἔγνωσαν δεῖν ἐς Φιλοκρήνην εἰσελθεῖν, ὥστε ἀναλαβεῖν σφᾶς αὐτοὺς καὶ ἀναμαχέσασθαι ἐνταῦθα. Ὡς ἐπὶ τὴν πόλιν ἐτράποντο, κατὰ νώτου γενόμενοι οἱ βάρβαροι καὶ ἐπικείμενοι συχνούς τε τῶν Ἑλλήνων διέφθειρον, καὶ τούς γε λοιποὺς ἐς τὴν [1.21] πόλιν συνελάσαντες ἐπολιόρκουν, ἐπεὶ δὲ παράλιος ἦν αὕτη ἡ πόλις, ὡς οὐδὲν προεχώρει τῷ Ὀρχάνῃ, αὖθις ἐπὶ Νίκαιαν ἐλθὼν ἐπολιόρκει τε ἐπί τινα χρόνον καὶ εἷλε τε οὐ πολλῷ ὕστερον ὁμολογίᾳ παραστησάμενος. Οὕτω Νίκαια ἐπὶ Ὀρχάνῃ ἐγένετο.

out against Mihail, having with him Mihail's nephew, Aleksandăr. He defeated Mihail in battle and put his nephew Aleksandăr on the throne. Citing the offense that the Greeks had given him in this matter, he then marched against them and seized some towns before returning home. Later they made a treaty, and agreed to be friends and allies.[66]

It was at this point that Andronikos learned that Orhan, 26
who was raiding the region of Bithynia and taking slaves there, was besieging Nikaia and was relentlessly attacking its walls. Andronikos raised an army, crossed over into Asia, and marched to Nikaia, intending to defend those in the city.[67] But when Orhan learned that a Greek army was coming against him, he assembled his forces and came out to meet them. He advanced with his army in battle formation and found the king of Byzantion encamped at Philokrene. Shortly afterward there was an evenly matched battle,[68] and the king himself was wounded in the leg. Many Greeks were also wounded and they decided that they should go into Philokrene, so that they could regroup and fight back from there. As they turned to go to the city, the barbarians came up from behind and attacked them, killing many of the Greeks. The Turks corralled the rest in the city and besieged them but, as this is a coastal city, Orhan could do nothing against it. So he went back to Nikaia and besieged it again for a while. Shortly afterward he captured it through a negotiated surrender. Thus Nikaia came under Orhan's control.[69]

27 Εἰσέβαλε δὲ καὶ εἰς Φιλαδέλφειαν, ἀλλ' οὐκ ἠδυνήθη παραστήσασθαι πολιορκῶν διὰ τὸ πλῆθος τῶν ἐπικούρων. Μετὰ δὲ ταῦτα διενεχθείς, ὥς φασι, πρὸς τοὺς ἐν τῇ Ἀσίᾳ βαρβάρους ἡγεμόνας, τούτων ἐνίους συμμάχους οἱ προσλαβόμενος τοῖς ἄλλοις πολεμῶν οὐκ ἀνίει. Ὕστερον μέντοι χρόνου συχνοῦ διελθόντος, Καντακουζηνοῦ βασιλέως Ἑλλήνων ἄρτι γενομένου ἔγημε θυγατέρα, καὶ ἐπιγαμίαν ποιησάμενος ταύτην εἰρήνην τε τοῖς Ἕλλησιν ἐποιήσατο, καὶ τοῦ λοιποῦ πρὸς τοὺς ἐν τῇ Φρυγίᾳ βαρβάρων ἡγεμόνας διενεχθεὶς ἐπολέμει. Ὡς τελευτήσαντος γὰρ Ἀνδρονίκου τοῦ βασιλέως, κατελείφθη τε αὐτῷ παῖς ἀμφὶ τὰ δυοκαίδεκα ἔτη γεγονώς, καὶ τόν γε Καντακουζηνὸν κατέλιπεν, ἄνδρα εὐδαίμονα καὶ μέγα δυνάμενον, τόν τε παῖδα ἐπιτροπεύειν, ἄχρι δ' ἂν ἐπὶ τὸ τῆς ἡλικίας ἀφίκηται ἐντελές, καὶ τὴν βασιλείαν περιέπειν, μέγα τε ὄλβιον, καὶ ἀρεσκόμενος τούτῳ ἐπέτρεψε τὰ ἀμφὶ τὴν βασιλείαν τε καὶ τὸν παῖδα, ἐμπεδώσας ὅρκοις ἦ μὴν ἀδόλως ἐπιτροπεύειν τῆς τε βασιλείας ἅμα καὶ τοῦ παιδός, καὶ ἀβλαβῆ τὸν παῖδα ἐς τὴν βασιλείαν καταστήσειν. Ὡς δὲ ἐτελεύτησεν ὁ βασιλεύς, χρόνου οὐ πολλοῦ {I.22} διελθόντος Ἑλλήνων τέ τινων ἐναγόντων ἐς τοῦτο καὶ συνεπιλαβομένων τήν τε βασιλείαν κατέσχε καὶ τὸν παῖδα κακὸν μὲν οὐδέν τι εἰργάσατο, κηδεστὴν δέ οἱ ποιησάμενος ὀλιγώρως τὰ τοῦ παιδὸς εἶχε, καὶ ἑαυτῷ ᾤετο τοὺς Ἕλληνας μᾶλλόν τι ἀνακτήσασθαι. Ὁ μὲν οὖν Καντακουζηνὸς τὴν βασιλείαν ἀφελόμενος τὸν παῖδα, πρὸς Ὀρχάνην τὴν ἐπιγαμίαν ποιησάμενος ἑαυτῷ ξένον τε καὶ φίλον ἐκτήσατο ἐς τὰ μάλιστα.

Orhan also attacked Philadelpheia, but was unable to take it by siege because it had too many defenders.[70] After this they say that he fell out with the barbarian rulers in Asia: taking some as his allies, he waged war relentlessly against the others. Much later, he married the daughter of Kantakouzenos, who had just become king of the Greeks.[71] Through this marriage Orhan made peace with the Greeks, and from that point on he fought against the barbarian rulers in Phrygia,[72] with whom he was in dispute. When King Andronikos [III] died, he left a son who was about twelve years old.[73] He also left Kantakouzenos, who was a wealthy and very powerful man, to act as the boy's guardian until he came of age and to supervise the realm. Given Kantakouzenos's great fortune, and because the king liked him personally, he entrusted him with both the kingdom and his son, but bound him with oaths to supervise honestly both the kingdom and the child and to keep his son safe until he should ascend to the throne.[74] But shortly after the king died, Kantakouzenos took the throne at the instigation of some of the Greeks who sided with him. Although he did no harm to the child and made him his son-in-law, he marginalized him, hoping to win the Greeks over to his side more. So Kantakouzenos deprived the child of the throne and made a marriage alliance with Orhan to acquire a powerful friend and ally.[75] 27

28 Ὀρχάνης μὲν δὴ βασιλεύσας ἔτη [. . .][6] ἐτελεύτησε, παῖδας καταλιπὼν Σουλαϊμάνην τε καὶ Ἀμουράτην. Σουλαϊμάνης μὲν οὖν ὁ Ὀρχάνεω τὴν βασιλείαν παραλαβὼν τοῖς τε Ἕλλησιν ἐπιὼν ἐπολέμει αὐτίκα, καὶ ἀνδράποδα ἀπὸ τῆς ἐς τὴν Ἀσίαν Ἑλλήνων χώρας ὡς πλεῖστα ἀγόμενος καὶ ἐς Εὐρώπην διαβάς, τῶν μετὰ Χαλίλεω πρότερον κατὰ τὴν Χερρόνησον πρὸς Ἕλληνας διενεχθέντων ἐναγόντων τε καὶ ἐξηγουμένων αὐτῷ τὴν διάβασιν, ὡς ἡ Εὐρώπη εἴη τε χώρα περικαλλὴς καὶ εὐχερὴς χειρώσασθαι ὑπὸ Σουλαϊμάνεω βασιλέως. Ἐντεῦθεν διαβιβάσας στρατὸν οὐ πολὺν τήν τε Χερρόνησον ληΐζεσθαι, καὶ τὸ πρότερον ἔτι φρούριον καὶ Μάδυτον κατασχόντες καὶ ἄλλ' ἄττα πολίσματα κατὰ τὴν Χερρόνησον, ἐπέδραμόν τε τὴν Θρᾴκην ἔστε ἐπὶ Τέαρον τὸν ποταμόν, καὶ τά τε ἀνδράποδα ἐς τὴν Ἀσίαν διεβίβαζον. Καὶ οἱ ἐν τῇ Ἀσίᾳ Τούρκων, ὅσοι ἐπυνθάνοντο ταῦτα, αὐτίκα ἐς τὴν Εὐρώπην παρὰ Σουλαϊμάνην διέβαινον, καὶ συνελέγοντο εἰς τὴν Χερρόνησον οὐκ ὀλίγοι· ἔνθα δὴ καὶ ἐπὶ γεωργίαν τῶν ἀπὸ τῆς [1.23] Ἀσίας φειδοῖ τῆς ἑαυτῶν χώρας ἐτράποντο. Ὕστερον μέντοι ὁ Ἑλλήνων βασιλεὺς διαπρεσβευσάμενος σπονδάς τε ἐποιήσατο πρὸς Σουλαϊμάνην τὸν Ὀρχάνεω, καὶ ἐνῆγεν ἐπὶ τοὺς Τριβαλλούς, ἐφ' ᾧ τε αὐτοὺς ξένους τε καὶ φίλους εἶναι ἀλλήλοις καὶ τὸν πρὸς τοὺς Τριβαλλοὺς πόλεμον συνδιαφέρειν ἅμα ἀμφοτέρους. Ἔνιοι μὲν οὖν φασιν, ὡς ἔτι περιόντος Ὀρχάνεω ἐν τῇ Ἀσίᾳ τὸν παῖδα αὐτοῦ Σουλαϊμάνην ἐς τὴν Εὐρώπην διαβῆναι μεταπεμπομένου ἐπὶ τοὺς Τριβαλλοὺς τοῦ τῶν Ἑλλήνων βασιλέως.

29 Τοὺς μέντοι Τριβαλλῶν ἡγεμόνας ὧδε ἐλθεῖν ἐπὶ τὰ τῆς

Orhan died after reigning for [. . .] years,[76] and left behind two sons, Süleyman and Murad. Süleyman, the son of Orhan, succeeded to the throne and immediately started waging war against the Greeks.[77] He took as many captives as he could from Greek territory into Asia, and he also crossed over into Europe. The followers of Halil[78] who had earlier fallen out with the Greeks in the Chersonese led him there and told him all about the crossing, saying that Europe was a very beautiful land and would easily fall to Sultan Süleyman. He transported a small army there and plundered the Chersonese. They took the fort that they had held previously[79] along with Madytos and some other towns in the Chersonese. Then they raided in Thrace as far as the river Tearos, and transported their captives to Asia. All the Turks in Asia who learned about this immediately crossed over into Europe to join Süleyman, and many of them gathered in the Chersonese. Here they turned to farming, sparing the lands in Asia, their own country.[80] Later on the king of the Greeks sent envoys and made a treaty with Süleyman, the son of Orhan, urging him against the Serbs. The terms were that they would be friends and allies to each other and provide mutual support in the war against the Serbs. Some even say that, while he was still alive in Asia, Orhan had sent his son Süleyman to cross over into Europe when the king of the Greeks summoned him against the Serbs.[81] 28

I have learned that the rulers of the Serbs became 29

Εὐρώπης πράγματα ἐπυθόμεθα. Στέπανος ἐγένετο βασιλεὺς Τριβαλλῶν, ὃς ὁρμώμενος ἦν ἀπὸ τῆς ἐς τὸν Ἰόνιον χώρας, τὰ περὶ Ἐπίδαμνον καταστρεψάμενος, καὶ ἐς τὴν Μακεδονίαν ἠλάσατο, καὶ ἐς τὴν τῶν Σκοπίων τὰ βασίλεια ἐποιήσατο. Εἶεν δ' ἂν οὗτοι, ὅσα γε ἔξεστι τεκμαίρεσθαι, ὅθεν προαγαγεῖν ἐπὶ τὴν τῆς Εὐρώπης ἡγεμονίαν ἀφίκοντο, Ἰλλυριῶν γένος, ἀπὸ τῆς πρὸς ἑσπέραν τῆς ἐς τὸν Ἰόνιον χώρας προελθόντες ἐπὶ τὴν τῶν Σκοπίων πόλιν, τῇ τε φωνῇ παραπλησίᾳ χρώμενοι ἐκείνοις, καὶ γένος δὲ ἐκεῖνο τῶν Ἰλλυριῶν μέγα τε καὶ ἐπὶ πλεῖστον διῆκον τοῦ Ἰονίου πελάγους ἔστε ἐπὶ Ἑνετούς, ὡς ἂν ἔχειν οὐ χαλεπῶς τεκμαίρεσθαι ἀπ' ἐκείνων δὲ τότε ἀνὰ τὴν Εὐρώπην σκεδασθέντας ἀχθῆναι. Φωνῇ τε γὰρ ἀμφότεροι τῇ αὐτῇ χρῶνται ἔτι καὶ νῦν, καὶ ἤθεσι τοῖς αὐτοῖς καὶ διαίτῃ, ὥστε οὐκ ὀρθῶς ἂν λέγοιεν οἱ γνώμην ἀποδεικνύμενοι περὶ Ἰλλυριῶν, ὡς εἴησαν οἱ [1.24] νῦν Ἀλβανοί. Ἀρχὴν δ' ἐγὼ οὐδὲ προσίεμαι τὸν λόγον, ὡς εἴησαν Ἰλλυριῶν γένος οἱ Ἀλβανοί. Ὡς μὲν οὖν ἀπ' Ἐπιδάμνου καὶ οὗτοι ὥρμηντο ἐς τὴν πρὸς ἕω χώραν τῆς Εὐρώπης ἐπὶ Θετταλίαν τε ἀφικόμενοι καὶ ἐπὶ Αἰτωλίαν καὶ Ἀκαρνανίαν, οὐκ ὀλίγα ἄττα τῆς Μακεδονίας χωρία ὑφ' αὑτοῖς πεποιημένοι ᾤκουν, οἶδά τε αὐτὸς ἐπιστάμενος, ἀπὸ πολλῶν τεκμαιρόμενος, καὶ πολλῶν δὴ ἀκήκοα. Εἴτε μὲν οὖν ἀπὸ Ἰαπυγίας, ὡς ἔνιοί φασιν, ἐς Ἐπίδαμνον διαβάντες ἐπὶ τὴν χώραν, ἣν ὑπηγάγοντο σφίσιν, ἄλλος ἄλλῃ ἀφίκοντο, εἴτε αὐτοῦ περὶ Ἐπίδαμνον τὴν ἀρχὴν Ἰλλυριῶν ὅμοροι προϊόντες κατὰ βραχὺ κατέσχον τὴν πρὸς ἕω τῆς Ἐπιδάμνου χώραν, οὐκ ἔχω, ὅπῃ συμβάλλωμαι ἀσφαλῶς. Ἧι μὲν

involved in the affairs of Europe in the following way. Stefan[82] became king of the Serbs and advanced from his territory by the Adriatic Sea. He conquered the area around Durrës, pushed into Macedonia, and made Skopje his royal capital.[83] As far as one may infer, the Serbs may well be an Illyrian people [i.e., the Slavs], given where they came from before they acquired dominion over Europe.[84] They thus came to Skopje from the lands to the west, by the Adriatic Sea, and speak a language similar to that of the Illyrians. The Illyrian people is populous and has spread far and wide along the Adriatic Sea, as far as the Venetians. It would, then, not be difficult to infer that it was from them that the Serbs came to be dispersed across Europe. Even today both of them speak the same language and have the same customs and way of life, so that those who venture an opinion about the Illyrians would be wrong were they to say that they are the present-day Albanians. I do not accept the premise of the argument, that the Albanians are an Illyrian [i.e., Slavic] people. I know perfectly well that they too came out of Durrës and moved to the more eastern lands of Europe, reaching Thessaly, Aitolia, and Akarnania, and that they inhabited many regions of Macedonia after they had conquered them. I have inferred this from much evidence and heard it from many people. But whether they originally came to Durrës from Apulia, as some say, after they had crossed to the territory which they subjected to themselves, each in a different place; or whether they were originally neighbors of the Illyrians right there, around Durrës, and set out from there, gradually taking over the lands to the east of Durrës, I cannot conclude with certainty. What I

ἄμφω τὼ γένεε τούτω, Τριβαλλοί τε καὶ Ἀλβανοί, ἀπὸ τῆς ἐς τὸν Ἰόνιον χώρας ὡρμημένω, τὸ μὲν πρὸς ἕω τῆς Εὐρώπης ἰόντες τὴν ταύτῃ χώραν ᾤκησαν καὶ οὐκ ὀλίγα σφίσιν ἐς τὴν ἀρχὴν ὑπηγάγοντο, τὸ δὲ πρὸς ἑσπέραν[7] ὡρμημένον σχεδὸν ἔστε Εὔξεινον πόντον ἀφίκοντο καὶ ἐπὶ Ἴστρον ἄχρι Θετταλίας ἐλάσαντες, ὧδέ μοι εἰρήσεται.

30 Ὁ βασιλεὺς ἀπὸ τῆς τῶν Σκοπίων πόλεως ὡρμημένος, ἔχων μεθ' ἑαυτοῦ ἄνδρας τε τὰ ἐς πόλεμον ἀγαθοὺς καὶ στρατιὰν οὐ φαύλην, πρῶτα μὲν τὰ περὶ Καστορίαν κατεστρέψατο χωρία, καὶ [1.25] ἐπὶ Μακεδονίαν ἐλάσας, πλὴν Θέρμης τὰ ἄλλα ὑφ' αὑτῷ ποιησάμενος, ἐπὶ Σάβαν τε προελαύνων καὶ ἐπὶ τὰ κατὰ τὸν Ἴστρον χωρία, μεγάλα ἀπεδείκνυτο ἔργα, καὶ τήν τε χώραν ταύτῃ σύμπασαν καταστρεψάμενος εἶχε. Τάξας δὲ ἀνὰ τὴν Εὐρώπην τῶν ὑποχειρίων ἄλλους ἄλλῃ ἐπὶ μέγα τε ἐχώρει δυνάμεως, καὶ ἐπὶ Ἕλληνας ἤλαυνε τὴν ἀρχὴν ἀφαιρησόμενος, καὶ πολλαχῇ ἐπὶ τὰ κατὰ τὸ Βυζάντιον χωρία στρατὸν ἐπαφεὶς ἀπέδραμέ τε καὶ ἀνεχώρει. Καὶ ἦν ἐπὶ τούτου τὰ Ἑλλήνων πράγματα προσδόκιμα ἐπὶ τὸν ἔσχατον ἀφίξεσθαι κίνδυνον, ὑπὸ σφῶν τε αὐτῶν περιτρεπόμενα κατὰ τὴν τῆς βασιλείας ῥᾳστώνην, ἐπὶ τὸ ἀκόλαστον καὶ ἀνειμένον τῆς διαίτης Ἀνδρονίκου, τοῦ πρεσβυτέρου βασιλέως φημί, τετραμμένου ταύτῃ. Ἐς μάχην μὲν οὖν τὸ Ἑλληνικὸν γένος ἀπελθεῖν καὶ διαπειρᾶσθαι γνώμην οὐκ ἐποιεῖτο, σώζειν μέντοι τὰ τείχη τρόπῳ, ὅτῳ ἂν δύναιντο, ἀσφαλεστάτῳ.

31 Ἤλασε μὲν οὖν καὶ ἐπὶ Αἰτωλίαν, καὶ Ἰωαννίνων τὴν πόλιν εἷλε. Καὶ τὰ μὲν κατὰ τὴν Μακεδονίαν περὶ Ἀξιὸν

will relate is how both of these peoples, the Serbs and the Albanians, set out from the lands by the Adriatic Sea, and how the latter went to the eastern parts of Europe, settled that land, and conquered a considerable realm for themselves, while the former pushed to the west[85] so that they almost reached the Black Sea, and advanced from the Danube all the way to Thessaly.

The king [Stefan Dušan] set out from the city of Skopje, 30
accompanied by his warriors and a large army. First he subjugated the region around Kastoria and then advanced into Macedonia, conquering all of it except for Thessalonike.[86] He pushed on to the Sava River and the region by the Danube, performing great deeds, and he conquered that entire land. After appointing other men among his subordinates to govern Europe, he became very powerful. He also attacked the Greeks in order to take over their realm, often sending armies against the areas near Byzantion,[87] and then withdrawing and racing back home. At this time the affairs of the Greeks seemed to have reached a state of ultimate peril, as they were undermining themselves by the indolence of their royalty. I am referring to the licentious and dissolute way of life to which the elder king Andronikos [II] had turned.[88] So the Greek people made a decision not to go out and attempt battle, but instead decided that the surest way to keep safe, whatever this might mean, was behind their walls.

Stefan raided into Aitolia and captured the city of Ioan- 31
nina.[89] He entrusted the region around the Axios River in

ποταμὸν Ζάρκῳ ἐπέτρεψεν, ἀνδρὶ ἐς τὰ πρῶτα τιμῆς ἀνήκοντι παρ' ἑαυτῷ, τὰ δὲ ἀπὸ Φερρῶν ἔστε ἐπὶ Ἀξιὸν ποταμὸν Μπογδάνῳ ἀνδρὶ ἀγαθῷ καὶ τὰ ἐς πόλεμον οὐκ ἀδοκίμῳ, τὰ δὲ ἀπὸ Φερρῶν ἔστε ἐπὶ Ἴστρον Κράλῃ τε καὶ Οὐγγλέσῃ τοῖν ἀδελφοῖν, ὧν θάτερος μὲν οἰνοχόος ἦν τοῦ βασιλέως, ὁ δὲ ἕτερος ἱπποκόμος. Τὰ μέντοι περὶ τὸν Ἴστρον Βούλκῳ τῷ Ἐλεαζάρῳ τοῦ Πράγκου ἐπέτρεψε, καὶ τὰ ἀμφὶ τὴν Τρίκκην καὶ Καστορίαν Νικολάῳ τῷ ζουπάνῳ, καὶ τὰ [1.26] περὶ Αἰτωλίαν Πρεαλούπῃ. Τὰ δὲ περὶ Ὀχρίδα τε καὶ Πριλαπαίων χώραν οὕτω καλουμένην ἐπέτρεψε Μλαδένῃ εὐθύνειν, ἀνδρὶ οὐκ ἀγεννεῖ. Τούτοις μὲν δὴ ἐπυθόμεθα ἐπιτετράφθαι τὰ κατὰ τὴν Εὐρώπην ὑπὸ Στεπάνεω τοῦ βασιλέως.

32 Ἐπεὶ δὲ ἐτελεύτησε βασιλεύς, ἕκαστος, ἣν κατεῖχε χώραν ἐπιτετραμμένος, ἦρχόν τε καὶ ἀλλήλοις εἰρήνην συνθέμενοι σφῶν μὲν αὐτῶν τοι ἀπείχοντο, τοῖς δὲ Ἕλλησιν, ὡς ἑκάστῳ προεχώρει, ἐπετίθεντό τε καὶ ἐπολέμουν. Μιχαῆλον μέντοι τὸν Μυσῶν ἡγεμόνα, ἀπὸ τὰ κάτω τοῦ Ἴστρου ἐπινεμόμενον ἐπὶ Εὔξεινον πόντον καὶ τὰ βασίλεια ἐν Τρινάβῳ ποιησάμενον, παλαιότερον γενόμενον Στεπάνεω, ἀναπυνθανόμενος εὑρίσκω, ὡς ταύτῃ Βουλγάρους μὲν τούτους, οὓς γε Μυσοὺς ὀνομάζομεν, Σέρβους δὲ ἐκείνους, οὓς καὶ Τριβαλλούς, διακεκρίσθαι ἀπ' ἀλλήλων ἐς τοὔνομα ξυνηνέχθη ἀπὸ τούτου. Τούτω δὲ ἄμφω τὼ γένεε ὡς παντάπασιν ἑτέρω ὄντε ἀλλήλων, καὶ διεστηκότε νομίζεσθαι. Ὡς μὲν ἕκαστος τούτων τήν τε ἀρχὴν ἀφήρηντο ὑπὸ τῶν βαρβάρων καὶ αὐτοί τε ἀπώλοντο, ἐς τὸ πρόσω τοῦ λόγου ἰόντι εἰρήσεταί μοι.

Macedonia to Žarko, a man he held in the highest honor;[90] the region from Serres to the Axios River to Bogdan, a good man and an experienced warrior;[91] and the region from Serres to the Danube to two brothers, the Kral and Uglješa, the former being the royal wine-pourer, the latter his groom.[92] As for the lands by the Danube, he entrusted them to Vuk Lazar, the son of Branko;[93] the area around Trikala and Kastoria to the *župan* Nikola;[94] and those in Aitolia to Preljub.[95] The governance of the region around Ohrid and the land called Prilep he entrusted to Mladen, a noble man.[96] It was to these men, we have ascertained, that King Stefan entrusted his European territories.

When the king {Stefan} died,[97] each man remained in 32
command of the territory that had been entrusted to him, and they agreed on a peace with each other and so avoided hostilities.[98] But they continually attacked the Greeks and fought a war against them, each one of them in whatever way he could. As for Mihail, the ruler of the Bulgarians who lived long before Stefan, he occupied the territory south of the Danube and toward the Black Sea, and established his royal court at Tărnovo.[99] I have discovered from my inquiries that this was how the Bulgarians, whom we call Mysians, and the Serbs, whom we call Triballians, came to be distinguished from each other with regard to their names from then on. These two peoples are regarded as entirely different from each other and separate. But how each of them was stripped of his realm by the barbarians and how they were themselves defeated, my narrative will later reveal.

33 Σουλαϊμάνης μὲν οὖν ἐπεί τε τὰ κατὰ τὴν Χερρόνησον πολίσματα πλὴν Καλλιουπόλεως κατέσχε τε καὶ ἐνηυλίζετο, ὥστε ἔχειν ὁρμώμενος ἀπὸ τούτων τὰ ἐπὶ τῆς Θρᾴκης χωρία ἐλαύνων καταστρέφεσθαι, ὡς τοῖς Ἕλλησιν εἰρήνην ἐποιήσατο, ἐστράτευεν [1.27] ἐπὶ Κράλην τε καὶ Οὐγγλέσην τοὺς Τριβαλλῶν ἡγεμόνας, οἳ δὴ τοῖς Ἕλλησιν ἐπετίθεντο καὶ χαλεποὶ ἦσαν διὰ τὸ μηδέποτε ἡσυχίαν ἄγειν, ἀλλ' ἀεὶ κακῶς ποιεῖν πολεμοῦντας τοῖς Ἕλλησιν. Οὗτοι μὲν οὖν ὡς ἐπύθοντο Σουλαϊμάνην διαβάντα ἐς τὴν Εὐρώπην δῃοῦν τε ἐπὶ τῇ Ἑλληνικῇ τὴν σφετέραν αὐτῶν χώραν καὶ διαρπάζειν μηδενὸς φειδόμενον, ἐστρατεύοντο ἐπὶ τοὺς Τούρκους, καὶ συμβαλόντες μάχῃ τε ἐκράτησαν καὶ διέφθειρον οὐκ ὀλίγους ἐν τῇ ἐπιδρομῇ. Μετὰ δὲ ταῦτα, ὡς ᾔσθοντο ἤδη τὰ Τούρκων πράγματα ταχὺ ἐπὶ μέγα προχωροῦντα δυνάμεως, καὶ τοὺς ἀπὸ Ἀσίας Τούρκους αἰεὶ διαβαίνοντας προσγίνεσθαι αὐτῷ, ὥστε καὶ ἐς πολιορκίαν τῶν κατὰ τὴν Εὐρώπην πόλεων καθίστασθαι, καὶ προϊόντας ἐπὶ τὴν μεσόγαιον τῆς Θρᾴκης, συνελέγοντό τε στράτευμα ἀμφότεροι. Οὐγγλέσης μὲν οὖν ὥρμητο ἀπὸ Φερρῶν ἐπὶ τοὺς Τούρκους, ἐν αἷς τὰ βασίλεια ἦν αὐτῷ· Κράλης τε ἅμα αὐτῷ ὁ ἀδελφὸς στράτευμα ἔχων ἀπὸ τῆς μεσογαίου τῆς Θρᾴκης συνῄει τῷ ἀδελφῷ ὡς στρατευσόμενοι ἅμα ἐπὶ τοὺς Τούρκους.

34 Ὁ μὲν οὖν Σουλαϊμάνης ἔτυχε πολιορκῶν πόλισμά τε παρὰ Τέαρον ποταμόν, διέχον ἀπὸ Ἀδριανουπόλεως σταδίους ὡσεὶ ἑβδομήκοντα, καὶ σκηνὰς μὲν αὐτοῦ οὐκ ὀλίγας ἀπὸ πίλων αἰγῶν ἐπήξατο, ἐν αἷς δὴ οἱ κατὰ τὴν Ἀσίαν Σκύθαι τε οἱ νομάδες καὶ Τούρκων οἱ πρὸς τόνδε τὸν βίον

After Süleyman acquired and then established himself in the towns of the Chersonese, except for Gallipoli, he used them as a base for pushing into the region of Thrace and subjugating it. As he had made peace with the Greeks, he marched out against the Kral and Uglješa, the rulers of the Serbs,[100] who were attacking the Greeks and were causing problems because they would never leave them alone. They were always up to no good, making war against the Greeks. When the Kral and Uglješa learned that Süleyman had crossed over into Europe and was ravaging their own lands in accordance with the Greek treaty,[101] and was plundering them, sparing no one, they marched out against the Turks and joined them in battle. They prevailed and slaughtered many in their assault.[102] After that, when they realized how the power of the Turks was rapidly growing and that Turks from Asia were constantly crossing over to join Süleyman, to the point where they could besiege cities in Europe, and that they were advancing into the interior of Thrace, both men assembled their armies. Uglješa advanced against the Turks from Serres, where he had his royal court, while his brother the Kral, who had an army from the Thracian interior, joined his brother so that they could campaign together against the Turks. 33

Süleyman happened to be besieging a town by the Tearos River, about seventy stades distant from Adrianople. He had pitched many tents there made of goat skins, in which the nomadic Skythians of Asia as well as the Turks who have adopted that way of life are accustomed to camp. He was 34

τετραμμένοι σκηνοῦν εἰώθασι, καὶ ἐπολιόρκει τὸ χωρίον προσέχων ἐντεταμένως. [1.28] Διατρίβοντα δὲ αὐτὸν λέγεται, ὡς τάχιστα ἐπύθετο ἐπιόντας οἱ τοὺς πολεμίους, λαβεῖν τε ἐπιλεξάμενον ἄνδρας ἐς ὀκτακοσίους τῶν ἀμφ' αὐτὸν ἀρίστων, καὶ νυκτὸς ἐπελάσαντα ἐς τὸ πολεμίων στρατόπεδον καταδυόμενον, ὡς ἤδη ἡ ἠὼς ὑπέφαινε, καὶ οὔτε φυλακὰς ἔχοντας τοὺς πολεμίους ἑώρα αὐτούς τε τὰ πολλὰ παρὰ Τέαρον ποταμόν, ὡς ὕδωρ κάλλιστόν τε παρέχεται πιεῖν καὶ ὑγιεινότατον, θέρους δὲ ἦν ὥρα, ὀλιγώρως τε τῶν ὅπλων σφίσιν αὐτοῖς καὶ τῶν ἵππων ἔχοντας, οἷα τοὺς πολεμίους ἐν οὐδενὶ λόγῳ ποιουμένους, ἐπὶ ῥᾳστώνην τετραμμένους, κατὰ Κερμιανὸν[8] χῶρον ἐπεισπεσεῖν τε ἄφνω σὺν τοῖς ὀκτακοσίοις καὶ διαφθεῖραι σύμπαντα τὸν στρατὸν κτείνοντας ἀφειδέστατα, ὥστε τοὺς πλείονας αὐτῶν πεσεῖν ἐς τὸν ποταμόν, καὶ ἐν ἀπορίᾳ εἴχοντο, ὅποι τράπωνται γενόμενοι, καὶ ταύτῃ διαφθαρῆναι. Ἔνθα ὅ τε Οὐγγλέσης ἀπώλετο καὶ ὁ Κράλης ὁ ἀδελφὸς αὐτοῦ ἐν ταύτῃ τῇ μάχῃ. Ὅτῳ δ' ἂν τρόπῳ διεφθάρη, οὐκ ᾔδει οὐδείς, ὥστε οἴεσθαι τοὺς προσήκοντας αὐτῷ περιεῖναι ἔτι αὐτὸν ἐπὶ πολύν τινα χρόνον.

Ὡς οὖν ταύτην τὴν νίκην εὐκλεῆ καὶ περιφανῆ ἀνείλετο Σουλαϊμάνης, τό τε πόλισμα, ὃ ἐπολιόρκει πρότερον, παρεστήσατο, καὶ Ὀρεστιάδα τὴν Ἀδριανούπολιν καλουμένην ἐλαύνων ἐπολιόρκει. Ἔτυχε δὲ τήν τε πόλιν περὶ ἀμητὸν πολιορκῶν, καὶ προσβάλλων τῷ τείχει θαμὰ οὐκ ἀνίει. Ἐν τούτῳ δὲ ὄντος Σουλαϊμάνεω τυχεῖν νεανίαν λέγουσι τῶν ἐν τῇ πόλει κατὰ ὀπήν τινα ἀπὸ τῆς [1.29] πόλεως φέρουσαν ἔξω λάθρᾳ τε ἐξιόντα νυκτὸς ἀμῶντα πυροὺς κατὰ

vigorously pressing the siege of the place. Although he was busy with this, it is said that as soon as he learned the enemy was coming against him, he took eight hundred men picked from the best of those who were with him and marched out at night. Creeping up to the enemy camp just as dawn was breaking, he observed that the enemy had not posted sentries. As it was summertime, most of them were by the river Tearos, which provides the purest and healthiest drinking water, and he saw that they were careless with their weapons and horses and had become lazy, because they held their opponents in low esteem. So there, at a place called Černomen, Süleyman and his eight hundred suddenly attacked the Serbs and destroyed the entire army, slaughtering them mercilessly. Most of them fell into the river and, not knowing which way to turn, died there. Uglješa perished in this battle, as did his brother the Kral. No one knew exactly how he died, however, so that his followers thought that he had survived for some time thereafter.[103]

After Süleyman had won this glorious and famous vic- 35
tory, the city that he had been besieging earlier surrendered, and he then pressed forward to besiege Orestias, which is called Adrianople. He happened to besiege the city at harvest time. He did not let up in his continual attacks on the walls but could not break them. While Süleyman was in this predicament, they say that a young man of the city snuck out at night through an opening that led to the outside,

τὴν ὀπὴν ταύτην διαφορεῖν ἐς τὴν πόλιν, καὶ τοῦτο συνεχῶς ποιοῦντα ὀφθῆναι ὑπό τινος τῶν ἐν τῷ στρατοπέδῳ. Ἰδόντα δὲ τὸν Τοῦρκον, ᾗ εἰσῄει ὁ νεανίας, ἐφεπόμενον κατόπιν γενέσθαι κατὰ τὴν ὀπήν, πειραθῆναί τε αὐτῆς, καὶ εἰσιόντα ἐς τὴν πόλιν αὖθις ἐς τὸ στρατόπεδον γενέσθαι, καὶ ἀφικόμενον παρὰ Σουλαϊμάνην ἐξειπεῖν τε τὴν εἴσοδον καὶ αὐτὸν αὐτίκα ἐξηγεῖσθαι. Πειραθέντα δὲ τῆς εἰσόδου τὸν ἡγεμόνα καταλαβεῖν τε τὴν πόλιν ταύτῃ καὶ ὑφ' αὑτῷ ποιήσασθαι. Μετὰ δὲ ταῦτα εἰς Φιλιππόπολιν ἐλαύνοντα ἑλεῖν τε καὶ ταύτην τὴν πόλιν καὶ παραστήσασθαι ὁμολογίᾳ. Λέγεται δὲ γενέσθαι τούτῳ τῷ βασιλεῖ ἄνδρα ἐπὶ στρατηγίας ἐπισημότατόν τε καὶ ἐξηγεῖσθαι δεινότατον ἐπὶ πόλεμόν τε καὶ ἐπιδρομάς. Καὶ οἱ μὲν λέγουσιν αὐτὸν τὰ πλείω ἀποδεικνύμενον πάμπολυ ταχύ τε καὶ παραχρῆμα ἐπιδεδωκέναι.

36 Νοσήσαντος δὲ Σουλαϊμάνεω καὶ ἐπὶ Ἀσίαν ἐπειγομένου τὴν νόσον οἱ χαλεπωτέραν γενομένην ἀπενέγκαι ἐκ τοῦ βίου αὐτόν. Τελευτῶντα δὲ ἐπιτεῖλαι τοῖς ἀμφ' αὐτὸν θάψαι τε τὸ σῶμα αὐτοῦ ταύτῃ, κατὰ τὸν τῆς Χερρονήσου ἰσθμόν, ᾗ δὴ καὶ συνέβη πρότερον τελευτήσαντα τὸν παῖδα αὐτοῦ θάψαι τε μεγαλοπρεπῶς καὶ ἐξήνεγκε· καὶ τῷ σήματι ταξάμενος φόρους, ὥστε παννυχίᾳ χρῆσθαι τοὺς ἱερεῖς αὐτῶν ἐπὶ τῷ μνήματι, αὐτόν τε ἐκέλευσεν αὐτοῦ θάψαι ἅμα τῷ παιδὶ αὐτοῦ.

37 Ἐπεί τε δὲ αὐτοῦ ἐτελεύτησεν, Ἀμουράτης ὁ Ὀρχάνεω παῖς, Σουλαϊμάνεω δὲ ἀδελφός, ὡς ἐπύθετό οἱ αὐτὸν τελευτήσαντα, τούς τε νεήλυδας καὶ ἄλλους τοὺς τῶν θυρῶν λαβὼν καὶ ἐς {1.30} τὴν Εὐρώπην διαβὰς παρέλαβε τὸ

harvested some grain, and took it back into the city through that opening; and he was seen doing this repeatedly by someone in the camp. The Turk who saw where the young man entered, followed him to the opening, tried it out, and, after going into the city, returned to the camp. He came before Süleyman, told him about the entrance, and led him there straightaway. His ruler tried out the entrance, captured the city in this way, and subjected it to himself.[104] After this he pressed forward to Philippopolis and took possession of this city too through a negotiated surrender.[105] But there is said to have been a man with this sultan who was a most remarkable military strategist and an extraordinary leader in battle and during assaults. Some say that he displayed extreme and almost instantaneous speed in the execution of most matters to which he gave his attention.[106]

Süleyman fell ill and, when he was rushed back to Asia, 36
his illness became worse and he died. When he was dying, he ordered his attendants to bury his body in the place at the isthmos of the Chersonese[107] where he had previously buried with appropriate magnificence the body of his own son. And this was done. He also imposed taxes for the tomb so that their priests would conduct all-night services at the monument, and he ordered that he be buried there together with his son.[108]

When Süleyman died, as soon as Murad, who was Orhan's 37
son and Süleyman's brother, learned of his death, he took the janissaries and the other men of the Porte, crossed over into Europe, and took command of the entire army. He

στράτευμα αὐτοῦ ἅπαν, καὶ ἐπὶ Ἀδριανούπολιν ἐλάσας τὰ βασίλειά οἱ αὐτοῦ ἐποιήσατο. Καὶ ἐντεῦθεν ὁρμώμενος ἐληΐζετο τὴν τῆς Μακεδονίας μεσόγαιον χώραν, καὶ ἀνδράποδα συχνὰ ἀγόμενος ἐπλούτιζε τοὺς μεθ' ἑαυτοῦ στρατιώτας, καὶ Τούρκων ὅσοι ἐπ' ἐλπίδι τοῦ κερδᾶναι ὁτιοῦν εἵποντο αὐτῷ, ἐδωρεῖτο ἀνδραπόδοις τε καὶ ὑποζυγίοις, ἃ ἡλίσκετο ἀπὸ Μυσῶν τε καὶ Ἑλλήνων. Λέγεται μέντοι καὶ τόδε, ὡς Σουλαϊμάνης, ἐπεί τε ᾔσθετο τῆς Τριβαλλῶν καὶ Μυσῶν δυνάμεως ἐπ' αὐτὸν ἀθροιζομένης, καὶ ἔπραττεν, ὥστε δοθῆναί οἱ ἑξάκις μυρίας δραχμάς, ὥστε ἀποδοῦναι αὐτοῖς, ὅσα τῶν πολισμάτων προσηγάγετό οἱ, καὶ αὐτὸν οἴχεσθαι ἀπαλλαττόμενον ἐς τὴν Ἀσίαν ἀποχωρήσειν τηνικαῦτα πολιορκοῦντα τὰ ἐν Θρᾴκῃ πολίσματα Ἑλλήνων. Ὡς οὖν πυθόμενοι οἱ Ἕλληνες ἀπεδέχοντό τε καὶ ἕτοιμοι ἦσαν ἐπὶ τούτοις σπένδεσθαι, ξυνενεχθῆναι σεισμόν τε μέγαν καὶ τὰ τείχη τῶν πόλεων διαρραγῆναι, ὥστε αὐτοὺς ἑλεῖν ἀπὸ τούτου τὰ πλέω, οἷς ἐπήλαυνον πολιορκοῦντες. Καὶ ἑλόντας παρὰ τῶν Ἑλλήνων τὰ πολίσματα ἔχεσθαι τοῦ λοιποῦ τῆς Εὐρώπης, μηδέν τι τοιοῦτον ἔτι προσιεμένους.

38 Μετὰ δὲ ταῦτα ἤλαυνεν ἐπὶ Μυσοὺς καὶ ἐπὶ Τριβαλλούς. Τὸ δὲ γένος τοῦτο παλαιότατόν τε καὶ μέγιστον τῶν κατὰ τὴν οἰκουμένην ἐθνῶν, εἴτε ἀπὸ Ἰλλυριῶν μοίρας ἀπεσχισμένον ταύτην ᾤκησε τὴν χώραν, εἴτε, ὡς ἔνιοι, ἀπὸ τῆς πέραν τοῦ Ἴστρου [1.31] ἐπ' ἐσχάτων τῆς Εὐρώπης, ἀπό τε Κροατίας καὶ Προυσίων τῶν ἐς τὸν ἀρκτῷον ὠκεανὸν καὶ Σαρματίας τῆς νῦν οὕτω Ῥωσίας καλουμένης ἔστε ἐπὶ χώραν τὴν διὰ τὸ ψῦχος ἀοίκητον, κἀκεῖθεν

traveled to Adrianople and established his royal court there.[109] Using it as his base, he plundered the interior of Macedonia, took many slaves, and enriched his soldiers. He made gifts of slaves and pack animals, which he had seized from the Bulgarians and the Greeks, to all the Turks who followed him in the hopes of personal gain. It is also said that when Süleyman realized the Serbs and Bulgarians were assembling against him in force, he negotiated [with the Greeks] and proposed that in exchange for sixty thousand drachmas he would give back to them the towns that he had appropriated and would leave and go back to Asia, and lift the ongoing sieges of the Greek towns in Thrace. When the Greeks learned this they accepted, and were prepared to make a treaty on these terms. But a major earthquake occurred and demolished the walls of the cities, so that in consequence the Turks captured most of those that they had under siege. Once they took these towns from the Greeks they were henceforth well established in Europe, and never made such an offer again.[110]

After this Murad marched against the Bulgarians and the 38
Serbs. This race [i.e., the Slavs] is the most ancient and largest among all the peoples in the world. They either broke away from the Illyrian tribe and settled in this land or, as some claim, came from beyond the Danube and the farthest ends of Europe, namely from Croatia[111] and the territory of the Prussians, by the Arctic Ocean and by Sarmatia (now called Russia), as far as the land that is uninhabitable on

ὡρμημένοι καὶ τόν τε Ἴστρον διαβάντες ἐπὶ τὴν ἐς τὸν Ἰόνιον χώραν ἀφίκοντο καὶ ταύτῃ ἐπὶ πολὺ ἐπὶ Ἑνετοὺς διήκουσαν καταστρεψάμενοι ᾤκησαν, εἴτε δὴ τοὐναντίον μᾶλλον εἰπεῖν ἄμεινον, ὡς ἐντεῦθεν ἀπὸ τῆς ἐς τὸν Ἰόνιον χώρας ὡρμημένοι καὶ Ἴστρον διαβάντες ἐπέκεινα ἐγένοντο τῆς οἰκουμένης, οὐκ ἂν δὴ λεγόμενον ἀσφαλῶς λέγοιτο ὑφ' ἡμῶν. Τοσόνδε μέντοι ἐπίσταμαι, ὡς τοῖς ὀνόμασι ταῦτα δὴ τὰ γένη διεστηκότα ἀλλήλων ἤθεσι μὲν οὐκέτι, γλώττῃ δὲ καὶ φωνῇ τῇ αὐτῇ χρώμενοι κατάδηλοί εἰσιν ἔτι καὶ νῦν. Ὡς μέντοι διέσπαρται ἀνὰ τὴν Εὐρώπην, πολλαχῇ ᾤκησαν, ἄλλῃ τε δὴ καὶ ἔν τινι τῆς Πελοποννήσου χώρας τε τῆς Λακωνικῆς ἐς τὸ Ταΰγετον ὄρος καὶ ἐς τὸ Ταίναρον ᾠκημένον. Ὧι δὴ καὶ ἀπὸ Δακίας ἐπὶ Πίνδον τὸ ἐς Θετταλίαν καθῆκον ἐνοικῆσαν ἔθνος. Βλάχοι δὲ ἀμφότεροι ὀνομάζονται· καὶ οὐκ ἂν δὴ ἔχω διεξιέναι, ὁποτέρους ἂν τούτων λέγοιμι ἐπὶ τοὺς ἑτέρους ἀφικέσθαι. Οὕτω δὴ κἀνταῦθα τούς τε Τριβαλλοὺς καὶ Μυσοὺς καὶ Ἰλλυριοὺς καὶ Κροατίους καὶ Πολάνους καὶ Σαρμάτας τὴν αὐτὴν ἐπίσταμαι ἱέντας φωνήν· εἰ δέοι ταύτῃ τεκμαιρόμενον λέγειν, εἴη ἂν τοῦτο τὸ γένος ταὐτό τε καὶ ἓν καὶ ὁμόφυλον ἑαυτῷ. Ὑπὸ δὲ τοῦ καιροῦ ἐς ἤθη τε διενηνεγμένα ἀλλήλων καὶ ἐπὶ χώραν ἄλλην ἀφικόμενοι ᾤκησαν. Οὐκοῦν δὴ λέγεται πρὸς οὐδένων, ὥστε σαφές τι περὶ αὐτῶν [1.32] ἔχειν ἡμᾶς ἐς ἱστορίαν ἀποδείκνυσθαι.

39 Βασίλεια μὲν ἔστιν αὐτοῖς κἀνταῦθα τοῦ Ἴστρου καὶ πέραν τε, τό τε γένος τοῦτο πολὺ μεῖζον καὶ ἐπὶ πολὺ μᾶλλον διῆκον, ὥστ' ἂν μᾶλλον ἐκεῖθεν φάναι κάλλιον

account of the cold. Advancing from there, they crossed the Danube and arrived at the lands by the Adriatic Sea before they spread out over most of it as far as the Venetians, conquering and then settling it. Or perhaps it would be better to say the exact opposite: that they moved out from the lands by the Adriatic Sea, crossed the Danube, and then went out beyond the inhabited world. But I could not state that with any certainty. This much I do know, however, that although these peoples have different names they do not have different customs, and it is quite clear that they speak the same language even now.[112] As they spread throughout Europe, they settled in many places, including some parts of Lakonia in the Peloponnese, on Mount Taygetos and at Tainaron, just as another group of this people settled from Wallachia about the Pindos range, extending down to Thessaly.[113] Both groups are called Vlachs, although I cannot provide any detailed argument for saying which of the two was first to arrive. But I know that Serbs, Bulgarians, Illyrians [here Bosnians], Croatians, Poles, and Russians speak one and the same language. So if we must draw a conclusion from this evidence, it would be that they are all one and the same people, being of the same race. But over time their customs began to deviate from each other and they settled in the different lands in which they had arrived. But nothing clear is said about them by anyone that we could present as reliable history.

The Slavs possess kingdoms both on this side of the Dan- 39
ube and beyond it, for their race is very large and very widely extended. As a result, it would be better to conclude that

παρέχον ἐπὶ τάδε ἀφικέσθαι τὸ γένος τοῦτο, καὶ οἰκῆσαι πρὸς τῇ κατὰ τὸν Ἰόνιον χώρᾳ, καὶ παρὰ τὸν Ἴστρον διαβῆναι, καὶ αὐτοῦ μᾶλλον οἰκῆσαι, ἢ ἐντεῦθεν ὡρμημένον ἐπὶ τὰ ἐκεῖ τῆς οἰκουμένης σχεδόν τι ἀοίκητα ἀφικέσθαι. Εἴτε μὲν οὖν ἀνάγκῃ τινὶ προηγμένον, εἴτε καὶ ἑκούσιον ἐπ' ἄμυναν στελλόμενον χωρὶς οὕτω ἀπ' ἀλλήλων ἀπῳκισμένον ἔτυχεν, ὡς ἔστιν ἰδεῖν, τεκμαίρεσθαι μᾶλλόν τι, ἢ διϊσχυρίζεσθαι δέοι ἄν. Ἐντεῦθεν μὲν οὖν καὶ τήν τε ἄνω Μυσίαν καὶ κάτω Μυσίαν φάναι καλῶς ἔχειν οἴονται ἔνιοι, ὡς τὴν ἄνω Μυσίαν οὐ τὴν ἐς τὰ ἄνω τοῦ Ἴστρου ἀλλὰ τὴν ἐς τὸ πέραν τοῦ Ἴστρου ᾠκημένην χώραν, τὴν δὲ κάτω Μυσίαν οὐ τὴν ἐς τὰ κάτω τοῦ Ἴστρου ἀλλὰ τὴν ἐπὶ τοῦτο τοῦ Ἴστρου χώραν, ἔστε ἐπὶ Ἰταλίαν καθήκουσαν. Τοὺς μέντοι Βουλγάρους, οὓς κάτω Μυσίαν καλοῦσιν οἱ ἄμεινον Ἑλληνικῆς ἐπαΐοντες φωνῆς, ἐπίσταμαι καθήκειν ἐπὶ τὸν Ἴστρον ἀπὸ Βιδίνης πόλεως ἔστε ἐπὶ Εὔξεινον πόντον ἐν Τρινάβῳ πόλει τὰ βασίλεια σφίσιν ἀποδεικνυμένους.

40 Τούτοις μὲν οὖν ὁπότε Ἀλέξανδρον ὁ τῆς Σερβίας κράλης, ὁ τῶν Τριβαλλῶν ἡγεμών, ἐς τὴν βασιλείαν κατέστησεν, [1.33] ἐβασίλευέ τε οὕτως, ἐς ὃ δὴ τελευτήσας κατέλιπε βασιλέα τοῦ γένους τὸν παῖδα αὐτοῦ Σούσμανον, ἐφ' ὃν δὴ ἐστρατεύετο Ἀμουράτης ὁ Ὀρχάνεω. Ἐπεὶ ἐς Τριβαλλοὺς ἐσέβαλε, καὶ μάχῃ κρατήσας αὐτῶν Φερράς τε ὑπηγάγετο πόλιν εὐδαίμονα, καὶ τὰ ἐς τὴν Ῥοδόπην χωρία καταστρεψάμενος μεγάλα ἀπεδείκνυτο ἔργα, Σαΐνῃ τε τὴν Φερρῶν ἐπιτρέψας πόλιν, ἀνδρὶ ἀγαθῷ, ἐστρατεύετο ἐπὶ Σούσμανον τὸν Μυσίας βασιλέα, καὶ συμβαλὼν

they set out from there and came here, and settled in the lands by the Adriatic Sea before crossing the Danube and also settling more there, rather than that they started out from here and arrived at those parts of the world that are virtually uninhabited.[114] Whether driven by some necessity, or motivated by choice in self-defense, they now happen to live separately from each other, as can be seen, based on the preponderance of the evidence; or, at any rate, one may reasonably assert it.[115] Therefore some think that it is appropriate to speak of upper Mysia and lower Mysia; upper Mysia being not along the upper Danube but the land that is inhabited beyond the Danube, and lower Mysia being not along the lower Danube but the land on this side of the Danube which extends as far as Italy. I know that the Bulgarians, whom those who understand the better sort of Greek call lower Mysians, inhabit the Danube area from the city of Vidin to the Black Sea, and have their royal court at the city of Tărnovo.

When the kral of Serbia, the ruler of the Triballians, es- 40
tablished Aleksandăr on the throne for them [the Bulgarians],[116] the latter reigned in this way until he died and left his son Šišman to reign over his people.[117] It was against him, then, that Murad, the son of Orhan, was campaigning. He attacked the Serbs, defeated them in battle, and captured the prosperous city of Serres.[118] He also subjugated the region by Rodope, performing great deeds. He entrusted the city of Serres to Shahin,[119] a good man, and marched against Šišman, the king of Bulgaria. He joined battle with him and

αὐτοῦ ταύτῃ ἐτρέψατό τε τοὺς Μυσούς, καὶ διέφθειρεν οὐ πολλούς, διασωθέντας ἐπὶ τὰ ἐς τὸν Ἴστρον χωρία. Διαπρεσβευσάμενος δὲ πρὸς Ἀμουράτην Σούσμανος ὁ Ἀλεξάνδρου σπονδάς τε ἐποιήσατο καὶ συμμαχίαν, ὥστε τὸν αὐτὸν ἐχθρόν τε καὶ φίλον νομίζειν, καὶ ἐπιγαμίαν ποιησάμενος θυγατέρα αὐτοῦ, κάλλει τε ὑπερφέρουσαν καὶ ἀπὸ Ἑβραΐδος, ἣν ἠγάγετο τρωθείς, γεννηθεῖσαν τῷ Ἀμουράτῃ, ἐξέδοτο μέντοι καὶ ἑτέραν τῷ Ἑλλήνων βασιλεῖ, ὃς τηνικαῦτα [τοῦ] Ἑλλήνων τὸν Καντακουζηνὸν ἀφελόμενος τὴν ἀρχὴν ἐβασίλευε γένους τοῦ Ἑλληνικοῦ.

41 Ὁ μέντοι Καντακουζηνός, ἐπεί τε ἐβασίλευε παῖδας ἔχων δύο, τὸν μὲν νεώτερον Ἐμμανουῆλον ἔπεμψεν ἐς Πελοπόννησον ἡγεμόνα τοῦ Μυζηθρᾶ, τὸν δὲ πρεσβύτερον καθίστησι βασιλέα τοῖς Ἕλλησιν. Ἰωάννης δὲ ὁ τοῦ Ἀνδρονίκου παῖς, ὡς ἐπὶ τὸ ἱκανὸν τῆς ἡλικίας ἀφίκετο, συνίστατό τε τοῖς [1.34] Ἕλλησι καὶ συνετίθετο αὐτοῖς ὡς ἐπὶ τὴν βασιλείαν ἀφιξόμενος. Ἔτυχε δὲ διαίτας ἔχων ἐν τῇ Μακεδονίᾳ. Οἱ δὲ Ἕλληνες ἀχθόμενοι τῇ διαίτῃ καὶ ὕβρει τοῦ βασιλέως, ὡς ἕκαστος εἶχεν αἰτίας αὐτῷ, ἐπαγόμενοι ἀπὸ Μακεδονίας τὸν νεανίαν ἐς τὴν βασιλείαν κατεστήσαντο. Ὡς δὲ ἐς τὴν βασιλείαν κατέστη, τὸν μέντοι Καντακουζηνὸν Ναζηραῖον ἐποιήσατο, Ματθαῖον τοὔνομα. Ὁ τούτου δὲ πρεσβύτερος παῖς, ὃν ἀπέδειξε βασιλέα τοῖς Ἕλλησιν, ἀφίκετο μὲν τὰ πρῶτα ἐς Ῥόδον παρὰ τὸν ταύτῃ αὐτοῦ ἀρχιερέα, δεόμενος ἐπικουρίας τυχεῖν, καὶ ἐδεῖτο κατάγειν αὐτὸν ἐς τὴν βασιλείαν. Καὶ πολλὰ προϊσχόμενος, ὥστε οἱ γενέσθαι τιμωρίαν τινά, ὡς οὐδὲν εὕρατο ἐπιτήδειον, παρῆν αὐτίκα μετὰ ταῦτα ἐς

routed the Bulgarians,[120] but did not kill many, as they fled to various regions along the Danube. Šišman, the son of Aleksandăr, then entered into negotiations with Murad, and made a treaty and an alliance with him whose terms were that they would have the same friends and enemies. He also made a marriage alliance with him by giving Murad his daughter, who was exceedingly beautiful and born of a Jewish woman whom he had married after falling in love with her.[121] He gave another daughter to the king of the Greeks, who at that time was reigning over the Greek people, having removed Kantakouzenos from power over the Greeks.[122]

Kantakouzenos had two sons: while he was reigning, he 41
sent the younger, named Manuel, to the Peloponnese to be the governor of Mistra,[123] while the elder he established as king over the Greeks.[124] But when Ioannes [V], the son of Andronikos [III], came of age, he organized the Greeks and prepared them for his accession to the throne.[125] He happened then to be residing in Macedonia.[126] The Greeks were discontent at the king's way of life and his overbearing manner, and each person had his own grievance against him, so they brought the young man back from Macedonia and set him on the throne. When he was set on the throne, he forced Kantakouzenos to become a monk with the name Matthaios.[127] Kantakouzenos's elder son, however, the one whom he had made king of the Greeks, went first to Rhodes and to the bishop there,[128] asking for his help and begging him to restore him to the throne. He made many promises to secure some aid, but obtained nothing useful. So he then

Πελοπόννησον παρὰ τὸν ἀδελφὸν αὐτοῦ Ἐμμανουῆλον, τὸν ἡγεμόνα τῆς Σπάρτης, καὶ παρ' αὐτοῦ τὴν δίαιταν ἐποιεῖτο. Ἰωάννης μὲν οὖν τῷ τε Ἀμουράτῃ νεωστὶ ἐς τὴν Εὐρώπην διαβάντι ξυμμαχίαν ἐποιήσατο, καὶ τὴν τοῦ Μυσῶν βασιλέως θυγατέρα ἠγάγετο ἐπὶ τῷ παιδὶ αὐτοῦ Ἀνδρονίκῳ, ἀφ' ἧς ἐγένοντο αὐτῷ παῖδες, πρεσβύτερος μὲν Ἀνδρόνικος, Δημήτριος δὲ καὶ Ἐμμανουῆλος οἱ νεώτεροι, καὶ Θεόδωρος. Καὶ εἵπετο τῷ Ἀμουράτῃ ὅποι ἂν στρατεύηται, καὶ φόρου τε ὑποτελεῖς ἅμα ὄντες τῷ Ἀμουράτῃ, ἐπισπόμενοι, ὅποι ἂν στρατεύοιτο.

42 Μετὰ δὲ ταῦτα ἐπὶ Δραγάσην τὸν Ζάρκου ἡγεμόνα τὴν ἐν τῷ Ἀξιῷ ποταμῷ χώραν στρατευσάμενος κατεστρέψατο, ἐς φόρου τε ἅμα ἐπαγωγήν, καὶ αὐτόν οἱ στρατευόμενον ἕπεσθαι ἐπὶ τοὺς πολεμίους, ἐς τοσούτους τὸν ἀριθμὸν ἔχοντα ἱππέας. Μετὰ ταῦτα [1.35] Μπόγδανον τὸν ταύτῃ ἡγεμόνα ὑπαγόμενος, ὥστε οἱ ἕπεσθαι σὺν τῇ αὐτοῦ στρατιᾷ, ἀπεδείξατο μεγάλα ἔργα, ἐπιείκειαν μὲν κατὰ τὴν Κύρου τοῦ Καμβύσεω ἐπιδεικνύμενος, καὶ ὡς μετριώτατά τε καὶ ἐλευθεριώτατα προσφερόμενος τοῖς ὑπ' αὐτὸν γενομένοις ἡγεμόσι Τριβαλλῶν καὶ Μυσῶν καὶ δὴ καὶ Ἑλλήνων.

43 Κατὰ μὲν οὖν τὴν Εὐρώπην διατρίβοντα συχνόν τινα χρόνον καὶ πρὸς τούτους ἔτι διαπολεμοῦντα ἀφίκετο ἀγγελία, τοὺς ἐν τῇ Ἀσίᾳ βαρβάρων ἡγεμόνας ἀλλήλοις συνθεμένους ἀποστῆσαί τε ἀπὸ Ἀμουράτεω χώραν οὐκ ὀλίγην αὐτοῦ, καὶ αὐτοὺς στρατιὰν συλλέξαντας, ὅσην ἠδύναντο, μάλιστα ταράξαι τε τὰ ἐν τῇ Ἀσίᾳ πράγματα αὐτοῦ, καὶ χώρας τῆς ἑαυτοῦ τὰ μὲν καταστρεφομένους

went straight to the Peloponnese, to his brother Manuel, the governor of Mistra, and lived there with him.[129] Ioannes then made an alliance with Murad, who had recently crossed over into Europe, and he arranged for the daughter of the king of the Bulgarians to marry his own son Andronikos [IV].[130] She bore him sons: the oldest was Andronikos and the younger ones were Demetrios, Manuel, and Theodoros.[131] He followed Murad wherever he was campaigning, for they too were Murad's tributaries, and attended upon him wherever he happened to be campaigning.

After that Murad attacked Dragaš, the son of Žarko,[132] 42
who ruled the lands by the Axios River. He conquered him, imposed the payment of tribute on him, and forced him to follow with a fixed number of cavalry when he campaigned against his enemies.[133] After that he subjected Bogdan, the ruler in that area, so that he too had to follow him with his army.[134] In all this he performed great deeds and displayed the same sort of decency as Cyrus, the son of Cambyses. He thus treated the rulers of the Serbs, the Bulgarians, and the Greeks whom he had subjected to his authority in the most equitable and liberal way.

When Murad had spent some time in Europe and was 43
still fighting against his enemies there, news reached him that the chiefs of the barbarians in Asia had made an alliance and had provoked a large part of his territories there to rebel against him. They had assembled as large an army as they could, and had seriously disrupted his affairs in Asia; they would not stop taking over his lands and besieging his

τὰ δὲ καὶ πολιορκοῦντας οὐκ ἀνιέναι. Ἐπεί τε δὴ τάχιστα ἐπύθετο, διαβὰς ἵετο ἐπὶ τοὺς ἡγεμόνας παρασκευασάμενος, καὶ ἐς τὰ ἔσχατα πειρασόμενος, ᾗ ἐδύνατο κράτιστα, ὡς διαμαχούμενος. Εὑρὼν δὲ τούτους ἐν Μυσίᾳ στρατοπεδευομένους, παρετάξατο ἐς μάχην. Οἷα δὲ μάχης ἐμπείρῳ πολλαχῇ γενομένῳ ἐμεμηχάνητο τοιόνδε. Λέγεται γάρ, ὡς ἐπεὶ θέρους ἦν ὥρα, καὶ ἠπίστατο μεσημβρίας ἐπιγιγνομένης ἐπιπνεύσειν ἐτησίαν ἄνεμον ἀπὸ ἑσπέρας, ταύτῃ δὲ παρεγγυῶν τῇ στρατιᾷ τὸ μέρος ἐκεῖνο κατὰ νώτου λαβεῖν, ἐς μάχην τε καθίστατο περὶ πλήθουσαν [1.36] ἀγοράν, καὶ συμμίξας τοῖς πολεμίοις ἐμάχετο ἰσχυρῶς. Μάχης δὲ ἀμφοῖν ἰσορρόπου γενομένης ἐπὶ λόφον τινὰ αὐτοῦ που λέγεται ἀναβῆναι, καὶ φωνῆσαι μέγα τοῖς ἑαυτοῦ τάδε. "Παῖδες ἐμοὶ στρατιῶται, μέμνησθε ὑμῶν αὐτῶν, ὅσα ἐπεπόνθειτε ἐν τῇ Εὐρώπῃ, τοσαῦτα ἔτη διαπολεμοῦντες. Τί δὴ ὑποχωρεῖτε; Οὐκ ἴστε, ὡς τὰ πάντα ἐφ' ἡμῖν ἔσται, τούτων περιγενομένοις; Ἄγετε δὴ ἐμοὶ ἕπεσθε, ὡς ἢν μὴ ἀρτίως ἕπησθε, ταχὺ περιεσομένων τῶν πολεμίων ἡμᾶς." Ταῦτα εἰπόντα τὸν βασιλέα ἐλαύνειν ὁμόσε τῷ ἵππῳ ἐπὶ τοὺς πολεμίους, ἐς τὸ μέσον στῖφος ἐμβάλλοντα· καὶ αὐτίκα ἐπιπνέοντα τὸν ἄνεμον ἀπὸ νώτου τῇ στρατιᾷ ἐνοχλεῖν ἐπὶ πρόσωπον τοὺς ἐναντίους, καὶ οὕτως ἅμα ἀλλήλοις διακελευσαμένους καὶ ἐς τὸ πρόσθεν ἰόντας καὶ βιαζομένους τέλος δὴ τρέψασθαί τε καὶ ἐπιδιώκειν ἀνὰ κράτος ἀπολοῦντας τοὺς πολεμίους. Καὶ διαφθαρῆναι μὲν λέγεται τὰ πλείω τοῦ στρατεύματος αὐτοῦ, διαφυγόντας δὲ τοὺς πολεμίους οἴχεσθαι ἀπαλλαττόμενον ἕκαστον ἐπὶ τὰ ἑαυτοῦ. Ἐνταῦθα διαπρεσβευσαμένους σπονδάς τε

cities.[135] As soon as he learned this, he crossed over and set about preparing himself against these rulers, going to the greatest possible lengths and exerting himself to the fullest in his struggle against them. He found them camped in Mysia and drew up his army for battle. As he had a great deal of experience in battle, he contrived the following stratagem. It is said that he knew, because it was summertime, that a seasonal wind would blow from the west at noon. He thus had his army position itself with their backs to that direction and he joined battle in the late morning: he engaged with the enemy and fought fiercely. The battle was hanging in the balance, however, when Murad is said to have climbed up on a hill there and to have shouted this loudly to his men. "My children! Soldiers! Remember who you are, what you have been through in Europe, your fighting for all these years! So why are you falling back? Don't you know that all will be ours, if only we can overcome them? Come on now and follow me, because if you don't follow me right now, the enemy are going to overpower us in no time." After saying this, the sultan charged straight at the enemy on his horse and hurled himself into the heart of their throng. And at that moment the wind starting blowing from behind his army's back right into the face of the enemy, and disconcerted them. At the same time, his men also encouraged each other and pushed forward. So they managed to overcome the enemy at last and, putting them to flight, gave chase with all their might and destroyed them. It is said that most of the army perished there, but the enemies who escaped went off, each going to his own home. They sent envoys and asked

αἰτεῖσθαι, καὶ συμβῆναι αὐτῷ, ἐφ' ᾧ ἕπεσθαι τούτους, ᾗ ἂν ἐξηγοῖτο τοῦ λοιποῦ στρατευόμενος.

44 Ἐν ᾧ δὴ κατὰ τὴν Ἀσίαν διέτριβε καὶ περιῄει καὶ τὰ ἐν τῇ Ἀσίᾳ καθίστη πράγματα καὶ τοῖς Τούρκων ἡγεμόσι σπονδὰς ἐποιεῖτο, Σαουζῆς ὁ πρεσβύτερος τῶν παίδων αὐτοῦ ἐν τῇ Εὐρώπῃ καταλειφθείς, ὥστε ἐφορᾶν τε τὴν ἀρχήν, καὶ ἤν τι ἐπίῃ [1.37] δεινὸν ἢ χαλεπὸν κατὰ τὴν ἀρχήν, ἐπὶ τὸ δοῦναι αὐτῷ ἀσφαλῶς ἔχειν, καταστησάμενος. Οὗτος δὲ συνίστη τε καὶ τοὺς κατὰ τὴν Εὐρώπην ἀριστέας, ὡς ἠδύνατο, μάλιστα εὖ ποιῶν τε καὶ ἀνακτώμενος, καὶ τοῦ Ἑλλήνων βασιλέως τῷ πρεσβυτέρῳ παιδὶ Ἀνδρονίκῳ, ὡς οἰχομένου τοῦ πατρὸς αὐτοῦ Ἀμουράτῃ τῷ Ὀρχάνεω ἐς τὸν κατὰ τὴν Ἀσίαν πρός γε ἡγεμόνας αὐτοῦ πόλεμον ἐγκατελείφθη ἐν τῷ Βυζαντίῳ καὶ ἐπετέτραπτο τὴν βασιλείαν, τούτῳ ἀφικόμενος ἐς λόγους ἔπειθέ τε ἀφίστασθαι ἀπὸ τῶν πατρῴων, καὶ ἄμφω κατασχεῖν τὴν πατρῴαν ἀρχήν, τὸν αὐτὸν σφίσιν ἐχθρόν τε καὶ φίλον ἡγουμένους, καὶ ἤν τις ἐπίῃ πολέμιος, ἀμύνοντας παραγίνεσθαι ἀλλήλοις κατὰ τὸ δυνατὸν πάσῃ δυνάμει. Ταῦτα ὡς αὐτοῖς ἐδόκει ποιητέα, ἐσπένδετό τε καὶ ὅρκια ἐποιοῦντο, ἐμπεδοῦντες ὡς μάλιστα τὰ τοιαῦτα σφίσιν αὐτοῖς, ᾗ ἀσφαλέστατα ἐδόκει ἀμφοῖν ἔσεσθαι. Ὡς δὴ ταῦτα ποιησάμενοι δῆλα ἐποιοῦντο, ἠσφαλίζοντο σφᾶς παρασκευαζόμενοι, ἢν ἐπίῃ ἐς τὴν Εὐρώπην Ἀμουράτης, ὡς ἀμύνεσθαι.

45 Ταῦτα ὡς ἐπύθοντο τάχιστα γενόμενα κατὰ τὴν Εὐρώπην, καλέσας Ἰωάννην βασιλέα Βυζαντίου ἔλεγε τοιάδε. "Βασιλεῦ Ἑλλήνων, ἐμοί τε νεωστὶ παρὰ τῶν ἐν τῇ Εὐρώπῃ

for terms and Murad agreed to them, on the condition that they follow him wherever he led his army in the future.

While Murad was spending time in Asia, going around, arranging his affairs in Asia, and making this treaty with the chiefs of the Turks, Savcı, his eldest son, had been left behind in Europe to look after his realm. If anything bad or dangerous were to happen concerning his realm, his task was to deal with this and thus hold it securely for him. But Savcı now brought together, as best he could, the leading men in Europe, treated them very well, and won them over. He also opened discussions with Andronikos, who was the eldest son of the king of the Greeks and whose father had gone off to Murad, the son of Orhan, for the war in Asia against his chiefs. Andronikos had been left behind in Byzantion and entrusted with the kingdom. Savcı approached him and persuaded him that they should rebel against their fathers and so both seize their fathers' realms.[136] They would have the same friends and enemies and, if someone should oppose them, they would be there to defend each other with all possible force. As this seemed a good thing to do, they made a pact and took oaths, binding themselves firmly to this plan, which seemed as if it would be the safest thing for them both. They did these things quite openly and prepared to secure themselves in the case that Murad should come to Europe to fight back. 44

As soon as these events in Europe became known, Murad summoned Ioannes, the king of Byzantion, and said this to him. "King of the Greeks, I have just now received news 45

πιστοτάτων ἀγγελία ἀφίκετο, ὡς Σαουζῆς ὁ ἐμὸς παῖς ὑπὸ τοῦ [1.38] σοῦ παιδὸς ἀναγκασθεὶς ἀνήκεστά μοι βουλεύονται πράγματα. Πῶς οὖν ἔχει μηδέν τι ἐπισταμένου σοῦ τούτων πέρι ἐς τοσοῦτον ἀφικέσθαι ἀφροσύνης, ὥστε μὴ μόνον ἐπιχειρῆσαι τὸν ἐμὸν παῖδα, ἀλλὰ καὶ τὸν παῖδα συνέπαινον γενέσθαι ἐς ταῦτα; Πῶς δ' ἄνευ σῆς γνώμης τὰ τοιαῦτα γενέσθαι ἐξείη λογίζεσθαι; Ἀλλ' εἰ μὲν δίκην ἐπιθήσων τῷ σῷ παιδί, ἥν τινα ἂν ἐπιτάττοιμεν, μηδ' ὁτιοῦν ὑπολογιῇ, εἴσομαι τότε σαφῶς, ὡς ἄκοντός σου ταῦτα ἐγένετο. Ἢν δὲ ἄλλῃ λογιζόμενος ἀλλοῖον, ἢ ἐμοὶ δόξει περὶ τοῦ ἐμοῦ παιδός, μὴ τιμησάμενος μὴ βούλοιο τίθεσθαι, ἴσθι δὴ σαυτὸν ἐν αἰτίᾳ ἕξων ἐς ὕστερον." Βασιλεὺς δὲ Ἑλλήνων ἀμείβετο τοῖσδε. "Ὦ βασιλεῦ, οὐκ ἂν δή ποτε τοῦ λοιποῦ ταύτην ἔμοιγε τὴν αἰτίαν αἰτιώμενος ἐπιθείης σὺν δίκῃ· ἢν γὰρ κἀμοὶ γένηται ὁ παῖς οὗτος, ὃν σὺ ἔφησθα ἐπὶ ταῦτα ὡρμῆσθαι, οὐδέν τι ἧττον ἐμοῦ συνειδότος, ᾔδει δὴ τότε σαφέστατα, ὡς ἔχοιμεν εὐνοίας τε καὶ φιλοφροσύνης περὶ σέ τε καὶ τὴν σὴν δυναστείαν. Ἢν δ' ἂν ἐπιτάττοις δίκην ἐκείνῳ ἐπιθεῖναί με, μὴ ἂν οὕτω μεμηνέναι δόξαιμι, ὥστε τῷ ἐμοί τε καὶ σοὶ ἐχθίστῳ τε καὶ πολεμιωτάτῳ διατεθειμένῳ χαρίζεσθαι ὁτιοῦν ἐνδιδόντα τῆς δίκης." Ταῦτα εἰπόντα τῷ βασιλεῖ, ἐδέδοκτο Ἀμουράτῃ τὴν αὐτὴν [1.39] ἀμφοῖν ἐπιθεῖναι τὴν δίκην, κατὰ ταῦτα ἄμφω τὼ πατέρε ἐπαιτιωμένω τοῖς παισίν, ἐξορύξαι τὼ ὀφθαλμὼ ἑκατέρῳ ἐκείνοις.

46 Ὡς δὲ ταῦτα ἐδέδοκτο, ἤλαυνεν ἐπὶ τὴν Εὐρώπην, στράτευμα ἀγόμενος, ᾗ ἐδύνατο, πλεῖστον. Καὶ διαβὰς ἐπὶ τὴν Εὐρώπην ἵετο ὁμόσε ἐπὶ τὸν παῖδα, ὅπου δὴ

sent by some of my most trusted men in Europe that my son Savcı was forced by your son into plotting something terrible with him against me. But how could your son have done something so stupid without your knowing anything about it? Not only did he make overtures to my son, but also got the boy to actually agree to this. How could anyone imagine that such things have happened without your approval? However, if you impose whatever punishment I decree on your son, and do not diminish it, then I will know for sure that there is no reason for me to suspect that you had a hand in this. But if you have other ideas and are not willing to inflict on your son the same punishment as it seems proper for me to impose on my own, then you should know that you yourself will then be considered guilty." The king of the Greeks replied as follows: "May you never again have cause to accuse me of being guilty of this crime, O sultan. For even if it is my son who you say has started this business, I could not possibly know less about it. It will become perfectly clear to him that I am your friend and a supporter of your regime. If you order me to punish him, I will not be crazy enough to show any favors in imposing punishment on someone who has made himself such a bitter enemy and opponent to us both." After Ioannes had said this to the sultan, Murad decided to impose the same punishment on both sons, as both fathers were accusing their sons of the same thing: each of them was to have his eyes gouged out.

When this was decided, Murad advanced on Europe 46
leading the largest possible army. He crossed over into Europe and moved against his son, having learned where he

ἐπυνθάνετο αὐτὸν ἐνστρατοπεδευόμενον σὺν τῷ Ἑλλήνων βασιλέως παιδί. Οἳ δὴ τὸ Εὐρώπης στράτευμα συλλέξαντες ἐστρατοπεδεύοντο ἐν χωρίῳ τινὶ Βυζαντίου τὰ Πικριδίου καλουμένῳ, οἳ δὴ τούς τε Ἕλληνας ἅμα καὶ τοὺς ἀρίστους ἀπ' Εὐρώπης συλλέγεσθαί οἱ ὡς μάλιστα ἐλογίζοντο. Ἐνταῦθα δὴ ἐπὶ χαράδρᾳ τινὶ ὡς ἐπὶ χάρακι ἐστρατοπεδεύετο Σαουζῆς Ἀμουράτεω παῖς, τὸν πατέρα ἐπιόντα οἱ ἐπιδεχόμενος. Ἀμουράτης δὲ ὡς ἐνταῦθα κατέλαβε τὸν παῖδα αὐτοῦ καὶ τοὺς Ἕλληνας στρατοπεδευομένους, συνταξάμενος ἐπῄει ὡς συμμίξων αὐτίκα τοῖς ἐναντίοις. Ὡς δὲ ὑπὸ τῆς χαράδρας διεκωλύετο, ἐστρατοπεδεύσατο καὶ αὐτός. Συνέβαλλον, ᾗ ἐνεχώρει, Ἑλλήνων τινὲς τοῖς τοῦ Ἀμουράτεω στρατιώταις, καὶ ἐτρέψαντο τούτους, ὡς λέγεται. Ὡς δὲ ἐφαίνετο χαλεπῶς ἔχειν τὸν χῶρον ἐκεῖνον μάχῃ συνάψαι τοῖς πολεμίοις, νυκτὸς ἐλάσας ἐναντίον τοῦ στρατοπέδου ἐπὶ τὸ χεῖλος τῆς χαράδρας, ὡς ἐγγυτάτω γενόμενος τοῦ στρατοπέδου τῶν πολεμίων, ὡς ῥᾷστα ἐπακούοιτο, φωνῇ τε μεγάλῃ ἐπικαλούμενος ὀνομαστὶ ἄνδρα ἕκαστον, ὡς εὐκλεΐζων ἅμα τῶν πεπραγμένων ἑκάστῳ, εἴ τῳ φιλότιμον πώποτε ἢ ἀγαθὸν ξυνηνέχθη γενέσθαι. Μετὰ δέ, εὐφημίζοντα ἕκαστον, παρὰ τὸ χεῖλος διϊππεύοντα λέγεται ἐπειπεῖν τοιάδε. [1.40] "Ἄνδρες ἥρωες, ποῖ δὴ οἴχεσθε, ἀπολιπόντες ἐμὲ τὸν πατέρα ὑμῶν; Ποῦ τοῦ διδασκάλου τῆς διδασκαλίας ὑμῶν ἀφέμενοι ἐπὶ παῖδα ἐτράπεσθε ἔτι ἁπαλὸν ὄντα, ὅν, ἐπειδὰν ἐς χεῖρα ἐμὴν ἀφίκηται, συλλαβὼν μαστιγώσω, οὐδέν τι ἄλλο λυμηνάμενος τὸν νεανίαν, ἂν μέντοι μόνον ὑμῖν βουλομένοις ἐξῇ ἐκεῖνον τοιαῦτα ποιῆσαι; Ἦν δὲ ἄλλο

was encamped with the son of the king of the Greeks. They had assembled the army of Europe and were encamped at a place near Byzantion called Pikridion.[137] They reckoned that they had assembled most of the Greeks and the leading men from Europe. Savcı, the son of Murad, was encamped by a ravine that acted as a defensive wall, waiting for his father to launch an attack against him. When Murad reached the place where his son and the Greeks were encamped, he drew up his army so as to engage the enemy at once. But the ravine caused him difficulty, so he had to encamp as well. It is said that, when they had the chance, some of the Greeks engaged Murad's soldiers and routed them. Because it seemed a bad place to engage the enemy in battle, Murad moved forward at night toward the edge of the ravine opposite the camp. When he was very close to the enemy camp, so that he could easily be heard, he called each man by name in a loud voice, praising the deeds of each one who had ever done anything noble or valiant. After praising each one, he rode to the lip of the ravine and, it is said, spoke the following words. "Men! Heroes! Why have you gone and abandoned me, your father? For some reason you have left the teacher who taught you and turned to his son, who is still immature. When he falls into my hands, I will take him and whip him, but I will inflict no worse injury upon the young man if indeed you decide, as you may, that it is possible to do this to him alone.[138] However, if you want to make a trial of

πειρώμενοι τῆς γνώμης ἐμοῦ ἐθέλητε διὰ μάχης ἰέναι, ἴστε δὴ ὡς ὑμῖν οὐδὲν ὑγιὲς ἐσεῖται τοῦ λοιποῦ. Δεῦρο δὴ οὖν ἰόντες παρ' ἡμᾶς μηδ' ὁτιοῦν ὑπολογίζεσθε αἰδοῖ τῆς ἡμετέρας ἀρετῆς, καὶ ὑπὸ παιδὸς μαστιγία αἰσχύνεσθε τοιαῦτα ἐπιτηδεύοντες. Καὶ ἐπόμνυμι τὸν τὴν ἀρχὴν τήνδε ἐμοὶ ἐπιτρέψαντα μηδένα μηδὲν ἔτι ἀνήκεστόν τι ἐργάσεσθαι."

47 Ταῦτα ἀκούσαντας τοὺς Σαούζεω στρατιώτας αἰδεσθῆναί τε λέγεται τὴν βασιλέως φωνήν, φωνεῖν τε γὰρ διάτορον μάλιστα δὴ ἀνθρώπων, καὶ περὶ σφῶν αὐτῶν δεδιέναι, τὴν τύχην αὐτοῦ καὶ ἀρετὴν ἐξεπισταμένους. Καὶ οὕτω πεισθέντας, ὡς ἐδίδοσαν σφίσιν αὐτοῖς λόγον ἐπὶ τῷ γεγονότι, νυκτὸς ἐκείνης ἀπαλλάσσοντο ἐκ τοῦ στρατοπέδου, ἀπιόντες, ᾗ ἑκάστῳ προεχώρει, τοὺς δὲ πλείους ἀφικομένους παρὰ τὸ Ἀμουράτεω στρατόπεδον παραιτεῖσθαι, ὡς ἀνάγκῃ προηνεγμένοι συνελέγησαν ἐς τὸ Σαούζεω στρατόπεδον. [1.41] Αἰσθόμενος δὲ ὁ Σαουζῆς ἀποδιδράσκοντας τοῦ στρατοπέδου τοὺς στρατιώτας αὐτοῦ, σὺν τοῖς ἀρίστοις, οἷς ἑώρα εὐνουστάτοις αὐτῷ, ᾤχετο ἐπὶ τὸ Διδυμότειχον, συνεπισπομένων καὶ τῶν παίδων ὅσοι ἐς τόνδε οἱ συνεπιλαβομένων τὸν πόλεμον ὡς προθυμότατα, καὶ συμπροθυμούμενος ἐδόκει τούτων ἀντιλαβέσθαι, ᾗ ἐδόκει ἐρρωμενέστατα.

48 Πυθόμενος δὲ Ἀμουράτης ἤλαυνε κατὰ πόδας, καὶ ἐπολιόρκει τὴν πόλιν. Οἱ δὲ σὺν τῷ Σαουζῇ λιμῷ πιεζόμενοι, ἅτε σίτου οὐκ εἰσενεχθέντος ἐς τὴν ἀκρόπολιν πρότερον καὶ ἐν βραχεῖ ἐπιλελοιπότος, παρεδίδοσαν σφᾶς αὐτοὺς χρῆσθαι, ὡς ἂν μάλιστα αὐτῷ δοκοίη. Ἀμουράτης δὲ τὴν

my resolve by going into battle, you should know that nothing good will come of it for you in the future. So come over here to me. Do not feel dishonored in taking advantage of my good nature,[139] or feel shame at the whipping of a child in this fashion when it is done to good purpose. I swear by him who entrusted him with my realm that I will do no serious harm to anyone else."

It is said that Savcı's soldiers were filled with shame when 47
they heard the sultan's voice, for he spoke more menacingly than anyone, and they feared for their own safety, because they well knew his good fortune and virtue. So they were won over and made a deal among themselves regarding what had to be done. That night they got away from the camp, each one leaving in whatever way he could. Most went to Murad's camp and appealed to him by saying that they had been forced to join Savcı's camp. When Savcı realized that his soldiers were deserting his camp, he took off for Didymoteichon with his leading men, whom he thought were most loyal toward him. He was also followed by the youths who had been most eager to join him in this war, and he seemed just as eager to accept them in turn, as heartily as he could.

When Murad learned this, he advanced as fast as he could 48
and besieged the city. Savcı's men were pressed by hunger, as they had not brought grain into the citadel in advance and so quickly ran out. They surrendered themselves to be treated in whatever way he decided. Thus Murad starved

πόλιν λιμῷ παραστησάμενος εἷλε τὸν παῖδα αὐτοῦ Σαουζῆν, καὶ λαβὼν ἐξέκοψε τὼ ὀφθαλμὼ αὐτοῦ. Τοὺς δὲ ἄλλους κελεῦσαι αὐτὸν δεδεμένους ἐπὶ κεφαλὴν κατὰ κρημνὸν κατενεχθῆναι ἀπὸ τῆς πόλεως ἐς τὸν ποταμόν. Τὸν δὲ ἐσκηνωμένον παρὰ τὸν ποταμὸν καὶ θεώμενον ἐπιφερομένους τούς τε ἀρίστους ἐπὶ κρημνὸν σύνδυό τε ἅμα καὶ σύντρεις ἀνακαγχάζειν ὡς ἐπισπεύδοντα κυσὶ λαγὼ ἐπιδιώκουσι, παῖδας τῶν παρ' ἑαυτῷ ἀρίστων σὺν τῷ Σαουζῇ ἀπιόντας, ἐκέλευσε τοὺς πατέρας αὐτῶν αὐτοχειρὶ διαχρήσασθαι. Δύο δὲ τούτων λέγεται, μὴ ἐθελήσαντας τοὺς παῖδας αὐτῶν ἀποκτεῖναι, αὐτούς τε ἅμα ἀνελεῖν καὶ τοὺς παῖδας αὐτῶν κελεῦσαι ἀνελεῖν. Γνώμη δ' ἔφασκε τῶν πατέρων ἀφικέσθαι τοὺς παῖδας ἐπὶ τὸν Σαουζῆν, καὶ ἀφικέσθαι ταλαντευομένων αὐτῶν [1.42] καὶ ἐπ' ἀμφότερα. Ταῦτα δὲ ποιησάμενον, ἐπιτεῖλαι πέμψαντα ἄγγελον, τῷ Ἑλλήνων βασιλεῖ τὸν παῖδα τὰ αὐτὰ τούτῳ ποιῆσαι, ᾗ συνέθετο αὐτῷ τὴν ἀρχήν. Κἀκεῖνον δέ φασι λαβόντα τὸν παῖδα αὐτοῦ ὄξει ζέοντι κατενέγκαι τὼ ὀφθαλμώ. Τότε μὲν οὖν οὕτως ἐτελεύτα ἀμφὶ τόνδε τὸν πόλεμον.

49 Μετὰ δὲ ταῦτα ὡς Ἐμμανουῆλος ὁ τῶν Ἑλλήνων βασιλέως παῖς Θέρμην τὴν ἐν Μακεδονίᾳ, Θεσσαλονίκην ἐπικαλουμένην, ἐπιτροπεύων διΐθυνε, καί τινος λαβόμενος ἐπιστάτου ἀμφὶ τήνδε τὴν χώραν τῇ Φερρῶν πόλει ἐπιβουλεύων ἑάλω, πρὸς δὲ καὶ νεώτερα πράττων πρὸς Ἀμουράτην, ἐπιπέμψας Χαρατίνην ἄνδρα μὲν μέγα δυνάμενον, διὰ σύνεσιν δὲ τὰ ἐς πόλεμον οὐδενὸς τῶν παρ' ἑαυτῷ λειπόμενον, ἐπέτελλε τὴν Θέρμην αὐτῷ παραστησάμενον ἥκειν, ἄγοντα τὸν τοῦ βασιλέως Ἰωάννου παῖδα. Χαρατίνης

the city into surrender and captured his son Savcı. He took him and cut out his eyes. He ordered that the rest be tied up and thrown headfirst over the precipice into the river from the city. He set up his tent by the river and watched as the leading men were brought to the precipice in twos and threes, and burst out laughing as though at a hare that rushes about when it is being chased by hounds. He ordered his own leading men, who were the fathers of the youths who had followed Savcı, to kill their sons with their own hands. It is said that when two of them did not want to kill their sons, he gave orders to kill them along with their sons. He maintained that the sons had gone over to Savcı with their fathers' consent, and that they had done so because they were playing both sides. After he had done this, he sent a messenger to the king of the Greeks [Ioannes V] ordering him to do the same to his own son, as they had agreed at the start. And they say that the king of the Greeks took his son [Andronikos IV] and poured scalding vinegar over his eyes. And that was how this war ended.

After that, when Manuel, the son of the king of the 49
Greeks, had been entrusted with the governorship of Therme, the city in Macedonia that is also called Thessalonike, he was exposed as plotting against the city of Serres after taking on a supervisor for that area, and he was also planning a rebellion against Murad.[140] So the latter sent Hayreddin, a very powerful man, whose grasp of military affairs was second to none among his men,[141] with orders to attack Thessalonike and subject it to his authority and so capture King Ioannes's son. Hayreddin set about his task.[142]

μὲν δὴ ἐν τούτοις ἦν· Ἐμμανουῆλος δὲ αἱρήσεσθαι τὴν πόλιν οἰόμενος ταχὺ ὑπὸ Χαρατίνεω, ἅτε τῶν πραγμάτων τῶν ἐν τῇ πόλει πονηρῶς ἐχόντων καὶ ἐπ' οὐδενὶ ἀγαθῷ οἱ ἀποβεβηκότων, αὐθαδέστερόν τε γὰρ αὐτῷ ἀχθόμενοι ἐχρῶντο οἱ τῆς πόλεως ἢ ὡς ἐχρῆν, ὡς εἶχε τάχιστα ἀπηλλάττετο διὰ θαλάττης ἐπὶ τὸν πατέρα αὐτοῦ ἐν νῷ ἔχων ἀπιέναι. Ὡς δὲ ἐπιπέμπων αὐτῷ ὁ πατὴρ προηγόρευεν ἄλλου πη ἀπιόντα ἀπαλλάττεσθαι, ὡς οὐκέτι αὐτῷ ἐνὸν δέχεσθαι διὰ δέος τοῦ Ἀμουράτεω, ἔγνω δεῖν ἐς αὐτὸν ἴεσθαι δὴ τὸν Ἀμουράτην παραιτησόμενον, εἴ τι μὴ ἐν δέοντι διαπραξαμένῳ αὖθις αὐτῷ μεμελέτηκεν.

50 Ἀμουράτης δὲ [1.43] πυνθανόμενος τὸν βασιλέως παῖδα ἐπ' αὐτὸν ἀφικνεῖσθαι ἠγάσθη τε αὐτὸν τῆς γενναιότητος, καὶ ἀπαντήσας, ᾗ πρότερον εἰώθει ποιεῖν αὐτῷ ἐπελαύνοντι, ἔπειτα προσεῖπε, καὶ ἐπισχών τι βραχὺ οὕτω διηλέγχθη μετ' αὐτοῦ. Μετὰ δὲ ταῦτα προσγελάσας αὐτῷ ἔλεγε τοιάδε. "Ὦ παῖ βασιλέως, ὡς μὲν σὺν δίκῃ τῇ ἐμῇ χώρᾳ νῦν, πρότερον δὲ ὑμετέρᾳ οὔσῃ ἐπιβουλεύων ἑάλως, καὶ ταῦτα, ὅσα διεπράξω, σὺν δίκῃ διαπεπραγμένος εἴης, ἐπισταμένῳ μοι ταῦτά ἐστι, καὶ ἤδη συγγνώμην σοι παρεχόμενος ἐν τῷ παρόντι, ὅρα, μὴ εἰσαῦθις ἁλοὺς τοιοῦτον ἐς ἐμὲ καὶ τὴν ἐμὴν ἀρχὴν διαπραττόμενος εἴης. Ἐμέ τε γὰρ καὶ Θεὸν ἅμα τὸν τοῦδε κηδόμενον, ἀποδεδειχὼς ἤδη φαυλότατά σε δὴ διαγενόμενον· ὡς ταύτῃ ἄμεινον ἔχει γενόμενα ἐφ' ἡμῖν[9] τὰ τῆς Εὐρώπης πράγματα." "Ἀλλ' ἐγώ," ἔφη ἐκεῖνος, "καὶ Θεὸν αὐτὸν παρὰ σοῦ, ᾗ ἔχει, ὡς ἄριστα διαιτῶντα αἰσθόμενος ἤϊα ἐπὶ σέ, ἐν τοσαύτῃ αἰτίᾳ γενόμενος. Ὡς ἂν μοι ἐπιτηδείως σχοίης, ἐφ' οἷς πεπλημμέληταί

Manuel, however, realized that Hayreddin would quickly take the city,[143] as conditions in the city were dangerously unstable and were not going to turn out well for him, for the citizens had grievances against him and had less respect for him than they should. So he quickly made his escape by sea, intending to go to his father. But when his father sent word, publicly telling him to go elsewhere to seek refuge, for he could no longer take him in out of fear of Murad, Manuel realized then that he had to go to Murad himself and beg forgiveness for anything that he had perforce plotted to do against his interests.[144]

When Murad learned that the king's son had come to 50
him, he admired Manuel for his courage. He received him just as he had done when he had come to him on previous occasions, and spoke with him. He paused briefly and then interrogated him. After that, he smiled as he said the following to him. "King's son, I know full well that you have justly been discovered to be intriguing for the territory that is now mine but used to be yours, but I also know that, whatever you plotted, you were plotting justly. I am offering you immediate forgiveness for now. But see to it that you are never again caught plotting anything like this against me or my realm. You are now convicted of having acted maliciously against both me and the God who protected me from this. It will be better for the affairs of Europe to be under our control."[145] "But yes," said Manuel, "I came to you even though I realize that God himself seems to be on your side, arranging matters in the best way, and I am guilty of such a great infraction. You can thus deal with me appropriately,

μοι ἐπὶ σὲ καὶ τὴν σὴν βασιλείαν." Οὕτω δὲ καὶ Ἀμουράτης συνέγνω τε αὐτῷ τὴν ἁμαρτίαν, καὶ τῷ πατρὶ αὐτοῦ ἐπιπέμπων ἐκέλευε τὸν παῖδα αὐτοῦ δέχεσθαι· ὁ δὲ ἐποίει τε, ᾗ ἐνετέλλετο, καὶ τὸν παῖδα αὐτίκα [1.44] προσίετο ἐς Βυζάντιον.

51 Χαρατίνης δὲ τήν τε Θέρμην παραλαβὼν καὶ τοὺς ξυναφεστῶτας δουλωσάμενος μέγα εὐδοκίμει παρ' Ἀμουράτῃ, καὶ πρόσθεν μέγας ὢν παρ' αὐτῷ καὶ μέγιστον δυνάμενος. Λέγεται μὲν περὶ Χαρατίνεω πολλὰ ἄξια λόγου, ὡς ὑποτιθεμένου Ἀμουράτῃ τὰ δέοντα καὶ τὰ πλείω ὑπηρετοῦντι διαπράττεσθαι μεγάλα ἄττα κατά τε Ἀσίαν καὶ Εὐρώπην· καὶ λόγοι δὲ αὐτοῦ πρὸς Ἀμουράτην ἀπομνημονεύονται, ἐρίζοντος αὐτῷ περὶ συνέσεως καὶ στρατηγίας. Ἐρομένου γὰρ αὐτοῦ λέγεται, "Ἀμουράτη ὦ βασιλεῦ, πῶς ἂν δὴ μάλιστα στρατηγῇ, ἕως, ἂν βούλοιτό οἱ γενέσθαι, τούτων ῥᾳδίως ἐπιτυγχάνοι;" Τὸν δὲ φάναι λέγεται, "εὖ τε στοχαζόμενος, καὶ τοὺς στρατιώτας ὡς οἷόν τε μάλιστα εὐεργετῶν." Τὸν δὲ ἐπανερέσθαι, "καὶ πῶς ἂν δὴ" εἰπόντα "στοχάζεσθαι ὀρθῶς;" Τὸν δὲ φάναι, "εἰ μετρῶν τὰ εἰκότα μὴ σφάλληται περὶ τὰ μέτρα." Ἐνταῦθα καγχάσαι λέγεται Χαρατίνην πάνυ μέγα, καὶ ἐπειπεῖν, "Ἀμουράτη ὦ βασιλεῦ, σωφρονεῖν ἄριστ' ἂν δοκοίης. Πῶς δ' ἂν μετροίη, ἂν μὴ παρὼν ἑκάτερα θεωρῇ, τά τε δέοντα καὶ τἀναντία τούτων, καὶ τῶν μὲν ἀπέχοιτο, τὰ δὲ αὐτῷ μεταδιώκοι ἑλόμενος, φθάνων τε τούτων τὰ δέοντα;" Διὰ ταῦτα δὲ ταχυτῆτα αἰνιττόμενος προφέρειν μέγα [1.45] τῶν ἄλλων ἀγαθῶν ἐς τὸ μεγάλα κατεργάζεσθαι, ὡς οὐδὲν ἄλλο πρὸ ταχυτῆτός τε καὶ σπουδῆς τόν γε στρατηγὸν χρῆναι ἐπιτηδεύειν, καὶ

given my crimes against you and your throne." So Murad forgave him this crime, and sent him back to his father, instructing the latter to receive his son. Ioannes did as he was told and allowed his son back into Byzantion.[146]

Hayreddin took over Thessalonike and enslaved the reb- 51
els.[147] He was held in high esteem by Murad, although previously too he had risen high in his service and wielded great power. Many worthwhile stories are told about Hayreddin, about how he would advise Murad on what needed to be done and accomplished great deeds in both Asia and Europe while serving him in most matters. Some of his sayings to Murad in discussions of judgment and strategy are recorded. It is thus said that he once asked, "O Sultan Murad, how should one best conduct a campaign so as to most easily accomplish one's goals?" It is reported that Murad answered, "By planning well and treating the soldiers as well as possible." Hayreddin asked again, "And how do you plan properly?" He said, "If you use the right calculations and do not make mistakes in them." At this point it is said that Hayreddin laughed loudly and said to him, "O Sultan Murad, you might seem to be most wise. But how could one make these calculations without being present to actually observe both what needs to be done and its opposite, and thereby avoid the latter while choosing to pursue the former, and so achieve what is necessary?" In this way he hinted that it was speed that accomplished great deeds, more so than other good qualities, and that there is nothing that a general should practice more than speed and swift application, and

πανταχοῦ παραγενόμενον, ὅποι ἂν δέοι πῃ παρεῖναι. Ταῦτα μὲν οὖν διειλεγμένους ἀλλήλοις ἀποδείκνυσθαι γνώμας οὐ τοῦ δέοντος ἐλλιπεῖς.

52 Ἀμουράτης μὲν οὖν διϊὼν ἁπανταχῇ ὡς τάχιστα, δέους τε ἐπλήρου ἅπαντα καὶ φυλακῆς, Χαρατίνῃ χρώμενος ὑπηρέτῃ τῷ πάντα ἀρίστῳ καὶ ἐς τὸ συλλαμβάνειν αὐτῷ καὶ ὁτιοῦν ξυνεπιλαβέσθαι, καὶ ἐπιτηδείως ἔχοντι ἐς τὰ μάλιστα, καὶ οὐκ ὀλίγα ἐς τὴν ἀρχὴν αὐτῷ ποιησαμένῳ κατὰ τὴν Εὐρώπην. Ὑπηγάγετο μὲν οὖν τοσάδε ἔθνη καὶ ἡγεμόνας τοὺς ἐν τῇ Εὐρώπῃ ἐς φόρων τε ἀπαγωγήν, καὶ συνεπομένους αὐτῷ, ὅποι ἂν στρατεύοιτο, Ἑλλήνων βασιλεῖς εἶχέ οἱ στρατευομένους. Ἐμμανουήλῳ δὲ ἠρέσκετο μάλιστα δὴ ξυμπάντων Ἑλλήνων. Εἶχε δὲ καὶ τῶν Μυσῶν βασιλέα, πρὸς δὲ καὶ Δραγάσην τὸν Ζάρκου παῖδα καὶ Μπόγδανον τὸν τὴν Ῥοδόπην κατέχοντα καὶ ἄλλους τοὺς ἐν τῇ Εὐρώπῃ ἡγεμόνας καὶ Τριβαλλῶν καὶ Ἑλλήνων καὶ Ἀλβανῶν. Τούτων δὲ ἁπάντων κατεστρατευμένων, καὶ τῶν ἐν τῇ Ἀσίᾳ ἡγεμόνων αὐτῷ συνεπομένων ἐς τοὺς πολέμους ἤλαυνε δὲ τελευτῶν. Ὡς μὲν οὖν Ἕλληνες κατεστραμμένοι ἐδεδούλωντο [1.46] Ἀμουράτῃ τῷ Ὀρχάνεω, καὶ πρότερόν μοι δεδήλωται. Καὶ νῦν δὲ τοσάδε ἂν λέγοιτο ἐς ὑπόμνησιν ἱκανῶς.

53 Ἰωάννης γὰρ ἐπεί τε κατέσχε τὴν βασιλείαν, συνελάσας Καντακουζηνὸν τὸν πρόσθεν βασιλεύοντα Ἑλλήνων ἐς τὴν Ναζηραίων δίαιταν, ἐνεώρα γε τὰ Τούρκων πράγματα ἐπὶ μέγα χωροῦντα δυνάμεως, ἀπέπλευσεν ἐς Ἰταλίαν. Καὶ πρῶτα μὲν ἐπὶ Ἑνετοὺς τραπόμενος, ἐπικουρίας μὲν οὐδέν τι ἀξίας λόγου τυχών, ἐδανείσατο χρήματα, ἐν νῷ ἔχων ἐπὶ

that he should be everywhere that he has to be. Conversing about such matters with each other, they showed that they did not lack judgment about what was required.

Murad would, then, travel everywhere with the greatest 52
speed, filling every place with fear and apprehension. He relied on Hayreddin, who served him superbly in all things, assisting him and supporting him in any matter that was at hand; he was extremely useful to him and contributed in no small way to the creation of his realm in Europe. Thus Murad subjected many peoples and rulers in Europe to the status of tributaries and made the kings of the Greeks attend him in arms whenever he went on campaign. However, he favored Manuel over all the Greeks. He also had with him the king of the Bulgarians; Dragaš, the son of Žarko;[148] Bogdan, who ruled over Rodope;[149] and, in Europe, other rulers of the Serbs, Greeks, and Albanians. In the end he was marching to war with all of them fighting under him, and attended by the Asian rulers as well. I also stated earlier that the Greeks were defeated and enslaved by Murad, the son of Orhan, but I say all this now by way of a brief reminder.

When Ioannes [V] had taken the throne, he forced Kan- 53
takouzenos, who had previously reigned over the Greeks, to become a monk.[150] Ioannes saw that the power of the Turks was greatly increasing, and sailed to Italy. He turned first to the Venetians but received no help worth mentioning, so he borrowed money with the intention of traveling to the king

τὸν Γαλατίας βασιλέα ἀπιέναι. Ἀφίκετο μέντοι καὶ ἐπὶ τοὺς λοιποὺς τῶν πρὸς ἑσπέραν ἡγεμόνας, δεόμενός τε ἐπικουρίας καὶ ἀποπειρώμενος ὡς οἷόν τε μάλιστα αὐτῶν. Παριὼν τε ἐπὶ τῶν Κελτῶν βασιλέα κατέλαβε μὲν τὰ οἴκοι αὐτῷ διεφθορότα καὶ πάνυ δὲ ἔχοντα μοχθηρῶς, τυχεῖν οὐδενός, ὧν ἕνεκα ἀφίκετο ἐπὶ Ἰταλίας. Ἐπανιὼν δὲ ἐπ' οἴκου, ὡς ἐγένετο κατὰ τοὺς Ἑνετούς, καὶ τὸ δάνειον οὐκ εἶχεν ἀπαιτούμενος ἀποδιδόναι, ὃ ἐδανείσατο ἀπιὼν ἐπὶ Γαλατίαν, κατεσχέθη τε αὐτοῦ ὑπὸ Ἑνετῶν, οὐ μεθιεμένων αὐτὸν ἀποπλεῖν οἴκαδε, ἄχρις ἂν μὴ ἐκτίσῃ τὸ χρέος τοῖς δανεισταῖς. Ὁ δὲ ἐν ἀπορίᾳ γενόμενος, ἐπιπέμπων ἐς Βυζάντιον παρὰ Ἀνδρόνικον τὸν παῖδα αὐτοῦ ἐπιτετραμμένον τὴν βασιλείαν, ἠξίου χρήματα ἐξευρόντα ἀπό τε τῶν ἱερῶν κειμηλίων καὶ ἄλλων τῶν κατὰ τὴν ἀρχὴν πέμψαι οἱ ἱκανὰ ἀπολῦσαι αὐτόν, καὶ μὴ [1.47] περιϊδεῖν αὐτὸν ἐν φυλακῇ ὄντα πάνυ πολὺν διατρίβειν χρόνον. Ὁ μὲν οὖν Ἀνδρόνικος ἐν ὀλιγωρίᾳ ἐποιεῖτο τὰ ἐπεσταλμένα αὐτῷ, οἷα περὶ τὴν βασιλείαν μαλακιζόμενος καὶ τῷ πατρὶ οὐ πάνυ τι ἀρεσκόμενος. Ἐπιστέλλων ἔφασκε μήτε τοὺς Ἕλληνας ἐπιτρέπειν αὐτῷ χρῆσθαι τοῖς ἱεροῖς, μήτε αὐτὸν ἄλλοθέν ποθεν οἷόν τ' εἶναι χρήματα ἐξευρεῖν, ἐκέλευέ τε ἄλλῃ τραπόμενον μὴ διαμέλλειν κήδεσθαι ἑαυτοῦ, ὅπως ἂν ἀπολύοιτο τοῦ χρέους.

54 Ἐμμανουῆλος δὲ ὁ νεώτερος βασιλέως παῖς πυνθανόμενος, οἷ ἀνάγκης ἀφίκετο ὁ πατὴρ αὐτοῦ βασιλεὺς ὑπὸ Ἑνετῶν, εὑρὼν χρήματα καὶ πορισάμενος ὅσα ἠδύνατο, ὅτι τάχιστα ἐπέβη νηός, καὶ διαπλέων ἐς τὴν Ἑνετῶν πόλιν ἀφίκετο, τά τε χρήματα φέρων ἀπέδωκε τῷ πατρί,

of France. In fact, he visited the rest of the western rulers, begging for aid and testing the limits of their willingness to help. But while he was with the king of the French, he realized that his domestic affairs were in bad shape and altogether unstable. He there accomplished none of the goals for which he had gone to Italy. As he was returning home, when he reached the Venetians he could not pay back the loan that he had taken out when he set out for France, which they were now demanding from him.[151] So he was detained there by the Venetians, who would not let him sail home before he had paid back the debt in full to his creditors. He was now at a loss, and sent word to Byzantion to his son Andronikos, to whom he had entrusted the kingdom,[152] asking him to find money from the holy treasures and other state properties, and send him enough to secure his release. He asked that he not be abandoned to spend a lot of time in prison. But Andronikos disregarded his instructions; he had grown self-indulgent on the throne and did not like his father much anyway. He replied by saying that the Greeks would not allow him to use sacred treasures for this purpose, nor could he raise money from any other source. He told his father to look elsewhere and not keep worrying himself about how to be rid of the debt.

When Manuel, the king's younger son, learned what a 54
tight spot his father, the king, was in with the Venetians, he raised money and, when he had procured as much as he could, immediately boarded a ship, set sail, and arrived at Venice. He handed over to his father all the money that he

ὅσα ἐπορίσατο κατὰ τὴν Θέρμην, ἥν τινα ἐπετέτραπτο καὶ κατελέλειπτο ἐπιτροπεύειν. Καὶ ἑαυτὸν δὲ ἄγων παρείχετο χρῆσθαι τῷ πατρί, ὅ τι ἂν βούλοιτο. Καὶ τὸ ἀπὸ τοῦδε ᾠκειῶσθαι Ἐμμανουῆλον τῷ πατρὶ ἐς τὰ μάλιστα συνήθη ὄντα, Ἀνδρόνικον δὲ ἀπεχθάνεσθαι τὸ ἐντεῦθεν μεγάλως· καὶ τὸ μέγα δὲ ἔχθος ἀρξάμενον ἀπὸ τούτου ξυμβῆναι ἀλλήλοις, τά τε ἄλλα σφίσι καὶ ἐς τὴν βασιλείαν διαφερομένοις.

55 Ὁ μὲν οὖν βασιλεὺς Ἑλλήνων, οἷς ἧκε φέρων χρήμασιν Ἐμμανουῆλος, τὰ χρέα ἀπελύετο πρὸς τοὺς Ἑνετούς, καὶ ἐπὶ τὸ Βυζάντιον ἐπανιὼν διεπρεσβεύετο πρὸς βασιλέα Ἀμουράτην, πέμπων τόνδε τὸν παῖδα αὐτοῦ τὸν νεώτερον ἐπὶ τὰς θύρας αὐτοῦ. Ἠξίου τε αὐτὸν ὡς οἷόν τε μάλιστα θεραπεύειν καὶ [1.48] συστρατεύεσθαι, ὅποι ἂν κελεύοι, καὶ προσέχειν τε αὐτῷ τὴν γνώμην, ὥστε φυλάττεσθαι ἐπιεικῶς μηδ᾽ ὁτιοῦν ἐς τὸν βασιλέα τοῦ λοιποῦ ἐξαμαρτεῖν. Ὕστερον μέντοι Θεόδωρον τὸν παῖδα αὐτοῦ ἐπιπέμπων ἐς Πελοπόννησον τελευτησάντων τῶν τοῦ Καντακουζηνοῦ παίδων ἐν τῇ Σπάρτῃ, ἐγένετο ἐν τῇ Θέρμῃ σὺν τῷ ἀδελφῷ Ἐμμανουήλῳ, καὶ αὐτόν τε τῆς Μακεδονίας καὶ Θετταλίας ἡγεμόνα. Ἀφικόμενοι ἐς λόγους ἀπόστασιν ἐβουλεύοντο ἀπὸ Ἀμουράτεω βασιλέως, τὸν μὲν οἴχεσθαι ἐπιόντα ἐπὶ Βυζαντίου μεταπεμπομένου αὐτὸν τοῦ πατρὸς ἐπὶ τὴν βασιλείαν, τὸν δὲ εἰσελθεῖν ἐς τὴν Πελοπόννησον καὶ ἐπιτροπεύειν τὰ κατ᾽ αὐτήν, ᾗ ἐδύνατο κράτιστα καὶ ᾗ ἐδόκει αὐτῷ ἕξειν ὡς ἀσφαλέστατα. Ταῦτα μὲν οὖν ξυνηνέχθη, πρὶν ἢ Ἀνδρόνικον τὸν παῖδα βασιλέως ἀφιστάμενον σὺν τῷ Ἀμουράτεω παιδὶ τῷ Σαουζῇ

had brought with him that he had raised in Thessalonike, which had been entrusted to him and left to him to govern.[153] He even offered himself to be used by his father in any way that he saw fit. And from that point on Manuel and his father became very close, and the latter began to hate Andronikos deeply. This was the origin of the great hatred that existed between them, and caused them to be at odds regarding the kingdom and other matters.

Thus the king of the Greeks paid back the loan to the 55
Venetians with the money brought by Manuel, and he returned to Byzantion.[154] He sent envoys to Sultan Murad, in fact sending his younger son for this purpose to the Porte. He asked his son to serve the sultan as best he could, to campaign with him wherever he commanded, to heed his opinion, and take every precaution against offending the sultan in any matter in the future. Later on[155] he sent his son Theodoros to the Peloponnese,[156] as Kantakouzenos's sons had died in Mistra.[157] When Theodoros was in Thessalonike with his brother Manuel, who had been sent as governor of Macedonia and Thessaly, they began to discuss how they might rebel against Sultan Murad,[158] but the one [Manuel] went to Byzantion, as his father had recalled him there to assume the throne, while the other [Theodoros] entered the Peloponnese and governed its affairs as best he could, making it as secure as he thought was possible. All this happened before Andronikos, the king's son, rose up with Savcı, the

ἐξενέγκαι πόλεμον ἄμφω τῷ Ἀμουράτῃ κατὰ ταῦτα. Ὕστερον μέντοι καὶ τὰ ὑπὸ Ἐμμανουήλου ἐς νεωτερισμὸν πρασσόμενα ἀνάπυστα ἐγένετο βασιλεῖ, καὶ τήν τε Θέρμην καὶ τὰ ταύτης χωρία Χαρατίνης ἀφείλετο αὐτόν. Καὶ ὕστερον ἀπαγορεύοντος τοῦ πατρὸς μὴ ἐπιβῆναι τῆς χώρας αὐτοῦ, καὶ δὴ καὶ ἐπὶ Λέσβον ἀφικόμενον περιδεῆ γενόμενον τὸν Λέσβου ἡγεμόνα προαγορεύειν ἀπαλλάττεσθαι ἐκ τῆς χώρας αὐτοῦ. Κατασχεῖν τριήρη ἐς Τροίαν διαβάντα ἐς τὴν Ἀσίαν, καὶ μισθωσάμενον ἵππους ἀφικέσθαι ἐς Προῦσαν παρὰ βασιλέα Ἀμουράτην. [1.49]

56 Μετὰ δὲ ταῦτα ἐστρατεύετο ἐπὶ Τριβαλλοὺς καὶ ἐπὶ Ἐλεάζαρον τῶν Τριβαλλῶν ἡγεμόνα, πρός τε τοὺς Παίονας τετραμμένον καὶ ἐξοτρύνοντα ἐκείνους στρατεύεσθαι ἐπ' αὐτόν. Ὁ μὲν οὖν Ἐλεάζαρος ὡς ἐπύθετο Ἀμουράτην ἐπιέναι ἐπ' αὐτόν, παρεσκευάζετο στρατιὰν συναγείρων, ᾗ ἐδύνατο, μεγίστην, καί, ᾗ ἐδύνατο, κράτιστα ἀμυνόμενος. Ἐλεάζαρος δὲ θυγατέρας ἔχων ἐπὶ μὲν τῇ μιᾷ τούτων Σούσμανον τὸν τῶν Μυσῶν βασιλέα κηδεστὴν ἐποιήσατο, ἐπὶ δὲ τῇ ἑτέρᾳ Βοῦλκον τὸν τοῦ Πράγκου τοῦ Μλαδένεω υἱόν, Καστορίας τε καὶ Ὀχρίδος τῆς ἐν Μακεδονίᾳ ἡγεμόνος. Ἐπικτησάμενος δὲ μετὰ ταῦτα τὴν ἐν Μακεδονίᾳ χώραν Νικόλεω τοῦ ζουπάνου ἐπὶ τῇ τελευτῇ Οὐγγλέσῃ τε καὶ Κράλεω τῶν ἡγεμόνων, τό τε Πρίστινον καὶ Νήστεαν[10] οὕτω καλουμένην χώραν ὑπαγόμενον ἄχρι ποταμοῦ Ἰλλυριῶν, Σάβα δὲ τὰ νῦν καλουμένου, προεληλυθέναι. Ἐπὶ τοῦτον ὡς ἐστρατεύετο Ἀμουράτης ὁ Ὀρχάνεω, κατέλαβε στρατοπεδευόμενον ἐν πεδίῳ Κοσόβῳ οὕτω καλουμένῳ τῆς Πριστίνου χώρας.

son of Murad, to wage war against Murad.[159] Later, when Manuel's rebellious plot became known to the sultan, Hayreddin removed Thessalonike and its surrounding territory from him.[160] And then, when his father {Ioannes V} prohibited him from entering his own territory, Manuel went to Lesbos, but the ruler of Lesbos became terrified and told him to depart from his territory.[161] He boarded a trireme and crossed over to Asia, to Troy. He hired horses and went to Sultan Murad at Prousa.[162]

After that Murad marched against the Serbs and against 56
Lazar, the ruler of the Serbs,[163] who had turned to the Hungarians and aroused them to campaign against the sultan. When Lazar learned that Murad was coming against him, he assembled and prepared as large an army as possible to defend himself as vigorously as he could. Lazar had two daughters, and he had married one to Šišman, the king of the Bulgarians, and the other to Vuk, the son of Branko, the son of Mladen, who was the ruler of Kastoria and Ohrid in Macedonia.[164] He then also acquired the lands of the *župan* Nikola in Macedonia after the deaths of the rulers Uglješa and the Kral, and, after subjugating Priština and the land called Nestea, advanced as far as the river of Illyria now called the Sava.[165] Murad, the son of Orhan, marched against him and found him camped in the region of Priština called

Καὶ ὡς ἐνταῦθα παρῆν, ἐς πόλεμον παρετάσσετο, ἔχων μεθ' ἑαυτοῦ καὶ τὼ παῖδε ἀμφοτέρω, Παιαζήτην τε καὶ Ἰαγούπην. Τὸ δὲ ἐντεῦθεν Τοῦρκοι μὲν οὖν φασιν Ἀμουράτην μαχεσάμενόν γε καὶ τρεψάμενον τοὺς περὶ Ἐλεάζαρον διώκειν ἀνὰ κράτος, διώκοντα δὲ καταλαβεῖν ἄνδρα Τριβαλλόν, καὶ ἐπικαταβάντα, τὸν δὲ ἐπιστρέψαντα πεζῇ [1.50] ἀκοντίσαι κατὰ τοῦ στήθους, καὶ οὕτω ἀνελεῖν βασιλέα Ἀμουράτην.

57 Ἕλληνες δὲ οὔ φασι μαχεσάμενον καὶ ἐπεξελθόντα, ὡς ἐτρέψατο τοὺς ἐναντίους, ἀποθανεῖν, ἀλλ' ἐν τῇ παρατάξει ἔτι μένοντος αὐτοῦ λέγουσιν ἄνδρα γενναιότατον ἐθελῆσαι ἑκόντα ὑποστῆναι ἀγῶνα κάλλιστον τῶν πώποτε γενομένων. Τοὔνομα δὲ εἶναι τἀνδρὶ τῷδε Μηλόην. Τοῦτον δὴ τὸν Μηλόην φασίν, αἰτησάμενον, ὅσα ἐβούλετό οἱ γενέσθαι ὑπὸ Ἐλεαζάρου τοῦ ἡγεμόνος, ὡπλισμένον ἐλαύνειν σὺν τῷ ἵππῳ ἐπὶ τὸ Ἀμουράτεω στρατόπεδον, ὡς ἂν αὐτομολοῦντα ἀπὸ τῶν ἐναντίων. Ἀμουράτην δὲ λέγουσιν, ἐλπίζοντα αὐτομολεῖν παρ' ἑαυτὸν τὸν ἄνδρα, κελεύειν ὑποχωρεῖν αὐτῷ ἐπιτρέπειν, ὥστε ἐλθόντα ἐπειπεῖν, ἃ βούλοιτο. Γενομένου δὲ ἀγχοῦ τῶν θυρῶν βασιλέως, ᾗ ἔμενε, παραταξάμενος ἄρασθαι τὸ δόρυ, καὶ ἐπιόντα ὁρμήσασθαι ὁρμὴν πασῶν δὴ καλλίστην, ὧν ἡμεῖς ἴσμεν, καὶ ἀνελόντα βασιλέα Ἀμουράτην αὐτόν τε ἅμα αὐτοῦ ἀποθανεῖν γενναιότατα. Ἕλληνες μὲν οὖν οὕτω λέγουσι γενέσθαι, Τοῦρκοι δὲ ἐπεξερχόμενον μετὰ τὴν νίκην ἀποθανεῖν ὑπ' ἀνδρὸς Τριβαλλοῦ.

58 Ἐτελεύτησε δὲ Ἀμουράτης ἐνταῦθα ἐν Κοσόβῳ. Καὶ τὸ μὲν σῶμα αὐτοῦ ἀπήγαγον ἐς Προύσην, ἐν ᾗ οἱ πρῴην

the Plain of Kosovo.[166] When he arrived there, he arranged his army for battle, with both of his sons at his side, Bayezid and Yakub. At this point, so the Turks say, Murad joined battle, routed Lazar's men, and pursued them with all his might. In the pursuit he overtook a certain Serb and sought to ride him down; but the latter, on foot, turned around and speared him in the chest, and so Sultan Murad was killed.

But the Greeks say that he did not die after he had gone 57
out and fought the battle, while he was routing the enemy. Rather, they say that while he was still waiting in battle formation, a most brave man wanted, of his own volition, to undertake the most valiant contest that had ever been attempted. The man's name was Miloš. They say that this Miloš, after asking permission and being allowed to do what he wanted by his ruler Lazar, armed himself and rode out to Murad's camp, pretending to be an enemy deserter. They say that Murad, hoping that the man was deserting to his side, ordered his men to stand aside and allow him to pass, so that he could approach and tell him what he wanted. Once he was close to the sultan's Porte, where Murad was waiting, he drew himself up, raised his spear, and launched himself in the most valiant charge of any that we know. He killed Sultan Murad and died himself at the same time in a most noble manner. This is how the Greeks say it happened, but the Turks say that he was killed by a Serb while he was in pursuit after winning the battle.[167]

So Murad died there in Kosovo. His body was brought 58
back to Prousa, where the tombs of the earlier Ottomans

τάφοι τῶν Ὀτουμανίδων πλὴν Σουλαϊμάνεω ἀποκεκλήρωνται, τὰ δὲ ἐντόσθια Ἀμουράτεω ἐν πεδίῳ Κοσόβῳ κείμενα ἐν τάφῳ αὐτοῦ βασιλικῷ. Ἐτελεύτησε δὲ βασιλεύσας ἔτη ἕν τε καὶ τριάκοντα, ὑπ' [1.51] ἀνδρὸς Τριβαλλοῦ, τελευτὴν οὐ κατὰ βασιλέα τοσαῦτα δὲ ἔτη διαπολεμοῦντα καὶ ἔργα μεγάλα ἀποδειξάμενον, ὃς τοὺς μεγάλους ἐν τῇ Ἀσίᾳ πολέμους καὶ ἐν τῇ Εὐρώπῃ διαπολεμήσας ἔτη ἕν τε καὶ τριάκοντα, ἐς τοσοῦτον αὐτῷ μετῆν τύχης τε ἅμα καὶ ἀρετῆς, ὥστε μηδέποτε ἡττηθῆναι ἐν μάχῃ, δύναμιν δὲ καὶ χώραν ἀξιόχρεων ὑπαγόμενος, κατ' ἄμφω δὲ τὼ ἠπείρω, γῆρας ἤδη βαθὺ ἀφικόμενος μὴ μεθίεσθαι τῶν πολεμίων μάχης, ἀλλ' αἰεὶ λυττῶντι ἐοικέναι ἐπὶ τὴν μάχην, ἄπληστον δὲ αἱμάτων γενόμενον ἁπανταχῇ. Ἦν δὲ αὐτῷ παῦλα τῶν πολεμίων ἡ τῶν κυνηγεσίων ἄγρα, μελέτη τε ἅμα καὶ τριβή. Καθῆστο δὲ οὐδαμῇ οὐδέποτε, ἀλλ' ὁπότε μὴ μάχοιτο, κυνηγῶν διετέλει. Πλεῖστα δὲ ἐς τοῦτο τῶν πρὸ αὐτοῦ βασιλέων δόξαντος αὐτοῦ ἐνευδοκιμεῖν, σπουδήν τε ἅμα καὶ ταχυτῆτα ἐνδεικνύμενος οὐδαμῇ ἐλάσσονα ἐπὶ γήρως ἢ ἐπὶ νεότητος. Ἦν δὲ πρὸ πολλῶν ἐπιφανῶν ἡγεμόνων τε καὶ βασιλέων, καὶ πάντῃ ἀοκνότατός τε καὶ σπουδαιότατος ἐς πάντα. Πάντων δὲ ἐφαπτόμενος οὐδ' ὁτιοῦν παρίει ὑπόλοιπον τῶν πράττεσθαι δεομένων.

59 Καὶ ἐπὶ φόνον ἐλάσαι μέγιστον δὴ τῶν πρὸ αὐτοῦ βασιλέων ἀκοῇ παρειλήφαμεν, λόγου μέντοι ἐπιεικείᾳ χρώμενον ἐς τὰ μάλιστα προσφέρεσθαι τοῖς τε ὑπὸ χεῖρα αὐτοῦ καὶ τοῖς ἡγεμόνων παισὶν ὡς μετριώτατα. Καὶ τιμῆσαι δὲ ἄνδρα ἕκαστον καὶ προσειπεῖν ἑτοιμότατος, καὶ τοὺς μεθ' ἑαυτοῦ ἐξοτρῦναι εἰς μάχην δεινότατος, χρῆσθαι τοῖς τε

were located, except for that of Süleyman.[168] But Murad's internal organs lie buried in a royal tomb on the Plain of Kosovo. He died after reigning for thirty-one years,[169] at the hands of a Serb, a death that was not fitting for a sultan who had waged war for so many years and performed such great deeds. For thirty-one years he waged major wars in Asia and Europe, and so great were both his good fortune and his virtue that he was never defeated in battle. He brought under his control a remarkable array of military force and territory in both continents, and he did not stop waging war against his enemies even when he reached the depths of old age; rather, he always seemed rabid for battle and insatiable when it came to spilling blood everywhere. He paused in his wars only to practice and study the art of hunting. He was always on the move: whenever he was not fighting, he was hunting. In this respect he seems to have gained greater glory than the sultans who reigned before him, displaying no less vigor and alacrity in his old age than when he was young. He surpassed many eminent rulers and kings by always being completely resolute and zealous in all matters. He involved himself in everything and never overlooked anything that had to be done.

We have also heard it said that he surpassed previous 59
kings in terms of the slaughter he caused. But he spoke very politely when dealing with those under his power and with great moderation to the sons of rulers. He honored each man and was very willing to speak with them. He was wonderfully effective at inspiring his men in battle and, they say,

πράγμασι δεινὸς ἁπανταχῇ γενόμενος ἦν, ᾗ φασιν, ὁπότε ἴοιτο ἐπὶ μάχην, χαρίεις τε ἰδεῖν καὶ ἐπιεικέστατος εἰς τὸ [1.52] διαλέγεσθαι. Καὶ τὸν μὲν ὁτιοῦν ἐξαμαρτόντα ἐτιμωρεῖτο ἀφειδέστατα, καὶ προσδιαλέγεσθαι μετριώτατος. Ἐμπεδοῦν λέγεται τὸν ὅρκον αὐτοῦ μάλιστα δὲ τῶν τοῦ γένους τούτου βασιλέων. Καὶ πολλοὺς διὰ ταῦτα αὐτίκα ἴεσθαι ἐς αὐτὸν θαρροῦντας, μηδ' ὁτιοῦν οἰομένους πείσεσθαι χαλεπόν, πρὶν ἢ ἐς χεῖρας αὐτοῦ ἐλθόντας διαπειρᾶσθαι τῆς δυνάμεως αὐτοῦ. Καὶ τόν γε μέγα φρονοῦντα καὶ αὐθαδέστερον αὐτῷ προσφερόμενον τῶν γε ἐς αὐτὸν ὁτιοῦν πεπλημμεληκότων μηκέτι χαίροντα ἀπαλλάττεσθαι. Φοβερώτατον δὲ γενόμενον τοῖς ὑφ' αὐτῷ φιλεῖσθαι μάλιστα δὴ ἡγεμόνων ἐπυθόμεθα αὐτόν, ὥστε μηδὲ κακῶς οἴεσθαι, ὡς ἦν ἐπὶ τόνδε τὸν ἄνδρα ἐστρατεύετο Τεμήρης ὁ βασιλεύς, μὴ ἂν οὕτω φαυλότατα θέσθαι τὸν πόλεμον, ἀλλ' ἢ μαχεσάμενον περιφανῶς μὴ περιγενόμενον τοῦ Τεμήρεω μὴ μέντοι μηδὲ ἡττηθῆναι, ἑλόμενον χώραν ἐς τὸ διαμαχέσασθαι, καθ' ἣν ἂν μὴ ἡττῷτο ῥᾳδίως, ἢ μὴ μαχεσάμενον μεγάλα ἂν βλάψαι τὸν Τεμήρεω βασιλέως στρατὸν ἐπιϊόμενον αὐτῷ καὶ ἐπιτιθέμενον, ᾗ αὐτῷ προχωροίη. Ὡς μὲν οὖν ἐτελεύτησεν Ἀμουράτης ὁ Ὀρχάνεω, αὐτίκα οἱ ἐν ταῖς θύραις ὄντες Ἀμουράτεω ἁρμοσταὶ Παιαζήτην τὸν νεώτερον αὐτοῦ παῖδα κατεστήσαντο βασιλέα.

wonderful also at organizing everything when he was going into battle. He was handsome and reasonable in discussion. While he was merciless in his punishment of wrongdoers, he was very fair in negotiations. It is said that he honored his oaths more than the other sultans of his family. That is why many came to him with high expectations, believing that they would suffer nothing bad, so long, that is, as it was before they had tested his strength and fallen into his hands. But anyone who had offended him and who spoke to him insolently and stubbornly would not be happy when he departed from him. We have learned that while he was terrifying to his subjects, he was especially loved by other rulers. Therefore, it would not be wrong to suppose that if King Timur had marched against this man, the war would not have been managed so badly. He would either have fought bravely against Timur and, even if he had not beaten him, at least he would not have been defeated by him, as he would have chosen a battleground where he would not have been defeated easily; or else, avoiding battle, he would have done a lot of damage to Timur's army by following him and attacking him, as opportunity presented itself.[170] When Murad, the son of Orhan, died, the officers at the Porte of Murad immediately appointed Bayezid, his younger son, sultan.[171]

Β'

[1.53] Ἐπεὶ δὲ ἐτελεύτησεν Ἀμουράτης ὁ Ὀρχάνεω ὑπ' ἀνδρὸς Τριβαλλοῦ, αὐτίκα οἱ ἐν ταῖς θύραις ὄντες τοῦ Ἀμουράτεω ἁρμοσταὶ Παιαζήτην τὸν νεώτερον αὐτοῦ παῖδα ἐστήσαντο βασιλέα. Ὁ δὲ αὐτίκα, ὡς ἔσχε τὴν βασιλείαν, μετάπεμπτον Ἰαγούπην τὸν ἀδελφὸν αὐτοῦ ἐποιήσατο ὡς ὑπὸ τοῦ πατρὸς καλούμενον τοῦ Ἀμουράτεω ἐπὶ τὰς βασιλείας θύρας, φοιτῶντα καὶ πρόσθεν, ὁπότε καλοῖτο. Οὐδ' ὁτιοῦν δὲ τῶν πραχθέντων ἐπιστάμενος ἀφίκετο καλούμενος ὑπ' αὐτοῦ, καὶ ὡς ἐγένετο παρ' αὐτοῦ, συνελήφθη τε καὶ ἐτελεύτησε. Καὶ ἐχρήσατο, ᾗ νομίζεται τοῖς τοῦ γένους τοῦδε βασιλεῦσιν ἐς τοὺς ἀδελφοὺς ποιεῖν, ὡς ἀγχόνῃ δέοι τελευτᾶν τὸν βίον ὑπ' αὐτοῦ, καὶ οὐ σιδήρῳ νενόμισται.

2 Ὡς μὲν οὖν τῷ βασιλεῖ τῷδε ἐξείργαστο τὰ ἐς τὸν ἀδελφὸν καὶ ἐβασίλευε, παρετάξατό τε αὐτίκα ἐς μάχην, καὶ συμβαλὼν ἐτρέψατό τε τοὺς Τριβαλλούς, καὶ ἐν τῇδε τῇ μάχῃ πολλά τε ἀπεγένετο τοῦ στρατεύματος. Ὡς γὰρ οἱ Τοῦρκοι ἐτρέψαντο, ἐπεξῆλθον διώκοντες ἀνὰ κράτος, καὶ διέφθειρον τοὺς Τριβαλλούς, ἱππεύειν τε ὄντες ἐκείνων ἀμείνους καὶ ἵππους πολὺ [1.54] βελτίους ἔχοντες, ὥστε καταλαμβάνειν τοὺς φεύγοντας. Ἧι μὲν οὖν ὑπ' Ἑλλήνων λέγεται, ταύτῃ ἐγένετο· ὡς δὲ αὐτοὶ Τοῦρκοι φασίν, οὐ

Book 2

When Murad, the son of Orhan, died by the hand of a Serb, the officers of his Porte immediately appointed Bayezid, his younger son, as sultan. As soon as he had assumed the throne, Bayezid sent for his brother Yakub and made it seem as though he was being summoned to the royal Porte by his father Murad. Yakub had spent time there in the past too, whenever he was summoned. Knowing nothing of what had happened, he came when he was summoned by him and, as soon as he arrived, was arrested and put to death. He was dealt with in the manner in which the sultans of this people customarily deal with their brothers: namely that they should be strangled to death, not put to the sword.

So when this sultan had dealt with his brother and se- 2
cured his rule, he immediately deployed his army for battle, attacked the Serbs, and routed them. The Serbs lost a large part of their army in this battle, for when the Turks routed them, they began to pursue and kill the Serbs with all their might, as they were better horsemen and had much better horses, so that they were able to overtake those who were fleeing. That, at least, is how the Greeks say it happened. The Turks, on the other hand, say that it was not Bayezid

Παιαζήτεω γενέσθαι τὴν νίκην τήνδε, ἀλλ' ἀπὸ Ἀμουράτεω τήν τε μάχην γενέσθαι καὶ νίκην ἐκείνου, καὶ Ἐλεάζαρον τὸν ἡγεμόνα [ἐκείνου] ὑπ' ἐκείνῳ στρατηγοῦντι ἀποθανεῖν ἐν τῇ μάχῃ. Τοῦρκοι μὲν δὴ οὕτω λέγουσι γενέσθαι, οὐκ ἔχω δὲ συμβαλέσθαι, ὡς ἐν τῇ παρατάξει ἐν βραχεῖ τινι χρόνῳ τόν τε ἀδελφὸν ἀνεῖλε καὶ ἐς μάχην καθίστατο αὐτίκα, ἀλλ' οὐδὲ ὡς ἀράμενος τὸ δόρυ ἕλοι τε ἐπὶ τὸν βασιλέα καὶ ἐξείη διαχρήσασθαι μηδενὸς αὐτῷ ἐμποδὼν γενομένου. Ἀλλὰ ταῦτα μὲν ἴτω, ὅπῃ ἑκάστῳ προσφιλὲς ἡγεῖσθαι περὶ αὐτῶν.

3 Ἐπεὶ δὲ Παιαζήτης παρέλαβε τὴν βασιλείαν, καὶ τῇ ἐς τοὺς ἐναντίους νίκῃ ἐχρήσατο περιφανεῖ, πολλῶν τε καὶ αὐτοῦ ἀποθανόντων ἐν τῇ μάχῃ καὶ τελευτήσαντος τοῦ ἡγεμόνος, ἐπέδραμέ τε σύμπασαν τὴν Τριβαλλῶν χώραν, καὶ ἀνδράποδα ὡς πλεῖστα ὑφ' αὐτῷ ποιησάμενος, καθίστησι τὰ ἐν τῇ ἀρχῇ αὐτῷ, ᾗ ᾤετο ξυνοίσεσθαι ἐπὶ τὸ ἄμεινον, καὶ Ἕλλησι σπονδὰς ἐποιήσατο. Καὶ τοῖς περὶ Μακεδονίαν ἡγεμόσιν εἰρήνην ποιησάμενος τὴν Σκοπίων ᾤκισε πόλιν, παμπόλλους τῶν Τούρκων ἀπό τε τῆς Εὐρώπης καὶ ἀπὸ τῆς Ἀσίας ἀγαγὼν σὺν γυναιξί τε ἅμα καὶ παισί. Ταῦτα δὲ ἐποίει, ὡς ἔχοι ἂν ἀπὸ ταύτης ὁρμώμενος ἄγειν καὶ φέρειν τὰ Ἰλλυριῶν πράγματα. Ἐπέδραμε μὲν οὖν καὶ τὴν Ἰλλυριῶν χώραν, [1.55] καὶ πολίσματα ἄττα ἑλὼν ἠνδραποδίσατο, καὶ τήν τε Ἀλβανῶν χώραν ἐπιπέμψας στράτευμα ἐληΐζετο ἔστε ἐπὶ τὴν ἐς τὸ Ἰόνιον παράλιον χώραν, καὶ τὴν περὶ Ἐπίδαμνον.

4 Καὶ Ἕλληνες μὲν αὐτῷ ἐφείποντο στρατευόμενοι ἅμα, ὅποι ἂν ἐλαύνοι, ὅ τε Ἰωάννου τοῦ βασιλέως Ἑλλήνων

who won this victory, but that the battle was fought and won by Murad, and that the ruler Lazar was killed in that battle while Murad was in command.[1] That is how the Turks say it happened.[2] But I cannot see either how, while he was in battle formation, Bayezid could have both killed his brother and joined battle in such a short time, nor how Miloš could have raised his spear, attacked the sultan, and been able to kill him without anyone trying to stop him. But let each person think what he likes about these matters.

When Bayezid became sultan and won this famous vic- 3
tory over his enemies, many of them died in the battle, including their ruler. So he overran the entire territory of the Serbs and seized as many captive slaves as he could. He then made arrangements for his realm that he believed would be in his best interest, and he made a treaty with the Greeks. After he had made peace with the rulers in Macedonia, he settled the city of Skopje by bringing a large number of Turks from both Europe and Asia, with their women and children. But he did this in order to use it as a base from which to plunder the belongings of the Illyrians [Bosnians]. He raided their land, captured some towns, and enslaved their inhabitants. He also sent an army to the land of the Albanians and ravaged it as far as the coast of the Adriatic Sea and the land around Durrës.[3]

The Greek army accompanied Bayezid on campaign, 4
wherever he went, including Manuel, the son of Ioannes

παῖς Ἐμμανουῆλος, καὶ Ἀνδρονίκου τοῦ πρεσβυτέρου παῖς Ἰωάννης. Τούτους γὰρ ὡς τὼ ὀφθαλμὼ ὄξει ζέοντι περιέχει, παρείχετο αὐτοῖς τὴν δίαιταν ἀμφοῖν. Οὗτοι δ' ὡς ἔγνωσαν ὁρῶντες ἐπὶ σφίσιν αὐτοῖς, καὶ ὅτι τῶν ὀφθαλμῶν ἐπὶ τὸ ἄμεινον διακέοιτο, χρόνου ἐπιγενομένου σφίσι, τῇ τε γυναικὶ καὶ ἀλλήλοις ἐς λόγους ἀφικόμενοι, καί τινων ἄλλων ἐς τὴν ἐσήγησιν ταύτην ἐξηγουμένων καὶ συνεπιλαβομένων, ἀπέδρασαν ἐς τὴν καταντικρὺ Βυζαντίου πόλιν Γαλατίην Ἰανυΐων. Ἐντεῦθεν δὲ ἀφίκοντο παρὰ βασιλέα Παιαζήτην, καὶ ἀφικόμενοι ἠξίουν σφίσιν ἐπικουρίαν δοθῆναι ὡς ἐπὶ τὴν ἑαυτῶν πόλιν ἐλαύνειν, καὶ ἐδέοντο κατάγειν σφᾶς. Ἔλεγε δὲ ἐς ὄψιν τῷ βασιλεῖ ἀφικόμενος τοιάδε.

5 "Ἐμοὶ μὲν οὖν, βασιλεῦ, συμφορᾷ πεπληγμένῳ τοιᾷδε, τύχῃ τῇ ἀμείνονι ἐπιτρέψας ἐμαυτὸν καὶ Θεῷ τῷ πάντα ἐφορῶντι βέλτιον ἔχω ἐμαυτοῦ, καί μοι χάριν ὁ δαίμων κατέθετο οὐκ ἀηδῆ· ὁρᾶν γὰρ ἤδη ἐμοὶ κατέλιπε βραχὺ πάμπαν τῆς ὄψεως ἀφελόμενος, τήν τε βασιλείαν ὑπισχνεῖται, καὶ τὴν βασιλείαν ἀνήκουσαν ἐμοὶ θέμις ἀποδιδόναι. Ταύτην δὲ τὴν βασιλείαν ἡμῶν, ἣν ἐμοὶ πείθῃ, ἕξεις τοῦ λοιποῦ χρῆσθαι, [1.56] ὅπως ἄν σοι δοκοίη, ἣν ἐμοὶ ταύτην ἀποδεδωκὼς ἔσῃ, ἢν ἱππέας τετρακισχιλίους μάλιστα παρεχόμενος ἕπεσθαί μοι ἐπὶ μῆνας δύο κελεύῃς. Εἰσὶ δὲ παρ' ἡμῖν σχεδὸν οἱ τοῦ ἄστεος γένει τε καὶ πλούτῳ προφέροντες, καὶ τούτων οὐκ ὀλίγοι εἵποντο ἄν μοι ἐνθάδε, εἰ μὴ εἰδείην ἐν τῷ ἄστει ἐμοὶ τυγχάνειν ὄντας καὶ ἐμοὶ τιμωροῦντας, ἐφ' ὅ τι ἂν γνοίην ἡμῖν ἐπιτήδειον ἔσεσθαι. Φόρον δὲ τῷ σῷ οἴκῳ πολλαπλάσιον ὑπισχνοῦμαι

[V], king of the Greeks, and Ioannes [VII], the son of Andronikos the elder [IV]. Having poured scalding vinegar on their eyes,[4] the king now provided for the livelihood of them both. But they had realized, between themselves, that they had regained some vision and that their eyes were improving. After some time had passed, they discussed things with their wives and each other, and, with the guidance and support of certain other people for this plan, they escaped to the Genoese city of Galatas, across from Byzantion.[5] From there they went to Sultan Bayezid[6] and, when they arrived before him, asked him to give them assistance so that they could march against their own city, and begged him to restore them. He [Andronikos] said the following when he came before the sultan.

"O sultan, since I had been struck by this misfortune, I 5
entrusted myself to Good Fortune and to God, who oversees all things, and now I find myself much better off, as that Power has granted me a most welcome favor. For even though I had completely lost my sight, he has now partially restored my vision and is promising me the kingdom, to restore to me the throne that is rightfully mine. If you agree to my proposal and give me back my kingdom, you will in the future be able to make use of it in whatever way you see fit. Give me four thousand cavalry and order them to follow me for two months. The richest and noblest men of the city are almost all on our side, and many would have followed me here were it not that I know that they remain in the city for my sake, to support me in whatever way I decide is best for us. I promise to render to your house a much greater tribute

ἀπάγειν ἔτους ἑκάστου, καὶ ἁρμοστὴν ἔχειν ἐν τῇ πόλει." Βασιλεὺς δὲ ἀμείβετο τοῖσδε. "Ἐμοί τε οὖν, ἐπεί τε ἐπυθόμην, ὡς ὁρᾶν ἤδη σοι καταλέλειπται, ἡδομένῳ τέ μοι ὁ λόγος ἐγένετο, καὶ χάριν οἶδα τῷ θνητῶν τε καὶ ἀθανάτων δημιουργῷ τήνδε σοι τὴν χάριν καταθεμένῳ· ἥκεις ἐπὶ ἄνδρας σοι προσφιλεῖς, καὶ ἀμυνοῦντάς σοι, εἰς ὅσον ἂν ἐξῇ διαπράξασθαι, ἐφ' ὅ τί περ ἴεσθαι ἀγωνιζόμενος. Τίσομαι δὲ βασιλέα τὸν σὸν πατέρα οὕτως, ὥστε μηδέποτε ἐσαῦθις βουλεύεσθαι περὶ ἐμὲ νεώτερα πράγματα. Ἴθι δὲ τούτους λαβών, οὓς σὺ ἔφησθα, χώρει δὲ ἐπὶ τὴν πόλιν πράσσων, ὅπως ὡς βέλτιστα ἔσοιτό σοι καταγομένῳ ἐπὶ τὴν πατρίδα."

6 Ὁ μὲν ταῦτα εἰπὼν ἑτοίμους παρείχετο τοὺς ἱππέας, Ἀνδρόνικος δὲ τούτους λαβὼν ἤλαυνεν ἐπὶ Βυζάντιον. Ἰωάννης δὲ καὶ Ἐμμανουῆλος ὁ παῖς αὐτοῦ, ὡς ἐπύθοντο τάχιστα Ἀνδρόνικον σὺν τῷ παιδὶ αὐτοῦ ἐλαύνοντα ἐπὶ σφᾶς, ἐσῆλθόν τε ἐς τὴν τῆς Χρυσέας οὕτω καλουμένην ἀκρόπολιν, καὶ παρεσκευάζοντο ὡς [1.57] πολιορκησόμενοι. Ἀνδρόνικος μὲν οὖν ἐλάσας ἐπολιόρκει, μετὰ δὲ ταῦτα ὁμολογίᾳ χρησάμενος εἷλε τὴν ἀκρόπολιν, εἴς τι κλωβίον ἐμβαλλομένω μετέωρον καὶ καθεῖρξεν ἄμφω ἐς πύργον τε, καὶ εἱρκτὴν βραχεῖαν συνελάσας ξυλίνην πεποιημένην ἐντὸς τοῦ πύργου, καὶ τήν τε βασιλείαν κατέσχε, τόν τε πατέρα καὶ ἀδελφὸν ἔχων ἐν φυλακῇ. Βασιλεύσας δὲ ἀπέδειξε καὶ τὸν παῖδα αὐτοῦ Ἰωάννην βασιλέα τοῖς Ἕλλησι. Κατεῖχε μὲν οὖν ἐπὶ ἔτη τρία ἐς τὴν εἱρκτὴν τήνδε, καὶ ἀνελεῖν οὐκ ἤθελε παραινοῦντος ἐς τοῦτο αὐτῷ συνεχῶς Παιαζήτεω. Τῷ δὲ τετάρτῳ ἔτει ἀναπείσαντες

every year, and accept one of your governors in the city." The sultan answered with these words: "When I learned that some sight still remained to you, the news brought me joy and I gave thanks to the Creator of mortals and immortals who had done you this favor. You have come to men who are well disposed toward you and will fight at your side for as long as it takes to achieve what you are contending for. I will take such vengeance on the king, your father, that he never again plans any opposition to me. Come now, take the men for whom you asked, and go to the city, and do whatever is best for your return to your homeland."

When Bayezid had said this he supplied the cavalry, all ready to go. Andronikos took them and marched against Byzantion. But as soon as Ioannes [V] and Manuel, his son, learned that Andronikos and his son [Ioannes VII] were marching against them, they entered the fortress that is named after the Golden Gate and prepared for a siege. Andronikos then arrived and besieged them. Later he took the fortress by surrender and incarcerated both of them in a cage suspended in a tower.[7] He had a small wooden cell constructed inside the tower and put them in it together, keeping his father and brother imprisoned in it while he held the throne. During his reign,[8] he also declared his son Ioannes [VII] as king over the Greeks. He kept them in this cell for three years, but he did not wish to kill them, although Bayezid was continually advising him to do so. In the fourth 6

ὑπηρέτην, ὃς αὐτοῖς τε προσήει καὶ τὰ ἀμφὶ τὴν τροφὴν ἐκόμιζεν ἐς τὴν εἱρκτήν, ἐπιδοῦναι σφίσι σίδηρον· καὶ κατὰ βραχὺ καταλῦσαί τε αὐτοὺς λέγεται τὴν εἱρκτήν, καὶ ἀποδράντας ἀφικέσθαι παρὰ βασιλέα Παιαζήτην, ὑπισχνουμένους δὲ φόρον ἀπάγειν καὶ στρατιάν, ὅσην ἂν ἐπιτάττοι σφίσιν αὐτοῖς. Ἐπιπέμψας ἄγγελον ἐς τὸ Βυζάντιον ἐπήρετο τοὺς Βυζαντίους καὶ τὴν γνώμην αὐτῶν, τίνα βούλοιντο σφίσι βασιλέα γενέσθαι, Ἐμμανουῆλον ἢ βασιλέα Παιαζήτην· διεπειρᾶτο γὰρ ταύτῃ καὶ περὶ ἑαυτοῦ τῆς γνώμης τῶν Βυζαντίων. Οἱ δὲ Βυζάντιοι αἱροῦντο Ἐμμανουῆλον, ἅτε ἀχθόμενοι ἤδη τῇ Ἀνδρονίκου ἀρχῇ. Ἐνταῦθα ἐρίζοντε ἄμφω τῶν Ἑλλήνων βασιλέε περὶ τῆς Βυζαντίου [1.58] βασιλείας, ἐτάξατο φόρον ἀπάγειν ὁ Ἐμμανουῆλος ἐς τρισμυρίους χρυσίνους, καὶ ἑαυτὸν ἄγοντα ἐπὶ στρατιὰν ἕπεσθαι συστρατευόμενον, καὶ οὕτω δὲ παραλαβεῖν ὑπὸ Παιαζήτεω τὴν Βυζαντίου βασιλείαν, καὶ ἐς θύρας φοιτῶντα τόν τε φόρον οἱ ἐτάξατο καὶ τὸν στρατὸν ἀπάγειν ἑκάστου ἔτους, ὡς ἔαρ ὑπέφαινεν. Ἀνδρόνικος μὲν οὖν καὶ Ἰωάννης ὁ παῖς αὐτοῦ ἐν ταῖς θύραις διατρίβοντες δίαιταν εἶχον παρὰ βασιλέως, Ἐμμανουῆλος δὲ ἐβασίλευε.

7 Παιαζήτης δὲ ὁ Ἀμουράτεω, ἔχων μεθ' ἑαυτοῦ τοὺς Ἑλλήνων βασιλεῖς ἐνάγοντας ἐς τοῦτο, ἐστρατεύετο ἐπὶ Φιλαδέλφειαν πόλιν Ἑλληνίδα. Ἐριζόντων γὰρ τῶν βασιλέων Βυζαντίου ᾐτεῖτο αὐτοὺς καὶ Φιλαδέλφειαν, οἱ δὲ ἔφασαν ἀποδοῦναι. Ὡς δὲ ἄγγελον ἐπιπέμποντος τοῦ βασιλέως Ἐμμανουήλου, ὅπως τοῦ λοιποῦ παραδόντες σφᾶς τῷ Παιαζήτῃ δέχοιντο ἄρχοντα καὶ ἁρμοστὴν Τοῦρκον,

year they managed to persuade a servant, who used to come to bring them food in the prison, to give them an iron tool. It is said that they quickly freed themselves from the cell.[9] When they had escaped, they went to Sultan Bayezid,[10] promising to deliver to him as much tribute and as many soldiers as he might demand from them. He sent a messenger to Byzantion and asked the Byzantines for their opinion too, about which of them they wanted as their king, Manuel or Sultan Bayezid. For he wanted to sound out the Byzantines' opinion about himself too in this way. The Byzantines chose Manuel, as they were already unhappy with the way Andronikos was governing. While the two kings of the Greeks were thus disputing possession of the throne in Byzantion, Manuel agreed to pay Bayezid thirty thousand gold coins as tribute and to accompany him personally with an army when he went on campaign. On these terms he was given the throne of Byzantion by Bayezid. Thereafter he attended the Porte each year, early in the spring, delivering to him the tribute and the army that he had agreed on. As for Andronikos and his son Ioannes, they resided at the Porte and were maintained by the sultan, but Manuel held the throne.[11]

Bayezid, the son of Murad, now campaigned against Phil- 7
adelpheia, a Greek city, having been led into doing this by the kings of the Greeks, whom he had with him. For while the kings of Byzantion were quarreling among themselves, Bayezid had also asked for Philadelpheia and they had said they would give it to him.[12] But when King Manuel sent a messenger asking them to surrender themselves to Bayezid in the future and accept a Turk as their lord and gover-

οὐκ ἔφασαν ἑκόντας εἶναι καταπροδοῦναι σφᾶς τῷ βαρβάρῳ, καὶ τὸ ἐντεῦθεν ἐπολιόρκει Φιλαδέλφειαν Παιαζήτης, ἔχων καὶ τοὺς Ἑλλήνων βασιλεῖς. Οἱ δὲ ἀριστεῦσαί τε αὐτοῦ λέγονται, καὶ ἀναβάντες οὗτοι πρῶτον εἷλον τὴν πόλιν. Οὕτω μὲν οὖν ἑάλω Φιλαδέλφεια ἡ τῆς Λυδίας πόλις εὐνομουμένη Ἑλληνίς.

8 Μετὰ δὲ ταῦτα Παιαζήτης ἤλαυνεν ἐπὶ Σκενδέρεα τὸν τῶν Ἀρμενίων βασιλέα, καὶ ἐπὶ Ἐρτζιγγάνην πόλιν, τὰ τῶν Ἀρμενίων βασίλεια, καὶ ἐπὶ Σαμαχίην πολίχνιον λεγομένην. Λέγεται δὲ [1.59] οὗτος ὁ Σκενδέρης τῶν βαρβάρων πολλῷ τῶν κατὰ τὴν Ἀσίαν ἀνδρειότατος καὶ τὰ ἐς πόλεμον τόλμῃ τε καὶ ῥώμῃ σώματος γενέσθαι οὐδενὸς δεύτερον, ὡς ἐπιόντων ποτὲ αὐτῷ τῶν Ἀσσυρίων πολλάκις ἔργα ἀποδείξασθαι ἄξια λόγου, τρεψάμενος τοὺς ἐναντίους σὺν ὀλίγοις τοῖς ἀμφ' αὐτόν. Τοῦτον δὲ τὸν Σκενδέρεα, ὡς ἀπήχθετο τῇ ἑαυτοῦ γυναικί, συλλαβοῦσα αὐτὸν σὺν τῷ παιδὶ διαχρήσασθαι καὶ τὴν βασιλείαν κατέχειν. Ἐπὶ τοῦτον δὴ Παιαζήτης ἐλάσας τήν τε Ἐρτζιγγάνην πόλιν πολιορκῶν παρεστήσατο καὶ τὸν παῖδα Σκενδέρεω εἶχεν ἐν φυλακῇ. Μετὰ δὲ ταῦτα τούς τε Τζανίδας καταστρεψάμενος, οἳ κατέχουσι τὰ τῆς Κολχίδος ἐπὶ Ἄμαστριν πόλιν καθήκοντα, ἤλαυνεν ἐπὶ Καραΐλούκην τὸν Λευκαμνᾶν Σαμαχίης ἡγεμόνα, καὶ ἐπεξελθόντα σὺν τῇ ἑαυτοῦ στρατιᾷ μάχῃ ἐκράτησε, καὶ ἐπολιόρκει Σαμαχίην πόλιν. Καὶ ὡς οὐδὲν προεχώρει ἡ τῆς πόλεως αἵρεσις, ἀπεχώρησεν ἀπαγαγὼν τὸν στρατόν, καὶ ἐπανέστησεν ἐπ' οἶκου.

9 Μετὰ δὲ ταῦτα ἐλαύνων ἐπὶ τοὺς ἐν τῇ Ἀσίᾳ λοιποὺς

nor, they said that they were not willing to hand themselves over to the barbarian. Thus Bayezid besieged Philadelpheia, while keeping the kings of the Greeks with him. It is said that they performed valiantly there, and that they were the first to scale the walls and take the city. Thus fell Philadelpheia, a well-governed Greek city in Lydia.

After this Bayezid moved against Iskender, the king of 8
the Armenians, against the city of Erzinjan, the royal court of the Armenians, and against a town called Shemakha.[13] It is said that this Iskender was by far the bravest of the barbarians in Asia, second to none in military daring and physical strength. At one time the Assyrians had attacked him and he had often performed notable deeds, routing the enemy with only the few men he had with him.[14] But this Iskender was hated by own wife who, along with his son, arrested him, put him to death, and held the throne herself.[15] Bayezid now moved against this man and captured the city of Erzinjan by siege, imprisoning Iskender's son.[16] Then he subdued the Janids, who occupy the lands of Kolchis as far as the city of Amastris.[17] He also marched against Kara Yülük, the White Sheep ruler from Shemakha. He advanced against him with his own army, defeated him in battle, and besieged the city of Shemakha. But as he was making little progress in taking the city, he left and led his army away, returning home.[18]

After that he moved against the remaining rulers in Asia, 9

ἡγεμόνας, τόν τε Ἀϊδίνην, Σαρχάνην, Μενδεσίαν, Τεκίην καὶ Μετίνην, τήν τε ἀρχὴν αὐτῶν ἀφείλετο, καὶ ἐκβαλὼν αὐτοὺς τὴν χώραν ὑφ' αὑτῷ ποιησάμενος εἶχεν. Οὗτοι δὲ ὡς ἀπελήλαντο τῆς σφῶν χώρας, [1.60] ἀνέβησαν παρὰ βασιλέα Τεμήρην ἐς Σκυθίαν. Ὡς μὲν οὖν ἀναβάντες οὗτοι ἐς ὄψιν ἦλθον τῷ βασιλεῖ, ὕστερόν μοι δεδήλωται. Πλὴν γὰρ Καραμάνου τοῦ Ἀλισουρίου ἐπίκλην καὶ Τουργούτεω τοῦ τῆς Φρυγίας ἄρχοντος, οἳ καὶ ἐπιγαμίας αὐτῷ ποιησάμενοι εἰρήνην ἦγον, οἱ λοιποὶ τῶν ἡγεμόνων ἐστερημένοι τῆς ἀρχῆς ἀνέβησαν ἐς Σαμαρχάνδην τὰ βασίλεια Τεμήρεω. Σαρχάνην μὲν τὴν πάραλον τῆς Ἰωνίας ἐπιτροπεύοντα, καὶ Μενδεσίαν τοῦ Καλάμεω ἀπόγονον, καὶ Τεκίην τὴν Μυσίαν κατέχοντα τῶν ἑπτὰ ἡγεμόνων ἀπογόνους γεγονέναι φαμὲν τῶν τοῦ Ὀτουμάνεω τὴν τῆς Ἀσίας ἀρχὴν κοινῇ συγκατεργασαμένων, οἳ καὶ Ἀλαδίνεω τοῦ βασιλέως γενέσθαι θεράποντες λέγονται. Μετίνην δὲ καὶ Ἀϊδίνην, ὅθεν τὴν ἀρχὴν ἐκτήσαντο, οὐκ ἔχω διασημῆναι. Τὸν δὲ Ἀϊδίνην λέγεται μόνον, τῆς ἀπὸ Κολοφῶνος ἔστε ἐπὶ Καρίαν ἦρχε χώρας. Τούρκων μέντοι γένος τούς τε ὑπὸ Τουργούτεω τελοῦντας καὶ ὑπὸ Καραμάνεω καὶ Μετίνῃ καὶ Ἀϊδίνῃ ἐπίσταμαι σαφῶς εἶναί τε καὶ ὀνομάζεσθαι. Καὶ ἐν Καππαδοκίᾳ ὑπαγόμενος τοῦτο μὲν τὴν ὑπὸ Καραϊσούφῃ χώραν, τοῦτο δὲ τὴν ὑπὸ τοῖς Ὀμούρεω παισί, καὶ τὰ πλέω τῆς Φρυγίας καταστρεψάμενος, [1.61] ἤλαυνεν ἐπὶ Ἐρτζιγγάνην τὰ τῶν Ἀρμενίων βασίλεια, καὶ ἐπὶ τὸν Σκενδέρεω παῖδα, ὃς ταύτης ἡγεῖτο τῆς χώρας ἔστε ἐπὶ Εὐφράτην καὶ τῆς τε Κολχίδος μοῖραν οὐκ ὀλίγην ὑφ' αὑτῷ ποιησάμενος ἦρχε.

namely Aydın, Saruhan, Menteşe, Teke, and Metin.[19] He stripped them of their realms, driving them out, and appropriating their territory. Driven from their own lands, they went off to King Timur, in Skythia. I will recount later how they went off there and came into the presence of the king.[20] Except for Karaman, who was also known as Alishur, and Turgut, the lord of Phrygia, who were related to Bayezid by marriage and so were at peace with him,[21] all the other rulers were deprived of their realms and went off to Samarkand, to the court of Timur. I should add that Saruhan, who governed the coast of Ionia; Menteşe, who was the descendant of Kalamshah; and Teke, who held Mysia, were descended from the seven rulers who jointly assisted Osman in conquering the realm of Asia, and they are said to have been servants of Sultan 'Ala' al-Din.[22] I have no specific information as to how Metin and Aydın obtained their realms. It is said only that Aydın ruled the land from Kolophon to Karia. I know clearly, however, that the subjects of Turgut, Karaman, Metin, and Aydın are Turks and are called that. In Kappadokia Bayezid took control of both the territory that was under Kara Yusuf and also that which was under the sons of Umur.[23] He conquered the larger part of Phrygia, marched against Erzinjan, the royal court of the Armenians, and against the son of Iskender, who ruled this land as far as the Euphrates, and he ruled a significant part of Kolchis after he had brought it under his power.[24]

10 Ταῦτα μὲν οὖν γενόμενος ἐν τῇ Ἀσίᾳ καὶ μεγάλα ἀπεδείκνυτο ἔργα· μετὰ δὲ ὡς τὴν Εὐρώπην διαβάς, στρατεύματα ἐπιπέμπων ἔστε Μακεδονίαν, τὴν πρὸς τὸν Ἰόνιον τοὺς ταύτῃ Ἀλβανοὺς καὶ τὴν χώραν ἐδῄου, καὶ πολίσματα ἄττα ἑλὼν τῆς Ἀλβανῶν χώρας ἐπὶ Ἰλλυριοὺς ἤλαυνέ τε καὶ ἐδῄου τὴν χώραν, λείαν τὰ ἐκείνων ποιούμενος. Μετὰ δὲ ταῦτα ἐστρατεύετο ἐπὶ Πελοπόννησον, τῷ μὲν λόγῳ ὡς ἐπὶ Φωκαΐδα καὶ ἐπὶ Θετταλίαν ἐλαύνων, καταστησόμενος τὰ ἐν τῇ Θετταλίᾳ, ὥστε ἐπιτηδείως ἔχειν αὐτῷ, τοῦ δὲ Φωκέων ἀρχιερέως ἐπαγομένου σφίσιν ἐπὶ χώραν κυνηγῆσαί τε κρατίστην καὶ λειμῶνας γεράνους παρεχομένους πλῆθος ἄπλετον καὶ πεδία ἐνιππεῦσαι τὰ κάλλιστα, τῷ δὲ ἔργῳ ἐπὶ Θετταλίαν τε καὶ τοὺς ταύτῃ ἡγεμόνας Ἐπικερναίους τοὔνομα καὶ ἐπὶ γυναῖκα τοῦ Δὲ Λουῆ ἡγεμόνος τοῦ Δὲ Σουλᾶ. Μετὰ δὲ ταῦτα καὶ ὡς Πελοπόννησον ἐμβαλών, ἔχων δὴ καὶ τὸν βασιλέως [1.62] Ἰωάννου παῖδα Θεόδωρον ἡγεμόνα, ἐστρατεύετο.

11 Ἀφικόμενος δὲ ἐς Θετταλίαν τήν τε Δομοκίην παρέλαβεν, ἐκλιπόντος τοῦ ἐν αὐτῇ ἡγεμόνος Ἐπικέρνεω, καὶ δὴ καὶ Φαρσάλων πόλιν, καὶ ταύτην ὑπὸ Ἐπικερναίων ἐπικρατουμένην ὑφ᾽ αὑτῷ ἐποιήσατο. Προέλαυνε δὲ ἐς τὸ πρόσω, τό τε Ζητοῦνιν τὸ ἐν Θερμοπύλαις καὶ Πάτρας τὰς ἐν τῷ πεδίῳ πρὸς τῇ ὑπωρείᾳ τῶν Λοκρῶν ὄρους κατεστρέψατο, καὶ αὐτῷ προεχώρησε· καὶ ἄλλα δὲ τῶν ταύτῃ πολισμάτων οὐκ ὀλίγα προσεχώρησεν αὐτῷ καθομολογίῃ. Μετὰ δὲ ταῦτα ἡ Δὲ Λουῆ τοῦ ἡγεμόνος γυνή, ἔχουσα θυγατέρα γάμου τε ὡραίαν καὶ ἐγγυημένην ἀνδρί, ὡς ἐπύθετο βασιλέα ἐπιόντα, ἡγεῖσθαι δὲ αὐτῷ ἐπὶ τάδε τῶν

These were the great deeds that Bayezid performed while he was in Asia. After that, when he crossed over into Europe, he sent armies as far as Macedonia, plundering the land by the Adriatic Sea and the Albanians there. He captured some towns in Albanian territory and then moved on against the Illyrians, plundering the land and taking their goods as loot.[25] After that he marched against the Peloponnese, but he pretended that he was going to Phokis and Thessaly in order to organize the affairs of Thessaly to suit him.[26] For the bishop of Phokis[27] had invited him to that land that was superb for hunting, with meadows which offered an extraordinary abundance of cranes, and plains that were most excellent for riding. In reality, Bayezid marched against Thessaly and its rulers, who were called Epikernaioi,[28] and against the wife of De Luis, the ruler of Salona.[29] After that he intended to invade the Peloponnese, with its ruler Theodoros [I] in tow, the son of King Ioannes [V]. 10

When he arrived in Thessaly, he seized Domokos in the absence of its Epikernian ruler. Then he also took and subjected to his authority the city of Pharsala, whose lords were also Epikernaioi. He advanced further and conquered Lamia by Thermopylai and Patras, the one on the plain by the foot of the mountain in Lokris. He then moved on to the plain. Many other towns in that area also went over to him through negotiated surrender. After that, when the wife of the ruler De Luis, who had a marriageable daughter already betrothed to a man,[30] learned that the sultan was coming against her and that the bishop of Salona was spurring him 11

Σαλόνων ἀρχιερέα, λαβοῦσά τε τὴν θυγατέρα καὶ δῶρα, ὅσα ἠδύνατο, ὑπήντα τῷ βασιλεῖ. Ὁ δὲ τήν τε θυγατέρα ἐδέξατο, καὶ αὐτὴν ἅμα τῇ θυγατρὶ ἐς τὰ ἑαυτοῦ ἤθη ἀπέπεμπε, τὴν δὲ χώραν παραλαβὼν ταύτῃ ἐπέστησεν ἄρχοντα.

12 Λέγεται δὲ περὶ ταύτης τῆς γυναικός, ὡς ἱερέως τινὸς Στράτεω ἐπικαλουμένου ἐρασθεῖσα καὶ ἐς τὸ πρόσω ἀναιδείας ἐλαύνων τήν τε ἀρχὴν ἐπέτρεψε τῷ ἱερεῖ, καὶ ἀναιδῆ πολλοὺς τοὺς τὴν Δελφῶν πόλιν ἐνοικοῦντας ἐργασαμένη. Διὰ ταῦτα ὑπὸ ἀρχιερέως ἐς βασιλέα διεβλήθησαν, ὡς αἰκία ἂν [1.63] εἴη γυναῖκα χώρας τοσαύτης ἡγουμένην, ὑπὸ ἱερέως μοιχευομένην, ἀνήκεστα κακὰ ποιεῖν τοὺς πολίτας, καὶ διὰ ταῦτα ἀπᾶραι βασιλέα ἐπιόντα στρατεύεσθαι ἐπ' αὐτούς. Λέγεται μέντοι περὶ τοῦ ἱερέως τούτου τοῦ τῇ γυναικὶ ταύτῃ συγγενομένου καὶ ἄλλα οὐκ ὀλίγα ἔστε γυναῖκας πλημμελῆσαι, κατεργαζόμενον δαιμονίῳ τρόπῳ, ὥστε ταύτας ἐφέλκεσθαι ἀπαγόμενον ἐπὶ συνουσίας. Δὲ Λουῆς δὲ ὁ τῆς γυναικὸς ἀνὴρ πρόσθεν ἐτετελευτήκει νόσῳ. Ἦν δὲ οὗτος γένος τῶν Ταρακωνησίων βασιλέων, καὶ ὁπότε οὗτος ἀπὸ Ἰταλίας ἀφικόμενος ἐπὶ Πελοπόννησον, κατέσχε τὴν Ἀττικὴν ἅμα καὶ Βοιωτίαν πρὸς τῇ Πελοποννήσῳ, καὶ δὴ καὶ Φωκαΐδα καὶ Πάτρας τὰς ἐκτὸς Θερμοπυλῶν. Οὗτοι μὲν οὖν ὕστερον χρόνῳ οὐ πολλῷ διελθόντι τήν τε ἡγεμονίαν ἀπέβαλον, καὶ οἱ μὲν ἀπενόστησαν ἐπὶ Ἰταλίας, οἱ δ' αὐτοῦ ἐνέμειναν, ἐς ὃ ἐτελεύτησαν. Τούτων δ' ἦν καὶ οὗτος ὁ Δὲ Λουῆς, ᾧ τὴν γυναῖκα ἀφελόμενος Παιαζήτης ὁ Ἀμουράτεω καὶ τὴν θυγατέρα ἔχων ἀπεχώρει.

on in this, she took her daughter and as many gifts as she could, and went to meet the sultan. He accepted her daughter and sent both her and her daughter to his own household while he took possession of the land and appointed a governor for it.[31]

This woman is said to have fallen in love with a priest 12
called Strates and become so shameless that she entrusted her realm to this priest. She also treated reprehensibly many people who lived in the town of Delphi [Salona]. For this reason they were denounced to the sultan by the bishop, as it was outrageous for such an extensive land to be ruled by a woman, one who was committing adultery with a priest and inflicting intolerable harm on the citizens. It was for this reason that the sultan set out to march against them. It is also said that this priest, who was living with this woman, had misbehaved with many other women as well by working some kind of demonic sorcery by which to attract them and lure them into having sex. De Luis, the woman's husband, had previously died of an illness.[32] He was of the family of the kings of Aragon and, when he came to the Peloponnese from Italy, he took over Attica and Boiotia bordering on the Peloponnese, and also Phokis and Patras, the one that is outside Thermopylai.[33] Shortly afterward, these men lost their rule; some of them went back to Italy, while others stayed there until they died. Among the latter was this De Luis, whose wife and daughter were taken away by Bayezid, the son of Murad, when he left.

13 Ὁ μὲν ἐς Πελοπόννησον ἐπέβαλεν. Ὁ μὲν οὖν τῆς Σπάρτης ἡγεμών, ὡς ἐς τὴν Θετταλίαν ἐσέβαλε τάς τε πόλεις ἐπὶ τὸ ἀσφαλὲς καταστησάμενος, ἀποδρὰς νυκτὸς ᾤχετο ἐς Πελοπόννησον, ὡς ἦν ἐπίῃ, ἀμυνούμενος ᾗ ἠδύνατο κράτιστα. Καὶ [1.64] ἐμέλησε μὲν οὐχ ἥκιστα διὰ τοῦτο εἰσβαλεῖν ἐς τὴν Πελοπόννησον, ἀγγελία δὲ ἀφίκετο αὐτῷ, ὡς οἱ Παίονες ἡγουμένου Σιγισμούνδου Ῥωμαίων βασιλέως τε καὶ αὐτοκράτορος καὶ Κελτοὶ καὶ Γερμανῶν οὐκ ὀλίγοι συνελέγησαν ὡς ἐπ' αὐτὸν ἐπιόντες, καὶ τόν τε Ἴστρον παρασκευάζοιντο διαβῆναι, καὶ Δᾶκας δέ, γένος οὐκ ἀγεννές, ἔχοιεν μετ' αὐτῶν, τῆς τε ὁδοῦ ἡγουμένους, τὴν ἐσήγησιν τοῦ στρατοῦ ποιουμένους. Σιγισμοῦνδος δὲ οὗτος ὁ ἐπὶ Παιαζήτην στρατευόμενος ἡγεμών τε Γερμανῶν τὴν ἀρχὴν ἐτύγχανεν ὤν, περὶ Βιέννην τὴν πόλιν τὰ πολλὰ διατρίβων, καὶ χώρας τῶν ταύτῃ Γερμανῶν ἄρχων οὐ φαύλης. Παιόνων μετὰ ταῦτα προσαγομένων σφίσιν αὐτὸς βασιλεύς τε ἅμα καθειστήκει Παιόνων καὶ τῆς Γερμανῶν χώρας ἡγεμών.

14 Ἡ δὲ Γερμανία ἄρχεται μὲν ἀπὸ τοῦ Πυρηνίου ὄρους, ὅθεν καὶ ὁ Ταρτησὸς ῥέων ἐπὶ τὸν πρὸς ἑσπέραν ὠκεανόν. Καὶ ἔστι μὲν ἡ ἄνω Γερμανία, ἐφ' ὅσον δὲ προϊοῦσα καθήκει ἔστε Κολωνίαν καὶ Ἀργεντίην, πόλεις οὕτω καλουμένας. Τὸ δὲ ἐντεῦθεν καθήκει ἐπὶ ὠκεανὸν τὸν περὶ Κελτικήν τε ἐπὶ δεξιὰ καὶ περὶ Δανίαν ἐπ' ἀριστερά, ὡς ἐπὶ τὰς Βρετανικὰς νήσους. Ἔστι δὲ [1.65] καὶ ἀπὸ Ἴστρου Γερμανία, ἀπὸ Βιέννης πόλεως ἐπ' αὐτὸν δὲ ἐς Ταρτησὸν προϊοῦσα χώρα, καὶ ἐπὶ Βράγαν, τοὺς Βοέμους. Εἴη δ' ἂν ἀπὸ Βιέννης ἐς ὠκεανὸν ἀνδρὶ εὐζώνῳ πεντεκαιείκοσιν

Bayezid now turned his attention to the Peloponnese. When he had invaded Thessaly and secured the cities there, the ruler of Mistra [Theodoros I] escaped at night and went to the Peloponnese to defend himself as best he could against an attack. This made Bayezid all the more eager to invade the Peloponnese. But news reached him that the Hungarians, under the leadership of Sigismund, the emperor of the Romans,[34] along with the French and a great many Germans, had assembled to attack him and were preparing to cross the Danube. They also had with them the Wallachians, a noble people who were showing them the way and guiding their army. This Sigismund who was marching against Bayezid was the ruler of the German realm, resided mostly in the city of Vienna,[35] and ruled a significant area of German territory from there. Later, when the Hungarians joined them, he was at once king of the Hungarians and ruler of the land of the Germans.[36] 13

Germany begins at the Pyrenees Mountains, from where the Tartesos River flows to the Ocean in the west.[37] There is upper Germany, which extends as far as the cities called Cologne and Strasbourg.[38] From there it extends to the Ocean that surrounds France on the right and Denmark on the left,[39] as far as the British Isles. There is also Danubian Germany, whose territory extends alongside that river from the city of Vienna to the Tartesos, and then to Prague and Bohemia. An active man could traverse its length from Vienna to 14

ἡμερῶν ἀνύσαι κατὰ μῆκος· κατὰ δὲ πλάτος εἴη ἂν καὶ πλέων τούτων, βραχὺ ἀπὸ τῆς Κελτικῆς ἰόντι ἐπὶ τὴν Δανίαν χώραν.

15 Εὐνομεῖται δὲ ἡ χώρα αὕτη μάλιστα δὴ τῶν πρός τε ἄρκτον τε καὶ ἑσπέραν πασῶν τῶν ταύτῃ χωρῶν ἅμα καὶ ἐθνῶν, ἔστε πόλεις περιφανεῖς καὶ εὐδαίμονας καὶ ὑπὸ σφῶν αὐτῶν ἐς τὸ ἰσοδίαιτον εὐθυνομένας διῃρημένους, καὶ ἐς τυραννίδας, καὶ ὑπὸ ἀρχιερεῦσι ταττομένας τοῖς ὑπὸ τοῦ Ῥωμαίων μεγάλου ἀρχιερέως καθισταμένοις. Καὶ πόλεις μὲν ἐς τὸ ἰσοδίαιτον εὐνομούμεναι εἴησαν αὗται ἔν τε τῇ ἄνω καὶ τῇ κάτω Γερμανίᾳ, Νορόβεργον πόλις εὐδαίμων καὶ Ἀργεντίη καὶ Ἀμπύργον, καὶ αἱ εἰς ἀρχιερεῖς ταττόμεναι Κολωνία, Βιέννη ἡ ἐς τὴν κάτω Γερμανίαν ἀνιοῦσα, καὶ ἄλλαι μὲν οὐκ ὀλίγαι πόλεις, ἀποδέουσαι τούτων ὀλίγῳ τινί, ἀμφὶ τὰς διακοσίας. Ἐς δὲ τυραννίδας τρεῖς μάλιστά πῃ διέλοι τις τῆς Γερμανίας ἡγεμόνας, τῆς τε Ἀτζιλείης[1] πόλεως [1.66] καὶ Ἀουστρίας καὶ Βρέμης τῆς ἄνω Γερμανίας γενομένης.

16 Ἔστι δὲ γένος τοῦτο μέγα καὶ ἐπὶ πολὺ διῆκον τῶν κατὰ τὴν οἰκουμένην, μετά γε Σκυθῶν τῶν νομάδων δεύτερον, ὡς εἰ ταὐτὸ φρονοίη, καὶ ὑφ᾽ ἑνὶ ἄρχοντι ἡγεμόνι, ἀμάχητόν τε ἂν εἴη καὶ πολλῷ κράτιστον. Ὑγιεινότατον δὲ ὂν ἅτε ὑπὸ τὴν ἀρκτῴαν μοῖραν τεταγμένον καὶ περὶ τὴν ταύτῃ μάλιστά πῃ μεσόγαιον, θαλάττῃ οὐ πάνυ τι προσχρωμένους, εὐνομεῖται μάλιστα δὴ ἐθνῶν, ὧν ἡμεῖς ἴσμεν, οὔτε λοιμοῦ, ὃς δὴ ὑπὸ τῆς τοῦ ἀέρος σήψεως ἐπιγενομένης μάλιστα ἐπιφοιτῶν τοῖς ἑῴοις ἀπόλλυσι πολύ τι μέρος τῶν ταύτῃ οἰκούντων, οὔτε ἄλλων δὴ νόσων

the Ocean in twenty-five days. Its width would take longer, but less if one were to go from France to the land of Denmark.

15 Germany is better governed than all the lands and peoples situated toward the north and west. It thus has widely known and prosperous cities, some of which are governed under their own authority by egalitarian regimes and some as tyrannies, while others are subject to bishops appointed by the great pontiff of the Romans. The cities that are well-governed in an egalitarian way in both upper and lower Germany are the following: Nuremberg, a prosperous city; Strasbourg; and Hamburg. Those which are subject to bishops are Cologne, Vienna, the one that belongs to lower Germany,[40] and a good many other cities, which are slightly less important than those two, in all about two hundred more. As for the tyrannies, one may distinguish three rulers in Germany, namely those of the city of Atzileia,[41] Austria, and Bremen in upper Germany.[42]

16 This people is populous and occupies a large part of the world, being second only to the nomadic Skythians. If they were to agree and be governed by one ruler, they would be invincible and by far the most powerful people. They enjoy good health as they are situated below the Arctic region and live mostly in its interior; they do not make much use of the sea. They are better governed than any of the peoples of which we know. They are not afflicted by plagues, which, produced by the corruption of the air, break out especially in the eastern regions and carry off a large part of their inhabitants, nor by the other illnesses that tend to break out

τῶν ἐς ἡμᾶς πάνυ τι εἰωθότων θέρους τε καὶ φθινοπώρου ἐπιφοιτᾶν ἐπιχωριαζόντων αὐτοῖς θαμά, ὥστε καὶ ἱκανόν τι ἀπογίνεσθαι τοῦ γένους τούτου, οὔτε σείει, ὅ τι καὶ ἄξιον λόγου. Ὕει δὲ θέρους μάλιστα δὴ ἐν ταύτῃ τῇ χώρᾳ. Πολιτεύεται δὲ κατὰ ταὐτὰ Ῥωμαίοις ἔς τε δίαιταν καὶ ἤθη τετραμμένον, συμφερόμενον τά τε ἄλλα Ῥωμαίοις, καὶ ἐς τὴν θρησκείαν Ῥωμαίων μάλιστα δὴ τῶν πρὸς ἑσπέραν δεισιδαιμονεῖν. Νομίζεται δὲ παρὰ τούτοις καὶ μονομαχία μάλιστα δὴ τῶν ἄλλων ἐθνῶν, ὥστε γῆθεν οὐδ' ἐφ' ἵππων ἀλλήλοις μονομαχεῖν. Τὸ δὲ γένος τοῦτο δεξιώτατον ἔστε [1.67] μηχανὰς ὂν καὶ ἐς τὰ πολεμικὰ ἔργα καὶ ἐς πάσας τὰς τέχνας πολύ τι εὐδοκιμεῖ. Φέρει δὲ ἡ χώρα αὕτη πλὴν ἐλαίου καὶ ἰσχάδων τἆλλα πάντα οὐκ ἐλάσσω τῶν ἐς τὴν ἄλλην χώραν φερομένων. Οἴονται δέ τινες καὶ τηλεβόλους τε καὶ τηλεβολίσκους ὑπὸ Γερμανῶν ἀρχὴν ἀποδεδειγμένους ἐς ἀλλήλους προελθεῖν καὶ ἐς τὴν ἄλλην οἰκουμένην.

17 Παιονία δὲ ἄρχεται ἀπὸ Βιέννης τῆς Γερμανῶν πόλεως, καὶ ἐπὶ μὲν ἕω τῷ Ἴστρῳ συμπροϊοῦσα καθήκει ἐπὶ Δᾶκας τε καὶ Τριβαλλούς, ἐπὶ δὲ ἄρκτον ἐπὶ Βοέμους, τοὺς Κεχίους καλουμένους, καθήκει. Ἔνεισι δὲ ἄρχοντες ταύτῃ τῇ χώρᾳ, ἄρχων δὲ ἕκαστος τῆς πατρῴας χώρας, καὶ ὑποτασσόμενος τῷ βασιλεῖ αὐτῶν, ἐς ὅσον νομίζεται σφίσι. Νομίζεται δὲ ἐπὶ ῥητοῖς. Καὶ ἐπιχωρίῳ μὲν βασιλεῖ οὐ πάνυ τι χρῶνται, ἐπάγονται δὲ ἢ ἀπὸ Βοέμων τοῦ βασιλείου οἴκου ἢ ἀπὸ Γερμανῶν ἢ Πολάνων ἢ καὶ ἄλλων τῶν ταύτῃ ἐθνῶν. Συμφέρονται δὲ Γερμανοῖς τά τε ὅπλα καὶ τὴν ἐς τὰ ἤθη αὐτῶν δίαιταν, ἐς τὸ ἁβροδίαιτον ἀποκλίνοντες, ἢ

often among us in the summer and autumn and carry off a good many people here. Nor are there earthquakes, at least not worth mentioning. It rains a great deal in this land, especially in the summer. As a political community they are organized in the same way as the Romans, whose customs and way of life they have adopted. They are also like the Romans in most other respects, and of all the people in the west they are the most pious followers of the religion of the Romans. They also practice duels more than other peoples do, so that they even duel with each other on foot, rather than on horseback. This people is very adept mechanically and so excels when it comes to warfare and all crafts. The land itself produces no less than what other lands do, except for olive oil and figs. Some believe that cannons and firearms were first invented among the Germans and spread to others and the rest of the world.

Hungary begins at the German city of Vienna and extends along the Danube to the east as far as the Wallachians and Serbs, while to the north it extends to the Bohemians, who are called Czechs. There are lords in this land, each the lord of his ancestral land, and they are subject to their king to the extent defined by their customs; for custom imposes certain conditions. They do not usually have local kings but bring them in either from the royal house of the Bohemians, or from the Germans, Poles, or other nations there.[43] They are like the Germans in terms of weaponry and in way of life and customs, and favor a luxurious life as, they say, the 17

φασι Κελτούς τε καὶ Γερμανούς. Νομίζει κατὰ ταὐτὸ Ῥωμαίοις τὰ ἐς θρησκείαν. Γένος δὲ τοῦτο ἄλκιμον καὶ ἐς μάχας τόλμῃ προσχρώμενον ἐπιεικεῖ. Ποιοῦνται δὲ καὶ ἐπιχώριόν τινα τῶν ἀρχόντων τὰ πρῶτα, ἐς τὴν βασιλείαν ἀνήκοντα, καὶ οἰκονόμον δὲ ὄντα, καὶ μηδὲ ἄρχοντα ὀνομάζουσι. Φωνῇ δὲ χρῶνται οὐδαμῇ παραπλησίᾳ ἑτέρῳ τινὶ τῶν γενῶν, ἀλλὰ ἄλλῃ τὸ παράπαν διενεγκούσῃ τε τῆς Γερμανῶν τε καὶ Βοέμων καὶ Πολάνων. Οἴονται δέ τινες τούτους οἱ μὲν Γέτας γενέσθαι τὸ [1.68] παλαιόν, καὶ ὑπὸ τὸν Αἷμον οἰκοῦντας, ὑπὸ Σκυθῶν κακουμένους, ἀναχωρῆσαι ἐς τήνδε τὴν χώραν, ἣν καὶ νῦν οἰκοῦσιν· οἱ δέ φασι Δᾶκας γενέσθαι. Ἐγὼ δέ, ὁποῖον ἄν τι εἴη τὸ γένος τοῦτο τὴν ἀρχήν, οὐκ ἂν οὕτω ῥᾳδίως εἰπεῖν ἔχοιμι· τοὔνομα μέντοι τοῦτο ὑπό τε σφῶν αὐτῶν καὶ ὑπὸ Ἰταλῶν καλουμένους, οὐ πάνυ τι καλῶς ἔχοιμι ἑτέρῳ τινὶ ὀνόματι καλεῖν τούτους. Ἔστι δὲ αὐτοῖς βασίλεια ἐν Μπούδῃ πόλει εὐδαίμονι παρὰ τὸν Ἴστρον.

18 Σιγισμοῦνδον δὲ τὸν Βιέννης τῆς Γερμανῶν πόλεως ἡγεμόνα ἐπαγόμενοι οὗτοι δὲ οἱ Παίονες βασιλέα τε σφίσιν αὐτοῖς καθίστασαν, καὶ τὰ κατὰ τὴν ἀρχὴν ἐπέτρεψαν αὐτῷ διαθεῖναι ὡς ἔχοι ἐπὶ τὸ ἀσφαλέστερον. Οὗτος μὲν οὖν ἐπεί τε τὴν Παιόνων παρέλαβε βασιλείαν, διεπρεσβεύετο πρὸς τὸν Ῥωμαίων ἀρχιερέα, συνήθη τε ὄντα αὐτῷ καὶ ἐπιτήδειον ἐς τὰ μάλιστα, ὥστε ἐπιψηφισθῆναι αὐτῷ αὐτοκράτορι Ῥωμαίων γενέσθαι. Τοῦτο μὲν οἱ τῆς Ῥώμης ἀρχιερεῖς τοῖς Κελτῶν βασιλεῦσι τὸ πρῶτον ἐπεδίδοσαν διὰ τοὺς πολέμους, οὓς θαμά τε καὶ ἀνδρειότατα πρὸς τοὺς ἀπὸ Λιβύης διαβάντας ἐπὶ Ἰβηρίαν βαρβάρους καὶ

French and the Germans do. They hold to the same religious practices as the Romans. Theirs is a hardy race that displays considerable daring in battle. They promote one of their local lords to the highest position and give him royal rank, but they call him governor and not lord.[44] They speak a language that is like that spoken by no other people and is entirely different from that of the Germans, Bohemians, and Poles. Some believe that they formerly used to be the Getai and lived beneath the Haimos range, but when they were oppressed by the Skythians, they moved to the land where they live now. But others say that they were Wallachians. For my part, I cannot easily decide what these people were originally. This name is what they use for themselves and what they are called by the Italians, and so it would not really be correct for me to call them by any other name.[45] Their royal capital is at Buda, a prosperous city on the Danube.

These Hungarians, then, brought in Sigismund, the ruler 18
of the German city of Vienna,[46] and made him their king. They entrusted their realm to him so that it would be more secure. When he received the kingdom of the Hungarians,[47] he sent envoys to the pontiff of the Romans, who was an associate and close friend of his, to ask for his support in becoming emperor of the Romans.[48] The pontiff of the Romans had originally given this title to the kings of the French on account of the wars that they fought, frequently and with great courage, against the barbarians who crossed over from North Africa to Iberia and who conquered large parts of

τὰ πολλὰ τῆς Ἰβηρίας καταστρεψαμένους αὐτοῖς. Μετὰ δὲ ταῦτα ἐπὶ τοὺς Γερμανῶν ἡγεμόνας μετενήνεκται ἡ ψῆφος τοῦ Ῥωμαίων [1.69] ἀρχιερέως. Σιγισμοῦνδον ὡς ὑπισχνοῖτο ὁ ἀρχιερεὺς τήν τε ἀξίαν ταύτην ἐπιτιθέναι, καὶ δὴ μετεπέμπετο ἐπὶ τοῦτο, ὥρμητο μὲν ἐπὶ Ἰταλίαν διὰ τῆς Ἑνετῶν χώρας. Οὗτοι μὲν οὖν ὡς ἐπύθοντο Σιγισμοῦνδον διὰ τῆς χώρας αὐτῶν τὴν πορείαν ποιούμενον, ἔπεμψαν ἄγγελον, προαγορεύοντες αὐτῷ μὴ διϊέναι διὰ τῆς χώρας αὐτῶν. Ὁ δὲ οὐκ ἔφη πείσεσθαι, ἂν μὴ γνῷ αὐτοὺς πειρωμένους ἔργῳ διακωλῦσαι διαπορευόμενον. Παρεσκευάζοντο μὲν οὖν οἱ Ἑνετοὶ στρατὸν καὶ διεκώλυον. Ὡς δὲ ᾔσθετο κωλυόμενος, παρετάξατο ἐς μάχην καὶ συνέβαλε τῷ Ἑνετῶν στρατῷ, καὶ ἀπεγένετο αὐτῷ οὐκ ὀλίγα τοῦ στρατεύματος, τραπομένῳ τε ἐς φυγὴν καὶ μόλις διαφυγόντι τοὺς ἐναντίους.

19 Οὗτος μὲν δὴ ἐπεί τε ἀπέγνω τὴν δι' Ἑνετῶν πορείαν, ἀπῄει διὰ τῆς ἄνω Γερμανίας ἐς τὸν Λιγυρίας τύραννον ἀφικόμενος. Ἐντεῦθεν δὲ ἐς Ῥώμην παρεγένετο, καὶ βασιλεύς τε καθειστήκει, ὑπὸ τοῦ μεγάλου ἀρχιερέως ἐς τοῦτο ἀποδειχθείς. Μετὰ δὲ ταῦτα ἐδεῖτό τε τοῦ ἀρχιερέως συμβαλέσθαι ἐς τὴν ἐπὶ τὸν βάρβαρον αὐτῷ ἐκστρατείαν γινομένην, ᾐτεῖτο δὲ αὐτὸν χρήματά τε καὶ ἄνδρας. Ὁ δὲ πρός τε τὸν Κελτῶν βασιλέα διαπρεσβευσάμενος καὶ πρὸς τὸν Βουργουνδίας τύραννον διεπράξατο δοθῆναι ἐς ὀκτακισχιλίους, καὶ στρατηγὸν τὸν Βουργουνδίας ἡγεμόνος ἀδελφόν. Παρεσκευάσατο μὲν οὖν καὶ αὐτός, συλλέξας στράτευμα ἀπὸ Γερμανῶν, ὅσον ἠδύνατο μισθωσάμενος. Ὡς ἤδη αὐτῷ τε τὰ εἰς τὸν πόλεμον παρεσκεύαστο,

Iberia. Afterward the support of the pontiff of the Romans was transferred to the rulers of the Germans.[49] The pontiff had promised to invest Sigismund with this rank and invited him to come for that purpose, and he set out for Italy through Venetian territory. But when the Venetians learned that Sigismund's journey would take him through their territory, they sent a messenger publicly warning him not to travel through their land.[50] He said that he would not agree to this unless he knew that they were actively trying to block his passage. So the Venetians prepared an army and blocked him. When Sigismund realized that he was blocked, he drew up his men for battle and engaged the Venetian army. He lost a large part of his army, was routed, and barely escaped from the enemy.

Abandoning his plan to pass through Venetian territory, 19
Sigismund went through upper Germany and came to the tyrant of Lombardy.[51] From there he reached Rome and was made king [i.e., emperor], being appointed by the great pontiff to this position. After that he asked the pontiff to contribute to the expedition against the barbarian that he was planning, requesting money and men from him. The latter sent envoys to the king of the French and the tyrant of Burgundy and managed to secure eight thousand men, under the command of the brother of the Burgundian ruler.[52] He made his own preparations too, assembling as large an army from among the Germans as he could afford to hire. When he was prepared for war, he set out, taking the Hungarians

ἐξήλαυνε, λαβὼν τούς τε Παίονας καὶ Δᾶκας [1.70] τῆς ὁδοῦ ἡγεμόνας, εὐθὺ τοῦ Ἴστρου ἐπὶ Παιαζήτην. Διεπρεσβεύσατο δὲ καὶ πρὸς τοὺς Ἰταλῶν καὶ Ἰβήρων ἡγεμόνας, χρηματίζοντος δὲ τοῦτο αὐτῷ τοῦ ἀρχιερέως, αἰτούμενος χρήματα καὶ ἄνδρας. Καὶ χρήματα μὲν ἐπεπόμφει αὐτῷ ἱκανὰ ὁ ἀρχιερεύς, ἄνδρας δέ [. . .][2]

Ὁ μὲν οὖν Παιαζήτης ὡς ἐπύθετο ἐπιόντα οἱ Σιγισμοῦνδον τὸν Ῥωμαίων αὐτοκράτορα, σὺν πολλῷ στρατεύματι ἐλαύνοντα, παραλαβὼν τὸν τῆς Εὐρώπης τε καὶ Ἀσίας στρατὸν ἅπαντα ἀντεπῄει ἐπὶ Ἴστρον, ᾗ ἐδύνατο τάχιστα πορευόμενος. Στρατοπεδευσαμένου δὲ αὐτοῦ ἀπὸ τοῦ Ἴστρου ἐπὶ σταδίους τεσσαράκοντα, οἱ Κελτοὶ αὐθάδεις τε ὄντες καὶ ἀγνώμονες ὡς τὰ πολλά, ἀξιοῦντες σφῶν αὐτῶν μόνων τὴν νίκην γενέσθαι, ὁπλισάμενοι ἐπῄεσαν πρότεροι ὡς ἀναρπασόμενοι τοὺς βαρβάρους. Μάχης δὲ καρτερᾶς γενομένης τρέπονται οἱ Κελτοί, καὶ φεύγοντες ἀνὰ κράτος καὶ οὐδενὶ κόσμῳ ἐπιπίπτουσι τῷ σφετέρῳ στρατεύματι, ἐπισπομένων τῶν Τούρκων. Ἐνταῦθα ἀναμὶξ γενομένων αὐτῶν, ὡς ἐπέκειντο οἱ βάρβαροι, τρέπονται ἅμα τούτοις οἵ τε Παίονες καὶ οἱ Γερμανοί. Ἐπειγομένων δὲ εἰς τὴν τοῦ Ἴστρου διάβασιν ἀπώλετο πολλὰ τοῦ στρατεύματος κατὰ τὸν ποταμόν. Ἐγένετο δὲ φόνος πολὺς ὀλλυμένων τῶν Κελτῶν καὶ Παιόνων ὑπὸ τῶν ἐναντίων, καὶ ὁ Βουργουνδίων στρατηγὸς ἑάλω, καὶ ἄλλοι οὐκ ὀλίγοι Παιόνων τε καὶ Κελτῶν. Ὁ μὲν οὖν Σιγισμοῦνδος διακινδυνεύσας τὰ ἔσχατα, καὶ παρὰ βραχὺ ἁλῶναι διαφυγών, ἐμβὰς ἐς τριήρη κατὰ τὸν ποταμὸν [1.71] ἔπλει ἐς Βυζάντιον παρὰ βασιλέα Ἑλλήνων. Ἐς λόγους δὲ ἀφικόμενος τῷ

and the Wallachians to lead him on the way, straight along the Danube against Bayezid. He also sent envoys to the rulers of the Italians and Iberians through the mediation of the pontiff, asking for money and men. The pontiff had sent him enough money, but men [. . .]

When Bayezid learned that Sigismund, the emperor of 20
the Romans, was coming against him, he set out with a large military force, taking the entire army of Europe and Asia, and rushed to the Danube as fast as he possibly could. He encamped forty stades away from the Danube. Yet the French, being impetuous and ignorant in most matters, wanted to gain the victory all by themselves. They armed themselves and advanced with the intention of storming the barbarians ahead of everyone else. In a fierce battle,[53] the French were routed; they fled with all their might and in complete disorder back to their own army, with the Turks at their heels. Then they all became mixed up together, as the barbarians pressed upon them, and the Hungarians and the Germans turned to flight as well. As they rushed to cross the Danube, a large part of the army perished by the river. A great slaughter ensued as the French and Hungarians were cut down by the enemy. The Burgundian general was captured and many other Hungarians and Frenchmen.[54] As for Sigismund, he ran all manner of extreme risks and barely managed to escape being captured. He embarked upon a trireme on the river and sailed to Byzantion to the king of the Greeks [Manuel II]. He held talks with the king of

Βυζαντίου βασιλεῖ, καὶ χρηματίσας αὐτῷ, ὅσα ἐβούλετο, ᾤχετο ἀποπλέων ἐπ' οἴκου.

21 Παιαζήτης δὲ ὁ Ἀμουράτεω, ὡς τούς τε Παίονας ἐτρέψατο καὶ Κελτούς, ἐληΐζετο τὴν χώραν αὐτῶν, ἀδεέστερον ἤδη χωρῶν ἐπ' αὐτοὺς καὶ ἀνδράποδα πάμπολλα ἀγόμενος. Καὶ δὴ ἐπελαύνων ἐπὶ Μπούδην, τὰ Παιόνων βασίλεια, ἔκαμνεν ὑπὸ τῆς νόσου· ποδαλγίαν δὲ ἐνόσει. Καὶ εἰ μὴ μέντοι ἐνωχλεῖτο ὑπὸ τῆς νόσου, οὐκ ἔχω λογίζεσθαι, ὅ τί περ ἂν γένοιτο αὐτῷ ἐμποδὼν ἐπὶ Μπούδην τε ἐλάσαι καὶ παραστήσασθαι Μπούδην, τὰ Παιόνων βασίλεια καὶ καταστρέψασθαι τὴν χώραν αὐτῶν· νῦν δὲ κάμνων ὑπὸ τῆς νόσου ἐπιεικῶς πάνυ ἀπενόστησέ τε αὐτὸς καὶ τὸν στρατὸν ἀπήγαγεν ὡς τὴν χώραν αὐτοῦ. Ὕστερον μέντοι ἐπιπέμπων στρατεύματα ἐπὶ Παιονίαν καὶ Παιονοδακίαν ἐδῄου τὴν χώραν. Χρόνου δὲ ἐπιγενομένου ἐπὶ Δᾶκας καὶ ἐπὶ Μύρξαν τὸν Δακίας ἡγεμόνα ἐστρατεύετο, αἰτιασάμενος αὐτόν, ὡς ὑπάρξαντά τε πολέμου καὶ σὺν τοῖς Παίοσιν ἐπ' αὐτὸν στρατευόμενον.

22 Ἔστι δὲ γένος τοῦτο, Δᾶκες ἄλκιμόν τε τὰ ἐς πόλεμον καὶ οὐ πάνυ τι εὐνομούμενον, κατὰ κώμας οἰκοῦν, πρὸς τὸ νομαδικώτερον τετραμμένον. Διήκει δ' αὐτῶν ἡ [1.72] χώρα ἀπὸ Ἀρδελίου, τῆς Παιόνων Δακίας ἀρχομένη ἔστε ἐπὶ Εὔξεινον πόντον. Ἔχει δὲ ἐπὶ δεξιᾷ μὲν καθήκουσα ἐπὶ θάλασσαν τὸν Ἴστρον ποταμόν, ἐπ' ἀριστερᾷ δὲ Βογδανίαν χώραν οὕτω καλουμένην. Διείργει δὲ αὐτοὺς ἀπὸ Παιονοδακίας ὄρος ἐπὶ πολὺ διῆκον, Πρασοβὸς καλούμενον. Ἔχει δ' ὁμόρους ἡ χώρα αὕτη καὶ Σκυθῶν τῶν νομάδων μοῖραν οὐκ ὀλίγην, γένος πολύ τι καὶ ὄλβιον,

Byzantion, negotiated what he wanted with him, and then departed and sailed back home.

After routing the Hungarians and French, Bayezid, the son of Murad, plundered their land, moved against them without fear, and captured countless slaves. He even marched against Buda, the court of the Hungarians, but on the way he fell ill; for he suffered from gout. And if he had not been afflicted by this illness, I have no reason for thinking that anything could have prevented him from reaching Buda and capturing Buda, the court of the Hungarians, and conquering their land. But as it was, he suffered greatly from this condition, and so he turned back and led his army to his own territory. Later he sent armies to ravage the land of Hungary and Hungarian Wallachia. After some time he campaigned against the Wallachians and against Mircea, the ruler of Wallachia,[55] accusing him of being at war and marching against him with the Hungarians. 21

This race, the Wallachians, is hardy in war but not well governed. They live in villages and tend to a more nomadic way of life. Their land extends from Ardeal in Hungarian Wallachia to the Black Sea. It has the Danube to its right as it extends down to the sea and to its left the land of Bogdania, as it is called [i.e., Moldavia].[56] They are separated from Hungarian Wallachia by a long mountain range called Brassó.[57] Their neighbors include a large number of nomadic Skythians, a populous and prosperous race, subject to King 22

ὑπὸ Καζημίρεω τῷ βασιλεῖ ταττόμενον· ὑφ᾽ ᾧ δὴ καὶ Σκύθαι οἱ νομάδες ταττόμενοι στρατεύονται, ᾗ ἂν ἐξηγῆται, αὐτός τε ἀρετὴν παρεχόμενος ἐς πόλεμον ἀξιόλογον. Τούτων δὲ ἔχονται Πολάνοι μὲν πρὸς ἄρκτον, Σαρμάται δὲ πρὸς ἕω. Δᾶκες δὲ χρῶνται φωνῇ παραπλησίᾳ τῇ Ἰταλῶν, διεφθαρμένῃ δὲ ἐς τοσοῦτον καὶ διενεγκούσῃ, ὥστε χαλεπῶς ἐπαΐειν τοὺς Ἰταλοὺς ὁτιοῦν, ὅτι μὴ τὰς λέξεις διασημειουμένων ἐπιγινώσκειν, ὅ τι ἂν λέγοιτο.

23 Ὅθεν μὲν οὖν τῇ αὐτῇ φωνῇ χρώμενοι ἤθεσι Ῥωμαίων ἐπὶ ταύτην ἀφίκοντο τὴν χώραν καὶ αὐτοῦ τῇδε ᾤκησαν, οὔτε ἄλλου ἀκήκοα περὶ τούτου διασημαίνοντος σαφῶς ὁτιοῦν, οὔτε αὐτὸς ἔχω συμβαλέσθαι, ὡς αὐτοῦ ταύτῃ ᾠκίσθη. Λέγεται μὲν πολλαχῇ ἐλθὸν τὸ γένος τοῦτο ἐνοικῆσαι αὐτοῦ, οὐ μήν, ὅ τι καὶ ἄξιον ἐς ἱστορίαν, ὁτιοῦν παρεχόμενον τεκμήριον. Συμφέρεται δὲ Ἰταλοῖς τά τε ἄλλα καὶ τῇ ἐς δίαιταν καταστάσει, καὶ ὅπλοις τοῖς αὐτοῖς καὶ σκευῇ ἔτι [1.73] καὶ νῦν τῇ αὐτῇ Ῥωμαίων διαχρώμενοι. Ἐς δύο μέντοι διῃρημένον ἀρχάς, ἔστε τὴν Βογδανίαν καὶ αὐτὴν παρ᾽ Ἴστρον χώραν οὐ πάνυ τι εὐνομεῖται. Νομίζουσι δὲ ἡγεμόσιν οὐ τοῖς αὐτοῖς διαμένοντες, ἀλλ᾽ ἐπὶ τὸ ἀεὶ σφίσι πρόσφορον συμμεταβάλλοντες καθιστᾶσιν ἄλλοτε ἄλλους σφίσι τυράννους. Μύρξαν μέντοι τοῦτον, ἄρχοντα τοῦ γένους τοῦδε τὸ παλαιὸν γενόμενον, ἐπικαλεσάμενοι τύραννον σφίσι κατεστήσαντο, συνανελόντες Δᾶνον τὸν πρόσθεν τυραννεύοντα αὐτῶν. Μύρξας μὲν οὖν οὗτος παλλακίσι ξυγγενόμενος οὐκ ὀλιγάκις, καὶ νόθους ἀπὸ τούτου σχὼν παῖδας ἀνὰ τὴν Δακίαν οὐκ ὀλίγους, ὕστερον προϊόντι τῷ χρόνῳ καὶ τελευτήσαντος

Casimir.[58] The nomadic Skythians, being subject to him, march with him wherever he may lead them, and he personally displays considerable valor in war. To the north their neighbors are the Poles, and the Russians to the east. The Wallachians speak a language that is similar to that of the Italians, but so corrupted and different from it that it is difficult for the Italians to understand anything they say, unless they recognize words that are spoken distinctly.

Regarding the question of where the Wallachians came 23
from when they arrived in this land and settled it, speaking the same language as the Romans and using their customs, I have heard no one else with anything clear to say nor have I myself anything to contribute on how it was settled by them. It is said that this race came to settle this land from many different places, but there is no proof of this, at least none worthy of being treated as historical. This people is like the Italians in its way of life and in other aspects. With respect to weapons and dress, they still, even now, use the same as the Romans do. Wallachia is divided into two realms, Moldavia and the land by the Danube, and is not well governed. It is not their custom to keep the same rulers for long but they are always replacing one tyrant with another based on what is advantageous for them. So they summoned this Mircea, who had formerly been a lord of this race, and established him as their tyrant, after they had joined forces to kill Dan, the previous tyrant.[59] Mircea had many concubines and left many illegitimate children throughout Wallachia. Later, when some time had passed

Μύρξεω ἀνεφύοντο τῇ Δακίᾳ θαμὰ ἡγεμόνες ἄλλοτε ἄλλοι ἔστε ἐπὶ τόνδε τὸν χρόνον καθιστάμενοι ἐς τὴν ἀρχήν.

24 Ἐπὶ τοῦτον δὴ τὸν Μύρξαν, ὑπάρξαντα πρότερον πολέμου ἐς τοὺς βαρβάρους συστρατευόμενον τῷ Σιγισμούνδῳ, Ῥωμαίων αὐτοκράτορι, αἰτιασάμενος Παιαζήτης ὁ Ἀμουράτεω ἐστρατεύετο, καὶ τόν τε Ἴστρον διαβὰς ἤλαυνεν ἐς τὸ πρόσω, τήν τε χώραν ἀνδραποδιζόμενος. Μύρξας δὲ συλλέξας στράτευμα ἀπὸ τῆς χώρας ἐπεξελθεῖν μὲν καὶ διαμάχεσθαι οὐκ ἐποιεῖτο βουλήν, τὰς δὲ γυναῖκας καὶ παῖδας ἐς τὸ ὄρος τὸ Πρασοβὸν κατεστήσατο περιποιούμενος. Ἐφείπετο δὲ ὕστερον καὶ αὐτὸς τῷ [1.74] Παιαζήτεω στρατεύματι διὰ τῶν δρυμώνων τῆς χώρας, οἳ δὴ πολλοί τε ἐνυπάρχουσι καὶ ἁπανταχῇ περιδέουσι τὴν χώραν μὴ βάσιμον εἶναι τοῖς ἐναντίοις, μηδὲ εὐπετῆ χειρωθῆναι. Ἐφεπόμενος δὲ ἀπεδείκνυτο ἔργα ἄξια λόγου, μαχόμενός τε, εἴ τι διασπασθὲν τῶν πολεμίων ἐπισιτιούμενόν πη τῆς χώρας τράποιτο ἢ ἐπὶ ὑποζύγια ληϊζόμενον, καὶ οὕτω τόλμᾳ μεγίστῃ ἐφεπόμενος τῷ στρατεύματι· περιφανῶς δὲ ἐφεπόμενον αὐτῷ διαμάχεσθαι. Καὶ δὴ λέγεται, διαπορευομένῳ τῷ στρατεύματι ἐπέκειτο ἐν λύπῃ πάνυ χαλεπῶς, καὶ ἐξετίθει, καὶ διαφθείρων οὐκ ἀνίει. Ἔνθα Βρενέζεω θεράποντος γνώμην ἀποδεικνυμένου, ὥστε ἐνστρατοπεδεύσασθαι τὸν στρατὸν αὐτοῦ καὶ ἀπαλλαγὴν εὕρασθαι, ἀπὸ τούτου μέγα τὸ ἀπὸ τοῦδε εὐδοκιμεῖν παρὰ τῷ βασιλεῖ, καὶ ἐς στρατηγίας χρηματίζοντα ὑπὸ βασιλέως ἐπὶ μέγα χωρῆσαι δυνάμεως. Τότε μὲν οὖν αὐτοῦ Παιαζήτης ἐνηυλίσατο, ἐπισχὼν τὴν ἡμέραν ἐκείνην· τῇ δ᾿ ὑστεραίᾳ διεπόρθμευσεν, ᾗ ἐδύνατο ἀσφαλέστατα,

and Mircea had died, many rulers emerged in Wallachia at one time or another, and they remain in power to this day.

It was against this Mircea that Bayezid, the son of Murad, marched, accusing him of having sided with Sigismund, the emperor of the Romans, during the previous war against the barbarians.[60] He crossed the Danube and pressed forward, reducing the land to slavery. Mircea assembled an army from his territory but decided not to march against him and offer battle; rather, he first safeguarded the women and children, settling them on Mount Brassó. Then he followed the army of Bayezid through the forests of that land, which are extensive and enclose it on all sides, making it inaccessible for invaders and not easy to occupy. Following him, then, Mircea performed remarkable deeds, giving battle if any contingent of the enemy broke away to seek supplies in the surrounding countryside or to plunder pack animals. Thus he followed the army with great daring and he fought conspicuously well in shadowing Bayezid. It is said that as the Turkish army was moving through this area, Mircea gave it a very hard time, as he isolated it and would not let up in killing its men. At that point Evrenos, the minister, expressed the opinion that the army should encamp there and seek relief. From then on he was held in high esteem by the sultan for this reason, was appointed by him to high military commands, and became powerful.[61] So at that time Bayezid encamped there for the rest of that day, and on the next day he ferried his army across the Danube in the safest

τὸν στρατὸν διὰ τοῦ Ἴστρου. Οὕτω μὲν οὖν αὐτῷ ὁ ἐπὶ Δακίᾳ στρατὸς ἐπεπρήγει.

25 Μετὰ δὲ ταῦτα ἐλαύνων ἐπολιόρκει Βυζάντιον, ἀπὸ αἰτίας τοιᾶσδε. Οἱ γὰρ δὴ Ἑλλήνων βασιλεῖς, ὡς αὐτῷ παραγενόμενοι ἐς τὰς θύρας παρῆσαν, καὶ ἐστρατεύοντο ἑκάστου ἔτους. Καί ποτε ὄντος βασιλέως ἐν Φερραῖς τῆς Μακεδονίας χώρας καὶ διατρίβοντος, καὶ τοῦ Ἑλλήνων βασιλέως φοιτῶντος ἐνταῦθα ἐπὶ τὰς θύρας καὶ τοῦ τῆς Σπάρτης ἡγεμόνος καὶ Κωνσταντίνου τοῦ Ζάρκου παιδὸς καὶ Στεφάνεω τοῦ Ἐλεαζάρου, ἀφικνεῖται ἀπὸ [1.75] Πελοποννήσου ὁ τῆς Ἐπιδαύρου τὸ παλαιὸν γενόμενος ἄρχων, τοὔνομα Μαμονᾶς, ὃς ἀφικόμενος παρὰ βασιλέα Παιαζήτην ἐνεκάλει τῷ τῶν Ἑλλήνων βασιλέως ἀδελφῷ ὡς ἀφελομένῳ τήν τε Ἐπίδαυρον καὶ ποιήσαντι αὐτὸν κακά. Ἤχθετό τε τῷ Ἑλλήνων βασιλεῖ Παιαζήτης. Ἐνῆγε δὲ ἐς τοῦτο καὶ Ἰωάννης ὁ Ἀνδρονίκου τοῦ βασιλέως παῖς, ὃς παρὼν αὐτοῦ τὴν δίαιταν εἶχεν ἀπὸ Παιαζήτεω. Καὶ δὴ λέγεται καὶ ἀνελεῖν ὡρμημένον περὶ ὁμιλίας ἔχοντα, μετέμελεν αὖθις οὐ πολλῷ ὕστερον. Ἐπήμυνε δὲ αὐτῷ τὸν ὄλεθρον Ἀλίης ὁ Χαρατίνεω παῖς, ὃς συνήθης αὐτῷ ἐτύγχανεν ὢν καὶ χρήμασιν ὡς τὰ μάλιστα ἐθεραπεύετο ὑπ᾽ αὐτοῦ.

26 Συνιόντες δὴ οὖν ἐς ταὐτὸ οὗτοι οἱ ἡγεμόνες ἐν τῷ τότε χρόνῳ περὶ τὰς θύρας τοῦ βασιλέως διατρίβοντες, ἐδίδοσαν σφίσι λόγους, ὡς μηκέτι τοῦ λοιποῦ ἀφίξεσθαι ἐπὶ τὰς θύρας. Ἐνταῦθα μὲν οὖν ἐγγυᾶται Κωνσταντῖνος ὁ Ζάρκου, Δραγάσεω ἀδελφός, ὃς ἐκείνου τελευτήσαντος τοῦ Ζάρκου ἦν ἀνδρῶν ἄριστος τὰ ἐς σύνεσίν τε καὶ πόλεμον,

way he could. And that is what the army did that he led against Wallachia.[62]

After that he set out to besiege Byzantion, for the follow- 25
ing reason. The kings of the Greeks would attend him at his Porte and campaign with him each year. One time,[63] when the sultan was residing at Serres in Macedonia, the king of the Greeks {Manuel II} was also there in attendance at the Porte along with the ruler of Mistra [Theodoros I]; Konstantin, the son of Žarko;[64] and Stefan, the son of Lazar.[65] At that time, the former lord of Monemvasia arrived from the Peloponnese. His name was Mamonas and he came before Sultan Bayezid and accused the brother of the king of the Greeks [Theodoros] of capturing Monemvasia and causing him harm.[66] Bayezid now became angry at the king of the Greeks {Manuel}, and he was spurred on by Ioannes {VII}, the son of King Andronikos [IV],[67] who was present as he was being maintained by Bayezid. It is said that Bayezid spoke about being ready to kill him, but shortly afterward changed his mind. He was saved from destruction by Ali, the son of Hayreddin,[68] who happened to be his close associate and was courted by him with much money.

The rulers who were then in attendance at the sultan's 26
Porte met and agreed among themselves that they would never again come to the Porte. One man who made a pledge there was Konstantin, the son of Žarko and brother of Dragaš. When Žarko had died, Dragaš, a most excellent man in counsel and war, second to none among his

οὐδενὸς λειπόμενος τῶν ἐς ἐκεῖνον τὸν χρόνον, καὶ πρός τε Ἀλβανοὺς καὶ Τριβαλλοὺς πολεμίους διαπολεμῶν χώραν τε αὑτῷ ὑπηγάγετο οὐ φαύλην, καὶ ἐπὶ τῇ τελευτῇ αὐτοῦ Κωνσταντῖνος ὁ ἀδελφὸς αὐτοῦ κατέσχε τὴν χώραν καὶ ἐφοίτα ἐς τὰς βασιλέως θύρας. Οὗτος ἐγγυᾶται τὴν θυγατέρα τῶν Ἑλλήνων βασιλεῖ, ὥστε ἐμπεδοῦνται σφίσιν αὐτοῖς, ὅσα συνέθεντο ἐς τὴν ἀπόστασιν. Ἠγάγετο μέντοι οὗτος [1.76] Ἐμμανουῆλος καὶ πρότερον τὴν τοῦ βασιλέως Κολχίδος θυγατέρα χηρεύουσάν τε, Ζετίνεω δέ τινος Τούρκων ἡγεμόνος γυναῖκα γενομένην, κάλλει τε διαφέρουσαν. Ταύτην γὰρ ὡς ἠγάγετο ἀπὸ Κολχίδος ἐς Βυζάντιον, θεασάμενος ὁ πατὴρ αὐτοῦ τότε βασιλεύων, ὡς ἐδόκει αὐτῷ κάλλει τε γυναικῶν πολλῶν εἶναι καλλίστη καὶ τοῖς ἄλλοις, ᾗ ἐγένετο, ὑπερφέρουσα, ἑαυτῷ τε ταύτην ἠγάγετο, ἀφελόμενος τοῦ παιδός. Ἦν δὲ καὶ ἐν νόσῳ τῇ ποδαλγίᾳ διεφθαρμένος, ὥστε μηδὲ ὀρθούμενον στῆναι οἷόν τ' εἶναι. Λέγεται δὲ οὗτος ταῖς γυναιξὶν ἐπιμαινόμενος κατὰ πολλὰ ἄττα ἀπρεπῆ ἐξενεχθῆναι, ἡδόμενος ταῖς τε ψαλτρίαις καὶ συγγενόμενος ἀποθέσθαι τὴν ἐργασίαν τῆς βασιλείας ἐν ὀλιγωρίᾳ πεποιημένος, γανύμενός τε περὶ τὰ τοιαῦτα.

27 Οἱ μὲν οὖν ἡγεμόνες ἐν ταῖς θύραις ὄντες τοῦ Παιαζήτεω συνετίθεντο ἀλλήλοις ὡς ἀποστησόμενοι γενομένης τῆς ἐπιγαμίας· μετὰ δὲ ταῦτα, ὡς εἶχεν ἕκαστος, ἀπηλλάττετο ἐπὶ τὴν ἑαυτοῦ χώραν. Καὶ βασιλεὺς μὲν Ἑλλήνων, διαφυγὼν βασιλέα Τούρκων, ἀφικνεῖται ἀπὸ Φερρῶν ἐς Βυζάντιον τεταρταῖος, ᾗ λέγεται, Θεόδωρος δὲ ὁ ἀδελφὸς αὐτοῦ ἀφίκετο ἐπὶ Πελοπόννησον. Καὶ οἱ

contemporaries, had subjugated a significant territory by fighting against his Albanian and Serb enemies. After his death,[69] his brother Konstantin held the land and attended the sultan's Porte. He now pledged his daughter in marriage to the Greek king in order to confirm their agreement about the rebellion.[70] This man, Manuel, had formerly married the daughter of the king of Kolchis, a widow, who had once been the wife of a certain Taj al-Din, a Turkish ruler, and was exceedingly beautiful.[71] When she was brought from Kolchis to Byzantion to be wed, his father {Ioannes V}, who was then reigning, saw her and thought that, when it came to beauty, she was the most beautiful of many women and superior in other respects as well. So he married her himself, taking her away from his son. He was also afflicted with gout, so that he was unable to stand up straight. It is said that he lusted after women and perpetrated many indecent acts. He was attracted to singers and spent time with them, setting aside the work of the kingdom and paying little attention to it while enjoying such things.

The rulers at the Porte of Bayezid agreed among them- 27
selves to rebel when the marriage took place. Then each returned to his own country by his own means.[72] The king of the Greeks escaped from the sultan of the Turks and is said to have arrived at Byzantion on the fourth day after he left Serres; and his brother Theodoros arrived in the

λοιποὶ δέ, ὡς ἕκαστος ἀπήλαυνεν ἐπὶ τὰ ἑαυτοῦ, ἐπιτραπέντες ἰέναι ὑπὸ βασιλέως ἐπὶ τὰ ἑαυτῶν ἤθη ἕκαστος. Ὕστερον μέντοι ὡς τοῦ ἐπιγιγνομένου θέρους, ὡς οὐ παρεγένετο Βυζαντίου βασιλεὺς ἐπὶ τὰς θύρας καὶ ἠγγέλλετο τῷ Παιαζήτῃ μηδὲ ἐλθεῖν τοῦ λοιποῦ ἔτι διανοούμενος, ἐπιπέμψας Ἀλίην τὸν Χαρατίνεω, [1.77] ἄνδρα δὴ τῶν παρ᾽ ἑαυτῷ μέγα δυνάμενον, ἐπέτελλε παρεῖναι αὐτὸν ἐς τὰς θύρας παραγενόμενον· εἰ δὲ μή, πόλεμον προαγορεύειν αὐτῷ βασιλεῖ. Ἐλθὼν μέντοι οὗτος ὁ Ἀλίης ἐς τὸ Βυζάντιον δημοσίᾳ μὲν ἔλεγε τὰ ἐπεσταλμένα αὐτῷ ὑπὸ βασιλέως, ἐχρημάτιζε δὲ αὐτῷ, ὡς ἔνιοι λέγουσιν, ἰδίᾳ συγγενόμενος μηδαμῶς ἐλθεῖν ἐπὶ τὰς βασιλέως θύρας. Ἐμμανουῆλος μὲν ἀπεκρίνατο, ὡς πείθεσθαί τε ἕτοιμος εἴη καὶ βασιλεῖ μὴ θαρρῶν οὐκέτι βιωτὸν τὸν βίον αὐτῷ ἡγήσατο, ἀλλ᾽ ὡς ἐν βραχεῖ παρεσόμενον ἑαυτὸν ὑποδέχοιτο τῷ βασιλεῖ, ᾗ ἂν παραγγέλλοι. Ὕστερον μέντοι ἀπιόντος Ἀλίεω, ὡς Παιαζήτῃ δῆλα καθειστήκει μηδὲ διανοεῖσθαι αὐτὸν ἰέναι ἐπὶ τὰς θύρας, ἐπήλαυνέ τε καὶ ἐπολιόρκει Βυζάντιον. Ἐπελαύνων δὲ τήν τε γῆν ἔκειρε καὶ τὴν χώραν ἑκάστην ἐδῄου, καὶ κώμας ἀνδραποδισάμενος τὰς προαστείους, ὡς οὐδὲν προεχώρει ἡ τοῦ ἄστεος αἵρεσις, ἀπεχώρησεν αὐτὸς ἐπ᾽ οἴκου. Ἐπιπέμπων δὲ στράτευμα πανταχῇ ἀνὰ πᾶν ἔτος ἐπολιόρκει τὴν μακρὰν γενομένην πολιορκίαν ἐπὶ δέκα ἔτη, ἐν οἷς πολλά τε τῆς πόλεως ταύτης ἀπεγένετο ὑπὸ λιμοῦ διαφθαρέντα καὶ ἐπὶ τὸν βάρβαρον ἀπιόντα.

28 Τὴν μὲν οὖν Σηλυβρίαν αὐτὸς κατεῖχε Παιαζήτης, ἐπετρόπευε δὲ ταύτης Ἰωάννης ὁ Ἀνδρονίκου παῖς, ὃς

Peloponnese.[73] As for the rest of them, each returned home, having been granted permission by the sultan to go to his own residence. But in the following summer, the king of Byzantion did not attend the Porte and sent word to Bayezid that it was not his intention to ever come again. Bayezid sent Ali, the son of Hayreddin, one of his most powerful men, to order him to attend the Porte; otherwise, he would declare war on the king himself. When Ali came to Byzantion, he spoke publicly the words that the sultan had instructed him to say, but some say that when Ali met with Manuel in private he advised him not to come to the sultan's Porte under any circumstances. Manuel replied that he was ready to obey and that his life would be unbearable if he did not enjoy the sultan's trust; he would shortly attend so that he could be received by the sultan, wherever he was told to go. But later, when Ali had gone and it became clear to Bayezid that Manuel had no intention of coming to the Porte, he set out to besiege Byzantion.[74] On his way he devastated the land and plundered each region, enslaving the inhabitants of the suburbs. He made no progress in taking the city, and so departed for home. But he sent an army every year and set up a siege all around it which lasted for ten years,[75] during which time many of the city's inhabitants died of starvation or went over to the barbarian.

Bayezid controlled Selymbria himself but had entrusted 28
it to Ioannes [VII], the son of Andronikos, who had fled

διαφυγὼν ἀπὸ Βυζαντίου τὸν πάτρων, ὡς οὐκ ἠδύνατο, παρεῖχεν αὑτόν, ἐς ὅ τί περ ἂν αὐτῷ χρήσαιτο ὁ πάτρως Βυζαντίου τότε βασιλεύων. Ὁ δὲ πέμπων αὐτὸν ἐς Ἰταλίαν, διαπραξόμενον αὐτόν, ὅσα γε δὴ ὑπετίθετο, ἔπεμπε παρὰ [1.78] Ἰανυΐους ἐπικουρίας δεησόμενον δῆθεν· κρύφα δὲ πέμπων τοῖς Ἰανυΐοις ἐπέτελλεν ἐν φυλακῇ τε ἔχειν αὐτὸν μηδαμῇ μεθιέντας. Ὁ δὲ χρόνου ἐγγινομένου διαφυγὼν τοὺς Ἰανυΐους, καὶ ἀπὸ Ἰταλίας ἀνέβη παρὰ βασιλέα Παιαζήτην, ὃς πολιορκῶν Βυζάντιον. Καὶ ἄγων αὐτὸν τήν τε Σηλυβρίαν παρεστήσατο ὁμολογίᾳ καὶ ἐπέστησεν ἄρχοντα. Μετὰ δὲ ταῦτα ἐλαύνων ἐπὶ Βυζάντιον, ὡς οὐ προεχώρει αὐτῷ ἡ Βυζαντίου αἵρεσις προσβάλλοντι, λιμῷ ἐξεπολιόρκει. Καὶ εἷλεν ἂν τὴν πόλιν, εἰ μὴ ὁ Τεμήρης ἐλαύνων μεγάλῃ χειρὶ ἠγγέλλετο ἐπ᾽ αὐτόν· ὅτε δὴ καὶ αὐτὸς ἑάλω ὑπὸ Τεμήρεω καὶ τὰ πολλὰ τῆς ἀρχῆς αὐτοῦ ἀπώλετο τῆς ἐν τῇ Ἀσίᾳ.

29 Ὡς μὲν οὖν τὸ Βυζάντιον Παιαζήτης πολιορκῶν οὐκ ἀνίει, καὶ ἔγνω βασιλεὺς Ἑλλήνων τόν τε λεὼν τετρῦσθαι ἐς τὸ χαλεπώτατον, καὶ οὐκ εἶχεν ὅπως τοῦ λοιποῦ ἐξαπαλλαγῇ, ἐπέτρεψέ τε τὸ Βυζάντιον τῷ ἀδελφιδῷ Ἰωάννῃ, τῷ Ἀνδρονίκου παιδί. Ὡς γὰρ οἱ ἤχθετο Παιαζήτης, ὅτι δι᾽ αὐτὸν οὐ προεχώρει ἡ Βυζαντίου αἵρεσις, καὶ ἐν ὑπόπτῳ καθειστήκει, ἀποφυγὼν βασιλέα ἐσῄει ἐς Βυζάντιον. Καὶ αὐτὸν ἄσμενός τε ἐδέξατο ὁ πάτρως βασιλεὺς Βυζαντίου, καὶ τὴν πόλιν ἐπιτρέψας ᾤχετο ἀποπλέων ἐπὶ Ἰταλίαν, ἐπικουρίας δεησόμενος ἐς τὴν ὑπὸ τῶν πολεμίων πολιορκίαν μακρὰν καθεστηκυῖαν, μὴ περιϊδεῖν τὴν πόλιν ἀπολλυμένην. Ὡς δὲ κατὰ τὴν Πελοπόννησον

from his uncle Manuel in Byzantion because he could not bear to make himself available to serve in whatever matter his uncle, who was reigning in Byzantion, wanted to use him.[76] Manuel thus sent him to Italy so that he could carry out his instructions: he was supposedly sending him to Genoa to seek aid, but he sent a secret message to the Genoese telling them to imprison him and not let him out under any circumstances. After some time had passed, Ioannes escaped from the Genoese and went from Italy to Sultan Bayezid, who was besieging Byzantion.[77] Bayezid took Ioannes with him, they made an agreement, and he entrusted Selymbria to him and made him its governor. After that Bayezid moved against Byzantion, but as his attempt to capture it by force was not making any progress, he tried to starve it into submission. And he would have taken the city had news not reached him that Timur was marching against him with a large army. Indeed, when he was captured by Timur he lost most of his dominion in Asia.

As Bayezid would not stop besieging Byzantion, the king 29
of the Greeks realized that his people had been ground down very badly. He could see no way by which they might be freed from the siege in the future, so he entrusted Byzantion to his nephew Ioannes, the son of Andronikos. Bayezid was displeased with Ioannes because he blamed him for the lack of progress in capturing Byzantion and so, having fallen under suspicion, the latter fled from the sultan and entered Byzantion.[78] His uncle, the king of Byzantion, received him gladly, and entrusted the city to him when he left and sailed for Italy, to solicit aid in regard to the protracted siege by the enemy; for he would not let the city fall.[79] When Manuel

ἐγένετο, κατέθετο μὲν αὐτοῦ ἐν Πελοποννήσῳ τὴν γυναῖκα αὐτοῦ παρὰ τῷ ἀδελφῷ, αὐτὸς δὲ ἀπέπλει ἐς Ἰταλίαν. Τραπόμενος δὲ ἐπὶ Ἑνετῶν καὶ [1.79] χρηματίσας αὐτοῖς ὅσα ἠβούλετο, ᾤχετο ἐπὶ τὸν Λιγυρίας τύραννον, Μεδιολάνου δὲ ἡγεμόνα· ὁ δὲ φιλοφρονησάμενός τε αὐτὸν τὰ εἰκότα, καὶ χρήματα παρεχόμενος, ἀπέπεμψεν ἐπὶ τῶν Κελτῶν βασιλέα, ἵππους τε αὐτῷ παρεχόμενος καὶ τῆς ὁδοῦ ἡγεμόνας. Ὡς δὲ ἐγένετο ἐπὶ τὸν Γαλατίας βασιλέα, ἐδεῖτο αὐτοῦ μὴ προέσθαι πόλιν βασιλίδα Ἑλλήνων ὑπὸ βαρβάρων πολιορκουμένην, προσήκουσαν ἀγχοτάτω τῶν βασιλέων Γαλατίας οἴκῳ. Τοῦτον οὖν μεμηνότα εὑρὼν καὶ ἐν φυλακῇ ὑπὸ τῶν ἀρίστων κατεχόμενον, ὥστε θεραπεύεσθαι τὴν νόσον αὐτοῦ, διέτριβεν αὐτοῦ ἐπὶ συχνόν τινα χρόνον.

30 Κελτῶν δὲ τὸ γένος τοῦτο μέγα τε ὂν καὶ ὄλβιον καὶ παλαιόν τε καὶ ἐφ' ἑαυτῷ μέγα φρονοῦν, ὑπερέχειν τε τῶν ἄλλων τῶν πρὸς ἑσπέραν ἐθνῶν, ἀξιοῦν ἑαυτῷ μετεῖναι τῆς ἡγεμονίας τε καὶ Ῥωμαίων βασιλείας. Ἔστι δ' ἡ χώρα αὐτῶν πρὸς ἕω μὲν τῇ Λιγύρων χώρᾳ, πρὸς μεσημβρίαν δὲ τῇ Ἰβηρίᾳ, καὶ πρὸς ἄρκτον τῇ Γερμανίᾳ, καὶ πρὸς ἑσπέραν τῷ ὠκεανῷ καὶ ταῖς Βρετανικαῖς νήσοις· διήκει δὲ ἀπὸ Ἄλπεων τῶν ἐκτὸς Ἰταλίας ἔστε ἐπὶ ὠκεανὸν καὶ ἐπὶ Γερμανούς, ὁδὸν ἡμερῶν μάλιστα ἑπτακαίδεκα ἀπὸ Ἰταλίας ἐς ὠκεανόν, ἀπὸ δὲ Ἰβηρίας ἐπὶ Γερμανίαν ὁδὸν μάλιστά πῃ ἐννεακαίδεκα. Ἔστι δὲ Παρίσιον πόλις, ἐν ᾗ τὰ Κελτῶν βασίλεια, εὐδαιμονίᾳ τε καὶ ὄλβῳ προφέρουσα. Καὶ πόλεις οὐκ ὀλίγαι τῆς Γαλατίας, ὑπ' αὐτῷ δὲ τῷ βασιλεῖ ταττόμεναι ἐς τὴν σφῶν διοίκησιν. Εἰσὶ δὲ ἡγεμονίαι

reached the Peloponnese, he left his wife there in the Peloponnese with his brother, while he sailed on to Italy. He turned to the Venetians and negotiated what he wanted with them. He then went to the tyrant of Lombardy, the ruler of Milan,[80] who received him in a friendly manner and gave him money, sending him on to the king of the French; he also gave him some cavalry and guides for the road. When he reached the king of France, he begged him not to leave the royal city of the Greeks to be besieged by barbarians, a city with such close ties to the kings of France. But as he discovered that the king was insane and under the close watch of his leading men in order to treat his illness, he spent a long time there.[81]

The French are a great people, prosperous, and ancient. 30
They think highly of themselves, believing that they are superior to the other western peoples and regarding themselves as having a rightful share in the hegemony and kingdom of the Romans. Their land is bordered to the east by the land of the Lombards, to the south by Iberia, to the north by Germany, and to the west by the Ocean and the British Isles.[82] It extends from the Alps that are outside of Italy as far as the Ocean and the Germans, a journey of about seventeen days from Italy to the Ocean and a journey of about nineteen days from Iberia to Germany. The city of Paris, the site of the royal court of the French, is prosperous and wealthy. There are a good many cities in France, and their governance is subject to the king. There are also

τε καὶ ἡγεμόνες δυνάμει τε προὔχοντες καὶ ὀλβιώτατοι, [1.80] ὑπ' αὐτῷ δὲ τῷ βασιλεῖ ταττόμενοι καὶ ἐς τὰ βασίλεια παραγενόμενοι αὐτῷ.

31 Ὅ τε τῆς Βουργουνδίας ἡγεμὼν χώρας πολλῆς τε καὶ μεγάλης, καὶ πόλεων ἄλλων τε καὶ τῆς Βρουγίων πόλεως καὶ Κλοζίων παραλίων καὶ Γαντύνης πόλεως εὐδαίμονός τε καὶ μεγάλης καὶ μεσογαίου. Ἔστι δ' αὐτῷ ἡ Βρουγίων πόλις πάραλος παρὰ τὸν ὠκεανόν, ἀντικρὺ τῆς Βρετανικῆς Ἀγγλίας οὕτω καλουμένης νήσου, ἐς ἣν ὁρμίζονται νῆες ἀπό τε τῆς ἡμετέρας τῆσδε θαλάσσης καὶ ἀπὸ τῶν ἐς τὸν ὠκεανὸν πόλεων τῆς τε Γερμανίας, Ἰβηρίας, Ἀγγλίας, Δανίας καὶ τῶν λοιπῶν δυναστειῶν. Διέχει δ' αὕτη ἡ πόλις ἀπὸ Ἀγγλίας σταδίους πεντήκοντα καὶ ἑκατόν. Ἡ δὲ χώρα αὕτη καλεῖται Φλανδρία, καὶ εἰσὶ τούτοις τοῖς ἡγεμόσι Βουργουνδίας ἔργα ἀποδεδειγμένα ἄξια λόγου ἐς τὴν Κελτικὴν χώραν πρός τε αὐτὸν βασιλέα τῆς Γαλατίας καὶ πρὸς τοὺς Βρετανούς. Μετὰ δὲ ταῦτα ἡγεμὼν ἐπὶ τῆς ἠπείρου Βρετανίας ἔχεταί γε τῆς γῆς τῆς τοῦ βασιλέως χώρας. Ἐπὶ δὲ τούτοις ἡγεμὼν τῆς [. . .] τούτων δὲ ἔχεται χωρῶν ἡγεμόνος Σαβοΐας χώρα, μεγάλη τε καὶ ὑπερκαλλής, ἐπὶ Λιγυρίαν καθήκουσα. Πρὸς δὲ τὴν πάραλον χώραν τῆς Γαλατίας ὧδε ἄν μοι διακέοιτο πρὸς ἱστορίαν. Ἡ μέντοι Ἰανύη πύλη τις οὖσα τῆς Γαλατίας ἐπέχει χώραν, ἐπὶ τὴν Προβεντίαν καθήκουσα, ἧς ἄρχει ὁ τοῦ [1.81] οἴκου τοῦ βασιλέως τῆς Γαλατίας Ῥαινέριος βασιλεύς. Ἦν μητρόπολις ἡ Νίτια Προβεντίας. Πόλεις δ' ἔχονται ἥ τε Ἀβινιὼν πόλις, καθ' ἣν γέφυρα ἐπέστη μεγάλη δὴ τῶν

principalities and rulers who are extremely powerful and very wealthy, but they are subject to the king and attend upon him at his court.

The ruler of Burgundy possesses a large and great land 31
and many cities, including Bruges and Sluis on the coast, and Ghent, a large, prosperous, and inland city. The city of Bruges that belongs to him lies on the coast of the Ocean and faces the island called British England; ships anchor there both from our sea and from the cities along the Ocean, namely from Germany, Iberia, England, Denmark,[83] and the other kingdoms. This city is one hundred and fifty stades distant from England. The land is called Flanders, and the rulers of Burgundy performed remarkable deeds in France both against the king of France and against the British. After that, the ruler of Britain holds some continental lands in the king's territory.[84] In addition to them, the ruler [. . .] next to these lands there is the land of the ruler of Savoy, a great and exceedingly beautiful land that extends to Lombardy. I will record the following regarding the coastal lands of France. Genoa, being the gateway to France,[85] controls the land that extends to Provence, whose ruler is King René of the royal house of France.[86] The metropolis of Provence is Nice. They have other cities there such as the city of Avignon, where there is one of the largest bridges in the

κατὰ τὴν οἰκουμένην ἔστε ἐπὶ Βαρκενώνην[3] χώραν ἐλθεῖν. Αὕτη μὲν οὖν ἡ χώρα τῆς Γαλατίας, ὡς συνελόντι διεξιέναι.

32 Τὸ δὲ γένος τοῦτο Κελτῶν λέγεται παλαιόν τε καὶ ἔργα πρὸς τοὺς ἀπὸ Λιβύης βαρβάρους ἀποδεδειγμένον λαμπρά, καθ' ὃν δῆτα χρόνον βασιλεῖς Ῥωμαίων καὶ αὐτοκράτορες ἀπεδεικνύοντο οἱ τῶν Κελτῶν βασιλεῖς. Κάρουλον δὲ μάλιστα δὴ τῶν βασιλέων τούτων τὸν πρὸς τοὺς Λίβυας πόλεμον ἀνελόμενον, συνεπιλαβομένου τοῦ τε ἀδελφιδοῦ αὐτοῦ Ὀρλανδίου, ἀνδρὸς τόλμῃ τε καὶ ἀρετῇ τὰ ἐς στρατὸν ἐπισήμου γενομένου, καὶ Ῥινάλδου καὶ Ὀλιβερίου καὶ ἄλλων τῶν ταύτῃ ἡγεμόνων, Παλατίνων καλουμένων, συνδιαφερόντων αὐτῷ τὸν πόλεμον, καὶ πολλαχῇ κατὰ τὴν Γαλατίαν μὲν πρῶτα, μετὰ δὲ ταῦτα κατὰ Ἰβηρίαν τρεψάμενον τοὺς ἐναντίους νίκας ἀνελέσθαι περιφανεῖς. Καὶ κλέος αὐτῶν ἀνὰ Ἰταλίαν καὶ Ἰβηρίαν καὶ δὴ καὶ Γαλατίαν μέγα ἐς τόνδε ἀεὶ εὐφημούμενον ᾄδεται ὑπὸ πάντων. Λίβυες γὰρ διαβάντες τὸν πρὸς Ἡρακλείους στήλας πορθμὸν κατέσχον τε κατὰ βραχὺ προϊόντες τὴν Ἰβηρίαν, μετὰ δὲ ταῦτα Ναβάρην τε [1.82] χειρωσάμενοι καὶ Πορτουγαλλίαν χώραν, ἔστε ἐπὶ Ταρακῶνα ἐλαύνοντες, τὰ ἐς τήνδε αὖ τὴν χώραν καταστρεψάμενοι ἐσέβαλλον ἐς τὴν Κελτικήν.

33 Κάρουλος μὲν οὖν καὶ οἱ σὺν αὐτῷ πόλεμον ἐξενεγκόντες πρὸς τούσδε τοὺς Λίβυας μεγάλα ἀπεδείκνυντο ἔργα, ἄνδρες γενόμενοι ἀγαθοί, καὶ τῆς τε Κελτιβήρων καὶ Κελτικῆς χώρας ἐξελάσαντες ἐς τὴν Γρανάτην πόλιν ὀχυρωτάτην ἐπὶ τοῦ ὄρους τοῦ ἐς ὠκεανὸν καθήκοντος.

world,[87] and then one comes to the territory of Barcelona. And that, in summary, is the land of France.

The French people is said to be ancient and they performed illustrious deeds against the barbarians from North Africa, at the time when the kings of the French were appointed kings and emperors of the Romans.[88] Charles especially, from among their kings, waged war against the North Africans with the help of his nephew Orlando, a man distinguished by his daring and virtue in military matters. He was also assisted in that war by Rinaldo, Oliviero, and the other rulers of that land who are known as Paladins. They routed the enemy first in various battles in France and afterward in Iberia, and won glorious victories. Their fame is greatly celebrated in song by everyone down to our time throughout Italy, Iberia, and especially France. For the North Africans had crossed the straits at the Pillars of Herakles, had conquered and quickly passed through Iberia, and after that had seized the land of Navarre and Portugal, advancing as far as Aragon. When they had conquered that land, they invaded France. 32

So Charles and his men waged war against these North Africans and performed great deeds, as they were noble men, and they drove them out of the lands of the French and Celtiberians and into Granada, a highly fortified city on a mountain by the Ocean. They quickly reached the straits 33

Παρ' αὐτὸν δὲ τὸν πορθμὸν κατὰ βραχὺ προϊόντες τήν τε Ἰβηρίας χώραν πολλὴν κατασχόντες ᾤκουν καὶ συνελαύνοντες ἐπολιόρκουν. Καὶ τήν τε χώραν ἀπέδοσαν τοῖς ἑαυτῶν προσήκουσι, τὴν Ἰβηρίαν καὶ Ναβάρην καὶ Ταρακῶνα, καὶ τοὺς σφῶν αὐτῶν προσήκοντας ὑπὸ βαρβάρων πολιορκουμένους ἀπέλυόν τε τῆς πολιορκίας, καὶ τὴν χώραν ἐπιδιελόμενοι σφίσιν ᾤκουν, ἀπολαβόντες ἕκαστος τὸ ἀνῆκον αὐτῷ μέρος. Καὶ οὗτοι μὲν ταύτῃ κάλλιστα θέμενοι τὸν πόλεμον ἐς τόδε ἀεὶ ὑμνοῦνται ὡς ἄνδρες γενόμενοι ἀγαθοί. Καὶ Ὀρλάνδον μὲν τόν γε στρατηγὸν ὑπὸ δίψους ἐκπολιορκηθέντα ἀποθανεῖν, Ῥινάλδον δὲ διαδεξάμενον τὸν πόλεμον καταλιπεῖν τοῖς Ἰβηρίας βασιλεῦσιν. Οἱ δὲ διαδεξάμενοι τόνδε τὸν πόλεμον ἐς ἔτι καὶ νῦν τοὺς Λίβυας τούτους ἄγειν καὶ φέρειν νομίζουσι. Τὸ δὲ γένος τοῦτο Λιβύων γλώττῃ μὲν διαχρῆται τῇ Ἀραβικῇ, καὶ ἤθεσι δὲ καὶ θρησκείᾳ τῇ Μεχμέτεω, ἐσθῆτι δὲ τοῦτο μὲν βαρβαρικῇ, τοῦτο δ' αὖ καὶ Ἰβηρικῇ. [1.83]

34 Οἱ μὲν οὖν Κελτοὶ ἐς τοῦτο παραγενόμενοι μέγα φρονοῦσιν ἐπὶ τούτοις, καὶ γένος οἴονται τὸ ἑαυτῶν εὐγενές τε καὶ διαπρέπον διὰ πάντων δὴ τῶν πρὸς ἑσπέραν γενῶν. Διαίτῃ δὲ χρῶνται οἱ Κελτοὶ ἁβροτέρᾳ τῆς Ἰταλῶν διαίτης καὶ σκευῇ τῇ ἐκείνων παραπλησίᾳ, φωνὴν δὲ προΐενται διενεγκοῦσαν μὲν τῆς Ἰταλῶν φωνῆς, οὐ μέντοι τοσοῦτον, ὥστε δόξαι ἑτέραν εἶναι τῆς Ἰταλῶν φωνῆς τὴν γλῶτταν ἐκείνων. Ἀξιοῦσι δὲ πρωτεύειν, ὅποι ἂν παραγένωνται τῶν ἐς τὴν ἑσπέραν γενῶν.

35 Ὑφίεντο μέντοι τῆς ἀγνωμοσύνης ἐπεί τε ὑπὸ Ἄγγλων τῶν τὴν Βρετανίαν οἰκούντων ἔθνος διαπολεμῆσαν τήν τε

and subjected most of the land of Iberia, settled it, and, pushing forward together, were laying sieges there. They gave the land, namely Castile, Navarre, and Aragon, over to their followers, and when those followers were besieged by the barbarians they freed them from the sieges. They divided up the land among themselves and settled it, each receiving his allotted portion. They are praised to this day as great men for managing the war so superbly. After the general Orlando was besieged and died of thirst, Rinaldo inherited the war and bequeathed it to the kings of Castile. And they who have inherited this war even today are used to harrying these North Africans. This race of North Africans speaks Arabic, practices the customs and the religion of Muhammad, and their clothes are partly in the barbarian and partly in the Iberian style.

Given their past, then, the French think highly of themselves on account of these things, and they believe that their nation is the most noble and distinguished of all the nations of the west. Their way of life is more luxurious than that of the Italians and their dress is similar. Their language differs from that of the Italians, but not so much that one might believe theirs is a different language from that of the Italians. They expect to be first wherever they find themselves among the western peoples. 34

Their arrogance abated, however, when the English, who inhabit Britain, fought a war against their country, 35

χώραν αὐτῶν κατεστρέψαντο καὶ αὐτούς, καὶ τὴν ἡγεμονίαν ἀφελόμενοι, ἐπὶ τὴν μητρόπολιν αὐτῶν Παρίσιον συνελάσαντες ἐπολιόρκουν. Τὴν δὲ αἰτίαν αὐτῶν τῆς διαφορᾶς φασι γενέσθαι ὧδε. Ἔστι πόλις Καλέση οὕτω καλουμένη ἐν τῇ παραλίῳ χώρᾳ τῆς Κελτικῆς, παρὰ τὸν ὠκεανόν, οὐ πάνυ τι ἐπίσημος, ἐν ἐχυρῷ δὲ ᾠκημένη, ἔς γε τὸν ἀπὸ Γαλατίας ἀπόπλουν ἐς τὴν Βρετανικὴν ἐπιτηδείως ἔχουσα, καὶ ἐν καλῷ τοῦ πορθμοῦ ᾠκημένη παρέχεται ἐντεῦθεν ὁρμωμένοις ἐς τὴν Κελτικὴν ἐσβαλεῖν. Ταύτην τὴν πόλιν ὁ τῶν Βρετανῶν βασιλεύς, τοῖς ἐν τῇ πόλει προδοσίαν συνθέμενος, εἷλεν ἐπιβουλῇ, καὶ κατασχὼν ἐτυράννευε ταύτης. Ἀπαιτοῦντι δὲ τὴν πόλιν ταύτην τῷ Γαλατίας βασιλεῖ οὐκ ἔφη ἑκὼν εἶναι ἀποδιδόναι, καὶ φρουρὰν ἔφαινον διαπορθμεύοντες ἀπὸ τῆς νήσου ἐπὶ τὴν πόλιν. [1.84] Τὴν μέντοι πόλιν ἐπελαύνων ἐπολιόρκει ἐπὶ συχνὸν χρόνον· μετὰ δέ, ὡς οὐ προεχώρει αὐτῷ οὐδὲν πολιορκοῦντι, ἀπήγαγε τὸν στρατὸν ἐπ' οἴκου ἀναχωρῶν.

36 Ὕστερον ὁ Βρετανῶν πολύ τι στράτευμα ἀθροίσας, καὶ διαβάντες ἐς Γαλατίαν τὴν χώραν ἐδῄουν, καί πῃ συμμίξαντες τῇ τῶν Κελτῶν μοίρᾳ οὐκ ὀλίγῃ καὶ μαχεσάμενοι διέφθειρον τὸ πλέον τῆς Κελτικῆς. Ἐγένετο δὲ ὧδε. Ὡς ἐπὶ διαρπαγὴν τῆς χώρας ἐτράποντο οἱ Ἄγγλοι, ἐπήλαυνον ὀπίσω ἀπάγοντες λείαν· καταλαβόντες δὲ αὐτοὺς οἱ Κελτοί, πρὶν ἢ φθῆναι διασωθέντας ἐς τὴν Καλέσην, περιστῆσαί τε αὐτοὺς κυκλωσαμένους ἔν τινι λόφῳ. Ὡς δὲ ἐν ἀπόρῳ τε εἴχοντο οἱ Βρετανοί, μὴ οὐκ ἔχοντες ὅποι τράπωνται γενόμενοι, διεμηνύοντο, ὥστε τὴν λείαν ἀποδοῦναι καὶ τὰ ὅπλα, ἐφ' ᾧ ἐπιτραπῆναι σφίσιν ἀσινέσιν

conquered it and them, and stripped them of their rule; they even marched against their capital Paris and besieged it.[89] It is said that the following was the cause of this conflict. There is a city called Calais on the coast of the land of France by the Ocean. It is not especially distinguished but it is built in a secure location, conveniently situated for sailing from France to Britain and, as it is located at a strategic point on the Channel, it provides a good base for anyone who wants to invade France. The king of the British took this city by treachery after arranging its betrayal with those inside, seized it, and controlled it.[90] When the king of France demanded this city back, the king of the British said that he was unwilling to give it back, and they revealed the garrison they had brought over from the island to the city. So the king of the French set out and besieged the city for a long time. But when he was not making any progress in the siege, he led his army away and went home.[91]

Later the king of the British assembled a large army, 36
crossed to France, and plundered the land. When they engaged in battle with a fairly large contingent of the French, they killed most of the Frenchmen. This happened in the following way.[92] After the English had engaged in plundering the land, they set out to return, taking their loot home with them. The French intercepted them before they managed to reach the safety of Calais, and had them surrounded on a hill. The British now were at a loss, not knowing which way to turn, and so they sent a message that they were willing to hand over the loot and their weapons on the condition that they be allowed to return to their own land

ἀπιέναι ἐς τὴν ἑαυτῶν. Οἱ δὲ οὐκ ἔφασαν ἐπιτρέπειν ἀπιέναι, εἰ μὴ δώσουσι δίκην, ὧν εἰς τοὺς Κελτοὺς ἐξυβρίσαντες τὴν χώραν αὐτῶν διαρπάζουσιν. Ἐνταῦθα, ὡς ἔγνωσαν οἱ Βρετανοὶ ἐς τὸ ἔσχατον τοῦ κακοῦ ἀφιγμένοι, μαχόμενοι τοῖς Κελτοῖς ὀλίγοι πρὸς πολλοὺς ἄνδρες ἐγένοντο ἀγαθοί· τρεψάμενοι δὲ τοὺς ἐναντίους ἐδίωκον φεύγοντας, καὶ διέφθειρον αὐτοῦ ταύτῃ πολλούς. Κελτοὺς δέ, φασί τινες, φεύγειν αὐτοὺς ἐν ταῖς μάχαις οὐ θέμις νομίζεται, ἀλλὰ μαχομένους αὐτοῦ τελευτῆσαι· καὶ ἀπὸ [1.85] τούτου Κελτοὶ σφᾶς ἀξιοῦσι προέχειν τῶν ἄλλων γενναιότητι καὶ ἐπισημοτάτους εἶναι ἁπάντων.

37 Τοὺς μέντοι Βρετανοὺς ἀπὸ τοῦδε ἀδεέστερον ἤδη χωρεῖν ἐπὶ τὰς πόλεις τῶν Κελτῶν πολιορκοῦντας καὶ κατὰ βραχὺ προϊόντας, μαχέσασθαί τε τὴν μάχην ἐν τῷ λύπης πεδίῳ οὕτω καλουμένῳ· ἐν ᾧ οὐδὲν πλέον ἔχοντες οἱ Ἄγγλοι τῇ προτεραίᾳ ἐνηυλίσαντο, καὶ μετὰ ταῦτα τῇ ὑστεραίᾳ μαχεσάμενοι ἐφόνευον τοὺς Κελτοὺς μαχομένους φύρδην τε καὶ ἀναμὶξ καὶ χωρὶς ὡς ἕκαστον ἐπιχωροῦντα, ὥστε ἀποθανεῖν, τὴν μέντοι χώραν σχεδόν τι σύμπασαν ὑπαγόμενοι οἱ Βρετανοὶ ἐχώρουν ἐπὶ τὰ βασίλεια, τὴν πόλιν αὐτοῦ τοῦ Παρισίου. Καὶ ἦσαν δὲ τὰ Κελτῶν πράγματα προσδόκιμα ἐπὶ τὸν ἔσχατον ἤδη ἀφίξεσθαι κίνδυνον. Δεισιδαιμονοῦσι τοῖς Κελτοῖς, ὡς τοιαύτῃ κατείχοντο συμφορᾷ, καθ' ὃν δὴ χρόνον ἄνθρωποι μάλιστα εἰώθασιν ὡς τὰ πολλὰ ἐπὶ δεισιδαιμονίαν τρέπεσθαι, γυνή τις τὸ εἶδος οὐ φαύλη, φαμένη ἑαυτῇ χρηματίζειν τὸν Θεόν, ἡγεῖτό τε τῶν Κελτῶν ἐπισπομένων αὐτῇ καὶ πειθομένων. Ἐξηγεῖσθαί τε τὴν γυναῖκα, ᾗ δὴ ἔφασκε

unharmed. But the others said that they would not let them leave before they paid the penalty for the offense they had committed against the French by plundering their land. Thus, when the British realized that they had reached the end of the road, they fought against the French, although there were only a few brave men facing many. But they routed the enemy and pursued them when they fled, killing many of them on the spot. Some say, however, that the French disapprove of fleeing from battle, and hold that one should die fighting. It is because of this that the French regard themselves as surpassing all others in bravery and distinction.

After this, the British moved with greater impunity 37
against the cities of the French and besieged them, advancing little by little, until they fought the battle that is called "the plain of sorrow."[93] The English, with no other choice, had made camp there the previous day and then, on the next day, joined battle and began slaughtering the French who were fighting against them in a chaotic melee, each man advancing by himself so that he perished. Thus the British took control of almost the entire land and moved against the royal court, the city of Paris itself. The affairs of the French looked as though they had reached their ultimate crisis. But, facing such catastrophe, the French now turned to religion—indeed, people generally turn to religion at such a time—when a certain woman of considerable beauty [Joan of Arc] claimed that she was in communication with God. She became the leader of the French, who followed her and obeyed her. This woman led them to a spot that, she

σημαίνεσθαι ἑαυτῇ ὑπὸ τοῦ θείου, προελθεῖν τε συλλεγομένους ἐπὶ τοὺς Βρετανοὺς καὶ ἀναμαχομένους. [Οὐδὲν πλέον ἐχόντων τῶν Ἄγγλων][4] ἐπηυλίσαντό τε αὐτοῦ, καὶ τῇ ὑστεραίᾳ αὖθις ἤδη θαρροῦντες τῇ γυναικὶ ἐξηγουμένῃ ἐπὶ τὴν μάχην ἐπῄεσαν, καὶ μαχεσάμενοι ἐτρέψαντό τε τοὺς πολεμίους καὶ ἐπεξῆλθον διώκοντες. Μετὰ δὲ ταῦτα ἥ τε γυνὴ ἀπέθανεν ἐν τῷ πολέμῳ τούτῳ, καὶ οἱ Κελτοὶ ἀνέλαβόν τε σφᾶς καὶ ἐρρωμενέστεροι ἐγένοντο πρὸς τοὺς Βρετανοὺς μαχόμενοι, καὶ τὰς πόλεις σφῶν ἀπολαμβάνοντες διεσώζοντο αὖθις τὴν βασιλείαν αὐτῶν, [1.86] ἄχρις οὗ πολλάκις διαβάντων ἐς τὴν Γαλατίαν στρατῶν πολλῶν καὶ μεγάλων ἀπὸ Βρετανίας. Μαχεσαμένους οἱ Κελτοὶ φέρονται πλέον τῶν Βρετανῶν, ἐς ὃ δὴ συνελαύνοντες αὐτοὺς ἐς τὴν Καλέσην ἐξελάσαι αὐτοὺς ἐκ τῆς χώρας.

38 Βρετανικαὶ νῆσοι καταντικρὺ τῆς Φλανδρίας τρεῖς οὖσαι, ἐπὶ μήκιστον δὲ τοῦ ὠκεανοῦ καθήκουσαι, ὁτὲ μὲν μία νῆσος τυγχάνει οὖσα, ὁπότε πλημμυρία, ὁτὲ δ' αὖθις τρεῖς, ὁπότε τὰ ὕδατα ἐς ἄμπωτιν γινόμενα ἀναστρέφοιτο. Δικαιοτέρα δ' ἂν λέγοιτο μία αὕτη ἡ νῆσος, ἐπεὶ καὶ μία τε οὖσα καὶ κατ' αὐτὸ διήκουσα πολιτεύεται, φρονοῦσά τε κατὰ ταὐτὸ καὶ ὑφ' ἑνὸς ἀρχομένη τὰ ξύμφορα ἑαυτῇ ἐπισκοπεῖ. Ἔστι δ' ἡ περίοδος τῆσδε τῆς νήσου ἐς πεντακισχιλίους μάλιστα σταδίους. Γένος δὲ ἐνοικεῖ τὴν νῆσον πολύ τε καὶ ἄλκιμον, πόλεις τε ἔνεισιν αὐτοῦ μεγάλαι τε καὶ ὄλβιαι, καὶ κῶμαι ὅτι πλεῖσται. Ἔστι δ' αὐτοῖς βασιλεύς, καὶ μητρόπολις αὐτῶν, ἐν ᾗ καὶ βασίλεια, Λόνδραι, τοῦ βασιλέως, ὑπ' αὐτὸν δὲ ἡγεμονίαι ἐν τῇ νήσῳ ταύτῃ

said, had been indicated to her by God. They advanced and assembled in order to fight the British again. [As the English had no choice,][94] the French encamped there and on the very next day, with their confidence restored by the woman who was leading them, they went to battle. They routed the enemy in the battle and set off in pursuit. Although the woman died after that in this war, the French recovered and grew stronger in fighting the British.[95] They reclaimed their cities and preserved their kingdom to the point where many large armies often had to cross over into France from Britain.[96] The French are prevailing over the British in their battles, to the point where they are driving them toward Calais in order to expel them from their land.[97]

The British Isles lie across from Flanders and are three 38
in number; they extend over a long stretch of the Ocean. Sometimes there is only one island, but then the tide comes in and there are three, whereupon the waters again ebb and recede.[98] It would thus be more correct to say that there is only one island and, because it is one, it is governed as such in its entirety, with the same purpose and looking after its own interests, being ruled by one man. The circumference of this island is about five thousand stades. The race that inhabits the island is populous and hardy; it contains large, prosperous cities, and a multitude of villages. They have a king and a capital, where the royal court of the king is, namely London. There are many subordinate principalities

οὐκ ὀλίγαι, κατὰ ταὐτὰ τοῖς Κελτοῖς διατιθέμεναι τῷ σφετέρῳ βασιλεῖ· οὔτε γὰρ ἂν ῥᾳδίως ἀφέλοιτο βασιλεὺς τούτων τινὰ τὴν ἡγεμονίαν, οὔτε παρὰ τὰ σφῶν ἔθιμα ἀξιοῦσιν ὑπακούειν τῷ βασιλεῖ. [1.87] Ἐγένοντο δὲ τῇ νήσῳ ταύτῃ ξυμφοραὶ οὐκ ὀλίγαι, παραπαιούσῃ αὐτῇ, ἐς διαφορὰν ἀφικνουμένων τῶν ἡγεμόνων πρός τε τὸν βασιλέα καὶ πρὸς ἀλλήλους.

39 Ἄλλα τε καὶ δὴ φέρει ἡ νῆσος αὕτη, οἶνον δὲ οὐδαμῇ, οὐδὲ ὀπώρας πάνυ τι, σῖτον δὲ καὶ κριθὰς καὶ μέλι. Καὶ ἔρια ἔστιν αὐτοῖς, οἷα κάλλιστα τῶν ἐν ταῖς ἄλλαις χώραις, ὥστε καὶ ὑφαίνεσθαι αὐτοῖς πάμπολύ τι πλῆθος ἱματίων. Νομίζουσι δὲ γλώσσῃ ἰδίᾳ πάμπαν, καὶ οὐδενὶ συμφέρεται ἐς τὴν φωνήν, οὔτε Γερμανοῖς, οὔτε Κελτοῖς, οὐδὲ ἄλλῳ οὐδενὶ τῶν περιοίκων. Σκευῇ δὲ τῇ αὐτῇ χρώμενοι τοῖς Κελτοῖς, καὶ ἤθεσί τε τοῖς αὐτοῖς καὶ διαίτῃ. Νομίζεται δὲ τούτοις τά τ' ἀμφὶ τὰς γυναῖκάς τε καὶ τοὺς παῖδας ἁπλοϊκώτερα, ὥστε ἀνὰ πᾶσαν τὴν νῆσον, ἐπειδάν τις ἐς τὴν τοῦ ἐπιτηδείου αὐτῷ οἰκίαν ἐσίῃ καλούμενος, κύσαντα τὴν γυναῖκα οὕτω ξενίζεσθαι αὐτόν. Καὶ ἐν ταῖς ὁδοῖς δὲ ἁπανταχῇ παρέχονται τὰς ἑαυτῶν γυναῖκας [ἐν] τοῖς ἐπιτηδείοις. Νομίζεται δὲ τοῦτο καὶ ἐς τὴν Φραντάλων χώραν, τὴν ταύτῃ πάραλον, ἄχρι Γερμανίας. Καὶ οὐδὲ αἰσχύνην τοῦτο φέρει ἑαυτοῖς κύεσθαι τάς τε γυναῖκας αὐτῶν καὶ τὰς θυγατέρας.

40 Λονδρῶν δὲ ἡ πόλις δυνάμει τε προέχουσα τῶν ἐν τῇ νήσῳ ταύτῃ πασῶν πόλεων, ὄλβῳ τε καὶ τῇ ἄλλῃ εὐδαιμονίᾳ οὐδεμιᾶς τῶν πρὸς ἑσπέραν λειπομένη, ἀνδρίᾳ τε καὶ τῇ ἐς τοὺς πολέμους ἀρετῇ ἀμείνων τῶν περιοικούντων

on the island, in the same relationship to the king as among the French. The king could not easily strip one of them of his realm, nor do their customs require them to obey the king. Many disasters have struck this island, which has fallen apart when its rulers have come into conflict with the king or with each other.

This island produces many goods—wheat, barley, and 39
honey—but not wine nor much by way of fruit.[99] And they do have wool, which is of a much finer quality than in other countries, so that they weave a vast quantity of garments. They speak their own particular language which does not sound at all like that of the Germans, the French, or any of their neighbors. They have the same dress, customs, and way of life as the French. They have a rather casual attitude when it comes to women and children so that throughout the island, whenever a man is invited to a friend's house, he is greeted with a kiss by the host's wife. Even in the streets they present their own wives everywhere to their friends. The same custom prevails in the land of the Flemish, a coastal land there which extends as far as Germany. It brings no shame upon them for their wives and daughters to be kissed in this way.

The city of London surpasses all the cities on this island 40
in strength and is generally second to no other city in the west in wealth and prosperity. In courage and valor in war, it is superior to its neighbors and to many others in the lands

καὶ πολλῶν ἄλλων τῶν πρὸς ἥλιον δύνοντα. Ὅπλοις δὲ χρῶνται θυρεοῖς μὲν [1.88] Ἰταλικοῖς καὶ ξίφεσιν Ἑλληνικοῖς, τόξοις δὲ μακροῖς, ὥστε καὶ ἱστῶντας ἐς τὴν γῆν αὐτοὺς τοξεύειν. Ποταμὸς δὲ παρ' αὐτήν γε τὴν πόλιν ῥέων, σφοδρός τε καὶ μέγας, ἐς τὸν πρὸς Γαλατίαν ὠκεανὸν ἐκδιδοῖ, ἀπὸ τῆς πόλεως ἐς σταδίους δέκα τε καὶ διακοσίους ἐπὶ θάλασσαν, καὶ πλημμυρίᾳ ἀναβαίνειν τὰς ναῦς εὐπετῶς πάνυ ἐπὶ τὴν πόλιν· κἂν μέντοι ἐπιστρέφῃ τὰ ὕδατα τὰ ἔμπαλιν γινόμενα, χαλεπῶς ἐπὶ τὰ ῥεύματα ἀνιόντα, ἀντικόπτειν ἐπὶ τὴν πόλιν ἰόντα. Κατὰ μέντοι ἄμπωτιν, ἔν τε τῇ παραλίῳ χώρᾳ τῆς γε Κεντίας καὶ ἐν αὐτῇ τῇ νήσῳ, ἐς ἄμπωτιν γινομένων τῶν ὑδάτων τὰς ναῦς ἐπὶ ξηρὰν γίνεσθαι, περιμενούσας, ἐς ὃ ἀναπλημμυρίζει αὖθις τὰ ὕδατα. Πλημμυρεῖ δὲ ἐς τὸ μέγιστον ἐπὶ πήχεις βασιλικοὺς πεντεκαίδεκα, τοὐλάχιστον δὲ ἐπὶ ἕνδεκα. Νυκτὸς μὲν οὖν καὶ ἡμέρας ἀπορρέοντα πλημμυρεῖ αὖθις ἐπανιόντα.

41 Σελήνης δὲ κατὰ μέσον οὐρανὸν γιγνομένης, ἔστε τὸν καθ' ἡμᾶς καὶ ἐς τὸν ὑπὸ τὴν γῆν ὁρίζοντα, τρέπεσθαι ἐπὶ τὴν ἐναντίαν τὰ ὕδατα κίνησιν. Χρὴ οὖν διασκοπεῖσθαι περὶ τῆς κινήσεως ταύτης τῶν ὑδάτων τῇδ' ἐπισκεπτομένους. Τὴν γὰρ σελήνην ἐπιτροπεύειν τε τὴν τῶν ὑδάτων φύσιν ὑπὸ Θεοῦ τετάχθαι οἰόμεθα. Οὐκ ἂν δὴ ἀσυμφώνως ἔχειν πρός τε τὴν φύσιν τε αὐτῆς καὶ τὴν κρᾶσιν, [1.89] ἣν εἴληχε τὴν ἀρχὴν ὑπὸ Θεοῦ τοῦ μεγάλου βασιλέως, πρὸς μὲν τὴν κίνησιν αὐτῆς μετεωρίζουσαν ἐφέλκεσθαί τε ἐφ' οἷ τὰ ὕδατα, ἐς ὃ ἐπὶ τὴν μεγίστην ἀνάβασιν γένηται τοῦ οὐρανοῦ, κἀντεῦθεν αὖθις κατιοῦσαν ἐπανιέναι τὰ ὕδατα,

of the setting sun. They use Italian shields, Greek swords, and long bows that they shoot by standing them upright on the ground. A river flows by this city, broad and with a mighty current, emptying into the Ocean toward France. The distance from the city to the sea is two hundred and ten stades, and when the tide is in the ships can easily sail up to the city. But when the waters change direction and flow back again, it is difficult to sail against the current and access to the city is prevented. At the low tide, in the coastal region of Kent and on the island itself, when the waters ebb the ships become grounded and must wait for the waters to flood again. At its maximum the tide rises to a height of fifteen royal cubits, at its minimum eleven. Day and night the tide ebbs and then rises again.

When the moon reaches the middle of the sky, coming to 41
both our horizon and the one beneath the earth, the waters turn and flow in the opposite direction. Those who observe the moon need to consider this motion of the waters. For I believe that the moon has been assigned by God to govern the nature of the waters. This would not be inconsistent with its nature and mixture of elements, which it received in the beginning from God the Great King. When the moon rises in the sky it draws the waters after it until it reaches the highest point in the sky; then, as it descends, the waters go

μηκέτι συνανιόντα αὐτῇ ἐς τὴν ἄνοδον· ἐπειδὰν δὲ αὖθις ἐς τὴν κάθοδον γινομένη ἄρξηται γίνεσθαι ἐς τὸ ἄναντες, τὸ ἐντεῦθεν αὖθις ἐπανιόντα πλημμυρεῖν.

42 Συμβαίνει μέντοι καὶ ὑπὸ πνευμάτων ἐς τοῦτο συμβαλλομένων κινεῖν ἔτι μᾶλλον τὰ ὕδατα, ὅθεν ἂν δεχόμενα ᾖ τὴν ἀρχὴν τῆς κινήσεως. Φέροιτο δ' ἂν ταῦτα κινούμενα διττὴν τήνδε τὴν κίνησιν ἐπὶ τὴν τοῦ παντὸς τοῦδε τοῦ οὐρανοῦ κίνησιν, τήν τε αὐθαίρετον καὶ δὴ βίαιον γενομένην, ὡς ἂν μὴ ἐς σύμφωνόν τινα ἁρμονίαν γινομένης τῆς κινήσεως, πολυειδῆ τε καὶ ὡς μάλιστα, ᾗ ἂν τὸ ἥδιστον ἐπί τε τῇ θεωρίᾳ καὶ ὄψει καὶ ἀκοῇ, καὶ ἐς ὅρον τινὰ σύμφωνον τῇ τοῦ παντὸς τοῦδε ψυχῇ, ὡς ἂν αἰσθομένη μᾶλλόν τι[5] ἐνεγκουσῶν τῶν κινήσεων καὶ ἀλλήλαις συμφερομένων ἔς τινα ὁμοειδῆ συμφωνίαν ἔχειν τὴν[6] ἄλλην τὸ ἥδεσθαι. Ἐντεῦθεν τήν τε ψυχῆς κίνησιν, τὴν ἀρχὴν ἐκεῖθεν λαμβάνουσαν, ἐπὶ τὴν διττὴν ἐκείνην φορὰν κινεῖν αὖθις τὰ σώματα, αὔξοντά τε δὴ καὶ φθίνοντα. Καὶ μὲν δὴ καὶ ἐπὶ κίνησιν τήνδε τὴν ὁρμὴν ὑποδέχεται τῷ παντὶ τῷδε συμφερομένην ἡ ἡμετέρα ψυχή. Τῇ μὲν αὐθαιρέτῳ τήν τε γένεσιν καὶ αὔξησιν ἕπεσθαι ἀνάγκῃ, τῇ δ' αὖ βιαίῳ καὶ ἀκουσίῳ κινήσει τήν τε φθίσιν αὖ καὶ τὴν τελευτὴν ἐπισπομένην συμβαίνειν τοῖς τῇδε οὖσι. [1.90]

43 Ταῦτα μὲν ἔστε τὴν τοῦ ὠκεανοῦ κίνησιν καὶ τὴν τῇδε αὖ διττὴν ζῴων ἐμψύχων κίνησιν, ὅσα τε ψυχὴν ἴσχει ἐνταῦθα καὶ κίνησιν κινεῖται ἡντιναοῦν. Τὰ μέντοι ἐς τήνδε τὴν θάλασσαν ὕδατα οὐ τὴν αὐτὴν ἐκείνην ἀνάγκῃ κινεῖσθαι κίνησιν, ἀλλ' ὡς ἔχει τε ἕκαστα πνευμάτων τε καὶ τόπων ἐς τὴν κίνησιν βιαζομένων αὐτά, ᾗ φύσεως ἔχοι ἂν

back, no longer following it in its ascent. And when, in turn, the moon has made its descent and begins to go back up again, the tide turns about and starts to rise again.

It happens that the winds contribute to this process too 42
and move the waters still more, from wherever the latter originally receive their motion. This movement of the waters may, then, feature a dual motion that goes against the motion of the totality of the sky, becoming both spontaneous and violent, so that if this motion does not attain a harmonious unison, it becomes extremely varied. This is most pleasant to contemplate, view, and hear, and is in accordance with one of the rules of the Soul of this Universe, namely that this Soul takes pleasure in perceiving how different motions may be conveyed and borne along with each other into a certain uniform harmony.[100] Therein lies also the source of the soul's motion, which in turn moves our bodies on this dual course, namely to grow and to decline. Moreover, our individual soul receives the impulse for its motion as it is borne along with the Universe. For all living things, birth and growth necessarily follow the spontaneous motion, while decline and death are caused by the violent and compulsive one.

So much, then, concerning the motion of the Ocean and 43
the dual motion of living beings with souls in relation to it, those here that have a soul and move in any way whatever. The waters of the sea, however, are not necessarily moved by that same motion, but, as they move in accordance with how the winds and places compel them individually, their

καὶ ῥοπῆς, πρὸς ἣν ἂν κινοῖτο δὴ ταῦτα κίνησιν. Ταῦτα μὲν οὖν ἐς τὴν τῶν ὑδάτων τοῦ ὠκεανοῦ κίνησιν καὶ ἐπὶ πλεῖστον δὲ τῆσδε τῆς θαλάσσης ἐς τοσοῦτον ἀπερρίφθω· ἐπάνειμι δὲ ἐπ' ἐκεῖνα τῆς ἀφηγήσεως, ὅθεν ταύτῃ ἀπετραπόμεθα.

44 Βασιλεὺς γὰρ δὴ Ἑλλήνων, ὡς ἐπὶ τὸν βασιλέα Κελτῶν ἀφίκετο, φρενίτῃ τε ὄντα δὴ κατέλαβεν, οὐκ ἐξεγένετό οἱ ὁτῳοῦν ἄλλῳ τῶν κατὰ τὴν Γαλατίαν ἡγεμόνων, ὧν ἕνεκα ἀφίκετο, χρηματίσαι· καὶ διὰ ταῦτα συμβουλευόντων τῶν αὐτοῦ ταύτῃ ἀρίστων ἐπέμενε θεραπευθῆναι τὸν βασιλέα, συχνόν τινα διατρίβων αὐτοῦ χρόνον. Ὡς δὲ ἐπετείνετο ἐπὶ μακρότερον τοῦ νοσήματος, οὐχ οἷός τε ἦν ἔτι ἐπιμένειν αὐτῷ, ὑπέστρεψε διὰ Γερμανίας τε καὶ Παιονίας. Παιαζήτης δὲ τό τε Βυζάντιον ἐπολιόρκει προσέχων ἐντεταμένως, καὶ ἐπὶ Πελοπόννησον πέμψας στρατόν, ἀποκρούων μυριάδας πέντε, καὶ Ἰαγούπην τὸν τότε αὐτῷ Εὐρώπης στρατηγόν, αὐτὸς εἶχεν ἀμφὶ τῇ ἑαυτοῦ ἀρχῇ τῇ περὶ τὸ Βυζάντιον. Ἰαγούπης μὲν σὺν τῷ Βρενέζῃ, τότε δὴ ἀρξαμένῳ εὐδοκιμεῖν, ἐσέβαλον ἐς τὴν Πελοπόννησον· καὶ Βρενέζης μὲν πολλάκις ἐσβαλὼν καὶ τότε καὶ μετὰ ταῦτα ἐδῄου τὴν Πελοπόννησον, ἀλλὰ καὶ τὰ περὶ Κορώνην τε καὶ Μεθώνην χωρία, Ἰαγούπης δὲ ὁ [1.91] τῆς Εὐρώπης ἡγεμὼν ἀφικόμενος ἐς τὸ Ἄργος ἐπολιόρκει.

45 Τὸ δὲ Ἄργος τοῦτον τὸν χρόνον κατεῖχον οἱ Ἐνετοί. Ἀπέδοτο δὲ Θεόδωρος ὁ τῆς Σπάρτης ἡγεμών, ὡς ἀπέγνω τοῖς Ἕλλησι τὴν σωτηρίαν τῷ τε Βυζαντίῳ, πρὸς δὲ καὶ τῇ Πελοποννήσῳ, καὶ ἐπὶ ξυροῦ ἀκμῆς ἤδη ἑστηκότα τὰ τῶν Ἑλλήνων πράγματα· τό τε Ἄργος ὅμορον ὂν Ναυπλίῳ,

motion is determined by whatever their nature and equilibrium may be. Having said all this, let us now set aside the topic of the motion of the waters of the Ocean and, especially, of this particular sea. I return to that point in my narration from where I digressed.

When the king of the Greeks came to the king of the French and realized that he was demented,[101] he was prevented from discussing the issues for which he had gone there with any other of the leading men in France. For this reason his leading men who accompanied him there advised him to persist in attending upon the king, and so he spent a considerable time there. But as the illness dragged on for a long time, he was unable to stay there any longer and so he returned through Germany and Hungary.[102] Meanwhile, Bayezid was vigorously pressing the siege of Byzantion, and he sent an army against the Peloponnese, detaching fifty thousand men and Yakub, who was then his general in Europe, while he himself retained command of operations around Byzantion. Yakub and Evrenos, who was then beginning to become famous, invaded the Peloponnese. Both then and later Evrenos often invaded and plundered the Peloponnese, including the regions around Korone and Methone, while Yakub, the governor of Europe, arrived at Argos and besieged it.[103] 44

At this time the Venetians held Argos. It was given to them by Theodoros, the ruler of Mistra, who had decided that the Greeks had no hope of safety in Byzantion, or for that matter in the Peloponnese, as the affairs of the Greeks already stood upon a razor's edge.[104] He sold Argos, which 45

πόλει τῶν Ἑνετῶν, ἀπέδοτο οὐ πολλοῦ. Καὶ Σπάρτην δὲ τοῖς ἀπὸ Ῥόδου Ναζηραίοις ἐς λόγους ἀφικόμενος ἀπέδοτο πολλοῦ τινός. Οἱ μὲν Σπαρτιᾶται, ὡς ᾔσθοντο προδεδομένοι ὑπὸ τοῦ σφῶν αὐτῶν ἡγεμόνος, ἀπῆν γὰρ τότε, ἐνάγοντος τοῦ Σπάρτης ἀρχιερέως κοινῇ τε συνιόντες σφίσι λόγον ἐδίδοσαν, καὶ συνίσταντο ἀλλήλοις, καὶ συνετίθεντο ὡς οὐδενὶ ἐπιτρέψοντες εἰσελθεῖν ἐς τὴν πόλιν τῶν Ναζηραίων, πᾶν δέ, ὅ τι ἂν δέοι, χαλεπὸν πεισομένους πρὸ τοῦ Ναζηραίοις τοῖς Λατίνων πείθεσθαι. Ἐστήσαντο δὲ σφίσι καὶ τόν γε ἀρχιερέα ἄρχοντα ἐπὶ τούτῳ. Καὶ ἐλθόντων τῶν Ναζηραίων προηγορεύοντο ἀπαλλάσσεσθαι τὴν ταχίστην· εἰ δὲ μή, περιέψεσθαι ὡς πολεμίους. Οὗτοι μὲν οὖν ᾤχοντο ἀπαλλασσόμενοι ὡς ἐπὶ τὸν ἡγεμόνα, ὡς οὐδὲν ἐς τοῦτο σφίσι προεχώρει· Θεόδωρος δὲ ὁ τῆς Σπάρτης ἡγεμών, ὡς ᾔσθετο τὸ πρᾶγμα, ὡς τοὐναντίον, ἢ ἐβούλετο, περιέστη αὐτῷ, λόγους τε ἔπεμπεν αὖθις παρὰ τοὺς Σπαρτιάτας, ἀποπειρώμενος, εἰ δέξαιντο ἔτι αὐτὸν αὖθις ἐπανιόντα. Ὡς δὲ διαπειρωμένου προσίεντο τοὺς λόγους, ἐσῄει δὲ τὴν πόλιν, ὅρκια ποιησάμενος [1.92] μηκέτι τοῦ λοιποῦ ἐπὶ νοῦν βαλέσθαι τοιοῦτον.

46 Τότε οἱ Οὐενετοὶ φρουρὰν ἐς τὴν ἀκρόπολιν ἀποφηνάμενοι κατεῖχον. Ἐπὶ τοῦτο δὲ τὸ Ἄργος Ἰαγούπης ὁ Παιαζήτεω βασιλέως στρατηγὸς ὡς ἐστρατεύετο, ἐπολιόρκει τε ἀνὰ κράτος, καὶ προσβάλλων τῷ τείχει θαμὰ οὐκ ἀνίει. Μετὰ δὲ οὐ πολὺν χρόνον, ὡς ἀπὸ δυοῖν ἅμα τόποιν προσβάλλων ἐπειρᾶτο τοῦ χωρίου, γίνεταί τι δεῖμα τοῖς ἐν τῇ πόλει πανικὸν τοῖς ἐπὶ τῷ εὐωνύμῳ τῆς πόλεως μέρει ἀμυνομένοις, ὡς δόξαν αὐτοῖς ἄνθρωπόν τινα τῶν

borders on Nauplion, a city of the Venetians, for a small price.[105] He also negotiated with the monks from Rhodes and sold Mistra to them for a large price.[106] But when the people of Mistra found out that they had been betrayed by their own ruler, for he was away at the time, they assembled at the instigation of the bishop of Mistra to discuss the matter.[107] They came to an agreement and decided that they would permit none of the monks to enter into the city. They were prepared to suffer any necessary hardship rather than obey the Latin monks. They appointed their bishop to be their leader in this matter. When the monks arrived they were told to leave as quickly as possible; otherwise, they would be regarded as enemies. So they departed and went back to the ruler, as they were making no progress there. When Theodoros, the ruler of Mistra, was informed that the matter had turned out in the opposite way to what he had planned, he sent word to the people of Mistra in an attempt to see if they would still accept him if he returned. When they accepted his overtures, he entered the city, taking an oath that he would never again entertain such an idea.[108]

The Venetians then installed a garrison in the citadel of 46
Argos and so held the city. Yakub, the general of Sultan Bayezid, marched against the city and besieged it with all his might. He attacked the walls often and would not let up. After a short time, because he was attempting to assault the place from two locations simultaneously, a fearful panic arose among those inside who were defending the left side of the city, as they came to believe, based on the report of

ἐπιχωρίων φήσαντα εἰπεῖν, ὡς ἑάλω ἡ πόλις ἀπὸ τοῦ δεξιοῦ, καὶ ἐκλιπόντας τὸ χωρίον τοῦτο ἰέναι δρόμῳ ἐπὶ τὸ δεξιόν, ἐνταῦθα δὲ ἀναβεβηκότας τὸ τεῖχος τοὺς πολεμίους ταύτῃ ἑλεῖν τε κατὰ κράτος τὴν πόλιν καὶ ἀνδραποδίσασθαι πόλιν περιφανῆ τε καὶ παλαιάν. Ἀνδράποδα δὲ λέγεται γενέσθαι ἐντεῦθεν τοῖς Τούρκοις ὡς τρισμύρια. Κατοικίσαι μὲν τούτους λέγεται βασιλεὺς ἐς τὴν Ἀσίαν· οὐκ ἔχω δὲ τοῦτο συμβάλλεσθαι, ὡς εἴη ἀληθές, οὐ δυνάμενος ἐξευρεῖν διαπυνθανομένῳ, ὅποι τῆς Ἀσίας οὗτοι κατῴκηνται ὑπὸ Παιαζήτεω βασιλέως. Ἰαγούπης μὲν οὖν, ὡς τὸ Ἄργος ἠνδραποδίσατο, ἀπήγαγε τὸν στρατόν.

47 Μετὰ δὲ ταῦτα Βρενέζης τε αὐτίκα ἐπὶ μέγα ἐχώρει δυνάμεως, ἐμβάλλων τε ἐς τὴν Πελοπόννησον καὶ ἐς τὴν παράλιον Μακεδονίαν ἐπὶ τοὺς Ἀλβανούς, μεγάλα καὶ ἐπίσημα ἔργα ἀποδεικνύμενος τῷ τοῦ βασιλέως οἴκῳ, στρατηγὸς μὲν οὐκέτι ἀποδειχθεὶς ὑπὸ βασιλέως, τῶν δὲ Τούρκων ἑπομένων αὐτῷ, [1.93] ὅποι ἂν ἐξηγοῖτο, ὡς εὐτυχεῖ τε γενομένῳ τὰ ἐς πόλεμον καὶ πλουτίζοντι τὰ στρατεύματα, ὅποι ἂν ἐπίοι στρατευόμενος. Τοὺς γὰρ δὴ ἱπποδρόμους καλουμένους τοῦ γένους τοῦδε, μήτε μισθόν, μήτε ἀρχὴν ἔχοντας ὑπὸ τοῦ βασιλέως, ἐπὶ διαρπαγήν τε καὶ λείαν ἀεὶ διωσθέντας ἕπεσθαι, ὅποι ἄν τις ἐξηγῆται αὐτοῖς ἐπὶ τοὺς πολεμίους, αὐτίκα ἕκαστον ἱππεύοντά τε καὶ ἕτερον ἀγόμενον ἵππον ἐς τὸν ὑπόδρομον τῆς λείας, ἐπὰν δὲ ἐν τῇ πολεμίᾳ γένωνται, σύνθημα λαμβάνοντες ὑπὸ τοῦ στρατηγοῦ, ἀναβάντες οὓς περιάγουσιν ἵππους, θεῖν ἀνὰ κράτος, μηδέν τι ἐπέχοντας, καὶ σκεδαννυμένους σύντρεις διαρπάζειν ἀνδράποδα, καὶ ὅ τι ἐς ἄλλο

a local man, that the city had been taken from the right side. Leaving their sector they rushed over to the side on the right, but the enemy scaled the walls there and captured the city, enslaving this proud and ancient city.[109] It is said that the Turks obtained thirty thousand slaves there. It is also said that the sultan settled them in Asia. I cannot ascertain whether this is true, nor am I able to discover through inquiry where in Asia they were settled by Sultan Bayezid. Having enslaved Argos, then, Yakub led his army away.

After that Evrenos immediately rose to great power when 47
he invaded the Peloponnese and coastal Macedonia, where he fought against the Albanians, performing great and distinguished deeds on behalf of the sultan's household. He had not yet been appointed as a general by the sultan, but the Turks followed him wherever he led them because he was fortunate in war and enriched his army, wherever he went on campaign. The cavalry raiders of this people, as they are called,[110] receive neither wages nor office from the sultan, but they are always striving for plunder and loot and thus follow wherever someone leads them against an enemy. Each rides one horse and brings along another to carry the loot. When they enter enemy territory, they receive a signal from the general to mount the horses that they have been leading, and they ride with all their might; nothing holds them back. Dispersing into groups of three, they seize

προχωροίη. Ταύτῃ ἐπίσταμαι τούς τε μετὰ Ἀμουράτεω τοῦ Ὀρχάνεω καὶ τοὺς τότε δὴ ἐπὶ Παιαζήτεω διαβάντας ἐς τὴν Εὐρώπην ὠθῆσαί τε καὶ ταύτῃ ἑλομένους σφίσι βιοτεύειν, καὶ ἐπιδόντας παραχρῆμα ἐνίους μέγα ὀλβίους ἐν βραχεῖ γίνεσθαι, ἁπανταχῇ τε τῆς Εὐρώπης οἰκήσαντας, ἀπὸ τῆς τῶν Σκοπίων πόλεως ἐπὶ τὴν Τριβαλλῶν χώραν καὶ Μυσῶν καὶ κατὰ τὴν Μακεδονίαν, μετὰ δὲ ταῦτα περὶ Θετταλίαν οἰκῆσαι πολλούς.

48 Ἐπὶ μὲν οὖν Παιαζήτεω λέγεται μοῖραν οὐκ ὀλίγην Σκυθῶν ἐπὶ Δακίαν ἐλθοῦσαν πρεσβεύσασθαι πρὸς Παιαζήτην, αἰτεῖσθαι αὐτῶν τοὺς ἡγεμόνας χρήματά τε καὶ ἀρχήν, ἐφ' ᾧ διαβάντας τὸν Ἴστρον συνδιαφέρειν αὐτῷ τοὺς ἐπὶ τῇ Εὐρώπῃ ἐναντίους [1.94] πολέμους. Τὸν δὲ ἡδόμενον τῷ λόγῳ προσίεσθαι τὴν αἴτησιν αὐτῶν καὶ ὑπισχνεῖσθαι μεγάλα. Διαβάντων δὲ ἐκείνων κατοικίσαι αὐτοὺς ἀνὰ τὴν Εὐρώπην, θεραπεύοντας τοὺς ἡγεμόνας αὐτῶν ἀνὰ μέρος ἕκαστον, καὶ σκεδασθέντας οὕτω αὐτοὺς χρησίμους γενέσθαι ἔστε ἱπποδρόμους καὶ ἐς πόλεμον. Ὕστερον μέντοι Παιαζήτης ὀρρωδῶν, μή τι νεωτερίσωσιν οἱ ἡγεμόνες αὐτῶν συνιόντες σφίσι, συλλαβὼν τούτους ἀπέκτεινε. Τῶν δὲ Σκυθῶν καὶ νῦν ἔτι ἀνὰ τὴν Εὐρώπην πολύ τι πλῆθος πολλαχῇ σκεδασθέντων ἔστιν ἰδεῖν.

49 Καὶ ὑπὸ Ἀμουράτεω μέντοι ἐν τῇ Μακεδονίᾳ ἡ περὶ Θέρμην καὶ παρὰ Ἀξιὸν ποταμὸν χώρα κατῴκισται, ἀγαγόντος μέγα τι πλῆθος Τούρκων τε ἐς τοῦτον τὸν χῶρον καὶ κατοικίσαντος. Καὶ τὸ τῆς Ζαγορᾶς πέδον οὕτω καλούμενον ὑπὸ Ἀμουράτεω κατῳκίσθη, καὶ ἡ Φιλιπποπόλεως χώρα. Ἡ μέντοι Χερρόνησος ἡ ἐν τῷ

captives and anything that might be useful. I know that this is how those with Murad, the son of Orhan, and those at this time who crossed over into Europe with Bayezid used to behave when they charged and so made their living, and some of them quickly became very wealthy by doing this. They settled throughout Europe, from the city of Skopje to the land of the Serbs and that of the Bulgarians, and throughout Macedonia, and after that many settled in Thessaly.

It is said that during Bayezid's reign a large contingent of 48
Skythians came to Wallachia and sent an embassy to Bayezid requesting money and positions for their rulers, in exchange for which they would cross the Danube and join him in his wars against his enemies in Europe.[111] He was pleased by their proposal, granted their request, and made great promises to them. When they crossed over, he settled them in various places in Europe, with each group following its own ruler in each place. Dispersed in this way, they became useful in cavalry raiding and in war. But later Bayezid became afraid that their leaders might conspire together and rebel against him, so he arrested them and killed them. But even now one can still see a very large number of Skythians dispersed in various places throughout Europe.

Under Murad, the land in Macedonia around Thessalo- 49
nike and the Axios River was also settled with colonies, as he brought a great multitude of Turks to this region and settled them. The plain called Zagora was also settled by Murad as was the land of Philippopolis. The Chersonese at

Ἑλλησπόντῳ καὶ πρότερον ὑπὸ Σουλαϊμάνεω κατῳκίσθη τοῦ ἀδελφοῦ. Θετταλία δὲ καὶ ἡ περὶ τὰ Σκόπια χώρα καὶ ἡ Τριβαλλῶν ἀπὸ Φιλιπποπόλεως ἔστε ἐπὶ τὸν Αἷμον καὶ τὴν Σοφίαν οὕτω καλουμένην κώμην, Παιαζήτης ὁ Ἀμουράτεω κατοικίσας τήν τε Ἰλλυριῶν καὶ Τριβαλλῶν ἐληΐζετο χώραν. Ἐπιδιδόασι μὲν οὗτοι οἱ χῶροι πρός γε πολεμίων, καὶ ὕστερον μετὰ ταῦτα ἑτέρων ἐκ τοῦ ταύτῃ ἐπιρρεόντων αὐτοῦ, ὥσπερ ἂν ἐπυνθάνοντο ἐπιτηδείως σφίσιν ἔχειν τὴν χώραν πρός τε ἀνδράποδα καὶ ἐς [1.95] τὴν ἄλλην οὐσίαν τὴν ἀπὸ τῶν πολεμίων, καὶ ὅπῃ ἂν μάλιστα μὴ ἀντικόπτῃ ὑπὸ τῶν πολεμίων. Παιαζήτης δὲ ὡς ἐς τὴν Ἀσίαν διαβὰς ἐπὶ Ἐρτζιγγάνην πολιορκῶν παρεστήσατο, προϊὼν Μελιτηνὴν τὴν ἐπὶ τῷ Εὐφράτῃ ἐπολιόρκει τε καὶ προσέβαλε μηχανὰς παντοίας προσάγων τῷ τείχει. Καὶ ἐπὶ χρόνον μὲν ἀντεῖχε, μετὰ δὲ ταῦτα προσεχώρησε καθ' ὁμολογίαν.

50 Ἐν ᾧ δὲ ἥ τε Μελιτηνὴ ἐπολιορκεῖτο ὑπὸ Παιαζήτεω καὶ ἠγγέλλετο τῷ βασιλεῖ, ὡς ἑάλω Μελιτηνή, παρόντες καὶ τότε οἱ Τούρκων τῆς Ἀσίας ἡγεμόνες ἔπραττον, ὅπως κατάγοιντο ὑπὸ Τεμήρεω βασιλέως ἐς τὴν ἑαυτῶν ἕκαστος χώραν, προϊσχόμενοι τήν τε ξυγγένειαν ἀπὸ παλαιοῦ σφίσιν οὖσαν πρὸς τὸ Τεμήρεω γένος καὶ τὴν θρησκείαν, ἐς ἣν τελοῦντες αὐτὸν πατέρα τε καὶ κηδεμόνα ἐπεποίηντο τῆς ἑαυτῶν χώρας. Ἔλεγον δὲ αὐτῷ, ὡς διὰ ταῦτα εἴη τε τῆς Ἀσίας βασιλεύς, ὥστε μηδενὶ ἐπιτρέπειν ἐξυβρίζειν ἐς τοὺς ὁμοφύλους, μὴ ὑπάρξαντας ἀδικίας πρότερον· ὅτι δὲ μὴ ἠδίκουν Παιαζήτην, μηδὲ παρὰ τὰς συνθήκας ὅτι πεπλημμεληκότες εἶεν, ἐπετράποντο αὐτῷ διαιτητῇ, ὥστε

the Hellespont had previously been settled by Süleyman, his brother. Bayezid, the son of Murad, settled colonies in Thessaly, in the land around Skopje, in the land of the Serbs, from Philippopolis to the Haimos, and in the town known as Sofia, and he raided the land of the Illyrians and the Serbs. These places devoted themselves to fighting the enemy, and later, after that, others flooded into this area for the same reason when they learned that they could conveniently plunder the land for slaves and property taken from the enemy, especially where the enemy put up no resistance. Bayezid crossed over into Asia, besieged Erzinjan, and took it.[112] He then advanced to Melitene on the Euphrates and besieged that too, attacking its walls with every manner of siege engine. For some time it held out, but afterward it submitted by agreement.[113]

While Melitene was being besieged by Bayezid and it was 50
announced to the sultan[114] that Melitene had fallen, the rulers of the Turks in Asia were at hand, negotiating to be restored by King Timur, each to his own land.[115] They invoked the ancient bonds of kinship that existed between them and Timur's people, and also their religion, practicing which they had made him the father and guardian of their land. They said to him that this was the purpose of his being the king of Asia, namely so as not to allow anyone to wrong their kinsmen when they had committed no prior injustice. Because they had not wronged Bayezid nor were they guilty of violating their agreements, they were thus turning to

δίκας ὑπέχειν, ἤν τι παρὰ τὰς σπονδὰς αὐτῶν κακὸν Παιαζήτην εἰργασμένοι εἶεν. Τεμήρης δὲ τέως μὲν Παιαζήτῃ πρὸς τοὺς πολεμίους σφῶν διαπολεμοῦντι καὶ ἀγωνιζομένῳ ὑπὲρ τῆς Μεχμέτεω θρησκείας (διακεκρίσθαι γὰρ ἐς δύο σύμπασαν θρησκείας τήν γε [1.96] ἐγνωσμένην ἡμῖν οἰκουμένην, τήν τε τοῦ Ἰησοῦ καὶ τὴν σφῶν αὐτῶν θρησκείαν, ἐναντίαν ταύτῃ πολιτευομένην· τὰς γὰρ λοιπὰς τῶν θρησκειῶν οὔτε ἐς βασιλείαν οὔτε ἀρχὴν ἡντιναοῦν καταστῆναι) Παιαζήτῃ τε πολεμοῦντι ἔφασκε πρὸς τοὺς τοῦ ἥρωος πολεμίους οὐχ ὅπως ἄχθεσθαι διὰ ταῦτα, ἀλλὰ καὶ χάριν εἰδέναι ξύμπαντας τοὺς τῆς Μεχμέτεω μοίρας. Ταύτῃ μὲν οὖν τὴν ἀρχὴν ἀπεδείκνυτο γνώμην Τεμήρης.

51 Μετὰ δὲ ταῦτα, ὡς ὑπὸ πολλῶν ἤδη παρ' ἑαυτὸν ἀναβεβηκότων ἐπυνθάνετο τήν τε φύσιν αὐτοῦ μήτε ἐπιεικῆ, ὥστε τῇ καθεστηκυίᾳ ἐθέλειν ἐμμένειν κατὰ τὴν Ἀσίαν ἀρχῇ, ἀλλὰ τήν τε ὁρμὴν αὐτοῦ διεξιόντες ὡς Λαίλαπα παραβάλλοιεν αὐτόν, καὶ ὡς ἐπὶ Συρίαν καὶ Αἴγυπτον καὶ ἐπὶ Μέμφιος βασιλέα ἐν νῷ ἔχει στρατεύεσθαι, ἀναπεισθεὶς ὑπὸ τούτων ἔπεμψε πρεσβείαν ἐς Παιαζήτην ὡς διαλλάξουσαν, ἢν δύνηται, αὐτὸν τοῖς ἡγεμόσι, καὶ ἐπιπέμπων ἐσθῆτα, ᾗ δὴ ᾤετο χαριεῖσθαι τῷ Παιαζήτῃ, ᾗ δὴ νομίζεται τὴν ἡγεμονίαν τῆς Ἀσίας κατέχουσιν. Οἱ δὲ πρέσβεις ἀφικόμενοι ἔλεγον τοιάδε.

52 "Ἡμᾶς ἔπεμψε βασιλεὺς Τεμήρης, δῶρά τε τήνδε τὴν ἐσθῆτα φέροντάς σοι, καὶ χάριν εἰδέναι σοι ἔφη, ὅτι τοῖς τοῦ ἥρωος πολεμίοις μαχόμενος τούς τε ἐπὶ μέγα τε ἡμετέρους φίλους ἀκκίζεις[7] ἀγωνιζόμενος καὶ τὴν ἡμετέραν θρησκείαν ἐπὶ τὸ ἄμεινον καθιστᾷς. Ὡς δὲ ταύτῃ σοι

Timur as an arbiter to assess the justice of their case, that is whether they had done anything wrong to Bayezid in violation of their treaties. Timur said that insofar as Bayezid was fighting against their common enemies and struggling on behalf of the religion of Muhammad—for the entire known world is divided between two religions, that of Jesus and their religion, which sets itself against the other; for no other religion apart from these is established in the form of a kingdom or any other type of state—they should not be upset with Bayezid, who was fighting against their hero's enemies, but instead, all who sided with Muhammad should give him thanks. This was the initial verdict that they received from Timur.

But after that, Timur learned from the many people who 51
had gone up to him by then that Bayezid's nature was too disagreeable to allow him to remain content with the state of his realm in Asia, and they explained to him how the onset of Bayezid's assault might be compared to a hurricane.[116] Moreover, it was Timur's intention to march against Syria and Egypt and against the king of Cairo,[117] and so he was persuaded by them and sent an embassy to Bayezid to reconcile him with the rulers, if he could. Timur also sent him a robe, thinking that this would please Bayezid, for this is customary among those who hold dominions in Asia. When the ambassadors arrived they said the following:

"King Timur sent us to bring you this robe as a gift and to 52
convey his thanks to you because, by fighting against the hero's enemies, you incite our friends to great deeds with your struggles and establish our religion on a stronger footing. But just as it is good that you fight off our enemies, so

ἔχει καλῶς τοὺς ἡμετέρους ἀμύνεσθαι πολεμίους, τούς γε φίλους τε καὶ ἐπιτηδείους καὶ ἐς τὰ μάλιστα καθημένους ἡμῖν πολεμίους ποιεῖσθαι μηδὲ ἀδικεῖν, ἀλλ' ἐς τούτους μὲν μηδ' ὁτιοῦν [1.97] ἐκφέρεσθαι κακὸν κἀκείνους. Ἢν δὲ μὴ ἐς τοὺς ὁμοφύλους ἐπιτηδείως ἔχῃς, πῶς ἂν τοῖς πολεμίοις προσφέροις; Διὰ ταῦτα δὴ κελεύει τήν τε ἀρχὴν τοῖς ἐν τῇ Ἀσίᾳ ἡγεμόσιν, ἣν ἀφελόμενος ἔχεις, ἀποδοῦναι, μηδ' ὁτιοῦν παραβαίνοντας τῶν σφίσι πρὸς τὴν σὴν ἀρχὴν ἐσπεισμένων. Καὶ ταῦτα ποιῶν ἐκείνῳ τε χαριῇ, καὶ τὸ ἐν τῇ Ἀσίᾳ γένος καὶ ἐν τῇ Εὐρώπῃ χάριν εἰσομένους σοι διὰ τοῦτο. Εἰ δέ τι παρὰ τὰς συνθήκας πεποιημένοι εἶεν, ἐπετράποντο διαιτητῇ τῷ βασιλεῖ Τεμήρῃ, ἐς ὅ τι ἂν λέγοις ὑπ' αὐτῶν ἠδικῆσθαι."

53 Τὸν μὲν οὖν Παιαζήτην διακηκοότα λέγεται τῶν πρέσβεων τὰ μὲν ἄλλα οὐ χαλεπῶς, ἀχθεσθῆναι δὲ μάλα ἐπιεικῶς διὰ τὴν ἐσθῆτα, καὶ μὴ ἀνασχόμενον εἰπεῖν ἐς τοὺς πρέσβεις, "ἀπαγγείλατε τοίνυν τῷ ὑμετέρῳ βασιλεῖ, ὡς ἔμοιγε ἀγωνιζομένῳ ὑπέρ τε τοῦ ἥρωος πρὸς τοὺς ἡμῖν πολεμιωτάτους χάριν ἂν εἰδείης σύ τε καὶ οἱ ἐν τῇ Ἀσίᾳ πρὸς τὴν ἡμετέραν τετραμμένοι θρησκείαν· καὶ σέ τε ἀντὶ τοῦ ὁτιοῦν ἡμῖν συλλαμβάνειν ἐς τὸν ἡμέτερον τοῦτον ἀγῶνα, στράτευμά τε καὶ χρήματα ἐπιπέμποντα, οὐκ ἂν δέοι δὴ τοιαῦτα ἡμῖν ἐξηγούμενον συμβουλεύεσθαι. Ἀφαιρεῖσθαι δὲ πειρώμενος χώραν, ἣν καταστρεψάμενος τοὺς ἐμοὶ ἐπιβουλεύοντας ἔχω, πῶς ἂν εἰδείης χάριν ἐμοί, ἢ ἔφησθα εἰδέναι; Ἐσθῆτα τοῦ λοιποῦ ἀπαγγείλατε [1.98] τῷ βασιλεῖ τῷ ὑμετέρῳ μὴ ἐπιπέμπειν ἀντὶ ἑαυτοῦ τό τε γένος καὶ τὴν τύχην ἀμείνονι."

too you should not wrong those who are our friends and associates, especially those who are devoted to us, and make them into enemies, but rather display no wrong behavior whatsoever toward them.[118] For if you are not on good terms with those of the same race, how will you attack your enemies? For this reason, Timur bids you to restore to the rulers of Asia the realms which you have taken from them, for they did not in any way violate the agreements that were made with them concerning your realm. If you do this, you will please him greatly; moreover, the people in Asia and in Europe will owe you a debt of gratitude on account of it. But if they should be in violation of the treaties, they have turned to King Timur as an arbiter for any injustice that you might say they have committed against you."

It is said that Bayezid calmly heard the other things that 53
the envoys said, but that he was especially annoyed by the robe and, being unable to bear it, said to the envoys: "Tell this to your king: both you and those in Asia who share our religion should indeed be grateful to me, who am fighting on the hero's behalf[119] against our most bitter enemies. It is not right for you to lecture me and give me advice on such matters instead of aiding me in some way in this struggle of ours, for instance by sending me an army and money. How exactly are you expressing your gratitude to me, as you have said you are doing, by trying to deprive me of lands which I hold after defeating those who plotted against me? Tell your king not to send a robe ever again to a man who is superior to him in race and fortune."

54 Ταῦτα ὡς ἀνηνέχθη παρὰ βασιλέα Τεμήρην ἐς Σαμαρχάνδην, τεθυμωμένον μεγάλως τῇ ἐσθῆτος ὕβρει, ἄγγελον λέγεται ἐπιπέμψαι προαγορεύοντα τήν τε ἀρχὴν ἐς τοὺς ἡγεμόνας ὀπίσω ἀποδοῦναι καὶ μὴ τὴν ταχίστην διαμέλλειν· εἰ δὲ μή, περιέψεσθαι ὡς πολέμιον. Ταύτην δὲ τὴν δίκην ἔφασαν αὐτὸν βασιλέα Τεμήρην ἐπιδικάσαι, ὡς ἠδικημένοι τε εἶεν οἱ Τοῦρκοι ἡγεμόνες ὑπ' αὐτοῦ δὴ τοῦ Παιαζήτεω, καὶ μὴ περιϊδεῖν αὐτοὺς ἐστερημένους τῆς σφῶν ἀρχῆς περινοστεῖν κατὰ τὴν Ἀσίαν, Τεμήρεω ἔτι περιόντος. Τὸν δὲ Παιαζήτην ὑπολαβόντα ἐς τὸν ἄγγελον φάναι, "εἰ τοίνυν μὴ ἐπίῃ μαχούμενος ἡμῖν, ἐς τρὶς τὴν ἑαυτοῦ γυναῖκα ἐχέτω ἀπολαβών." Τοῦτο δὴ οὖν ἐς ὕβριν φέρειν τῷ γένει τούτῳ, Μεχμέτην ἐξορκῶσαι ἐς τρὶς ἤδη ἀπολαβεῖν τὴν ἑαυτοῦ γυναῖκα, ἂν μὴ πείθηται. Τοῦτο δέ ἐστιν, ὅτι νόμος ἐστὶ τούτοις ἀποπεμπόμενον τὴν ἑαυτοῦ γυναῖκα ἕκαστον ἀπαγορεύειν τοῦ λοιποῦ αὖθις ἄγεσθαι ἐς τὰ οἰκεῖα, ὡς οὐ θεμιτὸν ὄν, ἐπειδὰν ἐς τρεῖς ἔφησε σπλῆνας διαστῆσαι τὸν γάμον αὐτῷ ὁ ἀνήρ, ἀρνησάμενον ἔτι ἐπὶ τὸν αὐτὸν γάμον ἐλθεῖν, εἰ μή τις τρὶς σπληνὸς ἐς μέσον ἐμβαλόντος αὖθις ἄγοιτο ὑπὸ ἑτέρου μοιχευομένην.

55 Ταῦτα μὲν οὖν ὡς ἤκουσεν ὁ ἄγγελος, ἤλαυνεν ὀπίσω τὴν ταχίστην παρὰ βασιλέα Τεμήρην. Λέγουσι δὲ τὴν γυναῖκα [1.99] Τεμήρεω δεισιδαίμονά τινα ἐς τὰ μέγιστα γεγονέναι, καὶ μὴ ἐᾶν Τεμήρην οὕτω προσφέρεσθαι ἐπαχθῆ ὄντα Παιαζήτῃ, ἀνδρί τε ἐπαίνου ἀξίῳ ἐς τὴν κατ' αὐτοὺς θρησκείαν, ἀγωνιζομένῳ πρὸς τὴν τοῦ Ἰησοῦ μοῖραν, ἀλλ' ἐᾶν αὐτὸν ἡσυχίαν ἄγειν, καὶ μὴ πράγματα παρέχειν οὐ δικαίῳ ὑφίστασθαι ὁτιοῦν ἀνήκεστον ὑπ' αὐτῶν. Ὡς δὲ τὰ

When this was reported to King Timur in Samarkand, he was extremely angry at the insult over the robe, and he is said to have sent a messenger to warn Bayezid that unless he gave the rulers their realms back without any delay, he would regard him as an enemy. This was the verdict that King Timur is said to have reached, namely that the Turkish leaders had been wronged by Bayezid and that he, Timur, for as long as he lived, would not allow them to remain stripped of their realms and wandering around Asia. Bayezid is said to have responded to the messenger as follows: "If he does not come to fight against me now, let him renounce his wife three times."[120] That is an insult among this race, for Muhammad ordained that one should renounce his wife three times if she is not obedient. This happens because there is a law among them that prohibits a person who has rejected his wife from taking her back into his household, for this is considered improper. When a man has said that his marriage is dissolved "on three spleens," the law prevents him from entering again upon the same marriage, unless he does so after she has committed adultery with another man in the meantime who has also "thrown spleen" three times.[121] 54

When the messenger heard this, he rushed back as quickly as possible to King Timur. They say that the wife of Timur was an especially devout woman[122] and would not allow Timur to attack Bayezid when he was upset with him, as Bayezid was a man who was worthy of praise in their religion and was fighting against the faction of Jesus; rather, Timur was to allow him to be at peace, as Bayezid had given no cause for offense that would justify an attack against 55

ὑπ᾽ ἀγγέλου ἐλέχθη, λέγεται ἐπικαλεσάμενον τὴν γυναῖκα αὐτοῦ κελεῦσαι ἐναντίον αὐτῆς τὰ παρὰ τοῦ Παιαζήτεω λεχθέντα ὑπ᾽ αὐτῷ ἀπαγγεῖλαι. Τοῦ δὲ ἀπαγγείλαντος τὰ ὑπὸ Παιαζήτεω ἐπεσταλμένα, ἐρέσθαι τὴν γυναῖκα αὐτοῦ, εἰ ἔτι δικαιοῖ Παιαζήτην ἐᾶν οὕτω ἐξυβρίζοντα. Καὶ ἀνεδήλου, ὡς, εἰ ἐπὶ θάτερα δικαιοῖ Παιαζήτην, οὐκέτι δέοι αὐτῷ ἐκείνην συνοικεῖν τοῦ λοιποῦ· εἰ δ᾽ ἐπὶ θάτερα γένοιτο ἡ γνώμη, ὥστε ἀμύνεσθαι τὸν πόλεμον, οὕτω δὲ νομίζεσθαι αὐτήν οἱ γυναῖκα, καὶ μεταδιώκειν, ὅ τι ἂν αὐτῷ γενέσθαι ἀναγκάζοι. Τὴν δὲ γυναῖκα τότε δὴ ὑπολαβοῦσαν φάναι λέγεται.

56 "Ἀλλ᾽ ὅτι μέν, ὦ βασιλεῦ, ὑπὸ ἀφροσύνης κατεχόμενος, συμφορᾷ χρώμενος τοιᾷδε, οὐκέτι ἔμπεδον ἔχει τὸν λογισμὸν ἐκεῖνος ἀνήρ, δῆλά ἐστι, καὶ ἔμοιγε ταύτῃ καταφαίνεται εἶναι, καὶ ἠπιστάμην, ὡς ἐκεῖνον σὺν δίκῃ τισάμενος σωφρονεῖς τε ὡς μάλιστα, καὶ ἐνδείξῃ αὐτῷ, οἵῳ ὄντι σοι οἷος ὢν ἐκεῖνος τοιαῦτα ἐπιπέμπει. Ἐκεῖνο μέντοι σαφῶς ἐπίστασο, ὡς ὅτ᾽ ἂν ὑπὲρ τοῦ ἡμετέρου ἥρωος ἀγωνιζομένῳ ἔστε τοὺς Ἕλληνας καὶ ἐς τὰ ἄλλα τὰ ἐς [1.100] τὴν ἄλλην ἤπειρον ἔθνη ὑπάρξαι πολέμου ἐς ἐκεῖνον οὔτε θέμις ἡγησάμην ἔγωγε εἶναι. Ἢν δέ τι ἐκεῖνος ἀφροσύνῃ μὴ διασκοποῖτο, οὐ δίκαιόν ἐστιν ἐπιτρέπειν ὑβριστῇ τοιούτῳ μέγα φρονεῖν. Ἀλλ᾽ ἴθι δὴ ἐπὶ τὸν πόλεμον, μήτε αὐτὸς μαχεσάμενος, ἀλλὰ πόλιν αὐτοῦ Σεβάστειαν ἢν καθέλῃς, ἱκανῶς τετιμωρημένος ἔσῃ ὑπέρ τε τῆς ἐν τῷ Εὐφράτῃ πόλεως Μελιτηνῆς καὶ ὑπὲρ τῶν ἡγεμόνων τῶν παρ᾽ ἡμῖν διατριβόντων."

him. When the messenger had made his report, it is said that Timur summoned his wife and ordered him to recite before her what Bayezid had said. When the messenger had recited Bayezid's message, Timur asked his wife whether she still thought that it was right to allow Bayezid to utter such insults. He made it clear that if, on the one hand, she still thought Bayezid right, he could no longer live with her in the future. If, on the other hand, she had changed her mind and would now favor war, she would be considered his wife and would assent to whatever it was that he was forced to do. The woman is then said to have given the following response:

"It is clear, O king, that this man has lost his mind, giv- 56
ing such offense! He is no longer mentally stable; that, at any rate, seems plain to me. And I know that you will impose a just punishment on him and bring him to his senses. You will show him exactly what kind of a person you are to whom he, being the kind of person he is, has sent these messages.[123] But know this well, that as long as he was fighting on behalf of our hero against the Greeks and the other peoples on the other continent, I, for my part, did not believe that it was right to wage war against him. But if he does not reconsider his foolishness, it is also not right to allow a man who gives such offense to think highly of himself. So go to war. Do not fight in it yourself, but if you take his city of Sebasteia you will be sufficiently avenged for the city of Melitene on the Euphrates and on behalf of the rulers who are at our court."

57 Οὕτω μὲν οὖν ἤλαυνε Τεμήρης ὁ βασιλεὺς ἐπὶ Παιαζήτην, προκαλεσάμενος αὐτὸν ἑκὼν εἰς τὸν πόλεμον. Φασὶ μὲν οὖν τινές, ὡς Τεμήρης διὰ μὲν τὴν Μελιτηνὴν καταβὰς ἐπὶ Σεβάστειαν, καὶ ἐπεί τε καθεῖλε τὴν πόλιν ταύτην, τότε δὴ πρεσβεύεσθαι πρὸς Παιαζήτην περί τε τῶν ἡγεμόνων, ὥστε τὴν χώραν αὐτοῖς ἀποδιδόναι, καὶ τὴν τοῦ βουτύρου αἴτησιν καὶ σκηνῶν. Ἠιτεῖτο γὰρ αὐτόν, ᾗ λέγεται, βουτύρου μὲν καμήλους δισχιλίους, σκηνὰς δὲ πιλίνους, αἷς χρῶνται οἱ νομάδες, δισχιλίας, καὶ αὐτὸν ἐν τοῖς ναοῖς αὐτοῦ διαμνημονεύειν ὡς βασιλέα, καὶ τὸν παῖδα αὐτοῦ ἐπὶ τὰς Τεμήρεω θύρας ἰέναι, καὶ νομίσματα δὲ αὐτοῦ ἐς τὴν χώραν αὐτοῦ νομίζεσθαι. Ταῦτα δὲ τὰ ἑπτὰ αἰτήματα γενέσθαι αὐτῷ αἰτούμενον Τεμήρην φασὶ μετὰ τὴν τῆς Σεβαστείας ἅλωσιν. Καὶ τότε δὴ καὶ τὸν Παιαζήτην θυμωθέντα μεγάλως ἐπιστεῖλαι ἐκείνῳ τὰ περὶ τὴν γυναῖκα.

58 Τεμήρης μέντοι ὥρμητο ἐπὶ Παιαζήτην, ὡς τήν τε χώραν αὐτοῦ ἐν τῇ Ἀσίᾳ καταστρεψόμενος καὶ ἐς τὴν Εὐρώπην διαβησόμενος, μὴ ἐπισχεῖν πρότερον ἀναχωροῦντα, πρὶν ἢ ἐπὶ τοῖς τέρμασιν αὐτῆς γένηται, ἔστε [1.101] ἐπ' ὠκεανὸν ἐλαύνοντα τὸν περὶ τὰς Ἡρακλείους στήλας, ἔνθα ἐπύθετο πορθμὸν ὡς βραχύτατον διείργειν τήν τε Εὐρώπην καὶ Λιβύην, ὅθεν ἐς τὴν Λιβύην περαιουμένῳ, καὶ ταύτην τῆς οἰκουμένης χώραν οἱ ὑπαγομένῳ ἐπ' οἴκου ἐντεῦθεν κομίζεσθαι. Ταῦτα μέντοι Τεμήρης ἐπενόει τε μεγάλα καὶ ἐς τύχην μᾶλλόν τοι ὑπὸ Θεοῦ δεδομένην ἀφορῶντα· Παιαζήτης δὲ ἄρα ἐλογίζετο ἐπιόντα ἀμύνεσθαι, ἀπό τε τῶν παλαιῶν συμβαλλόμενος, ὡς

Thus King Timur set out against Bayezid, deliberately challenging him to war. But some say that Timur went down to Sebasteia via Melitene,[124] and only when he had captured that city did he send envoys to Bayezid regarding the rulers—that they should be restored to their lands, and also demanding butter and tents. It is said that he demanded two thousand camel-loads of butter and two thousand tents, of the type that nomads use, made of felt; that he should be commemorated as king in Bayezid's shrines; that his son should come to Timur's Porte; and that Timur's currency should be used in his land.[125] They say that Timur made these seven demands after the fall of Sebasteia; and it was then that Bayezid became furiously angry and sent him the message about his wife. 57

So Timur set out against Bayezid in order to conquer his lands in Asia and to cross over into Europe, and he did not intend to turn back before he had reached its farthest ends, going all the way to the Ocean by the Pillars of Herakles, where, he learned, the narrowest of straits separates Europe and North Africa. He would cross over to North Africa there, subject that part of the world to himself, and then return home from there. These were the great ambitions of Timur, plans that fall rather under the jurisdiction of the fortune that is granted by God. Bayezid, for his part, planned to defend himself against this invader, reasoning, 58

οὐδέποτε τῆς γε Εὐρώπης οἱ τῆς Ἀσίας βασιλεῖς ἐν τοῖς πρόσθεν χρόνοις περιγένοιντο πώποτε, ἀλλὰ καὶ ὡρμημένους ἐπὶ τὴν Ἀσίαν τῇ τε βασιλείᾳ ἀφῃρῆσθαι τοὺς τῆς Ἀσίας ἡγουμένους. Ταῦτα διασκοπούμενος μέγα τε ἐφρόνει, καὶ ᾤετο ἐν βραχεῖ πολέμῳ ἅμα καθαιρήσειν τὴν Τεμήρεω βασιλείαν.

59 Ἐνταῦθα δὲ γενομένῳ μοι, καὶ τὴν ἐπὶ Παιαζήτην πρώτην τε καὶ δευτέραν ἔλασιν Τεμήρεω βασιλέως κατὰ τοῦτον τὸν χρόνον γενομένην διασκοπουμένῳ, ἐπῄει λογίζεσθαι, ὡς ἐπὶ μέγα ἂν ἀφίκοιτο δυνάμεως τὰ τῶν Τούρκων πράγματα, παρέχοιτ' ἂν εἰς τὴν ἑσπέραν ἀναστρέφεσθαι, εἰ μὴ οὕτω παραχρῆμα ἐπιδιδόντος ἀνεκόπτετο ὑπὸ Τεμήρεω βασιλέως. Οὔτε γὰρ ἂν δίχα γενομένης τῆς βασιλείας Ὀτουμανίδων καὶ ἐπὶ διαφορὰν σφίσι καθισταμένων ἐφθείρετο ὑπ' ἀλλήλων τὰ πράγματα αὐτῶν, ὄλεθρον μέγιστον δὲ τῶν ἐν μνήμῃ πώποτε ἐπενεγκόντα, ὡς μετὰ τὴν τελευτὴν τοῦ Παιαζήτεω συνηνέχθη γενέσθαι ἐς τοὺς παῖδας ἀλλήλοις διαφερομένους, καὶ τὴν χώραν ὑπ' ἀλλήλων [1.102] δῃουμένην ξυμφορὰν τῷ γένει ἐπινεῦσαι ὅσην δὴ βαρυτάτην καὶ χαλεπωτάτην. Νῦν δὲ ἐς ὑπερφυᾶ δύναμιν ἀφικόμενος, ὑπὸ τοῦ Θεοῦ ἐγένετο Παιαζήτῃ σωφρονισθῆναι, ὥστε ἐπὶ τὴν βασιλείαν μεγάλα φρονεῖν. Ὅθεν βασιλεὺς Τεμήρης ὁρμώμενος ἐπὶ τὰ τῆς Ἀσίας ἀφίκετο πράγματα καὶ ἐπὶ τὴν τῆς Σαμαρχάνδης βασιλείαν κατέστη, τῇδε ἄν μοι διεξιόντι ἐπίδηλα γένοιτο. Λέγεται μὲν πολλαχῇ τοῦτον ἀπ' ἐλαχίστου ὁρμώμενον κατὰ τὴν Ἀσίαν ἐπὶ μέγα χωρῆσαι δυνάμεως.

based on ancient history, that the kings of Asia had never prevailed over those of Europe in the past, while it was the latter who had set out against Asia and stripped its leaders of their kingdom. Bearing this in mind, he aspired to great things and thought that he would destroy Timur's kingdom in a brief war.

Now that I have reached this point, where I am about to 59
recount the first and then the second advance of King Timur against Bayezid that took place at that time,[126] it occurs to me upon reflection that the power of the Turks would have reached great heights and would have permitted them to turn back to the west had it not been so suddenly cut short by the advance of King Timur. The kingdom of the Ottomans would not have been split in two, nor would they have fallen out among themselves and so harmed their interests, causing a ruin greater than any which has ever been recorded before. For after Bayezid's death, his sons started to quarrel with each other and plundered each other's portion of the land, inflicting a very serious disaster on their people, one that it was hard for them to bear. But at that moment, when he had reached an extraordinary degree of power, it came about that Bayezid was chastened by God, as he had been presumptuous about his kingdom. In what follows, I am going to make clear King Timur's background before he came to rule the affairs of Asia and the kingdom of Samarkand. For it is said in many places that he came from very humble origins to advance to great power over Asia.

Γ'

[I.103] Τεμήρεω μέντοι ἡ πρώτη ἔλασις ἐγένετο ἐπὶ Σεβάστειαν, πόλιν τῆς Καππαδοκίας εὐδαίμονα. Ὡς γὰρ ἠγγέλλετο οὐδὲν ὑγιὲς Παιαζήτεω εἶναι ἔστε ἐπὶ τῶν τῆς Ἀσίας ἡγεμόνων Τούρκων καὶ ἐς τὴν πρὸς τοὺς ἡγεμόνας διαλλαγήν, οὓς τὴν χώραν σύμπασαν ἀφελόμενος ἐξήλασεν, ὡς γὰρ δὴ ἐπιπέμποντι οὐδὲν ἐπὶ πλέον προὐχώρει, ὧν ἐπέστελλεν αὐτῷ, ἀλλ' ἑώρα τε ἐς πολλά τε ἄλλα καὶ βλάσφημα ἐξενηνεγμένον, παρεσκευάζετο ἐλαύνειν ἐπὶ Σεβάστειαν. Ἀρχὴ δὲ αὐτῷ, ἥ τε ἐπὶ τὴν ἀρχὴν πάροδος, καὶ ὡς τὸν μὲν πολεμῶν, τὰ δὲ καὶ σπενδόμενος δέει τῷ ἀμφ' αὐτὸν ξύμπασαν ὑπηγάγετο ἑαυτῷ τὴν Ἀσίαν, ὧδε αὐτῷ ξυμβῆναι ἐπυθόμεθα.

2 Οὗτος μὲν δὴ ὁ Τεμήρης ἐγένετο πατρὸς Σαγγάλεω, ἀνδρὸς ἰδιώτου, ὃς ἐπεί τε ἠγάγετο τὴν γυναῖκα αὑτοῦ, λέγεται ξυμβῆναι αὐτῷ τοιόνδε. Ὡς δὴ ἐγένετο Τεμήρης, τήν τε τῆς πόλεως φορβὴν ἐπιτετραμμένος ἱπποφορβός τε ἦν, καὶ τοῖς τε περὶ αὐτὰ δὴ τὰ χωρία τὰς φορβὰς ἐπινεμομένοις συνιών τε καὶ διαλεγόμενος συνέθετο αὐτοῖς, ὡς ἀπὸ κλοπῆς σφίσιν, ἣν δύνωνται, χρημάτων κτῆσιν ποιησόμενοι ἐπ' ἄλλην ἴωσι χώραν· καὶ δεινὸς κλέπτειν γενόμενος ἵππους τε καὶ ὑποζύγια καὶ προβάτων πλῆθος [I.104] ἐληλακέναι. Οὐδὲν ὑγιὲς ἦν αὐτοῦ τὸ παράπαν.

Book 3

Timur's first campaign was against Sebasteia, a prosperous city of Kappadokia.[1] Timur had been informed that Bayezid was up to no good with regard to the rulers of the Turks in Asia and he had not been reconciled with those rulers, whom he had driven out after stripping them of all their lands. So, as Timur had made no progress through the messengers whom he had sent to him, and as he saw that Bayezid was behaving blasphemously in many other respects as well, he prepared to set out for Sebasteia. As for Timur's origins, how he came to power, and how he subjected all of Asia to himself, in some cases by fighting wars and in others by making treaties premised on the fear that he inspired, we have learned that it all happened in the following way.

Timur's father was Sangal, an ordinary man,[2] and it is said 2
that such a son was born to him when he married his wife. After Timur was born, he was entrusted with the city's herds of horses and so he became a horse-keeper. He approached those who grazed the herds in those lands, entered into a discussion with them, and reached an agreement with them that they would, if possible, make their living through robbery and then move on to another land. He became a formidable thief, taking off with horses, pack animals, and many sheep. He did not enjoy the best of health. It is said that

Καί ποτε ἐπὶ μάνδραν λέγεται ἀναβῆναι, καὶ ὀφθέντα ὑπὸ τῶν δεσποτῶν τοῦ οἴκου ἅλλεσθαι δὴ ἅλμα μέγιστον ἀπὸ τοῦ τείχους τῆς μάνδρας ἐς τὴν γῆν· τά τε γὰρ ὑποζύγια καὶ κτήνη ἐν τῇδε τῇ χώρᾳ περιβάλλεται τείχη, ὡς μέγιστα εἶναι καὶ μὴ ἀναβῆναι εὐπετῆ. Ὡς δὲ ἥλατο, ἐπιτριβῆναί τε αὐτῷ τὸν πόδα, καὶ χωλὸν γενέσθαι τὸ ἀπὸ τοῦδε. Λέγεται μὲν οὖν ὡς μαχόμενον πληγῆναί τε τὸν πόδα καὶ χωλεύοντα διαγενέσθαι τὸ ἐντεῦθεν.

3 Μάχης δὲ γενομένης πρὸς τοὺς περιοίκους, ἐλαύνοντα αὐτόν τε ἅμα καὶ οἳ συνέθεντο τὴν ἀρχήν, τὴν ἵππων φορβὴν οἴχεσθαι ἐπὶ τοὺς πολεμίους, ἐντεῦθεν προσλαβόμενον, ὅτῳ ἂν περιτύχοι, καὶ ἀναπείθοντα κατασχεῖν χώραν τε ἐρυμνήν, καὶ ὡς ἐπιτηδείως ἔχειν πρὸς ληστείαν. Ἐντεῦθεν δὲ ὁρμώμενον ληστεύειν τοὺς διϊόντας καὶ κατακρίνειν ἀφειδῶς. Καὶ χρήματα ἐπικτησάμενον ἑταίρους τε προσκτήσασθαι αὑτῷ ἄλλους τε δὴ καὶ ἄνδρε δύω, Χαϊδάρην τε καὶ Μυρζίην. Τὸ γένος, ᾗ δὴ λέγεται, γενέσθαι τούτω Μασσαγέτα. Τούτοιν δὲ ἑκατέρῳ προσχρώμενον περιτυχεῖν τε τοῖς πολεμίοις λῃϊζομένοις τὴν χώραν, καὶ τρεψάμενον ἐπεξελθεῖν διαφθείραντα τοὺς ἱπποδρόμους τῶν ἐναντίων. Τῆς δὲ φήμης ἐπὶ τὴν πόλιν ἐλθούσης, ἐπιτρέψαι τε αὐτῷ στρατιωτῶν μοῖραν οὐκ [1.105] ὀλίγην καὶ χρήματα, ὥστε θεραπεύειν τοὺς στρατιώτας. Καὶ δὴ τὸ ἀπὸ τοῦδε ἐπεγείραντα τὴν σὺν αὐτῷ στρατιὰν καὶ ἐξοτρύνοντα ἀμφὶ τῇ πολεμίων ἔχειν χώρᾳ, ἀνδράποδά τε καὶ ὑποζύγια ὡς πλεῖστα ἐπάγοντα ἐς τὴν πόλιν. Τὸν δὲ βασιλέα Μασσαγετῶν ἐνιδόντα τοῦτο ἐς τὸν Τεμήρην,

he was once climbing into a sheepfold and was seen by the owners of the house, so he had to jump a long distance from the wall of the pen to the ground. For in that land they enclose pack animals and beasts within walls that are high and not easy to scale. So when he jumped he broke his leg and was lame from that point on. But it is also said that his leg was wounded in battle and he was lame thereafter.[3]

In battle with his neighbors, he would ride out against 3
the enemy with his original band and they would drive away their herd of horses,[4] and from that point on he began to appropriate whatever he came across. He also persuaded his men to occupy a fortified location so as to have somewhere suitable for his robbery. Using that place as his base, he robbed passersby and passed merciless judgment upon them. He acquired money and attracted more followers to himself, including two men, Haydar and Mirza.[5] It is said that by race they were Massagetai.[6] With their assistance, he attacked his enemies while they were plundering the land, routed them in his attack, and killed his opponents' cavalry raiders. When his fame reached the city,[7] they entrusted him with a large contingent of soldiers and the money to maintain them. From this point on he stirred up and urged his army to take the land of the enemy, leading countless slaves and pack animals back to the city. When the king of the Massagetai saw this in Timur, he decided

ἀξιοῦντα παρ' ἑαυτῷ τιμῆς τῆς μεγίστης, καὶ στρατηγὸν ἀποδεδειχέναι ξυμπάσης ἤδη τῆς ὑπ' αὐτὸν στρατιᾶς.

4 Καὶ ἐντεῦθεν δὴ δρόμους τε ἀνύσαι μεγίστους τῶν πώποτε γενομένων σὺν τῇ στρατιᾷ, ὥστε καταλαμβάνειν τοὺς πολεμίους ἄφνω ἐπιπίπτοντα αὐτοῖς καὶ διαφθείροντα τὸν ἐκείνων στρατόν. Καὶ δὴ καὶ ἐς χεῖρας ἐλθόντα τοῖς ἐναντίοις φασὶν αὐτὸν μαχεσάμενον τρέψασθαι, καὶ ἐπιδιώκοντα ἐλάσαι τε ἐς Βαβυλῶνα, τὸ Παγδάτιν οὕτω καλούμενον, καὶ πολιορκοῦντα μεταπέμψασθαι τὸν ἑαυτοῦ δεσπότην βασιλέα. Μετὰ δὲ ταῦτα οὐ πολὺν χρόνον τελευτήσαντος τοῦ βασιλέως, γῆμαί τε τὴν γυναῖκα τοῦ δεσπότου αὐτοῦ καὶ ἐς τὴν βασιλείαν καταστῆναι. Ὡς δὲ ἐς τὴν βασιλείαν ἀφίκετο, ἐπιὼν τό τε Παγδάτιν καὶ τὸ Σαμαρχάνδιν ἐπολιόρκει. Καὶ οὐ πολὺ ὕστερον, ὡς ἔξοδον ποιησάμενοι οἱ τῆς πόλεως οὐδὲν πλέον ἔσχον, ἀλλ' ἡττημένοι ἐσῆλθον ἐς τὴν πόλιν καὶ ἐπολιορκοῦντο, προσεχώρησαν αὐτῷ καθ' ὁμολογίαν. Ὡς ἐπὶ τὴν τῆς Σαμαρχάνδης ἀρχὴν παρεγένετο, προδοσίαν συνθέμενον τοῖς ἐν τῇ Βαβυλῶνι αὐτόν, Χαϊδάρη ἐς τοῦτο χρησάμενον ὑπηρέτη.

5 Τὸν μέντοι Μυρζίην ἄνδρα ἐπιεικῆ τε ἅμα καὶ [1.106] συγκιρνῶντα τὸν Τεμήρεω, θυμοῦ κατέχειν ἐμφερόμενον, ἐφ' ὅ τι ἂν ἡγήσαιτο, μὴ προσήκειν αὐτῷ τὴν ἀρχήν. Ἐξηγεῖσθαί τε αὐτῷ τὴν ἐς τὰ συσσιτήρια Τεμήρεω ἐσήγησιν. Τήν τε γὰρ στρατιὰν αὐτῶν ξύμπασαν Μυρζίεω ὑποτιθεμένου ἐπιδιελόμενος ὁ Τεμήρης ἔστε δεκάρχας καὶ λοχαγοὺς καὶ δὴ καὶ ἐνωμοτίας, τὸν δεκάρχην παρεγγύα δίαιταν παρεχόμενον τοῖς μεθ' ἑαυτοῦ στρατιώταις

that he deserved the highest honors from him, and so he appointed him general over his entire army.[8]

Timur covered greater distances with his army than any- 4
one ever had done before, so that he took his enemies by surprise, attacked them suddenly, and destroyed their armies. It is said that he routed the enemy by fighting personally in battle, and he pursued them all the way to Babylon, which is called Baghdad. He besieged it and summoned his own master and king. Shortly after this the king died, so Timur married the wife of his master and ascended the throne. When he attained the throne, he marched out and besieged both Baghdad and Samarkand. Shortly afterward, the city's defenders became desperate and made a sally but they were defeated, returned to the city, and were again besieged; finally, they surrendered to him by offering terms. When he had control of Samarkand, he contrived the betrayal of Babylon by those inside the city, using Haydar as his agent in the matter.[9]

Mirza was a moderate man and would mollify Timur, re- 5
straining him when Timur was carried away by anger and believed, for whatever reason, that he was not fit to rule.[10] He also taught Timur how they should go into the mess tents. At Mirza's suggestion, Timur divided their entire army thus among leaders of ten men, captains, and division commanders. He ordered the leaders of ten to provide their soldiers with the means by which to live and to attend upon their

παρεῖναι αὐτίκα τῷ λοχαγῷ, τὴν ταχίστην παρεχόμενον τοὺς στρατιώτας, ἐπειδὰν παραγγέλῃ, τοὺς δὲ αὖ παραγενομένους τῷ σφετέρῳ. Γενομένους δὲ ἐς τὰ συσσίτια, οὐδένα λείπεσθαι, ὅτῳ μὴ εἴη χῶρος αὐτῷ ἀποδεδειγμένος. Καὶ τήν τε ἀγορὰν σιτίζεσθαι ἐκέλευε κατὰ τὰ δεδογμένα ἐπὶ τοῦ λοιποῦ στρατεύματος. Κινεῖν δὲ τούς τε ἄρχοντας αὐτῶν ἑκάστους θαμὰ ἐπὶ τὰ ὑπὸ τῶν μεγάλων στρατηγῶν παραγγελλόμενα, ὥστε ξυμβαίνειν κατάσκοπον εἰσιόντα ἐς τὸ Τεμήρεω στρατόπεδον λεληθέναι πώποτε, οὔτε ξένον, ὃς ἂν παρὼν τυγχάνῃ ἐν τῷ στρατοπέδῳ. Τούτους δὲ αὖ ἀνδρὶ ἑτέρῳ ἐπιτετράφθαι, καταλύειν παρ' ἑαυτῷ τοὺς ξένους, εἰ τυγχάνοιεν παραγενόμενοι ἐς τὸ στρατόπεδον σίτου δεόμενοι. Ὥστε νεύματι τοῦ μεγάλου βασιλέως κινεῖσθαι πάντα δὴ τὸν στρατόν, ἐφ' ὅ τι ἂν γένοιτο, καὶ ἐκείνου δὴ ἄγοντος τὰ πάντα ἐφ' ἑνὶ συνθήματι ἰέναι αὐτίκα, ἐν τάχει παραγενόμενος ἐπὶ τὴν χρείαν καθίστασθαι αὐτίκα μάλα ἰόντα. Ἑσπέρας δὲ γενομένης, ὁπότε τὸ σύνθημα λαμβάνοιεν οἱ στρατιῶται ὑπὸ τοῦ μεγάλου ἡγεμόνος, θεῖν δρόμον αὐτόν τινα ἕκαστον ἐπὶ τὴν ἑαυτοῦ σκηνὴν ἐς τοὺς συσκήνους ἰόντα. Γενομένων δὲ ἐν ταῖς σκηναῖς τῶν στρατιωτῶν, τὰς φυλακὰς [1.107] περινοστεῖν τε τὸ στρατόπεδον, εἴ τινά που ἴδοιεν ἐκτὸς τῶν σκηνῶν γενόμενον, τοῦτον λαβόντες ἐτιμωροῦντο. Εἰ δέ τις κατάσκοπος παρὼν τύχῃ ἐν τῷ στρατοπέδῳ, οὐκ ἔχων ὅποι τράποιτο, λείπεσθαι ἐκτὸς τῶν σκηνῶν καὶ οὕτως αὐτίκα ἁλίσκεσθαι. Ταύτῃ μὲν δὴ λέγεται γίνεσθαι τὰ Τεμήρεω συσσίτια.

captains, so that they could make their soldiers available as quickly as possible whenever they were ordered to furnish their men to their own captain. They were to be present in the mess tents and no one was to be absent to whom a place had been assigned. And he ordered the marketplace to provide supplies for the rest of the army at the usual prices. Each of their officers was rotated frequently on the orders of the senior generals, so that no spy who entered Timur's camp could ever escape detection, nor any foreigner who might happen to be present in the camp. If such foreign guests happened to be present in the camp and were in need of food, they were assigned to a specific man and stayed with him. Thus, the entire army was ready to move at the great king's nod, for whatever was going on. When he was in command, everything was set into motion immediately by one signal; when he was present, everything was quickly organized to move in whatever way was necessary. In the evening, the soldiers received a signal from the supreme leader and each of them rushed to his own tent and his tent mates. When the soldiers were supposed to be in their tents, patrols went around the camp, and if they saw someone outside the tents they seized him and punished him. If some spy happened to be present in the camp, he had nowhere to turn, as he was excluded from the tents, and was thus immediately apprehended. This is how it is said that Timur organized the mess tents.

6 Χαϊδάρην δὲ τόν γε ἑταῖρον αὐτῷ ὀξύν τε ἐς τὸ ὑπηρετεῖν αὐτῷ τὰ δέοντα γεγονέναι, ἐποτρύνειν τε αὐτὸν βασιλέα ἐπὶ τοὺς πολέμους, μηδαμῇ ἐς ῥᾳστώνην τρεπόμενον. Λέγουσι δὲ Μυρζίην, ἐπεί τε παρέλαβε τὴν τῆς Σαμαρχάνδης βασιλείαν, διαχρήσασθαι τρόπῳ τοιῷδε. Ἐπεί τε σὺν τούτοις ἅμα περιϊὼν Τεμήρης λῃστής τε καθειστήκει καὶ ἐχρηματίζετο, διαλεγομένων ἐπ' εὐτυχήματι τῶν ἑταίρων, καὶ εὐφημιζόντων Τεμήρην ὡς ἐν βραχεῖ ἤδη ἐς τὰ Σαμαρχάνδης βασίλεια παρεσομένου, ὑπολαβὼν ὁ Μυρζίης, "ἀλλ' ὦ τᾶν," ἔφη, "τοιαῦτά ἐστι τὰ Σαμαρχάνδης βασίλεια, ὥστε οὐκ εὐπετῆ χειρωθῆναι ὑπὸ Τεμήρεω, ἀνδρὸς λῃστοῦ καὶ ἰδιώτου. Εἰ δ' εἴη ποτὲ τοῦτο αὐτῷ γενέσθαι, ὥστε ἐπὶ τὴν Σαμαρχάνδης ἀρχὴν παριέναι, μὴ ἔτι περιὼν διαγενοίμην, ἀλλὰ τεθναίην αὐτίκα ἐψευσμένος." Ταῦτα μὲν σπουδῇ ἐῴκει ὑποδείκνυσθαι, συντυχίᾳ δέ τινι οὐκ ἀγαθῇ χρήσασθαι ἐς τὸ ἀπόφθεγμα.

7 Χρόνου δὲ ἐπιγενομένου, ὡς ἐς τὴν ἀρχὴν παρεγένετο τῆς πόλεως, τιμῆσαι μὲν ἀρετῆς ἕνεκα ὑπὲρ τὸν Χαϊδάρην, φάσκοντα δὲ αὐτῷ, ὡς ἐκεῖνο δὴ τὸ ἔπος ἐπὶ μαρτύρων ἄλλων εἰρημένον αὐτῷ δέοι μεταδιώκειν, ὅπερ [1.108] διϊσχυριζόμενος ὑπέβαλεν ἑαυτὸν θανάτῳ, ἀναμιμνήσκων, ὡς εἴπερ ἐς τὰ Σαμαρχάνδης βασίλεια παραγένοιτο, ψευσθείη τε αὐτὸς τῆς γνώμης, ἔνοχος εἶ τοῦ θανάτου ὑπὸ Τεμήρεω. Διηπόρει τε, ὅπως ἂν αὐτῷ θεραπεύοιτο τὴν δεξιὰν παρασχόντι τῷ βασιλεῖ, ἰδιώτῃ τότε ὄντι, μὴ παραβῆναι τὴν συνθήκην. Ἔλεγε δὲ πρὸς Μυρζίην τοιάδε.

8 "Οἶσθα, οἶμαι, ὦ Μυρζίη, σύ τε καὶ σύμπαντες οἱ ἄλλοι, ὅσοι ἐπὶ τήνδε τὴν ἀρχὴν τὰ πράγματα προηγάγομεν, δύο

Timur's other companion Haydar was energetic in serving him and accomplishing what had to be done, and he encouraged the king himself to wage war and avoid idleness at all costs. They say that after he had acquired the throne of Samarkand Timur treated Mirza in the following way. When Timur was still going around with them as a robber and he had established himself and was enriching himself, his companions began to discuss his good fortune and praised Timur, saying that he would soon acquire the palace of Samarkand. But Mirza responded, saying, "Good friends, the palace of Samarkand is such that it could not easily be taken by Timur, an ordinary man and a robber. If this should ever happen to him, I mean that he should become the ruler of Samarkand, may I then live no longer but die instantly as a liar." He seemed to say this in an offhand manner, but by some evil fortune his prediction came true for him. 6

When some time passed and Timur became the city's ruler, he honored Mirza for his bravery more than Haydar. But Haydar told him that he ought to follow through on what had been said in the presence of other witnesses: he argued that Mirza had consented to a death penalty, recalling that he had said that if the palace of Samarkand were taken and he thus turned out to have been wrong in his judgment, he would then be subject to death at Timur's hand. And Timur wondered how he might still be served by Mirza, a man who had given his right hand to the king as a pledge, when he was still an ordinary man, not to violate the agreement. Timur then said the following to Mirza: 7

"I believe that you, O Mirza, as well as all the others who have enabled us to reach this position of power, know that 8

τούτω ὡς μάλιστα ἡμῖν ἐπιβεβαιωσάμενοι ἐπὶ τὴν βασιλείαν παρήειμεν, σπουδήν τε ἅμα ὡς οἷόν τε μεταδιώκοντες, καὶ ἐμπεδοῦντες ἡμῖν, ὅ τι ἂν συνθέμενοι τοῖς τε ἐπιτηδείοις καὶ ἐναντίοις, οὐχ ὅπως δὴ ὅρκῳ, ἀλλὰ καὶ λόγῳ ἐψηφισμένοι ὦμεν αὐτοῖς, ὡς οὐδὲν ἔτι οὐδαμοῦ ὂν ἀσφαλέστερον οὐδὲ ἐχυρώτερον ἔρυμά τε καὶ ὅπλον ἐς τὸν βίον τόνδε ἀνθρώπῳ ἢ συμφώνῳ τε εἶναι ἐς τὰ πάντα καὶ μὴ διαφωνοῦντι φρονεῖν ἄλλοτε ἄλλως, ἐπειδὴ πολλάκις ἔφαμεν τούτῳ μόνῳ ἴσχειν ὁμοιότητα τῷ Θεῷ. Ὅτου δ' ἂν τῶν ἀνθρώπων μηδὲν ὑγιὲς εἴη λέγοντος, πῶς ἂν δὴ πράττοντος εὖ γένοιτ' ἂν πώποτε αὐτῷ; Μέμνησο δέ, ὡς ἐμοῦ τῆς δεξιᾶς λαβόμενος ἔφησθα τεθνάναι ἕτοιμος εἶναι, εἰ ἐπὶ τὰ βασίλεια πάριμεν; Καὶ ἐπὶ μαρτύρων δὲ τοῦτό σοι εἰρημένον συνθέσθαι. Ὥρα οὖν σοι τά τε λεχθέντα ἐπιτελέσαι, καὶ τὴν δεξιὰν τὴν ἡμετέραν ἀπολύσασθαι τῆς συνθήκης."

9 Μυρζίης δὲ ἀμείβετο τοῖσδε. "Ἀλλ' ὅπως μέν, ὦ βασιλεῦ, ἐπὶ [1.109] τήνδε τὴν ἀρχήν, ὅπως σοι γένοιτο, καὶ σὺ οἶσθα καὶ πάντες οὗτοι οἱ συμπαρόντες συνίσασι, καὶ ὡς πάντα τὰ ἔσχατα ὑποδυόμενος, ὥστε σοὶ εὖ γενέσθαι ὁτιοῦν. Καὶ τραύματα δὲ ἔστιν ἰδεῖν, ὅσα λαβὼν οὐδὲ πώποτε ὑπελογιζόμην δεινὸν πρὸ τοῦ χαρίζεσθαι. Εἰ δέ ἐστιν ὁτιοῦν ἡμῖν εἰρημένον, οὐκ ἀγαθῇ τύχῃ δέοι ἂν μὴ χαρίζεσθαι τοῖς ἐπιτηδείοις, ὑφ' ὧν μεγάλα εὖ πεπονθὼς εἴης; Ἐκεῖνο δή, βασιλεῦ, ἰδιωτέρῳ μὲν ὄντι τἀνθρώπῳ οὐ πάνυ τι ἐμπεδοῦν τὸ καὶ ἑαυτοῦ βίον. Ἐπειδὰν δέ σοι τὸ ἄρχειν ἑτέρως ἀφίκηται, τότε δὴ οὐ θεμιτὸν ἢ παραβῆναι, εἴ τι συνέθετο. Καὶ ἡμῖν ὁ Θεὸς πολλὰ ἀγαθὰ παρέχεται διὰ τὸ

we have attained kingship by being true to these two principles especially: pursuing our objectives as zealously as possible, and holding fast to the agreements we make with our friends and enemies. We hold them to be ratified not by oaths but by our word, as no fortress or weapon is anywhere more secure or strong in this life than for a man to be consistent in all things and not to keep changing his mind all the time. We have often said that in this alone are we similar to God. If a man does not say anything sound, how may his actions ever lead him to prosper? Do you remember how you once took my right hand and pledged that you would be ready to die if we gained the palace? You said so before witnesses. It is time now for you to do what you promised and make good on your pledge."

Mirza replied with the following words: "But, O king, 9
you know and all those present know as well how I have undertaken the most extreme perils so that you might come to this position of power, in fact so that you might prosper in any way at all. You can see the wounds I have received, as I have never considered the risk when it comes to pleasing you. But if there is something that I said in an unfortunate moment, should you not look kindly on your friends, through whom you have grown so mighty? As for that other matter, O king, an ordinary man's pledge is not binding for his entire life, although now that you are a ruler it would not be right to break an agreement that you have made. And

συγγνώμην ἴσχειν τοῖς ἐξαμαρτάνουσιν ἐς ἡμᾶς ὁτιοῦν. Ἦν δέ μοι καὶ ταύτην παραιτουμένῳ χαρίσαιο τὴν ἁμαρτίαν, καὶ πλείω τούτων σοι γένοιτο ἀγαθά.” Ταῦτα λέγων οὐκ ἔπειθε φάσκοντα δεῖν συγγνώμην ἴσχειν, οἷς ἂν μὴ ἑκούσια ᾖ τὰ ἁμαρτήματα. Πῶς δ’ ἂν σώζοιτο αὐτῷ ἡ τύχη, μὴ τὸν ἀντίπαλον διωσαμένῳ; Ταῦτα εἰπὼν τόν τε Μυρζίην διεχρήσατο, καὶ ἐπένθει αὐτὸν δημοσίᾳ ἐπὶ συχνόν τινα χρόνον, θάψας βασιλικῶς.

10 Μετὰ δὲ ταῦτα ἐπὶ Ὑρκανίους ἐστρατεύετο καὶ τὴν ταύτῃ θάλασσαν, καὶ ἔθνη τε οὐκ ὀλίγα ἐς τὴν θάλασσαν τήνδε Ὑρκανίαν ἐνοικοῦντα παράλια κατεστρέφετο. Λέγεται δὲ αὕτη καὶ Κασπία ἐς τὴν τοῦ ἔθνους τούτου ἐπωνυμίαν· διήκει δὲ κατὰ μεσημβρίαν Σάκας τε ἔχων καὶ Καδουσίους ἐπὶ σταδίους [1.110] τρισμυρίους, πρὸς ἕω δὲ καὶ βορρᾶν Μασσαγέτας, γένος ἄλκιμόν τε καὶ ἐν πολέμοις εὐδοκιμοῦν, ἐπὶ σταδίους δισμυρίους μάλιστα. Τοῦτο δὲ τὸ γένος ἐλαῦνον ἐπὶ τὴν Περσῶν χώραν λέγεται καταστρεψάμενον πολίσματα κατασχεῖν ἔστιν ἅ, καὶ Τεμήρην τοῦ γένους τούτου γενόμενον σὺν τοῖς Μασσαγέταις ὁρμᾶσθαι ἐπὶ τὴν Σαμαρχάνδης ἀρχὴν καὶ Ἀσσυρίων τὴν χώραν καταστρεψάμενον ἔχειν.

11 Τὴν μέντοι θάλασσαν ταύτην ὑπὸ ποταμῶν ἐς αὐτὴν οὐκ ὀλίγων ἐκδιδόντων μεγίστην τε γίνεσθαι καὶ ἐπὶ πολλοὺς σταδίους διήκειν, οὐδαμῇ ἐκδιδοῦσαν, ᾗ λέγεται, εἰς τὴν ἐκτὸς θάλασσαν. Διώρυχα μέντοι ἐπυθόμην ἔγωγε ἀπὸ ταύτης διήκειν καὶ ἐς τὴν Ἰνδικὴν θάλασσαν ἐκδιδοῖ. Ἐνοικοῦσι δὲ τὴν θάλασσαν τήνδε ἔθνη πολλά τε καὶ ἄλκιμα. Καὶ ἰχθύας μὲν φέρει αὕτη ἡ θάλασσα πολλούς τε

God offers many rewards when we forgive those who wrong us in any way. If you forgive this misdeed for me, as I ask of you, many more blessings will come to you." But he did not persuade him with these words, for Timur said that forgiveness is given to those whose transgressions are not of their choosing. How might his fortune be preserved when he had not refuted his opponent? Saying this, he killed Mirza, but he mourned for him in public for a long time and buried him royally.

After that he marched against the Hyrkanians and the re- 10
gions by their sea. He conquered many peoples who lived on the coasts of this Hyrkanian Sea.[11] It is also called the Caspian Sea after the name of this people. It extends to the south for thirty thousand stades, to the Sakai and Kadousioi; to the east and north it extends to the Massagetai, a hardy race that is famous in war, for twenty thousand stades. It is said that this race set out against the land of the Persians and that it conquered the towns, some of which it occupied; also that Timur was from this race and that it was with the Massagetai that he attacked the kingdom of Samarkand and conquered the land of the Assyrians.[12]

This sea is very large because many rivers flow into it and 11
it extends over many stades; it is said not to open out into the outer Ocean at any point. But I have learned that there is a channel that leads from it and flows out into the Indian Ocean. Many hardy people live around this sea. It produces

καὶ ἀγαθούς, φέρει δὲ καὶ ὄστρεα μαργαρίτας ἔχοντα, ᾗπερ δὴ καὶ ἡ Ἰνδικὴ θάλασσα. Καὶ πλοῖα πολλὰ πλεῖ τὴν θάλασσαν ταύτην, παρὰ ἀλλήλους ἐπιπλέοντα φορτίων πλέα. Ἔστι δὲ αὕτη ἡ θάλασσα πρὸς ἕω μάλιστα τῆς Ἀσίας, ἐς ἣν ἐκδιδοῖ ὅ τε Ἀράξης ποταμὸς μέγιστος καὶ Χοάσπης πρὸς ἕω ῥέων, καὶ ποταμοὶ δὲ ἄλλοι οὐκ ὀλίγοι. Τὰ μέντοι ἐς τήνδε τὴν θάλασσαν ἔθνη ὑπὸ Καδουσίων τε ἄρχεσθαι πρόσθεν ἔφαμεν, καὶ τούς γε φόρους αὐτῶν ἐς τὴν Καδουσίων πόλιν ἔτους ἑκάστου ἐπάγειν ἐπὶ τούτους.

12 Ὡς τοὺς Ὑρκανίους ὑπηγάγετο Τεμήρης καὶ τὸν βασιλέα τούτων ἀνεῖλεν, ἐστρατεύετο ἐπὶ Καδουσίους. Καὶ οὗτοι μὲν [1.111] συλλέξαντες στρατιὰν μεγίστην παρεσκευάζοντο ὡς ἀμυνούμενοι, ἣν ἐπίῃ Τεμήρης· Τεμήρης δέ, ὡς ᾔσθετο τούτους στρατευομένους, πέμπει Χαϊδάρην ἐπὶ τὴν πόλιν αὐτῶν ὡς ἑλοῦντα τὴν ταχίστην καὶ πολιορκήσοντα· αὐτὸς δὲ ἐπέμενεν ἐστρατοπεδευμένος παρεγγυτάτω τοῖς Καδουσίοις. Ἐνταῦθα δὲ ὡς ἐπύθοντο οἱ Καδούσιοι τοὺς πολεμίους ἐς τὴν πόλιν αὐτῶν ἰόντας, τὰ ἔμπαλιν γενόμενοι ἵεντο οὐδενὶ κόσμῳ ἐς τὴν πόλιν. Ἐνταῦθα ἐπιτίθεται αὐτοῖς ἰοῦσιν ἐπὶ τὴν πόλιν Τεμήρης σὺν τῷ ἑαυτοῦ στρατῷ, καὶ τεταραγμένοις ἐμβαλὼν ἐτρέψατο, καὶ διώκων ἐπὶ τὴν πόλιν ἤλαυνε, καὶ πολιορκήσας ἐπὶ χρόνον τινὰ παρεστήσατο.

13 Μετὰ δὲ ταῦτα ἐστρατεύετο ἐπὶ Ἀραβίαν. Γένος δὲ Ἄραβες μέγα τε καὶ ὄλβιον καὶ ἀνὰ τὴν Ἀσίαν οὐδενὸς τὰ εἰς εὐδαιμονίαν λειπόμενον, παλαιόν τε ὂν καὶ ἐπὶ πολὺ τῆς Ἀσίας διῆκον, προσχρώμενόν τε τῇ θαλάσσῃ τῇ Ἐρυθρᾷ καλουμένῃ. Ἔστι δὲ ἡ χώρα αὕτη μεγίστη τε καὶ

many good fish and has pearl oysters, just like the Indian Ocean. Many ships sail on this sea, carrying many cargoes to each other. This sea lies at the eastern edge of Asia; the Araxes, a great river, and the Choaspes flow into it from the west, along with many other rivers.[13] We said earlier that the peoples around this sea are ruled by the Kadousioi, and pay an annual tribute to them at their city.

When Timur had subjected the Hyrkanians and killed their king, he marched against the Kadousioi. They assembled a very large army and were preparing to defend themselves, should Timur attack. When Timur found out that they were going to fight, he sent Haydar against their city, to besiege it and take it as quickly as possible. But Haydar stayed encamped very close to the Kadousioi. When the Kadousioi learned that the enemy was coming against their city, they turned round and fled in disorder toward their city. Timur then attacked them with his army on their way to their city; striking them when they were in such disorder, he routed them and pursued them to their city. After besieging it for some time, he took it. 12

After that Timur marched against Arabia.[14] The race of the Arabs is populous and wealthy and second to none in its prosperity among all the people of Asia. It is ancient and has spread over a large part of Asia, making use of the so-called Red Sea. This land is extensive and the most pleasant to live 13

καλλίστη οἰκῆσαι τῶν κατὰ τὴν Ἀσίαν χωρῶν. Ὤικηται δὲ ὑπὸ ἀνδρῶν δικαιοτάτων καὶ τὰ ἐς θρησκείαν αὐτῶν σοφωτάτων. Καὶ βασιλέα νομίζουσιν οὐ τύραννον, ἀλλ᾽ ἐς τὸ ἰσοδίαιτον μᾶλλον καὶ ἰσόνομον καθιστάμενον σφίσιν. Ἔστι δ᾽ αὐτοῖς βασίλεια ἐν τῇ πόλει τῇ παρὰ τὴν θάλασσαν [. . .] καλουμένη, μεγάλη τε καὶ πλούτῳ προφέρουσα. Ὁμορεῖ δὲ τῇ τε Αἰγύπτῳ καὶ Περσῶν χώρᾳ καὶ Ἀσσυρίων. Ἀπὸ γὰρ Κολχίδος καὶ Φάσιδος χώρας ἐς τὴν θάλασσαν τὴν ἐς [1.112] κοίλην Συρίαν, ἐς τὴν Λαοδίκειαν καλουμένην πόλιν, εἴη δ᾽ ἂν ὁδὸς ἡμερῶν [. . .] ἀνδρὶ εὐζώνῳ πεζῇ διαπορευομένῳ τὴν χώραν, καὶ τὸ ἐντεῦθεν κάτω Ἀσίας ὡσεὶ χερρόνησον γεγενῆσθαι, καὶ τήν τε Ἀραβίαν ἐκτὸς γίνεσθαι τῆς Ἀσίας. Ἔστι δὲ ἡ χώρα αὕτη ἐπίφορος, δένδρων τε καὶ φοινίκων πεπληρωμένη, καὶ ἐν μέσῳ δυοῖν ποταμοῖν περίρρυτος γενομένη καρπούς τε ἐκφέρει ὑπερφυεῖς τῷ μεγέθει καὶ πολλαπλασίους, ὥστε εὐδαίμονα ὑπὸ τῶν παλαιοτέρων κεκλῆσθαι ἀνδρῶν.

14 Διὰ ταῦτα ἐπὶ ταύτην τὴν Ἀραβίαν, ὅτι Καδουσίοις ὑπ᾽ αὐτοῦ πολεμουμένοις συνεμάχει αἰτιασάμενος, ἐστρατεύετο. Καὶ δὶς μὲν ἐμαχέσατο τῷ Ἀράβων στρατεύματι, καὶ οὐδ᾽ ὣς ἠδυνήθη τρέψασθαι· μετὰ δὲ διαπρεσβευσάμενος, ὥστε στρατιὰν δοῦναι καὶ φόρον ἀπάγειν τοῦ ἔτους, ὅσον ἂν σφίσιν ἐπιτάττοι, σπονδάς τε ἐποιήσατο καὶ τότε ἐλθεῖν ἐπ᾽ αὐτὸν Ἀράβων πρέσβεις, οἳ καὶ ἀφικόμενοι προΐσχοντό τε τὴν χώραν τοῦ ἥρωος μὴ λεηλατεῖν, καὶ ἐδέοντο σφᾶς, ἅτε γένος τε ὄντας τοῦ νομοθέτου, καὶ πατέρας εἶναι τῶν ἐς τήνδε τοῦ ἥρωος τελούντων θρησκείαν. Νομίζεται δὲ τοῦτο τὸ γένος εὐαγές τε καὶ ἅγιον, ὅτι τε προῆλθεν ἐκ

in of all the lands that are in Asia. It is inhabited by men who are the most just and extremely wise in matters of their religion. By custom they have a king who is not a tyrant but is appointed by them on a footing of equality and equal rights. Their royal capital is in a city by the sea called [. . .], which is large and surpasses others in wealth.[15] It borders on Egypt, the land of the Persians, and that of the Assyrians. From Kolchis and the land of the Phasis to the sea by Koile Syria, at the city called Laodikeia, would be a march of [. . .] days for an active man walking through on foot, and from there he could reach Asia Minor, which is like a peninsula, and Arabia, which is outside of Asia. The land is fertile, full of trees and palms; situated between two rivers, it is irrigated on all sides and produces fruit that are enormous in size and vast in number, so that the land was called Felix by the ancients.

So Timur marched against Arabia, accusing the Arabs of 14
making an alliance with the Kadousioi when they were at war with him.[16] Twice he fought with the Arabs' army and was unable to rout them. He then sent an envoy and asked that they give him an army and pay an annual tribute, whatever sum he set for them. He made a treaty and then the envoys of the Arabs came to him. When they arrived they asked him not to plunder the land of the hero and they pleaded on their own behalf that they belonged to the lawgiver's race and were the fathers of all who worshipped according to the hero's religion. This race is believed to be

τῆς χώρας αὐτῶν Μεχμέτης ὁ νομοθέτης, καὶ σὺν τῷ Ὀμάρῃ τὴν νομοθεσίαν δεξαμένῳ ἐπὶ τὴν τῆς Ἀσίας ἀρχὴν προεληλύθεισαν, μεγάλα ἀποδειξάμενοι ἔργα.

15 Ὁ μέντοι νομοθέτης τούτων ὁ Μεχμέτης παῖς λέγεται [I.113] γενέσθαι Ἀλίεω, ἀπὸ Ἀραβίας τῆς εὐδαίμονος. Ἐκθέμενος δὲ τὴν νομοθεσίαν αὐτοῦ ἀρχὴν μέντοι μηδὲν βιάζεσθαι, ἀναπείθοντά τε τοὺς Ἄραβας καὶ Σύρους μετὰ ταῦτα· μετὰ δὲ ταῦτα προσλαβόμενον τοῦ Ἀλίεω δυνάστου τε τῆς χώρας καὶ ἐπιτηδείου αὐτῷ, ὡς μάλιστα ἐπιόντα προσάγεσθαι αὐτῷ ἐς τὴν νομοθεσίαν, ὅποι ἂν ἐπίῃ, τοὺς τὴν χώραν οἰκοῦντας. Ἀνίει τε τὴν νομοθεσίαν ἔστε τὴν ῥᾳστώνην καὶ τὴν τοῦ θείου βακχείαν μέντοι, συνεχῆ δὲ ὡς μάλιστα μελέτην. Νομίζεται γὰρ αὐτῷ τετράκις τῆς ἡμέρας προσεύχεσθαι τῷ Θεῷ, ὑπ' οὐδενὸς κωλυόμενον εἰς τοῦτο, ὥστε μὴ προσεύξασθαι. Τῇ δὲ τῆς Ἀφροδίτης ἡμέρᾳ κοινῇ τε ἅπαντας ἐς τοὺς ναοὺς ἰόντας προσεύχεσθαι· νομίζεται μηδ' ὁτιοῦν, μήτε ἄγαλμα, μήτε ἄλλο τι τῶν γεγραμμένων προσβαλόμενον σφίσιν ἐς τὴν προσευχὴν ἐν τοῖς ναοῖς. Ἱερεῖς τε σφίσιν καθιστῶντες, ὥστε πρὸ τοῦ ναοῦ ἐς περιωπήν τινα πύργον πεποιημένον ἀναβαίνοντα προσεύχεσθαι τῷ Θεῷ μεγάλῃ φωνῇ καὶ αἰεὶ τὰς νομιζομένας εὐχὰς ποιεῖσθαι κεκραγότα γεγωνότερον. Ἐς μὲν οὖν τὴν προσευχὴν αὐτοῦ γένος δὲ τοῦτο ἴσμεν ἐς τὰ μάλιστα ἐντεταμένον, μηδ' ὁτιοῦν ἀνιέναι προσδεχομένους.

16 Ἐς δὲ τὰ ἄλλα τά τε ἐς δίαιταν καὶ ἐς τὸν βίον αὐτοῖς οὔτε κεκολασμένον νομίζεται, ὥστε μὴ ἐς τὸ τοῦ βίου ἡδὺ πολιτεύεσθαι· οὕτω τὴν φύσιν μηδαμῇ βιάζεται. Γυναῖκας μὲν γὰρ ἄγεσθαι, παλλακίδας μέντοι ἀπὸ ἀνδραπόδων,

holy and sacred, as Muhammad the lawgiver originated from their land and, with ‘Umar, who received the law,[17] they took over the realm of Asia, performing great deeds.

Muhammad, their lawgiver, is said to have been the son 15
of Ali,[18] from Arabia Felix. When he first set out his lawcode, at least, he compelled no one by force, but used per-
suasion on the Arabs and later the Syrians. After that, with
the help of Ali, the chief of that land and his friend, he went
out with him and propagated his lawcode as widely as he
could among the inhabitants of any land which he visited.
This lawcode promotes indolent mildness yet also enthusi-
asm for God, and especially constant study. Their custom is
to pray to God four times a day[19] and they let nothing prevent them from praying. On the day of Aphrodite [Friday]
they all go into the shrines together to pray.[20] Their customs
prohibit introducing anything whatever, whether a statue
or any other image, into their prayer in their shrines. They
have priests who ascend to a conspicuous position in a tower
that is built in front of the shrine and there pray to God in a
loud voice and always recite the customary prayers, calling
them out in order to be heard. We know that this race is especially devoted to prayer and for no reason at all will they
agree to neglect it.

In other matters in their way of life and overall conduct 16
nothing is regarded as so reprehensible that it would prevent them from living pleasurably; thus, they do not curb
nature in any way. For they marry more than one wife and

ὅσαις ἂν ἕκαστος οἷός τε [1.114] εἴη τροφὴν παρέχεσθαι ἐς τὸν βίον. Γυναῖκας δὲ κουριδίας ἄγεσθαι ἐς τὰς πέντε, καὶ τούς τε ἀπὸ ἀνδραπόδων παῖδας νομίζεσθαι σφίσιν οὐ νόθους. Ἂν δὲ ἀπὸ παλλακίδων ἐλευθέρων γένωνται σφίσι παῖδες, νόθοι τε αὐτοῖς νομίζονται, καὶ οὐκ εἰς τὴν πατρῴαν οὐσίαν εἰσέρχονται. Ὠνοῦνται δὲ καὶ τὰς κουριδίας, ὅσου ἄν τις βούλοιτο ἐκδοῦναι τὴν ἑαυτοῦ θυγατέρα. Λαμπάδων δὲ προενηνεγμένων σφίσιν ἐς τοὺς γάμους ἄγονται τὰς γυναῖκας. Ἂν δὲ ἀχθεσθεὶς τῇ γυναικὶ ὁ ἀνὴρ ἐπείπῃ τοῦ λοιποῦ ἀπὸ τριῶν σπληνῶν ἀποσχέσθαι αὐτῆς, ἤδη ἠλλοτρίωται τῷ λόγῳ ἡ γυνὴ τοῦ ἀνδρός. Νομίζεται δὲ αἴσχιστον, ἣν ἄν τις ἀποπέμψηται, αὖθις αὐτὴν ἀγαγέσθαι· ἂν δὲ μὴ ὑπὸ ἑτέρου μοιχευθῇ, οὐκ ἔξεστιν ἀπάγειν.

17 Οἴνῳ δὲ χρῆσθαι ἀθέμιτον ἀπαγορεύει τῷ γένει τούτῳ, καὶ μὴ λουσάμενον μὴ ἐξεῖναι αὐτῷ ἐς τὴν προσευχὴν ἰέναι. Δεκατείαν δέ τινα ἐξελόμενος τῷ Θεῷ τοῦ ἔτους, ἐς νηστείαν αὐτοὺς προάγεται ἐς τριάκοντα καὶ ἐπέκεινα ἡμέρας. Τῆς μέντοι ἡμέρας ὅλης μηδ' ὁτιοῦν προσίεσθαι μήτε τροφῆς, μήτε πόσεως, ἑσπέρας δέ, ὅταν ἄστρα φαίνηται, σιτίζεσθαι· πάντων δὲ μάλιστα τὸν χρόνον τοῦτον μὴ ἐξεῖναι οἴνου πιέσθαι τὸ παράπαν. Περιτέμνεσθαι δὲ τὸ αἰδοῖον χρῆναι παντάπασιν. Ἰησοῦν δὲ Θεοῦ τε ἀπόστολον γενέσθαι νομίζει, καὶ ἐξ ἀγγέλου τοῦ Γαβριὴλ καὶ ἐκ τῆς Μαρίας, παρθένου τε οὔσης καὶ μηδενὶ [1.115] ἀνδρὶ συγγενομένης γεννῆσαι Ἰησοῦν, ἥρωά τινα μείζω ἢ κατὰ ἄνθρωπον· καὶ ἐς τὴν τελευτὴν τοῦδε τοῦ κόσμου, ἐπειδὰν

have concubines from among their captives, however many as each man is able to support and feed. They may lawfully marry up to five wives and they do not regard children born to their slaves as illegitimate, but if children are born to free concubines they are considered illegitimate and have no claim to an inheritance. They also buy their lawful wives, at whatever price their fathers are willing to sell their daughters. The women are led in procession to wedding ceremonies preceded by torches. If a man can no longer stand his wife and proclaims that henceforth because of "the three spleens" he is separated from her, the woman is thereby formally separated from the man. It is considered a great shame to remarry a woman whom one has sent away. It is not permitted to take her back again unless she has first committed adultery with another man.[21]

This race is forbidden to drink wine, as something un- 17
lawful, and is not permitted to go to prayer without having washed first. They offer an annual tithe to God and their fast lasts for thirty days and more [Ramadan]. During the entire day they are not allowed to touch any food or drink, but in the evening, when the stars come out, they may eat. Of all the times of the year, it is especially then that they are not allowed to drink wine. It is mandatory for all to circumcise their genitals. They believe that Jesus was an apostle of God, that he was born of the angel Gabriel and Maria, a virgin who had never known a man, and that he was a hero greater than a normal man. At the end of this world, when

ἐς κρίσιν τῶν σφίσι βεβιωμένων καθιστῶνται οἱ ἄνθρωποι, τόν γε Ἰησοῦν φασιν ἄγεσθαι διαιτητὴν τοῦ κόσμου. Συὸς δὲ μὴ ἅπτεσθαι θέμις εἶναι, καὶ τά γε ζῷα πάντα ἐσθίουσιν, ἂν μέντοι ἐπὶ σφαγὴν γένωνται. Θεὸν μὲν οὖν ἕνα ἐφιστῶσι τῷδε τῷ παντί, ὑπηρέταις δὲ χρώμενον τοῖς πυρίνοις, ᾗ φασί, νόοις. Πεπομφέναι δὲ Μεχμέτην ἐς τὰ ἐλλιπῆ τοῖς πρότερον ἐπιπεμφθεῖσιν ὑπὸ Θεοῦ ἐς τὴν οἰκουμένην νομοθέταις. Κάθαρσιν δὲ ἡγοῦνται τήν τε περιτομὴν σφίσι πάντων δὴ μάλιστα, ἐν ᾗ καὶ γάμους ποιοῦνται. Ταφὰς δὲ αὐτοῖς παρὰ τὰς ὁδοὺς νομίζεται γίνεσθαι, καὶ μηδὲν ἄλλῃ ἐξεῖναι θάπτειν. Θάπτουσι δὲ λούσαντες καὶ ξυρῷ ἅμα τὸ σῶμα.

18 Νομίζεται δ' ἔτι καὶ τόδε, ὃς ἂν μὴ πείθηται τῷ νόμῳ, τελευτᾶν τῷ σιδήρῳ. Ἀρμενίους δὲ μόνους τῶν ἄλλων ἐθνῶν διαφερομένων σφίσιν ἐς τὴν θρησκείαν οὐκ ἀνδραποδίζεσθαι, ὡς Ἀρμενίῳ τινὶ προειρηκότι τὸ γὰρ κλέος αὐτοῦ ἐς τὴν οἰκουμένην ἐσόμενον. Διὰ τοῦτο μὴ ἐπιτρέπειν ἀνδραποδίζεσθαι Ἀρμενίους. Ταῦτα μέντοι ἐς τὴν νομοθεσίαν ἀποδεδειγμένους αὐτῷ ὡς πλεῖστον τῆς οἰκουμένης κατέχειν μέρος, καὶ ἐπὶ μέγα ἐλθεῖν ἔστε τὴν Ἀσίαν καὶ ἐς τὴν Λιβύην καὶ ἐς μοῖραν τῆς Εὐρώπης [1.116] οὐκ ὀλίγην, τὴν ἐς Σκύθας τε καὶ τοὺς νῦν Τούρκους, καὶ ἐς τὴν Ἰβηρίαν τούς γε Λίβυας. Λέγεται δὲ τελευτῆσαι ἐπὶ παιδὶ Ἀλίῃ βασιλεύοντι Ἀραβίας· ἐκεῖνόν τε γὰρ ὡς νομοθέτην προσέμενόν τε, καὶ πειθόμενοι αὐτῷ, ἐφ' ὅ τί γε ἂν ἐξηγοῖτο, ἐπέτρεψάν τε αὐτῷ τὰ πράγματα καὶ σφᾶς αὐτοὺς χρῆσθαι, ὅπως ἂν βούλοιτο. Μετὰ δὲ ταῦτα στρατόν τε συναγείρας ὡς πλεῖστον, ἐπῄει τῆς τε Αἰγύπτου

all people who have ever lived are judged, they say that Jesus will judge the world. It is their custom not to touch pigs, but they eat all other animals, if they have been properly slaughtered. One God governs all, and as his servants he uses what they call "fiery minds."[22] Muhammad had been sent to complete the work of the other lawgivers previously sent by God into the world. They believe that circumcision purifies them more than anything else, and they combine it with weddings.[23] It is their custom to place graves next to the streets and they are not permitted to bury their dead anywhere else. They wash and shave the body before burying it.

They believe this too, that whoever does not obey the 18
law should die by the sword. Among all the peoples who differ from them in religion, the only people they do not enslave are the Armenians, for an Armenian foretold the glory that Muhammad would win throughout the world. For this reason they are not allowed to enslave Armenians.[24] Proclaiming these things in the lawcode, they took over for him the larger part of the world and rose to greatness in Asia, North Africa, and quite a large part of Europe, that which is near the land of the Skythians and the Turks today, and of the North Africans in Iberia. It is said that Muhammad died while his son Ali was king of Arabia. Muhammad was declared lawgiver and they obeyed him wherever he led them. They entrusted their affairs to him and allowed him to govern them in whatever way he deemed best. After that, he assembled the largest army he could and launched it against

καὶ τῆς ἄλλης Ἀραβίας ἔστιν ἃ καταστρεψόμενος, καὶ τὴν ψάμμον διαβὰς τῆς Ἀραβίας τὰ τῇδε αὐτοῦ ἔθνη ὑπηγάγετο. Βασιλεύσας ἔτη δέκα ἐτελεύτησε δὲ ἐν χωρίῳ τινὶ Μεκέ, οὑτωσὶ καλουμένῳ. Καὶ ὅ τε στρατὸς καὶ οἱ τὴν χώραν οἰκοῦντες ἔθαψάν τε μεγαλοπρεπῶς καὶ ἐπένθησαν μεγάλως. Καὶ τελετὰς αὐτῷ ποιοῦνται οἱ Ἄραβες ἀνὰ πᾶν ἔτος ὡς ἥρωί τε καὶ ὑπὸ Θεοῦ τάχα ἐς τὴν νομοθεσίαν σφίσιν ἀνδρὶ εὐαγεῖ ἀποδεδειγμένῳ. Τά τε ἐς τὴν νομοθεσίαν ἐπιεικεῖ τε καὶ οὐ τυράννῳ γενομένῳ οὕτως γεγενῆσθαι.

19 Ἐπεὶ δὲ ἐτελεύτησεν, Ὀμάρης ὁ τῶν μαθητῶν αὐτοῦ δοκιμώτατος, ὑπὸ τοῦ παιδὸς αὐτοῦ τὴν ἀρχὴν παραδεξάμενος, καὶ τὸν στρατὸν ἅμα ἀγόμενος, πρῶτον μὲν ἐπὶ Συρίαν ἐλαύνων τήν τε χώραν ὑπηγάγετο, τὰ μὲν πολεμῶν, τὰ δὲ ἀναπείθων τε, σπενδόμενος ἐπὶ ῥητοῖς. Μετὰ δὲ ταῦτα Κίλικάς τε ἐχειρώσατο καὶ Φρύγας καὶ Μυσούς τε καὶ Ἴωνας, πρὸς δὲ καὶ τὰ ἄνω τῆς Ἀσίας ἐπιὼν κατεστρέφετο, τήν τε νομοθεσίαν [1.117] ἐπιβεβαιούμενος τοῖς ἀνὰ τὴν Ἀσίαν ἔθνεσι τῶν βαρβάρων, καὶ τῶν ξυμμαθητῶν αὐτοῦ ἔς τινας ἄλλους ἄλλῃ διαπέμπων, πείθειν τε πειρώμενος.

20 Καὶ τάφον τῷ Μεχμέτῃ πολυτελῆ κατασκευασάμενος αὐτοῦ ὑπερεγένετο, τελετάς τε ἐπετέλει αὐτῷ μεγάλας τε ἀνὰ πᾶν ἔτος, καὶ τοὺς ἄλλους ἔπειθεν αὐτῷ τε προσεύχεσθαι καὶ ἐς τὸν τάφον αὐτοῦ φοιτῶντας δικαίους γίνεσθαι· καὶ νῦν ἀπό τε τῆς Ἀσίας καὶ τῆς Λιβύης καὶ ἀπὸ τῆς Εὐρώπης δὴ οὐκ ὀλίγοι ἰόντες ἐς τὸ μνῆμα τοῦ Μεχμέτεω μέγα τε σφίσιν οἴονται ἐς εὐδαιμονίαν αὐτοῖς φέρειν τὸ

Egypt and the rest of Arabia with the intention of conquering them. He crossed the Arabian desert and subjected the peoples there to him. After reigning for ten years,[25] he died in a place that is called Mecca.[26] The army and the inhabitants of that land buried him magnificently and mourned him deeply. The Arabs hold ceremonies every year honoring him as a hero and as a holy man appointed over them by God to bring the law. His lawcode bears the mark of a just man, not someone who became a tyrant.

When Muhammad died, ʻUmar, the most esteemed 19
among his disciples,[27] received power from Muhammad's son and led the army first against the land of Syria,[28] which he subjected partly by fighting and partly by conversion, making treaties with specific terms. After that he conquered the Kilikians, Phrygians, Mysians, and Ionians, and he also attacked Greater Asia and took it, establishing the lawcode firmly among the barbarian peoples throughout Asia. He dispatched his fellow disciples to various dispersed places in an attempt to convert others too.

ʻUmar built a magnificent tomb for Muhammad after he 20
succeeded him and instituted great celebrations in his honor to be held every year. He convinced the others to pray to him and to become righteous by regularly visiting his tomb. Even now many people from Asia, North Africa, and Europe come to Muhammad's shrine in the belief that doing this will contribute greatly to their own prosperity.[29] Some

τοιοῦτον. Πορεύονται δ' οἱ μέν, οἱ δὲ ἀργυρίου τελοῦσι τοῖς ὑπὲρ σφῶν αὐτῶν βουλομένοις ἰέναι. Ἔστι δὴ ὁδὸς χαλεπωτάτη ἴεσθαι διὰ τὴν ψάμμον, ἐπὶ καμήλων δὲ τὴν τροφὴν φερουσῶν καὶ τὸ ὕδωρ· ἀφθόνως γὰρ οὐκ ἔχουσι χρῆσθαι αὐτῷ τὸ παράπαν. Καὶ οὕτω δὴ τὰ ἐπιτήδεια συσκευασάμενοι σφίσιν ἀναβαίνουσί τε ἐπὶ τὰς καμήλους, σημείοις διαχρώμενοι ἐς τὴν πορείαν ταῖς τοῦ μαγνήτου ἀποδείξεσιν, ᾗ δὴ ἀπὸ τῆς ἄρκτου ἐπιλεγόμενοι, ὅποι τῆς οἰκουμένης ἴεσθαι δεῖ αὐτούς, τούτῳ τεκμαιρόμενοι τὴν ὁδὸν διαπορεύονται. Ἐπειδὰν δὲ ἀφίκωνται ἐς χώρας αὖθις τινάς, ἐν αἷς ἔνεστιν ὕδωρ, ὑδρευσάμενοι ταύτῃ ἐντεῦθεν ἀπιοῦσι, καὶ ἀφικνοῦνται ἡμέραις τεσσαράκοντα τὴν ψάμμον διαβάντες ἐς τὸ σῆμα τοῦ Μεχμέτεω. Λέγεται δὲ τὸ σῆμα τοῦτο ὑπὸ λίθων πολυτελεστάτων κατασκευασθῆναι, καὶ ἐν μέσῳ τοῦ ναοῦ τὸ σῆμα μετεωριζόμενον ἀπαιωρεῖσθαι· [1.118] ὅπερ ἀπίθανόν μοι δοκεῖ. Διέχει δὲ ἀπὸ τοῦ χώρου τούτου, ἐν ᾧ τὸ σῆμα αὐτοῦ, ἐπὶ τὸν [. . .] ὡσεὶ σταδίους ἐνενήκοντα, καὶ ἐξιόντες ἐντεῦθεν ἴενται ἐπὶ τὸν χῶρον τοῦτον. Τούς τε νόμους αὐτοῦ καὶ τὰ Ἀλκωρὰ ἐκτέθειται· τῇ τε ἀθανασίᾳ τιθέμενοι τῆς ψυχῆς, ἀγνωμοσύνης οὐδέν τι πάνυ οἴονται μετεῖναι τῷ θείῳ. Ταῦτα μὲν οὖν τὴν τοῦ Μεχμέτεω νομοθεσίαν ἐς τοσοῦτον ἀναγεγράφθω ἡμῖν.

21 Τεμήρης δ' ὡς τὴν χώραν ταύτην ληϊσάμενος, καὶ πόλεις ἑλὼν ἐνίας, ὑπεκομίζετο ἐπὶ Σαμαρχάνδης. Σκύθας δὲ ὡρμημένους ἐπυνθάνετο ἀπὸ Ταναΐδος τήν τε χώραν αὐτοῦ ἐπιδραμεῖν καὶ ληΐσασθαι οὐκ ὀλίγα· χαλεπῶς δὲ ἔφερεν. Ἐντεῦθεν δὲ αὐτίκα ἵετο ὁμόσε ἐπὶ τοὺς Χαταΐδας.

travel in person while others pay money to those who are willing to go on their behalf. The road through the desert is very difficult to travel; the food and water is carried by camels and it is not possible to consume much of either at all. Once they have packed their necessities they mount the camels and follow the directions of the compass to make the journey. They take their bearing from the north, so that, wherever in the world they need to go, they use it to deduce which way to go. Whenever they come to a place where there is water, they replenish their supplies before departing. They reach the tomb of Muhammad after forty days of travel through the desert. This tomb is said to be constructed of precious stones, and the tomb itself suspended in midair in the very middle of the shrine, but this seems unlikely to me.[30] The distance from this place, where the tomb is, to [. . .] is about ninety stades, and when they leave from there they go to that place. Muhammad's laws and the al-Quran are expounded[31] in public. They believe in the immortality of the soul and hold that God cannot be sinful. Let this account suffice, then, concerning Muhammad's lawcode.

When Timur had plundered this land and seized some 21
cities, he returned to Samarkand. He learned that the Skythians had set out from the Don, invaded his land, and plundered it extensively, which made him angry. But at that point he was setting out to deal with the Khataians.[32] It is said

Λέγονται δὲ οὗτοι εἶναι Μασσαγέται τὸ παλαιόν, καὶ διαβάντες τὸν Ἀράξην τῆς ἐπὶ τάδε τοῦ ποταμοῦ χώρας ἐπὶ πολὺ διεξελθεῖν, καὶ ὑφ᾽ αὑτοῖς ποιησαμένους ἐνοικῆσαι. Τούτους παρεσκευάζετο ὡς ἑλῶν, καὶ στράτευμα ποιησάμενος ἐς ὀγδοήκοντα μυριάδας ἐστρατεύετο ἐπ᾽ αὐτούς. Καὶ συμβαλὼν μάχῃ τε ἐκράτησε τοὺς Χαταΐδας, καὶ ἐπὶ τὴν ἀγορὰν αὐτῶν τούτων καὶ ἐπὶ τὰ βασίλεια ἐλαύνων ὁμολογίᾳ τε παρεστήσατο, καὶ μισθωσάμενος παμπόλλους αὐτῶν, τούς γε κρατίστους τὰ ἐς πόλεμον γενομένους, ᾤχετο ἄγων. Ὁμήρους δὲ λαβὼν καὶ τῶν ἀρίστων τοὺς παῖδας, καὶ φόρον ταξάμενος τούτοις ἀπάγειν τοῦ ἐνιαυτοῦ, ἀπήλαυνε. Τὰ δὲ Χατάϊα πόλις ἐστὶ πρὸς ἕω τῆς Ὑρκανίας μεγάλη τε καὶ εὐδαίμων, πλήθει τε ἀνθρώπων καὶ ὄλβῳ καὶ τῇ ἄλλῃ εὐδαιμονίᾳ [1.119] προφέρουσα τῶν ἐν τῇ Ἀσίᾳ πόλεων πλὴν Σαμαρχάνδης καὶ Μέμφιος, εὐνομουμένη δὲ τὸ παλαιὸν ὑπὸ Μασσαγετῶν.

22 Τῶν μέντοι Περσῶν τοὺς πλείστους μισθωσάμενος τούτους, οἷα τῶν τε Σκυθῶν ἐμπείρους ὡς τὰ πολλὰ γενομένους καὶ τὰ ἐς τὴν δίαιταν οὐκέτι ἁβροὺς ὄντας, ἐν νῷ ἔχων ἐπὶ Σκύθας στρατεύεσθαι, ἐπὶ τὴν ἀγορὰν αὐτῶν τὴν Οὐρδὰν καλουμένην, καὶ πυνθανόμενος, ὡς εἴη τε τὸ γένος τοῦτο παλαιότατόν τε τῶν κατὰ τὴν οἰκουμένην ἐθνῶν, καὶ οὐδένα ἔτι τῶν πρὸ αὐτοῦ βασιλέων χειρώσασθαι τοῦτο τὸ γένος, κακὰ δὲ ὡς πλεῖστα ἐργασάμενον ποιῆσαι τήν τε Ἀσίαν καὶ Εὐρώπην, ἐπιδρομῇ τὰ πλείω ταμιευόμενον τῇ χώρᾳ. Ταῦτα δὲ ἐπὶ νοῦν τιθέμενον, καὶ ὡς Δαρείῳ τῷ Ὑστάσπεω βασιλεῖ γενομένῳ Περσῶν καὶ

that in antiquity these were Massagetai who crossed the Araxes and spread over a considerable area of land along this side of the river; they subjected it to themselves and settled there. Timur had prepared to defeat them by assembling an army that was eight hundred thousand strong and marching against them. He engaged with the Khataians in battle and defeated them, before advancing against their assembly and royal court, which surrendered to him on terms. He hired a great number of their best warriors and left, taking them with him. He also took as hostages the sons of the notables and imposed an annual tribute on them, to be brought to him. Then he departed. The large and prosperous city of Khatai is to the east of Hyrkania. It surpasses the cities in Asia in the number of its inhabitants, in its wealth, and in its general prosperity, except for Samarkand and Cairo. In antiquity it was well governed by the Massagetai.

Timur hired a large number of Persians because they 22
were very experienced when it came to the Skythians, and their way of life is not a luxurious one.[33] It was his intention to march against the Skythians and against their chief assembly, which is called the Horde. He had learned that this race is the most ancient among all the peoples in the world and that no king before him had been able to conquer them. They had inflicted a great deal of harm on both Asia and Europe, as they controlled the land by raiding it. That was his intention, given especially that Darius, the son of Hystaspes, campaigned against them when he became king of the

ἐπιστρατεύσαντι αὐτοὺς οὐδέν τι προὐχώρησεν, ὥρμητο αὐτὸς ἐπὶ τοῦτο τὸ κλέος ἰέναι.

23 Ὥστε δὲ αὐτοῦ ἔχεσθαί τε τοῦ ἔργου ἐγγυτέρω τούτων γενόμενον, ἐς τὴν χώραν Χερίην[1] πόλιν κατοικίσας ἀπό τε τῆς Σαμαρχάνδης καὶ στρατιωτῶν καὶ τῶν ἀρίστων αὐτῷ στελλομένων ἐς τὴν ἀποικίαν ᾤκισε πόλιν Χερίην οὕτω καλουμένην, μεγάλην τε καὶ εὐδαίμονα ἅτε τοῦ βασιλέως ἐν αὐτῇ διατρίβοντος καὶ τῶν ἀρίστων αὐτοῦ, τῶν τε τῆς Ἀσίας στρατῶν ἐς αὐτὴν συνιόντων. Μεγάλη τε ἐν βραχεῖ ἐγένετο ἡ Χερίη, καὶ εὐνομήθη μέντοι καὶ ὕστερον, οὐχ ἥκιστα δὲ βασιλέως Τεμήρεω περιόντος. Ὅποι μὲν οὖν τῆς Ἀσίας ᾤκισται ἡ πόλις αὕτη, καὶ εἴτε ἐν τῇ Ἀσσυρίᾳ χώρᾳ, εἴτε καὶ ἐν τῇ Μήδων, οὐκ ἔχω τεκμήρασθαι. Λέγουσι [1.120] μέν τινες Νῖνον τὴν Χερίην γενέσθαι τὸ παλαιὸν καὶ ἐς τὴν Ἀσσυρίων χώραν τετάχθαι, τεκμαιρόμενοι τοῦτο ἀπὸ τῆς Παγδατίνης Βαβυλῶνος. Οἰκίσας δὲ Χερίην πόλιν, καὶ τὰ βασίλεια ἐν αὐτῇ ποιησάμενος, ἐπενόει ἐπὶ Αἴγυπτόν τε καὶ ἐπὶ Σκύθας στρατεύεσθαι καὶ τὴν τούτων ἀγορὰν Οὐρδὰν καλουμένην, καὶ στρατὸν μέγαν συναγείρας καὶ τοὺς Χαταΐδας· συμπαραλαβὼν ἤλαυνεν εὐθὺ Τανάϊδος. Ἐνταῦθα πυθόμενοι Σκύθαι Τεμήρην βασιλέα ἐπὶ σφᾶς ἐπιόντα μεγάλῃ παρασκευῇ, τήν τε εἴσοδον ἔπεμπον στράτευμα προκαταληψομένους τῶν ὀρέων, ᾗ ἔμελλε Τεμήρης σὺν τῷ στρατῷ αὐτοῦ διϊέναι.

24 Σκύθαι μὲν οὗτοι τὸ πάλαι ἐς μοίρας τινὰς διῃρημένοι ἐνέμοντο τὴν χώραν ἀπὸ Ἴστρου ἔστε ἐπὶ τοὺς ὑπὸ τὸν Καύκασον. Νῦν δὲ γένος μέντοι τούτων ἐς τὴν Ἀσίαν γενόμενον, τὰ πρὸς ἕω αὐτοῦ τε ἐνοικῆσαν τὴν ἐπὶ τάδε

Persians but achieved nothing. This made Timur all the more eager to secure the fame that would come with such a success.

In order to implement his project he moved closer to them and settled the city of Kherie with men from Samarkand; both soldiers and notables were sent by him to the colony. So he settled this city called Kherie, and it became large and prosperous, given that the king and his leading men lived in it and the armies of Asia assembled there. In a short time, then, Kherie became great and it was well governed both then and also in later times, but not least while King Timur was alive. But I have no evidence as to where this city was located in Asia,[34] whether in the land of Assyria or that of the Medes. Some say that Kherie was ancient Nineveh and belonged to the land of the Assyrians, and they cite Baghdad by Babylon as evidence. Anyway, Timur settled the city of Kherie, established his royal court in it, and planned to march against Egypt[35] and against the Skythians and their assembly that is called the Horde. He assembled a large army and, taking the Khataians with him, he advanced straight to the Don. When the Skythians learned that King Timur was coming against them with a large force, they sent an army to seize in advance the pass leading into the mountains, which Timur was about to cross with his army. 23

These Skythians were, in antiquity, divided into different branches and roamed the land from the Danube to the peoples beneath the Caucasus. One race of this people today, which is in Asia, settled in the land that is to the east on this 24

τῆς Ἀσίας χώραν, καὶ ἐπὶ πολλὰ τετραμμένον, Σαχαταῖοι ἐκλήθησαν, ὑπὲρ τὴν τῶν Περσῶν χώραν ἐς τοὺς Σάκας τε καὶ Καδουσίους· ἀφ' ὧν δὴ καὶ Τεμήρην αὐτὸν οἴονται γεγονέναι τινές. Ἔστι δὲ τοῦτο τὸ γένος ἄλκιμόν τε τῶν κατὰ τὴν Ἀσίαν καὶ πολεμικώτατον, καὶ σὺν τούτοις λέγεται Τεμήρης τὴν ἡγεμονίαν τῶν ἐν τῇ Ἀσίᾳ παραλαβεῖν, πλὴν Ἰνδῶν.

25 Οἱ δὲ λοιποὶ Σκύθαι κατὰ ταὐτὸ φρονοῦσί τε καὶ ὑφ' ἑνὶ ἄρχονται βασιλεῖ, κατὰ Οὐρδὰν τὴν καλουμένην ἀγορὰν τὰ βασίλεια ποιούμενοι, ἀποδεικνύμενοι σφίσι βασιλέα γένους τε ὄντα τοῦ βασιλείου τὸ παλαιότατον. Καὶ ἔστι δὴ καὶ ἀλλαχοῦ τῆς Εὐρώπης ἐς τὸν Βόσπορον μοῖρα τούτων οὐκ ὀλίγη, ἀνὰ τὴν χώραν ταύτην [1.121] διεσκεδασμένον, ὑπὸ βασιλεῖ ταττόμενον, οἴκου τῶν βασιλέων, ὄνομα δὲ τούτῳ Ἀτζικερίης. Οὗτοι μὲν οὖν ὡς ἐπετράποντο σφᾶς τούτῳ τῷ βασιλεῖ, ἐς τήνδε ἀφικόμενοι τὴν χώραν, ἐπελάσαντες ἐς τὸν Ἴστρον, καὶ δὴ καὶ τὸν Ἴστρον διαβάντες, μοῖρά τις οὐκ ὀλίγη τῆς Θρᾴκης λεηλατοῦντες ἐπέδραμον, καὶ ἀνεχώρουν ἀπὸ Σαρματίας ἐπὶ τὸν Τάναϊν ἰόντες. Καὶ πολλὰ μὲν τοῦ γένους τούτου αὐτοῦ παρὰ τὸν Ἴστρον ἐνέμειναν. Ὧν τὸ πλέον ἐπὶ Παιαζήτεω διαβὰν τὸν Ἴστρον [ἐνέμειναν] ᾠκίσθη χωρὶς ἕκαστον μέρος τοῦ γένους τούτου γενόμενον. Τὸ δὲ ὑπολειφθὲν μέρος αὐτοῦ πέραν τοῦ Ἴστρου παρὰ Καζιμήρῳ τῷ βασιλεῖ Λιτουάνων τὴν δίαιταν ἔχουσι, τὴν γῆν νεμόμενοι ἐς ἔτι καὶ νῦν, ἔς τε τὸν πρὸς τοὺς περιοίκους αὐτῷ πόλεμον συμβαλλόμενοι τὰ κράτιστα· ὅπου γὰρ ἂν τὸ γένος τοῦτο τυγχάνωσιν ὄντες, δοκοῦσί τε τὰ ἐς πόλεμον καὶ εἰσὶ κράτιστοι. Οἱ δὲ

side of Asia, and then went off in many directions. They were called Chaghadai, and they were above the land of the Persians, toward the Sakai and Kadousioi. Some think that Timur himself was one of them. This is the hardiest race of those in Asia, and they are most warlike; it is said that it was with them that Timur gained mastery over all the peoples in Asia, except for the Indians.[36]

25 The rest of the Skythians are united and are ruled by one king; they have their court at the so-called assembly of the Horde; and they appoint as their king a member of the most ancient royal family.[37] There is a branch of them elsewhere in Europe, toward the [Crimean] Bosporos; it is quite large and they are dispersed throughout that land, subject to a king from the royal family, whose name is Hajji Giray.[38] They entrusted themselves to this king and came to this land, reaching the Danube. Moreover, they crossed the Danube and a large group of them invaded and raided Thrace. Then they withdrew, going through Russia toward the Don. But a large number of this race stayed behind, by the Danube. During the reign of Bayezid, most of them crossed the Danube and then each part of this race was settled separately.[39] The remainder, who stayed on the other side of the Danube, have taken up with Casimir, the king of the Lithuanians.[40] To this day they still roam and live off the land and offer him powerful assistance in his wars against his neighbors. Wherever this race happens to be, they have a reputation for

περὶ τὸν Βόσπορον καὶ τὴν Ταυρικὴν νῆσον καλουμένην, διείργουσαν λίμνην τε τὴν Μαιώτιδα καὶ τόν γε Εὔξεινον πόντον, ὑπὸ τῷ βασιλεῖ Ἀτζικερίῃ τά τε ἔθνη τὰ ἐς γῆν ληϊζόμενοι κατεστρέψαντο ἐς φόρου ἀπαγωγήν, τούς τε Γότθους καλουμένους καὶ Ἰανυΐους τοὺς τὴν τοῦ Καφᾶ πόλιν ἐνοικοῦντας.

26 Καὶ Σαρματίας μέρος τι ἀπάγει τούτῳ τῷ βασιλεῖ φόρον. Σαρμάται μὲν οὖν οἱ πρὸς Εὔξεινον πόντον καὶ οἱ πρὸς ὠκεανὸν τῷ μεγάλῳ Σκυθῶν βασιλεῖ τῶν ἐν τῇ ἀγορᾷ [1.122] φόρον ἀπάγουσιν, ἐξ ὅτου τὴν Σαρματίαν ἐπιδραμόντες τὰ μὲν ἠνδραποδίσαντο, τὰ δὲ ληϊσάμενοι κατέσχον ἐπὶ συχνόν τινα χρόνον, καὶ ταύτῃ τὸ ἀπὸ τοῦδε φόρον τε ἐτάξαντο τῷ βασιλεῖ τῷ μεγάλῳ, καὶ ἔτους ἑκάστου ἀπάγουσι. Σαρματία μὲν οὖν διήκει ἀπὸ Σκυθῶν τῶν νομάδων ἐπὶ Δᾶκας τε καὶ Λιτουάνους, γένος τῶν Ἰλλυριῶν φωνῇ τὰ πολλὰ διαχρώμενον. Καὶ διαίτῃ τε καὶ ἤθεσι τοῦ Ἰησοῦ νόμοις ἐπήκοοι, ἐπὶ τοὺς Ἕλληνας μᾶλλον τετραμμένοι οὐ πάνυ συμφέρονται τῷ Ῥωμαίων ἀρχιερεῖ, Ἑλληνικῷ δὲ ἀρχιερεῖ χρῶνται, καὶ τούτῳ πείθονται τὰ ἐς θρησκείαν τε καὶ δίαιταν σφίσι. Καὶ ἤθεσι τοῖς αὐτοῖς Ἑλλήνων διαχρώμενοι, σκευῇ τῇ Σκυθῶν παραπλησίᾳ προσχρῶνται. Τὰ μέντοι πρὸς Εὔξεινον πόντον Σαρματῶν γένη, ἀπὸ Λευκοπολίχνης καλουμένης, ἡγεμονίαι τε διαλαγχάνουσι τὰ πολλά, τό τε Μοσχόβιόν τε καὶ Κίεβος καὶ Τοφάρι καὶ Χωρόβιον,[2] πόλεις ὑπὸ τυράννους εὐθυνόμεναι, ἐς τὴν μέλαιναν οὕτω ὑπὸ σφῶν αὐτῶν καλουμένην Σαρματίαν τελοῦσι. Τὰ δὲ πρὸς ὠκεανὸν ὑπὸ τὴν ἄρκτον οἰκημένα γένη λευκὴν Σαρματίαν καλοῦσι.

being powerful in war, as they actually are. Those by the Bosporos and the island called the Crimea, which separates the Sea of Azov from the Black Sea, attacked and raided the peoples in that land, under King Hajji Giray, to extract tribute from them, namely the so-called Goths and the Genoese who live in the city of Caffa.

Part of Russia also pays tribute to this king. The Russians 26
by the Black Sea and those by the outer Ocean pay tribute to the Great King of the Skythians of the Horde. They have done so ever since the latter invaded Russia and enslaved part of it while they plundered the rest and held it for some time,[41] and from that point on the Russians were assessed a tribute to the Great King, which they deliver every year. Russia extends from the nomadic Skythians to the Wallachians and Lithuanians. The Russians are a race that for the most part speaks the language of the Illyrians [i.e., Slavs]. In their customs and way of life they follow the laws of Jesus, and incline more to the Greeks and do not follow the pontiff of the Romans. They have a Greek bishop and obey him in matters of religion and in their way of life. They also use the customs of the Greeks but their dress is similar to that of the Skythians. The Russian races by the Black Sea starting from the so-called White Town[42] are divided into principalities, namely Moscow, Kiev, Tver, and Khorov,[43] cities that are governed by tyrants and extend as far as what they themselves call Black Russia. They call the races that live by the Ocean below the Arctic circle White Russia.

27 Πρὸς μέντοι ὠκεανὸν πόλις Οὐγκράτης καλουμένη, ἐς ἀριστοκρατίαν τετραμμένη, ὄλβον τε παρέχεται καὶ αὔτὴν εὐδαιμονίᾳ ὑπερφέρουσαν τῶν ἄλλων τῆς Σαρματίας πόλεων, τῆς τε λευκῆς καὶ μελαίνης οὑτωσὶ καλουμένης. Καὶ διήκει ἐπ' ὠκεανὸν αὕτη ἡ χώρα, Ἰνφλάντη καλουμένη. Ἔνθα δὴ ὁρμίζονται καὶ αἱ ἀπὸ Δανίας νῆες καὶ Γερμανίας, φορτία φέρουσαι Βρετανικά τε ἅμα καὶ Κελτικὰ ἐς τήνδε τὴν χώραν. Ἀπὸ μὲν οὖν [1.123] Ταναΐδος ἐς ὠκεανὸν τὸν Βρετανικὸν καὶ ἐπὶ τὴν Κελτῶν χώραν εἴη ἂν ὁδὸς τὸ μακρότατον ἡμερῶν πέντε καὶ τριάκοντα τὸ οἰκούμενον ἐπὶ μῆκος, ἐπὶ πλάτος δὲ τὸ μὲν ὑπὲρ τὸν Τάναϊν χώραν εἶναι μεγίστην, ἀπὸ Σαρματίας ἔστε ἐπὶ τὴν Ἀσσυρίων χώραν. Σκύθαι νέμονται τήνδε. Ἔστι μὲν οὖν, ὡς ἔμοιγε καταφαίνεται, τὰ ὑπὲρ τὸν Τάναϊν χώρα μεγίστη δὴ τῶν ἐν τῇ Εὐρώπῃ κατ' ἄμφω, μῆκός τε δὴ καὶ πλάτος ἐπὶ μήκιστον διήκουσα. Πέρμιοι δὲ οἰκοῦσι τὸ πρὸς βορρᾶν ὑπὲρ τοὺς Σαρμάτας, ὅμοροι δέ εἰσι Σαρματῶν, καὶ φωνὴν τὴν αὐτὴν ἵενται οἱ Σαρμάται τοῖς Περμίοις. Λέγεται δὲ περὶ Περμίων τάδε, ὡς ἔστι γένος ἀπὸ ἄγρας τὸ πλέον τοῦ βίου σφίσι ποιούμενον καί [. . .]

28 Ἡ μέντοι πρὸς ὠκεανὸν διήκουσα Σαρματία ἐπὶ Προυσίαν καλουμένην χώραν διήκει καὶ ἐπὶ τοὺς ταύτῃ λευκοφόρους Ναζηραίους καὶ ἱερὸν τὸ ἐν τῇδε τῇ χώρᾳ. Δοκοῦσι δὲ γένος τοῦτο εἶναι Γερμανοί, καὶ φωνῇ τῇ αὐτῶν ἐκείνων προσχρώμενοι καὶ διαίτῃ. Οἰκοῦσι δὲ πόλεις περικαλλεῖς καὶ εὐνομουμένας ἐς τὸ κράτιστον. Ἔστι δὲ τούτοις ἱερόν, ᾗ δὲ καὶ τὸ ἐν Ἰβηρίᾳ ἱερὸν νομίζεται καὶ ἐν τῇ Ῥόδῳ ἐνοικοῦν Ναζηραίων γένος. Ταῦτα γὰρ δὴ τὰ

The city of Novgorod, which is in the direction of the Ocean, has an aristocratic regime and is richer and more prosperous than the other cities in Russia, either of the White or the so-called Black Russia. This land, called Infland,[44] extends to the Ocean. Ships from Denmark and Germany anchor there, bringing British and French cargoes to this land. The journey from the Don to the British Ocean and from there to the land of the French, across the length of the inhabited region, would last thirty-five days at the longest, while in breadth the land above the Don is vast, from Russia to the land of the Assyrians. This is where the Skythians roam. It seems to me that the land above the Don is the largest in Europe with respect to both of its dimensions, stretching over the greatest distances in both length and breadth. The Permians live in the north beyond the Russians; they are neighbors of the Russians, and the Russians speak the same language as the Permians. It is said about the Permians that they are a race who live mostly by hunting and [. . .]. 27

The part of Russia that extends toward the Ocean reaches as far as the land called Prussia, toward the white-robed monks there and their holy order in that land.[45] The members of this race appear to be Germans, and they speak the same language as the Germans and have the same way of life. They live in beautiful cities that are well governed so that they are very powerful. They have a holy order there that is related to the holy order in Castile and the order of monks who live on Rhodes.[46] It is clear that these three holy 28

τρία ἱερὰ ἀνὰ τὴν οἰκουμένην ἐς τὴν τοῦ Ἰησοῦ θρησκείαν ἐπὶ τοὺς βαρβάρους ᾠκημένα δὴ καταφανῆ ἐστι, τό τε ἐν Ἰβηρίᾳ πρὸς τοὺς ταύτῃ τῶν Λιβύων διαβάντας, καὶ Προυσίων πρός τε τοὺς Σαμώτας καὶ Σκυθῶν τοὺς νομάδας, αὐτοῦ [1.124] ταύτῃ ἀγχοῦ τὸ παλαιὸν ᾠκισμένους, καὶ Ῥοδίων δὲ πρὸς τοὺς ἐν Αἰγύπτῳ τε καὶ Παλαιστίνῃ διὰ τὸν τοῦ Ἰησοῦ τάφον καὶ πρὸς τοὺς ἐν τῇ Ἀσίᾳ βαρβάρους.

29 Προυσίων δὲ ἔχονται Σαμῶται, γένος ἄλκιμόν τε καὶ οὐδενὶ τῶν περιοίκων ὁμοδίαιτον, οὐδὲ ὁμόγλωσσον. Νομίζει δὴ τοῦτο τὸ γένος θεοὺς Ἀπόλλω τε καὶ Ἄρτεμιν· διαίτῃ δὲ χρῶνται τῇ πάλαι Ἑλληνικῇ καὶ ἤθεσι, σκευῇ δὲ τῇ Προυσίων παραπλησίᾳ. Τούτων δὲ ἔχονται Βοέμοι, τῇ τε Σαμωτῶν δόξῃ τιθέμενοι καὶ τῇ Γερμανῶν οἱ ἐν τῇ χώρᾳ ταύτῃ ἐνοικοῦντες, σκευῇ τῇ τῶν Παιόνων παραπλησίᾳ ἐσκευασμένοι. Ἔνεστι δὲ αὐτοῖς μητρόπολις, πόλις εὐδαίμων τε καὶ πολυάνθρωπος, Βράγα οὑτωσὶ καλουμένη, καὶ πολλοὶ τῆς πόλεως ταύτης οὐ πολὺς χρόνος ἐπεὶ ἐπαύσαντο τῷ πυρὶ καὶ τῷ ἡλίῳ θρησκεύειν. Μόνον δὲ τὸ ἔθνος τοῦτο τῶν ἐν τῇ Εὐρώπῃ ἐκτὸς γενόμενον ταῖς ἐγνωσμέναις ἡμῖν ἐν τῷ παρόντι θρησκείαις, τῆς τε τοῦ Ἰησοῦ φημι καὶ τῆς τοῦ Μεχμέτεω καὶ Μωσέως· ταύτας γάρ τοι σχεδόν τι ἴσμεν διακατέχειν τήν τε ἐγνωσμένην ὡς τὰ πολλὰ ἡμῖν οἰκουμένην. Ἔστι μέντοι, ᾗ πυνθάνομαι, καὶ τὰ ὑπὲρ τὴν Κασπίαν θάλασσαν καὶ τοὺς Μασσαγέτας ἔθνος Ἰνδικὸν ἐς ταύτην τετραμμένον τὴν θρησκείαν τοῦ Ἀπόλλωνος. Νομίζει δὲ ἐκεῖνο τὸ γένος καὶ θεοὺς ἔτι

orders were established throughout the world to defend the religion of Jesus against the barbarians, the one in Castile against the North Africans who crossed over there; that of the Prussians against the Samogitians[47] and the nomadic Skythians, who formerly used to live in that region; and that of the Rhodians against those in Egypt and Palestine on account of the tomb of Jesus and against the barbarians in Asia.

Next to the Prussians are the Samogitians, a hardy race 29
whose way of life has nothing at all in common with that of its neighbors, nor its language. This race believes in the gods Apollo and Artemis.[48] They follow the ancient Greek way of life and customs, but their dress is similar to that of the Prussians. Next to them are the Bohemians who have the same beliefs as the Samogitians and the Germans who live in this land, but their dress is similar to that of the Hungarians. They have a capital city that is prosperous and populous; it is called Prague, and it has not been long since many of the inhabitants of this city stopped worshipping fire and the sun.[49] This is the only race in Europe that does not follow one of the religions that are recognized by us these days, I mean those of Jesus, Muhammad, and Moses; for we know that practically the majority of the known world adheres to them. But there is, so I have learned, an Indian race beyond the Caspian Sea and the Massagetai which practices that same worship of Apollo. That race believes in other gods

ἄλλους, Δία τε καὶ Ἥραν, ὡς προϊόντι πρόσω τοῦ λόγου δηλωθήσεται. Καὶ περὶ μὲν τούτων ταύτῃ ἐπὶ τοσοῦτον εἰρήσθω.

30 Πολάνοι [1.125] δὲ ἔχονται Σαρματῶν, καὶ τῇ φωνῇ τούτων νομίζουσι, καὶ ἤθεσι δὲ καὶ διαίτῃ τῇ Ῥωμαίων παραπλησίᾳ. Πολάνων δὲ ἔχονται Λιτουάνοι ἐπὶ Εὔξεινον πόντον καὶ ἐπὶ Σαρματίαν καθήκοντες καὶ οὗτοι. Ἡ μὲν μέλαινα Πογδανία, ἡ ἐν τῇ Λευκοπολίχνῃ καλουμένῃ τὰ βασίλεια ἔχουσα, ἀπὸ Δακῶν τῶν παρὰ τὸν Ἴστρον ἐπὶ Λιτουάνους καὶ Σαρμάτας διήκει. Γένος δέ ἐστι τοῦτο δόκιμον, ᾗ ἄν τις τεκμαίροιτο, τήν τε φωνὴν τὴν αὐτὴν ἱέμενον, καὶ ἀπὸ παλαιοῦ διεσχισμένον διχῇ τὸ γένος ἐς τυραννίδας καὶ ἡγεμονίας δύο κατέστη. Λιτουάνοι δὲ οὔτε Σαρμάταις εἰσὶν ὁμόγλωσσοι, οὔτε Παίοσιν, οὔτε μὲν Γερμανοῖς, οὐ μὴν οὐδὲ Δαξίν, ἰδίᾳ δὲ τὸ παράπαν νομίζουσι φωνῇ. Ἔστι δὲ αὐτοῖς βασίλεια πόλις μεγάλη τε καὶ πολυάνθρωπος καὶ εὐδαίμων. Καὶ δοκεῖ τοῦτο τὸ γένος εἶναί τε μέγα τῶν ἀμφὶ τήνδε τὴν χώραν ἐθνῶν καὶ ἀνδρειότατον, καὶ πρός τε τοὺς Προυσίους τοὺς Γερμανοὺς καὶ Πολάνους διαπολεμοῦν περί τε ὅρων τῶν ἐς τὴν χώραν. Ἔστι δὲ καὶ τοῦτο τὸ γένος πρὸς τὰ τῶν Ῥωμαίων ἔθη καὶ δίαιταν τετραμμένον, σκευῇ δὲ τῇ Σαρματῶν παραπλησίᾳ χρωμένους, καὶ τῇ μελαίνῃ Πογδανίᾳ ὅμορος τὰ πολλὰ οὖσα πρὸς τούτους ἀγωνίζεται. [1.126]

31 Σαρμάται δὲ φωνῇ διαχρῶνται παραπλησίᾳ τῇ Ἰλλυριῶν τῶν ἐς τὸν Ἰόνιον παροικούντων ἔστε ἐπὶ Ἐνετούς. Ὁπότεροι μὲν τούτων παλαιότεροι, καὶ τὴν ἑτέρων ὁπότεροι τούτων χώραν ἐπινέμονται, ἢ Ἰλλυριοὶ ἐπέκεινα τῆς

too, Zeus and Hera, as will be made clear later in the narrative.[50] Let this suffice on these matters.

The Poles are next to the Russians and speak their language, but their customs and way of life are like those of the Romans. Next to the Poles are the Lithuanians, and they too extend as far as the Black Sea and to Russia. Moldavia, whose royal court is in the so-called White Town,[51] extends from the Wallachians by the Danube to the Lithuanians and the Russians. This is an admirable race, insofar as one may ascertain, and while it speaks one and the same language it has, since ancient times, been divided between two tyrannies and rulers.[52] But the Lithuanians do not speak the same language as the Russians, the Hungarians, the Germans, or even the Wallachians; they use a language that is altogether unique to them. Their royal court is in a large, populous, and prosperous city.[53] This race seems to be the greatest among the peoples around this land and the most courageous, and they fight against Prussians, Germans, and Poles regarding the boundaries of their country. This race too has adopted the customs and way of life of the Romans but its dress is similar to that of the Russians. It borders for the most part on Moldavia and fights against its people. 30

The Russians speak a language similar to that of the Illyrians who live by the Adriatic Sea, up by the Venetians. As to which of them is more ancient and which settled in the lands of other people, that is whether the Illyrians crossed 31

Εὐρώπης διαβάντες Πολανίαν τε καὶ Σαρματίαν ᾤκησαν, ᾗ Σαρμάται δὲ ἐπὶ τάδε τοῦ Ἴστρου γενόμενοι τήν τε Μυσίαν καὶ Τριβαλλῶν χώραν καὶ δὴ καὶ Ἰλλυριῶν τῶν πρὸς τὸν Ἰόνιον ἄχρι δὴ Ἑνετῶν ᾤκησαν, οὔτε ἄλλου τινὸς ἐπυθόμην τῶν παλαιοτέρων διεξιόντος, οὔτ᾽ ἂν ἔχοιμι πάντη ὡς ἀληθῆ διασημήνασθαι.

32 Ἐπάνειμι δὲ ἐπὶ Σκύθας τοὺς νομάδας, ὃ δὴ γένος μέγιστόν τε καὶ ἰσχυρὸν καὶ γενναιότατόν ἐστιν, οἷον οὐδενὶ τῶν κατὰ τὴν οἰκουμένην ἐθνῶν παραβάλλειν, ἂν μὴ πολλαχῇ ἀνὰ τὴν οἰκουμένην κατά τε Ἀσίαν καὶ Εὐρώπην ἐσκεδασμένον ἄλλῃ τε τῆς αὐτῶν βασιλείας ᾠκίσθη, ὡς τῇ ἐπιδρομῇ τὰ πολλὰ χρησάμενον· ᾗ δὲ χώρᾳ ἠρέσκετο, ταύτῃ ἐναπολειφθὲν ᾤκησεν. Εἰ μὲν οὖν ἐφρόνει κατὰ τάδε, τὴν αὐτὴν ἐνοικοῦν χώραν, καὶ ὑφ᾽ ἑνὶ γένοιτο βασιλεῖ, οὐδένες οἱ τῶν ἐν τῇ οἰκουμένῃ ἐνίσταντο ἄν, ὥστε μὴ συνομολογεῖν αὐτῷ. Νῦν δὲ ἁπανταχῇ τῆς Ἀσίας ἐπινεμόμενον καὶ ἐν τῇ Εὐρώπῃ, ἐπὶ τῇ Θρᾴκῃ τε καὶ ἐς τὸν Βόσπορον ἐνοικοῦν, ἀπῴκισται τῆς σφῶν αὐτῶν βασιλείας τῆς ἐς τὸ Οὐρδάν. Οἱ μὲν οὖν ἐς τὸν Βόσπορον τὴν ταύτῃ χώραν ἐπινεμόμενοι καὶ τὴν ὅμορον λεηλατοῦντες, τήν τε Τζαρκάσων [1.127] καὶ Μιγκρελίων καὶ Σαρματῶν, καὶ ἀνδράποδα ὡς πλεῖστα ἀγόμενοι ἐπὶ τὸν Βόσπορον, ἐπὶ Καφᾶν πόλιν καὶ ἐς τὴν Μαιώτιδα καλουμένην λίμνην ἀπάγοντες, ὀλίγου τε αὐτὰ ἀποδιδόμενοι τοῖς τε Ἑνετῶν καὶ Ἰανυΐων ἐμπόροις, οὕτω δὴ βιοτεύουσι.

33 Σκύθαι δὲ οἱ ἐν τῇ ἀγορᾷ ἐπὶ ἁμαξῶν τε καὶ ὑποζυγίων τὸν βίον ποιούμενοι, γάλακτι τὰ πολλὰ ἵππων τε καὶ κρέᾳ διαχρώμενοι, οὔτε σίτῳ, οὔτε κριθῇ καταφανεῖς εἰσὶ

beyond Europe and settled in Poland and Russia, or whether the Russians came to this side of the Danube and settled Bulgaria and the lands of the Serbs and of the Illyrians who are by the Adriatic Sea as far as Venice, I have not been able to learn from any previous writer who covered this material, nor am I able to state an opinion that is categorically true.[54]

I return now to the nomadic Skythians, who are the larg- 32
est, most powerful, and bravest race. It would be impossible to compare them to any other people in the world had they not dispersed throughout the world to many parts of Europe and Asia and established their rule elsewhere, through their practice of widespread raiding. When they found a land they liked, they left the other one behind and settled there. If they had been unified, lived in the same land, and had one king, none of the people in this world could have stood in their way or refused to accept their terms. Now they roam everywhere in Asia and Europe, living in Thrace and by the [Crimean] Bosporos, and they have settled far from their kingdom at the Horde. Those by the Bosporos[55] roam that land and plunder the neighboring area, namely the land of the Circassians, Mingrelians,[56] and Russians. They take as many slaves as they can back to the Bosporos, taking them away to the city of Caffa and the Sea of Azov, where they sell them cheaply to Venetian and Genoese merchants, and thus make a living.

The Skythians of the Horde spend their lives on wagons 33
and pack animals, usually consuming the milk and meat of horses. They do not appear to consume wheat or barley, but

διαχρώμενοι, μελίνῃ δὲ τὸ πλέον καὶ σηκάλῃ, λινᾶς τε ἐσθῆτας φοροῦντες ἐς τὸν τῶν λίθων ὄλβον εὐδαιμονέστατοι καὶ πλουσιώτατοι νομίζονται. Τόξοις δὲ χρῶνται, τὸ σύμπαν εἰπεῖν, καὶ ξίφεσι βαρβαρικοῖς, καὶ θυρεοῖς τοῖς τῶν Δακῶν παραπλησίοις, πίλοις δὲ τὰ πολλὰ χρώμενοι, οὔτε ᾗ περὶ Σαρματίαν οἰκοῦντες, οὔτε ἱματίοις ἀπὸ ἐρίων, ὅτι μὴ λινοῖς νομίζουσι. Διήκει δὲ ἡ ἀγορὰ τούτων τῶν Σκυθῶν καὶ τοῦ μεγάλου βασιλέως ἐπὶ ὁδὸν πεντεκαίδεκα ἡμερῶν, ὥστε ἐπινέμεσθαι τὴν χώραν ἐς τὸ ἐπιτηδειότατον σφίσι καταστάντες, καὶ κατ' ὀλίγους διεσκεδασμένοι, ἀφ' ἑκατέρου πλαγίου καθιστάμενοι ἐφ' ἑνός· τήν τε ἀγορὰν ποιοῦνται ἐπὶ μήκιστον, καὶ διανέμονται τὴν χώραν, τοῖς ὑποζυγίοις ἄφθονον παρεχόμενοι, καὶ αὐτοί τε ἐς τάξιν τὴν ἀρίστην ὑπὸ σφῶν νομιζομένην καθιστάμενοι. Κατ' αὐτὸν δὲ μόνον τὸν βασιλέα καὶ τοὺς ταύτῃ ἀρίστους ἐπὶ κύκλους καταστάντες, καὶ περιόδους ποιούμενοι, βασίλειά τε παρέχουσι τῷ βασιλεῖ ἀπὸ ξύλων κατεσκευασμένα. Ἐπιδιελόμενοι [1.128] δὲ εἰς μοίρας ταύτην σύμπασαν τὴν ἀγοράν, ἄρχοντάς τε ἐφιστᾶσι τούτων, καὶ ἐπειδὰν παραγγέλῃ βασιλεύς, χωροῦσιν ἐφ' ὅ τι ἂν γένηται χρεία.

34 Τότε μὲν οὖν, ὡς ἐστρατεύετο Τεμήρης ἐλαύνων τὸν τῆς Ἀσίας στρατόν, καὶ ἐπύθοντο ἐπὶ σφᾶς στρατευόμενον, βασιλεὺς μέντοι τήν τε ἀγορὰν σύμπασαν ἐς στρατὸν ποιησάμενος ἐστρατοπεδεύετο, ἐπὶ πολλοὺς τὸ βάθος ποιησάμενος. Καὶ αὐτὸς μὲν ταύτῃ ταξάμενος ἵετο ὁμόσε ἐπὶ τοὺς πολεμίους, μοῖραν δὲ προέπεμψε τὴν πάροδον καταληψομένους, ᾗ ἔμελλε διαπορεύεσθαι Τεμήρης ὁ βασιλεύς, καὶ διακωλῦσαι ἐκέλευεν, ὅποι δύναιντο, ὡς

rather millet for the most part and rye; they wear linen garments and are considered the most prosperous and richest with regard to the wealth derived from precious stones. Generally speaking, they use bows, barbarian swords, and shields like those of the Wallachians. They usually wear felt hats, but not like those who live around Russia, nor garments made of wool because they do not use linen.[57] The Horde of these Skythians and the Great King extends for a fifteen-day journey, so that they are most adept at distributing the land among themselves, even though they are dispersed into small groups, and they come to one point from different directions. They extend their Horde out over the longest distance, distribute the land, provide abundant pasturage for their pack animals, and thus arrange things for themselves in the best way that accords with their customs. They set up circular forts only for the king himself and the notables and make circuit walls, providing their king with a court constructed out of wood. They divide this entire Horde into sections, appoint lords over them, and whenever the king bids them they depart upon whatever business is necessary.

At that time then, when Timur marched out leading the 34
army of Asia, and the Skythians learned that he was marching against them, their king turned the whole Horde into an army and made camp; this army had considerable depth in numbers.[58] He himself drew it up into formation there and set out against the enemy, sending a contingent in advance to hold the pass through which King Timur would come. He ordered them to block Timur however they could by

κράτιστα μαχομένους τῷ Τεμήρῃ. Οὗτος μὲν δὴ παραλαβὼν τὴν μεθ' ἑαυτοῦ μοῖραν, Τεμήρης δὲ ὡς ἐπῄει τὸν στρατόν, εὐθὺ Ταναΐδος ἐπορεύετο, ἐν δεξιᾷ ἔχων τὸν Καύκασον. Ἐπεὶ δὲ εἰσέβαλεν ἐς τὴν Σκυθικήν, εὗρε τοὺς Σκύθας ἐστρατοπεδευμένους. Καὶ ὡς ᾔσθοντο ἐπιόντα, παρετάσσοντο ὡς ἐς μάχην. Καὶ αὐτός τε ἀντιπαρετάσσετο, καὶ μάχην μέν τινα ἐποιήσαντο ἐν τῇ παρόδῳ, καὶ οὐδὲν πλέον ἔσχε Τεμήρης ἐν τῇ μάχῃ ταύτῃ. Μετὰ δέ, ὡς ἐπηυλίσατο, τῇ ὑστεραίᾳ αὖθις παρετάσσετο, καὶ ἐμαχέσαντο καὶ ἐξεκρούσαντο αὐτόν, ὥστε μηδ' ὁπωσοῦν ἐξεῖναι αὐτὸν παριέναι εἴσω καὶ ἐσβάλλειν ἐς τὴν χώραν. Καὶ αὐτοῦ τε διέφθειρε τοῦ στρατεύματος αὐτοῦ οὐκ ὀλίγους ὑπὸ τῶν Σκυθῶν. Μετὰ δέ, ὡς οὐχ οἷός τε ἐγένετο εἴσω παρελθεῖν διακωλυόμενος, ἀπήγαγε τὸν στρατὸν καὶ ἀνεχώρει ἐπ' οἴκου.

35 Τοῦ δ' ἐπιγενομένου θέρους στρατιὰν ὡς μεγίστην συλλέξας, καὶ ἐπὶ Αἴγυπτον ἐν νῷ ἔχων στρατεύεσθαι, μετὰ δὲ [1.129] συστρέψας, ἤλαυνεν αὖθις ἐπὶ Σκύθας, σταθμοὺς ἐλαύνων ὡς μεγίστους. Καὶ ἔφθη τε δὴ ἐσβαλὼν ἐς τὴν Σκυθικήν, καὶ συνέμιξε μοίρᾳ τινὶ αὐτοῦ ἐπὶ τὴν ἔφοδον ἐπειγομένοις, καὶ συμβαλὼν αὐτῇ ἐτρέψατο. Οὐ μέντοι γε ἀπεγένετο, ὅ τι καὶ ἄξιον λόγου, ἐν ταύτῃ τῇ συμβολῇ. Οἱ γὰρ Σκύθαι μέγιστον δὴ τοῦτο ἔχουσιν ἀγαθόν· ἐν τῇ τροπῇ συστρεφόμενοι αὖθις ἐλαύνουσιν ἐπὶ τοὺς πολεμίους, οὐδέν τι κατὰ τὴν τροπὴν χαλεπὸν ὑφιστάμενοι. Μετὰ δέ, ὡς ἐπὶ τὸν βασιλέα Σκυθῶν ἤλασε, παρετάξατό τε εἰς μάχην, καὶ οἱ Σκύθαι νυκτὸς ἀπεχώρουν ὡσεὶ σταδίους εἴκοσι καὶ ἑκατόν. Ὡς δὲ ἐπῄει Τεμήρης,

fighting vigorously against him. He took command of the contingent that was with him. Timur led his army and proceeded directly to the Don, keeping the Caucasus to his right. But when he invaded Skythia, he found the Skythians encamped. When they realized that he was approaching, they deployed for battle. He deployed in a counterformation, and a battle was fought at the pass in which Timur was unable to accomplish anything. After that he made camp and again deployed for battle on the next day. They fought and repelled him, so that it was impossible for him to gain entry and invade the country. A large part of his army was destroyed there by the Skythians. Afterward, as he was unable to pass through because he was being blocked, he led his army away and returned home.

The following summer he assembled a huge army with 35
the intention of invading Egypt. But then he wheeled around and advanced directly against the Skythians, covering the longest distances on each day's march. He arrived sooner than expected, invaded Skythia and engaged with a contingent that had hurried to meet his attack. He engaged them in battle and routed them. But he did not accomplish much by this battle, for the Skythians have this outstanding advantage: when they are routed, they wheel around and charge at the enemy again, and thus they do not suffer serious harm during routs. After that, when he advanced against the king of the Skythians, he deployed for battle, but the Skythians withdrew at night to a distance of about a hundred and twenty stades. Timur came against them, advancing

διημερεύων ἐπήλαυνε, νυκτὸς αὖθις ἀπεχώρουν οἱ Σκύθαι, ὥστε δὴ ταῦτα ποιούμενος ἔκαμνε τῷ Τεμήρῃ ὁ στρατός, καὶ προεκαλεῖτο ἐς μάχην τῶν Σκυθῶν βασιλέα.

36 Μετὰ δὲ ταῦτα στρατοπεδευσάμενος ἐς τὴν ὑστεραίαν παρετάξατο κατὰ ἴλας. Τεμήρης δὲ παρετάσσετο ἐπὶ πολὺ τὸ βάθος, ἔχων ἐπὶ τὸ δεξιὸν Χαϊδάρην σὺν τοῖς Μασσαγέταις, ἐπὶ δὲ τὸ εὐώνυμον τὸν παῖδα αὐτοῦ Σαχροῦχον σὺν τοῖς Πέρσαις τε καὶ Ἀσσυρίοις, καὶ Χαταΐων, ὅσοι εἵποντο. Ἐπεὶ δὲ συνέμισγον ἀλλήλοις τὰ στρατεύματα, καὶ ἐμάχοντο, μάχης τε καρτερᾶς γενομένης οὐδέν τι πλέον ἔσχον οἱ Σκύθαι. Μετὰ δέ, ὡς ὠσάμενοι εἴχοντο τοῦ ἔργου ἐντονώτερον οἱ Σκύθαι, οὐδ' ὣς ἐτρέψαντο τὸν Τεμήρεω στρατόν, [I.130] ἀπετράποντο, καὶ ἀπέβαλον ἐν ταύτῃ τῇ μάχῃ οὐκ ὀλίγους. Καὶ ἔπεσον ἀπὸ τοῦ στρατοῦ τῶν Περσῶν οὐκ ὀλίγοι. Ὕστερον μέντοι, ὡς οὐδὲν ἔπρασσον οἱ Σκύθαι μαχόμενοι τῷ Τεμήρεω στρατῷ, ἤλαυνον ἐς τὸ πρόσω ἐχόμενοι, ὡς ἐντὸς τῆς χώρας τοὺς πολεμίους ἀποληψόμενοι. Ὁ μέντοι Τεμήρης συστραφεὶς ἤλαυνέ τε αὐτὸς τὰ ἔμπαλιν γενόμενος, καί πως ἔφθη ἐς τὸν Τάναϊν ἀφικόμενος.

37 Μετὰ δὲ ταῦτα ἐς τὴν Ἰβηρίαν τὴν ἐν τῇ Ἀσίᾳ ἀφικόμενος ἀπεχώρει διὰ τῆς Κολχίδος, τὸν Φᾶσιν αὐτοῦ διαβὰς ποταμόν, τὸν ἀπὸ Καυκάσου ῥέοντα ἐπὶ Εὔξεινον πόντον. Ἐσβαλὼν δὲ ἐς τὴν Ἀρμενίων χώραν ἀπήλαυνεν ἐπὶ Χερίης. Ἐπεπράγει δὲ οὕτω αὐτοῦ τὸ στράτευμα ἐς τὴν ἐπὶ Σκύθαις ταύτην ἔλασιν. Τῷ δὲ τρίτῳ ἔτει παρασκευασάμενοι οἱ Σκύθαι ὡς ἀμυνούμενοι βασιλέα Τεμήρην, ἤλασάν τε καὶ ἐπέδραμον χώραν τὴν ὑπὲρ τοὺς Ἀσσυρίους.

during the day, but the Skythians again withdrew during the night, so that by doing this Timur's army was exhausted.[59] So he began to challenge the king of the Skythians to battle.

After that, he encamped and, on the following day, ar- 36
ranged his army by companies. Timur drew up in a deep formation, having Haydar on the right with the Massagetai and on the left his son Shahrukh[60] with as many Persians, Assyrians, and Khataians as were with the army. When the armies engaged with each other and fought, a furious battle ensued and the Skythians were unable to accomplish anything. After that, as the Skythians began to push back, they fought more vigorously, but they were unable to rout Timur's army. Instead, they were routed and lost many men in this battle. Many men from the Persian army also were slain. Later, as the Skythians failed to accomplish anything by fighting against the army of Timur, they withdrew further in order to deal with the enemy in the interior of the land. But Timur turned back and also withdrew, reaching the Don as quickly as he could.

After that, he left and went to Iberia, the one in Asia,[61] by 37
way of Kolchis, crossing over the river Phasis there, the one that flows from the Caucasus to the Black Sea. After invading the land of the Armenians, he marched back to Kherie.[62] That, then, was what his army did in this attack against the Skythians. In the third year the Skythians prepared to fight back against King Timur: they advanced and raided the land

Ἐπρεσβεύετο μὲν οὖν ὕστερον περὶ σπονδῶν πρός τε τὸν βασιλέα τοῦ Οὐρδὰν καὶ πρὸς σύμπασαν τὴν ἀγοράν, ἐπιγαμίαν τε ὑπισχνούμενος, καὶ σπονδάς τε ἐποιήσαντο, ἐφ' ᾧ ξένους τε καὶ φίλους εἶναι ἀλλήλοις.

38 Ὡς δὲ τὰ πρὸς τοὺς Σκύθας καθίστη, ἤλαυνεν ἐπὶ Συρίαν κοίλην. Ἐλάσας δὲ ἐπὶ Δαμασκὸν τήν τε πόλιν ἐπολιόρκει, καὶ μηχανὰς προσφέρων τῷ τείχει εἷλε τε κατὰ κράτος τὴν πόλιν καὶ ἠνδραποδίσατο, πόλιν μεγίστην δὴ τότε οὖσαν καὶ εὐδαιμονεστάτην, καμήλους τε ἐντεῦθεν ἀπήγαγεν ἐς ὀκτακισχιλίους τὰς [1.131] πάσας. Ὄλβον δὴ μέγιστον ἐν ταύτῃ τῇ πόλει ληϊσάμενος ἀπήλαυνεν ὀπίσω ἐπ' οἴκου, λείαν τε πολλὴν καὶ εὐδαίμονα ἀγόμενος. Ἐπρεσβεύετο μέντοι καὶ πρὸς τὸν τῆς Μέμφιος βασιλέα, Σουλδάνον οὕτω δὴ ἐξόχως καλούμενον, καὶ ἠξίου κοίλης Συρίας ὑποχωρῆσαί οἱ, ὥστε ἐς σπονδάς τε ἰέναι αὐτῷ καὶ εἰρήνην ἐπὶ τούτῳ ποιεῖσθαι. Ὡς δὲ προπέμποντι οὐ προεχώρει, ἤδη παρασκευασάμενος, ἑλών τε καὶ ἀνδραποδισάμενος τὴν Δαμασκὸν πόλιν εὐδαίμονα, ἀπεχώρει δι' αἰτίαν, ἥν τινα ἐς τὸ πρόσω τοῦ λόγου ἰὼν σημανῶ.

39 Ὁ δὲ τῆς Μέμφιος βασιλεὺς χώρας τε ἄρχει οὐκ ὀλίγης καὶ εὐδαίμονος· ἀπὸ Ἀράβων ἀρξάμενος Συρίαν τε κοίλην καὶ Παλαιστίνην καὶ σύμπασαν δὴ Αἴγυπτον ὑφ' αὑτῷ ἔχει. Βασιλεὺς δὲ καθίσταται τῆς Μέμφιος καὶ τῆς ἀρχῆς τῆσδε τρόπῳ τοιῷδε. Ὅσοι τῶν ἀνδραπόδων ἀρετῆς τι μεταποιοῦνται ἐν ταύτῃ τῇ χώρᾳ, ὑπὸ βασιλέως καθίστανται ἐς τοὺς στρατιώτας. Εἰσὶ δὲ οὗτοι δορυφοροῦντες βασιλέα, ἀμφὶ τοὺς δισμυρίους, Μαμαλούκιδες καλούμενοι. Ἀπὸ τούτων δέ, ὅσοι ἐπίσημοι ἐπὶ τὸ κατεργάζεσθαι

above the Assyrians.[63] But he later sent envoys to the king of the Horde and the entire Horde in order to make a treaty, offering a marriage alliance. And they made a treaty, agreeing to be each other's friends and allies.

Having settled his relations with the Skythians, Timur 38
set out against Koile Syria. He advanced against the city of Damascus and besieged it and, by bringing siege engines against the walls, he took the city by force and enslaved it.[64] At the time it was a huge city and very wealthy. He led away from there a total of eight thousand camels. Plundering a massive amount of wealth in that city, he marched back home, bringing a lot of valuable loot with him. He had sent an envoy to the king of Cairo, who bears the magnificent title of sultan,[65] and offered to withdraw from Koile Syria so that he could make a treaty with him and establish peace on that basis. It was when his overtures in this matter had failed, seeing as he was already prepared, that he captured and enslaved the prosperous city of Damascus, but he departed for a reason I will disclose in a later section of my narrative.[66]

The king of Cairo rules over a large and prosperous land. 39
Beginning from the land of the Arabs, he controls Koile Syria, Palestine, and all of Egypt. The king of Cairo and of this realm in general is appointed in the following way. All the slaves who display valor in that land are appointed by the king to the ranks of soldiers. These soldiers form the king's guard, about twenty thousand strong, and are called the Mamluks. Among them, those who distinguish them-

ότιοῦν τῶν ὑπὸ βασιλέως τεταγμένων, οὗτοι ἐς τὰς ἀρχὰς κατὰ βραχὺ καθιστάμενοι ἐπὶ μεῖζον χωροῦσι τύχης ἅμα κἀπὶ βασιλέως, καὶ ἐς τὰ πρῶτα τιμῆς ἀξιούμενοι ἐπὶ τοὺς καλουμένους Μελικαμηράδας καθίστανται, ἀφ' ὧν δὴ τῆς χώρας ἐπ' αὐτὴν ἤδη χωροῦσι τὴν βασιλέως χώραν, καὶ ἐπὶ τὴν τῆς Μέμφιος ἀρχὴν καὶ συμπάσης τῆς τε Αἰγύπτου Ἀραβίας τε καὶ Παλαιστίνης καὶ τῶν ἄλλων ἀρχῶν, ὅσαι ὑπὸ τούτῳ τῷ βασιλεῖ [1.132] τάττονται. Μελικαμηράδες εἰσὶν ἀρχαὶ ἐς τὰς πόλεις τὰς ὑπὸ τήνδε τὴν βασιλείαν ἐπισήμους, ἄρχοντες καθιστάμενοι ὑπὸ βασιλέως.

40 Τὴν δὲ πόλιν ταύτην τῆς Μέμφιος μεγίστην δὴ πασῶν τῶν κατὰ τὴν οἰκουμένην πόλεων ἔστε τὴν ἄλλην εὐδαιμονίαν καὶ τὸ πλῆθος τῶν ἀνθρώπων. Ὅ τε γὰρ περίβολος ταύτης τῆς χώρας ἐς ἑπτακοσίους μάλιστα σταδίους διήκων. Εὐνομεῖται δὲ κάλλιστα πασῶν δή, ὧν ἡμεῖς ἴσμεν, πόλεων. Οἰκίας δὲ ἔχειν καλλίστας λέγεται ἐς τὰς πεντήκοντα μυριάδας. Ῥεῖ δὲ διὰ μέσης τῆς πόλεως Νεῖλος ποταμός, κράτιστον ὕδωρ παρεχόμενος, ῥέων ἀπὸ ἀργυροῦ ὄρους. Αἴγυπτον δὲ σύμπασαν ἀρδεύει ἐς τὰ κάλλιστα κατὰ τὰς διώρυχας ὑπὸ τῶν ἑκασταχῇ χωρῶν κατεσκευασμένων, ὥστε τὴν χώραν ἄρδειν ἐπιτηδείως ἔχειν. Οἰκοῦσι δὲ τὴν χώραν ταύτην Μονοθελῆται καὶ Ἰακωβῖται, ἔθνη τε οὐκ ὀλίγα, καὶ τῶν ἐς τὴν τοῦ Ἰησοῦ τοῦ Θεοῦ θρησκείαν τελούντων τε καὶ φρονούντων ἄλλων ἄλλῃ, οὔτε κατὰ τοὺς Ῥωμαίους, οὔτε κατὰ τὰ Ἕλλησι δεδογμένα ἐς τὴν θρησκείαν φρονοῦντες· ἀλλ' ὅσοι μέν εἰσιν Ἀρμένιοι πλεῖστοι ἀνὰ τὴν χώραν ταύτην, Μονοθελῆται δὴ καὶ Ἰακωβῖται καὶ Μανιχαῖοι πάμπολλοι.

selves at carrying out any of the king's orders are soon promoted to higher ranks, advance to a higher fortune in the king's entourage, and claim the highest honor of the Melik *amirs,* as they are called, or the "royal *amirs.*" From that position they advance to the actual position of king and the realm of Cairo and all Egypt, Arabia, Palestine, and all the other dominions that are subject to this king. For the royal *amirs* are the authorities in charge of the distinguished cities of this kingdom, and are lords appointed by the king.

This city of Cairo is the largest of all the cities in the 40
world with respect to the size of its population and its general prosperity. The circumference of its territory is about seven hundred stades. It is the best governed city of all that we know. It is said that it has the most excellent houses, close to five hundred thousand of them.[67] The Nile River flows through the city, providing the best water, and it flows down from the Silver Mountain.[68] It irrigates all of Egypt in the most excellent way by means of the canals that are built through every district, so that it can efficiently irrigate the land. In this land live Monothelites, Jacobites, and many other groups whose religious customs and doctrines belong to those groups who practice and worship the religion of the God Jesus in other ways, that is, not according to the ways of the Romans or the Greeks. But the Armenians are very numerous in this land too, and there are countless Monothelites, Jacobites, and Manicheans.[69]

41 Διήκει δὲ ἡ χώρα τοῦ τῆς Μέμφιος βασιλέως ἀπὸ Λιβύης ἔστε πόλιν Χαλεπίην οὕτω καλουμένην κατὰ τὴν Ἀσίαν· νομίζεται δ' οὗτος ὁ βασιλεὺς ὑπό τε τῶν ἐν τῇ Ἀσίᾳ ἐθνῶν καὶ ὑπὸ τῶν τῆς Λιβύης καὶ δὴ καὶ ὑπὸ τῶν ἐν τῇ Εὐρώπῃ ἀρχιερεύς τε τὰ ἐς τὴν θρησκείαν αὐτῶν καὶ τὰ ἐς τοὺς νόμους τοῦ Μεχμέτεω, παμπόλλων αὐτοῦ ταύτῃ διδασκομένων τοὺς τῆς θρησκείας αὐτοῦ [1.133] νόμους, καὶ ὡς ἀπὸ τῶν παλαιοτέρων ἀρχιερεύς τε ἐνομίσθη, καὶ γράμμασι τοῖς τούτων ἀποδείκνυσθαι ἀκριβέστατα δὴ τὸν τοῦ Μεχμέτεω νόμον. Τὸν δὲ τάφον Ἰησοῦ κατὰ τὴν Παλαιστίνην κατέχοντες μέγα τε ἀποφέρονται κέρδος, καὶ ἄρχοντες μέγιστοι δὴ τοῦ βασιλέως οἴκου ἐς φυλακὴν τοῦ σήματος καθίστανται. Διήκει δὲ Αἴγυπτος ἀπὸ Φάρου τῆς Ἀλεξανδρείας ἔστε Ἰτουραίαν χώραν, ἐπὶ σταδίους μάλιστά πῃ [. . .] Ὁ δὲ Νεῖλος ὁ τῆς Αἰγύπτου ποταμὸς ἐκδιδοῖ ἐς θάλασσαν πρὸς βορρᾶν ἄνεμον κατὰ Ἀλεξάνδρειαν τῆς Αἰγύπτου. Ἐντεῦθεν ἄρχεται ἡ Παλαιστίνη διήκουσα ἔστε ἐπὶ κοίλην Συρίαν. Ἐν ταύτῃ δ' ἔστι τὸ τοῦ Κυρίου Ἰησοῦ σῆμα, κατὰ τὴν Ἱεροσολύμων πόλιν, ᾗ δὴ κατέσκαπται. Καὶ αὗται μὲν παράλιαι χῶραι· κοίλη δὲ Συρία διήκει ἐπὶ Ἀραβίαν ἐπὶ τὴν Ἐρυθρὰν θάλασσαν τῷ πρὸς ἕω ἰόντι. Διαβάντι δὲ τὴν θάλασσαν ψάμμος τε δέχεται αὐτοῦ ταύτῃ διαπορευομένων ἐπὶ τὸ σῆμα τοῦ Μεχμέτεω. Αὕτη δ' ἡ χώρα βασιλέως τῆς Μέμφιος οὖσα, πρὸς δὲ καὶ ἡ Φοινίκη.

42 Δύναμις δέ ἐστι τῷ βασιλεῖ τῷδε κατὰ θάλασσαν ἀξιόχρεως, ἔνθα δὴ ἐφίσταται Σάμος, πλοῖα τε καὶ τριήρεις. Κύπρον τε ὑπηγάγετο, καὶ ἐπὶ Ῥόδον καὶ Κύπρον

The territory of the king of Cairo extends from North Africa to the city that is called Aleppo in Asia. This king is regarded by the peoples of Asia, North Africa, and even Europe as the senior cleric of their religion and of the laws of Muhammad. Countless people have been taught his laws by him there, and he has been regarded as their religious leader from the early days, expounding the law of Muhammad with great precision in their script.[70] They control the sepulcher of Jesus in Palestine and derive much profit from it. The greatest lords of the royal house are appointed guardians of this tomb. Egypt extends from the Lighthouse of Alexandria[71] to the land of the Ituraeans,[72] a distance of about [. . .] stades. The Nile, the river of Egypt, flows northward and empties into the sea at Alexandria in Egypt. Here begins Palestine, which extends until Koile Syria. The tomb of the Lord Jesus is there, at the city of Jerusalem which has been razed to the ground.[73] And these are the coastal lands. Koile Syria extends to Arabia and the Red Sea for one traveling east. As one crosses the sea, the sand there greets those who are traveling to the tomb of Muhammad.[74] This is the land of the king of Cairo, in addition to Phoenicia. 41

This king possesses significant sea power in terms of ships and triremes, and Samos presides over them.[75] He subjected Cyprus and has sent his armies by ship against 42

πέμψαι τά τε πλοῖα καὶ στρατὸν σὺν αὐτοῖς. Διαπλεύσας δὲ τήν τε πόλιν ἐπολιόρκει, καὶ τὴν νῆσον [1.134] ληϊσάμενος προσέβαλέ τε τῷ τείχει ἐπὶ ἡμέρας ἱκανάς· καὶ ὡς οὐδὲν προὐχώρει ἡ τῆς πόλεως αἵρεσις, ἀπεχώρησεν ἐπ' οἴκου. Τὴν μέντοι Κύπρον ὑπηγάγετο, καὶ τόν τε βασιλέα Κύπρου ἄγων τε ᾤχετο· ἀφ' οὗ δῆτα χρόνου φόρον τε ἀπάγει ἡ Κύπρος τῷδε τῷ βασιλεῖ. Δοκεῖ δὲ ἡ νῆσος αὕτη ὑπὸ τόνδε γενέσθαι τὸν βασιλέα τὸ παλαιόν. Κελτοὶ δὲ ὡς ἀφίκοντο ἐπὶ τὸ τοῦ Ἰησοῦ τοῦ Θεοῦ σῆμα, δουλωσάμενοι τήν τε νῆσον ταύτην ὑπηγάγοντο σφίσι, στόλον ἐπαγόμενοι καὶ δύναμιν ἀξιόχρεων. Ἧι καὶ Ἑνετοὶ Ἀμαθοῦν πόλιν εὐδαίμονα χειρωσάμενοι ἐπὶ συχνόν τινα χρόνον διακατεῖχον, ὁρμητήριον τῆς πρὸς Αἴγυπτον ἐμπορίας αὐτῶν. Καὶ τὸ ἐντεῦθεν ἀπὸ Κελτῶν βασιλεῖς διαγενόμενοι βασιλεύουσιν ἐν ταύτῃ τῇ νήσῳ. Νέμονται μέντοι καὶ οἱ Ἄραβες μέρος τι τῆς νήσου ταύτης καὶ πόλιν καλουμένην Ἀμμοχώστην. Τῷ μὲν οὖν βασιλεῖ Μέμφιός τε καὶ Αἰγύπτου πόλεμός τέ ἐστι πρὸς τοὺς ἐν τῇ Ἀραβίᾳ καὶ πρὸς τοὺς ἀπὸ τῆς Λιβύης, διαφερομένους περὶ γῆς ὅρων, μαχεσαμένῳ τά τε ἄλλα καὶ δὴ διὰ Χαλέπιον. Χαλέπιον δὲ πόλις αὐτοῦ ἐν τῇ Ἀσίᾳ μεγάλη τε καὶ εὐδαίμων, καὶ ἐμπορίαν παρεχομένη τῆς τε Ἀσίας καὶ Αἰγύπτου καὶ Ἀραβίας. Ἵππους δὲ ἐκφέρει ἡ χώρα αὕτη γενναίους. Δοκεῖ δὲ καὶ ἥ τε Αἴγυπτος καὶ ἡ πρὸς Λιβύην χώρα φέρειν ἵππους τε ἀγαθοὺς καὶ καμήλους.

43 Τὴν μέντοι Χαλεπίην πόλιν Τεμήρης, ὅτε δὴ καὶ ἐπὶ [1.135] Δαμασκὸν ἐστρατεύετο, ὑπηγάγετο, καὶ κοίλης Συρίας οὐκ ὀλίγην χώραν καταστρεψάμενος ἀπεχώρει δι'

Rhodes and Cyprus. Sailing across, he besieged the city, plundered the island, and attacked the walls for many days. But as he was making no progress in taking the city, he departed for home. Nevertheless, he did eventually subject Cyprus and capture its king before leaving. Since that time Cyprus has paid a tribute to this king.[76] But it seems that this island had come under the power of this king long ago. When the French came to the tomb of the God Jesus, they enslaved this island and subjected it to themselves, bringing their fleet and significant forces.[77] The Venetians seized the prosperous city of Limassol and held it for a long time, making it their base for trade with Egypt. Then, the kings of the French reigned over this island. Nevertheless, the Arabs also hold part of this island and the city called Famagusta. The king of Cairo and Egypt has fought wars against those in Arabia and North Africa over their differences regarding borders; he has fought over other places but especially over Aleppo. Aleppo is his large and prosperous city in Asia and a trading center for Asia, Egypt, and Arabia. The land breeds noble horses. Egypt and the land toward North Africa also seem to produce good horses and camels.

Timur subjected the city of Aleppo when he marched 43
against Damascus,[78] and he conquered a large part of the land of Koile Syria, but then he departed for the following

αἰτίαν τήνδε. Ὁ γάρ τοι τῆς Χαταΐης βασιλεὺς τῶν ἐννέα καλούμενος, οὗτος δ' ἂν καὶ ὁ τῆς Ἰνδίας βασιλεύς, διαβὰς τὸν Ἀράξην τήν τε χώραν ἐπέδραμε τοῦ Τεμήρεω, καὶ ἀνδράποδα ὡς πλεῖστα ἀπάγων ᾤχετο αὖθις ἐπ' οἴκου ἀποχωρῶν. Ἤγαγε δὲ στρατόν, ᾗ λέγεται, ἐς τεσσαράκοντα καὶ ἑκατὸν μυριάδας. Τεμήρης δὲ ὡς ἤλαυνε τὴν ταχίστην, τῆς μὲν χώρας ὑφιέμενος, τῷ δὲ τάχει ἐπειγόμενος διαφυλάξαι, ὅσα τε ἦν αὐτῷ ὁμοροῦντα, τὴν Χαταΐων χώραν, καὶ ἐν τῇ Περσῶν αὖθις καὶ Καδουσίων ἀρχῇ οὐκ ἔφθη καταλαβὼν τὸν βασιλέα. Ἐντεῦθεν διαπρεσβευσάμενος, σπονδάς τε ἐποιήσατο, ἐν νῷ ἔχων ἐπὶ Παιαζήτην τὸν Ἀμουράτεω στρατεύεσθαι. Ἐποιήσατο οὖν σπονδάς, ἐφ' ᾧ ἀπάγειν φόρον ἱκανὸν ὑπὲρ τῆς τῶν Μασσαγετῶν χώρας, ἣν καταστρεψάμενος εἶχεν.

44 Ὡς δὲ πρὸς τοῦτον σπονδάς τε ἐποιήσατο καὶ εἰρήνην, ξυνηνέχθη αὐτῷ τὰ ἐς τοὺς ἀπὸ τῆς κάτω Ἀσίας Τούρκων ἡγεμόνας ἀφῖχθαί τε παρ' ἑαυτόν, καὶ τὰ περὶ τὴν Μελιτήνην. Ἐπολιορκήσαντο ταύτην τῷ Παιαζήτῃ. Παρασκευασάμενος δὲ στρατὸν μέγιστον ἤλαυνεν ἐπὶ Σεβάστειαν, πόλιν τῆς Καππαδοκίας εὐδαίμονα. Δοκεῖ δὲ αὕτη ἡ πόλις βασίλεια γενέσθαι τοῦ πρότερον βασιλέως [1.136] Τούρκων, καὶ ἀπὸ ταύτης ὁρμωμένους τοὺς Τούρκους τὸ παλαιὸν χώραν ὑπαγομένους τῆς τε Ἀσίας οὐκ ὀλίγην, ἐς τὸν Ἑλλήσποντόν τε καὶ ἀντικρὺ Βυζαντίου χώραν τὴν ἐς τὴν Ἀσίαν ἐπιδραμεῖν χειρὶ πολλῇ ἀφικομένους. Τεμήρης μὲν οὖν ὡς ἀφίκετο, ἐπολιόρκει τὴν πόλιν· Παιαζήτης δὲ ἀπῆν τότε, ἐπὶ Λεβάδειαν τῆς Βοιωτίας καὶ ἐπὶ Πελοπόννησον

reason. The king of Khatai, who is known as the "king of the nine" and is also the king of India, crossed the Araxes and raided Timur's land. He seized as many captives as he could and departed, returning home.[79] He led an army, it is said, that was one hundred and forty times ten thousand strong. Timur advanced as quickly as possible, abandoning that land and hurrying to defend his territories that bordered on the land of the Khataians. Coming to the kingdoms of the Persians and the Kadousioi, he was not in time to catch the king. At that point he sent an envoy and made a treaty, because he intended to march against Bayezid, the son of Murad. So he made a treaty, whose terms were that a substantial tribute would be paid on behalf of the land of the Massagetai, which he had conquered.

When he had made a treaty and peace with this king, he 44
became involved in the matter concerning the rulers of the Turks from Asia Minor who had come to him, and also the business of Melitene, which had been besieged by Bayezid.[80] He prepared a huge army and advanced to Sebasteia, a prosperous city in Kappadokia. It seems that this city had been the royal court of the previous sultan of the Turks, and it was from this city that the Turks had set out in the past to subject much of Asia.[81] With large forces, they had raided in Asia as far as the Hellespont and the land across from Byzantion. When Timur arrived, he besieged the city. Bayezid was absent at that time, campaigning against Lebadeia in Boiotia and against the Peloponnese and Thessaly. He had

καὶ Θετταλίαν στρατευόμενος. Κατέλιπε δὲ ἐν τῇ Σεβαστείᾳ στρατόν τε τὸν τῆς Ἀσίας καὶ παῖδα Ὀρθογρούλην, καὶ ταύτῃ καταστησάμενος αὐτὸς μὲν ἐπὶ Πελοπόννησον ἐστρατεύετο. Ἔνθα δὴ πυθομένῳ, ὡς Τεμήρης ἐλάσας πολιορκοίη Σεβάστειαν, ἤλαυνε τὰ ἔμπαλιν γενόμενος, καὶ οὐκ ἐξεγένετο αὐτῷ ἐσβαλεῖν ἐς τὴν Πελοπόννησον.

45 Ἐπειγόμενος δὲ τὴν ἐπὶ τὴν Ἀσίαν πορείαν ἐπύθετο ἁλῶναί τε τὴν πόλιν καὶ ἀνδραποδισάμενον οἴχεσθαι αὖθις ἀπιόντα ἐπὶ Χερίης. Ὡς γὰρ δὴ προσέβαλεν ἐπὶ ἡμέρας ἱκανάς, οἱ ἀπὸ τῆς πόλεως ἐξεκρούσαντο τὸν Τεμήρεω στρατόν. Ἐνταῦθα ἔχων μεθ' ἑαυτοῦ ὀρυκτὰς ἐς ὀκτακισχιλίους τὸν ἀριθμόν, ὑπώρυσσον ὑπὸ τὴν γῆν ὀρύγματα φέροντα ἐς τὸ τεῖχος τῆς πόλεως ἁπανταχῇ. Καὶ ἔνια μὲν οἱ τῆς πόλεως ᾔσθοντό τε, καὶ ἀντορύσσοντες καὶ αὐτοὶ ἐξεκρούσαντο· τὰ δὲ πλέω ἠνύετο αὐτῷ ἅτε πολυχειρίᾳ ἐργαζομένων. Ὡς δὴ ἤδη τὰ τείχη ὀρώρυκτο καὶ ἐπὶ ξύλων ἤδη ἦν μετέωρα, πῦρ ἐνιέντες κατεβλήθη τε τὰ τείχη αὐτόματα, καὶ [1.137] ἐπιπεσόντες ἐνταῦθα οἱ τοῦ Τεμήρεω στρατιῶται εἰσέπιπτον ἐς τὴν πόλιν, καὶ οὕτω κατέσχον αὐτήν.

46 Καὶ τοὺς μὲν ἄνδρας, παρεγγυήσαντος τοῦ βασιλέως, αὐτίκα ἑλόντες τὴν πόλιν διεχρήσαντο· παῖδας δὲ καὶ γυναῖκας τῆς πόλεως ἐς ἕνα χῶρον ἀγαγὼν τήν τε ἵππον ἐπαφεὶς κατεχρήσατο, ὥστε μηδένα τῶν τῆς πόλεως, μήτε ἄνδρα, μήτε γυναῖκα, μήτε παῖδα, περιγενέσθαι, οἰκτρότατα δὲ ξυμπάντων τῶν ἐν τῇ πόλει θανόντων. Λέγεται δὲ γενέσθαι ἀνθρώπους ἀμφὶ τὰς δώδεκα μυριάδας. Πρὸς δὲ καὶ ἐλεφαντιώντων ἐν ταύτῃ τῇ πόλει πλῆθος εὑράμενον

left the army of Asia in Sebasteia with his son Ertoğrul; having made that arrangement, he himself was campaigning in the Peloponnese.[82] When Bayezid learned that Timur had advanced to Sebasteia and was besieging it, he retreated and marched back, and so he did not manage to invade the Peloponnese.

As Bayezid was hurrying to Asia he learned that the city had been taken and that Timur had taken captives and left again to go back to Kherie. Timur had attacked it for many days, but the people of the city had repelled his army. He had with him about eight thousand sappers who dug underground tunnels that led up to the walls of the city on all sides. Some of the people inside realized this and dug countertunnels and themselves repelled the enemy. But Timur had completed more, given that he had a larger workforce. So, when the walls had been undermined and were propped up on wooden beams, they set fire to these and the walls collapsed of their own accord. At that point Timur's soldiers attacked the city, stormed it, and thus captured it.[83] 45

On King Timur's orders, the men were killed as soon as the city was taken. The women and children of the city were gathered in one place and the cavalry were let loose to cut them down, so that not one person from this city survived—not a man, woman, or child: everyone in this city died in a most pitiable way. It is said that its population was about one hundred and twenty thousand. It is also said that he found in this city a multitude of people suffering from 46

λέγεται κελεῦσαι ἀνελεῖν. Τούτους μὲν οὖν, ὅπῃ ᾔσθετο περιόντας, οὐκέτι εἴα ζῶντας περινοστεῖν, ἀλλ᾽ ὡς ᾔσθετο, τοῦ ζῆν ἀπήλλαττεν, οὐ θέμις εἶναι φάσκων εἰς τοιαύτην γενομένους τύχην περιϊέναι τούς τε λοιποὺς τῶν ἀνθρώπων διαφθείροντας καὶ αὐτοὺς ὡς τὰ πολλὰ παραπαίοντας. Λέγεται δὲ ταύτης τῆς πόλεως τὴν συμφορὰν ὑπερβαλέσθαι τὰς πώποτε γενομένας τῶν πόλεων ξυμφοράς.

47 Ὀρθογρούλην δὲ τὸν παῖδα Παιαζήτεω συλλαβὼν ζῶντα ἐπὶ ἡμέρας περιῆγε, μετὰ δὲ ταῦτα ἀνελεῖν ἐκέλευσε. Παιαζήτης δὲ ὡς ἐπύθετο ἕκαστα μετ᾽ οὐ πολύ, ἅτε δὴ ἡ πόλις ἁλοῦσα διεφθάρη, καὶ ὁ παῖς αὐτοῦ μετ᾽ οὐ πολὺ ἤγγελτο τελευτῆσαι ὑπὸ βασιλέως Τεμήρεω, ξυμφορᾷ τε ἐχρῆτο ὡς μάλιστα καὶ ἐν πένθει ἦν. Διαβάς τε γὰρ δὴ ἐς τὴν Ἀσίαν, ὡς βοσκόν τινα ἑωράκει αὐλοῦντα, λέγεται δὴ εἰπεῖν, [1.138] ἐπιδηλώσαντα τὸ πάθος αὐτῷ, οἷον ἦν, "αὐλεῖ δὴ ᾠδήν, οὔτε Σεβάστειαν ἀπώλεσεν, οὔτε παῖδα Ὀρθογρούλην." Ἦν γὰρ δή, ὡς λέγεται, Ὀρθογρούλης τῶν ἡλίκων τὰ πάντα κράτιστος, καὶ ἐξηγήσασθαι ἐπὶ πόλεμον ἱκανός· διὸ δὴ καὶ ἐν τῇ Ἀσίᾳ κατέλιπεν αὐτόν, ἐπιτρέψας τὴν ἀρχὴν αὐτῷ, ᾗ δοκοίη αὐτῷ ἐς τὸ ἐπιτηδειότατον καθιστάναι. Κατὰ μὲν οὖν τὴν ἐς τὴν Σεβάστειαν ἔλασιν Τεμήρεω τοσαῦτα ἐγένετο.

48 Μετ᾽ οὐ πολὺ δὲ καὶ ἡ πρεσβεία ἐφίκετο παρὰ τὸν Λαίλαπα Παιαζήτην, καὶ ἐκέλευσεν αὐτὸν ἀποδοῦναι τε τὴν χώραν τοῖς ἡγεμόσι, καὶ τάς τε δισχιλίας καμήλους βουτύρου, καὶ σκηνὰς δὴ δισχιλίας, αἷς εἰώθασιν οἱ νομάδες ἀνὰ τὴν Ἀσίαν χρῆσθαι, καὶ ἐν τοῖς ναοῖς τοῖς ὑπὸ τὴν Παιαζήτεω ἀρχὴν μνημονεύεσθαι αὐτὸν ὡς βασιλέα, καὶ

leprosy and he ordered them to be killed. In fact, wherever he discovered such people he would not permit them to go on living. As soon he discovered them he would take their lives, saying that it was not right for people who had fallen into such circumstances to go about causing the death of even more people, and that they were crazy, for the most part. It is said that the misfortune suffered by this city surpassed any misfortune that any city has ever experienced.

Timur captured Ertoğrul, the son of Bayezid, alive and 47
led him around for some days, but afterward he ordered his execution.[84] When Bayezid, shortly afterward, learned of each of these events—that the city had been taken and destroyed and that his son had been killed shortly afterward on the orders of King Timur—he regarded them as the greatest calamity and was stricken with grief. He crossed over into Asia, and there he saw a certain shepherd playing his pipes, and reportedly said something like this that revealed his sorrow: "He is playing the pipes, having lost neither Sebasteia nor his son Ertoğrul." For it is said that Ertoğrul was the most powerful among his peers and capable of waging wars. That is why Bayezid had left him in Asia and entrusted his realm to him, because he thought that he would manage it in the most efficient way. That is what happened during Timur's attack on Sebasteia.

It was shortly afterward that the embassy came to Baye- 48
zid the Hurricane, telling him to return the land to the rulers; to supply the two thousand camel-loads of butter; the two thousand tents, which the nomads in Asia typically use; that Timur should be commemorated as king in the shrines under Bayezid's authority; and that he should use the

νομίσματι δὲ χρῆσθαι τῷ βασιλέως Τεμήρη ἐς σύμπασαν τὴν ἀρχὴν αὐτοῦ, καθελόντα τὸ ἑαυτοῦ νόμισμα. Πρὸς δὲ καὶ τῶν παίδων αὐτοῦ ἕνα ᾐτοῦντο παραγίνεσθαι ἐς τὰς Τεμήρεω θύρας. Καὶ ἢν ταῦτα ποιῇ, φίλον τε καὶ ἐπιτήδειον ἔσεσθαι Τεμήρεω βασιλέως· ἢν δὲ μὴ ποιήσῃ, χρῆσθαι αὐτῷ ὡς πολεμίῳ βασιλέα Τεμήρην. Ἧι δὲ δὴ λέγεται θυμωθέντα τὸν Παιαζήτην ἐκεῖνο δὴ τὸ ἔπος εἰπεῖν, ὃ καὶ πρότερόν μοι δεδήλωται, ὡς ἢν μὴ ἐπικαταβὰς ἀφίκοιτο ἐπ' αὐτόν, τὴν γυναῖκα αὐτοῦ ἐς τρὶς ἀποπεμψάμενον [1.139] ἀπολαβεῖν αὖθις· ὃ δὴ αἰσχύνην φέρει μεγάλην, εἰρῆσθαι ὁτῳοῦν τὸ ἔπος τοῦτο.

49 Προθέμενος μὲν οὖν τὰ παρὰ τῆς πρεσβείας αὐτοῦ τὸ Παιαζήτεω ἔπος ὁ Τεμήρης οὐκέτι ἐς ἀναβολὴν ἐποιεῖτο τὴν ἔλασιν, καὶ αὐτίκα παρασκευασάμενος στρατὸν τόν τε παρ' ἑαυτῷ Σκυθῶν τῶν νομάδων καὶ Τζαχαταΐδων, ἐς ὀγδοήκοντα, ὡς λέγεται, μυριάδας, ἤλαυνεν ἐπὶ Παιαζήτην διὰ Φρυγίας τε καὶ Λυδίας τὴν πορείαν ποιούμενος. Παιαζήτης δὲ ὡς ἐξορκώσας Τεμήρην, ἢν μὴ ὡς ἠδύνατο κράτιστα παρεσκευασμένος ἐπήει, συναγείρας στρατὸν ὡς ἠδύνατο μέγιστον, συμπαραλαβὼν καὶ τοὺς Τριβαλλοὺς αὐτοῦ δορυφόρους, ἐς μυρίους μάλιστά που γενομένους τούτους, ἐφ' οἷς δὲ μέγα ἐφρόνει ὡς, ὅποι παρατυγχάνοιεν, ἀνδρῶν ἀγαθῶν γενομένων, καὶ προθέμενος ὡς Ἀλέξανδρος ὁ Φιλίππου τοὺς Μακεδόνας ἔχων μεθ' ἑαυτοῦ καὶ ἐς τὴν Ἀσίαν διαβάς, Δαρεῖον αἰτιασάμενος τῆς ἐς τοὺς Ἕλληνας Ξέρξεω ἐλάσεως, τῷ ἑαυτοῦ ἐλάσσονι δὴ στρατῷ ἐπιὼν κατεστρέψατο, καὶ τὴν Ἀσίαν ὑφ' αὐτῷ ἐποιήσατο, ἔστε ἐπὶ Ὕφασιν τῆς Ἀσίας

coinage of King Timur throughout his realm, and abolish his own coins.[85] In addition, the envoys demanded that one of his sons attend the Porte of Timur. If he were to do these things, he would be a friend and ally of King Timur, but if he were not to do them, then King Timur would treat him as an enemy. It was at this point, it is said, that Bayezid grew angry and spoke the words that I mentioned earlier,[86] that if he did not come and attack him, then he should renounce his wife three times and then take her back again. These words would bring great shame upon anyone to whom they are spoken.

Citing Bayezid's words that his envoys had reported back 49
to him, Timur no longer delayed his advance, and immediately prepared an army of the nomadic Skythians who were with him and the Chaghadai, a total, they say, of eight hundred thousand men. He advanced against Bayezid, making his way through Phrygia and Lydia. As Bayezid had bound Timur by oath to come against him as fully prepared as he might be,[87] he assembled the largest army possible, including his Serb bodyguards, who were about ten thousand strong. He took great pride in them because they were brave men in whatever circumstance they found themselves. He cited Alexander, the son of Philip, who took the Macedonians with him and crossed over into Asia, blaming Darius [III] for Xerxes's war against the Greeks. Alexander defeated him in an attack with a smaller army, subjected Asia to himself, and even reached the Hyphasis River in Asia. So

ἐληλάκει· ἐπίστευε δὲ καὶ αὐτὸς τῷ ἑαυτοῦ στρατεύματι ἐπιὼν καθαιρήσειν ταχὺ πάνυ τὴν Τεμήρεω βασιλείαν καὶ ἐπὶ Ἰνδοὺς ἀφικέσθαι.

50 Παραλαβὼν δὴ οὖν τό τε Εὐρώπης καὶ Ἀσίας στράτευμα, ἐς δώδεκα μυριάδας, ἵετο ὁμόσε ἐπὶ τὸν [1.140] Τεμήρην, φθῆναι αὐτὸν βουλόμενος ἐν τῇ χώρᾳ ἐστρατοπεδευμένον πρὸς τῷ Εὐφράτῃ, ἐν νῷ ἔχων βασιλεῖ Τεμήρῃ μαχέσασθαι. Τεμήρης δὲ ἐπῄει διὰ Φρυγίας ἐλαύνων. Παιαζήτης δὲ διὰ τῆς Καππαδοκίας ἐπείγετο, φθῆναι αὐτὸν πρὸς τῷ Εὐφράτῃ κατὰ τὴν Ἀρμενίων χώραν βουλόμενος. Ὡς δὲ ἐν τῇ Ἀρμενίων γενόμενος χώρᾳ ἐπύθετο Τεμήρην ἤδη ἐν τῇ ἑαυτοῦ ἀναστρέφεσθαι χώρᾳ, διὰ Φρυγίας ἐλάσαντα, τὰ ἔμπαλιν γενόμενος ἐπορεύετο εὐθὺ Φρυγίας, ὡς δὴ καὶ Τεμήρην αὐτὸν ἴεσθαι ἐπυνθάνετο. Ταχὺ δὲ ἐπειγομένων ἠνύετο ὁ δρόμος, ὥστε τὰ στρατεύματα αὐτοῦ πολλὴν διανύσαντα πορείαν δι᾽ ὀλίγου ἔκαμνέ τε χαλεπῶς φέροντα, καὶ ἤχθετο αὐτῷ, ὅτι μὴ ἐν δέοντι ἐχρήσατο τῇ ἑαυτοῦ τόλμᾳ. Ξυνέβαινε δὲ καὶ τῷ μηδενὶ ἐπιτρέπειν τοῦ στρατοῦ ἐπὶ πυροὺς καὶ κριθὰς ἐπὶ Προύσης, ὥρα ἦν παραβάλλειν τὸν ἵππον, χαλεπαίνειν τε αὐτῷ τὰ στρατεύματα καὶ ἀπαγορεύειν. Ἀπείρηται γὰρ μηδενὶ ἐξεῖναι εἰς πυροὺς εἰσιέναι· ὅν τινα δ᾽ ἂν λάβοι εἰσελθόντα, ἐτιμωρεῖτο.

51 Λέγεται δὲ αὐτῷ ἐστρατοπεδευμένῳ περὶ Καππαδοκίαν πνεῦμα βιαιότατον, ἐπιπνεῦσαν τῷ στρατεύματι αὐτοῦ, τάς τε σκηνὰς ἀπενεγκάμενον ἐπὶ πολὺ ἀποσπάσαι καὶ μετεώρους ποιησάμενον καταλαβεῖν, καὶ τοῦτο κατ᾽ αὐτοῦ γενέσθαι οἰωνὸν εἰς τὰ στρατεύματα. Μετὰ δὲ [1.141]

Bayezid too now believed that by attacking with his own army he would quickly destroy Timur's kingdom and go as far as the Indians.

Taking the army of Asia and Europe, then, which was one 50
hundred and twenty thousand strong, Bayezid marched against Timur, wanting to catch him encamped in the land by the Euphrates, and intending to engage King Timur in battle. But Timur marched against him, advancing through Phrygia. Meanwhile, Bayezid was hurrying through Kappadokia, wanting to catch him by the Euphrates, in the land of the Armenians. When he reached the land of the Armenians, he learned that Timur had already entered his own territories, advancing through Phrygia, and so he turned back and headed straight for Phrygia, as he learned that Timur was now there. As Bayezid was hastening, the pace was fast and his armies covered a great distance in a short time, so that they became exhausted and unhappy with him. They resented the fact that he was making bad use of his famous daring. His armies were also angry and losing patience with him because he allowed no one in the army to take wheat and barley at Prousa, even though it was time to fodder the horses. For no one was allowed to go into the town for wheat; whomever he caught going in he punished.

It is said that while Bayezid was encamped in Kappado- 51
kia a very violent wind blew on his army, and it ripped up the tents, lifted them away into the air, and dragged them over a great distance. This was construed by the army as a bad omen for him. After that, when he was marching in

ταῦτα ὡς ἀπελαύνοντι ἐπὶ τὴν Φρυγίαν ἐσκήνωτο, τήν τε σκηνὴν αὐτοῦ ἐς τρεῖς συστησαμένους τοὺς ἀμφ' αὐτὸν παῖδας αὐτόματον πεσοῦσαν, εἴτε τῆς γῆς μὴ δυναμένης κατέχειν τὰ σχοινία τῆς σκηνῆς, εἴτε καὶ ἄλλῃ πῃ ξυνέβη τοῦτο· τῇ τε γῇ ἀπειρῆσθαι αὐτῷ, μὴ ἐπιβαίνειν τῆς Φρυγίας, Ἑλλήνων τέ τινες αὐτοῦ παραγενόμενοι ἢ Τριβαλλῶν οἰωνίζοντο. Λέγεται μὲν οὖν καὶ πρὶν ἢ ἐπὶ τὴν Ἀσίαν διαβῆναι, Ἀλίην τὸν Χαρατίνεω παῖδα, ἄνδρα δὴ τῶν παρ' ἑαυτῷ τὰ ἐς σύνεσιν οὐδενὸς λειπόμενον, χρηματίσαι αὐτῷ μὴ στρατεύεσθαι ἐπὶ Τεμήρην, τρόπῳ δὲ ὅτῳ δύναιτο ἀσφαλεστάτῳ διαλύεσθαι αὐτῷ τὴν πρὸς Τεμήρην διαφοράν. Ἐκέλευε δὲ ἑαυτὸν πέμπειν, καὶ ὑπισχνεῖτο διαλλάξαι τε αὐτῷ βασιλέα Τεμήρην, ᾗ ἂν αὐτὸς βούλοιτο. Τὸν δὲ ὑπολαβόντα φάναι, ὡς οὐ τῇ ἐκείνου συνέσει πιστεύων ἀφίκοιτο ἐπὶ μέγα εὐδαιμονίας, ἡγεμόνας τοσούτους καταστρεψάμενον, ἀλλὰ τῇ ἑαυτοῦ ὁρμῇ τε καὶ γενναιότητι· τύχῃ δὲ εἰπεῖν καὶ τόλμῃ ἐπιτραπομένους τῶν βασιλέων πολλούς, καὶ δίχα συνέσεως μεγάλης, ἐπιδείξασθαι ἔργα, συνέσει δὲ τὸ πᾶν ἐπιτρέψαντας αἴσχιστα ἀπολέσθαι.

52 Μετὰ δὲ ταῦτα, ὡς ἐν τῇ Ἀρμενίων ἐγένετο ἐπὶ Τεμήρην στρατευόμενος, ἐβουλεύετο ὡς δὴ κράτιστα τὴν μάχην ποιήσαιτο. Μεταπεμψάμενος δὲ τοὺς ἀρίστους ἐς βουλὴν καθίστατο. Καί τινων γενομένων ἐπ' ἀμφότερα ταῖς γνώμαις, λέγεται Πραΐμην [I.142] τὸν Ἀλίεω, μέγιστον δὴ παρὰ τῷ Παιαζήτῃ δυνάμενον, βουλεύοντα λέξαι τοιάδε. "Ὦ βασιλεῦ, ἐπ' ἄνδρας παρασκευάζῃ στρατεύεσθαι τά τε πολέμια λεγομένους εἶναι ἀγαθοὺς ὑπὸ πάντων, ὅσοι δὴ

Phrygia he made camp, but his tent collapsed of its own accord on three boys who were part of his entourage; and this happened either because the ground could not hold down the tent ropes or for some other reason. Some Greeks who were there with him, or some Serbs, took this as an omen that the earth itself was preventing him from setting foot in Phrygia. It is said also that, before he crossed over into Asia, Ali, the son of Hayreddin, a man second to none in prudence among his retinue,[88] tried to persuade him not to march against Timur and to find the safest way that he could to settle his differences with Timur. Ali asked to be sent himself and promised to reconcile him with King Timur on whatever terms he wanted. But Bayezid responded by saying that it was not by relying on Ali's prudence that he had arrived at such great prosperity and had conquered so many rulers, but rather through his own boldness and bravery. He said that many of the kings who had entrusted themselves to chance and daring had accomplishments to show for it, even when they lacked great prudence, but those who staked everything on prudence had been shamefully destroyed.

After that, when he was in Armenian territory in his 52
march against Timur, Bayezid was deliberating on how best to fight the battle. He summoned his leading men and convened a council. Some of them had different opinions, and it is said that İbrahim, the son of Ali and a man who was highly influential with Bayezid,[89] gave the following advice: "O sultan, you are preparing to march against men who are said by all to be skilled in military matters, by all, certainly, who

τῆς τε γνώμης αὐτῶν καὶ ἀρετῆς ἐπειράσαντο. Τούτοις ἐγὼ εἰς λόγους ὡς τὰ πολλὰ ἀφικόμην, ἐπυθόμην τήν τε ἀρετὴν εἶναι παντὸς λόγου ἀξίαν, καὶ πλῆθος δὴ πολλαπλάσιον τοῦ ἡμετέρου στρατεύματος ἀγγέλλεται ἡμῖν εἶναι τὸ Τεμήρεω στράτευμα· ὥστε κατ' ἄμφω δὴ τούτω οὔτ' ἂν συμβουλεύσαιμι θαρροῦντα τῷ ἡμετέρῳ στρατῷ ἰέναι ὁμόσε ἐς τὸ Τεμήρεω στρατόπεδον. Ἀλλ' οὐδέν, εἰ μαχεσάμενοι περιγενοίμεθα, εἴη ἂν ἡμῖν ὄφελος ὁτῳοῦν. Εἰ μὲν γὰρ ἐς τὴν ἐκείνων ἐσβάλλοντες ἐμαχόμεθα, ἦν ἂν ὁμοῦ ξύμπαντα ἀγαθά, περί τε τῆς ἀρχῆς ἐκείνου ἀγωνίζεσθαι καὶ περὶ τῆς δυνάμεως. Νῦν δὲ καὶ ἢν εἰς μάχην καθιστάμενοι μαχεσώμεθα, οὐδὲν διὰ τοῦτο ἡμῖν ἔσται. Ἢν δέ, ὅπερ ἀπεύχομαι, ἐς τοὐναντίον ἡμῖν τὰ πράγματα περιστῇ, σκόπει δή, ὦ βασιλεῦ, ὁποῖον ἀποβήσεταί σοι ἀπὸ τούτου, τήν τε δύναμιν ἅμα καὶ βασιλείαν ἀποβαλόντι. Ξυμβαίνει δὴ οὖν σοι μὴ ἀπὸ τοῦ ἴσου ἀγωνίζεσθαι σοὶ κἀκείνῳ. Πείθομαι δὲ μηδὲ σύμπαντι τῷ στρατεύματι Τεμήρην βασιλέα, εἰ σωφρονεῖ, τὴν μάχην ποιήσασθαι, ἀλλ' ἐς μοίρας ἱκανὰς διελόμενος αὐτοῦ τὰ [1.143] στρατεύματα διαπειρᾶσθαι ἡμῶν· καὶ εἰ μὲν τῇ μιᾷ μοίρᾳ ἐναντία ἰόντες περιγενοίμεθα, τῇ ἑτέρᾳ αὖθις μετ' οὐ πολὺ χρησάμενος, ἐς ὃ δὴ ἀπαγορεύειν ἡμᾶς καμόντας μαχομένοις ἐκείνοις· οὐ γὰρ τοιοῦτόν ἐστιν τὸ ἐκείνου στράτευμα, οἷον ἐπειδὰν ἐς χεῖρας ἀφίκηται, αὐτίκα ἐς φυγὴν τραπόμενον οἴχεσθαι· ἀλλὰ καὶ ἐν τῇ τροπῇ βέλτιον ἡμῶν, ἀναλαμβάνειν τε σφᾶς συνιόντας πυνθάνομαι, καὶ ἀναμαχομένους μεγάλα ἀποδείκνυσθαι ἔργα. Δοκεῖ οὖν μοι ὁμόσε μέντοι μὴ ἴεσθαι ἐπὶ τὸ Τεμήρεω στράτευμα, διὰ δὲ

have made trial of their determination and valor. I myself have spoken with them many times and have ascertained that their valor is all that it is made out to be; moreover, we have been informed that Timur's army is many times larger than ours. Thus, for both these reasons, I would not advise that we place our hopes in our army attacking Timur's camp. Even if we should win the battle, we will derive no benefit whatsoever. If we were about to fight having invaded their land, then there would be every good reason for doing so, as we would be contesting his realm and his power. But now, even if it comes to a battle, there is nothing in it for us. Suppose that—and I pray this does not happen—it goes against us: consider, O sultan, what the outcome of this will be for you, when you lose your power together with your throne. Anyway, you are not even fighting him on equal terms. I am sure that King Timur, if he is sensible, will not commit his entire army to the battle, but he will test our strength by dividing his armies into large contingents. Then, even if we manage to overcome the one contingent that comes against us, he will quickly deploy the next one, and in that way will wear us down as we tire from fighting them. For his army is not the sort that is routed and flees when it comes to blows. Even in flight it is better than ours, for I have learned that they can regroup and recover, and fight again so as to perform great deeds. In sum, I believe that we should not attack Timur's army but follow it by traveling through the

τῶν ὀρέων πορευομένους ἐφέπεσθαι, ὅτι ἐγγύτατα γενομένους, καὶ ὅποι τε προχωροίη, κακοῦντας ἐν μέρει τὸ ἐκείνου στράτευμα. Δῆλα δ' ἂν γένοιτο ταύτῃ, ὡς οὔτε ἐπιδρομῇ χρήσαιτ' ἂν ἔτι τοῦ λοιποῦ ἐφισταμένων ἡμῶν καὶ ἐπισπομένων ἐγγύτατα, σιτίζεσθαί τε οὐκ ἂν ἔτι τοῦ λοιποῦ δύναιτο ἱκανῶς, ὥστε ἀποχρῶντα εἶναι αὐτῷ τὰ ἐπιτήδεια. Ἐπειδὰν δ' ἐν τῇ ἐκείνου γενώμεθα ἐπισπόμενοι τῷ Τεμήρεω[3] στρατεύματι, τηνικαῦτα δὴ ὁρμωμένῳ οἴκαδε τῷ στρατεύματι καὶ ἐχομένῳ τῆς οἴκαδε ὁδοῦ ἐπέχοιμέν τε ἂν καὶ ἀμυνόμενοι μαχεσαίμεθα."

53 Ταῦτα εἰπόντος τοῦ Πραΐμεω, ταύτῃ ἐτράποντο καὶ οἱ λοιποὶ τὴν ψῆφον τιθέμενοι. Βασιλεὺς δὲ Παιαζήτης λέγεται εἰπεῖν τάδε. "Τὸ πλῆθος ἔοικεν, ὦ ἄνδρες, ᾗ ἐγὼ τεκμαίρομαι, ὑμᾶς δεδίττεσθαι. Ἀλλ' ἐκεῖνο δὴ καὶ ὑμεῖς ἴστε, ὡς πλήθους οὐδὲν ὑγιές ἐστιν, ὅπου ἂν ἀρετὴ παραγένηται. Ἴστε δὴ καὶ Ξέρξην τὸν Δαρείου, βασιλέα Περσῶν, πλήθη ὁπόσα ἀγόμενος καὶ ἐς τὴν Εὐρώπην διαβὰς παρὰ βραχὺ ἐπῄει ἀποθανούμενος, εἰ μὴ [1.144] Μαρδόνιος ὑποστὰς ἐπήμυνεν αὐτῷ τὸν ὄλεθρον ἐπανιόντι ἐς Σοῦσα. Καὶ Ἀλέξανδρον ἴστε, ὡς Δαρείῳ μαχεσάμενος τήν τε βασιλείαν ἀφείλετο καὶ αὐτὸν ἀπέκτεινε. Καὶ πολλοὺς δὲ πυθέσθαι οἶμαι τῶν ἡμετέρων Τούρκων ὀλίγῃ χειρὶ μεγάλα ἀποδείξασθαι ἔργα. Καὶ ἡμεῖς δ' ἐν τῇ Εὐρώπῃ θαμὰ δὲ ἐπὶ τὰς μάχας ἰόντες γένη τε ἐτρεψάμεθα γενναιότατα δὴ γενόμενα τῶν ἐς τὴν οἰκουμένην ἐθνῶν, Κελτούς τε καὶ Παίονας. Καὶ διὰ ταῦτα μὴ οὕτω φαυλίζων ἡμᾶς ἐς γενναιότητα κακίους τε καὶ φαυλοτέρους ἀποφαίνου Σκυθῶν τε καὶ Τζαχαταΐων, οἳ ξίφει οὐδεπώποτε

mountains, come as close as we can to them, and then, when he advances, we can do damage to a part of his army. Clearly, if we operate in this way, Timur will no longer be able to make a sudden attack, as we will be watching and following closely, nor will he be able to gather abundant supplies in the future so as to have adequate provisions. And then, when we enter Timur's territory in pursuit of his army and he is hurrying to get his army back home and following the road that leads there, we can stop him and fight in retaliation."

When İbrahim spoke these words, the rest were swayed 53
by his opinion and gave him their support. But Sultan Bayezid reportedly said the following: "My men, it seems as though you are afraid of their numbers; that is how I interpret it. But you should know this too, that there is no safety in large numbers where valor can be found. You know how Xerxes, the son of Darius [I], the king of the Persians, led vast multitudes and crossed over into Europe, but would quickly have died in that attack had not Mardonios supported him and protected him from that calamity as he was returning to Susa.[90] You know Alexander too, who fought against Darius [III] and stripped him of his throne and killed him as well. I think that one can also learn about many of our Turks who have performed great deeds with only small numbers. We too in Europe have often gone into battle and routed the most courageous races in the world, the French and the Hungarians. Therefore, do not belittle our bravery or declare us to be worse and less significant than the Skythians and the Chaghadai, who have never ever used

οὐδαμῇ ἐχρήσαντο, ἀλλ' ἢ τόξῳ μόνῳ καὶ ὀϊστοῖς βάλλοντες ἐς χεῖρας ἰέναι οὐ πάνυ τι ἐθέλουσι."

54 Ταῦτα εἰπόντος τοῦ βασιλέως λέγεται τὸν Εἰενὲ ἄρχοντα ἐπειπεῖν τοιάδε. "Ἐπεὶ τοίνυν δοκεῖ σοι, ὦ βασιλεῦ, ἐπὶ τοὺς πολεμίους ἡμᾶς ὁμόσε ἰέναι, ἴθι δὴ πειθόμενος ἐμοὶ τούς τε θησαυροὺς ἀνεῳγὼς δίδου τῷ στρατεύματι πονήσαντι δὴ καὶ κεκμηκότι, ὡς ἐφ' ὅ τι ἂν γένοιτο τὰ πράγματα ἰόντα, τούτων δὲ τῶν σῶν θησαυρῶν οὕτω διδομένων τοῖς στρατιώταις ἐν κέρδει ἐσομένων ἡμῖν καὶ οὐκ ἀπολουμένων. Ἤν τε ἐφ' ἡμῖν γένηται, πολλαπλάσια ἕξομεν κερδανοῦντες· ἤν τε ἐπὶ τῷ Πέρσῃ, ἄμεινον ὂν ταύτῃ γενόμενον." Ταῦτα λέγων οὐκ ἔπειθε Παιαζήτην, ἔνθα γνώμην ἀποφηνάμενος ὡς τῇ Τεμήρεω σφραγῖδι ἐσφράγισται ἄρα τὰ [1.145] Παιαζήτεω χρήματα, καὶ διὰ ταῦτα οὐ τολμῴη αὐτὰ διανεῖμαι τοῖς στρατιώταις. Ταῦτα μὲν οὖν ἐς τοσοῦτον ἐβουλεύετο Παιαζήτῃ.

55 Μετὰ δὲ ταῦτα, ὡς ἐλαύνων οὐκ ἀνίει, ἀφίκετο ἐπὶ Οὔγκραν τῆς Φρυγίας πόλιν, ἔνθα δὴ καὶ Τεμήρης ἐστρατοπεδεύετο, ἐπὶ Μυσίαν ἐν νῷ ἔχων καὶ ἐπὶ Προῦσαν τὰ βασίλεια Παιαζήτεω στρατεύεσθαι. Ὡς δὲ ἀγχοῦ ἐγένετο τοῦ Τεμήρεω στρατεύματος, ἐστρατοπεδεύετο καὶ αὐτὸς ἐπὶ σταδίους πεντεκαίδεκα ἀπὸ τοῦ Τεμήρεω στρατοπέδου. Ἔνθα δὴ λέγεται τὸν Τεμήρην, ὡς ἐπιόντα στρατοπεδεύεσθαι ἐπύθετο, θαυμάσαι τε τὴν τόλμαν αὐτοῦ, καὶ ὡς ἀπὸ Ἀρμενίων ταχὺ παρεγένετο ἐπ' αὐτόν, καὶ ὡς οὕτω ἐκ τοῦ ἐμφανοῦς καθίστατο αὐτῷ ἐς μάχην, οὕτω δὴ ἐν τάχει σὺν τῷ στρατεύματι ἐλαύνων. Καὶ ἐφ' ἵππου δὴ λέγεται ἀναβάντα ἐλάσαι τε ὅτι ἐγγυτάτω τοῦ στρατοπέδου

swords but who only shoot with a bow and arrows, as they positively do not want to come to blows."

When the sultan had spoken these words, it is said that the lord Ine added the following: "Since you have decided, O sultan, that we should go to meet the enemy, come, trust me in this. Open your treasuries and give them to the army, which has labored hard and is tired, so that, however things turn out, we will benefit from having given your treasures to the army. We will not have lost them, for if it goes well for us, we will have made a profit many times over. But if it goes well for the Persian, well, it will be better to have happened in this way." Yet he did not persuade Bayezid by saying this, as he was declaring his opinion that Bayezid's money was actually stamped by Timur's stamp and it was for this reason that he did not dare distribute it to the soldiers.[91] That, then, was the extent of Bayezid's deliberations. 54

After that Bayezid did not let up in his advance and reached Ankara, a city of Phrygia, where Timur was encamped.[92] Timur's intention was to march against Mysia, specifically Prousa, the royal court of Bayezid. When the latter was close to Timur's army, he also encamped, at a distance of fifteen stades from Timur's camp. Whereupon it is said that Timur, when he learned that Bayezid had come against him and had encamped, admired his daring, the speed with which he had reached him from Armenian territory, and how he was about to offer him open battle after advancing with his army at such great speed. It is said that Timur mounted his horse and rode as close as he could to 55

Παιαζήτεω, καὶ τὰς φυλακὰς θεασάμενον καὶ τὸ στρατόπεδον, ὡς ἐσκήνωτο, ἀνακαγχάσαι τε καὶ εἰπεῖν· "ἄξιος ἡμῖν οὗτος λαίλαπι παραβάλλεσθαι τῆς τόλμης αὐτοῦ, οὐ μέντοι γε ἀρετῆς ἕνεκα χαίρων γε ἀπαλλάξεται. Ἔοικεν ὑπὸ δαίμονος πολεμίου ἐλαύνεσθαι οὕτω πάνυ· μελαγχολᾷ γὰρ δὴ ὁ κακοδαίμων καὶ οὐκέτι σωφρονεῖ." Ταῦτα εἰπόντα ἐλάσαι τε ἐπὶ τὸ ἑαυτοῦ στρατόπεδον.

56 Καὶ τῇ ὑστεραίᾳ αὐτὸν σὺν τοῖς ἀρίστοις αὐτοῦ, ἔχοντα ἀμφὶ τῇ [. . .], ἐπιπέμψαι Σαχροῦχον τὸν παῖδα αὐτοῦ ἐπὶ Παιαζήτην. Ἐνταῦθα ὡς ᾔσθετο ἐπιὸν τὸ Τεμήρεω στράτευμα κατ' αὐτοῦ, παρετάξατο καὶ αὐτὸς ἐπὶ λόφου τινὸς ὡς μαχούμενος. Καὶ τὸ εὐώνυμον αὐτοῦ μέρος τοῦ κέρατος εἶχεν ὁ τῆς ἕω στρατηγός, τὸ [1.146] δὲ δεξιὸν εἶχεν ὁ τῆς Εὐρώπης ἡγεμών· ἐν μέσῳ δὲ ἐπὶ τοῦ λόφου ἵδρυτο ὁ Παιαζήτης σὺν τοῖς νεήλυσι καὶ τοῖς ἀμφ' αὐτόν. Σαχροῦχος δὲ ἔχων τοὺς Τζαχατάϊδας καὶ τῶν Περσῶν τοὺς ἀρίστους ἐπῄει συντεταγμένῳ τῷ στρατεύματι ἐπὶ Παιαζήτην. Οὐ μέντοι γε ἐκυκλοῦτο, ἀλλὰ ἐδίδου χώραν ἀπιέναι, εἰ βούλοιντο, ὡς ἂν μὴ κυκλούμενοι σφῶν ἀμείνονες γένοιντο, περὶ ψυχῆς ἀγωνιζόμενοι. Συνέβαλέ τε κατὰ τὸ τῆς Εὐρώπης στράτευμα, καὶ ἐμάχετο. Ὡς ἐπὶ πολὺ μὲν τῆς ἡμέρας ἐμάχοντο, ὥστε μηδ' ἀναπαύεσθαι ἔχειν τὸ Παιαζήτου στράτευμα. Τριβαλλοὶ δὲ ἐνταῦθα ἄνδρες γενόμενοι ἀγαθοὶ ἐμάχοντο ἀξίως λόγου, καὶ ἐμβαλόντες ἐς τοὺς Τζαχατάϊδας τά τε δόρατα κατέαξαν, καὶ διηγωνίζοντο ἐντεταμένως ἐχόμενοι τοῦ ἔργου.

57 Παιαζήτης δὲ ὡς ἑώρα τὸ τῆς Εὐρώπης αὐτῷ στράτευμα κινηθὲν ἐς πρόσω καὶ μαχόμενον, ἀνεκαλεῖτο μὲν ἐν τῇ

Bayezid's camp, observed the sentries and how the tents were pitched in the camp, and laughed, saying, "I think it is right to compare his daring to a hurricane, but it will not go well for him here on account of his valor. He seems to be driven by a demon of war. This ill-starred man is brimming with bile and is no longer acting sensibly." Saying this, he rode back to his own camp.

On the next day Timur took his leading men and hav- 56
ing around [. . .] he dispatched his own son Shahrukh against Bayezid. When the latter realized that Timur's army was coming against him, he too deployed on a hill there to offer battle. The left wing of his army was commanded by the general of the east [i.e., Asia], while the right wing was commanded by the ruler of Europe;[93] in the middle, upon the hill, Bayezid took up his position with the janissaries and his retinue. Shahrukh moved against Bayezid with the Chaghadai and the leading Persians, keeping his army in formation. He did not surround them but gave them room to withdraw, if they wanted to, so that they did not become stronger than the enemy through being surrounded, in which case they would be fighting for their very lives. He engaged with the European army and battle was joined. They fought for most of the day so that Bayezid's army could take no rest. The Serbs proved their mettle there and fought worthily. They threw themselves upon the Chaghadai, broke their spears, and battled hard, sticking to their task in a determined fashion.

When Bayezid saw his European army move forward in 57
the fighting, he called back the general of Europe in the

ἀκμῇ τῆς Εὐρώπης τὸν στρατηγόν, ὀρρωδῶν μὴ παρασυρεὶς κυκλωθείη καὶ κινδυνεύσῃ διαφθαρῆναι, μετεπέμπετο δὲ ἐς τὸν χῶρον, ἐς ὃν ἵδρυτο τὴν ἀρχήν. Καὶ πρῶτα μὲν οὐχ ὑπήκουσε, δεδιὼς τὸ πρᾶγμα· μετὰ δέ, ὡς ἐπιφερομένου αὐτῷ τοῦ βασιλέως καὶ βλασφημοῦντος, ἀνεκαλεῖτο τὴν σύνταξιν. Ἐνταῦθα οἱ Τζαχατάϊδες ἐπεισπεσόντες τοῖς Τούρκοις ἐπέκειντο πάνυ φονεύοντες, ἐς ὃ δὴ ἐς φυγὴν κατέστησαν αὐτοὺς τραπῆναι. Ἐνταῦθα ὡς ὥρμηντο ἐς φυγήν, ἐπικειμένων τῶν πολεμίων καὶ τὸ ἀπὸ τῆς Ἀσίας στράτευμα αὐτίκα ἐς φυγὴν ὥρμητο. Καὶ αὐτίκα ὁ Παιαζήτης ἰδὼν ταῦτα οὐκέτι ἐνέμεινεν, ἀλλ' ἐπὶ ἵππον θήλειαν ἀναβὰς ἔφευγε κατὰ κράτος.

58 Ἐνταῦθα ὡς πρότερον κήρυγμα πεποιημένου Τεμήρεω [I.147] βασιλέως μηδένα κατακαίνειν τῶν τοῦ Παιαζήτου, μόνον δὲ ἀπεκδυόμενοι τούτους ἠφίεσαν· οὐ γὰρ ἐξῆν ὁμοφύλους ὄντας ἀνδραποδίζεσθαι. Παιαζήτης δὲ τἀναντία τούτων κηρύξας ἐς τὸ στρατόπεδον, ὡς ὃν ἂν λάβοιεν τοῦ Τεμήρεω στρατοῦ, πάντας κατακτείνειν. Σαχροῦχος μὲν οὖν ὡς ἐτρέψατο Παιαζήτην, ἤδη τὰ στρατεύματα Τεμήρεω, καὶ ὅσα ἐμάχοντο καὶ ὅσα ἐπὶ τοῦ στρατοπέδου ἐτύγχανεν ὄντα, ὥρμητο ἐπὶ τὸν Παιαζήτεω στρατὸν φθῆναι βουλόμενος. Καὶ ἐπὶ τὴν χώραν ἐτράποντο ἐπὶ διαρπαγήν, ἐπιδρομῇ χρησάμενοι, ἔστε τὴν Ἰωνίαν καὶ ἐς τὸν Ἑλλήσποντον, ἔνθα δὴ πολλαὶ μὲν κῶμαι ἐλήφθησαν, πολίσματα δὲ ἐρημώθη ὅτι πλεῖστα, τῶν ἱπποδρόμων τοῦ Τεμήρεω ἀνὰ τὴν χώραν τοῦ Παιαζήτεω διαθεόντων ἁπανταχῇ.

59 Περὶ δὲ τὸν Παιαζήτην τοιόνδε ξυνηνέχθη γενέσθαι.

thick of the battle, fearing that he might be carried away, become encircled, and risk being destroyed. He sent him back to the position to which he had originally been assigned. At first he did not obey, as he was afraid to do so. But when the sultan berated him and began to curse him, he recalled his formation. Thereupon the Chaghadai attacked the Turks and overpowered them, killing many, to the point that they routed them and put them to flight. And when they turned to flight with the enemy in pursuit, the army of Asia also immediately turned and fled. When Bayezid saw this he did not linger, but mounted his mare and fled as fast as he could.

According to the instructions that King Timur had given 58
in advance, they did not execute any of Bayezid's soldiers, but only stripped them bare and let them go. For it was not permissible to enslave men of the same race. But Bayezid had proclaimed the exact opposite in his camp, namely that they were to kill all whom they captured from Timur's army. When Shahrukh routed Bayezid, Timur's armies, both those that had fought and those that were in the camp, charged against Bayezid's army, trying to get there first. They also turned to plundering the countryside, making raids as far as Ionia and the Hellespont. Many villages were taken there and a multitude of towns was abandoned as Timur's cavalry raiders poured everywhere through Bayezid's territory.

As for Bayezid himself, the following happened to him. 59

Ὡς γὰρ ἔθει ἀνὰ κράτος οὗτος, ἐπέκειντό τε καὶ ἐπεδίωκον οἱ Τζαχατάϊδες, ἁμιλλώμενοι ἑλεῖν αὐτόν. Καὶ πολὺ μὲν προήλαυνεν ἅτε ἐπὶ ἵππῳ ταχυτάτῳ ἐπιφερόμενος· μετὰ δέ, ὡς ἐπὶ τὸν ποταμὸν ἀφίκετο, τὴν ἵππον λέγουσι διψήσασαν καρτερῶς ἐθελῆσαι τοῦ ὕδατος. Παιαζήτης γὰρ ἐνόσει τὼ χεῖρε καὶ τὼ πόδε ὑπὸ ποδάγρας, καὶ κατασχεῖν οὐχ οἷός τε ἐγένετο. Ἐνταῦθα δὴ ὑποχαλάσαι τὴν ἵππον ὑπὸ τοῦ ὕδατος καὶ λειφθῆναι τοῦ δρόμου, ὥστε τοὺς στρατιώτας Τεμήρη συλλαβεῖν τε Παιαζήτην, καὶ ἀγαγεῖν παρὰ βασιλέα Τεμήρην. Ἑάλωσαν μὲν οὖν ἐν τῇ μάχῃ ταύτῃ καὶ Μωσῆς καὶ πάντες σχεδὸν οἱ τοῦ Παιαζήτεω ἄρχοντες· οὐ μὴν χαλεπὸν ἔπαθον [1.148] ὁτιοῦν, πλὴν τῶν ἱματίων. Καὶ γὰρ Μωσῆς ἐδόκει τε τῶν ἄλλων κράτιστος γεγονέναι· καὶ διὰ τοῦτο περιῆγεν ἔχων τῷ στρατοπέδῳ καὶ δίαιταν παρεχόμενος. Ἑάλω δὲ καὶ ἡ γυνὴ τοῦ Παιαζήτεω ἐν Προύσῃ· καὶ γὰρ τήν τε Προῦσαν ἐπέδραμον, καὶ τὰς γυναικωνίτιδας ἀφείλοντο. Πρὸς δὲ καὶ τὴν Ἐλεαζάρου θυγατέρα, Παιαζήτεω δὲ γυναῖκα, ἑλόντες ἀπήγαγον παρὰ βασιλέα. Μουσουλμάνης μὲν οὖν καὶ Ἰησοῦς καὶ Μεχμέτης καὶ οἱ λοιποὶ τῶν Παιαζήτεω παίδων κατελείφθησαν, καὶ οἱ μὲν ἐν τῇ Εὐρώπῃ, οἱ δ' ἐν τῇ Ἀσίᾳ ὄντες διεσώζοντο, ὅποι ἑκάστῳ προὐχώρει.

60 Τῷ μέντοι Παιαζήτῃ, ὡς ἤχθη ἐναντίον βασιλέως, λέγεται εἰπεῖν αὐτῷ τοιάδε. "Ὦ κακόδαιμον, τί δὲ οὕτω πάνυ τὸν σαυτοῦ δαίμονα ἐβιάζου, προκαλούμενος ἡμᾶς ἐπὶ μάχην; Ἢ οὐκ ἐπύθου, ὡς τῷ ἐμῷ τῷδε στρατεύματι δυστήνων παῖδες ἀντέστησαν;" Παιαζήτης δὲ ὑπολαβὼν ἀμείβετο, ᾗ δὴ λέγεται, ὡς "οὐκ ἂν δὴ ἐς τοῦτο τύχης

He rode with all his might and the Chaghadai went after him and gave chase, competing with each other to catch him. He had a strong lead as he was riding a very fast horse. But later, when he reached the river, they say that the horse was thirsty and desperately wanted to drink. Bayezid's hands and feet were in pain because of gout and he was unable to restrain the horse. Thus the horse eased up because of the water and slowed down, with the result that Timur's soldiers apprehended Bayezid and brought him to King Timur. In this battle, Musa was captured along with almost all of Bayezid's officers,[94] but they suffered no harm beyond losing their clothing. Musa seemed to be more powerful than the rest, for which reason he was led around with the army and provided with necessities. Bayezid's wife was also captured at Prousa, for they raided Prousa too and removed the harem. They also captured Lazar's daughter, who was one of Bayezid's wives, and took her to the king.[95] Süleyman, İsa, Mehmed, and the rest of Bayezid's sons were left where they were: some found safety in Europe, others in Asia, each in whatever way he could.

It is said that when Bayezid was summoned before King 60
Timur, the latter said this to him: "You ill-starred man, why did you force the hand of fate in this way by challenging us to battle? Haven't you learned that only the sons of unhappy parents resist my army?"[96] Bayezid replied to him, it is said, that "I would not have fallen into such misfortune if Timur

ἀφικοίμην, ἂν μὴ αὐτῷ παρείχετο πράγματα ἐκεῖνος, τά τε ἄλλα καὶ ἀπὸ ἐθνῶν τῷ Μεχμέτῃ τῷ ἥρωι πολεμίων θαμὰ ἀνακαλούμενος." "Ἀλλ' ἢν μὴ ἐτετύφωσο," ἔφη Τεμήρης, "οὕτω μέγα πάνυ φρονῶν, οὐκ ἂν δὴ ἐς τοῦτο συμφορᾶς, οἶμαι, ἀφίκου· οὕτω γὰρ εἴωθε τὸ θεῖον τὰ πάνυ μέγα φρονοῦντα καὶ πεφυσημένα μειοῦν ὡς τὰ πολλὰ καὶ σμικρύνειν." Ἐνταῦθα δὴ ἐπιμέμψασθαι αὐτῷ λέγεται βασιλέα Τεμήρην τὴν {I.149} ἐπὶ τοὺς κύνας τε καὶ ἱέρακας φιλοτιμίαν, ὡς ἀνδρὶ κυνηγῷ ἐῴκει τὴν τέχνην, καὶ οὐκ ἄρχοντι ἄγοντι ἐς πολέμους· λέγεται γὰρ Παιαζήτης ἐς τοὺς ἑπτακισχιλίους κτήσασθαι ἱερακοφόρους καὶ κύνας ἀμφὶ τοὺς ἑξακισχιλίους. Ἐνταῦθα τόν τε Παιαζήτην φάναι ὑπολαβόντα, "ἀλλὰ σοὶ μὲν τῷ Σκύθῃ, ληστῇ ἔτι ὄντι καὶ ταύτην ἐπιτηδεύοντι τὴν τέχνην, οὐ πάνυ τι ἂν προσήκει ἄγρας οὐδὲ κυνηγεσίων· ἐμοὶ δὲ ἐς τοῦτό τε γεννηθέντι καὶ τεθραμμένῳ, τῷ Ἀμουράτεω τοῦ Ὀρχάνεω, βασιλέων παιδί, μετῆν καὶ κυνῶν καὶ ἱεράκων φιλοτιμίας." Ἐνταῦθα δὴ ἀχθεσθέντα τὸν βασιλέα περιαχθῆναι ἐς τὸ στρατόπεδον ἐκέλευσεν ἐπὶ ἡμιόνου, καὶ συριττόμενον ὑπὸ τοῦ στρατοπέδου περιαγαγεῖν. Ὡς δὲ περιαχθέντα ἤγαγον, ἔρεσθαι αὐτὸν λέγεται, εἰ τοῦ γένους ἐκεῖνα τυγχάνει ἐπιτηδεύματα, ὡς τὰ τῶν ἱεράκων τε καὶ κυνῶν. Μετὰ δὲ ταῦτα ἐν φυλακῇ ἐποιήσατο.

61 Καὶ ἄρας σὺν τῷ στρατεύματι ἤλαυνεν ἐπὶ Ἰωνίαν καὶ τὴν ταύτῃ πάραλον χώραν, ἐν νῷ ἔχων αὐτοῦ τε διαχειμάσαι καὶ ἦρος ἐπιφαινομένου ἐς τὴν Εὐρώπην διαβῆναι. Ἐπενόει γάρ, ὡς καὶ πρότερόν μοι δεδήλωται, ἐς τὴν Εὐρώπην διαβὰς πᾶσάν τε ὑφ' αὐτῷ ποιήσασθαι, ἐς ὃ

had not given me the grounds for it, among other things because he was called in so often to help people who were the enemies of the hero Muhammad." "But if you were not so arrogant," Timur said, "and did not think so highly of yourself, I believe you would not have reached such depths of misfortune. For God is accustomed to cut down to size those who think highly of themselves and are all puffed up." At this point it is said that King Timur reproached him for his passion for hounds and hawks, which made him look like a man who was a hunter by profession, not a lord and military leader. For it is said that Bayezid owned about seven thousand falconers and six thousand hounds. Bayezid replied by saying, "For you, a Skythian, who are still a bandit and practice that art, hunting with hounds and the chase would not be appropriate. Yet a passion for hounds and hawks does befit me, the son of Murad, grandson of Orhan, a son of sultans, who was born and raised to it." At this King Timur became angry and ordered him paraded through the camp on a mule, and he was mocked and taunted by the army as he was being led around. But as they were leading him around like this, he is said to have asked whether that race actually did engage in those pursuits, like those with hawks and hounds.[97] After that, Timur imprisoned him.

Timur broke camp and advanced with his army against 61
Ionia and its coastal lands. He intended to spend the winter there and to cross over into Europe in the spring. For he was planning, as I stated earlier, to cross over into Europe and

δὴ ἐπὶ τὰς Ἡρακλείους ἀφίκηται στήλας, ἐντεῦθεν δὲ αὖθις ἐς Λιβύην διαβῆναι, καὶ διὰ τῆς Λιβύης ἐπανιέναι ἐς τὴν ἑαυτοῦ χώραν, ξύμπασαν ὑπαγόμενος τὴν ταύτῃ ἤπειρον τῆς οἰκουμένης. Ἐπρεσβεύετο μὲν οὖν καὶ πρὸς τὸν Βυζαντίου βασιλέα, τήν τε διάβασιν αἰτούμενος αὐτὸν πλοῖά τε καὶ τριήρεις.

62 Λέγεται δὲ καὶ τόδε βασιλεὺς Τεμήρης ἐς Παιαζήτην. Ὡς [1.150] γὰρ ἀπήχθη ἡ γυνὴ αὐτοῦ, Ἐλεαζάρου θυγάτηρ, ἧς δὴ μάλιστα τῶν ἄλλων ἐραστὴς ἐτύγχανε Παιαζήτης, καὶ περιῆγε μεθ' ἑαυτοῦ ἔχων ἐν τῷ στρατοπέδῳ, ἐπιστῆσαί οἱ ἐναντίον τοῦ ἀνδρὸς αὐτῆς, οἰνοχοῆσαί οἱ. Τὸν δὲ εὖ μάλα ἀχθεσθέντα εἰπεῖν λέγεται, "ἀλλ' οὔτ' ἂν συμφώνως τῷ σῷ πατρὶ καὶ μητρὶ ἐργάζοιο· ἰδιωτῶν γὰρ τούτων καὶ πενήτων γενόμενος δίκαιος οὔτ' ἂν εἴης ὥστ' ἂν ἐπικερτομῆσαι βασιλέων παισί τε καὶ γυναιξί, καὶ ἐξυβρίζεις ἐς τοὺς σοὺς τῇ φύσει δεσπότας." Τούτῳ μὲν τοιαῦτα λέγοντι γέλωτά τε ἐποίει τοὺς λόγους, καὶ ἐπιχλευάζων ἐπέσκωπτεν οἷα οὐδὲν ὑγιὲς οὔτε φρονοῦντι οὔτε λέγοντι. Οἱ μέντοι Παιαζήτεω ἄρχοντες, ἐς λόγους ἀφικόμενοι τοῖς Τεμήρεω ὀρυκταῖς, ᾗ φασιν, ὑπέσχοντο ἀργύριον τελέσαι πάμπολυ, εἰ ὑφέλοιντο Παιαζήτην ὑπορύξαντες. Ἔνθα δὴ ὄρυγμά τε ποιησάμενοι ἐν τῷ στρατοπέδῳ, καὶ εἰς τὴν σκηνήν, ἐν ᾗ ἐσκήνου Παιαζήτης ἐν φυλακῇ ὤν, ἐξιόντες, ὤφθησαν ὑπὸ τῶν ταύτῃ φυλάκων καὶ ἑάλωσαν· οὐ γὰρ ἐντὸς ἐγένοντο τῆς σκηνῆς, ἀλλ' ἐκτός, ᾗ ἐφύλασσον πέριξ γενόμενοι ἄνδρες ὑπὸ Τεμήρεω ταχθέντες. Ταύτῃ ὡς ἐξῄεσαν καὶ ἑάλωσαν, ἀπετάμοντο τὰς κεφαλὰς ὑπὸ βασιλέως.

subject it all to himself until he reached the Pillars of Herakles, and from there to cross over to North Africa and to return to his own land across North Africa, subjecting the entire continent of the world in this way.[98] He sent envoys to the king of Byzantion [Manuel II], seeking transport ships and triremes from him for the crossing.

King Timur is also reported to have done the following 62
to Bayezid. When the latter's wife, the daughter of Lazar, whom he loved more than any of the others, had been taken away, and Timur was taking her around in the camp with him, he made her pour his wine in front of Bayezid, her husband. It is said that the latter grew very angry and said, "Your actions do not accord with the status of your father and mother. For they were ordinary people and poor, and so it is not right for you to mock the children and the wives of kings, and to insult those who are your superiors by nature." That is what Bayezid said, but Timur laughed at his words, mocked him, and ridiculed him for thinking and saying crazy things. Bayezid's lords, they say, approached Timur's sappers and promised to pay them huge amounts of silver if they could secretly get Bayezid out by digging a tunnel. They actually made a tunnel under the camp heading toward the tent in which Bayezid was being held under guard, but they were seen by the guards there as they emerged and were caught. For they did not emerge inside the tent, but outside, where the men stationed by Timur were keeping watch. As they emerged there, they were caught, and the king had them beheaded.

63 Ἐπὶ Σμύρνης μὲν οὖν ἀφικόμενος τήν τε Σμύρνην εἷλε τροχίσκοις, καὶ τὴν ἐν τῷ αἰγιαλῷ ἄκραν ὑπὸ Ῥωμαίων ταύτῃ κατεχομένην ὑπορύξας κατέβαλέ τε, καὶ ταύτην ἑλὼν πολίσματά τε ἄλλα τῆς χώρας ταύτης ἐπελαύνων ᾕρει, ὥς οἱ προὐχώρει [1.151] προσβάλλοντι ἐφ' ἕκαστον. Τριχῇ γάρ, λέγεται, διῄρει τὰς πόλεις Τεμήρης τοῖς τε τροχοῖς. Κύκλοι δὲ ὄντες οὗτοι καὶ κλίμακας ἔχοντες ἐντός, ὥστε ἀναβαίνειν ἐπὶ τὸ τεῖχος, ἐς τὴν τάφρον ἄγοντες ἐπετίθεσαν ἄνδρες διακόσιοι ἕκαστον τεταγμένοι, διὰ τοῦ τροχοῦ εἰσιὼν ἕκαστος, ἐς τὸ πέραν τε ἐγίγνετο τῆς τάφρου, στεγαζόμενοι ὑπὸ τοῦ τροχοῦ. Ὡς δὲ πέραν γίγνοιντο, ἀνέβαινον τὰς κλίμακας, καὶ οὕτω ᾕρουν τὴν πόλιν. Μετὰ δὲ πολλοὶ ὄντες αὐτῷ ἐν τῷ στρατοπέδῳ ἔχουν τὴν πόλιν, ὥστε ἐπὶ τὸ τεῖχος τὰ χώματα ἀναβαίνειν, καὶ ἄνω διὰ τῶν χωμάτων ἡλίσκετο αὐτῷ τὸ τεῖχος. Εἶχε δὲ καὶ ὀρυκτὰς ἐς μυρίους, καὶ ὀρύσσοντες τὰ τείχη ἐπὶ μετεώρων ξύλων καθειστήκεσαν. Μετὰ δὲ ταῦτα πῦρ ἐνιεὶς τὰ ξύλα, καὶ ὡς ἐκαίετο τὰ ξύλα, τὰ τείχη εὐπετῶς ἔπιπτον, καὶ ταύτῃ ἐσέπιπτον ἐς τὴν πόλιν. Οὕτω μὲν οὖν ᾕρει Τεμήρης τὰς πόλεις.

64 Ὡς δὲ ἤδη ἔαρ ὑπέφαινεν, ἀφίκετο παρ' αὐτὸν ἀγγελία, ὡς τοῦ Ἰνδῶν βασιλέως πρεσβεία ἀφικομένη ἐπὶ Χερίην μεγάλῃ χειρὶ δεινά τε τὴν πόλιν ἐργάσαιτο, καὶ ἐπὶ τοὺς θησαυροὺς παριὼν τοῦ βασιλέως τόν τε φόρον λαβὼν οἴχοιτο, καὶ ἀπειλοίη, ὡς οὐκέτι ἐμμένοι ταῖς σπονδαῖς ὁ Ἰνδῶν βασιλεύς. Ταῦτα ὡς ἐπύθετο, περιδεὴς γενόμενος μή, ἐπειδὴ ἀφίκοιτο ἡ πρεσβεία παρὰ βασιλέα τῶν Ἰνδῶν,

Timur came to Smyrna and captured it with his "little wheels."[99] He took the citadel by the shore, which was held by the Romans,[100] by tunneling under it. After he had taken it, he captured many towns in that region by marching against them, attacking each in turn as he advanced. It is said that Timur would break into the cities in three ways with his wheels. These were circular devices that had ladders inside them for scaling the walls: two hundred men were assigned to each, and they would bring it up to the ditch and make the attack. Each man would enter the ditch by means of the wheel and would cross to the other side of it, protected on top by the wheel. When they reached the other side, they would climb the ladders and thus take the city. In addition, he also had many men in his camp who used to throw up earth around the city so that they could climb the mound to the walls; thus, by reaching the top over the earthen mound, he could take the walls. Finally, he also had about ten thousand sappers who would dig tunnels under the walls and prop them up with wooden beams. After that they would set fire to the beams and, when the wood burned through, the walls would simply collapse and they would enter the city at that point. It was in these three ways that Timur would capture the cities. 63

With the arrival of spring, however, news reached him that envoys of the king of the Indians had arrived at Kherie with a large military escort and had done great harm to the city.[101] They had even entered the king's treasury and taken off with the tribute, and they also threatened that the king of the Indians would no longer abide by the treaty. When he learned this, Timur was frightened that when the envoys reached the king of the Indians, the latter would come 64

ἐπιὼν καταστρέφοιτο τὴν ἑαυτοῦ χώραν, σχόντος αὐτοῦ ἀμφὶ [1.152] τοὺς ἐπήλυδας πολέμους, καὶ ἅμα ἐσῄει αὐτὸν καὶ τὰ ἀνθρώπεια ἐν οὐδενὶ ἑστηκότα ἀσφαλεῖ, καὶ δεινὰ ποιησάμενος τοὺς Ἰνδοὺς πρέσβεις ἐξυβρίσαι ἐς αὐτὸν οὕτως ἀναίδην, ἤλαυνεν, ὡς εἶχε τάχιστα, ἐπὶ Χερίης, τόν τε Παιαζήτην ἔχων μεθ' ἑαυτοῦ καὶ τὸν παῖδα αὐτοῦ. Καὶ οὐδένα λόγον ἐποιεῖτο αὐτοῦ Τεμήρης, ἀπέδρα ἐπὶ τὴν πατρῴαν χώραν.

65 Παιαζήτην δὲ ὑπὸ λύπης νοσήσαντα τελευτῆσαι τὸν βίον ἔφασαν. Οὕτω μὲν οὖν ἐτελεύτησε Παιαζήτης ὁ Ἀμουράτεω, ἀνὴρ ὁρμήν τε καὶ τόλμαν ἐπιδειξάμενος, ὅποι ἂν παραγένοιτο, ἀξίαν λόγου, καὶ τόλμῃ μεγάλῃ ἀποδειξάμενος ἔργα κατά τε Ἀσίαν καὶ Εὐρώπην, βασιλεύσας ἔτη πέντε καὶ εἴκοσιν. Ἦν δὲ οὕτως αὐθάδης, ὥστε μηδενὶ πείθεσθαι, ὡς ἑαυτῷ θαρρούντως χωρεῖν ἐπὶ τοὺς πολεμίους. Ἐτελεύτησε δὲ ἐν τῇ Ἰωνίᾳ, διαχειμάζοντος αὐτοῦ Τεμήρεω τὸν στρατόν.

66 Ὁ δὲ Ἰνδῶν βασιλεὺς οὗτος ἐστὶν ὁ τῶν ἐννέα βασιλέων τοὔνομα ἔχων, Τζαχατάης βασιλεύς. Τῶν ἐννέα δὲ βασιλέων βασιλέα γενόμενον τοῦτον, τὸν διὰ τοὺς Μασσαγέτας στρατὸν μέγαν ἐπὶ Τεμήρην ἐπιπέμψαντα, λέγεται τόν τε Ἀράξην ἐπιόντα διαβῆναι, καὶ τὰ πλέω τῆς ταύτῃ χώρας καταστρεψάμενον ἐπ' οἴκου αὖθις ἀποχωρῆσαι. Σίνης τε βασιλεύει καὶ Ἰνδίας [καὶ] ξυμπάσης, καὶ διήκει αὐτῷ ἡ χώρα ἐπὶ Ταπροβάνην νῆσον, ἐς Ἰνδικὴν θάλασσαν, ἐς ἣν οἱ μέγιστοι τῆς Ἰνδίας χώρας ποταμοὶ [1.153] ἐκδιδοῦσιν, ὅ τε Γάγγης, Ἰνδός, Ἀκεσίνης, Ὑδάσπης, Ὑδραώτης, Ὕφασις, μέγιστοι δὴ οὗτοι ὄντες τῆς χώρας.

against him and conquer his territory while he was preoccupied with wars in neighboring lands. At the same time, he realized that human affairs are never secure, and he took to heart the way in which the Indian envoys had insulted him so shamelessly. So he marched to Kherie as quickly as he could, taking Bayezid and his son with him. Timur paid no attention to the latter, and so he escaped to his native land.[102]

They say that Bayezid died after becoming sick with 65
grief. Thus died Bayezid, the son of Murad, a man who, wherever he went, had shown great daring and remarkable boldness. He displayed great daring in his accomplishments in Asia and Europe, and reigned for twenty-five years.[103] But he was impetuous, so that he listened to no one else, and advanced confidently against the enemy. He died in Ionia, where Timur was spending the winter with the army.[104]

This king of the Indians is the one who is called "he of 66
the nine kings"; he is King Chaghadai. When he became king over the nine kings, he dispatched a large army against Timur on account of the Massagetai. It is said that he crossed the Araxes in his advance, conquered most of the land there, and then returned to his home. He reigns over China[105] and all of India. His land extends to the island of Taprobane [Sri Lanka] in the Indian Ocean, into which flow the largest of the rivers of India: the Ganges, Indus, Akesines, Hydaspes, Hydraotes, and Hyphasis, which are the

Φέρει δὲ ἡ Ἰνδικὴ χώρα ἀγαθὰ μὲν πολλὰ καὶ ὄλβον πολύν, καὶ ὅ τε βασιλεὺς ξυμπάσης τῆς χώρας ὑπ' αὐτὸν γενομένης. Ὁρμώμενος δὲ οὗτος ἀπὸ τῆς ὑπὲρ Γάγγην χώρας καὶ τῆς παραλίου Ἰνδικῆς καὶ Ταπροβάνης, ἐλθεῖν ἐπὶ τὸν βασιλέα Χαταΐης, τῆς χώρας τῆς ἐντὸς Γάγγου καὶ Ἰνδοῦ, καὶ καταστρεψάμενον τὴν ταύτη χώραν τὰ βασίλεια ἐν ταύτῃ δὴ τῇ πόλει ποιήσασθαι· ξυμβῆναι δὲ τότε γενέσθαι ὑφ' ἑνὶ βασιλεῖ ξύμπασαν τὴν Ἰνδικὴν χώραν.

67 Νομίζουσι δὲ οὗτοι θεούς, οἵ τε τὴν Χαταΐην χώραν οἰκοῦντες, Ἀπόλλω τε καὶ Ἄρτεμιν καὶ δὴ καὶ Ἥραν. Φωνὴν δὲ οὐ τὴν αὐτὴν σφίσιν ἵενται, ἀλλ' ἐς ἔθνη τε πολλὰ διῃρημένα εὐνομεῖται ἐπὶ πλεῖστον δὴ ἀνθρώπων κατά τε πόλεις καὶ κώμας. Θυσίας δὲ ἀνάγουσιν ἵππους μὲν τῷ Ἀπόλλωνι, βοῦς δὲ τῇ Ἥρᾳ· τῇ δὲ Ἀρτέμιδι θύουσι παῖδας ἀρτίως ἡβάσκοντας ἀνὰ πᾶν ἔτος. Φέρει δὲ ἡ χώρα αὕτη πυροὺς μὲν ἐπὶ πεντεκαίδεκα πήχεις, ὡς λέγεται, βασιλικούς, καὶ κριθὰς δὲ τὸν αὐτὸν τρόπον, καὶ μελίνην ἐς τὸ αὐτὸ μέγεθος. Καλαμίνοις δὲ πλοίοις χρώμενοι διαπορθμεύουσι τὸν ποταμόν. Φέρει δὲ ἡ Ἰνδική, ὡς λέγουσι, τοσοῦτον τὸ μέγεθος, ὥστε ἀπ' αὐτοῦ ναυπηγεῖσθαι πλοῖα μεδίμνων τεσσαράκοντα Ἑλληνικῶν.

68 Τὸ μὲν γένος τοῦτο οὐ πάνυ γνωστὸν ἡμῖν γενόμενον πολλὰς ἀπιστίας παρέχει μὴ πείθεσθαι περὶ αὐτῶν, ὅσα πυνθάνομαι. Ἥ τε γὰρ χώρα αὕτη πρόσω [1.154] ἐκποδὼν γενομένη οὐ πάνυ ἐπιτήδειος εἴσω ᾤκηται τε καὶ ὅποι ἔχει ἠθῶν τε καὶ διαίτης. Γένος μέντοι ἰσχυρότατον γενόμενον τὸ παλαιὸν τούς τε Περσῶν βασιλεῖς καὶ Ἀσσυρίων, ἡγουμένους τῆς Ἀσίας, θεραπεύειν μὲν τοὺς Ἰνδῶν βασιλεῖς,

largest in the land. India produces many goods and much wealth, and the king rules over the entire land.[106] Setting out from the land above the Ganges, as well as from coastal India, and Taprobane, he attacked the king of Khatai, the land between the Ganges and Indus, conquered that land, and established his own royal court in that city. It was at that time when all the land of India came under the control of one king.

The inhabitants of the land of Khatai[107] believe in the 67
gods Apollo, Artemis, and Hera. They do not all speak the same language but are divided into many races; it is the most well governed among all people, organized into cities and villages. They make sacrifices of horses to Apollo and oxen to Hera. To Artemis they sacrifice every year children who have just reached puberty. The land produces wheat that reportedly grows to a height of fifteen royal cubits, and barley in the same fashion, and millet to the same height. They cross the river in reed boats. India produces reeds of such a size, they say, that ships with a capacity of forty Greek *medimnoi* can be built from them.[108]

The fact that this race is not well known to us means that 68
there are many incredible stories told about them that are not to be believed, at least as far as I can ascertain. The land is very remote and so it is not easy to learn how it is settled in its interior and what its customs and way of life are. This race became very powerful in the past and the kings of the Persians and Assyrians, the rulers of Asia, served the kings

ἐπεί τε Σεμίραμις καὶ Κῦρος ὁ τοῦ Καμβύσου τὸν Ἀράξην διαβάντες μεγάλῳ τῷ πολέμῳ ἐχρήσαντο. Ἥ τε γὰρ Σεμίραμις τῶν Ἀσσυρίων βασίλισσα ἐπὶ τῶν Ἰνδῶν βασιλέα ἐλαύνουσα μεγάλῃ παρασκευῇ, ἐπεί τε τὸν ποταμὸν διέβη, ἐπεπράγει τε χαλεπώτατα καὶ αὐτοῦ ταύτῃ ἐτελεύτησε. Μετὰ δὲ ταῦτα Κῦρος ὁ Καμβύσεω, Περσῶν βασιλεύς, λέγεται δὴ τόν τε Ἀράξην διαβάς, καὶ διαγωνισάμενος πρὸς τοὺς Μασσαγέτας ἔπραξέ τε τὰ χαλεπώτατα, καὶ αὐτοῦ ὑπὸ γυναικὸς Τομύριος τῆς Μασσαγετῶν βασιλευούσης ἀποθανεῖν.

69 Τεμήρης μὲν οὖν ὡς ὑπὸ τοῦ ἀγγέλου ἐπύθετο τὰ περὶ τὴν πρεσβείαν τοῦ Χαταΐης βασιλέως, ἀπήλαυνεν, ὡς εἶχε τάχους, ἐπὶ Χερίης. Παιαζήτης δέ, ὡς εἴρηται, κατὰ τὴν ὁδὸν ἐτελεύτησεν, ὑπενεχθεὶς ἐς τὴν μέλαιναν ὑπὸ λύπης. Μωϋσῆς δὲ ὁ παῖς αὐτοῦ, ἀφεθεὶς ὑπὸ βασιλέως Τεμήρη, ἐπὶ τὴν πατρῴαν χώραν ἀφίκετο. Βασιλεὺς δὲ Τεμήρης ὡς ἐγένετο ἐς τὰ βασίλεια τὰ ἑαυτοῦ, τά τε ἐν τῇ ἀρχῇ αὐτοῦ καθίστη, ᾗ ἐδόκει κάλλιστα ἔχειν αὐτῷ, καὶ πρὸς τὸν Ἰνδῶν βασιλέα διενεχθεὶς ἐπολέμει. [1.155] Μετὰ δὲ ταῦτα εἰρήνην τε ἐποιήσατο, ἐφ᾽ ᾧ τε ξένοι τε καὶ φίλοι εἶναι ἀλλήλοις. Τούτῳ ἐγένοντο παῖδες Σαχροῦχός τε καὶ Παϊαγγούρης καὶ Ἀβδυλατούφης. Σαχροῦχον τὸν πρεσβύτερον παῖδα αὐτοῦ κατέλιπε βασιλέα ἀποδειξάμενος. Αὐτὸς δὲ περὶ ἔρωτας ἔχων καὶ ἐνταῦθα πολυπραγμονῶν ἐτελεύτησε. Λέγεται γὰρ δὴ Τεμήρης μάλιστα δὴ ἀνθρώπων ἐς τοσοῦτο ὑπὸ φύσεως ἀχθῆναι, ὥστε νεανίσκους ἐναντίον αὐτοῦ γυναιξὶ κελεύειν μίσγεσθαι, ὥστε καὶ τὴν φύσιν ἐρεθίζειν αὐτοῦ ἐπὶ τοῦτο. Ὡς δὲ ἀπὸ ἐρώτων

of the Indians, ever since Semiramis and Cyrus, the son of Cambyses, crossed the Araxes and found themselves involved in a major war. For Semiramis, the queen of the Assyrians, launched a major expedition against the king of the Indians and yet, when she crossed the river, she fared very badly and died there. After that it is said that Cyrus, the son of Cambyses and king of the Persians, crossed the Araxes and fought with the Massagetai. But he too fared very badly and was killed there by a woman, Tomyris, the queen of the Massagetai.[109]

So when Timur learned from the messenger about the 69
embassy sent by the king of Khatai, he marched, as quickly as he could, to Kherie. As I said, Bayezid died along the way, overcome by depression and grief. His son Musa was released by King Timur and returned to his native land.[110] When King Timur reached his palace, he arranged the affairs of his realm in the way that seemed best to him, and waged war against the king of the Indians over their differences. After that he made peace on the condition that they be friends and allies with each other.[111] The sons born to him were Shahrukh, Baysunqur, and ʻAbd-al-Latif.[112] He appointed the eldest son, Shahrukh, to be king after him,[113] while he himself indulged in sex and died preoccupied with that.[114] In fact it is said that Timur was tormented by his nature more than any other person, to such a degree that he ordered young men to copulate with women in front of him in order to become aroused enough himself for the act. But

γένοιτο, ἐπὶ πολεμίους αὐτίκα δὴ τρέπεσθαι, μηδέποτε ἡσυχίαν ἄγοντα. Καὶ ἐξυβρίσαι δὴ λέγεται τὴν φύσιν αὐτοῦ ἐς τὴν δίαιταν περὶ ἀφροδίσια γενόμενον.

70 Τούτου μὲν δὴ τελευτήσαντος ἔσχε τὴν βασιλείαν Σαχροῦχος, ἀνὴρ τά τε ἄλλα ἐπιεικής, καὶ τοῖς περιοίκοις τὰ πολλὰ σπενδόμενός τε καὶ ἡσυχίαν ἄγων διετέλει. Μετ᾽ οὐ πολὺ τελευτήσαντος Σαχρούχου τοῦ Τεμήρεω Παϊαγγούρης ὁ νεώτερος παῖς ἔσχε τὴν βασιλείαν, πρὸς τοὺς ἀδελφοὺς αὐτοῦ διενεχθείς. Οὐλίης μὲν γὰρ τήν τε Καδουσίων χώραν καὶ Ὑρκανίαν κατέχων πρὸς Ἀβδυλατούφην τὸν ἀδελφὸν διενεχθεὶς ἐπολέμει, καὶ ὡς Παϊαγγούρης ἐπαγόμενος, τήν τε χώραν ἀφείλετο, καὶ αὐτὸν ζωγρήσας εἶχεν ἐν φυλακῇ. Μετὰ δὲ ταῦτα τελευτήσαντος Παϊαγγούρεω Τζοκίης ἔσχε τὴν βασιλείαν. Πρὸς τοῦτον Μπαϊμπούρης [1.156] τῶν ἐννέα βασιλέων ἐπιγαμίαν ποιησάμενος καὶ ἐπιτραφθεὶς ἔσχε τὴν βασιλείαν· καὶ τὰ Σαμαρχάνδης πράγματα κατασχών, καὶ Ἰνδῶν συμμαχίαν ἐπαγόμενος, πρός τε τὸν Τζοκίην Παϊαγγούρεω ἐπολέμει παῖδα. Τζοκίης μὲν οὖν τούς τε Σκύθας ἐπαγόμενος, καὶ τῆς Ἀσσυρίων χώρας βασιλεύων ἐπὶ Παϊαγγούρην τὸν ἀδελφὸν τόν τε πόλεμον διέφερε καὶ στρατευσάμενος μάχῃ τε ἐκράτησε καὶ Σαμαρχάνδην παρεστήσατο.

71 Οὐ πολὺ δὲ ὕστερον τῶν ἐννέα βασιλεῖ συμμάχῳ χρησάμενος καὶ ἐν τῷ Ταβρέζῃ πόλει εὐδαίμονι Ἀσσυρίων τὰ βασίλεια ποιησάμενος πρός τε τοὺς Λευκάρνας πολεμῶν διετέλει καὶ Σαμαχίην πόλιν ἐπολιόρκει, τὰ τοῦ Καραΐλούκεω βασίλεια. Ταβρέζη δὲ πόλις εἶναι μεγάλη τε καὶ εὐδαίμων καὶ τῶν ἐν τῇ Ἀσίᾳ μετά γε Σαμαρχάνδην

when he set sex aside, he would immediately turn to war against his enemies, so that he was never at rest. It is said that he committed offenses against his nature with his sexual habits.

When Timur died, Shahrukh took the throne. He was a man who was generally reasonable and who, for the most part, made treaties with his neighbors and maintained peace. Shahrukh, the son of Timur, died shortly afterward, and Baysunqur, the younger son, took the throne and fell out with his brothers.[115] For Uluğ-Beg held the land of the Kadousioi and Hyrkania and fought against his brother 'Abd-al-Latif after falling out with him.[116] But Baysunqur came against him, stripped him of his land, captured him alive, and imprisoned him. After that, when Baysunqur died, Juki held the throne.[117] Babur "of the nine kings" made a marriage alliance with him, and so he held the throne after inheriting it.[118] He also took over the affairs of Samarkand, made an alliance with the Indians, and fought against Juki, the son of Baysunqur. Juki brought in the Skythians, reigned over the land of the Assyrians, and fell out in a war with his brother Baysunqur. He marched against him, defeated him in battle, and took over Samarkand.[119] 70

Shortly afterward, relying on the king of the nine as his ally and using Tabriz, a prosperous city of the Assyrians, as his royal capital, Juki waged war against the White Sheep and besieged the city of Shemakha, the palace of Kara Yülük.[120] Tabriz is a large city, prosperous, and, after Samarkand, first among all the cities in Asia in its income and 71

χρημάτων τε προσόδῳ καὶ τῇ ἄλλῃ εὐδαιμονίᾳ προέχουσα· σῆράς τε τρέφει ἡ χώρα αὕτη μέταξάν τε καλλίστην ποιουμένη καὶ τῆς Σαμαχίης ἀμείνω. Φέρει δὲ καὶ κριμίζιν σῆρα οὕτω καλούμενον πορφυροῦν, ἐπὶ τὰ ἱμάτια, τά τε ἀπὸ ἐρίων καὶ σηρῶν, βαφὴν ἐνδεικνύμενα ἀξίαν λόγου. Ἔστι δὲ πλέα τὰ ἐν τῇδε τῇ χώρᾳ Περσῶν τῶν Ἀτζαμίων καλουμένων· ὅσοι γὰρ τὴν Ἀτζαμίων φωνὴν προΐενται, Πέρσαι τε οὗτοι σύμπαντες καὶ τῇ Περσῶν [1.157] φωνῇ διαλέγονται. Οἰκοῦσί τε Ταβρέζην τε καὶ Καγινὸν καὶ Νιγετίην, πόλεις εὐδαίμονας τῶν Μήδων καὶ Ἀσσυρίων χώρας. Σαμαχίη δὲ πρὸς τῇ Ἀρμενίων χώρᾳ ᾠκημένη, πόλις εὐδαίμων τε καὶ πολυάνθρωπος.

72 Ἀπὸ δὲ τῆς θυγατρὸς Τζοκίεω, Καραϊσούφεω δὲ γυναικός, ἐγένετο Τζανισᾶς παῖς Καραϊσούφεω, Τζοκίεω δὲ ἀπόγονος. Οὗτος τε Παγδατίης τῆς Βαβυλῶνος ἐπῆρξε, καὶ Ἀσσυρίων τὴν χώραν καταστρεψάμενος Ταβρέζην τε ἑαυτῷ ὑπηγάγετο καὶ πρὸς τὸν Μπαϊμπούρεω παῖδα διεπολέμει. Ἐπελάσας δὲ πρὸς Ἐρτζιγγάνιν ἐπολιόρκει παραστησάμενος, καὶ τὴν Ἀρμενίων ἐντὸς Εὐφράτου χώραν ἐτύγχανεν οὖσαν ὑπηγάγετο. Μετὰ δὲ τοῦ Τζοκίεω παιδὸς ὡρμημένου ἀπὸ Σαμαρχάνδης τήν τε Βαβυλῶνα ἐπολιόρκει, καὶ αὐτὸν ἐπιόντα οἱ μάχῃ ἐπεκράτησε. Καὶ τὴν Βαβυλῶνα ἑλών, ἐπὶ Ταβρέζην ἐλαύνων, ἐς τόνδε συνδιαφέρει τὸν πόλεμον. Χασάνης μέντοι ὁ μακρός, Σκενδέρεω τοῦ τὸ Ἐρτζιγγάνιν διακατέχοντος ἀπόγονος ὢν καὶ τῆς Καραϊλούκεω μοίρας, ἐπὶ τὴν ἀρχὴν παρεγένετο τὴν Ἀρμενίων, συνελαυνομένων αὐτῷ τῶν τε Καραϊλούκεω παίδων. Οὗτοι γὰρ ὡς ὑπὸ τοῦ βασιλέως Τζανισᾶ,

other wealth. The land produces silkworms and the finest silk, better than that of Shemakha. It also produces a purple silk that is called "crimson," which highlights garments, those of both wool and silk, with a remarkable dye. Most things in this land are produced by Persians called Ajems; for all who speak the language of the Ajems are Persians and can converse in the Persian language.[121] They inhabit Tabriz, Kaginos, and Nigeti, prosperous cities of the land of the Medes and Assyrians. Shemakha is situated toward the land of the Armenians, and is a prosperous and populous city.

Jahanshah,[122] the son of Kara Yusuf and grandson of Juki, 72
was born to the daughter of Juki, the wife of Kara Yusuf.[123] He ruled Baghdad near Babylon and conquered the land of the Assyrians, subjecting Tabriz to himself and fighting against Babur's son. He advanced on Erzinjan, besieged it, and took it, and he subjected all the land of the Armenians bounded by the Euphrates.[124] When Juki's son set out from Samarkand, he besieged Babylon and, when Jahanshah came against him, he defeated him in battle.[125] He took Babylon and advanced on Tabriz, and is still waging this war. Meanwhile, Hasan the Tall, who was a descendant of Iskender who had once held Erzinjan and belonged to the tribe of Kara Yülük, came to power over the Armenians, and the sons of Kara Yülük marched with him.[126] For when they were besieged in Shemakha[127] by King Jahanshah, Kara

Καραϊσούφεω παιδός, ἐν Σαμαχίῃ πολιορκούμενοι ἐν ἀπόρῳ εἴχοντο, προσεδέοντο τοῦ Μπαϊμπούρεω ἐσβαλεῖν ἐς τὴν Μηδικήν, ὃς πεισθείς τε ἐσέβαλε, καὶ ἀπανέστη τε ὁ Τζανισᾶς ἀποχωρῶν πρὸς τὸν Μπαϊμπούρην, τὰ μὲν συμβάλλων, τὰ δὲ ληϊζόμενος τὴν χώραν ἐκείνου. Οἱ μέντοι ἡγεμόνες, ὅ τε Μενδεσίας, Ἀϊδίνης καὶ Σαρχάνης, ἁλόντος Παιαζήτεω τήν [1.158] τε χώραν κατέλαβον ἐπικελεύοντος Τεμήρεω, καὶ ἐς τὴν ἑαυτοῦ χώραν καθίστατο ἕκαστος. Ὁρῶν δὲ Χασάνης συμβαλλομένην αὐτῷ δύναμιν ἀξιόχρεων, τήν τε Ἀρμενίων χώραν ὑπηγάγετο καὶ τοὺς Τζάνιδας, καὶ πρὸς τοὺς Κολχίδος βασιλεῖς ἐπιγαμίαν ποιησάμενος εἰρήνην ἐποιήσατο.

Yusuf's son, they did not know what to do and so begged Babur to invade Media. He agreed and invaded, whereupon Jahanshah picked up and went against him, partly by engaging with him directly and partly by plundering his territories.[128] Meanwhile, the other rulers [of Asia Minor], Menteşe, Aydın, and Saruhan, reclaimed their lands at Timur's order when Bayezid was captured, so each of them was restored to his own land.[129] When Hasan saw that a significant force was attacking him, he subjected the land of the Armenians and Janids, and made peace with the kings of Kolchis through a marriage alliance.[130]

Δ'

[1.159] Μετὰ μὲν οὖν τὴν Τεμήρεω ἀναχώρησιν ἐπὶ Χερίης Ἰησοῦς ὁ πρεσβύτερος τῶν Παιαζήτεω παίδων τήν τε βασιλείαν κατέσχε, συλλέξας τε τοὺς ἀρίστους τῶν θυρῶν τοῦ πατρός, καὶ νεήλυδας προσαγόμενος, ὅσους δὴ ἠδύνατο. Τῷ γὰρ δὴ Παιαζήτῃ ἐγένοντο παῖδες οἵδε, Ἰησοῦς τε καὶ Μουσουλμάνης καὶ Μωσῆς καὶ Μεχμέτης καὶ Ἰησοῦς ὁ νεώτερος καὶ Μουσταφᾶς. Ἰησοῦς μὲν αὐτίκα μετὰ τὴν Τεμήρεω ἀναχώρησιν ἐν τῇ Ἀσίᾳ γενόμενος, ἔχων τούς τε νεήλυδας μετ' αὐτοῦ καὶ τῶν ἀρίστων, ὅσοι διέφυγον βασιλέα Τεμήρην, τά τε Προύσης βασίλεια ἔσχε, καὶ τὴν ἄλλην τῆς Ἀσίας ἀρχὴν ἑαυτῷ ὑπαγόμενος τάς τε ἀρχὰς διένειμε, καὶ ἐς τὴν Εὐρώπην διαβὰς τήν τε βασιλείαν κατέσχεν Ἑλλήνων ἐπὶ τὰ Εὐρώπης βασίλεια ὄντων. Καὶ ἄρχοντα δὲ ἐφίστησιν ἐν τῇ Εὐρώπῃ, ᾗ δὴ αὐτῷ ἐπιτηδείως ἔχειν ἐφαίνετο.

2 Μουσουλμάνης μὲν οὖν ὁρμώμενος ἀπὸ Βυζαντίου συνίστατο ἐπὶ τὸν Ἰησοῦν, καὶ τὰ πολέμια γενόμενος ἀνὴρ ἀγαθός, καὶ ἐπ' αὐτὸν προσγενομένων τῶν τῆς Εὐρώπης ἀρίστων καὶ νεηλύδων, ὅσοι τε αὐτοῦ ἐνῴκουν, ἐπῄει τε διὰ τῆς Εὐρώπης ἐπεξελθὼν καὶ ὑπαγόμενος ταύτην ἑαυτῷ, ἀπόντος τοῦ Ἰησοῦ ἐς τὴν Ἀσίαν καὶ διατρίβοντος. Μετὰ δὲ ταῦτα ἐς τὴν Ἀσίαν διαβάς, ἔχων τὸ ἀπὸ τῆς

Book 4

When Timur left for Kherie, İsa, Bayezid's eldest son,[1] took the throne, gathering to his side the leading men of his father's Porte, and securing the support of as many of the janissaries as he could. For Bayezid had the following sons: İsa, Süleyman, Musa, Mehmed, İsa the Younger,[2] and Mustafa. After Timur's departure, İsa was in Asia and, given that he had the janissaries with him and as many of the nobles as had escaped from King Timur, he took control of the palace at Prousa, assumed control of all the affairs of the realm in Asia, and distributed the offices.[3] He then crossed over into Europe and took over the kingdom while the Greeks held their capital in Europe.[4] He appointed a governor in Europe, someone whom he thought would be useful to him.

But Süleyman set out from Byzantion to engage with İsa. 2
He was a capable man when it came to war and was joined by the leading men and janissaries who lived in Europe. He advanced, marching through Europe and subjecting it to himself while İsa was absent and busy in Asia. After that he crossed over into Asia with the army from Europe and

Εὐρώπης στράτευμα, ἐστρατεύετο ἐπὶ Ἰησοῦν τὸν [1.160] ἀδελφὸν διατρίβοντα περὶ Καππαδοκίαν, ἐπεὶ συνεμάχουν οἱ τοῦ Σινωπίου ἡγεμόνες αὐτῷ καὶ οἱ τῆς συμμαχίας λοιποὶ τῶν τυράννων. Συμβαλὼν δὲ αὐτοῦ ταύτῃ τῷ ἀδελφῷ καὶ τρεψάμενος πολλά τε τοῦ στρατεύματος αὐτοῦ ἐν τῇ μάχῃ διέφθειρε, καὶ δὴ καὶ Ἰησοῦν ζωγρήσας διεχρήσατο βασιλεύσαντα ἔτη τέσσαρα. Οὗτος μὲν δὴ οὕτω καθαιρεθεὶς ὑπὸ Μουσουλμάνεω ἐτελεύτησεν.

3 Ὡς δὲ Μουσουλμάνης ἐς τὴν βασιλείαν κατέστη καὶ ἐβασίλευε, Μωσῆς μεμαθημένος καὶ ἀφεθεὶς ὑπὸ Τεμήρεω βασιλέως ἐκομίζετο ἐπὶ τὴν πατρῴαν χώραν καὶ ἐπὶ θαλάττης. Ἀφικόμενος δὲ ἐπὶ τοὺς Ὀμούρεω παῖδας τοὺς Μουσουλμάνεω πολεμίους διὰ τὴν πρὸς τὸν Ἰησοῦν αὐτῶν συμμαχίαν, ἐπὶ Σινώπην τε καὶ Καστάμονα, καὶ ἐντεῦθεν ἐπὶ Δακίαν διαβὰς διὰ τοῦ Εὐξείνου πόντου καὶ ἐπὶ Μύρξαν τὸν Δακίας ἡγεμόνα, αὐτῷ τε διελέχθη τά τε ἄλλα, καὶ ὡς ἢν ἐπὶ τὴν βασιλείαν συνεπιλάβηται, δοῦναι αὐτῷ πρόσοδον ἐν τῇ Εὐρώπῃ καὶ χώραν οὐκ ὀλίγην. Πρός τε γὰρ Ἕλληνας πολέμια ἦν αὐτῷ, ἐπεί τε Μύρξεω παῖδα αὐτοῦ ἐν Βυζαντίῳ ὑπεδέξαντο, καὶ ὑπέσχοντο τὴν ἀρχὴν αὐτῷ μετὰ Μουσουλμάνεω ἐπιτηδείου συγκατεργάσεσθαι. Οὗτος μὲν οὖν τόν τε Μωσῆν ὑπεδέξατο ἄσμενος, καὶ αὐτῷ παρείχετο τήν τε δίαιταν καὶ τὰ ἐπιτήδεια, καὶ τὸν στρατὸν δὲ αὐτῷ ἐδίδου.

4 Ἐντεῦθεν δὲ ὡς ἐς τὴν Ἀσίαν Μουσουλμάνης ἀπῆν, ἐπιρρεόντων αὐτῷ τῶν ἀπὸ τῆς Εὐρώπης, ὅσοι ἤχθοντο Μουσουλμάνῃ οὐκ εὖ φερόμενοι παρ' αὐτῷ, καὶ ὁρμώμενος λαβών τε τούτους καὶ ἀπὸ [1.161] Δακῶν στρατὸν

campaigned against his brother İsa, who was spending his time in Kappadokia, as the rulers of Sinope had allied with him along with the other tyrants of the alliance. Süleyman attacked his brother there, routed his army, and killed many of his men in the battle. He also captured İsa alive and killed him, after he had reigned for four years. İsa, then, was deposed in this way by Süleyman, and died.[5]

When Süleyman established himself on the throne and 3
began to reign, Musa, who had gained some experience and had then been released by King Timur, also returned by sea to his native land.[6] He went to the sons of Umur, who were enemies of Süleyman on account of their alliance with İsa, namely to Sinope and Kastamonu,[7] and from there he crossed the Black Sea to Wallachia and approached Mircea, the ruler of Wallachia.[8] He spoke with him about many matters, including how he might take over the throne with his help, for which he would give him an income in Europe and a lot of land. Mircea was hostile to the Greeks because they had received his son in Byzantion and had promised to assist the latter to gain the throne with the help of their ally Süleyman.[9] So he received Musa gladly, maintained him and provided him with necessities, and gave him his army.

At this point, when Süleyman went off to Asia, men from 4
Europe, who hated Süleyman because they had not been treated well by him, flocked to Musa. Musa set out with them and a large army of Wallachians, and Dan, a ruler of

ἱκανόν, ἐπισπομένου αὐτῷ καὶ Δάνου τοῦ Δακῶν ἡγεμόνος, τήν τε Εὐρώπην κατέσχε, καὶ ἐπὶ τὰ βασίλεια τῆς Ἀδριανουπόλεως παριὼν καθειστήκει τε βασιλεύς, καὶ ἐπὶ τὸν ἀδελφὸν ἐς τὴν Ἀσίαν παρεσκευάζετο στρατεύεσθαι. Μουσουλμάνης δὲ ἠπείγετο καὶ αὐτὸς φθῆναι πρότερος ἐς τὴν Ἀσίαν διαβάς· διέγνω γὰρ καὶ ἀμφοῖν ἄμεινον καὶ πρὸς τοῦ ἑτέρου εἶναι, ὁπότερος ἂν ἐπὶ τὴν τοῦ ἑτέρου ἀρχὴν διαβὰς τὴν μάχην ποιήσαιτο αὐτοῦ καὶ μὴ ἐπιμείνῃ τὸν ἀδελφὸν ἐπιόντα. Διαβάς τε ἐπὶ τὸ Βυζάντιον, ὥστε αὐτῷ φίλια εἶναι πρὸς τὸν Βυζαντίου βασιλέα, ἄγεται τὴν βασιλέως υἱϊδοῦν Ἰανυΐου τοῦ Ντόρια θυγατέρα. Υἱϊδοῦν δὲ τοῦ βασιλέως Ἑλλήνων ἀγόμενος Μουσουλμάνης ὁ Παιαζήτεω παῖς, καὶ ἐς Βυζάντιον διαβὰς ἐστρατεύετο ἐπὶ τὸν ἀδελφόν.

5 Μωσῆς δὲ ὡς τάχιστα ἐπύθετο παρὰ βασιλέα Ἑλλήνων καταλύειν ἐν Βυζαντίῳ, αὐτίκα ἐπήλαυνε, καὶ ἀπολαβὼν ἐν Βυζαντίῳ οὐκ εἴα ἐς τὴν Εὐρώπην ἐξελθόντα ἀναστρέφεσθαι. Μουσουλμάνης μὲν οὖν στρατόν, ὡς ἠδύνατο, μέγιστον ἀπὸ τῆς Ἀσίας διαπορθμεύσας ἐπὶ τὴν Βυζαντίου χώραν αὐτοῦ ἐστρατοπεδεύετο, καὶ τόν γε ἀδελφὸν ἐπιόντα ἐπέμεινεν. Ἐνταῦθα ὡς ἄμφω ἐς μάχην παρετάξαντο, συνέβαλον καὶ ἐμάχοντο. Μωσῆς μὲν τούς τε Δᾶκας καὶ Τριβαλλοὺς ἔχων μεθ᾽ ἑαυτοῦ καὶ [1.162] Στέπανον τὸν Ἐλεαζάρου παῖδα καὶ τὸ ἀπὸ τῆς Εὐρώπης στράτευμα Τούρκων παρετάσσετο. Βασιλεὺς μὲν δὴ πρὸς τοῦτον λόγους πέμψας συνεβουλεύετο αὐτῷ ἐν τῇ παρατάξει θαρροῦντα ἰέναι ἐπὶ τὸ Βυζάντιον παρὰ βασιλέα Μωσέως πολὺ ἀμείνω τε καὶ ἐπιεικέστερον· ἦν γὰρ δὴ Μωσῆς τά

the Wallachians, went with him.[10] He took over Europe and when he reached the palace at Adrianople he declared himself sultan,[11] and prepared to campaign against his brother in Asia. But Süleyman, who had crossed over into Asia, hastened to make the first move. For he realized that whichever of them crossed over into the other's territory and fought the war there, rather than waiting for his brother to attack him, would be at an advantage over the other. So he crossed over to Byzantion, given that he was on friendly terms with the king of Byzantion [Manuel II], and married the king's granddaughter, the daughter of the Genoese man Doria.[12] So Süleyman, the son of Bayezid, married the granddaughter of the king of the Greeks, crossed over to Byzantion, and marched against his brother.

As soon as Musa learned that Süleyman was staying in 5
Byzantion with the king of the Greeks, he advanced immediately and intercepted him at Byzantion, not allowing him to move into Europe and roll him back. Süleyman ferried the largest army he could from Asia over to Byzantine territory and encamped there, awaiting his brother's attack. Both sides deployed for battle, engaged, and fought.[13] Musa had the Wallachians and Serbs on his side along with Stefan, the son of Lazar,[14] and he also deployed the European army of the Turks. The king of the Greeks, however, sent word to Stefan and advised him, while he was in formation for battle, that it would be a much better and more reasonable choice for him to desert Musa and have every confidence in coming over to Byzantion; for Musa was generally

τε ἄλλα ἐπαχθὴς ἐς τοὺς συμμάχους καὶ ἐς ὀργὴν ταχύς. Στέπανος μὲν οὖν ἐν τῇ παρατάξει ὡς τῷ Ἑλλήνων συνέθετο βασιλεῖ τε καὶ Μουσουλμάνῃ, αὐτομολήσαντες ἀφίκοντο ἐπὶ Βυζάντιον.

6 Μωσῆς δὲ ὡς ἐμάχετο συμμίξας τῷ ἀδελφῷ, τούς τε ἀπὸ τῆς Ἀσίας ἐτρέψατο καὶ ἐπεξελθὼν ἐδίωκε. Μουσουλμάνης δὲ ὡς ἡττηθεὶς ἀνεχώρει ἐπὶ Βυζάντιον, ὡς ἐγένετο παρὰ τῇ πόλει, ἐπιλεξάμενος βουλὴν γενναιοτάτην καὶ ἔχων μεθ' ἑαυτοῦ ὡσεὶ πεντακοσίους ἄνδρας, ἐπιρρεόντων καὶ ἄλλων τινῶν, ὑποδυόμενος τὴν τῆς πόλεως τάφρον, ἔχοντος τοῦ ἀδελφοῦ Μωσέως ἀμφὶ τὴν δίωξιν καὶ διαφθείροντος σὺν τοῖς ἑαυτοῦ, ὡς ἐπεξέρχοιτο τοὺς πολεμίους, ἐπὶ τὸ στρατόπεδον αὐτοῦ ἀφικόμενος τό τε στρατόπεδον κατειλήφει, καὶ τοὺς ἐπιγινομένους ἀπὸ τῆς μάχης, οἳ καταφεύγουσί τε καὶ ἐπανῄεσαν, διέφθειρε. Καὶ ὡς ἐπανήκει τε αὐτὸς Μωσῆς ἐλαύνων ἐπὶ τὸ στρατόπεδον ἀπὸ τῆς μάχης, καὶ ἔγνω δὴ κατειλημμένον τὸ στρατόπεδον, αὐτίκα ἐς φυγήν τε αὐτὸς ἐτράπετο καὶ τοῦ στρατεύματος διέφυγε, καὶ ἄλλη ἄλλος, ᾗ ἑκάστῳ [1.163] προὐχώρει. Οἱ μέν τινες καὶ ἐπ' αὐτὸν αὐτίκα ἰόντες τὸν Μουσουλμάνην ὡς βασιλέα προσεκύνουν, καὶ ἐξελαύνοντι ἐφείποντο. Μουσουλμάνης μὲν δὴ οὕτω τὰ πράγματα ἔσχεν ἀμφὶ ταῖν ἠπείροιν, γενναιότατα δὲ πάντων, ὧν ἡμεῖς ἴσμεν, πρὸς τὸν ἀδελφὸν διαγωνισάμενος.

7 Ἐπελάσας μὲν οὖν ἐς τὴν Ἀδριανούπολιν τὰ βασίλεια, τήν τε βασιλείαν καὶ τὴν ἀρχὴν καθίστη αὐτῷ, ᾗ ἐδόκει κράτιστα ἔχειν. Μωσῆς μὲν οὖν ἐς τὴν παρίστριον χώραν ἀφικόμενος, καὶ συγγενόμενος Μύρξεω Δάνῳ τῷ Δακίας

detested by the allies and had a hot temper. Accordingly, Stefan agreed on the matter with the king of the Greeks and with Süleyman while he was in formation, deserted, and came over to Byzantion.

When Musa engaged with his brother in battle, he routed 6
the soldiers from Asia and began the pursuit. Süleyman, defeated, withdrew to Byzantion but, when he reached the city, he made a courageous decision: having about five hundred men with him, and with others coming to join him, he slipped down into the city's moat while his brother Musa was hard in pursuit with his men and killing them. To strike back against the enemy, he reached Musa's camp and occupied it, killing those who had survived the battle and who were fleeing there to seek shelter. When Musa himself arrived, as he returned to his camp from the battle and realized that it was occupied, he immediately turned to flight and ran away from his army, while his men scattered every which way. Some of them even went straight to Süleyman himself and did obeisance to him as their sultan, pledging to march with him on campaign. So this was Süleyman's situation on both continents, after he had fought against his brother more bravely than anyone else of whom we know.

He marched to the palace at Adrianople and established 7
himself in power on the throne in the way that seemed best to him. Musa, meanwhile, went to the Danubian region and met up with Dan, the son of Mircea and ruler of Wallachia,

ἡγεμόνι καὶ πρότερον ὄντι συνήθει αὐτῷ, διέτριβε παρὰ τῷ Αἵμῳ, παραμείβων ἄλλην ἐξ ἄλλης χώραν. Μουσουλμάνου δὲ ῥᾳθυμοῦντός τε καὶ περὶ ὁμιλίαν ἔχοντος τά τε πράγματα οἰδαίνετο. Οἵτε γὰρ ἄρχοντες αὐτῷ τε ἤχθοντο ὡς οὐδὲν ὑγιὲς ὂν αὐτοῦ, καὶ τῷ ἀδελφῷ αὐτοῦ προσγενομένων κατὰ βραχὺ τῶν Τούρκων οὐδένα λόγον ἐποιεῖτο. Ὡς μὲν οὖν ἐπὶ τὴν βασιλείαν ἀφίκετο, τήν τε Θέρμην τοῖς Ἕλλησιν ἀπέδωκε καὶ Ζητοῦνιν καὶ τὴν παράλιον τῆς Ἀσίας χώραν, καὶ ἐπιτήδειος ὢν ἐχαρίσατο αὐτοῖς, εἴ του δέοιντο, ὡς δυνατὸν ἦν αὐτῷ. Ἐπρεσβεύοντο μὲν οὖν αὐτῷ καὶ οἱ Ἕλληνες, βουλευόμενοι μὴ ἀνεῖναι αὐτὸν ἐς τὴν ὁμιλίαν οὕτω πάνυ, ὡς ἐπισφαλές τε ὂν αὐτῷ καὶ οὐδαμῇ ἐμπεδοῦν αὐτῷ τὴν βασιλείαν πρὸς τὸν ἀδελφόν. Τούτων μὲν οὐδένα λόγον ποιούμενος, ἕωθεν δὲ καὶ ἐς ἑσπέραν περὶ τὴν [1.164] ἀκρατοποσίαν διετέλει, προπίνων τοῖς ἀρίστοις, καὶ ὡς ἀναπαύοιτο, ἐπεγειρόμενος αὖθις ἐς ὁμιλίαν καθίστατο. Λέγεται δέ, ὡς ἔχοντος ἐν ταῖς χερσὶ τὴν φιάλην ἔλαφος ἐπὶ τὸ στρατόπεδον περιὼν διῄει, καὶ ἐπιθορυβούντων αὐτῷ τῶν στρατιωτῶν, ὡς ἡ ἔλαφος ἐπιπαρῇ, ἀγχοῦ γενόμενος ἐπειρᾶτο, εἰ φιάλην ἐπὶ τοῦ κέρατος φέροι, ὡς ταύτην ἀνακτησόμενος ἐπὶ τῆς ὁμιλίας. Ἦν μέντοι ἄλλως ὁ Μουσουλμάνης ἐπιεικὴς καὶ τὸ σῶμα ῥωμαλέος καὶ ὁρμὴν ἐς τὸ μάχεσθαι κράτιστος.

8 Μωσῆς δὲ τοὐναντίον θυμοῦ τε ἀκρατέστερος ὡς ἐπίπαν, καὶ ταχὺς δὲ μάλιστα ἐς ὀργήν, καὶ ἕπεσθαι τῷ δυσμενεῖ μηδὲν ἀνιέντα. Ἐπεί τε οὖν ἐπιγενομένων αὐτῷ οὐκ ὀλίγων ἐς τὸ πεδίον κατέβη καὶ ἐπὶ Μουσουλμάνην

who was his associate from before.[15] He spent time by the Haimos, moving from place to place. But Süleyman grew lazy and became preoccupied with banquets while his public affairs fell into disorder. The lords began to detest him and thought that he was unreliable, and he paid no attention to the fact that the Turks were gradually going over to his brother. When he gained the throne he returned Thessalonike to the Greeks along with Lamia and the coastal land of Asia.[16] He was their friend and granted them any favor that was in his power to give, if they asked it of him. The Greeks sent him envoys, advising him not to be so deeply engrossed in his banquets, as he was endangering himself and was doing nothing to secure his throne against his brother. But he paid no attention to them and spent all his time, from dawn to dusk, drinking heavily. He would start drinking before breakfast and, after resting in the afternoon, would rise and head straight back to the banquet. It is said that once, when he was holding the bottle in his hand, a stag wandered into the camp. The soldiers loudly alerted him that a stag was there, but he tried to get close enough to place the bottle in its antlers so that he might retrieve it during his banquet. In other respects, however, Süleyman was sensible, physically strong, and had a strong passion for fighting.

Musa, by contrast, had an altogether uncontrollable temper and quickly grew angry, and he would not let up in the pursuit of his enemies. After many had rallied to his side, he came down onto the plain and advanced against 8

ἤλαυνε, Χασάνης τε ὁ τῶν νεηλύδων ἄρχων καὶ Βρενέζης ἔχων ἱπποδρόμους τῆς Εὐρώπης ηὐτομόλησαν αὐτίκα παρὰ Μωσέα. Ὁ δὲ ὡς ᾔσθετο τοὺς νεήλυδας ἀφεστηκότας ἰέναι ἐπὶ τὸν ἀδελφόν, ἤλαυνεν εὐθὺ Βυζαντίου ἐπὶ τοῖς Ἕλλησι καὶ τὴν Βυζαντίου βασιλείαν ἐν νῷ ἔχων συμμῖξαι, ὡς ἐντεῦθεν αὖ ἐπὶ τὴν Ἀσίαν διαβὰς ἐπιχειροῖ τὰ ἐν τῇ Ἀσίᾳ πράγματα. Καὶ ὡς ἔχων τοῖς Τούρκοις ἐπίδηλος ἦν κατὰ τὴν ὁδὸν τὴν ἐς τὸ Βυζάντιον φέρουσαν, ἐνταῦθα συλλεγέντες οἱ τήνδε τὴν χώραν {1.165} οἰκοῦντες Τοῦρκοι τόν τε Μουσουλμάνην ἐζώγρησαν καὶ ἀπήγαγον παρὰ Μωσέα, χαριζόμενοι τῷ βασιλεῖ. Ὁ μέντοι Μωσῆς τόν τε ἀδελφὸν διεχρήσατο καὶ τούς γε Τούρκους πανοικί, οἳ συλλαβόντες ἧκον ἄγοντες, πυρὶ σὺν γυναιξί τε ἅμα καὶ παισὶν ἐνέπρησε, φάμενος ἀθέμιτα ἐργασαμένους, καὶ βασιλέα σφῶν αὐτῶν συλλαβόντες ταύτην τὴν δίκην ὑπέχοιεν.

9 Αὐτὸς δὴ ὑπέλαβε τὴν βασιλείαν, καὶ ἐς τὴν Ἀσίαν διαβὰς κατεστήσατο τὰ ἐκείνου πράγματα, καὶ ἐδόκει αὐτῷ ἀσφαλέστατα ἕξειν. Καὶ ἐπήλαυνεν ἐν νῷ ἔχων πολιορκήσειν Βυζάντιον, καὶ τῇ τε Θέρμῃ πόλεμον ἐπήνεγκε, καὶ τῷ Τριβαλλῶν ἡγεμόνι πολεμῶν διεγένετο, τήν τε χώραν αὐτοῦ θ' ἅμα ληϊζόμενος καὶ Σπενδερόβην τὴν μητρόπολιν αὐτοῦ πολιορκῶν. Στέπανος μὲν οὖν οὗτος Ἐλεαζάρου Παιαζήτεω τῆς γυναικὸς ἀδελφός, Βοῦλκος δὲ τοὔνομα ἔχων. Ὡς Ἐλεάζαρος ἐτελεύτησε, τήν τε ἡγεμονίαν παρέλαβε καὶ ἐτυράννευε, τῷ τε Παιαζήτῃ συστρατευόμενος, ᾗ ἂν παραγγέλλῃ. Καὶ τότε δὴ ἐν τῇ πρὸς Μουσουλμάνην γενομένῃ μάχῃ πρὸς τῷ Βυζαντίῳ μετέστη τε ἀπὸ Μωσέως

Süleyman. Hasan, the commander of the janissaries, and Evrenos, who led the cavalry raiders in Europe, immediately defected to Musa's side. When Süleyman realized that the janissaries had rebelled and gone over to his brother, he made straight for the Greeks of Byzantion with the intention of joining forces with the kingdom of Byzantion; then, from there he would cross over to Asia again and take care of his Asian affairs. But as he was doing this he was clearly identified by the Turks on the road that leads to Byzantion.[17] The Turks who lived in that area assembled, captured Süleyman alive, and took him off to Musa, hoping to ingratiate themselves with the sultan. Musa killed his brother but, as for the Turks who had arrested him and brought him there, he burned them alive with their entire households, including their women and children. He claimed that they had done something forbidden by arresting their own sultan, and so they should suffer this punishment.

Musa now ascended the throne and, after crossing to 9
Asia, set his affairs in order. It seemed to him that they would be most secure. He then set out with the intention of besieging Byzantion. He fought a war against Thessalonike and waged war against the ruler of the Serbs, plundering his land and besieging his capital, Smederevo. Now this Stefan, the son of Lazar, was the brother of Bayezid's wife, and was named Vuk. When Lazar died he had received the principality and became tyrant. He campaigned with Bayezid when ordered to do so. In the battle against Süleyman that had then taken place before Byzantion, Stefan had abandoned

ἐπὶ τὸν ἀδελφὸν καὶ ηὐτομόλησε· δι’ ἃ δὲ πόλεμον ἐπιφέρων τήν τε πόλιν αὐτοῦ ἐπολιόρκει καὶ τὴν χώραν ἐδῄου.

10 Ὡς δὲ ἐπελαύνων ἐπολιόρκει Βυζάντιον, ἐξηρτύετό τε ἅμα ἐπιφέρων τε καὶ ἐπέχων, ὅσα τῆς χώρας ἠδύνατο, καὶ τριήρεις καὶ πλοῖα, ὡς ἠδύνατο, πλεῖστα ναυπηγησάμενος ἐπῄει διά τε τῆς ἠπείρου καὶ διὰ θαλάσσης. [1.166] Ἐνταῦθα πληρώσαντες οἱ Ἕλληνες πλοῖα, ὅσα ἐπῆν αὐτοῖς, καὶ δὴ καὶ τριήρεις, ἡγουμένου Ἐμμανουήλου τοῦ νόθου Ἰωάννου τοῦ βασιλέως παιδός, ἀντανήγοντό τε καὶ ἐναυμάχησαν· καὶ ἐνίκησαν οἱ Ἕλληνες. Οὗτος δὲ ὁ Ἐμμανουῆλος, ὁ τοῦ βασιλέως παῖς, τὰ ἐς γνῶσιν καὶ φρόνησιν οὐδενὸς λειπόμενος, ἐπὶ τὸ ἐξηγεῖσθαι ἐς πόλεμον ἱκανός τε ἐδόκει ἐν τῷ τότε παρόντι καὶ ηὐδοκίμει. Δι’ ἃ δὴ εὐδοκιμῶν ἑάλω τε ὑπὸ τοῦ ἀδελφοῦ βασιλέως, καὶ ἐσπεσὼν ἐς εἱρκτὴν διεγένετο ἐπὶ ἔτη ἑπτακαίδεκα σὺν τοῖς παισὶν αὐτοῦ.

11 Μωσῆς μὲν οὖν ὡς ἐσφάλη τὴν κατὰ θάλασσαν δύναμιν, ἐπιὼν διὰ τῆς ἠπείρου ἐδῄου τε τὴν Βυζαντίου χώραν καὶ Θέρμην, ἣν ἐπολιόρκει καὶ Τριβαλλοῖς ἐπολέμει. Πρὸς μὲν οὖν τοὺς ἐν τῇ Ἀσίᾳ Τούρκων ἡγεμόνας σπονδὰς ποιησάμενος εἰρήνην ἦγε, καὶ ἐν τῇ Εὐρώπῃ τὰ πολλὰ διατρίβων ἐτύγχανεν. Ἕλληνες μὲν οὖν, ὡς ἐτελεύτησε Μουσουλμάνης, ἐπαγόμενοι τὸν παῖδα αὐτοῦ, τοὔνομα Ὀρχάνην, συνέστησαν ἐπὶ Μωσεῖ· μετὰ δὲ ταῦτα ἔπεμψαν ἐς τὴν Θέρμην, ὡς ἐντεῦθεν τῷ τε Μπογδάνῳ καὶ τοῖς ἄλλοις τοῖς ταύτῃ Τούρκων διὰ χρημάτων ἐπικούροις ὁρμώμενός τε ἐπὶ τὴν Εὐρώπην ἐπελαύνοι καὶ τὴν χώραν

Musa and defected to his brother. It was for this reason that Musa was making war against him, besieging his city, and plundering his land.[18]

Musa also marched out and besieged Byzantion.[19] He 10
equipped his army, brought it up, and positioned it as well as the terrain permitted; he also built as many triremes and ships as he could, and attacked the city both by land and sea. Then the Greeks manned all the ships they had, as well as their triremes, and put Manuel, the illegitimate son of King Ioannes, in command.[20] They attacked and fought a naval battle. And the Greeks won. This Manuel, the king's son, was second to none in his judgment and good sense, and seemed, at that time, to be very capable when it came to military leadership and was generally highly regarded. Because of this high regard, however, he was arrested by the king's brother and thrown into prison where he and his children stayed for seventeen years.[21]

When Musa's naval attack failed, he attacked by land and 11
plundered the hinterlands of Byzantion and Thessalonike, which he besieged; he also fought against the Serbs. He made a peace treaty with the rulers of the Turks in Asia and so spent most of his time in Europe. But the Greeks, when Süleyman died, had backed his son Orhan and set him up against Musa. After these events they sent Orhan to Thessalonike so that, using it as his base, he could attack Europe from there and subject the land with the help of Bogdan[22] and the other Turkish mercenaries. The boy was entrusted

κατάσχοι. Ὁ μέντοι παῖς ἐπετέτραπτο ἀνδρὶ Τούρκῳ ἀπὸ Ἀσίας, Παλαπάνῳ τοὔνομα, τὰ μὲν ἄλλα οὐκ ἀγεννεῖ, πιστῷ δὲ οὐ πάνυ. Καὶ ἐς τὴν Θέρμην ἀφίκετο, ἐξιὼν δ' ἐντεῦθεν ᾔει διὰ τῆς Μακεδονίας ἐπὶ Βέρροιάν τε καὶ τὴν ταύτῃ [1.167] χώραν, καὶ προσχωρούντων αὐτῷ τῶν ταύτῃ ἐπινεμομένων Τούρκων ἤλαυνεν ἐπὶ Θετταλίαν. Μωσῆς δὲ ὡς ἐπύθετο τὸν Μουσουλμάνεω παῖδα τήν τε χώραν ὑπαγόμενον καὶ ἐλαύνοντα ἐπὶ Θετταλίαν, συντίθεται προδοσίαν τῷ Παλαπάνῳ, ὥστε παραδοῦναι αὐτῷ τὸν παῖδα ἐπιόντι καὶ διασημῆναι ἑκάστοτε, ὅποι ἐλαύνοιεν περιϊόντες. Οὗτος μὲν οὖν ὡς ἑκασταχοῦ ποι τῆς χώρας ἐπίοι, διεσήμαινέ τε τῷ Μωσεῖ καὶ ἐδήλου, ᾗ ἐπιὼν σφίσιν τε περιτύχοι καὶ τὸν παῖδα παραδοίη αὐτῷ. Ἐγένοντο μὲν οὖν οἱ ἀμφὶ τὸν παῖδα ἐπὶ τὸ ἐς Θετταλίαν καθῆκον ὄρος τῆς Μακεδονίας, καὶ ἐνταῦθα ὡς ὑπεσημήνατο ὑπὸ Παλαπάνεω τῷ Μωσεῖ, ἐπιὼν τόν τε παῖδα ἐζώγρησε καὶ τὸν στρατὸν διέφθειρε. Μετὰ δὲ ταῦτα ἐπὶ τὴν Μπογδάνου χώραν ἀφικόμενος τήν τε χώραν αὐτῷ ταύτῃ ὑπηγάγετο, καὶ τοῖς Ἕλλησι διαπολεμῶν προσεῖχεν ἐντεταμένως. Ἕλληνες μὲν οὖν οὕτως ἐπολεμοῦντο.

12 Καὶ Ἰησοῦς ὁ νεώτερος τῶν Παιαζήτεω παίδων ἐπὶ τοὺς Ἕλληνας ἀφικόμενος ἔστε τὴν τοῦ Ἰησοῦ θρησκείαν μετέβαλλε, καὶ οὐ πολλῷ ὕστερον ἐτελεύτησε. Μεχμέτης μὲν οὖν, καὶ οὗτος Μωσέως μὲν ἀδελφός, παῖς δὲ Παιαζήτεω, ἀπὸ τῆς Καραμάνου χώρας ὁρμώμενος, ἐπειδὴ ἐν ἱκανῷ ἡλικίας ἦν, τούς τε συγγενεῖς τῶν Τούρκων μετήει, οἷς ἐπὶ τὴν ἀρχὴν ἐπιπαριών. Καὶ διαπρεσβευομένων, καὶ τῶν Ἑλλήνων ὑποδεχομένων καὶ αὐτῶν κατὰ δύναμιν ἐς

to a Turkish man from Asia by the name of Balaban, who was noble in other respects but not very trustworthy. Orhan reached Thessalonike and then went on through Macedonia to Berroia and the land there. Joined by the Turks who lived there, he advanced on Thessaly. When Musa learned that Süleyman's son was taking over the land and advancing on Thessaly, he came to a treacherous arrangement with Balaban: the latter would turn the boy over to Musa when he arrived and, meanwhile, keep him constantly informed of their movements. And Balaban did inform Musa of each stage of their journey and specified where he could meet them if he were to come, so that he could turn the boy over to him. So when the boy's retinue was near the mountain of Macedonia that borders on Thessaly, there, when Balaban gave the signal, Musa attacked them, captured the boy alive, and destroyed his army.[23] After that, Musa moved on to Bogdan's territory and subjected the land to himself. He also fought persistently against the Greeks. Thus the Greeks became involved in the war.

İsa, the youngest of Bayezid's sons, also came to the 12
Greeks and even converted to the religion of Jesus, and died shortly afterward.[24] As for Mehmed, who was also a brother of Musa and Bayezid's son, he set out from the land of Karaman when he came of age and sought out his Turkish relatives in the hope that they would assist him in claiming the throne.[25] They sent envoys whom the Greeks received well, promising all their help in raising him to the throne.

τὴν [1.168] βασιλείαν αὐτῷ συλλήψεσθαι, τήν τε Ἀσίαν ὑπηγάγετο, ἀχθομένων τῶν τῆς Ἀσίας ἀρίστων τῆς Μωσέως ἐν ἀρχῇ τυραννίδος καὶ προσχωρούντων τῷ Μεχμέτῃ, τῆς τε Ἀσίας ὑπῆρξε καὶ ἐπεὶ τὴν Εὐρώπην ὑπηγάγετο. Οὗτος μὲν δή, ὡς Μουσουλμάνης τε ἐβασίλευε καὶ Μωσῆς καὶ Ἰησοῦς, πρότερον οἱ τὸ παιδίον ἐπιτετραμμένοι, μὴ κατάδηλον, ὅποι τυγχάνοι ὂν τὸ παιδίον γενόμενον τοῖς ἀδελφοῖς, δεδοικότες, μὴ συλληφθείη τε καὶ ἀπόλοιτο, χορδοποιοῦ τινός, ἐν Προύσῃ παρεκατέθεντο, ὡς ἂν τὴν τέχνην ἐκμανθάνοι. Καὶ μετὰ ταῦτα, ὡς ἐνταῦθα τῆς ἡλικίας ἦν, ὅπῃ ἀντιλαβέσθαι τῶν πραγμάτων αὐτῶν οἷός τ' ἦν, ἐχώρει ἐπὶ Καραμᾶνον τὸν Ἀλισούριον. Καὶ ἐντεῦθεν δή, ὡς πρόσθεν μοι ἐδηλοῦτο, ὁρμώμενος τῆς τε Ἀσίας εὐπετῶς ἦρξε, συνεπιλαβομένου τοῦ Καραμάνου καί τινων ἄλλων ἡγεμόνων τῶν ἐν τῇ Ἀσίᾳ.

13 Καὶ ἐπὶ Βυζάντιον διαβὰς τῷ τε Ἑλλήνων βασιλεῖ ἐς λόγους ἀφίκετο, καὶ ὅρκια ποιησάμενοι, ᾗ ἐδόκει αὐτοῖς ἐπιτηδείως ἔχειν, ἤλαυνεν ἐπὶ τῶν Τριβαλλῶν ἡγεμόνα, τὰ τῆς Θρᾴκης, ὡς συμμίξων τε ἐκείνῳ καὶ προσλαβὼν τὴν ἐκείνου δύναμιν ἐπίῃ μαχούμενος τῷ ἀδελφῷ. Μωσῆς μέντοι, ἐπεὶ ἐπύθετο τάχιστα διαβαίνοντα ἀπὸ τῆς Ἀσίας, ἐπήλαυνε σὺν πολλῷ τῷ στρατεύματι ἐπ' αὐτόν, [1.169] καί ποι τῆς χώρας διελαύνοντι κατὰ Χαριούπολιν προσέμιξε τῷ ἀδελφῷ καὶ ἐς μάχην καθίστατο. Συνταξάμενος δὲ ἐπῄει· καὶ ὁ ἀδελφὸς αὐτοῦ Μεχμέτης ἀντεπῄει συντεταγμένῳ τῷ στρατεύματι. Καὶ ὡς ὁμόσε ἐγένοντο τοῖν ἀδελφοῖν τὰ στρατεύματα, τὸ μὲν τῆς Ἀσίας διαβὰν σὺν τῷ Μεχμέτῃ, τὸ δὲ ἀπὸ τῆς Εὐρώπης, συνέμισγον καὶ

Mehmed subjected Asia, as the leading men detested Musa's tyrannical rule and went over to him. And so Mehmed came to rule Asia and then subjected Europe. Regarding Mehmed, then: while Süleyman was reigning and then Musa and İsa, those who had earlier been entrusted with the boy feared that his brothers might learn where he was, in which case he would be taken and killed. So they entrusted him to a rope maker in Prousa, that he might learn this skill.[26] Later on, when he came of age and was fit to make his own decisions, he went to Karaman Alishur.[27] It was from there, as I mentioned above, that he set out and easily took over Asia, with the help of Karaman and some of the other Asian rulers.

Mehmed crossed over to Byzantion and entered into ne- 13
gotiations with the king of the Greeks [Manuel II]. They swore oaths on terms that seemed advantageous to them and then he went to the ruler of the Serbs, in Thrace, so that by joining up with him and gaining his forces he could go and fight against his brother. But when Musa learned that he had quickly crossed over from Asia, he advanced against him with a large army. He engaged with his brother while the latter was passing through the land somewhere near Charioupolis and forced him to battle. He deployed his soldiers in formation and then attacked him. And his brother Mehmed returned the attack with his army also in military formation. When the armies of the two brothers came together, the one that had crossed over with Mehmed from Asia and the other that was from Europe, they engaged and

ἐμάχοντο. Μετ' οὐ πολὺ δὲ ἐτράπετο τὸ ἀπὸ τῆς Ἀσίας στράτευμα, καὶ ὥρμητο ἐς φυγήν. Μεχμέτης μὲν δὴ ὁ χορδίνης ἐπὶ Ἀλίην Παιαζήτεω παῖδα ἐς Βυζάντιον διεσώζετο, καὶ τὰ στρατεύματα διεσώζοντο. Ἐντεῦθεν αὖθις ἐπὶ τὴν Ἀσίαν διαβάντα ἐπερρώννυντό τε αὖ καὶ ἀνελαμβάνοντο σφᾶς, ὡς αὖθις ἐπιόντες καὶ ἀναμαχούμενοι τῷ Μωσεῖ περὶ τῶν ἄλλων πραγμάτων.

14 Χρόνου δὲ οὐ πολλοῦ διελθόντος συναγείρας τὸ τῆς Ἀσίας στράτευμα διεπορθμεύετο ὑπὸ τῶν Ἑλλήνων ἐς τὴν Εὐρώπην. Ἐς μὲν οὖν τὴν Ἀσίαν διαβῆναι τὸν Μωσέα διεκώλυον Ἕλληνες, ἐπεὶ ἐπεκράτουν τὴν τῆς θαλάττης διάβασιν, καὶ τόν τε Ἑλλήσποντον ἐπετήρουν καὶ τὸ ἐν Προποντίδι Ἱερόν. Μεχμέτης μὲν οὖν, ὡς ἐς τὴν Εὐρώπην διέβη αὐτῷ τὰ στρατεύματα, ἵετο εὐθὺ Τριβαλλῶν ὡς τὴν δύναμιν ἐκείνων προσληψόμενος ἀξιόχρεων οὖσαν. Ὡς δὲ ἠπείγετο συμμῖξαι Μωσῆς, ὡς ἐγένετο ἐν Πανίου χώρᾳ οὕτω καλουμένῃ τῇ ὑπὲρ τὸν Αἶμον χώρᾳ, ἐνταῦθα καταλαμβάνει ἐπίπροσθεν γενόμενος διὰ τοῦ ὄρους ὁ Μωσῆς τοῦ ἀδελφοῦ. Καὶ ὡς ᾔσθετο [1.170] ἐπιόντα τὸν ἀδελφὸν ἐγγυτάτω οἱ γενέσθαι, παρετάξατό τε καὶ εἰς μάχην καθίστη. Μετ' οὐ πολὺ δὲ ἐτράπετο, καὶ φεύγων ᾤχετο ἐπὶ τῶν Τριβαλλῶν ἡγεμόνα.

15 Καὶ ἐπειδὴ διέτριβεν αὐτοῦ, ἔπεμπε λόγους παρὰ τῶν Τούρκων τοὺς ἀρίστους περὶ ἀποστάσεως, πρός τε Χασάνην τῶν ἐπηλύδων ἄρχοντα καὶ ἐπὶ Βρενέζεα καὶ Ἀμουράτην. Οἱ δὲ τούς τε λόγους προΐεντο καὶ σφίσι λόγον ἐδίδοσαν περὶ ἀποστάσεως. Ἐντεῦθεν Βρενέζης αὐτός τε αὐτομολεῖ παρὰ Μεχμέτην, ἔχων παρ' ἑαυτῷ Τούρκους τε

fought. The army from Asia was soon routed and put to flight.[28] Mehmed the rope maker sought refuge with Ali, a son of Bayezid,[29] in Byzantion, and his armies were also saved. At that point they crossed over into Asia again, gathered their strength, and regrouped so that they could again attack Musa and fight him over the rest of the realm.

Not much time passed before Mehmed had assembled 14
the army of Asia and was ferried by the Greeks to Europe. The Greeks had prevented Musa from crossing over into Asia, as they controlled the straits and patrolled the Hellespont and Hieron in the Propontis.[30] Mehmed, then, when his armies had crossed over into Europe, went straight to the Serbs so that he could gain their forces, which were substantial. But Musa was eager to engage with him when he reached the land of Panion,[31] which is what the land above the Haimos is called. There, by going over the mountain, Musa intercepted his brother. When Mehmed realized that his brother was close by and about to attack him, he deployed and prepared for battle. But he [presumably Mehmed] was quickly routed and fled, going to the ruler of the Serbs.[32]

While Mehmed was residing there, he sent messages to 15
the leading Turks urging them to rebel, to Hasan, the commander of the janissaries, to Evrenos, and to Murad.[33] They replied, giving their word that they would rebel. Then Evrenos personally defected to Mehmed, taking with him as

ὡς πλείστους καὶ δὴ καὶ τοὺς παῖδας Χασάνεω[1] σὺν τῶν νεηλύδων τοῖς ἀρίστοις. Ἐντεῦθεν ὡς τῷ Μεχμέτῃ προσεγένετο δύναμις, ὥστε διαπειρᾶσθαι ἱκανὸς εἶναι τοῦ ἀδελφοῦ, λαβὼν καὶ τὸν Τριβαλλῶν ἡγεμόνα μεθ' ἑαυτοῦ ἤλαυνεν ἐπὶ τὸν ἀδελφὸν ὡς μαχούμενος. Μωσῆς μὲν οὖν διανοούμενος ἐμποδὼν γενέσθαι τῷ ἀδελφῷ, ὥστε μὴ ἐξελαύνειν εἰς τὴν Εὐρώπην καὶ προσάγεσθαι αὐτῷ τὴν χώραν, ἔχων τάς τε θύρας καὶ τὸ τῆς Εὐρώπης στράτευμα ἅπαν πλὴν τῶν παρὰ Μεχμέτην αὐτομολησάντων, διέτριβε κατὰ τὴν τῶν Μυσῶν χώραν.

16 Ἐνταῦθα ἐξελθὼν ὁ Μεχμέτης ἐστρατοπεδεύετο. Ὡς δὲ ἀγχοῦ γενόμενος τῷ στρατεύματι Μωσέως, παρετάξατο εἰς μάχην· καὶ εἶχε μὲν τὸ εὐώνυμον αὐτοῦ κέρας ὁ τῶν Τριβαλλῶν ἡγεμών, τὸ δεξιὸν δὲ Βρενέζης σὺν τοῖς παισὶν αὐτοῦ· παρῆσαν γὰρ αὐτῷ παῖδες γενόμενοι ἀγαθοὶ Βαράμος τε καὶ Ἀλίης καὶ Βείκης καὶ Ἰησοῦς. Ἐπειδὴ [1.171] δὲ καὶ Μωσῆς παραταξάμενος εἶχεν ἐν τάξει τὰ στρατεύματα αὐτοῦ, καὶ παριὼν ἐπεσκόπει καὶ καθίστη, ὡς αὐτῷ ἐδόκει, παρελαύνων ἁπανταχῇ. Ἐνταῦθα Χασάνης ὁ τῶν νεηλύδων ἄρχων αὐτομολήσας, τότε δὴ προσελάσας τῷ ἵππῳ ἐπὶ τὸ Μωσέως στράτευμα ἐφώνει πρὸς τοὺς νεήλυδας. "Ὦ παῖδες, τί διαμέλλετε καὶ οὐκ ἐξέρχεσθε ὅτι τάχιστα ἐπὶ τὸν βασιλέα ὑμῶν, ἄνδρα τε τῶν τοῦ γένους Ὀτουμανίδων δικαιότατόν τε καὶ ἐπιεικέστατον καὶ πάντας δὴ τοῦ γένους αὐτοῦ ὑπερβαλλόμενον ἀρετῇ, ἀλλὰ ἀνέχεσθε ὑβριζόμενοι καὶ κακῶς πράττοντες ὑπ' ἀνδρὸς ὑβριστοῦ τῇ φύσει καὶ ἀλαζόνος καὶ ἑαυτῷ καὶ τοῖς ἐπιτηδείοις αὐτοῦ οὐδὲν ὑγιὲς ἔχοντος;"

many Turks as he could, including the sons of Hasan and the leading janissaries. Then, when Mehmed had assembled substantial forces to make trial of his brother, he took the ruler of the Serbs with him and advanced to fight his brother. Musa's plan was to block his brother from marching into Europe and taking over that land, so he took the Porte and the entire army of Europe, except for those who had defected to Mehmed, and made his base in Bulgarian territory.

Mehmed marched off there and made camp.[34] When he 16
came near to Musa's army, he deployed for battle. The ruler of the Serbs held his left wing, and Evrenos the right, with his sons; for his sons were present, and they were good men, Barak, Ali, Beyce, and İsa. Then Musa deployed and placed his armies in formation; going along the ranks, he inspected them and set them in order, as seemed best to him, and he rode along the entire length. At that point, Hasan, the commander of the janissaries who had defected, rode his horse up to Musa's army and called out to the janissaries: "My sons! What are you waiting for? Why are you not coming forward as quickly as you can to your sultan, a man of Ottoman lineage, who is most just, reasonable, and surpasses his entire family in virtue? Why instead do you endure insults and maltreatment at the hands of a man who is offensive by nature, arrogant, and completely unreliable to himself and his friends?"

17 Ταῦτα λέγοντος τοῦ Χασάνεω, ὥσπερ ἐλαύνων ἐπὶ τὰς συντάξεις ἤκουεν, ὅ τι λέγοι ὁ ἀνὴρ οὗτος, ὑπολαβὼν δέ τις ἔφασκεν. "Ἀλλ', ὦ βασιλεῦ, οὐχ ὁρᾷς Χασάνην τὸν νεηλύδων ἄρχοντα, μέγα τιμηθέντα ὑπὸ σοῦ, ὡς ἐξυβρίζει τοὺς νεήλυδας ἐπικαλούμενος ἐπὶ ἀπόστασιν;" Ἐνταῦθα ὡς ἤκουσε ταῦτα Μωσῆς, οὐκέτι ἐπέσχεν αὐτόν, ἀλλὰ ἐπαφεὶς τὸν ἵππον ἐκέντει ἐπὶ τὸν Χασάνην ὡς ἀναιρήσων, καὶ ἔθει ἀνὰ κράτος. Χασάνης μὲν οὖν ἐπεί τε τάχιστα ᾔσθετο Μωσέα ἀνὰ κράτος ἐλαύνοντα ἐπ' αὐτόν, ἔφευγέ τε αὐτὸς κατὰ δύναμιν, Μωσῆς δὴ ἐφείπετο διώκων. Ἐνταῦθα καταλαβὼν φεύγοντα καθαιρεῖ τῷ ξίφει τὸν ἄνδρα, ἄνωθεν καθεὶς τὸ ξίφος. Θεράπων [1.172] δὲ τοῦ Χασάνεω, ὡς ἐπεῖδε τὸν δεσπότην αὐτοῦ ἀναιρεθέντα, καὶ ὡς τὸ δεύτερον Μωσῆς ἐπανατεινόμενος τὸ ξίφος παίσων αὖθις, κατῆρεν ὁ Χασάνεω θεράπων, καὶ τὴν χεῖρα ἐπανατεινόμενος τὴν χεῖρα ἀφεῖλε τῷ ξίφει. Ὁ δὲ ὡς ᾔσθετο τῆς χειρὸς αὐτοῦ πεσούσης, ἤλαυνε μέντοι ἐπὶ τὸ στρατόπεδον. Καὶ ὡς ᾔσθοντο αὐτὸν τὰ στρατεύματα λελωβημένον, φεύγοντες ᾤχοντο πρὸς τὸν ἀδελφόν. Ἐνταῦθα δὴ καὶ αὐτὸς οὐδὲν ἐπέχων δρόμῳ ᾤχετο φεύγων ἐπὶ τὴν Δακίας χώραν. Μεχμέτης μὲν οὖν αὐτίκα, ὡς τὰ στρατεύματα ἤει ἐπ' αὐτὸν καὶ τὰ πράγματα αὐτῷ ἐγένετο, αὐτίκα ἐδόκει τὸν ἀδελφὸν ἐπιδιώκειν. Καὶ κάμνοντα αὐτὸν καὶ σὺν τῇ μιᾷ χειρὶ ἐλαύνοντα καὶ ἔς τι ἕλος ἐμβαλόντα συλλαμβάνουσι, καὶ ἄγοντες παρὰ τῷ ἀδελφῷ, κατεχρήσατο αὐτίκα ἀγχόνῃ τὸν λαιμὸν βιασάμενος.

18 Ἐνταῦθα Μεχμέτης ὁ Παιαζήτεω τὴν βασιλείαν παραλαβών, τούς τε Ἕλληνας ἐπιτηδείους ὄντας αὐτῷ, τῷ

As Hasan was saying this, Musa, who was riding along the ranks, heard what that man was saying, and someone then said this in response: "O sultan, do you not see how Hasan, the commander of the janissaries, whom you so greatly honored, is insulting the janissaries by inciting them to rebel?" When Musa heard that, he could no longer restrain himself; giving his horse free rein, he spurred it against Hasan with all his might to kill him, galloping at full speed. When Hasan realized that Musa was charging at him as fast as he could, he fled with all his might, and Musa followed in pursuit. He caught up with the man as he was fleeing and struck him down with his sword, bringing his sword down on him from above. When Hasan's servant saw that his master had been struck down and that Musa had raised his sword to strike him again, this servant swooped down, swung his arm, and severed Musa's arm with his sword. When Musa saw that his arm had been cut off, he rode back to the camp. But when his soldiers saw that he was wounded, they left and went over to his brother. Then he too gave up and left quickly, fleeing for Wallachian territory. Mehmed, as soon as the armies came over to him and he had control of the situation, immediately decided to pursue his brother. The latter grew tired, riding as he was with one arm, and when he entered a swamp he was captured. They brought him to his brother who had him killed immediately by strangulation. 17

Thus Mehmed, the son of Bayezid, came to the throne. 18
The Greeks were his friends and he granted to the ruler of

Τριβαλλῶν ἡγεμόνι χώραν ἐδωρήσατο ἱκανὴν τῇ παροίκῳ αὐτοῦ. Μετὰ δὲ ταῦτα στράτευμα ἐπιπέμψας ἐπὶ τὴν Δακίας χώραν ταύτην τε ἐδῄου. Ἐς ὃν δὴ πρέσβεις πέμψας ὁ τῶν Δακῶν ἡγεμὼν σπονδάς τε ἐποιήσατο, ἐφ' ᾧ ἀπάγειν φόρον, ὅν τινα ἐτάξατο αὐτῷ Μεχμέτης ὁ βασιλεύς. Ἕλλησι μέντοι φιλία ἦν αὐτῷ διὰ τέλους. Διὸ καὶ Ἐμμανουῆλος ὁ Βυζαντίου βασιλεὺς ἐπὶ Πελοπόννησον ἀφικόμενος τόν τε Ἰσθμὸν ἐτείχισε, καὶ τοὺς Πελοποννησίους αὐτοῦ μεταπεμψάμενος, ἐπειδὴ ἐτείχισε τὸν Ἰσθμόν.

19 Ὁ δὲ Ἰσθμὸς οὗτος ξύμπασαν τὴν Πελοπόννησον, ὥστε νῆσος γενέσθαι, διείργει, ἐς δύο [1.173] καὶ τεσσαράκοντα σταδίους ἀπὸ θαλάττης εἰς θάλατταν καθήκων, καθ' ὃν δὴ χῶρον καὶ Ἴσθμια ἐτελεῖτο τοῖς Ἕλλησι. Διήκει δὲ ἀπὸ Κορίνθου πόλεως σταδίους πέντε καὶ εἴκοσι. Τοῦτον τὸν Ἰσθμὸν ἐλαύνοντος Ξέρξεω τοῦ Δαρείου ἐπὶ τὰς Ἀθήνας ἐτειχίσαντο Πελοποννήσιοι, διακωλύειν βουλόμενοι μὴ παριέναι εἴσω τῆς Πελοποννήσου τὸν βάρβαρον. Μετὰ δὲ ταῦτα Ἰουστινιανὸς ὁ Ῥωμαίων βασιλεὺς τὸ δεύτερον ἐτείχισε. Καὶ οὗτος δή, ὡς εἰρηναῖα αὐτῷ πρὸς Μεχμέτην τὸν Παιαζήτεω, ἐς Πελοπόννησον ἀφικόμενος τόν τε ἀδελφὸν αὐτοῦ καθίστη ἐπὶ τὴν ἀρχὴν τῆς Πελοποννήσου καὶ τὸν Ἰσθμὸν ἐτείχισεν, ὥστε αὐτῷ τελέσαι τοὺς Πελοποννησίους ἐπὶ τὴν τοῦ Ἰσθμοῦ φυλακὴν χρήματα. Προηγόρευε μὲν οὖν ἐς τὸν Ἰσθμὸν συλλέγεσθαι. Οἱ δὲ ἐπείθοντο καὶ συλλεχθέντες ἐτείχιζον, συμβαλλόμενον ἕκαστον τὴν ἑαυτοῦ δύναμιν. Ἐπεί τε δὴ ἐς τέλος ἤγαγε τὸ τείχισμα, ἐνταῦθα συλλαμβάνει τοὺς Πελοποννησίων ἄρχοντας, οἳ πολὺν κατέχοντες χρόνον τὴν χώραν οὐδέν

the Serbs [Stefan] extensive lands bordering on his own.[35] After that he sent an army against the land of Wallachia and plundered it. As a result, the ruler of the Wallachians sent envoys to him and made a treaty according to which he had to pay as tribute whatever sum Sultan Mehmed set for him.[36] Mehmed's friendship with the Greeks, however, lasted to the end. Because of it Manuel, king of Byzantion, was able to go to the Peloponnese and build a wall across the Isthmos,[37] and he summoned the Peloponnesians when he was walling off the Isthmos.

This Isthmos cuts off the entire Peloponnese so that it is effectively an island, and it extends about forty-two stades from sea to sea. It was here that the Greeks used to celebrate the Isthmian Games. It is twenty-five stades from the city of Corinth. The Peloponnesians fortified this Isthmos when Xerxes, the son of Darius, marched against Athens, wanting to prevent the barbarian from entering the Peloponnese.[38] After that Justinian, the king of the Romans, fortified it a second time.[39] Manuel too, then, as he was at peace with Mehmed, the son of Bayezid, came to the Peloponnese, established his brother as the ruler of the Peloponnese, and fortified the Isthmos.[40] He thus had the Peloponnesians pay him money to make the Isthmos secure, and he proclaimed that they should assemble at the Isthmos. They obeyed, assembled, and built the wall, each one contributing in proportion to his means. When the wall was completed, he then arrested the lords of the Peloponnesians, who had held the land for a long time but had shown little 19

τι πάνυ πείθεσθαι τοῖς Ἑλλήνων ἡγεμόσι βούλοιντο, ὅ τι μὴ σφίσιν αὐτοῖς δοκοῦν ἔς τι ὠφελεῖν αὐτούς. Τότε μὲν δὴ συλλαβὼν τούτους ἐκομίζετο ἐπὶ Βυζάντιον, ἔχων καὶ τοὺς Πελοποννησίους ἐν φυλακῇ. Τούτους μὲν ᾤχετο ἄγων.

20 Μεχμέτης δὲ ὡς ἐβασίλευε, χρόνου ἐπιγινομένου ἐστρατεύετο ἐπὶ τὸν Ἰσμαήλην Σινώπης ἡγεμόνα, ὅτι τῷ Μωσεῖ φίλος τε ἐδόκει καὶ ἐπιτήδειος ὡς συμβαλέσθαι ἐς τὸν καθ' ἑαυτοῦ πόλεμον. Πρεσβείαν δὲ πέμψας καὶ ταξάμενος ἀπάγειν φόρον τὴν τοῦ χαλκοῦ πρόσοδον (δοκεῖ γὰρ [1.174] τοῦτο τὸ χωρίον τῶν κατὰ τὴν Ἀσίαν φέρειν μόνον, ὧν ἡμεῖς ἴσμεν, τὸν χαλκόν). Τούτου δὲ τὴν πρόσοδον παραδοὺς τῷ βασιλεῖ Μεχμέτῃ σπονδάς τε ἐποιήσατο καὶ τὸν πόλεμον κατελύσατο. Πρὸς μέντοι τοὺς Οὐενετοὺς διενεχθεὶς ἐπολέμησε διά τε τὴν πρὸς Ἰόνιον χώραν τῶν Οὐενετῶν, ἣν ἐπιπέμψας στρατεύματα ἐδῄου. Ἔνθα δὴ διαπρεσβευσάμενοι, ὡς οὐδὲν εὕραντο ἐπιτήδειον, ἐπολέμουν αὐτῷ.

21 Δοκεῖ δὲ τοῦτο τὸ γένος παλαιόν τε γενέσθαι καὶ τῶν κατὰ τὸν Ἰόνιον εὐγενῶν[2] κράτιστον δὴ εἶναι καὶ γενναιότατον. Ὤικουν δὲ τὸ πρῶτον χώραν τὴν πρὸς τῷ μυχῷ τοῦ Ἰονίου ἀπὸ Ἰλλυριῶν καθήκουσαν ἐπὶ Ἰταλίαν, καὶ Ἕνετοι μὲν τὸ παλαιὸν ὠνομάζοντο, μετὰ δὲ ταῦτα Οὐενετοὶ ἐκλήθησαν. Ὁρμώμενοι δὲ ἀπὸ τῆς ἠπείρου, τὰ μὲν προαιρέσει, τὰ δὲ καὶ ἀνάγκῃ, δῃουμένης τῆς χώρας αὐτῶν, ὥστε ἐν ἀσφαλεῖ μᾶλλον ᾠκῆσθαι, ἐπὶ νῆσόν τινα βραχεῖαν καὶ τεναγώδη ἀπὸ τῆς ἠπείρου ἐς πεντεκαίδεκα σταδίους ᾤκησαν. Ἀπὸ σμικροῦ δέ τινος ὁρμώμενοι,

inclination to obey the rulers of the Greeks because they believed it was not in their interest to do so.[41] So he arrested them and transported them to Byzantion, where he held the Peloponnesians under guard. So Manuel left, taking them away.

After Mehmed began to reign and some time had passed, 20
he marched against İsmail, the ruler of Sinope, because he had apparently been a friend of Musa who had supported him in the war against Mehmed. But this ruler[42] sent an envoy and set a tribute to be paid from the income from his copper, for it seems that this place alone in Asia, as far as we know, produces copper. So he paid the income from this to Sultan Mehmed, made a treaty, and ended the war.[43] Mehmed then fell out with the Venetians and waged war against them over the Venetians' territory by the Adriatic Sea, and he sent armies and plundered it. They sent envoys to him but did not find him receptive at all, and so they went to war against him.[44]

This people [the Venetians] seems to be ancient and the 21
most powerful and brave of the noble peoples around the Adriatic Sea. At first they dwelled in the land by the innermost part of the Adriatic Sea, the land which extends from the Illyrians to Italy, and they used to be called Enetoi, but afterward they were called Venetians. But they moved away from dry land, in part by choice and in part because of necessity, as their land was being plundered, so that they could live in greater security on a small shoal-water island on which they settled some fifteen stades from the mainland. They had small beginnings but, when others who lived

συλλεγομένων ἐς αὐτοὺς καὶ τῶν ἀπὸ τῆς ἠπείρου περιοίκων, ὑπὸ τῶν πολεμίων ὅτι μάλιστα κακουμένων, καὶ προσγινομένων ἀεὶ ἀπὸ τῆς ἠπείρου, ᾠκίσθη τε ὁ χῶρος οὗτος καὶ εὐνομήθη. Ἐς μέγα δυνάμεως ἐχώρει δὲ ἡ πόλις αὕτη εὐνομουμένων τε τῶν ἐς αὐτὴν συνεληλυθότων.

22 Ἀπό τε τῆς ἠπείρου ἐπισήμων ἀνδρῶν εἴ τινα τήν τε χώραν ἀφελόμενοι οἱ πολέμιοι ἐπιδιώκοιεν, ἐνταῦθα γενόμενος ᾤκει. Μεγάλης δὲ τῆς [1.175] πόλεως ἐν βραχεῖ γενομένης πολλοί τε Ἑλλήνων τε καὶ Ῥωμαίων καὶ ἄλλων συχνῶν γενῶν ἄνδρες, γένους ὄντες περιφανοῦς, ἤν τις ἐν τῇ πατρίδι αὐτοῦ μὴ εὖ φέροιτο, εἴτε ὑπὸ τῶν ἀντιστασιωτῶν διωκόμενοι, εἴτε ὑπὸ τῶν πολεμίων ἐξελαυνόμενοι, ἐς ταύτην δὴ τὴν πόλιν συνελέγοντο, ἄνδρες ἐπίσημοί τε καὶ ἀγαθοὶ καὶ παῖδες ἀνδρῶν τε ὄντες ἐπιφανῶν καὶ χώρας ἀρχόντων οὐ φαύλης. Τοῦτο μὲν ἐκ τῆς κατὰ τὸν Ἰόνιον χώρας καὶ τῆς Ἑλλάδος, τοῦτο δὲ καὶ ἐκ τῆς Ἰταλίας ἐξελαυνόμενοι καὶ ἐνταῦθα ἀφικόμενοι ᾤκουν δὴ ἀσφαλέστερον. Ἐχούσης δὲ τῆς πόλεως ἐμπορίαν, ὅτι μάλιστα ἀνάγκης ἀποδεικνυμένης ἐς τοῦτο τρέπεσθαι ἕνα ἕκαστον, διὰ τὸ μηδαμῇ τῆς ἠπείρου τοὺς ἐποίκους ἀντέχεσθαι, μηδέ, ὅσα φέρει ἡ ἤπειρος, ἐργαζομένων τὴν γῆν, ἀλλὰ καὶ ἀπὸ θαλάττης ἐσκομιζομένων τὰ ἐπιτήδεια ἐς τὴν πόλιν.

23 Χρήματα μεγάλα ἐργασάμενοι ἀπὸ τούτου τήν τε δύναμιν ἀξιόχρεω ἀπεδείκνυντο ἁπανταχῇ, καὶ τὴν πόλιν διῴκουν οἰκημάτων τε τῷ πολυτελεῖ καὶ μεγαλοπρεπείᾳ οἰκιῶν καὶ ναῶν. Τριήρεις δὲ ναυπηγησάμενοι οὐκ ὀλίγας, καὶ δυνάμεις περιβαλόμενοι ἰσχυράς, πρός τε τοὺς ἐν τῇ

around there on the mainland joined them, as they were suffering badly at the hands of their enemies, and as more people always kept coming from the mainland, the place was settled and was well governed. So this city attained great power, as those who emigrated to it were well governed.

If ever a notable man on the mainland was deprived of his 22
land by his enemies and they pursued him, he came to settle here. The city quickly became large and many men from the Greeks, Romans, and various other peoples, men who came from proud families, would come to this city if they were not faring well in their own countries, whether because they were being persecuted by their political rivals or driven out by foreign enemies. These men were notables and of good class and were the sons of men who were notables, the lords of substantial lands. Whether they were driven out from the lands around the Adriatic Sea and from Greece, or from Italy, they came and settled here in greater security. The city had trade, in fact everyone had of necessity to turn to it, as the settlers had no foothold on the mainland, nor could they work the land for the products that the mainland could offer, but instead they had to import necessities for their city by sea.

They made a great deal of money from this and rose to 23
great power in all ways. They adorned their city with sumptuous buildings and magnificent houses and churches. They built numerous triremes and invested themselves with powerful forces. Out of envy, they attacked those who had a

θαλάττη δυνατοὺς δοκοῦντας γενέσθαι προσενηνεγμένοι φθόνῳ διεπολέμουν, δέει ἐπ' αὐτοὺς τὸν πόλεμον ἐπιφερόντων τῷ δοκεῖν ἐπὶ μέγα ἤδη χωρῆσαι δυνάμεως. Τήν τε πρὸς τὸν Ἰόνιον χώραν ἐκπλέοντι ἐπ' [1.176] ἀριστερά, ἀπ' αὐτοῦ δὴ τοῦ μυχοῦ, χώραν τε οὖσαν οὐ φαύλην καὶ πόλεις εὐδαίμονας ὑπηγάγοντο· ἐπὶ δὲ τὸ Αἰγαῖον πέλαγος ἀφικέσθαι· τούς τε παράπλους αὐτοῦ ταύτῃ καταστρεψάμενοι Κέρκυράν τε ἐχειρώσαντο σύμπασαν καὶ Εὔβοιάν τε καὶ Κρήτην καὶ Πελοποννήσου τὰς πόλεις. Καὶ ἐπὶ Συρίαν δὲ ἀφικόμενοι στόλῳ καὶ Κυρήνην πόλιν ὑφ' αὐτοῖς ποιησάμενοι μεγάλα ἀπεδείκνυντο ἔργα, πρός τε τοὺς βαρβάρους ταύτῃ πολλαχῇ διαναυμαχήσαντες καὶ τῆς θαλάσσης τῆς ἐντὸς Ἡρακλείων στηλῶν ἐπικρατήσαντες. Κατά τε Εὐρώπην πρὸς τοὺς ἐν τῇ θαλάττῃ δοκοῦντας δύνασθαι ὁτιοῦν διεπολέμουν. Καὶ Ἰταλίας μέντοι τῆς παράπλου οὐδέν, ὅ τι καὶ ἄξιον λόγου, ὑπηγάγοντο σφίσιν, ὅτι μὴ Ῥαβέννην πόλιν εὐδαίμονα τελευτήσαντος τοῦ ἐν αὐτῇ ἡγεμόνος, διὰ τὸ μὴ ἐς τὸ ὁμόφυλον ἰέναι πολέμῳ, ἀλλ' ἐπὶ τοὺς ἀλλοφύλους διαναυμαχεῖν.

24 Ἐπολέμησαν δὲ οὗτοι πρός τε τοὺς Ἕλληνας, καὶ ναυμαχίαις περιγενόμενοι τήν τε μητρόπολιν ἐχειρώσαντο ἐπισπομένων σφίσι καὶ ἑσπερίων συχνῶν, ἐξηγουμένων δ' αὐτῶν ἐπὶ τοὺς Ἕλληνας. Καὶ ὡς τῆς ἠπείρου ἀντέχεσθαι ἤρξαντο, ἐν βραχεῖ δὴ χώραν τῆς ἠπείρου ἐκτήσαντο ἀγαθήν, καὶ ὀχυρὰν τὴν πόλιν αὐτῶν παρείχοντο, κατ' ἄμφω τὼ δυνάμεε ἐπὶ μέγα αὔξοντες. Πρός τε τοὺς τῆς ἠπείρου ἡγεμόνας διενεχθέντες ἐπολέμησαν ἐπὶ πολλὰς γενεὰς τὸν πόλεμον, καὶ διέφερον χρημάτων προσόδῳ

reputation for having become powerful at sea, and fought wars against them; they brought war against them out of fear, to all appearances,[45] and thus they advanced to great power. They subjected the land to the left as one sails out of the Adriatic Sea from its innermost bay, a land that is important and has prosperous cities, and they reached the Aegean Sea. They subdued its coastal regions, seized all of Kerkyra, Euboia, Crete, and the cities of the Peloponnese. They reached Syria with their fleet and subjected the city of Kyrene to themselves, performing great deeds.[46] They fought naval engagements with the barbarians there on many occasions and dominated the sea within the Pillars of Herakles. They were able to carry out wars against those in Europe with a reputation for naval power. They did not, however, subject to themselves any significant portion of coastal Italy—except for Ravenna, a prosperous city, when its ruler died[47]—so as not to wage war against their own people and to fight naval wars only against foreigners.

These people [the Venetians] fought against the Greeks, 24
defeated them in naval battles, and seized their capital; many westerners were with them then, but they were the leaders of the campaign against the Greeks.[48] As they began to claim the mainland [of Italy], they soon acquired good lands there and fortified their city, thereby greatly increasing their power on both land and sea. They fell out with the rulers on the mainland and fought a war with them that lasted for many generations. They excel at making their city

τὴν πόλιν μεγάλην ἑαυτοῖς παρασκευασάμενοι. [1.177] Μετὰ δὲ ταῦτα καὶ ὑπὸ βαρβάρων[3] βασιλέως τῆς Ἰταλίας πρὸς ἑσπέραν χώρας [πρὸς] τὸν Ῥώμης ἀρχιερέα ἐκπεσόντα τε τῆς ἀρχῆς καὶ τῆς Ῥωμαίων πόλεως, κατήγαγόν τε τὸν ἀρχιερέα, καὶ πρὸς τὸν βασιλέα πολεμήσαντες, ὥστε ἐμπεδῶσαι τῷ ἀρχιερεῖ τὴν ἀρχήν, ναυμαχίᾳ τε ἐπεκράτησαν καὶ κατήγαγον.

Καὶ πρός τε τοὺς Ἰανυΐους, δοκοῦντας τῆς κατὰ τὰ χωρία ἐκεῖσε καὶ τὴν πάραλον τῆς Ἰταλίας ἐπικρατεῖν, πόλεμον ἐξενεγκόντες μεγάλα ἀποδείξασθαι ἔργα, πολλαχῇ διαναυμαχήσαντες καὶ περιγενόμενοι. Οὗτοι τοιγαροῦν τὸν πρὸς τοὺς Οὐενετοὺς πόλεμον ἀναιρούμενοι ὀλίγου δεῖν τὴν πόλιν αὐτὴν ἐχειρώσαντο, ἐπιπλεύσαντες τριήρεσι καὶ ναυσὶν ἐπὶ τὸν Οὐενετῶν λιμένα, καὶ εἰσελθόντες κατὰ τὸ ἐπὶ Κλιζόην.[4] Πόλις δὲ αὐτῶν ᾤκηται, ὅπῃ δὴ ὁ λιμὴν μέγας τε ὢν καὶ πεντακοσίους σταδίους διήκων λήγει ἐς τὴν κατὰ τὸν Ἠριδανὸν χώραν· ταύτῃ γὰρ Ἠριδανός, μέγας τε τῶν κατὰ τὴν Ἰταλίαν ποταμῶν καὶ ναυσὶ πλόϊμος, πρὸς ταύτῃ δὴ ἐκδιδοῖ ἐς τὴν θάλασσαν, ταύτῃ δὴ οὖν εἰσελθοῦσαι αἱ νῆες τῶν Ἰανυΐων ἐπὶ τὸν Οὐενετῶν λιμένα τήν τε Κλιζόην κατέσχον καὶ ἠνδραποδίσαντο. Μετὰ δὲ ταῦτα πρὸς τὴν πόλιν διεπρεσβεύοντο. Καὶ ἐν ἀπόρῳ δὲ ὄντες οἱ ἐν τῇ πόλει, καὶ οὐκ ἔχοντες, ὅ τι γένωνται, ὑπακοῦσαί τε τοῖς Ἰανυΐοις ἔφασαν ἕτοιμοι εἶναι, καὶ [1.178] ὡς ἂν δοκοίη αὐτοῖς ξύμφορον εἶναι καὶ ἐπιτήδειον πολιτεύεσθαι, καὶ αἰτεῖσθαι σφᾶς ἐκέλευον, ὅ τι βούλονται, ὡς παρεχομένων ἑτοίμως αὐτοῖς ταῦτα.

great by bringing in revenues. After that, when the pontiff of Rome was removed from his position and from the city of the Romans by the king of the barbarians in the land to the west of Italy, they restored the pontiff; having fought against the king in order to confirm the pontiff in his position, they prevailed in a naval battle and restored him.[49]

They also waged a war against the Genoese, who had 25
risen to a position of dominance in the nearby regions and the Italian coast, and they performed great deeds, fighting many naval battles and winning. But the Genoese too, taking up the war against the Venetians, came close to capturing the city itself, sailing their triremes and ships against the Venetian harbor and entering at the point by Chioggia.[50] This city of theirs is built where the harbor, which is large, extending for five hundred stades, ends by the regions near the Po. For this is where the Po, one of the great rivers of Italy and one that is navigable to ships, flows into the sea. So it was from there that the ships of the Genoese sailed in against the harbor of the Venetians, when they seized and enslaved Chioggia.[51] After that they sent envoys to the city. The people of the city were at a loss and did not know where to turn, and so they said that they were prepared to obey the Genoese and govern themselves in whatever way seemed advantageous and useful to them, and they asked to be told what they wanted, so that they could carry it out for them.

26 Οἱ δὲ ὡς τὰ παρὰ τῆς πόλεως ἤκουσαν, οἰόμενοι τὴν πόλιν καταλήψεσθαι αὐθαδέστερόν τε ἀπεκρίναντο τῇ πρεσβείᾳ, φάμενοι αἰτεῖσθαι αὐτοὺς ἐπὶ τρεῖς ἡμέρας ἐξεῖναι σφίσι διαρπάζειν τὴν πόλιν. Οἱ μέντοι πρέσβεις ὡς ἀπεχώρησαν καὶ τὰ ἐπεσταλμένα τῇ πόλει ἀπήγγελον, ἥ τε σύγκλητος καὶ ὁ δῆμος ὑπεραχθεσθεὶς τῇ τῶν πολεμίων αὐθαδείᾳ τε καὶ ἀκολασίᾳ ναῦς τε αὐτίκα ἐπλήρωσαν, ὅσας ἠδύναντο, καὶ αὐτοὶ ἐς τὰς ναῦς ἐμβάντες ἀνήγοντο ἐς τὸν λιμένα. Οἵ τε Ἰανύϊοι ἀντανήγοντο, καὶ αὐτίκα ἐν τῷ λιμένι ἐναυμάχησαν, καὶ οὐδὲν πλέον ἔσχον οἱ πολέμιοι. Ἐνταῦθα ὡς ἐπετράποντο ἡττημένοι εἰς Κλιζόην, αὐτίκα οἱ Οὐενετοὶ ναῦν φέροντες μεγίστην τῶν παρὰ σφίσι νεῶν ἐς τὸ τοῦ λιμένος στόμα, ᾗ δὴ εἰσῄεσαν οἱ πολέμιοι, κατέδυσαν αὐτοῦ ταύτῃ (ἔστι γὰρ τοῦτο στενώτατον), καὶ τὸ στόμα ἐπικλείσαντες λιμῷ τοὺς Ἰανυΐους ἐν τῇ Κιόζῃ ἐξεπολιόρκησαν.

27 Ἀπεπειρῶντο μὲν οὖν καὶ τῆς διώρυχος, ἣ ἐκ τοῦ Ἠριδανοῦ ἐς τὸν λιμένα ἀφικνεῖται, διορύσσοντες, ὥστε ἐκπλόϊμοι γενέσθαι ταῖς ἑαυτῶν ναυσὶν ἐπὶ τὸν Ἠριδανόν· ἀλλ' οὐχ οἷοί τε ἐγένοντο ἀνύσαι τοὖργον. Ἐδόκει δὲ καὶ ὁ Παταβίου ἡγεμὼν συμβαλέσθαι αὐτοῖς ἐς τόν τε πόλεμον, διάφορος ὢν τοῖς Οὐενετοῖς. Οὗτοι μὲν λιμῷ ἐκπολιορκηθέντες ὑπὸ τῆς Οὐενετῶν πόλεως παρέδοσαν σφᾶς χρῆσθαι σφίσιν, ὅ τι βούλονται, καὶ ταύτῃ αἴσχιστα ἀπώλοντο, οὐκέτι παρὰ τὸ [1.179] δέον σωφρονισθέντες. Οἱ δὲ Οὐενετοὶ τὸ ἀπὸ τοῦδε στρατευόμενοι ἐπὶ τὴν Ἰανυΐων πόλιν πολλαχῇ τε ἐναυμάχησαν καὶ ἐπεκράτησαν, δύναμίν

When the Genoese heard the city's response, they thought that they would be able to seize the city and replied harshly to the embassy, demanding the right to plunder the city for three days. But when the envoys went back and announced this message to the city, the senate and the people were extremely distressed by their enemies' haughtiness and impudence, and so they manned as many ships as they could, boarded them themselves, and sailed to the harbor. The Genoese advanced against them and a naval battle was joined in the harbor. The enemy had the worst of it. Defeated, they retreated to Chioggia, whereupon the Venetians immediately brought their largest ship into the entrance to the harbor, through which the enemy had entered, and sank it there—for this was a very narrow point. Blocking the harbor mouth in this way, they besieged the Genoese in Chioggia to starve them out.[52] 26

The Genoese then made an attempt to widen the canal that leads from the Po to the harbor so that they could sail their ships to the Po, but they were unable to accomplish this task. It seems also that the ruler of Padua had joined them in this war, as he was at odds with the Venetians.[53] Defeated in this siege and starved out by the city of the Venetians, they surrendered to be treated in whatever way the Venetians deemed fit. But even though they were so shamefully defeated, they still did not learn their lesson as they should have. From that point on the Venetians campaigned against the city of the Genoese, fought many naval battles 27

τε περιποιούμενοι τὸ ἀπὸ τοῦδε, καὶ τῆς θαλάσσης εἴργοντες τῆς κατ' ἐκείνην τὴν χώραν.

28 Ἔνθα δὴ ξυμφορᾷ περιέπεσεν ἡ πόλις αὕτη οὐ τῇ ἐπιτυχούσῃ διὰ τὰς ναυμαχίας ταύτας. Ὕστερον μέντοι τόν τε τοῦ Παταβίου ἡγεμόνα τισάμενοι, τήν τε πόλιν ἐπολιόρκησαν, καὶ ὑπαγόμενοι τῆς ἠπείρου ἀντείχοντο βεβαιότερον ἐς σφᾶς ἐχυροῦντες τὴν ἀρχὴν τῆς ἠπείρου. Καὶ πρότερον μέντοι ἀρχήν τινα ἐς τὴν κατὰ τὴν ἤπειρον κτησάμενοι, καὶ Ταρβίζιον πόλιν εὐδαίμονα ἐπικτησάμενοι, προήγαγον τὴν χώραν αὐτῶν, ἐπαγομένων τῶν τῆς πόλεως ἔχθει τῷ σφετέρῳ πρὸς τοὺς σφῶν ἡγεμόνας. Καὶ ὑστερούμενοι, ὡς τὸ Πατάβιον ἐχειρώσαντο τοῦ ἡγεμόνος Καραρίων τῆς οἰκίας πρὸς τούτους διενεχθέντος, ὁρμώμενοι ἀπὸ τούτου πόλεις τε ἄλλας οὐκ ὀλίγας κατεστρέψαντο τῶν κατὰ τὴν Ἰταλίαν χώραν καὶ ἐς τὴν Λιγυρίαν, ἄλλας τε δὴ καὶ Οὐηρώνην πόλιν εὐδαίμονα, ἐξελάσαντες τοὺς ἡγεμόνας αὐτῆς Κλιμακίων τῆς οἰκίας οὕτω καλουμένους, καὶ Οὐικεντίαν καὶ Πρηξίαν, ὀλβίας τε πόλεις καὶ ἐπισήμους τῶν νῦν κατὰ τὴν Ἰταλίαν.

29 Μετὰ δὲ ταῦτα πρὸς τὸν Λιγυρίας τύραννον διενεχθέντες ἐπολέμουν ἐπὶ συχνὰ ἔτη. Ἔστι δ' ὁ ἡγεμὼν οὗτος οἰκίας τῶν [1.180] Μαριαγγέλων, ἄρχων δὲ Μεδιολάνου πόλεως. Ἦν δὲ ἐπιτηδεύμασί τε ὀλβιωτάτη, καὶ τῇ ἄλλῃ εὐδαιμονίᾳ προέχει τῶν ἐν τῇ Ἰταλίᾳ πόλεων, καὶ πολυάνθρωπος οὖσα παλαιοτάτη τε δοκεῖ γενέσθαι καὶ αἰεί τε, ἐξ ὅτου ᾠκίσθη, εὐδαιμονῆσαι τοῖς τε ἐπιτηδεύμασι τοῖς πολεμικοῖς καὶ ὅπλων κατασκευῇ. Μεσόγαιος δ' οὖσα ἡ πόλις αὕτη διέχει ἀπὸ θαλάσσης τῆς Ἰανυΐων σταδίους

with it, and prevailed. From then on the Venetians preserved their power and closed off the sea that is by that land.[54]

That city,[55] then, suffered a serious misfortune because 28
of these naval battles. The Venetians later set out to punish the ruler of Padua and besieged his city.[56] They brought the mainland under their control and secured their position by establishing a firmer hold on it. Of course, they had previously acquired holdings on the mainland when they took over the prosperous city of Treviso.[57] They had extended their territory when the people of that city called them in out of hatred for their own rulers. They later seized Padua when its ruler, who was from the house of Carrara, fell out with them, and they used it as a base to conquer many other cities in the land of Italy and Lombardy, including Verona, a prosperous city, whose rulers, of the house that is called Scaligeri, they expelled;[58] and Vicenza and Brescia, both wealthy and famous cities in Italy today.[59]

After that they fell out with the tyrant of Lombardy and 29
fought a war with him for many years. This ruler was from the house of Mariangeli and was lord of the city of Milan.[60] In its achievements, wealth, and general prosperity, Milan surpasses all the cities in Italy. It is populous and appears to be very ancient and, ever since its foundation, it has fared well in its military endeavors and the manufacture of arms. The city is situated inland, about six hundred stades from

ἀμφὶ τοὺς ἑξακοσίους, ἀγχοῦ δὲ ᾤκηται τῆς Γαλατίας, ἥτις καὶ Σαβόϊα χώρα κέκληται. Ῥεῖ δὲ ποταμὸς διὰ τῆς πόλεως, καὶ ἐκδιδοῖ οὗτος ἐς Τεσίνην ποταμὸν πρὸς Παβίῃ πόλει. Τεσίνης δ᾿ αὖ ἐπιρρεῖ ἐς τὸν Ἠριδανὸν πρὸς Πλακεντίῃ πόλει μεγάλῃ τῆς Λιγυρίας· οὗτος μὲν ᾗ ἐκδιδοῖ, πρότερόν μοι δεδήλωται.

30 Λέγονται δ᾿ οἱ τῆς οἰκίας ταύτης ἐς τὴν Μεδιολάνου καὶ τῆς ἄλλης Λιγυρίας ἀρχὴν καταστῆναι τρόπῳ τοιῷδε. Δράκων ἀπὸ ὄρεος φοιτῶν ἐς τὴν πόλιν ἀνθρώπους διαφθείρων οὐκ ἐπαύσατο, τούς τε ἐπὶ τὰ ἔργα ἐπιόντας καὶ ἐπὶ τοὺς ἀγρούς, γυναῖκα μέν, ᾗ λέγεται, οὐδέν τι ποιούμενος, καὶ τούς γε ἄνδρας ἐπὶ συχνὸν χρόνον διελυμαίνετο. Καὶ πολλοὶ δὴ ἐπ᾿ αὐτὸν ἐπελθόντες πολλά τε καὶ ἀνήκεστα πρὸς τοῦ θηρὸς ἐπεπόνθεισαν· ἤνυον δὲ οὐδέν. Οὗτος δὴ ὁ Μαριάγγελος, πρῶτος τῆς οἰκίας ταύτης, Βρετανὸς δὲ τὸ γένος, θεράποντα ἐξοπλίσας πανοπλίᾳ καὶ αὐτὸς ἐνεδύσατο πανοπλίαν. Μετὰ δέ, ὡς ᾖσαν ἐπὶ τὸν θῆρα, τὸν μέντοι θεράποντα χανὼν κατὰ μέσον ἐσεφόρει ἐς τὸν λαιμὸν [1.181] αὐτοῦ· ὡς δ᾿ ἤδη χανὼν οὔτε ἐντὸς λαβεῖν οἷός τε ἐγένετο, οὔτε ἐς τοὐπίσω ἐξορμῆσαι, πελέκει τὴν κεφαλὴν τοῦ δράκοντος καταίρων διέτεμε. Καὶ ὁ μέντοι δράκων ταύτῃ ἔπεσε, καὶ ἡ πόλις ἠλευθέρωτο τοῦ θηρὸς πολεμοῦντος αὐτῇ. Καὶ οὕτω δὴ στρατηγόν τε σφίσιν οἱ τὸ Μεδιόλανον ἐνοικοῦντες ἐστήσαντο, καὶ ἡγεῖσθαι ἐκέλευον ἐπὶ τοὺς πολεμίους ὡς ἄνδρα ἀγαθὸν γενόμενον. Μετ᾿ οὐ πολὺν δὲ χρόνον ἡγεμών τε κατέστη, δορυφόρους ἔχων ἀμφ᾿ αὐτὸν καὶ τοὺς ἐν τῇ πόλει πείθεσθαι ἀναγκάζων. Οὕτω δὴ ἄρξαντος ταύτης τῆς χώρας ἐπὶ τέσσαρας γενεὰς

the Gulf of Genoa. It is not far from France and the region that is called Savoy. A river runs through the city and empties out into the Ticino River by the city of Pavia. The Ticino flows into the Po by Piacenza, a large city in Lombardy. I have already stated where the Po flows out.[61]

This family [the Mariangeli] is said to have come to 30
power over Milan and Lombardy in the following way. A dragon would come regularly from the mountain to the city and relentlessly kill its people as they were going to their work and to the fields, but, so it is said, it would do no harm to the women. So for a long time it preyed on the men. Many set out to destroy it but the beast horribly injured them, and they accomplished nothing. Mariangelo, then, the first of this house, who was of British origin,[62] equipped his servant with a full array of armor and then put on armor himself. When they had encountered the beast, the latter, its maw gaping open, swallowed up the servant into his throat down to his waist. With its mouth wide open like this, however, it was unable to swallow the rest of him or spit him back out, so Mariangelo brought his ax down onto the dragon's head and cut it off. The dragon fell there and the city was liberated from the beast that had been attacking it.[63] Thus the inhabitants of Milan made him their general and urged him to lead them against their enemies, as he had shown himself to be a formidable man. But shortly afterward he made himself ruler, surrounded himself with bodyguards, and forced the people of the city to obey him. Thus this land was ruled

ἐς τὸν Φίλιππον ἡ ἀρχὴ περιῆλθε, πρὸς ὃν δὴ οἱ Οὐενετοὶ ἐπολέμουν διενεχθέντες.

31 Τά τε ἄλλα καὶ στρατηγοὺς ἑλόμενοι σφίσιν ἐς τὸν πόλεμον ἄνδρας τε ἀγαθοὺς καὶ χώρας ἄρχοντας οὐκ ὀλίγης. Πρῶτον μέντοι Καραμινιόλαν στρατηγὸν εἵλοντο ἐπὶ τὸν Λιγυρίας ἄρχοντα. Καὶ ὡς αὐτοῦ συνίεσαν καταπροδιδόντος τὴν χώραν καὶ συντιθεμένου τῷ Μεδιολάνου ἡγεμόνι, συλλαβόντες ἀνεῖλον, καὶ Φραγκίσκον τὸν Φορτίαν ἐπίκλην μεταπεμπόμενοι ἡγεῖσθαι τε αὐτῶν ἐκέλευον καὶ ἐτίμων μεγάλως, τά τε ἄλλα εὐδοκιμοῦντα καὶ πόλεις τῆς Λιγυρίων χώρας οὐκ ὀλίγας παραστησάμενον, τήν τε ἀρχὴν τῆς ἠπείρου ἐπὶ μέγα προήγαγε δυνάμεως. Ὡς μὲν οὖν πρὸς τούτους πολεμοῦντας ἀλλήλοις ξύμπασα ἡ Ἰταλία διέστη πρὸς ἑκατέρους, καὶ ὡς ἐπολέμησαν, ἐς τὸ πρόσω ἰόντι τοῦ λόγου δηλοῦταί μοι, ὡς ἐγένετο.

32 Ἐπάνειμι δὴ ἐπὶ τὴν Οὐενετῶν πόλιν, ὡς ταύτῃ τῇ πόλει ἐγένετο τύχη ἐπ' ἀμφότερα τῇ πόλει ἐναλλὰξ συμβάν. Καὶ [1.182] αὕτη ἐς τόνδε τὸν πόλεμον ἑλομένη ἑαυτῇ στρατηγοὺς τὰ πολέμια ἀγαθούς, ἐν δὲ δὴ καὶ ὃν ἐσήμηνα Καραμινιόλαν, κηδεστὴν γενόμενον τοῦ Λιγύρων τυράννου. Τοῦτον μέντοι ὡς ἐπιβουλεύοντα σφίσι λαβόντες ἀπέκτειναν, Φορτίαν δὲ μεταπεμψάμενοι ἐστήσαντο σφίσι στρατηγὸν ἑλόμενοι. Ὡς μὲν οὖν ἔργα ἀποδεικνυμένους μεγάλα τε καὶ ἄξια λόγου, ἐπὶ χίλια ἔτη εὐδαίμονας διαγενομένους, ἄλλοις πολλαχῇ κατὰ τὴν Ἰταλίαν ἐνευδοκιμῆσαι κατάδηλόν ἐστι. Καὶ ἐμπεδῶσαι αὐτῇ τὰ κατὰ τὴν ἀρχήν, ὡς ἐλάχιστα ἐσφάλλετο ὑπὸ τῶν πολιτῶν, τῇδέ πῃ

for four generations until power came to Filippo,[64] with whom the Venetians fell out and were fighting.

The Venetians appointed good men as their generals in war and as governors of their extensive territories. At first they appointed Carmagnola as general to fight against the lord of Lombardy. When they realized that he was betraying their country and making deals with the ruler of Milan, they arrested him and killed him.[65] Then they called in Francesco, known as Sforza, urged him to lead them, and paid him great honor.[66] He was particularly successful and subdued many cities in Lombardy, and turned their mainland empire into a great power. While they were fighting each other, all of Italy took sides, and my account will later on reveal how they fought.[67] 31

I return now to the city of the Venetians and to how this city's fortunes fluctuated. In this war it chose for itself generals who were skilled at warfare, among whom was Carmagnola, as I said, who was related by marriage to the tyrant of the Lombards.[68] When they discovered that he was plotting against them, they arrested and killed him. They called in Sforza and decided to appoint him their general. It is perfectly clear that they have performed great and remarkable deeds, have enjoyed a thousand years of prosperity, and have acquired a good reputation among others throughout Italy. The way in which they have firmed up their power, so that it is least open to being put at risk by the citizens, clearly 32

ἂν κατάδηλος γένοιτο ἡ τῆς πόλεως διοίκησις, ὡς ἐν βραχεῖ διασημῆναι.

33 Ἦν γὰρ αὕτη ἡ πόλις τὸ παλαιὸν δημοκρατία, καὶ ὑπὸ δήμοις τε ἅμα ἐν ταῖς ἀρχαῖς αὐτῶν, ἃς ᾑρεῖτο, τὴν πόλιν, ᾗ ἐδόκει καλῶς ἔχειν σφίσι, διῴκουν. Μετὰ δὲ ταῦτα, ὡς ἐπὶ τὰ ἔργα σφῶν οἱ δημόται ἐτρέποντο, καὶ οὐκέτι σχολὴν ἦγον, ὥστε ἐπὶ τὴν διοίκησιν λόγον ποιεῖσθαι, ὡς ἑκάστοτε ἀναγκάζοι βουλεύεσθαι ὁ χρόνος, ἐπιλεξάμενοι τοὺς ἀρίστους, εἴτε τύχῃ τινί, εἴτε δὴ καὶ ψήφῳ ἑλόμενοι, οὕτω περὶ τούτους ἐς ἀριστοκρατίαν τὸ παράπαν ἐτράπη, καὶ τὸ ἀπὸ τοῦδε εἰσέτι καὶ νῦν ἀσφαλῶς διῳκημένη ἐπὶ μέγα δυνάμεως ἐχώρησε.

34 Διοικεῖται δὲ κατὰ τάδε. Ἔστιν ἡ μεγάλη βουλὴ καλουμένη αὐτοῖς, ἐν ᾗ ἐπὶ ἡμέρας ὀκτὼ σχολὴν ἄγουσιν. Ἐν ταύτῃ δὲ τῇ βουλῇ τάς τε ἀρχὰς τῶν πόλεων αἱροῦνται, ψήφους τιθέμενοι, καὶ τὰς ἐν τῇ πόλει αὐτῇ ἀρχάς, ὅπῃ ἂν καθιστῶνται. Νομίζεται δὲ ἐξεῖναι, ὡς ἔτη [1.183] τέσσαρα καὶ εἴκοσι γεγονὼς εἴη, εἰσιέναι ἐς ταύτην τὴν βουλήν, ἣν αὐτῷ τὴν ἀρχὴν συνεχωρήθη γε εἰσιέναι, κἂν συγκλητικὸς ᾖ. Εἴησαν δ' ἂν οὗτοι ἀμφὶ τοὺς δισχιλίους, οἱ τάς τε ψήφους τιθέμενοι καὶ τὰς ἀρχὰς ξυμπάσης ἤδη τῆς ἀρχῆς αἱρούμενοι. Ἡγεμὼν δὲ τούτων ἐστίν, ὃν ἂν ἕλωνται, τὸν παρ' αὐτοῖς κράτιστον δοκοῦντα γενέσθαι. Φέρει δ' οὗτος δύο ψήφους, τιθέμενος ᾗ ἂν βούλοιτο προστίθεσθαι. Μένει δ' οὗτος ἡγεμὼν τιμώμενός τε τὰ πρῶτα ὑπὸ τῶν συγκλητικῶν καὶ ἐν τοῖς βασιλείοις ἐπιμένων, ἔχων τήν τε δαπάνην ὑπὸ τῶν τῆς πόλεως προεστηκότων. Πάρεισι δ' αὐτῷ βουληφόροι ἄνδρες ἓξ τὸν ἀριθμόν, ἑταῖροί τε αὐτῷ

reveals how the city is administered, which can now be explained briefly.

This city used to be a democracy of old, and they governed the city as they thought best through their demes as well as by their elected offices. After that, as the demesmen turned to their private affairs and no longer enjoyed the leisure required for public administration, whenever circumstance required them to make decisions they would choose the leading men, either by lottery or by electing them in a vote, and thus the government turned entirely into an aristocracy that revolved around these men. From then on and to this day, Venice is securely governed and has advanced to great power. 33

It is governed in the following way. They have the so-called Great Council, which meets for an eight-day session. In this Council they appoint the magistrates in charge of the cities by casting votes, and they also decide on the appointment of the magistracies of the city itself. Their custom is that one may enter this Council upon reaching the age of twenty-four if he has been granted entry to a magistracy and is a senator. There are about two thousand members, who cast votes and appoint the magistracies of the entire government. Their ruler,[69] whomever they appoint, is the one who seems to have become most powerful among them. He holds two votes, and may cast them however he wants. This ruler is honored by the senators above anyone else, and he resides in the palace, maintained at the expense of the leading men of the city. He has advisors, six in number, 34

ὄντες καὶ τὴν τιμὴν τῆς ἡγεμονίας συγκατεργαζόμενοι, ἐπὶ μῆνας ἓξ ἀπαλλαττόμενοι τῆς σφῶν οὗτοι ἀρχῆς.

35 Μετὰ δὲ τὴν μεγάλην βουλὴν ἔστιν ἡ βουλὴ γερουσία κλητῶν καλουμένη, ἀμφὶ τοὺς τριακοσίους. Αἱροῦνται δὲ τούτους ἤδη καὶ τὰς λοιπὰς ἀρχὰς ἐν τῇ μεγάλῃ βουλῇ, ἐπιλεξάμενοι τοὺς τἀμείνω φρονοῦντας. Κἀν ταύτῃ δὴ τῇ τῶν κλητῶν ἐπονομαζομένῃ βουλῇ περί τε πολέμων καὶ εἰρήνης βουλεύονται καὶ πρεσβειῶν, ὅ τι ἂν ᾖ δεδογμένον τούτοις, πείθεσθαι αὐτίκα τὴν πόλιν, καὶ ἐς ὅ τι ἂν δόξῃ ταύτῃ τῇ βουλῇ, ξύμπασαν τὴν πόλιν ἰέναι. Ἐπὶ δὲ τοῖς τῶν ὅλων ἐγκλήμασιν ἐφεστᾶσιν ἄρχοντες δέκα, οἵ τινες τά τε ἐγκλήματα καὶ τὰς ποινὰς ἐπιφέρουσιν ἑνὶ ἑκάστῳ. Ἔξεστι δὲ τούτοις τόν τε ἡγεμόνα λαβόντες θάνατον ἀπάγεσθαι, ὑπὸ μηδεμιᾶς τῶν ἀρχῶν ἀπαιτουμένους τὴν αἰτίαν τῆς δίκης. Διαιτῆσαι γὰρ οὕτως, καὶ καθίστανται ἤδη ξυμπάσης τῆς πόλεως [1.184] ἐς τὰς εὐθύνας τῶν ὁτιοῦν περί τινα ἐξαμαρτόντων ἢ περὶ τὴν πόλιν ἢ ἐς ἀλλήλους· ἄγονται δὲ θανάτου, ὅντινα ἂν ὑπόδικον εὕρωσι, καθίστανται δὲ καὶ ἐς τὰς ἄλλας δίκας δικασταί, τῶν τε ἐπιχωρίων ἄλλοι καὶ ἐς τοὺς ξένους ἄλλοι. Ἐπὶ τούτοις ἐφιστᾶσιν ἄρχοντας τεσσαράκοντα, ἐς οὓς ἐπειδὰν αἱ δίκαι ἀνενεχθῶσιν, εὐθύνουσι τὰς ψήφους ἐς τὸ σφίσιν ἐπὶ τὸ ὡς κράτιστα ἔχειν δοκοῦν. Ἢν δὲ μὴ συμφέρωνται ἐς τὴν δίκην, ἐπὶ τὴν τῶν κλητῶν βουλὴν ἀναφέρεται, κἀκεῖ πολυπραγμονεῖται καὶ τὴν ἀπόβασιν ἴσχει.

36 Εἰσὶ μὲν οὖν καὶ ἄλλαι ἀρχαὶ οὐκ ὀλίγαι τῆς πόλεως, φυλακῆς τε πέρι καθήκουσαι, καὶ ἐς τοὺς νυκτὸς ἀστασίαν τινὰ ἐς τὴν πόλιν πράσσοντας. Καὶ ἀγορανόμοι ἕτεροι

who are his companions and assist him in the dignity of the principality.[70] After six months these advisors are relieved of their position.

After the Great Council is the so-called Senate-Council 35
of the Avogadori [Attorneys], with about three hundred members.[71] They are chosen, along with the other magistracies, in the Great Council, and they select the most sensible men to serve there. In this so-called Council of the Avogadori they deliberate regarding war and peace and also embassies, and whatever they decide the city then obeys: whatever this Council decides must be done, the entire city does it. Ten magistrates are in charge of accusations concerning the whole state, and these men bring the indictments and impose punishments in each case.[72] They are permitted to arrest and execute even the ruler himself, as their verdicts are accountable to no other magistracy. In this way they administer justice, and they have jurisdiction over the entire city to punish those who have committed any offense, whether against the city or each other. They can impose the death penalty on whomever they find guilty, but they preside as judges over other trials too, some over the locals and others over the foreigners. In addition to these men, they appoint forty magistrates and, whenever trials are referred to them, they cast their votes directly for what seems to them to be the most powerful case.[73] If they do not agree in the verdict, they refer the case to the Council of the Avogadori, and it is there scrutinized closely and resolved.

There are many other magistracies in the city, which per- 36
tain to security and deal with those who create disturbances in the city at night. Other men are appointed officials of the

καθίστανται τοὺς φόρους τῶν ἐπί τινι πραγμάτων καὶ ἐς τὰς προσόδους τῆς πόλεως ἀπαιτήσεις· οἱ δὴ τὰς προσόδους πράττοντες καθιστάμενοι, ἐφ᾽ οὓς δὴ τὰ τῆς ξυμπάσης πόλεως χρήματα καὶ οἱ φόροι ἀναφέρονται. Ἄρχοντες δὲ οἱ γεραιρότεροι τε καὶ ἀξιώματι προέχειν δοκοῦντες καθίστανται διὰ βίου ὡς ἐργῶδες ὂν κατ᾽ ἐνιαυτὸν λογίζεσθαι τὰς προσόδους τε καὶ ἐξόδους τῆς πόλεως, ὅ τι ἂν ἀπογένοιτό τε καὶ περιγένοιτο αὐτῶν τῶν χρημάτων. Ἀπὸ μὲν οὖν τούτων αἱροῦνται σφίσιν ἡγεμόνα, ἐπειδὰν σφίσι τελευτήσῃ. Ἐς τὰ πρῶτα τιμῆς ἀνήκουσιν ἐς ταύτην τὴν πολιτείαν· τούς τε γὰρ θησαυροὺς καὶ τὰς προσόδους ἐφορῶσιν οὗτοι καὶ ἐπιτροπεύουσι. Χρηματίζουσι δὲ σφίσιν ἐς [1.185] τὴν ἀρχὴν αὐτῶν, σὺν τῷ ἡγεμόνι παραγενόμενοι ἔστε ἀκρόασιν πρέσβεων καὶ τῶν μεγάλων εἴτε βασιλέων εἴτε καὶ ἡγεμόνων ἀναφοράς. Καὶ ἄνδρες οὗτοι ἡ τῆς πόλεως ὅλη ἐξουσία, ὀνομάζεται δὲ καὶ ἡγεμονία.

37 Προέχει δ᾽ αὕτη ἡ πόλις δυοῖν τῶν ἐν τῇ Ἰταλίᾳ πόλεων, οἰκιῶν τε εὐπρεπείᾳ καὶ κατασκευῇ τῶν ἐπὶ τῆς θαλάσσης οἰκοδομημάτων, ὡς τὸ ἐπίπαν τῆς πόλεως, καὶ πλούτῳ τῶν ἐν τῇ πόλει ἐνοικούντων, ἅτε τῆς πόλεως ἐπὶ ἐμπορίαν ἐπιτηδείως ἐχούσης ὡς μάλιστα καὶ χρήματα εὐπετῶς ποριζομένης. Κεκόσμηται δὲ ἡ πόλις αὕτη τά τε ἄλλα, καὶ ἐπινείῳ ἐντὸς τῆς πόλεως ᾠκοδομημένῳ, καλλίστῳ τε ἰδεῖν καὶ εὐπρεπεστάτῳ, ταῖς τριήρεσιν ἐξηρτυμένῳ ὡς πλείσταις καὶ πλοίοις ἄλλοις παμπόλλοις, καὶ τῇ κατασκευῇ τούτων ἀφθόνως τε ἐχούσῃ αὐτοῦ ἀπό τε ὅπλων καὶ ἄλλων, ὅσα ἐς χρείαν φέρει ταῖς ναυσί. Διήκει δὲ ἐπὶ πέντε σταδίους, καὶ ἄνδρες ὡς πλεῖστοι ἐργαζόμενοι

market and have jurisdiction over the taxes that are levied on transactions and the city's demands for revenue. The business affairs and taxes of the entire city are referred to those who have been given jurisdiction over revenue matters. These magistracies are given for life to older men who seem most suitable, as it is a difficult task to calculate, over a whole year, the income and expenditures of the city, what has been spent and what remains of the city's money. It is from among these men that they choose their new ruler, whenever the old one dies. They have the highest rank and honor in this system of government, for they supervise and manage the treasury and the revenues. They negotiate with sovereign power, as they are present with the ruler to hear the petitions of embassies and powerful men, whether these are kings or rulers. These men are, in sum, the sovereigns of the city, and they are known as the Signoria.[74]

This city surpasses the cities in Italy in two respects, in 37
the elegance of its houses and the construction of waterfront buildings, which is the city's very being, as well as by the wealth of its inhabitants, given that this city is favorably situated for trade and has a knack for making money. The city is adorned in many ways, including an Arsenal that has been built within the city and that is very beautiful to behold and very elegant. It harbors very many triremes and a multitude of other ships, and there is abundant equipment there, consisting of weapons and other gear, that serves the ships' needs. It is five stades long, and a great number of

αὐτοῦ καθ' ἑκάστην ἐς τὰς ναῦς. Ἄρχοντας δὲ αἱροῦνται τοῦ ἐνιαυτοῦ δύο ἐς τὸ ἐπίνειον τοῦτο καὶ ἐς ξύμπασαν τὴν κατασκευήν. Ἵπποις δὲ οὐδέν τι χρῆται ἡ πόλις αὕτη, ἀλλὰ πεζῇ τε ἐπ' ἀλλήλους φοιτῶσι καὶ πλοιαρίοις, τῇ μὲν τῆς θαλάσσης διὰ τῶν οἰκιῶν διηκούσης, τῇ δὲ καὶ ἀκτῶν κατεστρωμένων πλίνθοις ἁπανταχῇ τῆς πόλεως. Τείχει δὲ οὐδὲν περιβέβληται ἡ πόλις.

38 Τὰς μέντοι ἀρχὰς τῶν σφετέρων πόλεων ἔστε τὴν ἤπειρον [1.186] τῆς Ἰταλίας καὶ ἐς τὴν παράλιον χώραν αὐτῶν διὰ τέλους δὲ ὡς ἐπὶ τὸ πολὺ αἱροῦνται. Ἐπειδὰν δὲ ἐπανίωσιν ἐς τὴν πόλιν, ἥν τι μὴ ὀρθῶς πεπραγμένον ᾖ αὐτῷ, τάς τε εὐθύνας δίδωσι καὶ δίκην, ἐφ' οἷς μὴ καλῶς πεπολιτευμένα τυγχάνει αὐτῷ. Καὶ αἱροῦνται μὲν οὗτοι στρατηγὸν σφίσιν οὐκ ἐπιχώριον ἐς τὰ στρατεύματα τῆς ἠπείρου, δεδιότες μὴ προσαγόμενοι τοὺς στρατιώτας περὶ τὴν ἀρχὴν νεωτερίσωσι καὶ κινδυνεύσῃ αὐτοῖς διαφθαρῆναι τὰ πράγματα. Ἐς μέντοι τὴν ἀρχὴν τῆς θαλάσσης οὐκ ἔχοντες, ὅπως ἐπάγωνται ἀλλοτρίους, καθιστᾶσί τε ἐκ τῶν ἐπιχωρίων αὐτοκράτορας, ἐπειδὰν πολεμεῖν ἐξέρχωνται, καὶ ἰδίᾳ κατ' ἐνιαυτὸν τὰς δέκα τριήρεις, ἃς ἐπιπέμπουσιν ἔτους ἑκάστου ἔστε τὸν Ἰόνιον καὶ ἐς τὸ Αἰγαῖον, τῶν νεῶν αὐτῶν, αἳ ἐπὶ ἐμπορίαν ἀφικνοῦνται ἐπὶ Αἴγυπτον καὶ Λιβύην καὶ ὠκεανὸν καὶ Εὔξεινον πόντον. Καὶ καθαιροῦντες τὸ ληστρικόν, ὅποι ἂν περιτύχωσιν, αἱ δέκα αὗται τριήρεις διατρίβουσιν ὅλον ἐνιαυτόν, ἐς ὅπερ αἱ δέκα ἀφικνούμεναι ἀπαλλάττουσι ταύτας τῆς φυλακῆς. Ἐπιπέμπουσι δὲ καὶ τριήρεις ἐπὶ ἐμπορίαν ἡ πόλις, ἐξωνουμένων τῶν πολιτῶν ταύτας, ἔστε Ἀλεξάνδρειαν καὶ

men work on the ships there every day. They choose two magistrates each year for the port and the entire shipyard. The city does not use horses, for the Venetians visit each other on foot and by small boats, because the sea extends between the houses, and the waterfront is paved with stone throughout the city. The city is not surrounded by walls.

They appoint the magistrates for their own cities on the 38
mainland of Italy and their coastal territories, mostly in order to collect the taxes due to them. But when the magistrates return to the city, if there is something that they have not done right, they are called to account and pay a penalty for those matters in which they have not governed well. They do not choose a local general for their mainland armies, because they are afraid that he might suborn the soldiers, incite sedition against the state, and have the means to endanger their affairs. When it comes to command at sea, however, they do not bring in foreigners but appoint commanders from their own countrymen whenever they sail out to war. Every year, through private means, they send out ten triremes to the Adriatic Sea and the Aegean from among their ships that travel for trade as far as Egypt, North Africa, the Ocean, and the Black Sea. These ten ships spend an entire year rooting out piracy wherever they find it; afterward, the ten return home and are relieved of the duty to provide security. The city also sends out for trade triremes, for which their citizens pay, and they go to Alexandria, Syria, the Don

Συρίαν καὶ Τάναϊν καὶ ἐς τὰς Βρετανικὰς νήσους καὶ ἐς τὴν Λιβύην. Εἴησαν δ' ἂν αἱ τριήρεις αὗται δύο καὶ εἴκοσι, μείζους τῶν ἄλλων τριήρεων, ἅτε ἐπὶ ἐμπορίαν κατεσκευασμέναι. Νομίζεται δ' αὐτοῖς ἐφ' ἑκάστης νεὼς καὶ παῖδας συγκλητικῶν ἀνδρῶν ἐπὶ τὴν ἐμπορίαν ἀφικνεῖσθαι, μεμισθωμένους καὶ τούτους σὺν τῇ νηὶ ἐπὶ τὴν ἐμπορίαν.

39 Ἐξεύρηται μὲν οὖν τούτοις τοῖς Οὐενετοῖς πρὸς τὸν [I.187] Λιγυρίας τύραννον διαπολεμοῦσι χρήματα τῇ τε ἄλλῃ καὶ δὴ καὶ τῶν πολιτῶν ἑκάστου τῆς οὐσίας ὁ δεκατισμός, πρὸς οὓς δὴ τάττει ἡ πόλις ἐτήσιον πρόσοδον οἷα τοῦ χρέους ἀπόδοσιν. Καὶ ἅττα δ' ἂν ἐπαγγέλῃ λαμβάνειν τοὺς πολίτας, τρία δὴ ἕκαστον ἐπαγγέλλει ἀποδιδόναι ἔτους ἑκάστου. Οὐκ ἔστιν, ὅτε ἐπὶ τοὺς παῖδάς τε καὶ ἐγγόνους οὐκ ἀφικνεῖται ἡ τοιαύτη πρόσοδος. Ἐξωνοῦνται μὲν ἔνιοι ταύτας οὐκ ὀλίγου τινὸς παρὰ τῶν ἐνδεῶς τοῦ βίου σφίσιν ἐχόντων καὶ εὐδαιμονοῦσι.

40 Δοκεῖ δὲ ἡ πόλις αὕτη Οὐενετῶν ἀπὸ παλαιοῦ εὐνομουμένη μηδένα φθῆναι ἐπὶ νεωτερισμὸν ἀφικέσθαι, πλὴν δὴ Βαϊμοῦνδον νεανίαν, ὀλβιώτατον δοκοῦντα γενέσθαι, ἀνακτώμενον τὸ πλῆθος ἐπὶ τοῦτο ὡρμῆσθαι· ἀπὸ οἰκίας δέ τινος βληθέντα ὑπὸ γυναικὸς ἄνωθεν, ἐν τῇ ὁδῷ προϊόντα ἐπὶ τὰ βασίλεια ἐπισπομένου αὐτῷ τοῦ πλήθους καὶ δεσπότην σφῶν καὶ τῆς πόλεως ἀποδεικνυμένου, καὶ ταύτῃ βληθέντα λίθῳ ἀποθανεῖν. Ὕστερον μέντοι οὐδένες, ὅ τι καὶ ἄξιον λόγου, ἐς νεωτερισμὸν περὶ τὴν πόλιν ταύτην ἐξηνέχθησαν, δεινῶς τοῦτο φυλαττομένης τῆς πόλεως μὴ συμβῆναι αὐτῇ, ὅτι μὴ τὸν παῖδα τοῦ ἡγεμόνος τῶν Φουσκαρέων οἰκίας φασὶ νεωτερίζοντα ἑαλωκέναι ὑπὸ τῶν

River, the British Isles, and North Africa. These triremes can be up to twenty-two in number and they are larger than other triremes because they have been built for trade. It is their custom to place the sons of senators aboard each ship so that they learn the business of trade, and they too are hired, along with the ship, for the trade run.

When the Venetians were fighting against the tyrant of 39
Lombardy they raised money in many ways, including a contribution of one tenth of the property of each citizen, and the city fixed for them an annual income to pay back the contribution. Whatever sum it announces that the citizens will receive, it specifies that each will be repaid three times each year. But this annuity is not inherited by sons and grandsons. Some even purchase this credit at a high price from those who are in need, and they prosper.

The city of the Venetians appears to have been well gov- 40
erned since ancient times and no one has managed to instigate sedition in it, except for a young man, Bajamonte. He had grown rich and suborned the crowd to attempt this. But he was struck from above by a woman in a house as he was processing through the street to the palace, with the crowd following behind him and acclaiming him as their master and master of the city; he was struck by that rock, and died.[75] After that no attempts worth mentioning were made at revolution in this city, as it took every precaution to prevent that from happening, unless we include the son of the lord of the Foscari family who, they say, was convicted by the

τῆς πόλεως δικαστῶν, καὶ ἐς ἀνάγκας ἀφικόμενον μεγάλας μηδ' ὁτιοῦν εὑρίσκειν ἐν ἑαυτῷ. Καὶ τὸν μὲν νεανίαν ἐκπεπτωκέναι διὰ τὴν [1.188] ἑαυτῷ ἐπενεχθεῖσαν αἰτίαν· ὅθεν καὶ εὐφροσύνην εὐπορησάμενον κατελθεῖν. Καὶ αὖθις ἁλῶναι διαφθείραντα τὸν ἄνδρα ἐκεῖνον, ὃς ἀπῆγεν αὐτὸν προδοσίας. Ἐς ἀνάγκας ἰόντα τὸν οὕτως ἐκπεπτωκότα διατρίβειν ἐν Κρήτῃ. Ἐπιφερομένης δ' ἐς αὐτὸν αὖθις αἰτίας, ἐπὶ τοῦτο μεταπεμψαμένους τοὺς δέκα τῆς πόλεως πολυπραγμονεῖν, καὶ οὐχ εὑρόντας ἀποπέμψαι τε αὖθις ἐς Κρήτην, καὶ μετ' οὐ πολὺ αὐτοῦ τελευτῆσαι.

41 Ὡς μὲν οὖν τῇ πόλει ταύτῃ πόλεμον ἐπαγγείλας Μεχμέτης ὁ Παιαζήτεω παῖς, καὶ τριήρεις ἐπλήρωσαν ἐπὶ ταῖς προφυλακαῖς ἄλλας ἀεὶ καὶ δύο γενομένας, ἔπλεον αὗται εὐθὺ Ἑλλησπόντου, ἡγουμένου Πέτρου τοῦ Λαυρεδάνων οἰκίας, ἐς ὕστερον καὶ τὴν ἐπὶ τοὺς Ἰανυΐους στρατηγίαν, καὶ στρατηγικῶς εὐδοκίμησεν. Οὗτος δὴ οὖν σὺν ταῖς ναυσὶν ἀφικόμενος ἐς τὸν Ἑλλήσποντον ἐπὶ τῆς Καλλιουπόλεως ἀνεκώχευε μετεώρους τὰς ναῦς ἐν τῷ πελάγει, ἑκὼν μὲν οὐχ ὑπάρχων πολέμου· ἐδόκει τε γὰρ εἰρήνην τε εἶναι καὶ τὰς σπονδὰς μὴ λελύσθαι, καὶ ἀμύνειν μέντοι ἐπηγγέλλετο αὐτῷ, ὑπάρξαι δὲ πολέμου μηκέτι. Ἐδόκει τε γὰρ καὶ μὴ πολεμεῖν, τῶν πόλεων σφίσι ἐν τῇ τοῦ Μεχμέτεω χώρᾳ ὑπὸ Τούρκων μὴ κακῶς πάσχειν, ἔν τε τῇ πρὸς τὸν Ἰόνιον καὶ ἐν τῷ Αἰγαίῳ πελάγει. Τούτῳ μὲν οὖν οὕτω ἐπιτέτακται ὑπὸ τῆς συγκλήτου, ἀμυνόμενον μὲν διαναυμαχῆσαι, [1.189] ἑκόντα δὲ εἶναι μὴ ὑπάρξαι πολέμου.

42 Ὡς δὲ ἀφίκετο ἐς τὸν Ἑλλήσποντον καὶ ἀπὸ τῆς Ἀσίας ἑδραιοῦντο αἱ τριήρεις, ὁ τῆς Καλλιουπόλεως ὕπαρχος

city's judges for attempting a rebellion, as he had fallen into great need and could not earn anything. The young man was exiled because of the charge brought against him, but he came back from there, having found a way to procure favor.[76] He was arrested again for killing the man who had indicted him for treason. Exiled and in need, he went to live on Crete. When an accusation was again laid against him, the Ten of the city brought him back for a detailed investigation, but as they could not find [anything against him], he was sent back to Crete. Shortly afterward he died there.[77]

It was on this city, then, that Mehmed, the son of Bayezid, declared war. The Venetians manned their triremes, those that were always on guard duty plus two more, and these ships sailed straight for the Hellespont under the command of Pietro of the Loredan family; he later had command of the campaign against the Genoese, and enjoyed considerable military success.[78] When he arrived with his ships at the Hellespont, by Gallipoli, he kept them riding at anchor out at sea, as he was unwilling to start the war, for it seemed that the peace was still holding and the treaty had not been broken. His orders were to defend himself, not to start a war. The Venetians had decided against a war, as their cities in Mehmed's territory were not being harmed by the Turks, in either the Adriatic or Aegean Sea. The senate had ordered him to fight a naval battle only in self-defense, but not to actively provoke a war. 41

But when Loredan arrived at the Hellespont and his triremes were sitting there off the coast of Asia, the governor 42

οὐκέτι ἀνασχετὸν ἐποιεῖτο τοὺς Οὐενετοὺς οὕτω περιφανῶς ὑβρίζειν ἐς τὴν βασιλέως χώραν καὶ αὐτὸ τὸ ἐπίνειον αὐτοῦ, καὶ ὡς ἐπλήρου δὲ τὰς ναῦς, ἀντανήγετο καὶ οὗτος, ἔχων τριήρεις πέντε καὶ εἴκοσι, νῆας δὲ ἄλλας ἀμφὶ τὰς ὀγδοήκοντα, ὡς δεδιττόμενος τοὺς Οὐενετοὺς τῷ βασιλέως ναυτικῷ. Οὗτοι μὲν προήεσαν ἐπὶ Προικόνησον, μετεώρους ἔχοντας τὰς ναῦς αὐτῶν. Ἡ δὲ Πελοποννησία ὑπολέλειπτο ὡς ὕστερον ἀναγομένη. Ἐνταῦθα ὡς ἀγχοῦ ἐγένετο τριήρης μία τοῦ βασιλέως, μετεπέμπετο ὁ ἡγεμὼν τῶν Οὐενετῶν σημεῖον ἐπάρας, κελεύων ἕπεσθαι καὶ μὴ ἐμβάλλειν. Οἰόμενος δ' ὁ τῆς τριήρους ἄρχων τῆς Πελοποννησίας ὡς κελεύοι ἐμβάλλειν, τὸ σύνθημα οἰόμενός οἱ γενέσθαι ὑπὸ τοῦ στρατηγοῦ, ἐμβάλλει τε τῇ τοῦ βασιλέως νηῒ καὶ καταδύει. Αἱ δὲ λοιπαὶ τῶν βαρβαρικῶν νεῶν ἰδοῦσαι ὡς ὑπῆρκτο πολέμου καὶ ἐς μάχην καθίστανται, ἐπείγονται ἐπαμύνειν βουλόμεναι ἐπὶ τὴν Πελοποννησίαν ναῦν. Ἐνταῦθα δὴ αἱ λοιπαὶ τῶν Οὐενετῶν τριήρεις κατιδοῦσαι τὸ γεγονός, ὡς ἐπὶ τὴν σφετέραν αἱ βαρβαρικαὶ νῆες ἐπείγονται, ἀντανήγοντο καὶ αὗται ἐπὶ ναυμαχίαν. Καὶ ὡς ἐναυμάχουν, διέκπλουν τε ἐποιήσαντο, καὶ καταδύσαντες ναῦς τέ τινας καὶ ζωγρήσαντες τὰς λοιπὰς ἐς τὴν γῆν ἐτρέψαντο καὶ ἐνίκησαν Οὐενετοί, ναῦς λαβόντες τῶν βαρβάρων τρισκαίδεκα, κενὰς δὲ τὰς πλείους· οἱ [I.190] γὰρ Τοῦρκοι, ὡς ἁλίσκοιτο ἡ ναῦς, ἐς τὴν θάλασσαν ἔπιπτον καὶ ἐξένεον ἐπὶ τὴν γῆν.

43 Ἐνταῦθα ὡς ἤδη πόλεμον τοῖς Οὐενετοῖς ἀνελομένοις πρὸς βασιλέα Μεχμέτην, τήν τε Λάμψακον πολιορκίᾳ παρεστήσαντο καὶ φυλακὴν ἐγκατέλιπον, καὶ αὐτοὶ

of Gallipoli could not bear the fact that the Venetians were so brazenly insulting the territory of the sultan and his port. He manned his ships and sailed against them in person, taking twenty-five triremes and about eighty other ships, to scare off the Venetians with the sultan's fleet. The Venetians then advanced to Prokonnesos and anchored their ships at sea. But a Peloponnesian ship was left behind to catch up later. When one of the sultan's triremes came near, the Venetian commander summoned the Peloponnesian ship by raising the signal flag, ordering it to follow and not to engage. But the captain of the Peloponnesian trireme thought that the signal he was being given by the general was an order to engage, and so he attacked the sultan's ship and sank it. The rest of the barbarian ships saw that war had begun; so they prepared for battle and hurried to defend themselves against the Peloponnesian ship. When the rest of the Venetian triremes saw what was happening, namely that the barbarian ships were rapidly advancing against their own, they too sailed into battle. In the fight they broke the enemy line, sank some ships, captured others, and ran the rest aground. The Venetians won, capturing thirteen barbarian ships, although most of them were empty. For when a ship was captured, the Turks would jump into the sea and swim to shore.[79]

As the Venetians were now at war with Sultan Mehmed, 43
they took Lampsakos by siege, left a garrison, and went

ᾤχοντο ἐπ' οἴκου ἀποπλέοντες. Ἐνταῦθα μέντοι οἵ τε Οὐενετοὶ τοῦτον τὸν στρατηγόν, ὃς περιεγένετο τοῦ τῶν βαρβάρων στόλου, ἦγοντο θανάτου ὡς πρότερον ὑπάρξαντα ἀδικίας καὶ λελυκότα τὰς σπονδὰς παρὰ τὰ ἐπεσταλμένα αὐτῷ. Καὶ ἐν δίκῃ γενόμενος παρὰ δικασταῖς ἀπελύθη μὴ αὐτὸς πρότερος ὑπάρξαι τοῦ πρὸς βάρβαρον πολέμου. Μετ' οὐ πολὺν δὲ χρόνον διεπρεσβεύσαντο καὶ σπονδὰς ἐποιήσαντο. Ἐς τούτους μὲν οὖν οὕτως ἔσχε τῷ βασιλεῖ Μεχμέτῃ.

44 Τοῖς δὲ Ἕλλησιν ἐπιτήδειός τε καὶ συνήθης ἠξίου θεραπεύειν, ὅτου ἂν δεήσαιντο παρ' ἑαυτῷ, δι' αἰτίαν τήνδε. Μουσταφᾶς γάρ τοι ὁ τῶν Παιαζήτεω παίδων, μιμησάμενος Μωσέα τὸν ἀδελφόν, καὶ πρὸς τὸν Σινώπης ἄρχοντα πολέμιον ὄντα τῷ ἀδελφῷ Μεχμέτῃ ἀφικόμενος, καὶ ὅρκια ποιησάμενος, ὥστε ξένους εἶναί τε καὶ φίλους ἀλλήλοις, καὶ πρὸς τὸν Δακίας ἡγεμόνα διαπρεσβευσάμενος, ὡς αὐτὸν ἄσμενος ὑπεδέχετο καὶ τἆλλα ὑπισχνεῖτο συγκατεργάζεσθαι τὰ ἐς τὴν βασιλείαν, διέβη τε εἰς τὴν Δακίαν Μουσταφᾶς, καὶ χρόνον αὐτόθι διατρίψας συχνόν, ἔχων ἄνδρας τριακοσίους ἔπρασσε πρὸς τοὺς Τούρκων ἀρίστους, μετιὼν ἕκαστον. Ὡς δ' οὐδὲν προεχώρει (ἦν γὰρ Μεχμέτης τά τε ἄλλα ἐπιεικὴς καὶ ἐς τὸ θεραπεύειν τοὺς ἀρίστους τῶν Τούρκων οὐκ [1.191] ἀδόκιμος, τρόπου τε ἡσυχίου), ψευδῆ τε παῖδα ἐνέφηνεν εἶναι τοῦ Παιαζήτεω τὸν Μουσταφᾶν, καὶ ὡς οὐδαμῇ καταφανῆ σχόντες τὴν διατριβὴν αὐτῷ· τὸν δὲ παῖδα τούτου τελευτῆσαι παρ' ἀνδρὶ ἐπιτηδείῳ καὶ τὸν τρόπον δικαιοτάτῳ, ὃς ἀφῖκτο παρ' ἑαυτὸν τὸν θάνατον τοῦ παιδὸς διασημῆναι.

away, sailing for home. But there the Venetians put this general, who had defeated the barbarian fleet, on trial for his life, as he had been the first to commence hostilities and break the treaty in contravention of his orders. When he stood trial, however, he was acquitted by the judges because he had not initiated hostilities against the barbarian.[80] Shortly afterward they sent envoys and concluded a treaty.[81] That is how Sultan Mehmed stood in relation to them.

Mehmed was a friend to the Greeks and was usually ready 44
to provide them with whatever they requested from him, for the following reason. One of Bayezid's sons, Mustafa, following the example of his brother Musa, went to the ruler of Sinope, who was at war with his brother Mehmed, and they swore oaths to be each other's friends and allies.[82] He also sent an envoy to the ruler of Wallachia,[83] and, when he was well received—he promised to support him to gain the throne—Mustafa crossed over to Wallachia and spent quite some time there. He had three hundred men and began to negotiate with the leading Turks, approaching each one individually. But he made no progress, for Mehmed was generally reasonable and especially adept at winning the favor of the leading Turks, and he kept calm. Mehmed claimed that Mustafa was not a true son of Bayezid and that no one knew anything certain about his career: the son of that name had died, and he knew this from an associate of his, a most upright man who had visited him precisely to announce the death of the child.[84]

45 Ἐνταῦθα Μουσταφᾶς, ὡς οὐδὲν αὐτῷ κατὰ νοῦν ἐπέβαινεν ἀπὸ Δακίας, καὶ οἰόμενος ἑαυτῷ ἄμεινον ἐξεῖναι, ἢν ἐπὶ τοὺς Ἕλληνας ἀφίκηται ἐν μέσῳ τῆς ἀρχῆς Μεχμέτεω ἱδρυμένους. Ἐλαύνει ἀπὸ Δακίας διὰ μέσης τῆς Θρᾴκης ἐπὶ τὴν Θέρμην, πόλιν Ἑλληνίδα. Καὶ ἐς λόγους ἀφικόμενος τῷ Ἑλλήνων ἄρχοντι εἰσῄει τε εἰς τὴν πόλιν καὶ κατελήφθη. Μεχμέτης δὲ ὡς ἐπύθετο τάχιστα ἐς τὴν Θέρμην ἀφικέσθαι τὸν ἀδελφόν, αὐτίκα οὐδὲν ἐπισχὼν δρομαῖος ἐπῄει ἐπὶ τὴν Θέρμην, παραλαβὼν στρατόν, καὶ ἐζήτει τὸν ἀδελφὸν τοὺς Ἕλληνας. Ὁ μέντοι τῆς Θέρμης ἄρχων ἄγγελον πέμψας ἐπὶ τὸν Βυζαντίου βασιλέα ἐδήλου τε, ὡς ἔχει αὐτῷ περὶ τοῦ παιδὸς Παιαζήτεω Μουσταφᾶ, καὶ ὡς Μεχμέτης ἐπελαύνων ἐξαιτοῖτο τὸν ἀδελφὸν οἷα ψευδῆ ὄντα καὶ διαφθείροντά γε αὐτοῦ. Βασιλεὺς δὲ πρέσβυν τε ἔπεμψε πρὸς Μεχμέτην, καὶ συνέθετο αὐτῷ τὸν Μουσταφᾶν ἐς φυλακήν τε ποιήσασθαι καὶ μηδαμῆ μεθιέναι τε ἀπιόντα. Καὶ ἐπὶ τούτῳ ὅρκιά τε ἐποιήσαντο, καὶ Μουσταφᾶν ἐν Ἐπιδαύρῳ τῆς Πελοποννήσου καὶ ἐν τῇ ἄκρᾳ τῆς πόλεως καθείρξαντες, αὐτόν τε τὸν Μουσταφᾶν, καὶ τὸν Σμύρνης ἄρχοντα Ζουναΐτην, ἅμα αὐτῷ ἀπὸ Δακίας ἐπὶ τὴν Θέρμην ἀφικόμενον καὶ συνεπιλαβόμενον τοῦ πρὸς Μεχμέτην πολέμου. [1.192] Τούτους μὲν οὖν Ἕλληνες εἶχον ἐν φυλακῇ ἐπὶ συχνόν τινα χρόνον, μετὰ δὲ ταῦτα ἤγαγον ἐς τὴν Λῆμνον καὶ ἐς τὴν Ἴμβρον, καὶ αὐτοῦ εἶχον ἐν φυλακῇ, ἐς ὃ δὴ ἐτελεύτησε Μεχμέτης ὁ Παιαζήτεω. Τότε μὲν δὴ χαριζόμενοι τῷ βασιλεῖ οἱ Ἕλληνες, καὶ τὴν ὁμοίαν ἀνταποδιδόντες, κατέθεντο τούτους ἐν Ἐπιδαύρῳ τῆς Πελοποννήσου· καὶ οὐκ ἔστιν,

At this point Mustafa, who could see that he was making 45
no progress in Wallachia, believed that it would be better for him if he went to the Greeks, who were established in the very middle of Mehmed's territory. He set out from Wallachia and went through central Thrace to Thessalonike, a Greek city. He negotiated with the governor of the Greeks, entered the city, and was arrested.[85] As soon as Mehmed learned that his brother had arrived at Thessalonike, he let nothing prevent him from rushing there, taking an army with him, and demanding that the Greeks surrender his brother. The governor of Thessalonike, however, sent a messenger to the king of Byzantion [Manuel II] and explained how matters stood with Mustafa, the son of Bayezid, and that Mehmed had marched there and was demanding his brother as an impostor who was trying to overthrow him. The king sent an envoy to Mehmed and they agreed that Mustafa would be put in prison and would not be released under any circumstances. They swore oaths upon it and Mustafa was imprisoned in the citadel of the city of Monemvasia in the Peloponnese. Along with Mustafa went Junayd, the lord of Smyrna, who had come with him to Thessalonike from Wallachia and had joined in the war against Mehmed.[86] The Greeks held them in prison for a long time, transferring them afterward to Lemnos and Imbros, where they were also kept in prison, until the death of Mehmed, the son of Bayezid.[87] At that time, then, the Greeks were in favor with the sultan and they paid him back when they placed these men at Monemvasia, in the Peloponnese. For

ὅτου ἀποτύχοιεν διὰ ταῦτα παρὰ βασιλεῖ Μεχμέτη. Τότε μὲν οὖν παρασχὸν σφίσιν ἐν βελτίονί τε τῆς πρόσθεν ἐπὶ πολὺν χρόνον ἀεὶ καταστάσει ἐτύγχανον ὄντες, εὖ πράττοντες, καὶ τήν τε Πελοπόννησον καθίστασαν ἐπὶ τὸ σφίσι δοκοῦν ἕξειν ὡς συμφερώτατα.

46 Ἐμμανουήλῳ μέντοι ἐγένοντο παῖδες ὅ τε Ἰωάννης ὁ πρεσβύτερος, ὃν δὴ τοῖς Ἕλλησιν ἀπεδείξατο βασιλέα, καὶ Ἀνδρόνικος καὶ Θεόδωρος μετὰ τοῦτον καὶ Κωνσταντῖνος καὶ Δημήτριος καὶ Θωμᾶς. Τῷ μέντοι Ἰωάννῃ τῷ πρεσβυτέρῳ, πάντων τῶν ἄλλων κρατίστῳ δοκοῦντι γενέσθαι, τήν τε βασιλείαν ἐπέτρεψε, καὶ ἀπὸ Ἰταλίας ἀγόμενος αὐτῷ γυναῖκα τοῦ Μονφεράτου ἡγεμόνος θυγατέρα, ἐπιεικῆ μὲν τὸν τρόπον, ἀηδῆ δὲ τὴν ὄψιν, διαδήματι ταινιώσας ἀρχιερέα τε καὶ βασιλέα ἐστήσατο τοῖς Ἕλλησι. Ταύτην μὲν οὖν, ὡς οὔτε συνῴκει οὔτε συνεγένετο, ἐς ἔχθος ἀφικόμενος καὶ ἀηδῶς ἔχων αὐτῇ ἐπί τινα χρόνον, καὶ ἥ τε γυνὴ τοῦ βασιλέως ἐνεώρα ἐς αὐτὴν τὸν ἄνδρα ἀηδῶς ἔχοντα, καὶ αὐτὴν ἀπεχθάνεσθαι τῷ ἀνδρὶ ἐς τὰ μάλιστα, ἐπιβᾶσα νεὼς [1.193] ἐχώρει ἀποπλέουσα ἐπὶ Ἰταλίας παρὰ τοὺς προσήκοντας. Ἠγάγετο δὲ γυναῖκα τὴν ἀπὸ Σαρματίας, τοῦ Σαρματῶν ἡγεμόνος θυγατέρα. Οὗτος μὲν οὖν οὕτω διατεθεὶς ἐβασίλευεν.

47 Ἀνδρονίκῳ μὲν τήν τε Θέρμην ἐπέτρεψεν οἰκεῖν, ἀνδρὶ οὐκ ἀγεννεῖ μετά γε Ἰωάννην τὸν βασιλέα. Καὶ ἐπί τινα χρόνον διαγενόμενος ἐς νόσον περιῆλθεν ἐλεφαντίασιν, καὶ τὴν Θέρμην ἀπέδοτο τοῖς Οὐενετοῖς, ὡς τῆς τε πόλεως οὐκ ἐπιτηδείως ἐχούσης ἐς φυλακὴν αὐτῆς, καὶ σφίσι τὰ πράγματα πονήρως ἤδη ἔχοντα. Καὶ ὡς ἐδέδοκτο ἤδη

this reason they could not go wrong as far as Sultan Mehmed was concerned. So things were much better for them at that time than they had been for a long time previously; they did well and arranged their affairs in the Peloponnese in a way that they thought would work to their advantage in the future.

Manuel had the following sons: the eldest was Ioannes 46
[VIII], whom he appointed king of the Greeks, then Andronikos, and after him Theodoros [II], Konstantinos, Demetrios, and Thomas.[88] Manuel entrusted the kingship to Ioannes, the eldest, who seemed to be the strongest of the lot, and brought a woman over from Italy for him to marry, the daughter of the ruler of Montferrat. She was a good match but was unattractive. Crowning him with a diadem, Manuel made him bishop and king of the Greeks.[89] But as Ioannes would not live or sleep with his wife, after a while he came to hate her and was on bad terms with her. The king's wife saw that her husband was treating her badly and that she had become loathsome to her husband, so she boarded a ship and sailed for Italy to return to her relatives. Ioannes then married a woman from Russia, a daughter of the ruler of the Russians.[90] And so he reigned with his affairs settled in this way.

Manuel entrusted the management of Thessalonike to 47
Andronikos,[91] a man no less noble than King Ioannes. After some time passed Andronikos fell ill with leprosy, and he gave Thessalonike to the Venetians as the city was unable to defend itself properly and its affairs were already in disorder. As they decided there that this course would be better both

αὐτοῖς ταύτῃ σφίσι τε αὐτοῖς καὶ τῇ πόλει ἄμεινον ἔσεσθαι, ἀπέδοτο ταύτην τοῖς Οὐενετοῖς οὐ πολλοῦ τινός. Ἀνδρόνικος μέντοι ἐς Πελοπόννησον παρὰ τὸν ἀδελφὸν ἀφικόμενος τήν τε δίαιταν εἶχεν ἐν Μαντινείᾳ τῆς Λακωνικῆς, ἐς ὃ δὴ ἐπικρατοῦντος τοῦ νοσήματος ἤδη τελέως ἐτελεύτησε.

48 Τὸν δὲ Θεόδωρον τούτον[5] παῖδα ὄντα βασιλεὺς Ἐμμανουῆλος ἐπεπόμφει παρὰ ἀδελφὸν αὐτοῦ Θεόδωρον τὸν πορφυρογέννητον, ἐφ᾽ ᾧ διάδοχόν τε τὸν παῖδα καταλιπεῖν ἐπὶ τῇ Πελοποννήσῳ. Καὶ ὡς ἐδέξατο τοῦτον ἀδελφοῦ τε παῖδα καὶ ἐπιτηδείου, εἶχέ τε παρ᾽ ἑαυτῷ, καὶ ὡς ἐτελεύτα, κατέλιπε τὴν ἀρχὴν αὐτῷ. Οὗτος δὲ ὡς ἐπὶ τὴν ἡγεμονίαν κατέστη, ἔγημέ τε γυναῖκα ἀπὸ Ἰταλίας, θυγατέρα Μαλατέστα τοῦ Μάρκης ἡγεμόνος, τῷ τε κάλλει διαπρέπουσαν καὶ τῇ ἄλλῃ κοσμιότητι. Ὕστερον μέντοι, ὡς ἐς μῖσός τε ἀφίκετο τῇ γυναικὶ καὶ ἐς ἔχθος ἀφικόμενος ἐς διαφορὰν κατέστη, ἐς τὴν Ναζηραίων δίαιταν ὥρμητο γενέσθαι, καὶ τόν [I.194] τε ἀδελφὸν αὐτοῦ μετεπέμπετο ἐπὶ τὴν ἀρχήν, ὡς ἐπεί οἱ ἐδόκει ἰέναι ἐς τὸ Ναζηραίων σχῆμα, τήν τε ἀρχὴν ἐπιτρέψων αὐτῷ καὶ τὴν οὐσίαν. Οὗτος μέντοι οὐκ εἰς μακρὰν αὖθις μετέβαλλεν, ἀποτρεπομένων τῶν ἀρίστων αὐτοῦ ἀπὸ τούτου καὶ οὐκ ἐπιτρεπόντων ἰέναι αὐτῷ, εἰς ὃ ὥρμητο.

49 Τῷ μὲν οὖν πρεσβυτέρῳ Θεοδώρῳ τῷ πάτρῳ παῖς οὐκ ἐγένετο ἀπὸ τῆς Ῥαινερίου θυγατρός, νόθοι δὲ ἐγένοντο. Ἠγάγετο γὰρ οὗτος τὴν τοῦ Ἀθηνῶν τυράννου θυγατέρα, πασῶν δὴ λεγομένην εἶναι καλλίστην τῶν εἰς ἐκεῖνον τὸν χρόνον κάλλει διενεγκουσῶν. Ῥαινέριος δὲ οὗτος

for themselves and for the city, they gave it away to the Venetians in exchange for a small sum.[92] Andronikos went to his brother in the Peloponnese and lived in Mantineia, the one in Lakonia, until the illness worsened and he finally died.[93]

As for Theodoros {II}, while he was still a child, King 48
Manuel sent him to his own brother, Theodoros {I} the Porphyrogennetos, for the boy to be his successor in the Peloponnese. The latter received the boy, who was the son of his brother and friend, kept him by his side, and, when he died, left the principality to him.[94] When this Theodoros, then, succeeded to the principality, he married a woman from Italy, the daughter of Malatesta, the ruler of Marche, who was distinguished for her beauty and good manners.[95] But later, as he came to hate his wife and bitter differences emerged between them, he became eager to take monastic orders and summoned his brother to the principality so that, when he decided to take on the monastic habit, he might entrust the principality to him along with his property. But shortly afterward he changed his mind, as his nobles dissuaded him from doing this and they would not allow him to proceed with his plan.[96]

The elder Theodoros, his uncle, had no sons from his 49
wife, the daughter of Nerio, but he had illegitimate ones. He had married the daughter of the tyrant of Athens, who was said to be the most beautiful of all the women who at that time were renowned for their beauty. This Nerio was the

Κορίνθου τε ἐτυράννευε καὶ Ἀθηνῶν, τῆς τε Βοιωτίας ἐπῆρξεν ἔστε ἐπὶ Θετταλίαν χωρῆσαι. Ἐπῆρξε δὲ τρόπῳ τοιῷδε. Ὁπότε ἐπὶ τοὺς Ἕλληνας ἐνάγοντος τοῦ Ῥωμαίων ἀρχιερέως ἐστρατεύοντο οἱ ἀπὸ τῆς ἑσπέρας Κελτοί τε ἅμα καὶ Οὐενετοί, τότε δὴ καὶ οἱ ἀπὸ Νεαπόλεως τοῦ βασιλέως καὶ ἀπὸ Τυρρηνῶν ὥρμηντο ἄνδρες καὶ Ἰανυΐων μέγα δυνάμενοι ἐπὶ τὴν τῆς Πελοποννήσου τε ἅμα καὶ τῆς ἄλλης Ἑλλάδος καταστροφήν. Καὶ τὴν μέντοι Πελοπόννησον κατεστρέψαντο ἄλλοι τε καὶ ἀπὸ τῆς Ἰανυΐων μοίρας, τοῦ οἴκου Ζαχαριῶν, τήν τε Ἀχαΐαν καὶ Ἤλιδος τὰ πλείω καὶ δὴ καὶ Πύλον καὶ Μεσήνης χώραν οὐκ ὀλίγην, ἔστε ἐπὶ Λακωνικὴν ἐλάσαι. Τὴν μέντοι μεσόγαιον τῆς Πελοποννήσου κατεῖχον αὐτοὶ τότε Πελοποννήσιοι Ἕλληνες. Ξύμπασαν δὲ τὴν παράλιον τῆς Πελοποννήσου οἱ ἀπὸ τῆς ἑσπέρας καταστρεψάμενοι εἶχον, Κελτοί τε δὴ καὶ [1.195] Κελτίβηρες, καὶ τῶν Ἰανυΐων καὶ Τυρρηνῶν ἄλλοι τε καὶ δὴ καὶ Ῥαινέριος ἀπὸ Φλωρεντίας ἀφικόμενος ἐπὶ τῇ στρατιᾷ ταύτῃ, τοῦ οἴκου τῶν Ἀζαϊόλων, τήν τε Ἀττικὴν κατέσχε καὶ Βοιωτίαν, ὡς καὶ πρότερόν μοι δεδήλωται, καὶ Φωκαΐδος χώρας τὰ πλείω.

50 Λίγυρες μέντοι τὴν Εὔβοιαν πολλῷ ἔτι παλαιότερον κατέσχον· ἀφ' ὧν ἐπιτραπέντες οἱ Οὐενετοὶ ἐπὶ ῥητῷ τῆς νήσου ἐπέβησαν. Μετὰ δὲ ταῦτα κατὰ βραχὺ προϊόντες ξύμπασάν τε τὴν Εὔβοιαν κατέσχον, ἐς διαφορὰν σφίσι τῶν Λιγύρων ἀφικνουμένων, καὶ τήν τε χώραν καὶ προσόδους αὐτῶν, ὅσοι τοῖς Οὐενετοῖς ἐπιτήδειοι ἐτύγχανον ὄντες, εἰσέτι καὶ νῦν διατελοῦσιν ἔχοντες, καὶ κατὰ ταῦτα ἐμμένοντες, ἐφ' οἷς σπενδόμενοι αὐτοῖς ξυνέβησαν κατὰ

tyrant of Corinth and Athens and he also ruled over Boiotia as far as Thessaly.[97] He came to rule in the following way. When, at the instigation of the pontiff of the Romans, the French and Venetians marched from the west against the Greeks,[98] men from the kingdom of Naples, from Tuscany, and from Genoa also set out with great forces to conquer the Peloponnese and the rest of Greece. They did in fact conquer the Peloponnese, and among the conquerors was a contingent of Genoese from the house of Zaccaria, who took Achaïa, most of Elis, Pylos, and much of the territory of Mesene, and they advanced as far as Lakonia.[99] The Peloponnesian Greeks held on to the interior of the Peloponnese. But the entire coast of the Peloponnese was conquered and held by the westerners, the French, Celtiberians,[100] and other Genoese and Tuscans, including Nerio, from the house of Acciaiuoli, who arrived from Florence with this army and held Attica and Boiotia, as I said earlier, and most of Phokis.[101]

Long before this the Lombards held Euboia, but the Ve- 50
netians took over the island when it was ceded to them by the Lombards under an agreement. After that the Venetians gradually advanced and took the whole of Euboia when they fell out with the Lombards.[102] Even to this day those who sided with the Venetians remain in possession of their land and revenues, and they are still there on the terms that they worked out with the Venetians when the latter arrived on

τὴν νῆσον οἱ Οὐενετοί. Ὁ μέντοι Ῥαινέριος καὶ οἱ Κελτίβηρες, καὶ Κελτῶν ὅσοι ἐπὶ τὴν τῆς Ἑλλάδος καταστροφὴν ἐγένοντο, πολλῷ ὕστερον τούτων φαίνονται ἀφικόμενοι ἐπὶ τὸν χῶρον τοῦτον. Ῥαινέριος δὲ καὶ πολλῷ ἔτι νέηλυς ὤν, ἐπιγαμίαν τε πρὸς τοὺς ἐν τῇ Εὐβοίᾳ Λιγύρων ποιησάμενος καὶ Προθυμοῦ τινος θυγατέρα ἔγημε, καὶ τήν τε χώραν κατασχὼν Κόρινθόν τε ἐχειρώσατο, καὶ τὴν Πελοπόννησον ἐπενόει ὅτι τάχιστα ὑφ' αὑτῷ ποιήσασθαι. Ὕστερον μέντοι ἀφικομένου τοῦ Ἑλλήνων βασιλέως ἀδελφοῦ, ἐπιγαμίαν πρὸς τοῦτον ἐπεποίητο, καὶ θυγατέρα ἡρμόσατο τούτῳ τῷ ἡγεμόνι Θεοδώρῳ, κάλλει, ὡς ἔφην, πασῶν τῶν τότε διαφέρουσαν, καὶ τήν τε Κόρινθον ἐπὶ τῇ ἑαυτοῦ τελευτῇ κατέλιπεν· ὑπέσχετο γάρ, ὁπότε αὐτῷ τὴν θυγατέρα ἡρμόσατο, ἐς φερνὴν αὐτῷ ταύτην, ἐπειδὰν τελευτήσῃ. [I.196]

51 Ἡρμόσατο δὲ καὶ ἑτέραν αὑτοῦ θυγατέρα Καρούλῳ τῷ Ἀκαρνανίας τε καὶ Αἰτωλίας ἡγεμόνι. Οὗτος γάρ, ὡς οἱ τῆς χώρας ταύτης ἄρχοντες πρότερον προσήκοντές τε ἦσαν τοῦ Παρθενόπης τῆς Νεαπόλεως καλουμένης βασιλέως, καὶ ὡς ὑπό τε τῶν περιοίκων καὶ τῶν ταύτῃ ἐθνῶν ἀπελαύνοντο ἐκ τῆς χώρας ἄρχοντες ἀπαλλαττόμενοι ἐπὶ Ἰταλίας. Κεφαλληνία δὲ καὶ Ζάκυνθος καὶ αἱ Ἐχινάδες νῆσοι, ὅσαι ταύτῃ ᾠκημέναι ἐτύγχανον, ἐς τουτονὶ τὸν βασιλέα τετραμμέναι ἁρμοστήν τε ἐδέχοντο καὶ ἄρχοντα τοῦ βασιλέως Παρθενόπης. Ἀφίκοντο μὲν δὴ καὶ ἄλλοι πρόσθεν ἁρμοσταὶ εἰς τὰς νήσους ταύτας, ἐν δὲ δὴ καὶ Κάρουλος οὑτοσίν, ὁ τῆς οἰκίας Τόκων καλούμενος, ἔχων ἑταίρους μεθ' ἑαυτοῦ ἄνδρας ἀγαθούς, τόν τε Ῥῶσον καὶ

the island. As for Nerio, the Celtiberians, and those French who came to conquer Greece, it appears that they arrived much later in this region. Nerio had only just arrived when he made a marriage alliance with the Lombards in Euboia, by marrying the daughter of a certain Prothymos.[103] He took over the land, fortified Corinth, and made plans to bring the Peloponnese under his authority as quickly as possible. Later, however, the brother of the king of the Greeks [Theodoros I] approached him and made a marriage alliance: Nerio's daughter, who was, as I said, the outstanding beauty among the women of that time, was to marry the ruler Theodoros. Nerio would then cede Corinth upon his own death, for he promised, when she was married, that he would cede it upon his death, as her dowry.[104]

Nerio also married another one of his daughters to Carlo, 51
the ruler of Akarnania and Aitolia.[105] Regarding the latter, then, the former lords of that land had belonged to the retinue of the king of Parthenope, which is also called Naples, and, when they were driven from those lands by their neighbors and the peoples who lived there, these lords went back to Italy. Now it happened that the islands of Kephallenia, Zakynthos, and such of the Echinades as are inhabited,[106] were under this king's authority and used to have a governor and ruler appointed by the king of Naples. Other governors had come to these islands earlier, among whom was this Carlo, named after the house of Tocco.[107] He had good men with him as his companions, including Rosso, Guido,

Γυΐδον καὶ Μυλειαρέσην. Καὶ ὡς ἐν τῇ Κεφαλληνίᾳ διατρίβοντες προσέσχον τε τῇ Ἠπείρῳ, ἐπαγομένων τῶν Ἠπειρωτῶν, τήν τε χώραν ἐκτήσαντο σφίσιν ὑπήκοον καὶ κατὰ βραχὺ τήν τε Ἀκαρνανίαν.

52 Ἀλβανοὶ δὲ ὡρμημένοι ἀπὸ Ἐπιδάμνου καὶ τὸ πρὸς ἕω βαδίζοντες Θετταλίαν τε ὑπηγάγοντο σφίσι καὶ τῆς μεσογαίου Μακεδονίας τὰ πλέω, Ἀργυροπολίχνην τε καὶ Καστορίαν. Ἀφικόμενοι δὲ ἐπὶ Θετταλίαν τήν τε χώραν σφίσιν ὑποχείριον ποιησάμενοι, καὶ τὰς πόλεις ἐπιδιελόμενοι, κατὰ σφᾶς ἐνέμοντο τὴν χώραν, νομάδες τε ὄντες καὶ οὐδαμῇ ἔτι βέβαιον σφῶν αὐτῶν τὴν οἴκησιν ποιούμενοι. Ἐπεὶ δὲ καὶ ἐς Ἀκαρνανίαν ἀφικόμενοι γνώμῃ τοῦ [1.197] ἡγεμόνος Ἀκαρνανίας, ἀφιεμένου αὐτοῖς τῆς χώρας, ἐνέμοντό τε τήνδε τὴν χώραν. Μετὰ δὲ ταῦτα συνίσταντο ἀλλήλοις ὡς τοῖς Ἕλλησιν ἐπιθησόμενοι, ὅπως ἂν αὐτοῖς προχωροίη. Καὶ δή ποτε τοῦ ἡγεμόνος (Ἰσαάκιος δ' ἦν τοὔνομα) ἐπὶ ἄγραν φοιτῶντος ἀφικνουμένου, ἐπέθεντό τε αὐτῷ οἱ Ἀλβανοί, ἡγουμένου αὐτοῖς Σπάτα, ἀνδρὸς ὁρμήν τε καὶ τόλμαν ἐπιδεικνυμένου σφίσιν ἐν τῷ τότε παρόντι ξύμφορον ἐς τὰ παρόντα αὐτοῖς καὶ οὐκ ἀδόκιμον. Καὶ τὸν μὲν ἡγεμόνα αὐτοῦ ταύτῃ ἀνεῖλον, τὴν δὲ χώραν αὐτίκα ὑπελαύνοντες κατέσχον τε καὶ ἐζώγρησαν τοὺς ἐν τοῖς ἀγροῖς, συλλαμβάνοντες, ᾧ ἂν περιτύχοιεν. Μετὰ δὲ ταῦτα πολιορκοῦντές τε Ἄρτην τῆς Ἀκαρνανίας πόλιν παρεστήσαντο, καὶ τὴν χώραν ταύτην ὑφ' αὐτοῖς ποιησάμενοι τὴν τῶν ἑσπερίων χώραν ἐδῄουν, οὐδὲν ἔτι ἐς ἡσυχίαν ἐνδιδόντες.

53 Μετὰ δὲ ταῦτα οἱ τῆς Νεαπόλεως ἄρχοντες, ἀπὸ

and Meliaresi.[108] They lived on Kephallenia but turned their attention to Epeiros and, with the assistance of the Epeirots, they acquired the land and soon after also subjected Akarnania to themselves.[109]

The Albanians, however, set out from Durrës and moved slowly eastward, subjecting Thessaly to themselves as well as most of inland Macedonia, Argyrokastron, and Kastoria. When they arrived in Thessaly they brought it under their control and divided up the cities, distributing the land among themselves, for they were nomads and did not establish permanent dwellings for themselves.[110] When they came to Akarnania with the consent of its ruler, he abandoned his land to them, and so they distributed this land among themselves too.[111] After that they came to an agreement with each other to attack the Greeks whenever they had the opportunity. On one occasion, when the ruler—his name was Isaakios[112]—was returning from the hunt, the Albanians attacked him. Their leader was Shpata, a man who displayed a boldness and daring that was advantageous to them at that time; he was quite formidable. They killed the ruler there, seized the land by raiding it, and enslaved those who worked the fields, capturing anyone they chanced upon. After that they took Arta, a city of Akarnania, by siege and, having brought that land under their control, they plundered the land of the westerners, without ever pausing to rest.[113] 52

After that the lords of Naples set out from the island 53

Κερκύρας τῆς νήσου ὁρμώμενοι (εἶχον δὲ τότε τὴν νῆσον οἱ Παρθενόπης βασιλεῖς) καὶ παρασκευασάμενοι στρατόν, ἵεντο ἐπὶ τὴν Ἀκαρνανίαν ὡς τούς τε Ἀλβανοὺς τὴν χώραν ἀφαιρησόμενοι καὶ Ἄρτην τῆς Ἀκαρνανίας καταστρεψόμενοι λαβόντες. Ἀφικόμενοι δὲ ἐς Ἄρτην τήν τε πόλιν ἐπολιόρκουν καὶ μηχανὰς προσέφερον τῷ τείχει ὡς αἱρήσοντες. Σπάτας δὲ ὁ τῶν Ἀλβανῶν ἡγεμὼν (οὐ γὰρ εἰσῄει ἐς τὴν πόλιν, ἀλλ' ἐκτὸς περιῄει τὴν χώραν) τούς τε Ἀλβανοὺς συλλέξας ἐς ταὐτὸ καὶ βουλευσάμενος, ὡς αὐτῷ εἵποντο ἑτοίμως [1.198] εἰς τὸν κίνδυνον, ἄφνω ἐπεισπίπτουσι τῷ Ἰταλῶν στρατεύματι, ὃ ἐπολιόρκει τὴν πόλιν, καὶ τρεψάμενοι ἐς φυγὴν πολλοὺς μὲν διέφθειραν, τοὺς δὲ πλείους ἐζώγρησαν. Συνεπελάβετο δὲ αὐτοῖς ἐς τόνδε τὸν πόλεμον καὶ Πρεάλουπας ὁ τῆς Αἰτωλίας ἡγεμών, ἀνὴρ Τριβαλλός, ὃς ἐπιγαμίαν πρὸς τὸν Σπάταν τῆς Ἄρτης ἡγεμόνα ἐπεποίητο. Οὕτω μὲν οὖν κατέσχον οἱ Σπαταῖοι τὴν χώραν τῆς Ἀκαρνανίας.

54 Μετὰ δὲ ταῦτα ὡρμημένου τοῦ Καρούλου ἀπὸ τῶν νήσων σὺν τοῖς ἑταίροις αὐτοῦ καί τινων τῶν τῆς χώρας ἅτε δὴ ἀχθομένων τῇ Ἀλβανῶν τυραννίδι, τήν τε χώραν κατεστρέψαντο τῆς Ἀκαρνανίας, πρὸς δὲ καὶ τὴν Αἰτωλίαν, ἀφελόμενοι Ἰζάουλον τὸν τότε ἡγεμονεύοντα Ἀκαρνάνων τε τῆς πόλεως καὶ χώρας τε τῆς Αἰτωλίας ἤδη. Ἡ δὲ ἀρχὴ τῆς Αἰτωλίας οὖσα τὸ πρότερον Θωμᾶ τοῦ Πρεαλουπῶν Τριβαλλοῦ, περιῆλθεν ἐς τοῦτον δὴ τὸν Ἰζάουλον τρόπῳ τοιῷδε. Ὡς συνεπελάβετο ὁ Πρεάλουπας τῷ τε Σπάτᾳ καὶ τοῖς Ἀλβανοῖς ἐς τὸν πρὸς Ἰταλοὺς πόλεμον, πολιορκοῦντας Ἄρτην μητρόπολιν τῆς Ἀκαρνανίας χώρας, ἑάλωσαν

of Kerkyra—for the kings of Parthenope then held that island[114]—prepared an army, and headed for Akarnania in order to deprive the Albanians of that land and take Arta, the city of Akarnania, by force. They arrived at Arta and besieged the city, bringing engines against the walls in order to capture it. But Shpata, the ruler of the Albanians, was not in the city at that time, and was moving around in the land outside. He assembled the Albanians in one place and advised them to follow him eagerly into danger. So they made a sudden attack on the Italian army that was besieging the city. They turned them to flight and killed many, but captured even more.[115] Preljubović, the ruler of Aitolia who was a Serb and had made a marriage alliance with Shpata, the ruler of Arta, had joined them in this war.[116] Thus the followers of Shpata held on to the land of Akarnania.

After that Carlo set out from his islands with his com- 54
panions and some of the locals who hated the tyranny of the Albanians, and they conquered the land of Akarnania in addition to that of Aitolia, stripping Esau, who was then the ruler, of the city of the Akarnanians and the land of Aitolia.[117] The principality of Aitolia had belonged previously to Thomas the Serb, of the Preljubović family, but it came to this Esau in the following way. When Preljubović aided Shpata and the Albanians in the battle against the Italians who were besieging Arta, the capital of the land of

δὴ ἐν τῇ μάχῃ ταύτῃ ἄλλοι τε πολλοὶ τῶν παρὰ σφίσιν εὐδοκιμούντων τῷ γένει καὶ δὴ καὶ Ἰζάουλος, εἷς τῶν ἀρίστων λεγόμενος γενέσθαι τοῦ Παρθενόπης βασιλέως νεανίας, τὸ μὲν εἶδος οὐκ ἀηδής, ἐπιεικὴς δὲ τὸν τρόπον καὶ ἡσύχιος. Τοῦτον σὺν πολλοῖς {1.199} ἄλλοις ἀγόμενος ὁ Πρεάλουπας εἰς τὰ οἰκεῖα ὡς ἀνδράποδά τε περιεῖπε καὶ εἶχεν ἐν φυλακῇ. Ἐς τὰ βασίλεια διατρίβων κατεῖχεν ὡς χρημάτων ἐς τοὺς προσήκοντας ἐσαῦθις ἀποδιδόμενος, ἢν αἰτοῖντο αὐτούς.

55 Ἡ δὲ γυνὴ τούτου ὡς ἑώρα τὸν νεανίαν, ἠράσθη τε αὐτοῦ· ἦν γὰρ καὶ ἐς ἄλλους πρότερον φοιτῶσα ἄνδρας καὶ ἀκόλαστος. Συγγινομένη τοίνυν τῷ νεανίᾳ, καὶ ἐπιμαινομένη αὐτῷ ἐς τὸν ἔρωτα, συντίθεται αὐτῷ ἐπὶ τῷ ἀνδρὶ ἐπιβουλήν. Καὶ ἐξηγουμένης τῆς γυναικὸς ἐς τὴν κοίτην, ὡς ἀνεπαύετο Πρεάλουπας ὁ ἡγεμών, ἀνεῖλέ τε αὐτὸν ἅμα σὺν τῇ γυναικί. Καὶ ἅμα συγκατίσχει τὴν ἡγεμονίαν αὐτῷ. Ἐπειδὴ ἐτυράννευεν, οὐδενὶ τῶν ἐν τῇ πόλει ἄλλῳ ἢ τῇ γυναικὶ ἀρεσκόμενος. Ἡ μέντοι δίκη τοῦ Πρεαλούπη οὐκ εἰς μακρὰν κατέλαβε τὸν παῖδα αὐτοῦ ἀπὸ ταύτης δὴ τῆς γυναικὸς γενόμενον αὐτῷ· τοῦτον γάρ τοι, ὡς ἐφοίτα παρὰ βασιλέα Μωσέα αἰτούμενος συμμαχίαν τε καὶ ἐπικουρίαν ἐπὶ Κάρουλον τὸν τότε δὴ Ἀκαρνανίας τύραννον, συλλαβὼν ὥστε τὴν χώραν αὐτοῦ κατασχεῖν, ἐξέκοψε τὼ ὀφθαλμώ. Τὴν μέντοι χώραν οὐδεὶς κατεστρέψατο τῆς Ἰωαννίνων πόλεως. Ἐπαγομένη τοῦτον δὴ τὸν Κάρουλον ἐπὶ σφίσιν ἄρχοντα, καὶ ἐπιτετραμμένου αὐτῷ διέπειν τὰ τῆς πόλεως πράγματα καὶ ἀντεχομένου ἐς τὸν πόλεμον κράτιστα. Ἡ μέντοι ἀρχὴ αὕτη Τριβαλλῶν

Akarnania, many were captured in the battle who were regarded as nobles by them, among whom was Esau, a young man who is said to have been one of the king of Parthenope’s [Naples’] very best men. He was very good looking and had a pleasant, calm manner. Preljubović led him back to his own domain along with many others as slaves, and kept them under guard. While he stayed in his palace, he held them for ransom, hoping to return them to their relatives, if they claimed them.

But Preljubović’s wife[118] saw the young man and became 55
infatuated with him, for she had a history of taking up with other men, and was insatiable. So she took the young man to bed and, having fallen madly in love with him, formed a plot with him against her husband. She brought Esau into the bedroom where Preljubović, the ruler, was sleeping, and he killed him with her help. And she took over the principality with him.[119] But the new tyrant pleased no one else in the city other than this woman. Shortly afterward, Preljubović’s fate also overtook the son that had been born to him from this woman. For when he[120] visited Sultan Musa to request an alliance and aid in attacking Carlo, who was then the tyrant of Akarnania, Musa arrested him so as to take over his territories, and gouged out his eyes.[121] As for the land of the city of Ioannina, no one conquered it. The city brought in Carlo to be its lord and they entrusted him to manage the city’s affairs and give it his strongest support in times of war.[122] Thus this principality, which formerly used to belong

οὖσα τὸ παλαιὸν οὕτω ἔστε Ἰζάουλον καὶ ἐπὶ Κάρουλον τὸν ἡγεμόνα περιῆλθεν.

56 Οὕτω δὲ ἄμφω τὼ χώρα [1.200] κατασχὼν οὗτος, καὶ τὴν πρὸς τῷ Ἀχελῴῳ χώραν τό τε Βάλτον καλούμενον καὶ Ἀγγελοπολίχνην ἔστε ἐπὶ Ναύπακτον τὴν καταντικρὺ Ἀχαΐας, ἐπεκράτει τῆς χώρας καὶ ἐτυράννευεν ἐπὶ μέγα χωρήσας δυνάμεως, ἀνὴρ τά τε ἐς ἀρχὴν καὶ ἐς τὸν πόλεμον δοκῶν γενέσθαι οὐδενὸς τῶν τότε ἡγουμένων λειπόμενος. Καὶ ἐν πολέμοις πρὸς τοὺς περιοίκους μέγα εὐδοκιμῶν ἠγάγετο, ὡς πρότερόν μοι ἐλέγετο, τοῦ Ἀθηνῶν τε καὶ Κορίνθου ἡγεμόνος θυγατέρα ἐς γάμον. Τούτῳ τῷ ἡγεμόνι παῖς ἐγένετο νόθος· ἀπὸ γὰρ τῆς Εὐβοΐδος αὐτῷ γυναικὸς ἄρρενος οὐκ ἔτυχε γόνου. Νόθῳ δὲ τῷ παιδὶ ἦν ὄνομα Ἀντώνιος. Τούτῳ τῷ Ἀντωνίῳ τήν τε Βοιωτίαν κατέλιπε καὶ τὴν Θηβῶν πόλιν· τὴν γὰρ Κόρινθον κατέλιπε τῷ κηδεστῇ αὐτοῦ Θεοδώρῳ τῷ βασιλέως ἀδελφῷ. Τὴν δὲ Ἀθηνῶν πόλιν, ἀφελόμενος ταύτην τὸ πρόσθεν τοὺς Κελτίβηρας ἀπὸ Ναβάρης (εἶχον γὰρ δὴ καὶ ταύτην οἱ Ἴβηρες καταστρεψάμενοι) κατέλιπε τοῖς Οὐενετοῖς.

57 Ὁ μέντοι παῖς αὐτοῦ Ἀντώνιος οὗτος, ὡς παρὰ τοῦ πατρὸς παρεδέξατο τὴν τῆς Βοιωτίας ἀρχὴν (τὴν γὰρ δὴ Φωκαΐδα[6] χώραν ἄλλην καὶ Λεβάδειαν ὑπηγάγετο Παιαζήτης ὁ Ἀμουράτεω, προσθέμενος τῇ ἑαυτοῦ ἀρχῇ, ὡς πρότερόν μοι δεδήλωται), οὗτος δὴ οὖν ἐπὶ τοὺς Οὐενετοὺς ἐξήνεγκε πόλεμον, καὶ τὰς Ἀθήνας ἐπολιόρκει προσέχων ἐντεταμένως. Οἱ μέντοι Οὐενετοὶ δεινὸν ποιησάμενοι πολιορκεῖσθαι τὴν πόλιν αὐτῶν, καὶ ἀμύνειν βουλόμενοι, καὶ ἐπὶ τὴν Θηβῶν διανοούμενοι πόλιν ἰέναι,

to the Serbs, fell into the hands of Esau and then the ruler Carlo.

In this way Carlo came into possession of both lands, namely the land toward the Acheloös River which is called the Baltos[123] and Angelokastron, as far as Naupaktos,[124] which is across from Achaïa. He dominated this land, became one of the most powerful tyrants, and seemed second to no other ruler of that time in statecraft and war. He did very well for himself in his wars against his neighbors and, as I mentioned earlier, married the daughter of the ruler of Athens and Corinth.[125] Now, the latter ruler [Nerio] had an illegitimate son, for he had no male child from his Euboian wife. The name of this illegitimate son was Antonio, and to this Antonio he left Boiotia and the city of Thebes, for Corinth he left to Theodoros [I], his son-in-law and the king [of the Greeks'] brother.[126] The city of Athens, which he had previously taken from the Celtiberians of Navarre—for the Iberians had held this city too after they conquered it—he left to the Venetians.[127] 56

When this son of his, Antonio, received the principality of Boiotia from his father (for Bayezid, the son of Murad, had subjected the rest of the land of Phokis and Lebadeia, adding them to his own territories, as I stated earlier),[128] he went to war against the Venetians and invested and besieged Athens vigorously.[129] The Venetians considered it an outrage that their city was being besieged and chose to fight back. They decided to attack the city of Thebes, and so they 57

στρατόν τε τὸν ἀπὸ τῆς Εὐβοίας, ὅσον ἠδύναντο, [1.201] συλλέξαντες καὶ ὁπλισμόν, ἀπὸ τῆς Εὐβοίας ἐχώρουν ἐπὶ τὴν Βοιωτίαν καὶ ἐπὶ τὴν πόλιν. Ἀντώνιος δὲ πυθόμενος τοὺς Οὐενετοὺς στρατευομένους ἐπ' αὐτόν, λόχους ποιησάμενος διττοὺς κατὰ τὴν ὁδόν, ᾗ ἐπύθετο μέλλοντας διαπορεύεσθαι τούς τε Εὐβοέας ἅμα καὶ Οὐενετούς, τὸν μὲν ἐνεδρεύσας ἐς τὸ πρόσω τῆς ὁδοῦ, τὸν δὲ ἐς τὸ ὄπισθεν, ἐπέμενεν ἐμβαλεῖν ἐς τὸ μέσον τοὺς πολεμίους. Ἐνταῦθα οὖν ὡς οἱ Οὐενετοὶ ἐπορεύοντο ἐπὶ τὴν Θηβῶν πόλιν (διέχει δ' ἡ πόλις αὕτη ἀπὸ Εὐβοίας σταδίους ὡσεὶ ρν'), καὶ ᾖεσαν ἐξωπλισμένοι τε ἅμα καὶ πολλοὶ ὄντες ἐπὶ τὰς Θήβας (ἦσαν δὲ ἀμφὶ τοὺς ἑξακισχιλίους), ἐπιπεσὼν τούτοις ἄφνω ὁ Ἀντώνιος, ἔχων κατὰ τοὺς λόχους οὐ πλείους τῶν τριακοσίων, καὶ ἐπ' ἀμφοῖν ἅμα ἐπιφανεὶς τοῖς Οὐενετοῖς ἐς φυγήν τε ἐτρέψατο, καὶ πολλούς τε αὐτῶν διέφθειρε, τοὺς δὲ ἐζώγρησε, καὶ τοὺς τότε ἡγεμόνας τῆς χώρας αὐτῶν ἐζώγρησε. Καὶ ἀπιὼν αὖθις ἐς τοὐπίσω ἐπολιόρκει τὴν Ἀθηνῶν πόλιν, ἐς ὃ δὴ προδοσίαν συνθεμένων αὐτῷ τῶν Ἀθηναίων τήν τε πόλιν κατέσχε, καὶ οὐ πολλῷ ὕστερον πολιορκῶν τὴν ἀκρόπολιν παρεστήσατο, καὶ ἐτυράννευε τῆς τε Ἀττικῆς ἅμα καὶ Βοιωτίας.

58 Καὶ ἀφικόμενος ἐς τὰς Παιαζήτεω μὲν πρῶτα θύρας, τοῦ πατρὸς αὐτοῦ ἔτι περιόντος, μετὰ δὲ ταῦτα ἐς τὰς Μωσέως τε καὶ Μουσουλμάνεω καὶ δὴ καὶ Μεχμέτεω θύρας, ἐθεράπευέ τε χρήμασι τὰς βασιλέως θύρας, καὶ κατὰ τὴν χώραν ἄρχων ἀδεῶς τοῦ λοιποῦ διῃτᾶτο. Λέγεται μὲν δὴ καὶ οὗτος καὶ δοκεῖ γενέσθαι ἀνὴρ τά τε ἄλλα

assembled as large an army and as many armaments as they could from Euboia and set out from Euboia for Boiotia and the city. Antonio learned that the Venetians were marching against him, so he set up two ambushes along the road by which he learned that the Euboians were going to march with the Venetians, the one lying in ambush further along the road, the other further back, and he delayed his attack until the enemy were in the middle. Then, as the Venetians were marching toward the city of Thebes (this city is about one hundred and fifty stades from Euboia), and they were coming in full armor and in great numbers against Thebes (there were about six thousand of them), Antonio suddenly attacked them, although he had no more than three hundred men in his ambushes. By appearing on both sides of the Venetians, he put them to flight. He killed many of them, captured others, and took the rulers of their land alive. He returned immediately to the siege of the city of Athens, and he took the city by arranging with the Athenians for its betrayal to him.[130] Shortly afterward he took the acropolis too after a siege,[131] and he held the tyranny of Attica as well as Boiotia.

Antonio first came to the Porte of Bayezid while his 58
father was still alive, and afterward to the Porte of Musa, Süleyman, and Mehmed; he curried favor with the sultan's Porte with gifts of money, and so he governed his land henceforth without fear. It is said that this Antonio acquired a reputation for general prosperity and, when he

εὐδοκιμῶν, καὶ ἐπεί τε παρέλαβε τὴν [1.202] Ἀθηνῶν πόλιν, ἐπί τε τὰς βασιλέως θύρας οὐδέν τι πολλῷ ἀφικόμενος, ἐπιτηδείους τε αὐτῷ σχεῖν καὶ συνήθεις τοὺς ἀμφὶ τὸν βασιλέα. Ἐτυράννευε δὲ γήμας γυναῖκα ἀνδρὸς ἰδιώτου ἀπὸ Θηβῶν. Ὡς γὰρ ἀνῆγον οἱ Θηβαῖοι χοροὺς ἐπὶ γάμῳ τινί, καὶ ἦν ἱερέως θυγάτηρ ὑπ' ἀνδρὶ γεγενημένη, οὐκ ἀηδὴς μέντοι, τὸν δὲ τρόπον ἐπιεικής τε ἅμα καὶ σώφρων, ἠράσθη τε αὐτῆς ἐν τῷ χορῷ ἅμα, καὶ ἐρασθεὶς ἀπάγεται ταύτην. Ἐπιμανεὶς δὲ τῷ ἔρωτι οὐ πολλῷ ὕστερον ἔγημέ τε αὐτήν, καὶ εὐδαιμόνως βιοτεύων ἐτύγχανεν, ἐξοικονομῶν τε τὴν ἀρχὴν ἐπὶ τὸ ὡς κάλλιστα ἔχειν δοκοῦν ἅμα τοῖς τε ἐν τῇ χώρᾳ καὶ τοῖς ἄλλοις.

59 Οὗτος μὲν οὖν καὶ πρὸς τὸν ἐν τῇ Αἰγίνῃ ἄρχοντα Γαλεώτου παῖδα, τοῦ ἐπὶ ῥώμῃ σώματος ἐπισήμου ὄντος, ἐπιγαμίαν ποιησάμενος ἐπὶ θετῇ αὐτοῦ θυγατρί, καὶ ἀπὸ Εὐβοίας νεανίαν τῆς Γεωργίου οἰκίας κηδεστὴν ἐπὶ ἑτέρᾳ αὐτοῦ θετῇ ποιησάμενος, πρός τε τοὺς Οὐενετοὺς σπονδάς τε ποιησάμενος ἡσυχίαν ἦγε. Καὶ Γαλεώτου τὸν παῖδα, Αἰγίνης δὲ ἄρχοντα, ἐπιτήδειον ἔχων, παρ' αὐτὸν φοιτῶντα ἐθεράπευε, καὶ σωφρονῶν ἐπὶ πολὺ δὴ τοῦ χρόνου διεγένετο εὐδαιμονῶν, ἀπό τε τῆς κατὰ τὴν ἀρχὴν οἰκονομίας πλοῦτον ἑαυτῷ περιποιούμενος καὶ τὴν πόλιν ὡς οἷόν τε μάλιστα κοσμῶν.

60 Τούτων μὲν πέρι ἐς τοσοῦτον ἐπιμνησάμενος, ἐπάνειμι δὴ ἐπὶ Θεόδωρον τὸν βασιλέως παῖδα, ἡγεμόνα Σπάρτης τε καὶ ἄλλης Πελοποννήσου, ὃς ὑπὸ Θεοδώρου τοῦ πάτρωος ἐξετρέφετο ἅμα καὶ ἐπαιδεύθη, μετὰ δὲ ταῦτα κατελείφθη ἐς τὴν ἀρχὴν αὐτοῦ ἡγεμών. Ἐς τοῦτον δὲ

took over the city of Athens, he rarely went to the sultan's Porte, having friends and associates in the sultan's inner circle. While he was tyrant he married the daughter of a commoner from Thebes. For at one time the Thebans were celebrating a wedding with dances, and the daughter of a priest was getting married; she was pretty, well mannered, and chaste. He fell in love with her during the dance and carried her off in his infatuation. He fell madly in love with her and married her shortly after, and they lived happily.[132] He administered the principality in a way that best benefited those who lived in it as well as others.

Antonio also made a marriage alliance with the ruler of 59
Aigina, the son of Alioto,[133] who was famous for his physical strength, by giving him his adopted daughter. He gave another adopted daughter to a young man from Euboia, of the Giorgio family, and made him his son-in-law too.[134] He made a treaty with the Venetians and was at peace with them. The son of Alioto, the ruler of Aigina, was his friend and he looked after him well when he visited. Antonio's wisdom and moderation ensured a long era of prosperity for him, and he acquired great wealth through his management of the principality and he embellished the city as much as possible.

Having said so much about these matters, I return to 60
Theodoros [II], the king's son and the ruler of Mistra and the rest of the Peloponnese. He had been raised and educated by his uncle Theodoros [I], and later succeeded him as

ἀφικόμενος ὁ πατὴρ αὐτοῦ [1.203] Ἐμμανουῆλος ὁ Βυζαντίου βασιλεὺς τόν τε παῖδα καθίστη ἐς τὴν ἀρχὴν βεβαιότερον, καὶ ἐπὶ τῷ ἀδελφῷ ἤδη τετελευτηκότι λόγον ἐπικήδειον ἐξετραγῴδει διεξιὼν ἐπὶ τῷ τάφῳ αὐτοῦ, ἀπολοφυρόμενός τε ἅμα τὸν ἐπιτήδειον ἀδελφόν. Καὶ μετὰ ταῦτα μεταπεμπόμενος τοὺς Πελοποννησίους ἐς Ἰσθμὸν τόν τε Ἰσθμὸν ἐτείχισε καὶ φυλακὴν καταστησάμενος αὐτοῦ ἀπῄει ἀποπλέων ἐπὶ Βυζαντίου, ἔχων μεθ' ἑαυτοῦ καὶ τοὺς Πελοποννησίων ἄρχοντας ἐν φυλακῇ.

61 Ταῦτα μὲν οὖν κατὰ τοὺς τῶν Ἑλλήνων βασιλεῖς συνηνέχθη ἐς ἐκεῖνον τὸν χρόνον· ἐπὶ δὲ Μεχμέτεω ἄμεινον σφίσιν ἔχοντες ἔστε τὴν ἀρχὴν καὶ ἐς τὴν ἄλλην αὐτῶν βιοτήν, ἐπεὶ ἠσφαλίζοντο τὴν πρὸς βασιλέα Μεχμέτην εἰρήνην τε καὶ σπονδὰς ἐμπεδοῦντες, ὡς οἷόν τε μάλιστα αὐτοῖς. Δι' ἃ δὴ καὶ ὁ βασιλεὺς Μεχμέτης ἐνέργει, ὡς περὶ πλείστου ποιοῖντο τὴν ἑαυτοῦ εἰρήνην, καὶ πᾶν ὁτιοῦν μᾶλλον πεισομένους, ὥστε τὴν ξενίην σφίσι μὴ διαλύεσθαι, ἐχαρίζετό τε αὐτοῖς, ὅ τι ᾤετο ἐν χάριτι ποιεῖσθαι αὐτοῖς, τά τε ἄλλα καὶ ἐπὶ τῷ παιδὶ αὐτοῦ Ἀμουράτῃ. Ἤστην γὰρ αὐτῷ δύω παῖδε, Ἀμουράτης μὲν ὁ πρεσβύτερος, Μουσταφᾶς δὲ ὁ νεώτερος καὶ ἔτι παῖς ὤν. Τούτοιν τὸν μὲν Ἀμουράτην ἐς τὴν Εὐρώπην διενοεῖτο καταλιπεῖν, τὸν δὲ ἕτερον ἐς τὴν Ἀσίαν βασιλέα. Καὶ ἐπιδιελόμενος τούτοις τὴν ἀρχὴν ἐγκατέλιπεν, ὥστε παῖδας ἐμμένειν, οἷς ἐπέτρεψε, τῷ Βυζαντίου βασιλεῖ κατὰ ταῦτα συλλαμβάνειν, ἤν τις ἀδικῇ, μὴ ἐπιτρέπειν, ἀλλὰ τῷ ἀδικουμένῳ τιμωρεῖν κατὰ δύναμιν.

ruler of the principality. For this reason his father Manuel, the king of Byzantion, came and confirmed his son's position. He also declaimed a funeral oration for his brother, who had already died, while visiting his tomb, lamenting his dear brother.[135] It was after this that he summoned the Peloponnesians to the Isthmos, fortified the Isthmos, installed a garrison there, and sailed away to Byzantion, taking with him, under guard, the Peloponnesian lords.[136]

So that was how things stood with the kings of the 61
Greeks at that time. Under Mehmed they fared better politically and with regard to their living conditions, as they had secured peace with him and strengthened their treaties with him as much as they could. For this reason, Sultan Mehmed also made sure that they valued peace with him highly and would endure anything rather than break their alliance with him. He also granted them whatever he thought would make them grateful to him, especially as it concerned his son Murad. He had two sons, of whom Murad was the elder[137] and Mustafa the younger, who was still a child.[138] Mehmed was planning to leave Europe to Murad and to make the other sultan in Asia. So he divided the kingdom between them, leaving it to them. To ensure that his sons would abide by these terms he entrusted them to the king of Byzantion, to stop them if one were to break this arrangement, and to avenge the victim with all his power.[139]

62 Τὴν μέντοι Δακίαν στρατεύματα ἐπιπέμψας τήν τε χώραν [1.204] ἐληΐζετο καὶ Παιονοδακίαν, Βρενέζεω τοῦ Χοτζαθερίζεω θεράποντος ἡγουμένου τε καὶ ἔργα μεγάλα ἀποδεικνυμένου, πρὸς δὲ καὶ Μιχαήλεω τοῦ τῆς Εὐρώπης αὐτῷ στρατηγοῦ στρατιάν τε ἄγοντος ἐπὶ τοὺς Παίονας καὶ Παιονοδακίαν καὶ δὴ καὶ Ἰλλυριούς. Βρενέζῃ μέντοι ἔργα ἐστὶν ἀποδεδειγμένα ἄξια λόγου κατὰ τὴν Εὐρώπην, ἄλλα τε καὶ ἐπὶ Ἰλλυριοὺς καὶ Παίονας καὶ ἐπὶ Πελοπόννησον στρατευσαμένῳ, πλεῖστα δὲ τοῦ γένους τούτου ἐπὶ στρατηγίας καθισταμένου, σὺν τοῖς Εὐρώπης ἱπποδρόμοις, ὥστε αὐτῷ αὐτίκα ἑπομένους, ὅποι ἂν ἐξηγοῖτο, ἀποφέρεσθαι κέρδη ὡς μέγιστα, καὶ ἐπὶ τῶν Ἑνετῶν χώραν ἀφικόμενον καὶ ἀνδραποδισάμενον τὴν χώραν, ἀνδράποδα ἀπαγαγόμενον πλουτίσαι τοὺς ἐφεπομένους Τούρκων καὶ μέγα ὀλβίους ἀποδεικνύναι ὡς ἐν βραχεῖ.

63 Ἔστι δὲ καὶ οἰκοδομήματα ἀνὰ τὴν Εὐρώπην ἁπανταχῇ οὐκ ὀλίγα Βρενέζῃ πεποιημένα, ὥστε ὡς μνημόσυνα ἐς τοὺς ἐπιγιγνομένους καταλιπεῖν. Ὕστερον μέντοι ἐπὶ Μωσέως τοῦ Παιαζήτεω συνέβη τε αὐτὸν μεταστησάμενον ἐπὶ Μεχμέτην τὸν ἀδελφὸν τοῖς γε παισὶν αὐτοῦ ὑφέσθαι τῆς στρατηγίας, καὶ τὸ ἐντεῦθεν ἡγουμένους τοὺς Βρενέζεω παῖδας, Ἰησοῦν καὶ Βαράμον καὶ δὴ καὶ Ἀλίην, ἐπὶ μέγα δόξης ἀφίκοντο ἀνὰ τὴν Εὐρώπην. Ὤικει δὲ Βρενέζης τὰ Ἰανιτζὰ πόλιν, ἣν δὴ αὐτὸς οἰκῆσαι παρὰ βασιλέως ἐδωρήθη, ἑαυτῷ τε καὶ τοῖς παισὶν ἀνήκειν τὴν πόλιν, αἰεί, ὁτουοῦν ἂν δέοιτο, ὑπηρετοῦντας τῷ βασιλεῖ. Τὰ δὲ Ἰανιτζὰ πόλις ἐστὶ παρὰ τῷ Ἀξιῷ ποταμῷ, καὶ [1.205] κῶμαι παρ᾽ αὐτὴν τὴν πόλιν Βρενέζεω οὐκ ὀλίγαι. Ἐπὶ

Mehmed sent armies to plunder Wallachia and Hungarian Wallachia under the command of his minister Evrenos Hajji Therizes,[140] who had performed great deeds. In addition, Michael, his general in Europe, led an army against the Hungarians, Hungarian Wallachians, and Illyrians.[141] Evrenos's remarkable deeds in Europe are well known, including his campaigns against the Illyrians, Hungarians, and against the Peloponnese.[142] When he was appointed general, many members of that race, including the cavalry raiders of Europe, would immediately join up to follow him wherever he might lead them, and they carried off huge profits. He attacked Venetian territory and enslaved their land, leading away so many slaves that he enriched his Turkish followers and made them very wealthy in a short time. 62

There are many buildings throughout Europe that were constructed by Evrenos, which he left as memorials to future generations. When, under Musa, the son of Bayezid, he transferred his allegiance to Mehmed, Musa's brother,[143] he also transferred his command to his sons, and after that the sons of Evrenos led the wars: İsa, Barak, and Ali, who achieved great glory throughout Europe. Evrenos lived in the city of Giannitsa,[144] a city that he was allowed to found as a gift from the sultan and keep for himself and his sons in perpetuity so long as they served the sultan in whatever he should request. Giannitsa is by the Axios River and Evrenos owned numerous villages around it. Under Mehmed, 63

μέντοι Μεχμέτεω μετὰ δὲ Βρενέζη Τουραχάνης παρὰ Τούρκοις εὐδοκιμῶν ἐπὶ στρατηγίας τε ἐξῄει ἐπισπομένων αὐτῷ τῶν ἱπποδρόμων, καὶ τύχῃ χρώμενος ἀγαθῇ τὴν πολεμίων ἐληΐζετο χώραν. Εἶχε δὲ Βυδίνην τότε ὑπὸ Μεχμέτεω ἐπιτετραμμένος ἄρχειν, καὶ ἐς Παιονίαν διαβαίνων, μέγα εὐδοκιμῶν ἐν τῇ Εὐρώπῃ.

Turahan was the most highly regarded general after Evrenos among the Turks, and he went out on campaigns followed by the cavalry raiders. He had good fortune in plundering enemy territory. He was entrusted by Mehmed with the governance of Vidin. He invaded Hungary and was highly esteemed in Europe.[145]

Ε'

[2.1] Ἐπεὶ δὲ ἐτελεύτησεν ὁ Παιαζήτεω Μεχμέτης βασιλεύσας ἔτη δυοκαίδεκα, διεδέξατο τὴν βασιλείαν Ἀμουράτης ὁ Μεχμέτεω, παῖς αὐτοῦ πρεσβύτερος γενόμενος. Ἐτύγχανε δὲ ὢν ἐν Προύσῃ κατὰ τὴν Ἀσίαν, καὶ καθίστη τὰ ἐν τῇ ἀρχῇ. Ἕλληνες δὲ ὡς ἐπύθοντο τελευτήσαντα Μεχμέτην καὶ Ἀμουράτην ἐς τὴν βασιλείαν καταστῆναι, μετεπέμποντο ἀπὸ Λήμνου Μουσταφᾶν τὸν Παιαζήτεω λεγόμενον παῖδα γενέσθαι. Ἔτυχε δὲ διατρίβων ἐν Λήμνῳ, ὑπὸ Ἑλλήνων ὡς μετριώτατα φυλαττόμενος. Ἐπεὶ δὲ μεταπεμπόμενοι τοῦτον διεκωλύοντο ὑπὸ πνευμάτων ἐν τῷ τότε δὴ παρόντι βιαζομένων τὴν ἐπὶ Ἑλλήσποντον ἀπὸ Λήμνου ἄνοδον, καὶ ἔδει ἐν τῇ Εὐρώπῃ αὐτοὺς καθιστάναι βασιλέα (τριήρεσι γὰρ διεκώλυον τὴν διάβασιν Ἀμουράτεω ἐπὶ τὴν Εὐρώπην, καὶ τήν γε Προποντίδα τε καὶ Ἑλλήσποντον εἴργοντες ἐς τὴν διάβασιν), κατέπλευσαν ἐπὶ Καλλιούπολιν τῆς Χερρονήσου, πόλιν εὐδαίμονα, ὡς ἐνταῦθα τῷ τε Μουσταφᾷ ἐσπλέοντι συγγένοιντο, καὶ ἀποδεικνύμενοι αὐτὸν βασιλέα Εὐρώπης τήν τε Καλλιούπολιν σφίσιν ἀποδοῦναι πείσαιεν Μουσταφᾶν. Ἐνταῦθα μὲν οὖν Ἕλληνες ἀπὸ ἀφροσύνης σφᾶς τε αὐτοὺς καὶ τὰ πράγματα ἵεντο διαφθεροῦντες ὡς τὸ ἐπίπαν, καὶ παρὰ βραχὺ δὲ τὴν πόλιν [2.2] αὐτῶν ὑπὸ Ἀμουράτεω ἀνδραποδισθῆναι.

Book 5

Mehmed, the son of Bayezid, died after a reign of twelve years, and was succeeded on the throne by Murad, his elder son.[1] The latter happened to be at Prousa in Asia and was established in power. When the Greeks learned that Mehmed had died and Murad had succeeded to the throne, they summoned from Lemnos Mustafa, he who was said to be the son of Bayezid.[2] He was then residing on Lemnos, being guarded by the Greeks as indulgently as possible. They summoned him but were hindered by the winds that were then blowing against the route from Lemnos to the Hellespont. They had to install him as sultan in Europe, for with their triremes they were blocking Murad from crossing over into Europe, and were hindering his crossing at both the Propontis and the Hellespont. So they sailed to Gallipoli on the Chersonese, a prosperous city, to meet with Mustafa there when he sailed in, acknowledge him as sultan of Europe, and persuade him to return Gallipoli to them. In this matter, out of sheer folly, the Greeks moved closer to utterly destroying their affairs and themselves, and they came very close to seeing their city enslaved by Murad.

2 Ὡς γὰρ δὴ οἱ τοῦ Ἀμουράτεω ἄρχοντες καταλειφθέντες ἐν τῇ Εὐρώπῃ ὑπὸ Μεχμέτεω τοῦ πατρός, ὥστε αὐτῷ πείθεσθαι διαδεχομένῳ τὴν βασιλείαν, ἀφίκοντο ἐπὶ Βυζαντίου βασιλέα πρεσβευόμενοι ἐς τὰ παρόντα σφίσι μὴ ἀξυμφώνους γενέσθαι τοὺς Ἕλληνας, καὶ περὶ σφᾶς νεωτερίσαι παρ' ἃ καὶ ἐπηγγελμένοι εἶεν τῷ βασιλεῖ Μεχμέτῃ. Ἦν δὲ Παιαζήτης τῶν ἀρίστων τοῦ βασιλέως, πρύτανίς τε καὶ στρατηγὸς τῆς Εὐρώπης γενόμενος. Οὗτος οὖν ἀγχοῦ ἐλάσας τῷ Βυζαντίου βασιλεῖ διεπρεσβεύετο ἐπὶ τὰς σπονδὰς παρακαλῶν, ὥστε σφίσιν αὐτὸν ἐπιτήδειον εἶναι, ἐδίδου ὁμήρους τῶν ἀρίστων παῖδας δυοκαίδεκα, χρυσοῦ δὲ μυριάδας εἴκοσι καὶ χώραν πολλὴν Καλλιουπόλεως, ὅσην ἂν ἕλωνται παρὰ σφίσι. Ταῦτα δὲ ὑπισχνεῖτό τε καὶ ἐδίδου, ὥστε αὐτὸν Μουσταφᾶν μὲν ἐᾶν χαίρειν, μηδετέροις δ' ἐπιβοηθεῖν, ἀλλ' ἐᾶν αὐτοὺς μαχομένους, ὁπότεροι ἂν περιγένωνται, τὴν βασιλείαν περιέπειν.

3 Ταῦτα μὲν οὖν διεκηρυκεύετο πρὸς τὸν τότε βασιλέα Ἑλλήνων Ἰωάννην, νέον τε ἔτι ὄντα καὶ οὐδὲν μικρὸν ἐπινοοῦντα αὐτῷ ἐς τὴν ἀρχήν· ἐδόκει τε γὰρ αὐτῷ ἄμεινον ἔχειν ἐς σφᾶς αὐτοὺς περιπίπτοντας, καὶ δίχα γενομένης αὐτοῖς[1] τῆς ἀρχῆς τὰ πράγματα αὐτοῦ ἐν βελτίῳ τε ἔσοιτο τοῦ καθεστηκότος, καὶ ἐπὶ μεῖζον ἀφίξοιτο εὐδαιμονίας, δεομένων ἀμφοῖν, καὶ τῆς γε ἀρχῆς ἐπ' ἀμφότερα γινομένης πλέον τι περιγενέσθαι ἀπ' ἀμφοῖν, ὥστε [2.3] μηδετέρῳ δὴ ταλαντεύεσθαι. Τοῦτο δ' εἶναι, ἐπειδὰν τὴν ἀρχὴν ἄμφω ἐπιδιελόμενοι σφίσι βασιλεύωσιν. Ὕστερον μέντοι οὐδὲ τοῦτο ταύτῃ προδιετίθετο, ἀλλ' ἐπὶ τὸν Μουσταφᾶν δῆλος ἦν τῷ παντὶ γινόμενος ὁ βασιλεὺς οὑτοσί.

Murad's lords who had been left in Europe by his father Mehmed to obey him as the successor to the throne came to the king of Byzantion [Manuel II or Ioannes VIII] as envoys to argue that the Greeks should neither break with the present agreement nor seek to make revolutionary changes in their status contrary to their promises to Sultan Mehmed. There was also Bayezid, one of the sultan's leading men, the vizier and general of Europe. He drew near and, through an envoy, pleaded on behalf of the treaty to the king of Byzantion, so that he would remain their friend. Bayezid gave as hostages twelve sons of leading men, two hundred thousand gold pieces, and as much of the land around Gallipoli as they might take for themselves. He promised these things and gave them so that they might abandon Mustafa, help neither side, and allow them to fight it out so that the winner could claim the throne. 2

These proposals were conveyed by envoy to Ioannes [VIII], who was then king of the Greeks,[3] still a young man with ambitious plans for his kingdom. He had decided that it would be better for him if the Turks fell out with each other and, with their kingdom split in half, his affairs would improve compared with their current state and attain a greater degree of prosperity. While both sides were seeking his support and with the kingdom split between them, he would obtain greater benefit from both, so that the balance of power would fall to neither side. He thought this would happen when they would divide the kingdom between them and reign in this way. But he proved inconsistent in pursuit of this policy: this king later declared himself openly and wholeheartedly in support of Mustafa. His father, who was 3

Βασιλεύων δὲ ὁ πατὴρ αὐτοῦ, τἀναντία τούτου φρονῶν, ἠξίου μὴ παραβαίνειν τὰς σπονδάς, ὡς οὐδενὶ ὅτῳ παραβαίνοντι τὰς σπονδὰς ἔσοιτ' ἂν ὑγιὲς ὁτιοῦν ἢ ἔμπεδον, ὥστε μὴ σφαλλομένῳ ἐπιτρίβεσθαι. Καὶ τοῦτ' ἔφασκε λογίζεσθαι δεῖν, ὁποτέρῳ γε δέοι προστίθεσθαι, ἔνθα τά τε χρήματα τῆς βασιλείας καὶ νεήλυδες πάρεισι. Καὶ τοῦτο μέντοι ἀναμφιλόγως ἔχον ἐμπεδοῦν ἔφασκε τὴν αἵρεσιν, ἥντινα ἂν ἕλοιτο. Ἐκεῖνα δ' αὖ ἐνδοιασμὸν παρεχόμενα, ὅποι τε καὶ ᾗ ἐπὶ τὴν βασιλείαν ἀφίκοιτο, κίνδυνον σφίσι τὸν μέγιστον παρέχεσθαι.

4 Ταῦτα μέντοι τοῖς Ἕλλησιν ἐπ' ἀμφότερα γινομένοις ταῖς γνώμαις, ἅτε τοῦ νέου βασιλέως τὸ κράτος ἔχοντος τότε τῶν Ἑλλήνων, ταύτῃ τῇ γνώμῃ ἐτίθεντο, καὶ αἱρούμενοι τὰ πράγματα, ᾗ ἐξηγεῖτο, ἐπὶ τὴν Μουσταφᾶ ἐτράποντο τύχην, ὥστε καθιστάναι αὐτὸν βασιλέα καὶ τὴν Καλλιούπολιν σφίσιν ἀποδίδοσθαι. Ὥς τε ταῦτα ἐδέδοκτο, καὶ ἐπλήρουν τὰς ναῦς. Ἀφίκετο οὖν ὁ βασιλεὺς ἐπὶ τὴν Καλλιούπολιν, καὶ ὡς οὐδὲν παρεγένετο ἀπὸ Λήμνου ὁ Μουσταφᾶς, προαγόμενος πράσσειν τι ἐς τὴν ἀρχὴν τῆς Εὐρώπης καὶ πολιορκεῖν τὴν Καλλιούπολιν, Ζουναΐτην τὸν τῆς Σμύρνης ἄρχοντα, παρόντα δὴ τότε σφίσιν ἅτε ἑταῖρον ὄντα τοῦ Μουσταφᾶ, ὡς παρεσομένου δὴ αὐτίκα κἀκείνου, ἐξεπιδεικνύντες τοῖς Τούρκοις, ἐπολιόρκουν τὴν ἄκραν τῆς Καλλιουπόλεως. [2.4] Μετ' οὐ πολὺν δὲ χρόνον παρεγένετό τε καὶ αὐτὸς Μουσταφᾶς, καὶ τά τε ἄκρα τῆς πόλεως προσεχώρησεν αὐτῷ, καὶ ἡ Χερρόνησος αὐτίκα ἐδέξατο βασιλέα καὶ εἵπετο, ὅπου ἐξηγεῖτο. Τὴν

still reigning, held the opposite position, namely that they should not violate the treaty, as nothing good or lasting happens to one who violates a treaty, so as to prevent him from being destroyed by his own mistake. He also said that they should make the rational decision to join the side that had control over the monies of the realm and the janissaries. He said that one's choice had to be unambiguously based on that, whatever that choice was. Those things caused him concern, regardless of how they brought one to the throne,[4] and held out the greatest danger to them.

Thus were the opinions of the Greeks divided, but as the 4
young king was in charge of the state of the Greeks, they sided with his opinion and adopted the policy that he expounded, namely to tie their fortunes to that of Mustafa, establish him as sultan, and receive Gallipoli in return. This was decided, and they manned their ships.[5] The king arrived at Gallipoli and, as Mustafa had not arrived from Lemnos, he led the way and took the first step in claiming power over Europe by besieging Gallipoli. They displayed to the Turks Junayd, the lord of Smyrna who was present there and was a companion of Mustafa,[6] as proof that the latter would soon be there too, and they besieged the acropolis of Gallipoli. Shortly afterward Mustafa himself arrived and the citadel of the city surrendered to him. Then the Chersonese accepted him as sultan and was ready to follow him, wherever

μέντοι Καλλιούπολιν ὁ Ἑλλήνων βασιλεὺς ἠξίου ἀποδίδοσθαι. Ὁ δὲ ἕτοιμος μὲν εἶναι ἀποδώσειν καὶ μὴ ἀντιτείνειν, τοὺς μέντοι Τούρκους χαλεπῶς τε οἴσειν, καὶ σφίσι μὴ ἐν καλῷ, οὔπω ἔτι κατεργασμένης τῆς ἀρχῆς, ἀποβαίνειν τὰ πράγματα. Ὑπέσχετο μέντοι, ἐπειδὰν ἐς τὴν ἀρχὴν παραγένηται, τήν τε πόλιν ἀποδιδόναι, καὶ εἴ τι ἄλλο ἐπιτήδειον αὐτοῖς οἴοιτο ἔσεσθαι, μήτε τοῦ λοιποῦ ἂν στερῆσαι αὐτούς ποτε.

5 Πείσας μὲν οὖν τότε τοὺς Ἕλληνας ἤλαυνεν ἐς τὸ πρόσω τῆς Εὐρώπης, καὶ προσεχώρει τε αὐτῷ σύμπαντα ὡς βασιλεῖ τε ὄντι σφῶν καὶ Παιαζήτεω παιδὶ γενομένῳ. Ἐπεὶ δὲ Παιαζήτης ᾔσθετο ἐπιόντα ἐπὶ Ἀδριανούπολιν (ἐπετρόπευε δὲ τῆς πόλεως, καταλειφθεὶς ὑπὸ Μεχμέτεω βασιλέως ἐπὶ τῇ τελευτῇ αὐτοῦ), συνήγειρέ τε τὸ ἀπὸ τῆς Εὐρώπης στράτευμα, καὶ ὑπήντα τῷ Μουσταφᾷ ἀγχοῦ τῆς Ἀδριανουπόλεως, ὡς διὰ μάχης ἐλευσόμενος καὶ μὴ ἐπιτρέπων, ἣν δύναιτο, ἐπὶ τὰ βασίλεια πορεύεσθαι. Ὡς μέντοι συνταξάμενος ἐπῄει, οἱ Τοῦρκοι οὖν αὐτίκα ᾔεσαν ἅμα πάντες ἐπὶ τὸν Μουσταφᾶν καὶ προσεκύνουν ὡς βασιλέα, καὶ αὐτός τε Παιαζήτης προσεκύνησε καὶ τὰ πράγματα παρεδίδου τῷ Μουσταφᾷ, χρῆσθαι αὐτοῖς, ὅ τι ἂν βούλοιτο. Τοῦτον μὲν οὖν λαβὼν αὐτίκα αὐτοῦ διεχρήσατο, καὶ ἀπελαύνων τήν τε πόλιν ἔσχε καὶ ἐπὶ τὰ βασίλεια παρεγένετο.

6 Μετὰ δὲ ταῦτα συστραφεὶς ἵετο ἐπὶ τὴν Ἀσίαν, ὥς τε καὶ τὴν τῆς Ἀσίας βασιλείαν ἑαυτῷ προσκτησόμενος. Διαβὰς δ᾽ ἐς τὴν Ἀσίαν, ἔχων τό τε [2.5] Εὐρώπης στράτευμα καὶ ἀζάπιδας τοὺς Τούρκων πεζοὺς οὕτω καλουμένους,

he might lead them. The king of the Greeks demanded that Gallipoli be restored to him. Mustafa said that he was ready to hand it over and would not resist, but that the Turks would take it badly. Matters would not then go well for them, especially when his authority had not yet been established. But he promised, when he ascended the throne, to hand over the city, and if there were anything else that he thought would benefit them, he would never again deprive them of it.

He persuaded the Greeks at that time and advanced farther into Europe. Everyone went over to his side, accepting him as their sultan in truth and as a genuine son of Bayezid. But when the vizier Bayezid realized that he was moving against Adrianople—he was governing the city, having been left there by Sultan Mehmed upon his death—he called up the army of Europe and met Mustafa near Adrianople with the intention of joining battle and preventing him, if that proved possible, from reaching the palace. He attacked him in formation, but then all the Turks went together over to Mustafa and bowed to him as their sultan. Bayezid himself also bowed and surrendered his authority to Mustafa for him to use as he deemed fit. Mustafa had him seized and killed on the spot, and then advanced, took the city, and installed himself in the palace. 5

After that Mustafa assembled his forces and went against Asia, so as to acquire the kingship of Asia as well. He crossed over into Asia,[7] taking the army of Europe and the Turkish infantry called the *azaps.* He ferried his army over into Asia, 6

καὶ ἐς τὴν Ἀσίαν διεπόρθμευσεν ἔχων μεθ' ἑαυτοῦ καὶ τὸν Ζουναΐτην Σμύρνης ἄρχοντα, ἐπὶ Ἀμουράτην ἤλαυνε τὸν Μεχμέτεω. Τὸν μέντοι βασιλέα Ἑλλήνων πέμπων πρέσβεις ἠξίου μηδὲν ἐς τὴν ξενίαν αὐτοῦ νεωτερίζειν, ὡς τὴν Καλλιούπολιν αὐτίκα ἀποδώσοντος, ἐπειδὰν τὴν Ἀσίαν αὐτῷ ὑπάγηται, καταστρεψάμενος τὸν ἀδελφιδοῦν. Παρῆσαν δὲ καὶ Ἀμουράτεω παρὰ βασιλέα Βυζαντίου ἀφικόμενοι, χρηματίζοντες καὶ οὗτοι ἐπὶ σφίσι γενέσθαι βασιλέα, καὶ ὑπισχνούμενοι δώσειν, ὅ τι ἂν βούλοιντο. Οἱ μὲν οὖν Ἕλληνες ἀνεβάλλοντο μὲν ἐπὶ χρόνον τινὰ τὰς πρεσβείας, τέλος δὲ τὴν μὲν Ἀμουράτεω ἀπεπέμψαντο πρεσβείαν, τὰ δὲ Μουσταφᾶ ἑλόμενοι πράγματα προσίεντό τε καὶ ἐπέσχον, ὥστε αὐτοῖς σπένδεσθαι κατὰ πᾶν δεδογμένον αὐτοῖς.

7 Ἡ μὲν οὖν Ἀμουράτεω πρεσβεία ἀφικομένη παρὰ τὸν στρατὸν τοῦ Ἀμουράτεω διεφήμισαν, ὡς τοὺς Ἕλληνας σφίσι προσκτήσαιντο συμμάχους. Ἐτύγχανον δ' ἐν Λοπαδίῳ τῇ λίμνῃ ἐστρατοπεδευμένοι, καὶ τήν τε χώραν διέλυσαν τοῦ Μιχαλικίου αὐτοῦ, ᾗ ἐς τὴν θάλασσαν ἐξιοῦσα ἡ λίμνη διὰ στενοῦ ἐπὶ πολὺ προϊοῦσα ἐκδιδοῖ, γέφυρα δέ ἐστι. Μουσταφᾶς δὲ καὶ αὐτὸς ἐλάσας ἀγχοῦ ἐστρατοπεδεύετο παρὰ τὸ χεῖλος τοῦ ποταμοῦ τῆς λίμνης. Ἐνταῦθα ὡς ἀφίκοντο οἱ πρέσβεις Ἀμουράτεω, τύχῃ τινὶ ἀγαθῇ χρησάμενοι διεφήμιζον ὡς συμμαχομένους σφίσι τοὺς Ἕλληνας ἔχοντες ἥκοιεν, καὶ ἐπὶ τὸ στρατόπεδον τοῦ Μουσταφᾶ ἐφώνουν [2.6] ἐπαπειλοῦντες ὡς ἀπειλημμένῳ ἐν τῇ Ἀσίᾳ. Ἐνταῦθα φήμης παρὰ τὸ στρατόπεδον τοῦ Μουσταφᾶ γενομένης, ὡς σφίσιν οὐ παρῆσαν οἱ πρέσβεις,

having also with him Junayd, the lord of Smyrna, and marched against Murad, the son of Mehmed. He sent envoys to the king of the Greeks [Ioannes VIII] requesting that he not do anything that would undermine his friendship, as he was prepared to hand Gallipoli over to him as soon as he had subjected Asia to himself and conquered his nephew. Present also were men who had been sent to the king of Byzantion by Murad, and they too were negotiating over who their sultan would be and promising to give them whatever they might want. The Greeks stalled the embassies for some time, but in the end they dismissed that of Murad, choosing to side with and support the interests of Mustafa so that he would make a treaty with them that would include all the terms on which they had decided.

Now, the embassy of Murad arrived back at the army of 7
Murad and reported that they had concluded an alliance with the Greeks. They happened to be encamped by lake Lopadion and ravaged the land there of Michalikion,[8] where the lake flows into the sea through a long and narrow channel, and where there is a bridge. Mustafa advanced in person and encamped near the bank of the lake's river. Then Murad's envoys returned and, by a lucky chance, they spread the word that they came bearing an alliance with the Greeks. They cried this out to Mustafa's camp with the threat that he would now be cut off in Asia. Thereupon the rumor spread throughout Mustafa's camp, as his envoys had not

καὶ δεδιότες, μὴ οἱ Ἕλληνες τὸν Ἑλλήσποντον κατασχόντες τοῦ λοιποῦ μὴ ἐπιτρέπωσι διαβαίνειν καὶ αὐτοῦ ταύτῃ ἀπόλοιντο. Λόγον τε σφίσιν ἐδίδοσαν, καὶ νυκτὸς ἐπιγενομένης αὐτὸς ὁ Ζουναΐτης ὁ τῆς Σμύρνης ἡγεμὼν ἀπέδρα ἐπὶ τὴν πατρῴαν ἀρχήν, καὶ οἱ λοιποὶ τῶν ἀρχόντων ἀπεδίδρασκον οὐδ' ὁπωσοῦν ἐπισχόντες, τύχῃ τοῦ Μουσταφᾶ οὐκέτι ἀγαθῇ πιστεύοντες.

8 Ὡς δὲ Μουσταφᾶς διϊδὼν τὰ στρατεύματα αὐτῷ ἀποδιδράσκοντα, περὶ αὐτῷ δεδιὼς ἀπέδρα καὶ αὐτὸς ἐπὶ θάλασσαν. Ἕλληνες μέντοι, ὡς ἑλόμενοι Μουσταφᾶν σφίσι σύμμαχον εἶναι, ἐπλήρωσαν τὰς ναῦς καὶ ἐπέπλεον ἐπὶ Ἑλλήσποντον. Βασιλεὺς δὲ αὐτὸς Βυζαντίου ἐν Προικονήσῳ γενόμενος ἐσχόλαζέ τε περὶ γυναικὸς ἔρωτα, ἧς ἐρῶν ἐτύγχανεν, ἦν γὰρ ἱερέως θυγάτηρ, καὶ οὐκ ἐν δέοντι παρεγένετο, ὥστε διακωλῦσαι Ἀμουράτην ἐς τὴν Εὐρώπην ἀφικέσθαι. Ἀμουράτης μὲν δή, ὡς τάχιστα ἡμέρα ἐγεγόνει, καὶ κατεῖδε τὸ στρατόπεδον τῶν πολεμίων κενόν, καὶ ὑπὸ τὴν οἰχομένην νύκτα ἀποδρᾶν τε, καὶ τούς τε ἀζάπιδας χεῖρα ὀρέγοντας, ὅτι ὑπὸ τῶν σφετέρων προδεδομένοι εἶεν ἱππέων, τόν τε ῥοῦν τῆς λίμνης ἔζευξε, καὶ διέβη ὡς εἶχε τάχους, καὶ τούς τε ἀζάπιδας διεχρήσατο ἅπαντας αὐτοῦ.

9 Μετὰ δὲ ταῦτα ἐδίωκε κατὰ πόλεις τὸν Μουσταφᾶν. Μουσταφᾶς μὲν οὖν ἔφθη διαβὰς ἐς Καλλιούπολιν, Ἀμουράτης δὲ ἐντυχὼν νηῒ μεγίστῃ τῶν Ἰανυΐων αὐτοῦ ταύτῃ ὁρμιζομένῃ, συντίθεται τῷ νεὼς δεσπότῃ διαπορθμεῦσαι αὐτόν τε ἅμα καὶ τοὺς νεήλυδας [2.7] καὶ τοὺς τῶν θυρῶν αὐτοῦ καὶ ἅπαν τὸ στράτευμα ἐς τὴν Εὐρώπην, καὶ

yet returned and they feared that the Greeks would occupy the Hellespont and no longer allow them to cross back, and thus they would perish right there. They held talks among themselves and at night Junayd himself, the lord of Smyrna, fled to his ancestral realm.[9] The rest of the lords then escaped too without any hesitation or delay, no longer trusting in Mustafa's good fortune.

When Mustafa saw that his armies were deserting him, 8
he feared for himself and likewise escaped to the sea. The Greeks, who had chosen to ally themselves to him, manned their ships and sailed to the Hellespont. But the king of Byzantion [Ioannes VIII], who came in person to Prokonnesos, was spending his time in an affair with a woman with whom he was infatuated, the daughter of a priest, and did not take the necessary steps to prevent Murad from arriving in Europe. As for Murad, as soon as day broke he saw that the enemy camp was empty and that they had escaped during the previous night. He saw also that the *azaps* were stretching out their hands in supplication, as they had been betrayed by their own cavalry. He threw a bridge across the stream of the lake, crossed over in haste, and had all the *azaps* killed on the spot.

After that Murad pursued Mustafa from city to city. Mus- 9
tafa managed to cross over to Gallipoli, but Murad happened upon the largest ship of the Genoese that had moored there, and he made an agreement with the ship's captain[10] to ferry him, the janissaries, the men of his Porte, and his entire army over to Europe. He paid him a large sum of silver,

ἐτέλεσεν αὐτῷ ἀργύριον ἱκανόν, ὅσον δὴ ᾐτήσατο. Καὶ διεπόρθμευσεν αὐτῷ τε ἅμα καὶ τῷ στρατῷ ἅπαντι. Ὁ μὲν οὖν Μουσταφᾶς, ὡς ἐπύθετο διαβεβηκότα Ἀμουράτην ἐς τὴν Εὐρώπην, καὶ ᾗ, ὅποι σῴζοιτο, ἀνεώρα ἐπισφαλὲς ὂν ἤδη ἁπανταχῇ, ἅτε Ἀμουράτεω καταλαβόντος αὐτόν, ἐσῴζετο ἐπὶ τὸ ὄρος τοῦ Γάνου οὕτω καλούμενον. Ὁ δὲ ὡς ἐδίωκε, καὶ ἐπισχών, πάντα ζητῶν οὐκ ἀνίει, σαγηνεύσας τε τὸν χῶρον αὐτοῦ, ᾗ ἐδόκει καὶ ἤδη ὑποψίαν παρεῖχεν ἐνταυθὶ κρύπτεσθαι, εὗρεν αὐτὸν ὑπὸ θάμνῳ τινὶ κεκρυμμένον, καὶ ζωγρήσας ἀγχόνῃ τε τὸν λαιμὸν αὐτοῦ ἐχρήσατο. Ἐτελεύτησε δὲ Μουσταφᾶς βασιλεύσας ἐν τῇ Εὐρώπῃ ἔτη τρία.

10 Ἀμουράτης δὲ ὡς ἔσχε τὴν ἀρχὴν ἀμφοῖν ταῖν ἠπείροιν, ἐς τὴν βασιλείαν κατέστη. Οὐ πολλῷ δὲ ὕστερον ἐστρατεύετο ἐπὶ Βυζάντιον καὶ ἐπὶ τοὺς Ἕλληνας. Προέπεμψε δὲ Μιχαλόγλην, πρυτανέα τε ἅμα καὶ στρατηγὸν τῆς Εὐρώπης. Καὶ λαβὼν οὗτος τὸ ἀπὸ τῆς Εὐρώπης στράτευμα ἅπαν, ἐπέδραμέ τε τὴν Βυζαντίου χώραν. Μετὰ δὲ ταῦτα ἐστρατοπεδεύετο, καὶ αὐτίκα ἀπήλαυνεν Ἀμουράτης ὁ Μεχμέτεω, τούς τε νεήλυδας ἔχων καὶ τὴν θύραν ἅμα, ὅσοι βασιλεῖ ἕπονται, ὅποι ἂν στρατεύηται. Καὶ τὰ Ἀσίας στρατεύματα ἔχων παρεγένετο, καὶ ἐστρατοπεδεύετο ἀπὸ θαλάσσης εἰς θάλασσαν.

11 Αἱ μὲν οὖν θύραι ὧδέ πῃ ἔχουσαι. Πεζοὶ πάρεισι τῷ βασιλεῖ ἀμφὶ τοὺς ἑξακισχιλίους καὶ ἐνίοτε ἀμφὶ τοὺς μυρίους· ἀπὸ [2.8] γὰρ τούτων φρουράν τε φαίνει ἐν ταῖς ἀκροπόλεσι, καὶ αὖθις ἑτέραν ἐς τὴν χώραν ἐκείνων καθίστησι. Παρεγένοντο δ' αὐτῷ τῇδε. Παῖδας λαβὼν

as much as he asked for. So he and his entire army were ferried across. When Mustafa learned that Murad had crossed over into Europe, he realized that every place where he sought refuge would be dangerous for him seeing that Murad had caught up with him, and he sought salvation upon a mountain called Ganos. Murad pursued him relentlessly and did not let up in his search for him: he swept that whole area with a dragnet, having a prior suspicion that he might have been hiding there, and found him hiding under a bush. He took him alive and strangled him. Mustafa died after a reign in Europe of three years.[11]

Murad now held sway over both continents and his hold 10
on the throne was secured. Shortly afterward he marched against Byzantion and the Greeks. He sent ahead Mihaloğlu, his vizier and general of Europe.[12] The latter took the entire army from Europe and raided the territory of Byzantion. After that he made camp, and then Murad himself, the son of Mehmed, set out too, having the janissaries and all the men of the Porte who follow the sultan when he goes on campaign. He arrived with the armies of Asia as well, and their camp stretched from sea to sea.[13]

The Porte is ordered in the following way. There are 11
about six thousand infantry present with the sultan, and sometimes as many as ten thousand. From among them garrisons are appointed to the citadels, but he appoints a different one to their native lands. They are procured for him in

αἰχμαλώτους, ὅσους ἂν τύχῃ ἀνδραποδισάμενος, κατατίθεται ἐς τὴν Ἀσίαν παρὰ τοῖς Τούρκοις, ὥστε τὴν φωνὴν ἐκμαθεῖν ἕνα ἕκαστον. Καὶ ἐπὶ δύο ἢ καὶ τρία ἔτη διαγενόμενοι τήν τε γλῶσσαν ἐκμανθάνουσι, καὶ συνιέντες τῆς φωνῆς, ὅσα ἂν δυνηθῶσιν, αὖθις συλλέγει, ἀφ᾽ ὧν κατέθετο, ἐς δισχιλίους καὶ πλείους τούτων. Ἄγει δ᾽ αὐτοὺς ξύμπαντας ἐς τὴν Καλλιούπολιν, καὶ καθίστησιν αὐτοὺς ἐς τὰ πλοῖα, ναυτίζεσθαί τε καὶ διαπορθμεύειν ἐς τὴν Ἀσίαν ἀπὸ τῆς Εὐρώπης τοὺς βουλομένους διαβαίνειν. Ὀβολὸν δ᾽ ἔχει ἕκαστος ἐνταῦθα, καὶ χιτῶνα τοῦ ἐνιαυτοῦ. Μετ᾽ οὐ πολὺν δὲ χρόνον μεταπέμπονται ἐς τὰς θύρας αὐτοῦ, παρέχων τε μισθόν, ὅσος ἂν ἱκανὸς εἴη ἐς τὸ ἀποζῆν αὐτούς, ἐνίοις ἄλλοις δὲ πλείω παρέχεται.

12 Καὶ ἐς δεκαδάρχας τε καὶ πεντηκοντάρχας καὶ ἐνωμοτίας καὶ λόχους τεταγμένοι τε καὶ διακεκριμένοι στρατεύονται, κατὰ τὰ συσσίτιά τε καὶ τῇ δύσει ἡλίου εἶναι σὺν τῷ δεκαδάρχῃ ἐς τὴν σκηνήν. Σκηνοῦσι δὲ οὗτοι ἀμφὶ τὸν βασιλέα, ἐς τὸν ἑαυτοῦ χῶρον ἕκαστος ἐχόμενος τοῦ ἑτέρου. Ἐντὸς μέντοι τούτων οὐδενὶ ἔξεστι σκηνοῦν, πλὴν τῶν τοῦ βασιλέως παίδων καὶ τῶν θησαυρῶν τοῦ βασιλέως καὶ τοῦ κοιτῶνος. Σκηνὴ δὲ ἐρυθρὰ αὐτῷ. Ὁτὲ μὲν δύο, ὁτὲ δὲ καὶ τρεῖς ἵδρυνται αὐτῷ τῷ βασιλεῖ, ἀπὸ πίλου ἐρυθροῦ χρυσόπαστοι, καὶ σκηναὶ ἕτεραι ἀμφὶ τὰς πεντεκαίδεκα, πᾶσαι ἐντὸς τῶν νεηλύδων. Ἐκτὸς δὲ σκηνοῦσιν οἱ λοιποὶ τῶν [2.9] θυρῶν ἄνδρες, οἵ τε ἀμουραχόριοι καὶ οἰνοχόοι οἱ λεγόμενοι παρ᾽ αὐτῶν σαραπτάριοι, καὶ σημαιοφόροι οἱ λεγόμενοι ἐμουραλάμιοι, καὶ οἱ τῶν θυρῶν πρυτανεῖς, βεζίριδες οὕτω καλούμενοι, τοῦ βασιλέως

the following way. He takes all the captive children whom he has happened to enslave and assigns them to Turks in Asia so that each can learn the language. They spend two or even three years learning the language, and when they can speak it, to whatever extent they are able, he then collects some two thousand or more from the group that he had originally assigned. He leads them all to Gallipoli and places them in the ships to man them and ferry those who wish to cross over from Europe into Asia. Each receives payment for this and one cloak per year. Shortly afterward they are summoned to his Porte and he gives some of them a living wage; to others he gives more.

They are organized under the command of leaders of ten 12
men, fifty men, divisions, and companies, and they march according to these distinctions. For common meals and at sunset they have to be with their leader of ten, in the tent. They pitch their tents around the sultan, each one in his own designated place, one next to the other. No one is allowed to pitch his tent among them, except for the sultan's sons, the sultan's treasury, and his sleeping chamber. His tent is red. Sometimes two and sometimes three tents are pitched for the sultan himself, which are of red felt embellished with gold, and about fifteen other tents as well, all of them within the janissary encampment. The rest of the Porte's men pitch their tents outside, including the *amir ahor*[14] and the wine pourers, whom they call *şaraptars;* the standard-bearers called *amir al-a'lam;*[15] the presiding officers of the Porte called the viziers; and the sultan's messengers.

ἀγγελιαφόροι. Οὗτοι μὲν οὖν μεγάλοι τε ὄντες, καὶ ὡς πλείους ἐπαγόμενοι θεράποντας, πληθὺν παρέχοντας ἄπλετον.

13 Μετὰ δὲ συλικτάριδες ἔνεισι τῶν βασιλέως θυρῶν ἀμφὶ τῶν τριακοσίων, οἳ ἱππεῖς ὄντες ἀπὸ τῶν νεηλύδων ἐπὶ ταύτην παραγίνονται τὴν χώραν. Μετὰ δὲ τούτους καρίπιδες οἱ ἐπήλυδες καλούμενοι, ἀπό τε Ἀσίας καὶ Αἰγύπτου καὶ δὴ καὶ Λιβύης αὐτῷ ἐς τὰς θύρας παραγενόμενοι, καὶ ἀρετῆς ἀντιποιούμενοι ἔναντι βασιλέως, μεμισθωμένοι αὐτῷ, ὁ μὲν πλείονος, ὁ δὲ ἐλάττονος. Τούτων δὲ ἔχονται ἀλοφατζίδες οἱ μισθωτοὶ καλούμενοι, ἀμφὶ τοὺς ὀκτακοσίους. Τούτων δὲ αὖθις ἔχονται οἱ σπαχίδες καλούμενοι, ἀμφὶ τοὺς διακοσίους. Οὗτοι δ' εἰσὶν οἱ τῶν ἀρχόντων παῖδες, ὧν τοὺς μὲν ἀπὸ τοῦ κοιτῶνος ἐκβαλὼν ἐς ταύτην αὐτοὺς καθίστησι τὴν χώραν, τοὺς δὲ ἐπιλεξάμενος ἐνταῦθα ἔχει ὡς ἀνδρῶν παῖδας ἀγαθῶν γενομένους. Καὶ αἱ μὲν θύραι, ὡς ξυνελόντι μοι φάναι, οὕτω τετάχαται.

14 Δύο δὲ ὑπὸ βασιλέως ἐς ξύμπασαν αὐτῷ τὴν ἀρχὴν καθίστανται στρατηγοί, ὁ μὲν τῆς Εὐρώπης, ὁ δὲ τῆς Ἀσίας. Καὶ τούτων ἑκατέρῳ ἕπονται τά τε στρατεύματα καὶ οἱ ἄρχοντες, ὅποι ἂν ἐξηγῶνται, ἐπειδὰν ἐπαγγείλῃ αὐτοῖς ὁ βασιλεύς. Ἕπονται δὲ αὐτοῖς καὶ οἱ ὕπαρχοι παρ' αὐτοῖς σημαιοφόροι καλούμενοι· ἐπειδὰν γὰρ ἐς τὴν ἀρχὴν ταύτην ὑπὸ βασιλέως καθίστηται, [2.10] σημαίᾳ τε δωρεῖται αὐτὸν ὁ βασιλεὺς ὡς στρατηγῷ γενομένῳ καὶ πολλῶν ἄρχοντι πόλεων. Τούτῳ δ' αὖ τῷ ὑπάρχῳ ἕπονται οἱ τῶν πόλεων ἄρχοντες, ὅποι στρατεύηται. Χωροῦσι δὲ ἅπαντες κατὰ ταῦτα ἑπόμενοι τοῖς σφετέροις αὐτῶν

These are all important men, and, as they are accompanied by many servants, they make for a vast multitude.

Then, at the sultan's Porte, there are about three hundred *silahdars,*[16] who are cavalry drawn from the janissaries and have this rank. After them are the *garips,*[17] foreigners so-called, who come to the Porte from Asia, Egypt, and North Africa, and contend for virtue before the sultan; they are salaried by him, and some receive more, some less. They are followed by the *ulufecis,* the mercenaries so-called,[18] about eight hundred of them. Then come the so-called *sipahis,* about two hundred in number. They are the sons of lords, some of whom he has dismissed from the sleeping chamber and assigned to this rank, while others he has selected to maintain here as the sons of noble men. The Porte, then, is so ordered, to put it briefly. 13

Two generals are appointed by the sultan over his entire territory, one for Europe and one for Asia. Each of them, wherever he may go on the sultan's orders, is followed by the armies and the lords. They are also followed by the prefects, which is what they call the standard-bearers. Whenever a general is appointed by the sultan to this position, the sultan gives him a standard to indicate that he is now a general and the lord of many cities. The governors of the cities follow this prefect during campaigns. They come to the sultan's 14

ἄρχουσί τε καὶ στρατηγοῖς, ἐπειδὰν ἐς τὸ βασιλέως παραγένωνται στρατόπεδον. Αὕτη σχεδὸν ἡ τῶν στρατευμάτων αὐτῷ διάταξις. Οἱ μέντοι ἱπποδρόμοι τάττονται καὶ οὗτοι ἐς τοὺς σφῶν αὐτῶν ὑπάρχους. Οἱ δὲ ἀζάπιδες ὑφ' ἑνὶ ἄρχοντι ἑπόμενοι, ἐς ταὐτὸ γιγνόμενοι στρατεύονται.

15 Ἀμουράτης μὲν οὖν ὡς ἐπέλασε, καὶ ἐπολιόρκει Βυζάντιον ἀπὸ θαλάττης εἰς θάλατταν, τηλεβόλοις τε ἔτυπτε τὸ τεῖχος καὶ ἐπειρᾶτο, οὐ μέντοι κατέβαλέ γε. Εἷλκον δὲ οἱ λίθοι τῶν τηλεβόλων σταθμὸν τρία ἡμιτάλαντα, ὥστε ἀντεῖχε τὸ τεῖχος ὀχυρόν τε ὂν πρός τε τούτους τοὺς τηλεβόλους, καὶ οὐδαμῇ ὑπεῖκον. Δοκεῖ μὲν οὖν ὁ τηλεβόλος οὐ πάνυ παλαιὸς εἶναι, ὥστε συνιέναι ἡμᾶς ἐπὶ νοῦν ἐληλυθέναι τοῖς παλαιοῖς τὸ τοιοῦτον. Ὅθεν μέντοι ἀρχὴν ἐγένετο, καὶ τίνες ἀνθρώπων ἐς τὴν τοῦ τηλεβόλου ἀφίκοντο πεῖραν, οὐκ ἔχω διασημῆναι ἀσφαλῶς· οἴονται μέντοι ἀπὸ Γερμανῶν γενέσθαι τε τούτους, καὶ τούτοις ἐπὶ νοῦν ἀφῖχθαι ταύτην τὴν μηχανήν. Ἀλλ' οἱ μὲν τηλεβολίσκοι ἀπὸ Γερμανῶν καὶ ἐς τὴν ἄλλην κατὰ βραχὺ ἀφίκοντο οἰκουμένην· οἱ δὲ τηλεβόλοι, οὐκ ἂν εἰδείην σαφῶς ἰσχυρίζεσθαι, ὅθεν ἐγένοντο τὴν ἀρχήν.

16 Τὴν δὲ ἰσχύν τε καὶ φορὰν τὴν ἀμήχανον, ᾗ ἐπιφερόμενος ὁ λίθος, ὅποι ἂν γένοιτο, μεγίστην τοῖς σώμασιν ἐπιφέρεται βλάβην, ἥ τε κόνις παρέχεται τῷ παντί, καὶ ἀπὸ ταύτης ἐνήνεκται. Τῆς δὲ κόνεως τὸ νίτρον ἔχει τὴν δύναμιν, ἄνθρακί τε καὶ θείῳ ἐπιμιγνυμένη. Οὕτω δὲ ὡς ἄμεινον ἔχει τὰ τῆς οἰκουμένης ἐς τὰ ὅπλα· διὸ καὶ ἀρετῆς ἔλαττον [2.11] ἴσχει αὐτῇ τὴν δαιμονίαν ἐκείνην φοράν. Δοκεῖ δὲ γενέσθαι σιδηρήεις μὲν τὸ πρῶτον, μετὰ δὲ τὴν

camp and then, according to this arrangement, all of them depart in the train of their own lords and generals. This, then, is how the sultan's armies are ordered. As for the cavalry raiders, they too are assigned to their own respective prefects. The *azaps* follow one commander and campaign as a unit.

Murad, then, set out and besieged Byzantion from sea to 15
sea, striking at the walls with cannons. Yet despite his efforts, he did not bring them down. The rocks thrown by his cannons weighed three half-talents each, but the walls were fortified against such cannons and withstood them; nowhere did they give way. The cannon does not appear to be a very ancient invention and it seems to us that the ancients did not conceive of such a weapon. I cannot indicate with any certainty where they were invented and which people were the first to use them. However, it is believed that they originated among the Germans and that they were the ones who contrived this device. Firearms certainly spread gradually from the Germans to the rest of the world. But as for cannons in general, I cannot say where they originated on the basis of secure knowledge.

It is the powder that imparts all the force and irresistible 16
momentum to the rock, wherever it may go in its trajectory, and it inflicts maximum damage upon all bodies; this is all conveyed by the powder. And, within the powder, it is the niter that has all the power, which comes from a mixture of carbon and sulfur. The world considers this substance as the best for weapons. Valor is hardly able to resist their demonic force. It seems that at first cannons were made of iron, but

τοῦ χύματος καλουμένου ἐπιφράσασθαι πεῖραν, τοῦ χαλκοῦ σὺν τῷ κασσιτέρῳ μεμιγμένων, εὐδοκιμεῖν ἐς τὸ ἀφιέναι τὸν λίθον ἄμεινόν τε καὶ βιαιότερον. Τὸ μέντοι σχῆμα διεξιέναι οἷόν ἐστι, περίεργον μέντ' ἂν εἴη πᾶσι καθορῶσιν ἁπανταχῇ. Ἐπίμηκες δ' ὄν, ὅσον δ' ἂν εἴη ἐπιμηκέστερον, τοσούτῳ ἐπὶ μήκιστον ἀφίησι τὸν λίθον, ὥστ' ἂν γενέσθαι τηλεβόλον, ᾗ ἐπυθόμεθα, ἀφιέντα τὸν λίθον ἐπὶ ἑβδομήκοντα σταδίους, πέριξ σειομένην τὴν γῆν κατ' ἄμφω τὼ διαστήματε. Δοκεῖ δ' ἡ τοῦ πυρὸς αὕτη δύναμις τόν τε ψόφον ἀπεργάζεσθαι καὶ τὴν φοράν, ᾗ ὁ λίθος φέρεται· βιαζόμενον γὰρ τὸ στοιχεῖον τοῦτο πάμμεγα καὶ δαιμόνιόν τι δύνασθαι δοκεῖ, ᾗ δὴ καὶ τὸν σκηπτὸν ἀπεργάζεται τὸ πνεῦμα εἰς τὸ πῦρ μεταβάλλον. Εἴτε μὲν οὖν τὸ μὴ κενὸν συγχωρεῖσθαι, τόν τε ψόφον γίνεσθαι καὶ τὴν φοράν, εἴτε ταύτῃ τοῦ πυρὸς τιθεμένου τῇ δυνάμει, ἐπειδὰν προσβιαζόμενον ὕλης ἐπιλάβηται, ἀνάγκη ταῦτα ἀπεργαζόμενον, ἴσχειν ἄμφω ταῦτα. Δοκεῖ δὲ τοῦ πυρὸς τὴν δύναμιν εἶναι ταύτην ξύμπασαν, καὶ τὴν κόνιν αὔξειν πεφυκυῖαν τὴν τοῦ πυρὸς δύναμιν διὰ τοῦ πυρὸς κινεῖν τε ἀμήχανον καὶ βάλλειν μακρότατα.

17 Τότε μὲν οὖν Ἀμουράτης ὁ Μεχμέτεω τηλεβόλοις καὶ ἄλλαις μηχαναῖς πειρασάμενος τοῦ τείχους περὶ ἡμέρας ἱκανὰς [2.12] προσέβαλε τῷ τείχει ἁπανταχῇ καὶ ἑλεῖν ἐπειρᾶτο. Ἐξεκρούσαντο δὲ αὐτὸν ἀπό τε τῶν κλιμάκων καταβαλόντες οἱ Ἕλληνες τοὺς βασιλέως νεήλυδας, καὶ ἐνίων ἀποταμόμενοι τὰς κεφαλὰς ἀπηνέγκαντο. Ἀμουράτης δ', ὡς οὐδὲν προεχώρει ἡ τοῦ ἄστεως αἵρεσις, ἤσχαλλέ τε καὶ ἠθύμει, ᾤετο δὲ αἱρήσειν τὴν πόλιν. Διατρίβοντι δὲ

later they tried fashioning them from the so-called alloy, wherein copper is mixed with tin,[19] and they succeeded at making the rock fly better and more powerfully. To describe its shape in detail would be superfluous for it is available everywhere for all to see. It is long and the longer it is the farther the rock will go, so that there was once a cannon, or so we have learned, that shot a rock to a distance of seventy stades, shaking the earth all around at both ends of its trajectory. It seems that it is the force of fire that creates both the blast and the impetus with which the rock flies, for under pressure this element seems to be capable of extraordinary and almost supernatural effects, as the gas, being changed into fire, causes the thunder. The blast and impetus are created either because a vacuum cannot be allowed or because, when the fire brings its power to bear as it uses force against the matter with which it comes into contact, it produces these effects by necessity, and so both of them come about. It seems, then, that all this is in the power of fire and that it is in the nature of the powder to enhance the power of the fire; it is thanks to the fire that it shoots irresistibly and over such great distances.

Murad, then, the son of Mehmed, made trial of the walls 17
with his cannons and other engines, assaulting the walls for many days and at many places in an attempt to capture them. The Greeks repulsed him by throwing the sultan's janissaries down from their ladders, and they cut off the heads of some and took them away.[20] As he was making no progress toward capturing the city, Murad grew angry and despondent, for he had thought that he would take the city.

αὐτῷ ἐπεκηρυκεύοντό τε οἱ Ἕλληνες· ἀλλ' οὐδ' ὣς ἤθελεν αὐτοῖς σπένδεσθαι. Μετ' οὐ πολλὰς δὲ ἡμέρας ἀπεχώρει ἐπ' οἴκου, καὶ τὰ στρατεύματα αὐτῷ διῆκεν. Οἱ μὲν οὖν Ἕλληνες πρέσβεις τε ἔπεμπον παρὰ Ἀμουράτην καὶ ἐδέοντο· ὁ δὲ ἀπεπέμπετο καὶ οὐ προσίετο τὴν ἀξίωσιν.

18 Μετὰ δὲ ταῦτα, ὡς πειρωμένοις τοῖς Ἕλλησι τῶν σπονδῶν οὐδὲν προεχώρει, τρέπονται ἐπὶ τὸν Μουσταφᾶν τὸν Μεχμέτεω παῖδα. Ἔτυχε δὲ διατρίβων παρὰ τῷ Καραμάνῳ τὴν δίαιταν ποιούμενος. Πρέσβεις δὲ πέμψαντες μετεπέμποντο ἐπὶ Βυζάντιον τὸν παῖδα, γεγονότα ἀμφὶ τὰ τρισκαίδεκα ἔτη. Ἐπεὶ δὲ ἀφίκετο ἐς Βυζάντιον ὁ παῖς, ἔπεμπε λόγους παρὰ τοὺς Τούρκους, μεγάλα τε ὑπισχνούμενος, καὶ μετιὼν ἕκαστον ἐπηγγέλλετο διπλασίω πάντων, ὧν εἶχεν ὑπὸ Ἀμουράτεω. Καὶ ηὐτομόλησαν μέν τινες Τοῦρκοι παρὰ τὸν παῖδα, οὐ πολλοὶ δέ. Ὁ μέντοι παῖς τὴν Ἀσίαν διαβάς, συνεπιλαβομένου καὶ τοῦ Ἑλλήνων βασιλέως, τό τε Ἱερὸν καλούμενον ἐξεπολιόρκησε. Καὶ προσελαύνοντι αὐτῷ διὰ τῆς Ἀσίας προσεχώρουν τε οἱ τῆς Ἀσίας Τοῦρκοι ἅτε βασιλέως παιδὶ ὄντι.

19 Ἐνταῦθα Ἀλιάζης ὁ οἰνοχόος ἐπίκλην, τοῦτον τὸν παῖδα ἐπιτετραμμένος ὑπὸ Μεχμέτεω, συντίθεται προδοσίαν τῷ Ἀμουράτῃ, ὥστε καταπροδοῦναι αὐτῷ τὸ παιδίον. Καὶ ὡς συνέθετο αὐτῷ, ἔπρασσεν, ὥστε τὸν παῖδα αὐτῷ παραδοίη, διεσήμαινέ τε πέμπων [2.13] ἄγγελον, ὅποι διατρίβων τυγχάνοι ὁ παῖς. Ὡς μὲν οὖν ἐς Νίκαιαν ἀφίκετο ὁ παῖς, τήν τε Νίκαιαν ὑπηγάγετο, καὶ ἐνταῦθα διατρίβων ὁ παῖς μετῄει τοὺς κατὰ τὴν Ἀσίαν ἀρίστους. Καὶ ὡς ἤδη χειμὼν ἦν, διεκωλύετο ἐς τὸ πρόσω τῆς Ἀσίας

The Greeks sent envoys to him while he was there, but he did not want to make terms with them. A few days later he departed for home and dismissed his army.[21] The Greeks sent envoys to Murad and pleaded with him, but he sent them back and would not grant their request.

After that, as the Greeks had made no progress in their 18
attempts to secure a treaty, they turned to Mustafa, the son of Mehmed. He happened to be with Karaman and was maintained by him.[22] The Greeks sent envoys to summon the boy to Byzantion; he was about thirteen years old. When the boy arrived at Byzantion, he sent word to the Turks, making grand promises, and he sent to each man and announced that he would get double what he was receiving from Murad. Some Turks did defect to the boy's side, but not many. Meanwhile, the boy crossed over into Asia accompanied by the king of the Greeks and took the place called Hieron by siege. The Turks of Asia went over to him as he advanced through Asia, as he was the son of a sultan.

At this point, İlyas, who was called the Wine Pourer and 19
had been entrusted with this boy by Mehmed, made a treacherous agreement to betray the boy to Murad. He did what he promised to do, namely surrender the boy to him by sending a messenger who would signal to him where the boy happened to be at any time. When the boy reached Nikaia, subjected it, and took up residence there, he made advances to the leading men in Asia. As it was winter,[23] he was prevented from going deeper into Asia. Murad now

ἰέναι. Ἐνταῦθα πυθόμενος Ἀμουράτης παρὰ Ἀλιάζεω τοῦ σαραπτάρη τήν τε διατριβὴν τοῦ παιδὸς ἐν τῇ πόλει, λαβὼν ἀμφὶ τοὺς ἑξακισχιλίους τῶν θυρῶν, ὡς εἶχε τάχους, ἀφικόμενος ἐπὶ τὸν Ἑλλήσποντον καὶ διαβὰς ἤλαυνεν εὐθὺ Βιθυνίας. Ἐπιπεσὼν δὲ ἄφνω ἐς τὴν πόλιν συλλαμβάνει τε τὸν παῖδα αὐτοῦ ταύτῃ, παραδιδόντος αὐτῷ τοῦ Ἀλιάζεω. Ὁ μὲν γὰρ παῖς, ἅτε τοῦτο πυθόμενος, κατέφυγεν ἐπ' αὐτόν, ὡς ἐπὶ σωτηρίαν σφίσι τράπωνται· ὁ δὲ κελεύων μὴ δεδοικέναι τὸν παῖδα, ἐπέμενε τὸν ἀδελφὸν τοῦ παιδός, καὶ ἐλθόντι ἐς τὰ βασίλεια τῆς πόλεως ἐνεχείρισε τὸν παῖδα αὐτῷ. Τοῦτον μέντοι ὁ Ἀμουράτης λαβὼν ἀγχόνῃ ἀνεῖλεν, ᾗ νομίζεται παρ' αὐτοῖς.

20 Λέγεται δὲ Τεζετίνην ἄνδρα γένους τοῦ βασιλείου τοῦ Ἐρτζιγγάνης βασιλέως, ἀφικόμενον τῷ παιδὶ σύμμαχον, ὡς ἐπύθετο τοὺς πολεμίους ἐπὶ τὴν πόλιν ἀφῖχθαι, ἐλάσαντα ἐς μέσους τοὺς πολεμίους τόν τε Μιχαλίην τὸν τῆς Εὐρώπης στρατηγὸν καὶ πρυτανέα ἀνελεῖν, πολέμιον αὐτῷ ὄντα, καὶ συχνοὺς ἄλλους ἀνελόντα καὶ αὐτὸν τελευτῶντα ἀποθανεῖν. Τότε μὲν δὴ Ἕλληνες οὕτω ἐπεπράγεισαν, ἑλόμενοι αἵρεσιν ἐναντίαν τῷ Ἀμουράτῃ.

21 Τὴν μέντοι Θέρμην τῆς Μακεδονίας ἀπέδοντο Ἐνετοῖς, ἀδύνατα εἶναι νομίζοντες σφίσι παραδοῦναι [2.14] τὴν πόλιν ἐς τὸν περιόντα τότε Ἀμουράτην.[2] Ἀμουράτης μὲν δὴ ἐπὶ Θέρμην μετὰ ταῦτα ἐστρατεύετο, καὶ ἐπολιόρκει τὴν πόλιν προσέχων ἐντεταμένως, καὶ προσῆγε τῷ τείχει μηχανάς. Καὶ οὐδὲν προὐχώρει αὐτῷ ἡ τῆς πόλεως αἵρεσις. Ἐνταῦθα, ὡς λέγεται, συντίθεται τοῖς ἐν τῇ πόλει προδοσίαν· ᾧ, λέγεται, ὑπορύσσοντες ἀπὸ τῶν οἰκιῶν

learned from İlyas the *şaraptar*[24] that the boy was resident in the city. He took about six thousand men of the Porte, came to the Hellespont as fast as he could, crossed it, and marched straight into Bithynia. He attacked the city suddenly and captured the boy there, when İlyas surrendered Mustafa to him. For the boy, when he learned what was happening, had turned to him for protection so that they could both be saved. He urged the boy not to fear, and awaited the arrival of the boy's brother. When Murad entered the city's palace, İlyas handed the boy over to him. Murad took him and had him killed by strangulation, as is their custom.[25]

It is said that Tâjettinoğlu,[26] a man of the royal family of 20
the king of Erzinjan, came to the boy as an ally, and when he learned that the enemy had come to the city, he charged into the midst of the enemy and killed Michalies, the general of Europe and vizier, who was his enemy.[27] He killed many others too before he himself was finally killed. That, then, was how the Greeks fared when they chose to oppose Murad.

The Greeks sold Thessalonike, in Macedonia, to the Ve- 21
netians,[28] believing that it would be impossible for them to surrender the city to Murad, who was then encircling them. After that Murad marched against Thessalonike and vigorously besieged it, bringing engines against the walls. But he made no progress toward capturing the city. There, it is said, he formed a plot with those inside the city to have it betrayed to him. According to what is said, they dug tunnels

ὀρύγματα ἐκτὸς φέροντα καὶ ἑάλωσαν ὑπὸ Οὐενετῶν, ᾗ λέγεται. Καὶ οἱ ὀρύσσοντες ἀπέδρασαν ἐς τὸ τοῦ Ἀμουράτεω στρατόπεδον, καταβάντες ἀπὸ τοῦ τείχους. Ὕστερον μέντοι ἀπὸ τῆς ἄκρας ὡς προσέβαλεν, εἷλέ τε κατὰ κράτος τὴν πόλιν καὶ ἠνδραποδίσατο.

22 Τοὺς μέντοι νεήλυδας πυνθάνομαι ἀναβάντας ἐς τὸ τεῖχος ἑλεῖν τε τὴν πόλιν, καὶ ἐπισπομένων τῶν ἄλλων ἁλῶναί τε τὴν πόλιν καὶ ἐπὶ ἀνδραποδισμῷ πρὸς τοῦ βασιλέως γενέσθαι. Ἀνδραποδισάμενον μέντοι τὴν πόλιν ταύτην οὐδένα ἐξελέσθαι τοῦ ἀνδραποδισμοῦ ἐπυθόμεθα Ἀμουράτην, ὥστε λογίζεσθαι ἡμᾶς ἔχειν, διὰ τὴν προδοσίαν ἐξείλετο αὐτούς. Ἐγένετο μὲν οὖν αὕτη μεγίστη δὴ τοῖς Ἕλλησι καὶ οὐδεμιᾶς τῶν πρόσθεν γενομένων αὐτοῖς συμφορῶν λειπομένη. Οἵ τε ἄνδρες τῆς πόλεως ἀνὰ τὴν Ἀσίαν τε καὶ Εὐρώπην, αἰχμάλωτοι γενόμενοι, περιήγοντο ἀνδραποδισθέντες. Ἡ μέντοι Οὐενετῶν φυλακὴ ἐν τῇ πόλει οὖσα, ὡς ᾔσθετο ἁλῶναι ἤδη τὴν πόλιν, ὥρμητο φυγεῖν ἐπὶ τὴν θάλατταν καὶ ἐπὶ τὰς ναῦς, καὶ ἐμβάντες εἰς ταύτας, ὅσαι σφίσι παροῦσαι ἐτύγχανον, ᾤχοντο ἀποπλέοντες. Ἡ μὲν δὴ πόλις αὕτη Ἑλληνὶς μεγάλη τε οὖσα καὶ εὐδαίμων ἑάλω ὑπὸ Ἀμουράτεω. Τὴν μέντοι πόλιν ἐπέτρεπε τοῖς αὐτοῦ ταύτῃ τῶν περιοίκων ἐνοικῆσαι. [2.15]

23 Αὐτὸς δὲ οἴκαδε ἐπανιὼν ἔπεμψε τὸν τῆς Εὐρώπης στρατηγὸν Καρατζίαν, ἐπὶ Ἰωάννινα πόλιν τῆς Αἰτωλίας, τὸ τῆς Εὐρώπης στράτευμα αὐτῷ παραδούς. Ὁ δὲ ὡς ἀφίκετο ἐπὶ τὴν Αἰτωλίαν, τήν τε χώραν ἐπέδραμε, καὶ ἐληΐσατο, ὅσα ἔφθη καταλαβεῖν ἄφνω, μετὰ δὲ ταῦτα ἐλάσας ἐπολιόρκει τὴν πόλιν. Κάρουλος μέντοι ὁ ἡγεμὼν

leading outside from within their houses but were captured by the Venetians; so it is said. The sappers escaped to Murad's camp, climbing down from the walls. But then he attacked from the direction of the citadel, took the city by force, and enslaved it.[29]

I have learned that the janissaries took the city after they scaled the walls, whereupon the others followed them and the city fell and was enslaved by the sultan. We have learned that when Murad was enslaving this city he spared no one from that fate, so that we may conclude that he displaced them on account of the betrayal. This was the biggest calamity suffered by the Greeks, second to none that had happened before. The men of the city were led as captives throughout Asia and Europe, and sold into slavery. As for the garrison of Venetians in the city, when they realized that the city was lost, they rushed to the sea to flee upon their ships; embarking upon as many as they had available, they sailed away. Thus this great and prosperous Greek city was taken by Murad. He allowed his men who lived in its vicinity to settle in the city. 22

Murad himself returned home and sent Karaja, the general of Europe, against Ioannina, a city of Aitolia, giving him the army of Europe.[30] When he arrived in Aitolia, he raided the land and plundered as much of it as he was able to take by surprise; after that, he advanced and besieged the city. 23

τῆς πόλεως ἤδη ἐτελεύτησε· καὶ ἐπειδὴ παῖς αὐτῷ ἐκ τῆς γυναικὸς αὐτοῦ τῆς Ῥαινερίου θυγατρὸς οὐκ ἐγένετο, νόθοι δὲ ἐγένοντο παῖδες, ὅ τε Μέμνων καὶ Τύρνος καὶ Ἑρκούλιος οἱ πρεσβύτεροι, διένειμε τούτοις μὲν τὴν ἐντὸς τοῦ Ἀχελῴου χώραν Ἀκαρνανίας ἐπινέμεσθαι, τὸν δὲ ἀδελφιδοῦν αὐτοῦ, τὸν Λεονάρδου παῖδα, κατέλιπε διάδοχον ξυμπάσης ἤδη τῆς ἀρχῆς αὐτοῦ, καὶ τήν τε Ἄρτην τῆς Ἀμπρακίας μητρόπολιν καὶ Αἰτωλίαν τε καὶ τὴν πόλιν κατέλιπε Καρούλῳ τῷ ἀδελφιδῷ. Οἱ μέντοι νόθοι παῖδες αὐτῷ οὐκ εἰς μακρὰν διενεχθέντες ἀφίκοντο ἐπὶ τὰς βασιλέως θύρας. Μέμνων δ' αὖ ἀφικόμενος, ὡς ἐδόκει τε τῶν ἄλλων συνέσει τε καὶ ἀξιώσει προέχειν, οὗτος δὲ ἀφικόμενος παρὰ τὸν βασιλέα προὐκαλεῖτο τε καὶ ἠξίου ἐπὶ τὴν χώραν σφᾶς τὴν πατρῴαν κατάγειν. Διὸ δὴ ἐλάσας σὺν τῷ τῆς Εὐρώπης στρατεύματι εἰσῄει.

24 Ὁ δὲ τῆς Εὐρώπης στρατηγὸς τὴν τῶν Ἰωαννίνων πόλιν ἐπολιόρκει, καὶ χρόνον ἐνδιατρίβων τῇ πολιορκίᾳ, ὡς οὐδὲν ἀνίει πολιορκῶν, ὁρῶντες οἱ τῆς πόλεως καὶ ὁ τῆς χώρας ἡγεμών, ἐντὸς ἀπειλημμένος καὶ πολιορκούμενος, προὐκαλεῖτο τὸν στρατηγὸν ἐπὶ ξύμβασιν, καὶ αἰτεῖτο αὐτὸν δοθῆναι αὐτῷ τήν τε ἄλλην χώραν [2.16] τῆς Ἀκαρνανίας καὶ τῆς Ἠπείρου παρὰ βασιλέως, καὶ σπονδὰς αὐτῷ ἐπὶ τούτῳ γενέσθαι, καὶ οὕτω παραδιδόναι τὴν πόλιν. Τούτου δὴ γενομένου τήν τε πόλιν παρέλαβε τὸ τοῦ βασιλέως στράτευμα, καὶ αὐτῷ συνεχώρει τὴν Ἀκαρνανίαν καὶ τὴν ἄλλην Ἤπειρον ἐπινέμεσθαι, φόρον ἀπάγοντα τῷ βασιλεῖ τοῦ ἐνιαυτοῦ, καὶ αὐτὸν φοιτῶντα ἐς τὰς βασιλέως θύρας.

Carlo, the ruler of the city, had already died.[31] As he had no son by his wife, the daughter of Nerio, but had illegitimate sons of whom the eldest were Memnon, Torno, and Ercole, he had divided up the land of Akarnania that is within the Acheloös and distributed it to them. But he left his nephew, the son of Leonardo, as heir to the principality as a whole. Arta, then, the capital of Ambrakia, Aitolia, and the city of Ioannina he had left to his nephew Carlo [II].[32] But shortly afterward his illegitimate sons fell out with his nephew and went to the sultan's Porte. Memnon also went, who seemed to surpass the others in intelligence and had the stronger claim, and when he arrived before the sultan he appealed to him and requested that he restore them to their native land. That is why he marched and invaded with the army of Europe.

The general of Europe besieged the city of Ioannina and 24
spent some time pressing the siege, without letting up at all in his efforts. The people of the city and its ruler [Carlo II], who were besieged inside and cut off, saw this and they appealed to the general for an agreement. The ruler asked to be given the rest of Akarnania and Epeiros by the sultan, and on that basis he would make a treaty with him and thus surrender the city. This was granted and so the sultan's army took possession of the city, while he [Carlo II] was granted Akarnania and the rest of Epeiros to rule, paying an annual tribute to the sultan and personally attending the sultan's Porte.[33]

25 Ὕστερον δὲ ἀφικόμενοι οἱ τοῦ Καρούλου ἡγεμόνος παῖδες, ὅ τε Ἑρκούλιος καὶ Μέμνων, καὶ οὐκ ὀλίγα κατασχόντες τῆς χώρας ἐπαγομένων τῶν ἐποίκων αὐτούς, πράγματά τε παρεῖχον τῷ ἀνεψιῷ αὐτῶν, καὶ ἦγον καὶ ἔφερον τὴν χώραν καὶ ἐπολέμουν. Ὁ μέντοι Κάρουλος καὶ ἀπὸ τῶν θυρῶν τοῦ βασιλέως στράτευμα ἐπαγόμενος ἐπὶ τούτους καὶ ἀπὸ Ἰταλίας, ὡς οὐδὲν ἤνυεν, ἐσπένδετό τε αὐτοῖς καὶ καθυφίετο τῆς χώρας, ἧς ἦρχον, ἐφ' ᾧ μηκέτι αὐτῷ τοῦ λοιποῦ παρέχειν πράγματα. Αἰτωλία μὲν δὴ οὕτω ἐγένετο ὑπὸ βασιλεῖ Ἀμουράτῃ.

26 Μετὰ δὲ ταῦτα ὡς Ἕλληνες ἰόντες ἐς τὰς θύρας ἠξίουν σφίσι σπένδεσθαι, εἰρήνην μέντοι ἐποιήσαντο, ἐφ' ᾧ τόν τε Ἰσθμὸν καθελεῖν καὶ μηδὲν ἔτι νεωτερίζειν τοῦ λοιποῦ. Τὸν μέντοι Τουραχάνην ἐπὶ Πελοπόννησον πέμψας τήν τε Οὐενετῶν χώραν ἐδῄου, καὶ τὸν Ἰσθμὸν καθεῖλε καὶ πολίσματα ἄττα ἑλὼν τῶν Οὐενετῶν ἠνδραποδίσατο. Ἐνταῦθα μὲν οὖν ἐξιόντι ἀπὸ Πελοποννήσου συνελέγοντο οἱ τῆς Πελοποννήσου Ἀλβανοὶ περὶ τὴν μεσόγαιον, Δαβίην καλουμένην χώραν, καὶ σφίσι στρατηγὸν ἐστήσαντο, καὶ ἀπόστασιν ἐβουλεύοντο ἀπὸ Ἑλλήνων, ὡς τὸ Τουραχάνεω στράτευμα διαφθείρωσι. Τουραχάνης μέντοι ὡς ἐπύθετο τοὺς Ἀλβανοὺς ἐπ' αὐτὸν ὁμόσε ἰόντας ὡς διὰ μάχης, ὡς οὐκ ἠδύνατο [2.17] διαφυγεῖν, παρετάξατό τε εἰς μάχην. Καὶ οἱ Ἀλβανοὶ συνταξάμενοι καὶ αὐτοὶ ἐπῄεσαν, καὶ ἐς χεῖρας ἐλθόντες οὐδὲ ἐδέξαντο τοὺς Τούρκους, ἀλλ' ἐτράποντο ἐς φυγήν. Ἐνταῦθα ἐπεξελθὼν ὁ Τουραχάνης ἐπιδιώκων πολλούς τε ἀνεῖλεν ἐν τῇ διώξει, καὶ οὓς

Then Ercole and Memnon, the sons of the ruler Carlo [I], arrived and took over much of the land at the instigation of the local inhabitants. They caused great difficulties to their cousin, troubled the land far and wide, and made war. Carlo [II] led an army against them from the sultan's Porte and from Italy, but he accomplished nothing, so he made a treaty with them and ceded the land that they already held on the condition that they no longer cause him any trouble. Thus did Aitolia come under the power of Sultan Murad. 25

After that the Greeks came to the Porte and requested that he make a treaty with them, and they did conclude a peace on condition that they dismantle the Isthmos fortification and never again rebel against him. He dispatched Turahan to the Peloponnese to plunder Venetian territory, and he dismantled the Isthmos fortifications and captured some towns of the Venetians, enslaving them.[34] Whereupon, as he was departing from the Peloponnese, the Albanians of the Peloponnese assembled in the interior, at a place called Davia, appointed a general of their own, and decided to break with the Greeks and destroy the army of Turahan. When Turahan learned that the Albanians were coming together against him to do battle, he also deployed for battle, seeing as he was unable to escape. The Albanians also deployed and attacked, and when they came to blows they did not withstand the Turks, but turned to flee. Turahan then advanced in pursuit, killing many in the pursuit. He 26

ἐζώγρησεν ἀμφὶ τοὺς ὀκτακοσίους, αὐτοῦ ἅπαντας διεχρήσατο, καὶ ταῖς κεφαλαῖς αὐτῶν πυργία ἐποικοδομησάμενος ἀπῄει ἐξελαύνων. Τούτῳ μὲν οὖν τἀνδρὶ ἔστι καὶ ἄλλα ἀποδεδειγμένα ἔργα ἐς ἀφήγησιν οὐκ ἀχρεῖα, δι᾿ ἃ δὴ εὐδοκιμῶν παρὰ βασιλεῖ ἐπὶ τὴν τοῦ Βρενέζεω χώραν ἐχώρει. Καὶ ἐπὶ Δακίαν οὐ πολλῷ ὕστερον πεμφθεὶς ὑπὸ Ἀμουράτεω τήν τε χώραν ἐδῄωσε, καὶ στρατὸν αὐτοῦ συλλεχθέντα οὐ σμικρὸν ἐτρέψατο, καὶ νίκην ἀνείλετο περιφανῆ ἀνδράποδά τε καὶ λείαν πολλήν.

27 Τοῖς μὲν οὖν Ἕλλησι θαμὰ ἰοῦσιν ἐπὶ τὰς θύρας αὐτοῦ, καὶ ἄνδρας τοὺς παρὰ σφίσι πρωτεύοντας ἄλλους τε δὴ καὶ Νοταρᾶν τὸν Λουκᾶν ὄλβιον ἐπιπέμψασι, σπονδὰς ἐποιήσατο. Ὁ μὲν οὖν Ἑλλήνων βασιλεύς, ὡς εἰρήνη ἐγένετο, ἔπλει ἐπὶ Πελοπόννησον, μεταπεμπομένου τοῦ ἀδελφοῦ Θεοδώρου τοῦ Σπάρτης ἡγεμόνος, ὅς, ὡς καὶ πρότερον λέξεως, διὰ τὸ πρὸς τὴν γυναῖκα αὐτοῦ τὴν ἀπὸ Ἰταλίας ἔχθος αὐτῷ γενόμενον ὥρμητο ἐπὶ τὴν Ναζηραίων ἰέναι δίαιταν. Ὡς μέντοι ἐς Πελοπόννησον ἀφίκετο ὁ Βυζαντίου βασιλεύς, τόν τε ἀδελφὸν αὐτοῦ Κωνσταντῖνον ἐπαγόμενος ὡς διαδεξόμενον τὴν ἀρχήν, μετεμέλησέ τε [2.18] αὐτίκα καὶ οὐκ ἔφασκεν ἰέναι ἔτι, μὴ ἐπιτρεπόντων τῶν τῆς χώρας ἀρίστων. Διηλλάγη μέντοι καὶ τῇ γυναικὶ μετὰ ταῦτα, καὶ ἐβίου ἡδέως συνὼν αὐτῇ τοῦ λοιποῦ.

28 Ὁ μέντοι Ἑλλήνων βασιλεὺς πρός τε τὸν τῆς Ἠπείρου ἡγεμόνα τὸν Κάρουλον πόλεμον ἐξήνεγκε, καὶ Κλαρεντίαν τῆς Ἤλιδος μητρόπολιν ἐπολιόρκει. Μετ᾿ οὐ πολὺν δὲ χρόνον, ὡς οὐδὲν αὐτῷ προεχώρει πολιορκοῦντι,

captured about eight hundred alive, all of whom he killed on the spot.[35] He erected towers with their heads and then departed. There are other deeds carried out by this man that are worth relating, through which he came to be esteemed by the sultan and advanced to the status of Evrenos.[36] Shortly afterward he was dispatched by Murad against Wallachia and plundered the land. He routed a large army that was assembled there and gained a glorious victory along with many slaves and much loot.[37]

So Murad made a treaty with the Greeks, who were coming often to his Porte and sending their leading men, including the wealthy Loukas Notaras.[38] As for the king of the Greeks [Ioannes VIII], when the peace had been established, he sailed to the Peloponnese when he was summoned by his brother Theodoros [II], ruler of Mistra. As I mentioned earlier, he had decided to assume the monastic habit out of hatred for his Italian wife.[39] When the king of Byzantion arrived in the Peloponnese, he brought his brother Konstantinos to succeed as ruler there,[40] but then Theodoros suddenly changed his mind and said he would not do it, as the leading men of the land would not permit it. After that he was reconciled to his wife as well, and he lived with her happily ever after. 27

The king of the Greeks then made war against Carlo [I], the ruler of Epeiros, and besieged Glarentsa, the capital of Elis. Shortly afterward, as he was making no progress in the siege, he married the ruler's niece, the daughter of 28

ἡρμόσατο τὴν ἀδελφιδοῦν ἡγεμόνος, Λεονάρδου δὲ θυγατέρα, ἐπὶ τῷ ἀδελφῷ Κωνσταντίνῳ, ὥστε καὶ ἡ πόλις αὕτη ἐδόθη αὐτῷ ἐς φερνήν. Καὶ βασιλεὺς Ἑλλήνων ἐπολιόρκει Πάτρας τῆς Ἀχαΐας, μετὰ δὲ ταῦτα καταλιπὼν τὸν ἀδελφὸν αὐτοῦ Κωνσταντῖνον ᾤχετο ἀποπλέων ἐπὶ Βυζαντίου. Τῷ μέντοι ἀδελφῷ αὐτοῦ Κωνσταντίνῳ ὡς τὰ περὶ τὴν πόλιν προσεχώρησε καὶ πολιορκῶν οὐκ ἀνίει τὴν πόλιν, συντίθενται οἱ τῆς πόλεως ἄνδρες προδοσίαν αὐτῷ, καὶ ἐπαγόμενοι τὴν πόλιν παρεδίδοσαν, ἀπόντος τοῦ ἀρχιερέως αὐτῆς ἐν Ἰταλίᾳ, ὅσον διατρίβοντος χρόνον, ἐπικουρίας δεόμενον παρὰ τοῦ Ῥωμαίων ἀρχιερέως.

29 Ταύτην μὲν οὖν τὴν πόλιν Ἀχαΐας οἱ ἀπὸ Ἰταλίας Πελοποννήσου ἡγεμόνες, τοῦ Ζαχαριῶν οἴκου, διϊόντες, ὁ μὲν ἄρχων τε καὶ ἡγεμὼν κατελείφθη τῆς χώρας, τῷ δὲ ἑτέρῳ διατρίβοντι παρὰ τῷ Ῥωμαίων ἀρχιερεῖ ταύτην ἐπέδωκε τὴν πόλιν ἀρχιερεῖ γενομένῳ ἐπιτροπεύειν. Ἡ μέντοι πόλις παρελθοῦσα ἐς τὸν Ῥωμαίων ἀρχιερέα ἐλάμβανεν ἀρχιερέα, ὃν ἂν ἐπιπέμψει ἐς σφᾶς [2.19] τοῦ ἐπιτροπεύειν τὴν πόλιν· καὶ τότε δὴ Μαλατεσταίων τοῦ οἴκου ἐπεπόμφει τοῖς ἐν τῇ πόλει ἀρχιερέα. Ταύτην μὲν οὖν τὴν πόλιν ἐπεί τε παρέλαβε Κωνσταντῖνος, τήν τε ἀκρόπολιν ἐπολιόρκει ἐπ' ἐνιαυτόν· μετὰ δὲ ταῦτα προσεχώρησεν αὐτῷ. Τὴν μέντοι Ἤλιδος μητρόπολιν εἷλον αἱ τοῦ ἀρχιερέως τριήρεις. Ἐπεί τε γὰρ ἐπύθετο τὴν πόλιν τῆς Ἀχαΐας ἁλῶναι ὑπὸ Ἑλλήνων, ἔπεμψε δέκα, εἰ δύναιντο τὴν πόλιν αὐτῷ παραστήσασθαι. Αὗται μὲν οὖν ἐπὶ Ἀχαΐαν οὐκέτι ἀφίκοντο, ἐπὶ δὲ τὴν Κλαρεντίαν ἀφικόμεναι ἀπόντος αὐτῇ τοῦ ἄρχοντος, καὶ φρουρᾶς οὐκ ἐνούσης ἐν τῇ πόλει,

Leonardo, to his brother Konstantinos, so that this city was given to him as a dowry.[41] The king of the Greeks also began the siege of Patras, in Achaïa, and after that he left his brother Konstantinos there and sailed away to Byzantion. When the areas around the city joined his brother Konstantinos and he would not let up in his siege of the city itself, the men of the city entered into discussions with him to betray the city to him and, inviting him in, they surrendered it to him while their bishop was away in Italy, spending time there while he sought help from the pontiff of the Romans.[42]

The Italian rulers of the Peloponnese, from the house of Zaccaria, had passed through this city of Achaïa, and one stayed behind as lord and ruler of the land while the other visited the pontiff of the Romans, who entrusted the city to him to supervise as its bishop.[43] So the city had passed to the pontiff of the Romans and received from him its own bishop, whomever he sent to them to supervise the city.[44] At that time he had sent as bishop to the citizens a member of the Malatesta family.[45] When Konstantinos took over this city, he continued to besiege the acropolis for one year. After that, it surrendered to him. But the triremes of the pontiff took the capital of Elis. For when he learned that the city of Achaïa [Patras] had been taken by Greeks, he sent ten of them in the hope that they would take the city back for him. But they did not go to Achaïa, for when they reached Glarentsa, the ruler was absent and there was no 29

εἰσελθόντες λάθρᾳ τὴν πόλιν κατέσχον καὶ ἠνδραποδίσαντο. Ὕστερον δὲ ἀποδιδόμενοι ταύτην τῷ βασιλέως ἀδελφῷ πεντακισχιλίων χρυσίνων ἀπέπλευσαν ἐπὶ Ἰταλίας.

30 Ξυνέβησαν δὲ τῇ πόλει ταύτῃ καὶ τύχαι ἄλλαι πρότερον γενόμεναι. Ὀλιβέριος γὰρ δὴ ἀπὸ Ἰταλίας ὁρμώμενος, ἔχοντος ταύτην τοῦ τῆς Ἀχαΐας ἡγεμόνος, ἐπεισελθών τε ἄφνω καὶ καταλαβὼν τὴν πόλιν ἠνδραποδίσατο, καὶ τὴν θυγατέρα ἡγεμόνος ἐς γυναῖκα αὐτῷ ἠγάγετο. Καὶ ταύτην μέντοι οὗτος ἀποδόμενος τῷ τῆς Ἠπείρου ἡγεμόνι ᾤχετο ἐς Ἰταλίαν. Καὶ τότε μὲν δὴ ἁλοῦσαν ὑπὸ τῶν ἀρχιερέως τριηρῶν αὖθις ἐξωνησάμενος ἀπέλαβε. Διέφερον μὲν οὖν καὶ πρὸς τὸν τῆς Ἀχαΐας ἡγεμόνα Ἰταλικὸν, Κεντηρίωνα, οἱ Ἕλληνες τὸν πόλεμον ἐπὶ συχνόν τινα χρόνον· μετὰ δὲ ταῦτα ἐπιγαμίαν ποιησάμενοι ἐπὶ τῷ βασιλέως παιδὶ τῷ νεωτέρῳ Θωμᾷ, ἁρμοσάμενοι τὴν θυγατέρα τοῦ ἡγεμόνος, καὶ τήν τε χώραν ἐς φερνὴν αὐτοῦ ἐπέδωκαν τῆς Μεσήνης τε [2.20] καὶ Ἰθώμης, πλὴν τῆς παραλίου Ἀρκαδίας, σπονδάς τε ἐποιήσαντο. Καὶ ταύτην μὲν οὖν, ἐπεί τε ἐτελεύτησε, παρέλαβε Θωμᾶς ὁ τοῦ βασιλέως ἀδελφός, καὶ τήν τε γυναῖκα τοῦ Κεντηρίωνος εἶχεν ἐν φυλακῇ, ἐς ἣν δὴ καὶ ἐτελεύτησε. Οὕτω μὲν οὖν ἡ Πελοπόννησος ἀπὸ Ἰταλῶν ἐς τοὺς Ἕλληνας περιῆλθεν. Ἕλλησι μὲν οὖν οὕτω προσέφερε τὰ πράγματα, ὑπαγομένοις σφίσι τὴν Πελοπόννησον.

31 Ἀμουράτης δὲ ὁ Μεχμέτεω ἐστρατεύετο ἐπὶ τὴν Τριβαλλῶν χώραν. Καὶ πρότερον μέν, ἐπεί τε ἐξήνεγκε πόλεμον, στρατεύματα ἐπιπέμψας ἐδῄου τὴν χώραν. Καὶ τότε

garrison in the city, so they entered that city by stealth, captured it, and enslaved it. Later they sold it to the brother of the king [Thomas?] for five thousand gold coins, and sailed back to Italy.[46]

The city [Patras] had previously experienced other vicis- 30
situdes of fortune as well. For Oliverio had set out from Italy when the city was being held by the ruler of Achaïa, and he attacked it suddenly, took it, and enslaved it. He took the ruler's daughter as his wife. He then sold it to the ruler of Epeiros [Carlo I] and departed for Italy.[47] When it was taken by the pontiff's triremes, he[48] bought it and took it back again. Thus the Greeks were at war with the Italian ruler of Achaïa, Centurione, for a long time. After that they made a marriage alliance: Thomas, the king's younger son, married his daughter and received as dowry the territories of Mesene and Ithome, except for coastal Kyparissia; and so they made a treaty. And when he [Centurione] died, this land too was received by Thomas, the king's brother, who kept Centurione's wife in prison, where she died.[49] Thus the Peloponnese passed from the hands of the Italians into those of the Greeks. And this was the situation for the Greeks, who had now subjected the Peloponnese to themselves.

Murad, the son of Mehmed, now marched against the 31
land of the Serbs. He had brought war to them earlier, when he sent armies to plunder their land.[50] At this time, then,

δὴ οὖν, ὡς ἐπύθετο ὁ τῶν Τριβαλλῶν ἡγεμὼν ἐπιέναι ἐπ' αὐτὸν βασιλέα, πρέσβεις τε ἐπεπόμφει, καὶ ἠξίου σπονδὰς ποιεῖσθαι, ἐφ' ᾧ ἂν ἀπάγειν φόρον, ὃν ἂν τάξηται αὐτῷ βασιλεύς, καὶ πείσεσθαι, ὅ τι ἂν κελεύοι αὐτῷ. Ἐνταῦθα Ἀμουράτης ἄγεται τὴν θυγατέρα τοῦ Τριβαλλῶν ἡγεμόνος. Ἐπιπέμψας δὲ Σαραζίην τὸν τῶν θυρῶν ἡγεμόνα ἠγάγετό τε τὴν γυναῖκα, τοῦ Χαλίλεω ἀνάγοντος, παρ' αὐτῷ μέγα εὐδοκιμοῦντος, κατὰ τὰ βασίλεια αὐτοῦ.

32 Μετὰ δὲ ταῦτα ἤλαυνεν ἐπὶ Καραμᾶνον τὸν Ἀλισούριον, ἡγεμόνα τῆς Καρίας, τά τε ἄλλα αἰτιασάμενος, καὶ ὅτι τὸν ἀδελφὸν αὐτοῦ τὸν νεώτερον ἔχων παρ' ἑαυτῷ ἔπεμψεν ἐπὶ τοὺς Ἕλληνας. Ἐπιὼν δὲ σὺν στρατεύματι πολλῷ τὴν χώραν ἐδῄου, ἐκλελοιπότος αὐτὴν τοῦ Καραμάνου καὶ τὰ ἄκρα [2.21] κατέχοντος τῶν ὀρέων. Ἐστὸν δὲ αὐτῷ δύο πόλεε, ἡ μὲν Λάρανδα λεγομένη, ἡ δὲ τὸ Ἰκόνιον, πόλις μεγάλη τε οὖσα τὸ παλαιὸν καὶ εὐδαίμων, ἐν ᾗ καὶ βασιλὶς ἦν τῶν πρόσθεν βασιλέων τοῦ γένους τούτου· ἅτε γὰρ τῶν ὀρέων τῆς χώρας ἰσχυρῶν ὄντων καὶ οὐκ εὐπετῶν ἐπιβῆναι, ὁρμώμενοι τὴν ταύτῃ χώραν περίοικον ἦγον καὶ ἔφερον καὶ κατὰ βραχὺ προϊόντες κατεστρέφοντο. Ἔστι δ' ἡ πόλις αὕτη εὐνομουμένη ἀπὸ τοῦ πάνυ παλαιοῦ. Λάρανδα δὲ ἡ πόλις ᾤκηται μὲν αὕτη ὑπὸ τὴν ὑπώρειαν τῶν ταύτῃ ὀρέων, καὶ οὐ πάνυ ἑάλω τινὶ ὀχυρώματι. Ἡ δὲ χώρα ἐπιόντος τοῦ Ἀμουράτεω ὑπέμενέ τε καὶ οὐκ ἐξέλιπεν· οὐ γὰρ δὴ νομίζεται Τούρκους γε ὄντας αὐτοὺς ἀνδραποδίζεσθαι, ἐς τὰ αὐτά τε ἅμα ἤθη καὶ ἐς τὴν αὐτὴν δίαιταν καθισταμένους.

33 Ὁ μέντοι Καραμᾶνος οὗτος ὅμορός ἐστι τῇ Πισιδῶν

when the ruler of the Serbs learned that the sultan was attacking him, he sent envoys asking to make a treaty and proposing that he pay whatever tribute the sultan set for him, and obey him in all matters. Thereupon Murad married the daughter of the ruler of the Serbs.[51] After dispatching as envoy Saraja, the lord of the Porte, he married the woman once Halil, who was held in high esteem by him,[52] escorted her to his palace.

After that Murad set out against Karaman Alishur, the 32
ruler of Karia,[53] accusing him, among other things, of keeping his own younger brother [Mustafa] by his side and then sending him to the Greeks.[54] He went against him with a large army and plundered his land, after Karaman abandoned it, withdrawing to the mountain heights. He had two cities, one called Laranda and the other Ikonion, which formerly used to be a large and prosperous city, and the palace of the former kings of his family was there. Because the mountains of this land are formidable and inaccessible, Murad's army invaded the surrounding territory, raided far and wide, and, advancing by stages, conquered it. This city has been well governed since the most ancient times.[55] As for the city of Laranda, it is settled at the foot of the mountains there and cannot be captured by any kind of counterfortification. When Murad attacked them, the people of this land stayed put and did not flee, for it would not have been according to tradition to enslave them, given that they too were Turks, with the same customs and way of life.

Karaman shares borders with the land of the Pisidians 33

χώρᾳ καὶ τῇ Τουργούτεω. Οἱ δὲ Πισιδῖται οὗτοι καὶ Βαρσάκιδες καλούμενοι νομάδες μέν εἰσι καὶ γλώττῃ τῇ Τούρκων διαχρώμενοι, ληστρικώτερον δὲ βιοτεύουσι, τήν τε Συρίαν ληϊζόμενοι καὶ τὴν ἄλλην σφίσιν χώραν, καὶ δὴ τὴν Καραμάνου διαπολεμοῦντες ληΐζονται. Ἄρχοντες δὲ σφίσιν ἐφεστῶτες καὶ ληϊζόμενοι τῆς τε λείας τὸ ἐπιβάλλον [2.22] μέρος αὐτοί τε διαλαγχάνουσι, καὶ τοῖς οἴκοι ἐπὶ ταῖς γυναιξὶν ἐπιμένουσιν ἐπιδιελόμενοι διδόασι τὸ ἄλκιμον μέρος. Τουργούτης δὲ τῆς Φρυγίας χώρας ἐπάρχει τε, καὶ ἐπὶ Ἀρμενίαν ἥκει καὶ Καππάδοκας ἡ χώρα αὐτοῦ. Τὸ δὲ Τουργούτεω γένος δοκεῖ νεώτερον γεγονέναι ὑπὸ Ἀμουράτη,[3] καὶ ἐπικαταβὰν ἐς τὴν ταύτῃ τῆς Φρυγίας χώραν ἐπικρατῆσαί τε τὸ ἀπὸ τοῦδε τῆς χώρας, καὶ ἐς δεῦρο διαγενόμενον πρός τε τοὺς παῖδάς τε καὶ Καραμᾶνον διαπολεμεῖν. Διεπολέμησε μὲν οὖν τὸ παλαιὸν καὶ πρὸς τοὺς Λευκάρνας Καραϊλούκεω παῖδας. Τὸ μέντοι Κανδυλόρον ἡ πόλις τῆς Καρίας ὑπὸ ἀνδρὶ τοὔνομα [. . .]

34 Καὶ τὴν χώραν καταστρεψάμενος Ἀμουράτης ὁ Μεχμέτεω τήν τε θυγατέρα αὐτοῦ ἔσχεν ἐς τὴν γυναικωνῖτιν, καὶ τὸν παῖδα αὐτοῦ κατέλιπεν ἄρχειν τῆς χώρας. Τοὺς μέντοι ἡγεμόνας, τόν τε Κερμιανὸν καὶ Ἀϊδίνην, ἐλαύνων ἐπὶ Καραμᾶνον, καὶ τόν τε Σαρχάνην τῆς τε χώρας ἐξήλασε, καὶ ἐπιὼν τὰ βασίλεια αὐτῶν ἠνδραποδίσατο. Ὁ μέντοι Ἀϊδίνης ἐτελεύτησεν ἄπαις ὤν, Σαρχάνης δὲ καὶ Μενδεσίας ἐπὶ τὰς ὁμόρους αὐτῶν χώρας διεσώζοντο, ἀποφυγόντες Ἀμουράτην ἐπιόντα. Μενδεσίας μέντοι ἐς Ῥόδον ἀφικόμενος διέτριβε, μετὰ δὲ ταῦτα κηρυκευσάμενος ἀφίκετο παρὰ βασιλέα, δεόμενος τυχεῖν ἀγαθοῦ τινος

and that of Turgut.[56] The Pisidians, who are also called Barsakids, are nomads and speak the language of the Turks; they make their living through brigandage, plundering Syria and the rest of the land there.[57] They also attack the land of Karaman with their raids. When the leaders placed over them go raiding, it is they who divide up the portions from the loot, giving the better shares to those who were assigned to stay at home with the women. Turgut rules over the land of Phrygia and his territory extends as far as Armenia and the Kappadokians. The family of Turgut would appear to be more recent than that of Murad.[58] They descended upon this part of the land of Phrygia and have held sway over it since that time. They have survived down to this day, fighting against their children and Karaman.[59] In the past this clan also fought against the White Sheep, the sons of Kara Yülük.[60] Kandyloron, the city of Karia,[61] [. . .] under a man named [. . .]

After conquering the land, Murad, the son of Mehmed, 34
took the daughter [of Karaman] for his own harem and placed his son in charge of the land. During his march against Karaman, he drove the rulers out of that land, Germiyan, Aydın, and Saruhan. He advanced against their royal capitals and enslaved them.[62] Now Aydın died without children, but Saruhan and Menteşe sought refuge in neighboring lands, and so escaped from Murad's advance. Menteşe went to Rhodes and spent some time there, but after that he sent a herald and went to Sultan Murad, asking to receive

πρὸς τοῦ βασιλέως, καὶ [2.23] ἐς δεῦρο ἔτι διατρίβων τὴν δαπάνην ἔχει ὑπὸ τῶν θυρῶν. Ὁ μέντοι Καραμᾶνος, ὡς τό τε Ἰκόνιον κατειλήφει καὶ τὴν χώραν αὐτοῦ κατέχων διέτριβεν, ἔπεμπε πρέσβεις παρ' Ἀμουράτην, ὑπισχνούμενος τήν τε θυγατέρα δοῦναι αὐτῷ εἰς γυναῖκα καὶ τὸν παῖδα αὐτοῦ ἐπιπέμπειν συστρατευόμενον ἐπὶ τὰς Ἀμουράτεω θύρας. Ὁ μὲν δὴ Ἀμουράτης ἐπείθετο, τὰς σπονδὰς καὶ ὅρκια ποιησάμενος ἀπήλαυνεν ἐπὶ τῆς Εὐρώπης.

35 Μετὰ δὲ ταῦτα χρόνου ἐπιγιγνομένου αἰτιασάμενος Ἰσμαήλην τὸν Σινώπης καὶ Κασταμωνίας ἡγεμόνα ἐστρατεύετο ἐπ' αὐτόν. Οὗτος μὲν οὖν ὡς ἐπύθετο ἐπ' αὐτὸν ἐπιέναι Ἀμουράτην, πρέσβεις ἔπεμψε, καὶ τὴν μὲν τοῦ χαλκοῦ πρόσοδον ὑπέσχετο ἀποφέρειν τοῦ ἐνιαυτοῦ, ὅση ἂν αὐτῷ τυγχάνοι οὖσα, καὶ τόν γε παῖδα ὑπισχνεῖτο ἐπιπέμπειν καὶ οὗτος ἐς τὰς βασιλέως θύρας. Τὸν μέντοι Τουργούτεω παῖδα καὶ πρότερον ἔτι παραγενόμενον ἐπὶ τὰς βασιλέως θύρας ἐπυθόμεθα ἐπαγαγέσθαι βασιλέα, καὶ ἐπιτρέπειν τὴν χώραν αὐτῷ διαθεῖναι, ᾗ ἂν αὐτῷ δοκοίη. Ταῦτα μὲν αὐτῷ ἐς τὴν Ἀσίαν ἐπέπρακτο, λαμπρὰ ἀποδεδειγμένα ἐς τὴν ἀρχὴν αὐτῷ. Καὶ πρός τε τοὺς Λευκάρνας ἐπολέμει συχνόν τινα χρόνον.

36 Ἐγένετο δὲ ἐκ τοῦ Ἀμουράτεω ἔλευσις ἐπὶ Τριβαλλῶν ἡγεμόνα καὶ ἐπὶ τὸν ἡγεμόνα Γεώργιον τὸν κηδεστὴν αὐτοῦ δι' αἰτίαν τήνδε. Στέφανον γὰρ τὸν νεώτερον [2.24] παῖδα ἔχων παρ' ἑαυτῷ διατρίβοντα, ὡς μέντοι ἐπήλαυνεν ἐπιὼν ἐπὶ Σπενδέροβον, ἐν ᾗ τὰ βασίλεια ἦν αὐτοῖς. Ὁ μέντοι ἡγεμὼν καταλιπὼν τὸν παῖδα αὐτοῦ Γούργουρον ἐπιτροπεύειν τε τὴν πόλιν καὶ φυλάττειν τὰ τείχη, ἣν

some benefit from him, and to this day he is still in attendance, being maintained by the Porte.[63] As for Karaman, when Ikonion was captured and Murad was spending time in his land, which he had occupied,[64] he sent envoys to Murad, promising to give him his daughter in marriage and to send him his son to campaign with Murad's Porte. Murad agreed, concluded a treaty with sworn oaths, and then marched back to Europe.

A year after that Murad leveled accusations against 35
İsmail, the ruler of Sinope and Kastamonu, and marched against him.[65] When the latter learned that Murad was coming against him, he sent envoys and promised to pay the annual income from the copper, whatever it happened to be, and he also promised to send his son to the sultan's Porte. I have learned that the son of Turgut[66] had, even before this, attended the sultan's Porte to win the sultan's favor, and entrusted him to govern that land, however he thought best. These, then, were his deeds in Asia, and they brought glory to his rule. He also fought against the White Sheep for a long time.

Murad then advanced against the ruler of the Serbs and 36
against the ruler Đurađ,[67] his relation by marriage, for the following reason. Stefan, the ruler's younger son, was attending upon Murad as he marched against Smederevo, where their royal court was. The ruler had left his son Grgur to supervise the city and guard the walls, in case the enemy

ἐπίωσιν οἱ πολέμιοι, αὐτὸς ἐπὶ Παιονίας ἀπῄει ἐπικουρίας δεησόμενος· ὑπῆν γὰρ αὐτῷ καὶ ἐν τῇ Παιονίᾳ χώρα τε οὐ φαύλη καὶ πόλεις πολλαὶ καὶ ἀγαθαί, ἃς ἠλλάξατο Ἐλεάζαρος πρὸς τὸν Παιόνων βασιλέα Σιγισμοῦνδον ἀντὶ τῆς Μπελογράδης πόλεως, ἧς ἐδεδώκει τῷ βασιλεῖ ὥστε τῷ πορθμῷ καλῶς ἔχοντος τοῦ χωρίου. Ὁ μὲν οὖν παῖς αὐτοῦ καταλέλειπτο ἐπιτροπεύων τὴν πόλιν, καὶ παρεσκευάζετο ὡς πολιορκησόμενος. Ὡς δὲ ἐπιὼν ὁ Ἀμουράτης ἐπέδραμέ τε τὴν χώραν καὶ ἐπολιόρκει τὴν πόλιν, ἐπειρᾶτο μηχανὰς παντοίας προσάγων τῷ τείχει ἑλεῖν τὴν πόλιν. Ὡς δ' οὐδὲν αὐτῷ ἠνύετο, ἐδεδίττετο τὴν πόλιν τηλεβόλοις μεγίστοις δὴ τοῖς εἰς ἐκεῖνον τὸν χρόνον γενομένοις, καὶ τά γε τείχη τύπτων οὐκ ἀνίει. Ἐνταῦθα ὁ τοῦ ἡγεμόνος παῖς Γούργουρος, δεδιὼς μὴ ἁλῷ ἡ πόλις ὑπὸ τῶν τηλεβόλων, ἐδέχετο λόγους παρὰ βασιλέως περὶ συνθηκῶν, καὶ ἐσπένδετο, ἐφ' ᾧ παραδιδόναι τε τὴν πόλιν τῷ βασιλεῖ, καὶ αὐτοὺς ἐς τὰς θύρας αὐτῷ φοιτῶντας τυγχάνειν, ὧν ἂν δικαιοῖ αὐτὸς βασιλεὺς ἀποφέρεσθαι. Οὗτος μὲν οὖν τὴν πόλιν παρέδωκε, καὶ ἐς τὸ στρατόπεδον ἐξελθὼν διέτριβε παρὰ [2.25] βασιλέα σὺν τῷ ἀδελφῷ αὐτοῦ Στεφάνῳ.

37 Μετ' οὐ πολὺν δὲ χρόνον, ὡς ἐπύθετο τὸν πατέρα αὐτῶν ἐπαγόμενον ἐπὶ Ἀμουράτην καὶ τούς γε παῖδας παρὰ τοῦ πατρὸς λόγους τε δεχομένους καὶ κρύφα διακηρυκευομένους περὶ ἀποστάσεως, λαβὼν ἄμφω τὼ παῖδε ἐξώρυξε τὼ ὀφθαλμὼ ἑκατέρων. Ὡς μὲν οὖν Σπενδέροβον τὰ Τριβαλλῶν βασίλεια παρεστήσατο, καὶ φρουρὰν ἐγκατέλιπε τῇ πόλει ἱκανήν, αὐτίκα ἐπιὼν ἤλαυνεν ἐπὶ Μπελογράδην τὴν Παιόνων πόλιν. Ἔστι δ' αὕτη ἡ πόλις

attacked them, while he went off to Hungary to seek aid. For he had substantial territory in Hungary with many fine cities, which Lazar had received from Sigismund, the king of the Hungarians, in exchange for the city of Belgrade, which he had given to the king because the place had a good transit point.[68] So his son was left there to supervise the city and he prepared to be besieged. As Murad advanced he raided the land and besieged the city, attempting to take it by bringing every kind of engine against the walls. As he was accomplishing nothing, he terrorized the city with the largest cannons that existed at that time, and he did not let up in his battery of the walls. Thereupon the ruler's son Grgur, fearing that the city would be taken as a result of the cannon bombardment, agreed to negotiate with the sultan regarding terms, and he made a treaty according to which he would surrender the city to the sultan and they themselves would attend upon the sultan at the Porte, and would obtain whatever maintenance the sultan himself deemed appropriate. So after surrendering the city, he went out to the camp and attended upon the sultan together with his brother Stefan.[69]

Shortly afterward, when Murad learned that their father 37
[Đurađ] was coming against him and that the sons were in communication with their father and secretly putting out word of a rebellion, he took both young men and gouged their eyes out.[70] When he took over Smederevo, the royal capital of the Serbs, he left a large garrison in the city and then set out to march against Belgrade, the city of the Hungarians. This city is washed on both sides by two rivers, on

ἀμφοῖν τοῖν ποταμοῖν περίρρυτος γινομένη, ἀφ' ἑνὸς μὲν μέρους τοῦ Ἴστρου ῥέοντος, ἀφ' ἑτέρου δὲ τοῦ Σάβα, ὃς ἐς τὸν Ἴστρον αὐτοῦ παρὰ τῇ πόλει ταύτῃ ἐκδιδοῖ. Ἡ μὲν οὖν Σπενδέροβος καὶ αὕτη [. . .] ὡς δὲ ἐς Μπελογράδην ἐπελάσας ἐπολιόρκει τὴν πόλιν Ἀμουράτης ὁ Μεχμέτεω, ἔτυπτε μὲν τὸ τεῖχος τηλεβόλοις καὶ κατέβαλε μέρος οὐκ ὀλίγον, ἐπεπόνθει δὲ τὰ στρατεύματα πρὸς τῆς πόλεως ἀνήκεστα ὑπό τε τηλεβόλων καὶ τηλεβολίσκων παμπόλλων ἐς τὸ βασιλέως στρατόπεδον ἀφιεμένων ἐπὶ τοὺς ἄνδρας καὶ μυρία ὅσα βέλη ἀφικνουμένων ἐπὶ τὸ στρατόπεδον.

38 Ἐνταῦθα Ἀλίης ὁ τοῦ Βρενέζεω ἤκουσεν ἄριστα ἐν τῷ στρατοπέδῳ, ἀνήρ τε γενόμενος τὰ ἐς τειχομαχίαν σὺν τοῖς ἑαυτοῦ πρῶτος, καὶ τάφρον ὀρύξας ὡς ἐγγυτάτω τῆς πόλεως ἐσκήνου σὺν τῷ στρατεύματι αὐτοῦ. Ὡς μὲν οὖν τὸ τεῖχος κατεβέβλητο, εἰσεχέοντο δὲ εἰς τὴν πόλιν οἱ νεήλυδες, καὶ τῆς μὲν πόλεως πολὺ μέρος [2.26] κατεκράτησαν. Μετὰ δὲ ταῦτα τῶν ἐν τῇ πόλει ἀθροιζομένων, ἐς χεῖρά τε τοῖς νεήλυσιν ἀφίκοντο, καὶ ὠσάμενοι ἐξεώσαντο καταβαλόντες ἀπὸ τοῦ τείχους. Καὶ ὡς ἐξεκρούσθη τὰ στρατεύματα καὶ οὐ προεχώρει αὐτῷ ἡ τῆς πόλεως αἵρεσις, ἀπήγαγε τὸν στρατὸν καὶ ἀπήλαυνεν ἐπ' οἴκου. Ὕπαρχον δὲ ἐπιστήσας τῇ Σκοπίων τε καὶ Ἰλλυριῶν χώρᾳ ἄνδρα τῶν παρ' αὐτῷ μέγα τε δυνάμενον καὶ αὐτῷ ἐπὶ τῇ ἀδελφῇ γαμβρὸν γενόμενον, καὶ στρατόν τε ἐπιτρέψας πεζόν τε ἅμα καὶ ἱππικόν, ὥστε ἐς τὴν Ἰλλυριῶν ἐσβαλεῖν χώραν, διῆκεν ἐνταῦθα τὰ στρατεύματα.

39 Ὁ μὲν οὖν Ἰλλυριῶν βασιλεύς—Πόσθνη δὲ ἡ χώρα αὕτη καλεῖται, καὶ ἔστιν ἡ χώρα αὕτη τραχεῖά τε καὶ

the one side by the Danube and on the other by the Sava, which flows into the Danube right there by that city. Smederevo too [. . .] When he marched to Belgrade, Murad, the son of Mehmed, besieged the city, battered the walls with cannons, and demolished a large part of them. But his army suffered terrible losses from the hail of cannon shot and small arms fire that came from the city and struck the men in the sultan's camp, and by the thousands of arrows that were also loosed upon the camp.[71]

It was there that Ali, the son of Evrenos, achieved the greatest reputation in the camp. He and his men were the best at storming walls. He dug a trench as close to the walls as he could and camped in it with his soldiers. When the walls collapsed, the janissaries poured into the city and occupied most of it. But then the men of the city regrouped and engaged with the janissaries, repelled them, and pushed them down from the walls. As his army was repulsed and he was making no progress toward taking the city, Murad led his army away and returned home. He appointed one of his most influential men [İsa] as prefect of the land of Skopje and the Illyrians [Bosnians], a man who was his brother-in-law through marriage to his sister, and entrusted him with an army of both infantry and cavalry so that he could invade the land of the Illyrians.[72] He then disbanded his armies. 38

Now the king of the Illyrians[73]—this land is called Bosnia, and it is a rugged and very mountainous land that 39

ὀρεινὴ πάνυ, διήκει δὲ ἐπὶ Ἰλλυριούς, τοὺς πρὸς τὸν Ἰόνιον ᾠκισμένους παρὰ τὴν θάλασσαν. Ἔστι δὲ αὐτῷ βασίλεια καὶ πόλις Γαΐτια καλουμένη, καὶ ποταμὸς παρ' αὐτῇ ῥέων ἐκδιδοῖ ἐς Ἴστρον—οὗτος μὲν δὴ ὁ τῶν Ἰλλυριῶν βασιλεύς, ὡς δῃουμένης αὐτῷ ὑπὸ Ἰσάμου τῆς χώρας, ὡς στρατόν τε συναγαγὼν ἤνυεν οὐδέν, οὐδὲ ἐς χεῖρας ἐλθεῖν ἠνέσχετο τῷ βασιλέως στρατῷ, πρέσβεις τε ἔπεμψε παρὰ βασιλέα, καὶ ἐτάξατο φόρον ἀπάγειν τοῦ ἐνιαυτοῦ μυριάδας δύο χρυσοῦ καὶ πεντακισχιλίους. Βασιλεὺς δὲ προσίετο καὶ σπονδὰς ἐποιεῖτο αὐτῷ.

40 Τούτου δὲ τῆς χώρας ἔχεται ἡ Στεφάνου τοῦ Σανδάλεω χώρα, Ἰλλυριῶν τὸ γένος, καθήκουσα ἐπὶ θάλασσαν ἐς τὸν [2.27] Ἰόνιον παρὰ [. . .] καλουμένη. Τὸ μὲν δὴ γένος τοῦτο Ἰλλυρικὸν ὂν ἀπὸ παλαιοῦ διέσχισται ἀπὸ τοῦ λοιποῦ τῶν Ἰλλυριῶν γένους· ἤθεσι μὲν γὰρ καὶ διαίτῃ τῇ αὐτῇ διαχρῶνται, νόμοις δὲ οὐ τοῖς αὐτοῖς. Κουδούγεροι δ' ὀνομάζονται σύμπαντες οἱ ἐς τὴν Σανδάλεω χώραν τελοῦντες. Μεταξὺ μέντοι τῆς Ἠπείρου καὶ αὐτοῦ τῆς χώρας πόλεις τε ἔνεισιν αὐτῶν τε τῶν Οὐενετῶν καὶ ἡ τοῦ Ἰβάνεω χώρα τοῦ Καστριώτου, μετὰ δὲ ταύτην ἡ τοῦ Κομνηνοῦ χώρα, τὰ πολλὰ παράλιος οὖσα· ἐπὶ μεσόγαιον μέντοι ἐς βραχύ τι παρατείνει ἐπὶ τὴν περίοικον τῆς Ἀργυροπολίχνης, αὐτοῦ ταύτῃ ᾠκισμένης, ἐν ᾗ ὁ τῆς χώρας ὕπαρχος διατρίβων τήν τε Ἰβάνεω χώραν καὶ Κομνηναίων ἐληΐζετο. Τούτων μέντοι ὅ τε Ἰβάνης ἐπὶ τὰς θύρας ἰὼν τοῦ βασιλέως ἐστρατεύετο σὺν τῷ βασιλεῖ, ᾗ ἂν ὑφηγοῖτο τὰ βασιλέως στρατεύματα. Καὶ Ἀριανίτης δὲ ὁ Κομνηνός,

extends as far as the Illyrians who inhabit the regions by the Adriatic Sea; he has a royal court and city named Jajce, and a river flows by it and lets out into the Danube—this king of the Illyrians, then, when his land was being plundered by İsa,[74] could accomplish nothing even though he raised an army, nor was he willing to come to grips with the sultan's army. He sent envoys to the sultan and pledged to pay an annual tax of twenty-five thousand gold coins. The sultan accepted his offer and made a treaty with him.

The land that borders his own belongs to Stjepan, the son 40
of Sandalj,[75] an Illyrian by origin, and it extends to the Adriatic Sea by the [. . .] called [. . .] This people is Illyrian [i.e., Slav] and broke away from the rest of the Illyrian people a long time ago. They have the same customs and way of life, but not the same laws. All the inhabitants of the land of Sandalj are called Koudougeroi.[76] Between this land and Epeiros there are cities of the Venetians and the land of Gjon Kastrioti,[77] and after that the land of Komnen, which, for the most part, is coastal.[78] In the interior, a small part of it extends toward the vicinity of Argyrokastron, which is located in that region. It was here, then, that the prefect of that territory made his base and plundered the land of Gjon and the Komnens. Gjon came to the sultan's Porte and campaigned along with him, wherever the sultan's armies might lead him, while Komnen Arianiti,[79] whose ancestral principality

ὡς ἀπῆν καὶ αὐτῷ ἡ πατρῴα ἀρχὴ ὑπὸ βασιλέως, ἀφικόμενος ἐς τὰς θύρας τὴν δίαιταν εἶχε παρὰ βασιλέως. Ὕστερον δὲ τελευτήσαντος Ἰβάνεω τοῦ Καστριώτου τόν τε παῖδα αὐτοῦ λαβὼν ἐς τὰ βασίλεια καὶ τὴν χώραν ὑφ' αὐτῷ ποιησάμενος εἶχε.

41 Μετὰ δὲ ταῦτα οὐ πολὺν χρόνον, ὡς διατρίβων Ἀριανίτης ἱκέτης ἐγένετο ἀπὸ τῶν θυρῶν τυχεῖν ἀγαθοῦ τινος πρὸς τοῦ βασιλέως, λόγους τε δοὺς ἐπιπέμψαι ἐπὶ τοὺς τῆς χώρας αὐτοῦ, καὶ ὑπισχνουμένων αὐτῷ ἀπόστασιν, ἢν ἀφίκηται ἐπ' αὐτούς, ἀποδιδράσκει τε ἀπὸ τῶν θυρῶν, καὶ κατιὼν ἐπὶ τὴν πατρῴαν ἀρχὴν συντίθεται τοῖς βελτίοσι τῆς χώρας. Καὶ ὑποδεχομένων ἀσμένως ἀπέστησαν ἀπὸ βασιλέως, καὶ τούς γε ἄρχοντας τῆς χώρας Τούρκους ἀνελόντες ἐπέδραμον τὴν [2.28] βασιλέως χώραν καὶ ἦγον καὶ ἔφερον, χώραν τε ἐρυμνὴν κατέχοντες αὐτοὶ καὶ ὀρεινὴν τὴν σύμπασαν καὶ τραχεῖαν. Ὡς μὲν οὖν ταῦτα ἠγγέλλετο βασιλεῖ, ἔπεμπεν Ἀλίην τὸν Βρενέζεω, στρατηγὸν ἀποδείξας· καὶ παραδοὺς αὐτῷ στράτευμα, ὅσον τε παρὰ Ἀξιὸν ποταμὸν καὶ τῆς Ἀργυροπολίχνης, καὶ ἱπποδρόμους, ὅσοι τήνδε τὴν χώραν ἐνοικοῦσιν, ἐκέλευεν ἐπιόντα τήν τε χώραν αὐτῷ τὴν Ἀλβανῶν καταστρέψασθαι, καὶ ἀνδραποδισάμενον ἥκειν αὐτῷ ἄγοντα τὸν Κομνηνοῦ παῖδα.

42 Οὗτος μὲν οὖν λαβὼν τὸν στρατὸν ἅπαντα ἐσέβαλεν ἐς τὴν χώραν, καὶ πεζὸν ἅμα εὑράμενος οὐκ ὀλίγον. Ὡς δὲ ἐσέβαλον, ἐδῄουν τε τὴν χώραν καὶ ἐνεπίμπρων οἰκίας τε καὶ ἀγρούς, οὐδενὸς φειδόμενοι. Ὁ μέντοι Ἀριανίτης συναγαγὼν τοὺς τῆς χώρας ἱππέας τε καὶ πεζοὺς καὶ ἀφικόμενος καταλαμβάνει τὰ ἄκρα, ᾗ ἔμελλεν ἀναζεύξας Ἀλίης ὁ

had also been removed by the sultan, arrived at the Porte and was maintained by the sultan. Later, when Gjon Kastrioti died, Murad brought his son to the royal court and subjected his land to himself.[80]

Shortly after that, while Arianiti was in residence at the Porte, a suppliant hoping for some benefit from the sultan, he entered into negotiations with the people of his land and they promised to rebel if he went to them. So he escaped from the Porte, returned to his ancestral principality, and banded together with the leading men of the land.[81] They received him gladly and rebelled against the sultan, killing the Turkish lords of the land, and raiding the sultan's territory far and wide. They occupied fortified locations in that thoroughly mountainous and rugged land. When this was reported to the sultan, he sent Ali, the son of Evrenos, appointing him general. He also gave him the army that was stationed by the Axios River and Argyrokastron and all the cavalry raiders who lived in that land, and instructed him to advance against the land of the Albanians, conquer it, and, after enslaving the land, he was to return, bringing back to him the son of Komnen. 41

Ali, then, took the entire army and invaded the land, having found many infantry forces to take with him. When they invaded, they plundered the land and set fire to homes and fields, sparing nothing. Arianiti assembled the cavalry and infantry of his land and took command of the heights which Ali, the son of Evrenos, would have to climb and pass 42

τοῦ Βρενέζεω ἐξελαύνειν. Καὶ ὡς ἐπειρῶντο μετὰ ταῦτα οἱ τοῦ Ἀλίεω διελθεῖν, οὐκ ἠδύναντο, ἐνισταμένων τῶν ταύτῃ μετὰ Ἀριανίτου καὶ οὐκ ἐπιτρεπόντων διεξιέναι. Ἐνταῦθα οἱ Τοῦρκοι ἄλλοι μὲν ὡς ἀπελήφθησαν ἐν τῇ χώρᾳ, ἄλλοι δὲ κατὰ τὴν χώραν ἐτράποντο, ὅποι ἑκάστῳ προὐχώρει διασώζεσθαι. Τούτων οἱ πλεῖστοι διεφθάρησαν ὑπὸ τῶν Ἀλβανῶν, οἱ δὲ ἄλλοι ἑάλωσαν παριόντες. Οἱ δὲ σὺν τῷ Ἀλίῃ ἀποτραπόμενοι ταύτην τὴν πορείαν πεδινωτέραν ἐποιήσαντο καὶ ἐπιμήκη, καὶ ἐξελθόντες ἐς τὴν Ἤπειρον τὴν κατὰ Κέρκυραν ᾠκημένην ἐκ πολλῶν ἀπενόστησαν διαφυγόντες μὴ ἀπόλλυσθαι. Ἐνταῦθα δὴ ἀνείλετο δόξαν περιφανῆ Ἀριανίτης ὁ Κομνηνοῦ, ἀποδειξάμενος ἔργα λόγου ἄξια καὶ τὸ ἐντεῦθεν εὐδοκιμῶν. [2.29] Οὕτω μὲν δὴ Ἀλίῃ τῷ Βρενέζεω, ὡς εἰσεβάλλοντο ἐς τὴν πρὸς Ἰόνιον χώραν, ὁ στρατὸς χαλεπώτατα ἐπεπράγει.

43 Οἱ μέντοι τῶν πρὸς τὴν Ἀργυροπολίχνην οἰκούντων Ἀλβανῶν οἱ λοιποί, ὡς εἶδον Ἀριανίτην νεωτερίσαντα περὶ τὴν βασιλέως ἀρχήν, ἔργον λαμπρὸν σφίσι κατεργασάμενον, ἐβουλεύοντο καὶ αὐτοὶ ἀπόστασιν ἀπὸ βασιλέως Ἀμουράτεω, καὶ ἐπεκαλοῦντο μὲν Δέπαν τὸν ἡγεμόνα αὐτῶν. Τούτου γὰρ δὴ τὸν πατέρα ἐξελάσας ἐκ τῆς χώρας Παιαζήτης ὁ Ἀμουράτεω, καὶ Μύρξαν τῶν Κανίνων ἡγεμόνα καὶ συχνοὺς ἄλλους ἄρχοντας τῆς τῇδε χώρας, τήν τε χώραν κατέσχε καὶ ἑαυτῷ κατεπροστήσατο. Τὸν δὴ οὖν Δέπαν τοῦτον περιόντα καὶ περινοστοῦντα ἄλλοτε ἄλλῃ τῆς Ἰταλίας, καὶ ἐν Κερκύρᾳ τῇ Ἑνετῶν νήσῳ τὰ πολλὰ διατρίβοντα, ἐπεκαλοῦντο οἱ περὶ τὴν Ἀργυροπολίχνην οἰκοῦντες καὶ σφίσι βασιλέα τε ἐστήσαντο. Καὶ

through. And when, after that, Ali's men attempted to pass, they could not, as they were opposed there by the men with Arianiti who would not let them pass. At that point, some Turks were cut off in that land while others fled across the land, each seeking safety wherever he could. Most of them were killed by the Albanians, the rest captured as they fled. Those who turned back with Ali journeyed along a long, flat valley and emerged in Epeiros, in the parts of it that are settled near Kerkyra. They were the few from that large army who returned and escaped death. Arianiti, the son of Komnen, was glorified for accomplishing such remarkable deeds and was thereafter held in high esteem. And thus did the army of Ali, the son of Evrenos, suffer most wretchedly when it invaded the land by the Adriatic Sea.[82]

When the rest of the Albanians who lived at Argyrokastron saw that Arianiti had rebelled against the authority of the sultan and performed a glorious feat on their behalf, they too deliberated on a rebellion against Sultan Murad and called in Depas, their ruler. For Bayezid, the son of Murad, had expelled his father from his territory along with Mrkša, the ruler of Kanina, and many other lords of this land, and had occupied the land and annexed it for himself.[83] This Depas, then, went around looking for a home in various places that belonged to Italy, and he spent much time on Kerkyra, an island of the Venetians. The inhabitants of Argyrokastron now called him in and made him their king. 43

στρατὸν ποιησάμενοι ἐπήλαυνον ἐπὶ τὴν Ἀργυροπολίχνην, τὴν βασιλέως τότε δὴ πόλιν, ἀνήκουσαν δὲ προὔθεντο τουτῳὶ τῷ Δέπᾳ, καὶ ἐπολιόρκουν τὴν πόλιν μηχαναῖς τε τῷ τείχει προσφέροντες. Ἦσαν δὲ αὐτοῦ ἐν τῇ πόλει νεήλυδές τε τοῦ βασιλέως φρουρᾷ καί τινες ἄλλοι οὐ πολλοὶ τῶν Τούρκων διαφυγόντες ἐς τὴν πόλιν, καὶ ἠμύνοντο τὸν στρατόν. Ὥς τε δὴ ταῦτα πράσσοντες οἱ Ἀλβανοὶ τήν τε πόλιν ἐπολιόρκουν, μηδὲν ἀνιέντες ἐς τὴν πολιορκίαν, καὶ τὴν χώραν τὴν περίοικον [2.30] τοῦ βασιλέως ἐπέδραμον, βασιλέως ἔχοντος καὶ ἀπόντος ἐς τὴν Ἀσίαν καὶ πολεμοῦντος Καραμάνῳ τῆς Κιλικίας τε καὶ Καρίας ἡγεμόνι.

44 Ἐνταῦθα ὡς ἐπύθετο Τουραχάνης ὁ τῶν Τρικκάλων καὶ Θετταλίας ὕπαρχος τότε δὴ ὤν, τούς τε Ἀλβανοὺς ἀφεστηκότας ἀπὸ βασιλέως καὶ τὴν μητρόπολιν πολιορκοῦντας, συλλέξας στράτευμα ὡς ἠδύνατο μέγιστον, συμπαραλαβὼν καὶ τοὺς τῆς παραθαλασσίας χώρας τῶν Τούρκων, ὅσους ἠδύνατο, ἐλαύνων διὰ τῆς χιόνος (χειμών τε γὰρ ἦν μέγας), δευτεραῖος ἀφικνεῖται ἐπὶ τὴν χώραν, καὶ καταλαμβάνει ἐπιστρατευομένους ἐν τῇ πόλει τοὺς Ἀλβανούς. Καὶ ἐπεισπεσὼν ἄφνω τοὺς πλείστους τε αὐτῶν διέφθειρε, καὶ τόν τε Δέπαν τὸν ἡγεμόνα ζωγρήσας ἀνεῖλε, καὶ τὴν πόλιν τῆς πολιορκίας ἠλευθέρωσε. Λέγεται δὲ ἐν ταύτῃ τῇ Τουραχάνεω ἐφόδῳ πλείους τῶν χιλίων διαφθαρῆναι. Καὶ οὕτω αὖθις κατεδεδούλωντο οἱ Ἀλβανοὶ ἀφεστηκότες ἀπὸ βασιλέως. Οἱ μὲν τῆς χώρας εὖ γεγονότες, ὅσοι μὴ διέφυγον τότε ἐπιόντος Τουραχάνεω, ἄλλος ἄλλῃ ἀπώλετο, ὀλέθρῳ τῷ κακίστῳ παραδοθέντες ὑπὸ τῶν βασιλέως ὑπάρχων.

They assembled an army and marched against Argyrokastron, which was then a city of the sultan but they claimed that it belonged to this Depas. They besieged the city and brought engines against its walls. Present in the city were the sultan's garrison of janissaries and a small number of Turks who had fled to the city and were resisting this army. This was how the Albanians besieged the city, and they did not let up in their efforts; they raided the sultan's surrounding territory, as the sultan himself was away in Asia, fighting against Karaman, the ruler of Kilikia and Karia.[84]

When Turahan, who was then the prefect of Trikala and 44
Thessaly, learned that the Albanians had revolted against the sultan and were besieging the capital, he assembled as large an army as he could and took with him as well the Turks who lived by the sea, as many as he could. After marching through the snow (for there was a bitter winter storm), he arrived in that land on the second day and found the Albanians encamped beside the city.[85] He attacked them suddenly and killed most of them, capturing Depas, their ruler, putting him to death, and freeing the city from the siege. It is said that in this attack by Turahan more than a thousand men were killed. Thus the Albanians who rebelled against the sultan were again enslaved. Those in this land who were well off and did not escape from Turahan's attack were killed, one here and another there, delivered over to a most awful death by the sultan's prefects.

45 Ἀμουράτης δὲ ὡς ἐγένετο ἐπανιὼν ἀπὸ Καραμάνου ἐς τὰ βασίλεια, Μεζέτην τὸν τῆς Εὐρώπης αὐτῷ στρατηγὸν ἐκέλευε, λαβόντα στρατόν, ὅσον ἂν βούληται, καὶ πεζὸν ἅμα καὶ ἱππικόν, ἀγαγέσθαι τε καὶ ἐλαύνειν ἐπὶ Παιονοδακίαν ὡς καταστρεψόμενον αὐτῷ τὴν χώραν. Ὁ δὲ λαβὼν τό τε Εὐρώπης στράτευμα καὶ ἀζάπιδας τῆς Εὐρώπης καὶ ἱπποδρόμους τοῦ βασιλέως, ὅσοι ἐν τῇ Εὐρώπῃ ἐγένοντο, ἀφίκετο ἐπὶ τὸν Ἴστρον, διαβὰς δὲ τὸν [2.31] Ἴστρον ἐπὶ Παιονοδακίαν τὴν Ἀρδέλιον χώραν καλουμένην. Τὸ δὲ Ἀρδέλιον τοῦτο ἀπὸ Πρασοβοῦ τοῦ ὄρους ἐπὶ Παιονίαν διήκει, ἐντὸς δρυμῶνος γενομένη ἅπασα ἡ χώρα, καὶ πόλεις ἔνεισιν ἐν ταύτῃ τῇ χώρᾳ οὐκ ὀλίγαι, μητρόπολις δὲ αὐτῶν τὸ Σιβίνιον καλούμενον. Γλώττῃ δὲ χρῶνται οὗτοι τὰ μὲν τῇ Παιόνων τὰ δὲ καὶ Δακῶν, διαίτῃ τε καὶ ἤθεσι τοῖς Παιόνων. Καὶ ὑπὸ τῷ Παιόνων βασιλεῖ οὖσα ἡ χώρα αὕτη ἄρχοντά τε δέχεται, ὃν ἂν αὐτοῖς ἐφιστῴη ὁ βασιλεὺς Παίονα. Αὐτόνομοι δὲ αἱ πόλεις οὖσαι, καὶ ὑπὸ τὴν μητρόπολιν τὸ Σιβίνιον εὐθυνόμεναι, παρὰ δὲ τῷ ἄρχοντι σφᾶς, ὅποι ἂν κελεύοι ἐπὶ ἐκστρατείαν, καὶ τὰς προσόδους ἀποδιδόντες, ἀξιοῦσι πολιτεύεσθαι σφίσιν αὐτοῦ ἐς τὸ ἐπιχώριον πάτριον ἔθος.

46 Ἐπὶ ταύτην οὖν δὴ τὴν πόλιν τὸν Ἴστρον διαβὰς ὁ Μεζέτης ἤλαυνεν ὡς πολιορκήσων, καὶ ἀγχοῦ ἐπὶ τῇ πόλει γενόμενος ἐστρατοπεδεύετο. Ἐνταῦθα δὲ ὡς ἐπολιόρκει τὴν πόλιν, τηλεβόλῳ βληθεὶς ὁ τοῦ στρατοῦ ἡγεμὼν ἐτελεύτησε. Μετὰ δὲ ταῦτα, ὡς ἀπεχώρει ἐντεῦθεν ὁ στρατὸς ἐπειγόμενος ἐπὶ τὴν διάβασιν τοῦ Ἴστρου, συλλεχθέντες οἱ τοῦ Ἀρδελίου ἄνδρες, ὡς ἠδύναντο φθῆναι τὸν στρατὸν

When Murad returned to the palace from his expedition against Karaman, he ordered Mezid, his general for Europe, to take as large an army as he wished, including both infantry and cavalry, and lead it on campaign against Hungarian Wallachia, to conquer that land for him. So he took the army of Europe, the *azaps* of Europe, and all the sultan's cavalry raiders who were in Europe, and came to the Danube. He crossed the Danube and went into Hungarian Wallachia, in the land called Ardeal. This Ardeal extends from Mount Brassó to Hungary. All the land of the interior is forested and has many cities in it; their capital is called Sibiu. These people speak the language of the Hungarians in part and in part also that of the Wallachians, and they have the same customs and way of life as the Hungarians. This land is subject to the king of the Hungarians and receives as its lord whatever Hungarian the king appoints over them. The cities have their own laws and are governed from the capital Sibiu. They follow their lord wherever he orders them to campaign and pay their revenues, but they demand to be ruled according to their local, ancestral ways. 45

Mezid, then, crossed the Danube and marched to besiege this city, and he made camp when he drew near the city. But while he was besieging the city, he, the leader of his army, was struck by cannon shot and died. After that, when the army departed from there in haste to cross the Danube, the men of Ardeal assembled and tried their best to catch up 46

ἔτι ἐν τῇ χώρᾳ διατρίβοντα, πολλούς τε κατέβαλλον τοῦ στρατεύματος, καὶ τρεψάμενοι ἐδίωκον φεύγοντας ἐπὶ τὸν Ἴστρον. Μεζέτης μὲν οὖν ἀφικόμενος ἐπὶ Ἀρδέλιον οὕτως ἐτελεύτησε, καὶ ἀπεγένετο οὐκ ὀλίγον τι τοῦ στρατεύματος.

47 Βασιλεὺς δὲ ὡς ἐπύθετο τὸν Μεζέτου θάνατον, συμφοράν τε ἐποιεῖτο, καὶ παρεσκευάζετό τε αὐτὸς ἐπὶ Παιονοδακίαν στρατευσόμενος, καὶ [2.32] κήρυκας πέμπων περιαγγέλλοντας τὴν ἐξέλευσιν αὐτοῦ ἅμα ἦρι ἐδόκει ἐξελαύνειν. Μετὰ δὲ συμβουλεύσαντος Σαβατίνεω εὐνούχου, ἀνδρὸς τὰ ἐς πόλεμον αὐτοῦ πολλαχῇ γενομένου, ἐπέτρεψέ τε τὸν στρατὸν αὐτῷ, καὶ ἐκέλευσε λαβόντα ἐξηγήσασθαι ἐπὶ Παιονοδακίαν, καὶ μὴ ἀνιέναι πρὶν ἢ καταστρεψάμενον ἀπελαύνειν. Οὗτος μὲν δὴ παραλαβὼν τὸν βασιλέως στρατὸν καὶ νεήλυδας τῶν θυρῶν ἀμφὶ τοὺς τετρακισχιλίους, τόν τε Ἴστρον διέβαινε καὶ τὸν στρατὸν αὐτοῦ σύμπαντα διεπορεύετο ἐς τὴν Ἀρδελίου χώραν. Ἤλαυνε δὲ διὰ τῆς Παιόνων χώρας ἡμέρας τινάς.

48 Ἰάγγος δὲ ὁ Χωνιάτης, ἀνὴρ τότε δὴ εὐδοκιμῶν παρὰ τοῖς Παίοσι καὶ τό τε Ἀρδέλιον ἐπιτετραμμένος ὑπὸ τῆς Παιόνων βουλῆς, συνήγαγέ τε στρατὸν ὡς μέγιστον, ὡς ἠδύνατο, ἀπὸ Ἀρδελίου, καὶ Παιόνων συμπαραλαβὼν ἐπῄει, ἑπόμενος τῷ Σαβατίνῃ κατὰ τὸ ὄρος. Σαβατίνης μὲν δή, ὡς ἐντὸς τῆς χώρας ἤδη ἄλλος[4] γενόμενος, ἐνόμιζε καλῶς ἔχειν αὐτῷ τὴν χώραν ἐπιδραμεῖν. Ἐπαφεὶς τοίνυν τοὺς ἱπποδρόμους καὶ τοῦ στρατοῦ πολύ τι μέρος ἐπὶ διαρπαγὴν τῆς χώρας, ὡς ἀφαρπάσαιντό τε τὴν χώραν αὐτοῦ σύμπασαν καὶ κερδανοῖ μέγιστα, κατελείφθη ὀλίγοις

with the army while it was still in their land. They killed many of the army's men, routed them, and pursued those who fled as far as the Danube. Thus did Mezid die when he came to Ardeal, and a large part of his army perished as well.[86]

When the sultan learned of Mezid's death, he considered 47
it a great misfortune and prepared to campaign in person against Hungarian Wallachia. He sent around heralds announcing his expedition, namely that he had decided to set out at the beginning of spring. But then he consulted the eunuch Şihabeddin, a man with much experience of warfare in that area, and entrusted his army to him. He ordered him to take the army, lead it on campaign against Hungarian Wallachia, and not to let up or return before he had conquered it. He, then, took the sultan's army and about four thousand of the janissaries of the Porte, crossed the Danube, and advanced with his entire army to the land of Ardeal. And for some days he advanced through the land of the Hungarians.[87]

But Janko Hunyadi, a man held in high esteem by the 48
Hungarians who had been entrusted with Ardeal by the council of the Hungarians, assembled as large an army as he could from Ardeal and the Hungarians and, having brought them together, set out, following Şihabeddin along the mountain. Şihabeddin, when he entered the land, believed that he was in a good position to raid it. So he released the cavalry raiders and a large part of the army to go and plunder the land, hoping to profit greatly by stripping bare the entire

τοῖς ἀμφ' αὐτὸν ἐν τῷ στρατοπέδῳ. Ἐνταῦθα ὡς ᾔσθετο Ἰάγγος τό τε στρατόπεδον ἔρημον ἀνδρῶν καταλειφθῆναι, καί οἱ καλῶς ἔχειν ἡγούμενος ἐπεισπεσεῖν ἐς τὸ στρατόπεδον τῶν πολεμίων, ἐπικαταβὰς ἀπὸ τοῦ ὄρους ἐμβάλλει τε ἐς τὸ στρατόπεδον τοῦ Σαβατίνεω. Καὶ ὁ μὲν Σαβατίνης ἐπεξελθεῖν μέντοι οὐκ εἶχεν, ὅτι καὶ ἄξιον λόγου μαχέσασθαι, φυλάξαι δὲ τὸ στρατόπεδον [2.33] πειρώμενος καὶ οὐκ ἠδύνατο, βιασαμένων τῶν μετὰ τοῦ Ἰάγγου Παιόνων, ἐς φυγήν τε ἐτράπη καὶ ἐπὶ τὸν Ἴστρον ἐπείγετο φθῆναι ὡς διαβησόμενος. Ἰάγγος δὲ τὸ στρατόπεδον παραλαβών, καὶ λόχους ὑπείσας αὐτοῦ ταύτῃ, ὥστε τοὺς ἐπανιόντας σὺν τοῖς ἀνδραπόδοις συμπαρελάμβανε διαφθείρων ἅπαντας. Καὶ οὕτω δὴ τὰ πλείω τοῦ στρατεύματος αὐτοῦ ταύτῃ κάκιστα διεφθάρη, καὶ νίκην νικᾷ ἀρίστην ἐς τῶν πρὸς αὐτοῦ[5] Ἰάγγος ὁ Χωνιάτης.

49 Οὗτος γένους ὢν οὐ πάνυ τι φαύλου, ἀπὸ Χωνιάτης πόλεως Ἀρδελίου ὡρμημένος ἐπὶ τὸν Τριβαλλῶν ἀφίκετο ἡγεμόνα, μεμισθωμένος δὲ αὐτοῦ διέτριβε συχνόν τινα χρόνον, τόλμαν τε ἐπιδεικνύμενος ἀξίαν λόγου καὶ σπουδήν, ὡς ὅ τι ἂν ἐπιπεμφθείη ὑπὸ τοῦ ἡγεμόνος. Καὶ δὴ λέγεται καὶ τόδε. Ὡς ἐξήλαυνεν ἐπὶ ἄγραν ὁ τῶν Τριβαλλῶν ἡγεμών, καὶ λύκου ἐπιφανέντος τῷ ἡγεμόνι ἐπεκάλει τὸν Ἰάγγον, ὡς ἐπὶ τῷ λύκῳ γένοιτο. Ὁ δ' ὡς παρεληλύθει, τὸν θῆρα ἤλαυνεν ἀνὰ κράτος. Πεσόντος δὲ τοῦ θηρὸς ἐς τὸν ποταμὸν καὶ νηχομένου, ἐπεισπεσεῖν τε ἅμα ἐς τὸν ποταμὸν καὶ αὐτὸν καὶ διανηχομένου τοῦ ἵππου διαβῆναι, διαβάντα δὲ ἐπιδιώκειν οὐδαμῇ ἀνιέντα, τελευτῶντα δὲ καταλαβεῖν τε τὸν λύκον καὶ ἀνελεῖν, μετὰ δὲ

land. He was left with only a few of his men in the camp. When Janko realized that the camp had been left empty of men and believed that he was in a good position to attack the enemy camp, he came down from the mountain and attacked Şihabeddin's camp. It was now not possible for Şihabeddin to come out and meet him or put up any kind of a fight. Still, he tried to defend the camp, but failed, as the Hungarians with Janko forced their way through, and so he turned to flight and hastened to reach the Danube in order to get across.[88] Janko took the camp and placed an ambush in it, so that he captured the men who were returning with slaves and killed them all. Thus the majority of Şihabeddin's army was wretchedly destroyed there, and Janko Hunyadi won a most excellent victory over his enemies.[89]

Janko came from a not undistinguished family. Setting 49
out from Hunyad, a city of Ardeal,[90] he came to the ruler of the Serbs,[91] who hired him for a while as a mercenary. He displayed a remarkable daring and zeal on whatever mission he was sent by this ruler. And the following is reported too. While the ruler of the Serbs was out hunting, a wolf appeared before him, and he challenged Janko to go after the wolf. Janko gave chase and pursued his prey with all his might. When his prey fell into a river and began to swim, he too jumped into the river and swam across on his horse. After he crossed the river, he did not let up at all in his pursuit until he finally caught up with the wolf and killed it; then

ἀφελόμενον τὸ δέρμα τοῦ θηρὸς ἐλαύνειν ὀπίσω ἐπὶ τὸν ἡγεμόνα, διαβάντα δὲ αὖθις τὸν ποταμὸν καὶ προεχόμενον τοῦ λύκου τὸ δέρμα εἰπεῖν, "ὦ δέσποτα, ἐγένετο, ᾗ ἐπέταξας, καὶ τόν τε λύκον ἀνεῖλον, καὶ τὸ δέρμα ὧδέ σοι παρέστη, ὑπουργεῖν ὅ τι ἂν δέοι χρῆσθαι." Τότε μὲν δὴ τὸ [2.34] θαῦμα ἀγασθέντα τὸν Τριβαλλῶν ἡγεμόνα εἰπεῖν λέγεται, ὡς οὐκ ἔστιν, ὅπως ὁ ἀνὴρ οὗτος ἐπὶ μέγα δυνάμεως οὐκ ἀφίξεται. Τότε μὲν δὴ οὕτως εἰπὼν τὸ ἐντεῦθεν χρήμασί τε ἐθεράπευε, καὶ διατρίψας αὐτοῦ χρόνον συχνὸν ἀφίκετο ἐπὶ τοὺς Παίονας.

50 Λέγεται μὲν δὴ καὶ πρὶν ἐπὶ τὸν Τριβαλλῶν ἡγεμόνα ἐλθεῖν, Ἀλίεω τοῦ Βρενέζεω γενέσθαι θεράποντα, καὶ θητεῦσαι παρ' αὐτῷ ἱπποκόμον γενόμενον. Οὐκ ἔχω δέ, ὅπῃ τοῦτο ἀληθὲς εἶναι συμβάλλωμαι· τήν τε γὰρ ἂν φωνὴν ἐξέμαθε τὴν Τούρκων. Ὡς μὲν οὖν ἐτράπετο ἐπὶ τοὺς Παίονας, καὶ συμπαραλαβών τινας μεθ' ἑαυτοῦ παρῄει ἐπὶ τὰ βασίλεια, μισθὸν φάσκων ἥκειν αὐτοῖς σὺν τοῖς ἀμφ' αὐτὸν ληψόμενος, ἐλάμβανέ τε τὸν μισθόν, καὶ ἐς διαφορὰν καθισταμένων τῶν Παιόνων πρὸς τοὺς Γερμανοὺς μεγάλα ἀπεδείκνυτο ἔργα, ὁπότε ἔδει αὐτίκα παρόντα, ἐν τάχει τε παραγενόμενος καὶ μαχόμενος ἀξίως λόγου. Μετὰ δὲ ταῦτα ἐπισπομένων αὐτῷ καὶ πολλῶν ἄλλων εὐδοκιμῶν ἐφαίνετο πανταχῇ, δι' ἃ δὴ καὶ ἐπετέτραπτο τὴν τῆς Ἀρδελίου χώρας ἀρχὴν ὑπὸ τῆς Παιόνων βουλῆς. Καὶ ἄρχων ταύτης τῆς χώρας τόν τε Σαβατίνην εὐνοῦχον τοῦ βασιλέως στρατηγὸν καθεῖλέ τε καὶ ἐτρέψατο, νίκην ἀνελόμενος εὐδοξοτάτην, ἀφ' ἧς δὴ τὰ Παιόνων πράγματα ἐπανῆκεν ἐπὶ τὴν πρότερον σφῶν κατάστασιν γενόμενα,

he removed its skin and turned back toward the ruler. He crossed the river again, presented the wolf's skin to the ruler, and said, "Lord, what you ordered has been done. I have killed the wolf, and here is its skin for you to use in whatever way you require." It is reported that the ruler of the Serbs was amazed at this feat, and said that there was no way this man would not rise to great power. Thus he spoke, and henceforth he courted him with gifts of money. Hunyadi spent a long time there and then went to the Hungarians.

50 It is also said that before he went to the ruler of the Serbs, he had attended upon Ali, the son of Evrenos, and had served him as a groom. But I cannot ascertain whether this is true, for he would in that case have learned the language of the Turks.[92] He turned to the Hungarians and, taking some men with him, went to their royal court and asked that he, and the group he assembled around himself, be given a salary. And he received the salary. When the Hungarians fell out with the Germans, he performed great deeds whenever his presence was required: he appeared quickly and fought admirably.[93] After that he was joined by many others and seemed to be held in high esteem everywhere, which is why he was entrusted with command over Ardeal by the council of the Hungarians.[94] It was when he was ruling this land that he destroyed and routed Şihabeddin, the eunuch-general of the sultan, winning a most glorious victory, after which the affairs of the Hungarians returned to their previous

ἀφ' οὗ κατὰ χρόνον Παιαζήτεω τὸν βασιλέα Παιόνων [ἐς] Σιγισμοῦνδον τρεψαμένου, τήν τε χώραν ἐπελαύνοντες ἐδήουν θαμὰ [2.35] ληϊζόμενοι οἱ Τοῦρκοι, καὶ ἀνδράποδα ὡς πλεῖστα ἀγόμενοι ἐνέπλησαν τήν τε Ἀσίαν καὶ Εὐρώπην ἀνδραπόδων Παιονικῶν.

51 Ἐπεί τε Ἰάγγος ἀφικόμενος ἐπὶ τὴν Ἀρδελίου χώραν τόν τε εὐνοῦχον ἐτρέψατο καὶ τοὺς περὶ αὐτὸν ἐτρέψατο Τούρκους, τόλμῃ τε ἐχρήσαντο οἱ Παίονες ἀπὸ τοῦδε, καὶ ἔργα ἀπεδείκνυντο ἐς τοὺς Τούρκους ἄξια λόγου. Τόν τε γὰρ Ἴστρον διαβάντες πολλάκις διέφθειρον, καὶ ὅποι περιτύχοιεν ὀλίγοι πολλοῖς οὖσι τοῖς Τούρκοις, εὐπετῶς τε περιεγένοντο καὶ οὐδὲ εἰς χεῖρας ἀφικομένους σφίσιν ἐτράποντο. Τότε μὲν δὴ περιγενόμενος ἐπὶ μέγα ἐχώρει δυνάμεως. Καὶ στρατηγὸς δὲ μετὰ ταῦτα ἀποδειχθεὶς ὑπὸ τῆς Παιόνων βουλῆς πρὸς τοὺς Τούρκους τε καὶ Γερμανοὺς τὸν πόλεμον διέφερε, γενναιότατα διαγωνιζόμενος.

52 Οἱ μέντοι Παίονες πρός τε τοὺς Γερμανοὺς διενεχθέντες τε ἐπολέμουν, ἀπὸ αἰτίας τῆσδε ἐς διαφορὰν ἀλλήλοις ἀφικόμενοι. Μετὰ δὲ ταῦτα καὶ πρὸς τοὺς Τζέχους, τοὺς Βοεμίους καλουμένους, ἐπὶ συχνόν τινα χρόνον τὸν πόλεμον διαφέροντες μεγάλα κακὰ ἐποίουν ἀλλήλους. Τρέπονται δὴ οὖν διὰ ταύτην αὐτῶν τὴν διαφορὰν ἐπὶ τοὺς Πολανίους, καὶ ἐπαγόμενοι τὸν βασιλέως ἀδελφιδοῦν παῖδα βασιλέα τε σφίσιν ἐστήσαντο, καὶ τοῖς Πολανίοις χρησάμενοι συμμάχοις τοῖς τε Γερμανοῖς καὶ Βοεμίοις ἐπέκειντο χαλεπῶς, καὶ ἐδήουν τὴν χώραν, καὶ πόλεις αὐτῶν ἐπιόντες ἐνεπίμπρων οὐκ ὀλίγας. Καὶ δὴ καὶ ἐς μάχην καταστάντες ἐμάχοντο· καὶ ὁτὲ μὲν περιεγένοντο οἱ Παίονες, ὁτὲ δὲ καὶ

condition, that is, since the time when Bayezid routed Sigismund, the king of the Hungarians,[95] and the Turks advanced into the land and plundered it often, leading away as many slaves as they could and filling Asia and Europe with Hungarian slaves.

When Janko arrived in the land of Ardeal, routed the eu- 51
nuch, and routed also the Turks with him, the Hungarians henceforth became more daring and performed remarkable deeds against the Turks. They crossed the Danube often and killed them, and wherever a few of them encountered a large body of Turks they would easily overcome them and rout them without even having to come to blows with them. At any rate, after that victory he became very powerful, was appointed general by the council of the Hungarians against the Turks and the Germans, and he waged war, fighting most bravely.

The Hungarians fell out with the Germans and went to 52
war with them, and they quarreled with each other for the following reason.[96] After that they also waged a war for a long time against the Czechs, the so-called Bohemians, and inflicted great harm upon each other. On account of this dispute they turned to the Poles and brought in the king's young nephew, making him their king.[97] With the Poles as their allies they put terrible pressure on the Germans and the Bohemians, plundered their land, and attacked and burned many of their cities. They even fought pitched battles. Sometimes the Hungarians would win and sometimes

ἡττῶντο, καὶ ἐπὶ βραχὺ αὖθις [2.36] ἀναλαμβάνοντες σφᾶς ἐμάχοντο.

53 Τήν τε γὰρ μάχην ποιοῦνται τάδε τὰ γένη κατὰ τὸ καρτερόν, οὐδενὸς φειδόμενοι, ἀλλὰ δόρασί τε ἐπιόντες καὶ τηλεβόλοις καὶ σιδηρείοις καταπέλταις ἱππικοῖς καὶ ἑτέροις βέλεσι διαμαχόμενοι κατακαίνουσί τε ἀλλήλους. Ἐπειδὰν δὲ ἐς φυγὴν γένωνται, οὐκέτι ἀνήκεστον συμβαίνει σφίσιν ἐς τὴν φυγήν, ἀλλ' ἢν παραδιδῷ τις ἑαυτὸν καὶ ὁμολογίᾳ χρῷτο ὡς ἡττημένος, ἀφίησιν αὐτὸν ἀπιέναι, ἐφ' ᾧ τοῦ λοιποῦ μὴ διαμάχεσθαι αὐτῷ, ἐπειδὰν συνίωσι τὰ στρατεύματα ἀλλήλοις καθιστάμενα ἐς τὴν μάχην. Ταύτῃ μὲν δὴ ἐς ἀλλήλους κατὰ τὰς μάχας χρῶνται καταστάσει, ὥστε ἐπειδὰν τρέποιτο ἐς φυγὴν τὰ στρατεύματα, οὐ πολύ τι μέρος αὐτῶν τὸ ἐντεῦθεν ἀπογίγνεσθαι.

54 Τὴν μέντοι Δακίαν αὐτοὶ οἱ Παίονες ἐπελθόντες, ἡγουμένου τοῦ Χωνιάτου, καθίστασαν Δᾶνον ἡγεμόνα αὐτοῖς καὶ πείθεσθαι αὐτὸν ἐκέλευον. Οὗτος μὲν οὖν ἐξελαυνομένου τοῦ Δρακούλεω ἡγεμόνος αὐτῶν, καὶ ἐπὶ τὰς βασιλέως θύρας ἰόντος, τήν τε χώραν κατέσχεν ὁ Δᾶνος, καὶ τοὺς ἐπιτηδείους Δρακούλεω τοῦ ἡγεμόνος διειργάζετο, ὅποι πυνθάνοιτο αὐτῶν τινα περιεῖναι. Οὗτοι μὲν δὴ λέγονται παῖδες γενέσθαι τοῦ Μύρξεω νόθοι, καὶ τούτων ἐνίους πλαττομένους ὑπὸ τῶν τῆς χώρας γένει τε καὶ πλούτῳ εὐδοκιμούντων καθίστασθαι ἐς τὴν τῆς Δακίας ἡγεμονίαν, ὡς ξύμφορά τε ἅμα καὶ λυσιτελῆ ἔσοιτο σφίσιν ἐς τὴν [2.37] ἀρχὴν καθισταμένων. Ὧν δὴ ἕνα τε καὶ δύο ἀναπυνθανόμενος εὗρον, καὶ ἐξέμαθον τό τε γένος αὐτῶν

they would lose, but they would quickly regroup and fight again.

These peoples fight ferocious battles, sparing no one. 53
They attack with spears, cannons, iron catapults drawn by horses, and other projectiles, and they fight with these and cut each other down. But when they flee, no harm is done to them in flight, for if someone surrenders and concedes defeat they let him go, on the condition that they never again have to fight him whenever the armies engage in battle with each other. This is how they treat each other in battles, so that whenever an army is routed and flees, only a small part of it is thereby lost.

The Hungarians came to Wallachia under the leadership 54
of Hunyadi, appointed Dan as its ruler and urged the Wallachians to obey him.[98] When their ruler [Vlad II] Dracul marched out and went to Sultan Murad's Porte, Dan occupied the land and killed off the associates of the ruler Dracul, wherever he learned that one of them could be found. They are said to have been the illegitimate sons of Mircea,[99] and some of them pretended to be his sons and were appointed to rule over Wallachia by the noble and rich men of the land, thinking that it would be good and profitable for them to be established in power. One or two of them I found by making careful inquiries and I learned who

καὶ τοὺς πατέρας· ἀλλ' οὐκ ἐξοίσω ἐς τοὺς πολλοὺς τοὔνομα διασημήνας.

55 Δᾶνος μὲν οὖν τότε ὑπὸ Παιόνων κατήχθη ἐς τὴν [Παιόνων] ἀρχήν, καὶ ἔσχε τὴν χώραν, θεραπεύων τε ἀπὸ τοῦδε διετέλει τοὺς Παίονας. Καὶ ὡς ἐπέκειντο τὴν χώραν διαβαίνοντες κρύφα οἱ τοῦ βασιλέως αὐτοῦ παρὰ τὸν Ἴστρον καθεστῶτες ὕπαρχοι, πρέσβεις τε ἔπεμπεν ὡς βασιλέα, καὶ εἰρήνην αἰτούμενος ἔπρασσεν, ὅπως αὐτῷ γένοιτο, ἀπαιτηθεὶς ἀπάγειν ἐς τρισχίλια τόξα καὶ θυρεοὺς τετρακισχιλίους τοῦ ἐνιαυτοῦ, σπονδάς τε ἐποιήσατο. Καὶ οὕτω δὴ ἐπὶ κατάστασιν εὖ ἔχουσαν ἑαυτῷ ἀφικόμενος ἡγεμόνευέ τε τῆς Δακίας, καὶ πρὸς τὸν Μπογδανίας τῆς μελαίνης ἡγεμόνα ἄγγελον πέμψας εἰρήνην τε ἐποιήσατο, καὶ ἐπιγαμίαν αὐτῷ ποιησάμενος συνεβάλλετο αὐτῷ ἐς τὸν πρὸς τὸν Δρακούλην μετὰ ταῦτα πόλεμον. Ταῦτα μὲν δὴ ἐς τὴν ἀρχὴν οὕτως ἔσχεν αὐτῷ τὰ πράγματα.

56 Ἀμουράτης δὲ μετὰ ταῦτα ἐπὶ Κολχίδα γῆν τριήρεις ἔπεμψε, τήν τε χώραν δῃῶσαι καὶ ἀνδραποδίσασθαι τὴν πόλιν, ἢν δύνωνται, καὶ ἐπὶ Γοτθίαν ἐπιπλεῦσαί τε, καὶ ὅπῃ παρείκοι, τὴν χώραν ληΐσασθαι ἀποβάντας. Καὶ ἐπιπλέουσαι μὲν αἱ τριήρεις προσέσχον ἐς γῆν τε τὴν Κολχίδα, καὶ ἐπὶ τοὺς Γότθους ἀφικόμενοι ἐλεηλάτουν τὴν χώραν, ἀνδραποδισάμενοι οὐκ ὀλίγην. Ἐπανιόντι δὲ τῷ στόλῳ χειμὼν ἐγένετο ἰσχυρός, καὶ ἄνεμος [2.38] ἀπαρκτίας ἐπιβαλὼν ἐξήνεγκεν ἐς τὴν Ἀσίαν κατὰ τὴν Ποντοηράκλειαν, καὶ φερόμεναι αὐτοῦ ἔνιαι τῶν τριηρῶν διεφθείροντο καὶ ἐν ξυμφορᾷ ἔσχοντο τοιαύτῃ.

57 Πρὸς Ἰανυΐους μέντοι αὐτῷ φιλια ἦν διὰ τέλους καὶ

their families and fathers were. But I will not divulge their names publicly.

So Dan was installed by the Hungarians as ruler and held 55
the land. Henceforth he served the interests of the Hungarians. But as the prefects who were appointed there to the Danube region by the sultan were crossing over and secretly infiltrating the land, Dan sent envoys to the sultan and negotiated, asking that he be at peace with him, and he was requested to deliver three thousand bows and four thousand shields annually. He made the treaty. Thus on these terms, that were good for him, he came to rule over Wallachia.[100] He sent a messenger to the ruler of Moldavia to make peace, and he also concluded a marriage alliance with him which brought him assistance for the war that he fought later against Dracul.[101] And that was how matters stood in his principality.

After that Murad dispatched triremes against Kolchis 56
to plunder the land and enslave the city, if they could; they were also to sail against Gotthia and, wherever they could obtain a foothold, to disembark and plunder the land.[102] The triremes sailed to Kolchis and put in there, and they went against the Goths and plundered their land, enslaving a large part of it. As the fleet was returning, a violent storm blew up and a wind from the north forced them toward Asia, by Herakleia on the Black Sea coast. Tossed in that direction some of the triremes were destroyed, and suffered such a fate.

Murad preserved his friendship and peace with the 57

εἰρηναῖα. Ἰανύϊοι μὲν δὴ τότε πρός τε σφᾶς αὐτοὺς περιπεσόντες μεγάλως τε ἐσφάλλοντο περὶ τὴν πόλιν αὐτῶν, καὶ δὴ καὶ τῶν στασιωτῶν ἐπαγομένων Φίλιππον τὸν Λιγύρων ἡγεμόνα τήν τε πόλιν ἐπέτρεψαν, καὶ οἳ ἂν ἐξηγοῖτο, εἵποντο τῷ ἡγεμόνι. Πυνθάνομαι γενέσθαι δὴ τοῦτο αὐτοῖς καὶ τὸν δῆμον ἑλόμενον ἐπαγαγέσθαι τοῦτον σφίσι τύραννον καταστησαμένους διὰ τὸ πρὸς τοὺς Οὐενετοὺς ἔχθος καὶ τὴν πρὸς ἐκείνους αὐτῶν διαφοράν, καὶ ὅτι καὶ τὸν Μεδιολάνου τοῦτον ἡγεμόνα ᾔσθοντο πολεμοῦντα τοῖς Οὐενετοῖς κατὰ τὸ καρτερὸν καὶ διαφέροντα τὸν πόλεμον ἐκτεταμένως.

58 Ἔστι δ᾽ ἡ πόλις αὕτη πρὸς τὸ ἄκρον τῆς Ἰταλίας κατὰ τὴν Γαλατίαν· Τυρρηνῶν δὲ τῆς χώρας ἔχεται τὸ πρὸς ἕω ἰόντι, καὶ Τυρρηνικοῦ πελάγους ἅπτεται, ταύτῃ τετραμμένη τὸ πρὸς ἀνίσχοντος ἡλίου ἡ πόλις· πρὸς δὲ ἑσπέραν ἀπαλλαττομένης τῆς χώρας Ἰανυΐων ἐπιβαίνειν ἔστι τῆς Προβεντίας, ἥτις Γαλατία ἐστὶ καὶ ὑπὸ τῶν Κελτῶν βασιλεῖ τεταγμένοι διατελοῦσιν. Ὀνομάζεται δὲ διὰ ταύτης πύλη Ἰταλίας, ὡς αὐτίκα ἀπὸ τούτων ἐμβάλλει ἐς Γαλατίαν. Πολιτεύεται δὲ οὔτε ἐς δημοκρατίαν τὸ παράπαν τετραμμένη ἡ πόλις, οὔτε ἐς ἀριστοκρατίαν· ἐπιμεμιγμένη δὲ ἀμφοῖν ταῖς καταστάσεσι, τοῦτο μὲν [2.39] ἐς δημοκρατίαν δοκεῖ ἀποκλίνειν, τοῦτο δ᾽ αὖ ὑπὸ ἀρίστων τινῶν διϊθύνεσθαι, τὰ ἐς τὴν ἀρχὴν αὐτὴ διατιθεμένη. Ἔστι γὰρ δύο γένη ἐν τῇ πόλει ταύτῃ ἀπὸ παλαιοῦ προεστῶτες τῆς πόλεως, καὶ πρωτεύοντες οὕτως, ὥστε ξύμπαντα τὸν δῆμον ἐπὶ τούτους τετράφθαι, τῷ παντὶ θάτερα ταλαντευόμενον. Τὸ μὲν δὴ τοῖν γένοιν καλεῖται Ντόρια, τὸ δὲ

Genoese to the end. At that time the Genoese had turned against each other and their city was experiencing great instability as one faction had brought in Filippo, the ruler of the Lombards, entrusted the city to him, and were ready to follow him upon whatever course he led them.[103] I have learned that this happened, and that the people chose to bring him in and made him their tyrant, on account of their hatred of the Venetians and their struggle against them. They realized that this ruler of Milan was fighting the Venetians fiercely and prosecuting the war on a broad front.

This city of Genoa is located at the edge of Italy in the 58
direction of France. To the east it borders on Tuscany, and it touches the Tyrrhenian Sea. The city is turned toward the rising sun. If one goes west from the land of the Genoese one enters Provence, which is in France and its inhabitants are subject to the king of the French. Because of this it is named "the Gates of Italy," because at this point it borders directly on France.[104] The city government is not entirely democratic but nor again is it an aristocracy: it is a mixture of both regimes, but seems to incline in part to the democratic side, but on the other hand it is governed by its nobility, and thus orders its public affairs. From of old there have been two leading families in this city and their prominence is such that the entire populace supports them, but they are evenly balanced on either side. One of these two families is

ἕτερον Σπίνουρα. Ἐπὶ τούτους ὁ δῆμος διῃρημένος τὸ μὲν αὐτοῦ αἱρεῖται τὴν Σπίνουρα αἵρεσιν, τὸ δὲ αὖ τοῦ Ντόρια. Ἄγοντες δὲ οὗτοι τὸν δῆμον, καθιστάναι μὲν ἀπὸ σφῶν αὐτῶν ἡγεμόνας τῇ πόλει οὐκ ἔξεστιν, οὐδὲ ἐπιτρέπει ὁ δῆμος· ἀλλ' ἐστὸν δύο ἑτέρω γένεε, δημόται ὄντες, καὶ τὸ μὲν τῶν γενῶν τούτων πρὸς τὸ γένος τῶν ἀρίστων τετραμμένον ἐστὶ καὶ ἐπιτήδειον, τὸ δὲ αὖ πρὸς τὸ ἕτερον. Καλεῖται δὲ τούτων τὸ μὲν Ἀδόρνοι, τὸ δὲ Φρεγούσιοι. Ἀπὸ δὲ τούτων τῶν οἰκιῶν νομίζεται αὐτοῖς, ὁποία δὴ τῶν ἀρίστων μοῖρα ἐπικρατοίη, ἐγκαθιστάναι τῇ πόλει ἄρχοντα. Καὶ τῶν μὲν Ἀδόρνων ὁ οἶκος ᾠκείωται τῷ Σπίνουρα γένει, τὸ δὲ Φρεγουσίων τῷ Ντόρια ἐπιτήδειόν τέ ἐστι καὶ ἐγκαθιστάμενον ὑπ' αὐτοῦ ἐς τὴν ἀρχήν.

59 Τῷ δὲ ἡγεμόνι τούτῳ, ἐπειδὰν ἐς τὴν ἡγεμονίαν καταστaίη, ἐπιτέτραπται κατὰ τοὺς νόμους, ἐπιλαβομένῳ καὶ τῶν ἀρίστων τινῶν, τρέπειν ὡς ξυμφερώτατα. Περὶ μὲν οὖν τῶν προσόδων τῆς πόλεως τούτους νομίζεται ἐπιτροπεύειν, διαθεῖναι, [2.40] ᾗ ἂν αὐτοῖς δοκοίη· περὶ πολέμου δὲ καὶ εἰρήνης νομίζεται τὸν δῆμον παρελθόντα ἐς μέσον αἱρεῖσθαι, ὅ τι ἂν αὐτῷ δοκοίη, ἑλόμενον δὲ ἐπιτρέπειν τῷ ἡγεμόνι πράσσειν ὡς λυσιτελέστατα. Ἐς δὲ τὰς δίκας τῆς πόλεως ἐγκαθίστανται δικασταὶ ὑπὸ τοῦ ἐπικρατοῦντος γένους, καὶ δικάζουσι κατὰ τὰ σφῶν αὐτῶν. Τῆς δὲ δίκης ἔφεσίς ἐστιν ἐπὶ τὸν δῆμον, ἐπειδάν τις αὐτῶν μὴ κατὰ τοὺς νόμους δικάσηται.

60 Διενεχθέντε δὲ τὼ γένεε τούτω, Ντόριά τε καὶ Σπίνουρα, καὶ ἐς διαφορὰν σφίσι καθισταμένω, μεγάλα τε τὴν

named Doria and the other Spinola. The people are divided between them, with one part choosing the faction of Spinola and the other the faction of Doria. They may lead the people but are not permitted to be appointed as rulers over the city, nor would the populace allow it. Yet there are two additional families and these come from the people. One of these two supports the noble families and sides with them, while the other favors the other side; the first of them is called Adorni, while the second are the Fregosi. It is their custom to appoint a lord for the city from these two families, depending on which faction of the nobility prevails. For the house of Adorni is affiliated with the family of Spinola, while the Fregosi are the friends of Doria and are installed by them in power.[105]

59 When a ruler is appointed and takes on some of the leading men, he is entrusted by the laws to act in the best interests of the city. Typically, it is the rulers who supervise the city's income and dispose of it as they see fit. Still, in matters of war and peace it is the populace that has the right to choose openly whatever it wants to decide, but it may choose to entrust matters to the ruler to handle in the most advantageous way. The dominant family appoints the judges for the trials that take place in the city, and they judge in accordance with their ways. It is possible to appeal a verdict to the people, whenever one of them is not judged in accordance with the laws.

60 When these two families, the Doria and Spinola, are at odds with each other and fall out between themselves, they

πόλιν κακὰ εἰργάσαντο, τυράννους τε ἐς τὴν πόλιν ἐγκαθιστάντες, καὶ ἐπαγόμενοι ἀθέμιτα ἐπὶ τὴν πόλιν πράγματα. Τῶν δὲ γενῶν τούτων τὸ μὲν πρὸς τοὺς Λίγυράς τε καὶ Ἰταλίαν τετραμμένον αἱρεῖται ἑαυτῷ τοὺς Ἰταλοὺς καὶ συμμάχους ἐπάγεται, τὸ δὲ τῶν Κελτῶν βασιλέα ἐπὶ τὴν πόλιν. Ξυμφοραῖς μὲν οὖν πολλαχῇ περιέπεσεν ἡ πόλις αὕτη, ἐς ἀνήκεστα κακὰ προαγομένων τῶν τῆς πόλεως γενῶν ἐπ' ἀλλήλους, καὶ τοὺς σφῶν αὐτῶν πολεμιωτάτους ἐπαγομένων ἐπ' ἀλλήλους· ἐπειδὰν μέντοι ἀνάγκῃ περιπίπτοντες ἀνηκέστῳ παρὰ τὰ σφῶν ἔθιμα ἀναγκάζοιντο πολιτεύεσθαι ὑπὸ τῶν τυράννων, δαιμονίως ὁμοφρονοῦντες ἀλλήλοις κατὰ τὸ ἰσχυρὸν ἐξελαύνουσί τε αὐτίκα, ὃς ἂν τύχῃ ἐν τῇ πόλει διαιτητὴς οὐκ ἀγαθός. Ἐπαγόμενοί τε γὰρ πολλάκις τῶν Κελτῶν βασιλέα, ἐπιτρέψαντες τὴν πόλιν, αὖθις ἐξήλασαν ὁμοφρονοῦντες ἀλλήλοις, ὥστε μὴ πάνυ ἐνδιατρίβειν ἐῶντες παρὰ σφίσι τὴν [2.41] τυραννίδα ὁ δῆμος ἐπὶ τὴν ἐλευθερίαν ἐπανίασι, τὰ παρόντα σφίσι καινοτομοῦντες καὶ ἐξελαύνοντες, αὖθις καθιστᾶσι τῶν ἀστῶν ἡγεμόνας καὶ κατὰ τὰ πάτρια πολιτεύονται.

61 Διάφοροι δέ εἰσι μάλιστα τοῖς ἀπὸ Ταρακῶνος καὶ τοῖς Ταρακονησίοις τὸ παλαιόν, καὶ πολέμους διέφερον ἐπὶ πολλαῖς γενεαῖς ἐς τούτους τε καὶ τὴν χώραν αὐτῶν, καὶ ἰδίᾳ τε καὶ δημοσίᾳ, ὅποι ἀλλήλοις περιτύχωσιν, ἐς μάχην αὑτοὺς καθίστανται, ὥστε ἀνελεῖν ἀλλήλους, ἢν δύνωνται. Ταρακονησίοις μὲν οὖν ἐς διαφορὰν καθεστῶτες αἰεί τε πολέμιοί εἰσιν, ἐξ ὅτου ἐγένοντο· πρὸς δὲ τοὺς Οὐενετοὺς διηνέχθησαν μὲν καὶ πάλαι διὰ τὰς ἐν τῷ Αἰγαίῳ πελάγει νήσους Χίον τε καὶ Λέσβον, οὐχ ἥκιστα δὲ καὶ διὰ

do great harm to the city, installing tyrants over it and introducing radical innovations. One of these families inclines to the Lombards and to Italy and brings in the Italians as its allies, while the other brings the king of the French into the city.[106] This city has often been struck by misfortune as the city's families inflict unspeakable evils upon each other and they unleash their own worst enemies against each other. But whenever they reach a point of dire necessity, contrary to their own customs they are forced to be governed by tyrants, but then they reach an extraordinary degree of agreement among each other and drive them out forcefully, if there happens to be an evil arbiter in the city. They have often brought in the king of the French and entrusted their city to him, but then they expelled him when they came to an agreement with each other. Thus, the populace does not allow tyrannies to last long among them and regains its liberty, introducing radical solutions to their problems and driving those tyrants out again. Then they appoint rulers from among the citizens and govern themselves according to their ancestral traditions.

The Genoese have long been at odds with Aragon and 61
the Aragonese, and have fought wars against them and their territories for many generations. Wherever they chance upon each other, whether in private or in public, they join battle with them with the intention of killing each other, if possible. For as long as they have existed, they have always been at odds with and enemies of the Aragonese.[107] They also fell out with the Venetians a long time ago on account of the Aegean islands Chios and Lesbos, and not least on

τὸν Λιγύρων ἡγεμόνα, ὃν σφίσιν ἐπαγόμενοι τύραννον ἐγκατέστησαν καὶ ἐν στάσει γενόμενοι τὴν πόλιν ἐπέτρεψαν ἐπιτροπεύειν τε, καὶ Οὐενετοῖς ἐπολέμουν καὶ τῷ Ταρακονησίων βασιλεῖ. Καὶ ναῦς μὲν ἐπλήρουν ἐς τὸν πρὸς Οὐενετοὺς πόλεμον, καὶ ἐπιπλέοντες τάς τε ἐς τὸν Ἰόνιον πόλεις ἐκάκουν καὶ τὰς ἐπὶ τῷ Αἰγαίῳ. Ταῦτα δὲ ἔπραττον τοὺς Οὐενετοὺς τιμωροῦντές τε τῷ Λιγύρων τυράννῳ τῷ Φιλίππῳ. Καὶ τήν τε Κέρκυραν πῦρ ἐνιέντες ἐς τὰ προάστεια κατέκαυσαν, καὶ ἔβλαπτον, εἴ τι προχωροίη αὐτοῖς.

62 Ὕστερον μέντοι, ὡς πρὸς τὸν Ταρακόνων βασιλέα ᾧ ὄνομα Ἀλφόνσον διενεχθέντες, ἐμάχοντο πρὸς Γαέτην πόλιν τῆς Ἰταλίας· ἐνταῦθά τε γὰρ καθορμιζομένων τῶν τοῦ [2.42] βασιλέως Ἀλφόνσου νεῶν μεγίστων, καὶ ὡς ἐπύθοντο οἱ Ἰανύϊοι τόν τε στόλον αὐτοῦ ἐνταῦθα ὡς ἐπ' αὐτοὺς παρασκευαζόμενον τὸν βασιλέα, πληρώσαντες ναῦς μεγίστας δὴ ὧν ἡμεῖς ἴσμεν, τῶν ἐπὶ τὴν ἐμπορίαν ἀφικνουμένων, καὶ ἐξοπλισάμενοι ἀπὸ τῆς πόλεως ἀνήγοντο ἐπὶ τοὺς Ταρακονησίους, καταλαβόντες δὲ αὐτὸν ἐν τῷ Γαέτης λιμένι διεναυμάχουν ταῖς τοῦ βασιλέως ναυσὶν ἐπὶ πολὺν χρόνον. Ἔτυχε δὲ αὐτοῦ τότε παρὼν ἐν τῇ πόλει ὁ βασιλεύς, καὶ τὴν μάχην θεώμενος ἤσχαλλέ τε καὶ ἠθύμει, ὅτι πλειόνων ἐν ταῖς ἑαυτοῦ ναυσὶν ὄντων ἀνδρῶν οὐχ οἷαί τ' ἂν εἶεν ὑπερβάλλεσθαι τὰς τῶν πολεμίων ναῦς. Καὶ δὴ καὶ ἐμβὰς αὐτὸς ἐς τὰς ναῦς, ὥστε ἐποτρῦναι αὐτοὺς ἐπὶ τὸν πόλεμον, μάχης οὖν καρτερᾶς γενομένης ἥ τε ναῦς ἑάλω, καὶ σὺν αὐτῇ τε ἅμα ἑάλω καὶ ὁ Ταρακόνων βασιλεύς. Εἷλε δὲ καὶ τὴν ναῦν γραμματιστὴς τοῦ Ντόρια, ναυαρχοῦντος τότε τοῖς Ἰανυΐοις.

account of the ruler of the Lombards [Filippo Maria Visconti], whom they brought in and installed as their tyrant. They were in a state of civil strife and entrusted the supervision of their city to him, and fought against the Venetians and the king of the Aragonese [Alfonso V].[108] They manned their ships in the war against the Venetians and set sail, harassing the cities both of the Adriatic and Aegean Sea. They did this to the Venetians on behalf of Filippo, the tyrant of the Lombards. They set fire to the suburbs on Kerkyra and burned them down, and generally caused harm wherever they had the opportunity.[109]

Later the Genoese fell out with the king of the Ara- 62
gonese, whose name was Alfonso,[110] and fought against Gaeta, a city of Italy, where the largest ships of King Alfonso were harbored. When the Genoese learned that the king was preparing his fleet against them there, they manned the largest ships of which we have knowledge, ships that were designed for trade. Thus equipped, they set sail from their city and attacked the Aragonese, attacking the enemy in the harbor of Gaeta and fighting a protracted naval battle with the king's ships. The king happened to be present at that time in the city and, as he watched the battle, he was distressed and was becoming despondent because his ships were unable to overcome the enemy ships even though they had more men. So he embarked in person upon a ship to encourage them in the battle. The battle became fierce and his ship was captured and along with it the king of the Aragonese was captured too.[111] The ship was captured by the secretary of Doria, who was the Genoese admiral at the time.[112]

63 Οἳ ἐπεί τε περιεγένοντο καὶ αὐτὸν εἷλον τὸν βασιλέα, ἀπέπλεον ἐπ' οἴκου. Ὡς δὲ ἀγχοῦ τῆς πόλεως ἐγένοντο, πρὶν ἢ ἐς τὴν πόλιν αὐτὸν καθορμίσασθαι, ἀποστρέψας ἔπλει ἐπὶ τὴν τοῦ Λιγύρων ἡγεμόνος χώραν, ὡς αὐτόν τε ἐκείνῳ ἄξων αἰχμάλωτον τὸν βασιλέα Ἀλφόνσον, καὶ οἰόμενος μέγα τι ἀποίσεσθαι αὐτῷ κέρδος ἀπὸ τοῦ ἡγεμόνος. Ἐπιβὰς δὲ τῆς χώρας αὐτοῦ ἧκεν ἄγων τὸν βασιλέα αἰχμάλωτον παρὰ τὸν Λιγυρίας τύραννον. Ἐνταῦθα ὁ Μεδιολάνου ἡγεμὼν οὗτος τόν τε βασιλέα ὑπεδέξατο ἐν τιμῇ, καὶ μεγάλως τιμήσας αὐτὸν ἀπέπεμψεν ἐπὶ τὴν ἀρχὴν αὐτοῦ. Καὶ τὸ ἀπὸ τοῦδε οἵ τε Ἰανυΐων ἄνδρες γνώμῃ διενεχθέντες [2.43] πρὸς τοῦτον οὐ πολλῷ ὕστερον ἀπέστησαν καὶ τὸν ἄρχοντα ἐξήλασαν, καὶ τοὺς ἐς τὴν τῆς πόλεως ἀκρόπολιν καταφυγόντας ὁμολογίᾳ παραστησάμενοι· καὶ αὐτοὶ ἐς τὰ πατρῷα σφίσι τοῦ λοιποῦ τὴν πόλιν διῴκουν, ἐγκαθιστάντες δὲ ἡγεμόνας τῶν ἀστῶν ἐπὶ τῇ ἡγεμονίᾳ, ᾗ καὶ πρότερον αὐτοῖς ἐνομίζετο.

64 Ὁ μέντοι Ἀλφόνσος ἀπολυθεὶς ὑπὸ τοῦ Μεδιολάνου ἡγεμόνος εὔνως τε αὐτῷ εἶχε, καὶ ἐπιτηδείως ὑπουργῶν, ἅττ' ἂν αὐτῷ πρὸς χάριν ἡγήσαιτο, ἥδεσθαι οὐκ ἐπαύσατο διὰ παντός, ἐς ὃ δὴ ὁ τοῦ Μεδιολάνου ἡγεμὼν ἐτελεύτησεν. Οὗτος δὲ ὁ Ταρακονησίων βασιλεὺς τῆς τε Βαλεντίας βασιλεύων καὶ Ταρακῶνος καὶ τῆς τε Σαρδόνος νήσου καὶ Κύρνου, καὶ ἐπάρχων τῆς Βαρκενώνης πόλεως εὐδαίμονος κατὰ τὴν Ἰβηρίαν, ἀφίκετο ἐς Σικελίαν μὲν τὸ πρῶτον, μετὰ δὲ ταῦτα ἐς Ἰταλίαν καὶ ἐπὶ Παρθενόπην, καὶ τὴν βασιλείαν κατέσχε τρόπῳ τοιῷδε· τὴν γὰρ Νεάπολιν ταύτην τῆς Ἰταλίας προσελθοῦσαν τὸ παλαιὸν ἐς τὸν

The Genoese prevailed in that battle, capturing the king himself, and sailed back home. When they came near the city, before harboring there the admiral turned away and sailed to the territory of the ruler of the Lombards [Visconti], in order to bring King Alfonso to him as a captive, and hoping to receive some great reward from the ruler. So he entered his territory and went there, bringing the captive king to the tyrant of Lombardy. Thereupon the ruler of Milan received the king with honors and, after greatly honoring him, sent him back to his realm. From this point on the men of Genoa turned against the ruler of Milan and not much later they rebelled and drove that lord out.[113] They subjected those who sought refuge in the city's citadel through a negotiated surrender. Henceforth they governed the city according to their own customs and installed rulers from among the citizens in the highest position, as they had done in the past. 63

Released by the ruler of Milan, Alfonso was well disposed toward him and assisted him as a friend in whatever manner he could bestow favors upon him, and he never ceased to gratify him, until the ruler of Milan died.[114] This king of the Aragonese reigned over Valencia, Aragon, and the islands of Sardinia and Corsica. He was also the governor of Barcelona, a prosperous city in Iberia.[115] He first went to Sicily and then to Italy and Parthenope, and occupied its kingdom in the following way.[116] Italian Naples used to belong of old 64

Κελτῶν βασιλέα, ἀπεδείκνυτο ἀπὸ οἴκου τοῦ βασιλέως ἐς τήνδε τὴν χώραν τῆς Ἰταλίας βασιλέα καὶ ἄρχοντα. Ἡ δὲ βασιλεία ἄρχεται μὲν ἀπὸ Ἰαπυγίας ἄκρας καὶ Μεσαπίας, καὶ ἐπὶ πολὺ προϊοῦσα κατὰ τὸν Ἰόνιον κόλπον ἐπ᾽ ἀριστερὰ εἰσπλέοντι ἀμείβει τε τὴν χώραν τῆς Βάρης οὕτω καλουμένης, καί γε τὴν βασιλικωτάτην ἐπέχει λόγου ἀξίαν οὕτω χώραν. Μετὰ δὲ τὴν Γήπονον οὕτω καλουμένην διήκει ἐπὶ Γαέτην καὶ ἐπὶ Κιετίην, πόλιν ὁμοροῦσαν τὸ πρὸς ἑσπέραν [2.44] τῇ Ῥωμαίων χώρᾳ, τὸ δὲ πρὸς ἕω τῷ Ἰονίῳ. Ἔχει δὲ καὶ τὴν πρὸς Σικελίαν τετραμμένην χώραν, Ἑλλάδα τὸ παλαιὸν καλουμένην, τὰ νῦν δὲ Καλαβρίαν.

65 Ὡς δὴ οὖν ἐπὶ τῶν Κελτῶν βασιλέα περιελήλυθεν ἡ τῆς Νεαπόλεως βασιλεία, ἐπέστησεν αὐτῇ βασιλέα τῶν προσηκόντων αὐτοῦ, ἕνα οἴκου τοῦ βασιλέως. Ὃς δὲ ἀφικόμενος ἐς τὴν Νεάπολιν (Λαντίσλαος δ᾽ ἦν ὄνομα αὐτῷ) ἐβασίλευέ τε τῆς χώρας, καὶ ἐπὶ μέγα δυνάμεως τῶν κατὰ τὴν Ἰταλίαν[6] ἐπί τε τὴν Τυρρηνῶν ἀρχὴν ἐστρατεύετο καὶ ἐπὶ τὴν λοιπὴν Ἰταλίαν, μεγάλα ἀποδεικνύμενος ἔργα. Καὶ δὴ καὶ ἐπὶ τὴν τῶν Τυρρηνῶν μητρόπολιν Φλωρεντίαν στρατὸν ἐπαγόμενος καὶ προσκαθεζόμενος ἐπολιόρκει. Ὡς δὲ χρονιωτέρα ἐγένετο ἡ πολιορκία, λέγεται, ὡς ἐς τὸ ἔσχατον κακοῦ ἀφικόμενοι οἱ τῆς πόλεως λόγους προσέφερον περὶ εἰρήνης, φάσκοντες πείσεσθαι αὐτούς, ὅ τι ἂν κελεύοι, καὶ ἐπὶ τούτοις διαλύεσθαι. Τὸν δὲ ξυμβαίνοντα αἰτεῖσθαι τῶν ἀστῶν τινὸς θυγατέρα, εὐπρεπῆ τε οὖσαν καὶ πασῶν τῶν ἐν τῇ πόλει λεγομένην[7] εἶναι καλλίω, ταύτην ὡς ἐπύθετο κάλλει διενεγκεῖν τῶν ἐν τῇ πόλει.

to the king of the French, and the lord and king of this territory in Italy was appointed from his royal house.[117] The kingdom begins from the ends of Apulia and Salento and extends a long distance along the Adriatic Sea, along the left coast as one sails into it, where it meets the territory of Bari, as that place is called. It contains the most royal and noteworthy lands. Beyond the Terra di Lavoro, as it is called,[118] it extends to Gaeta and Chieti, a city that borders on the land of the Romans to the west, while to the east it borders the Adriatic Sea. It also has the land that is turned toward Sicily, which was formerly called Greece[119] but is now Calabria.

When the kingdom of Naples came under the king of the 65
French, he appointed over it as king one of his relatives from his own house. His name was Ladislao and he went to Naples and reigned over that territory.[120] When he attained great power among the Italians, he campaigned against the principality of the Tuscans and the rest of Italy and performed great deeds.[121] He also led an army against the capital of the Tuscans, Florence, and invested the city to besiege it. As the siege was dragging on, it is said that the people of the city reached the limit of their endurance and made peace overtures, saying that they would obey him no matter what he asked so long as they could be reconciled. He agreed and asked for the daughter of one of the citizens, who was decorous and said to be more beautiful than all the women in the city; for he had learned that she surpassed in beauty all of the city's women.

66 Φέρει δὲ αὕτη ἡ πόλις μάλιστα δὴ γυναῖκας κάλλει διαφερούσας τῶν ἐν Ἰταλίᾳ, μετ' αὐτῶν γε παρθένους. Ταύτην δὲ ἀναπυνθανόμενος οὕτω ἔχειν ἐς κάλλος (ἦν δὲ ἄλλως ὁ βασιλεὺς οὗτος καὶ ἐς γυναῖκας ἐπιμανὴς καὶ ἀκόλαστος), [2.45] αἰτούμενος ταύτην αὐτῷ δοθῆναι τὴν γυναῖκα, ἐπὶ τῇ ξυμβάσει αὐτὸν συναινέσαι τοὺς Τυρρηνούς, καὶ κελεῦσαι τὸν πατέρα ἐνσκευασάμενον τὴν θυγατέρα αὐτοῦ τῷ καλλίστῳ δὴ κόσμῳ, ἐκδοῦναι τῷ βασιλεῖ. Τυχεῖν δὲ ἰατρὸν τὸν τῆς παιδὸς ταύτης πατέρα, ἥκοντά τε ἐς τὰ πρῶτα τῆς τέχνης καὶ ἐπὶ πεῖραν πολλῶν ἀφικόμενον. Ὡς δ' οὐκ ἠδύνατο διαφυγεῖν, ὥστε μὴ ἐκδοῦναι τὴν θυγατέρα, ἐγκερασάμενον κόνειον ὡς ἠδύνατο ἰσχυρότατον (ἐν δὲ ταύτῃ τῇ πόλει μάλιστα δὴ τῶν ἐν Ἰταλίᾳ πόλεων ἐγκιρνῶνται τὸ κόνειον ἄμεινον τῶν ἐν ταῖς ἄλλαις πόλεσι) καὶ ἐμβάψαντα τὸ λέντιον ἐς τὸ κόνειον, φέροντα δοῦναι τῇ θυγατρί, ὡς ἐπειδὰν αὐτῇ ἐπιμίσγοιτο ὁ βασιλεύς, μετὰ τὴν συνουσίαν ἐκμάσσειν τὸ αἰδοῖον τῷ λεντίῳ ὡς εὐπρεπέστατα· ταύτην δὲ λαβοῦσαν τὸ λέντιον, θέας τε ἄξιον καὶ χρυσῷ κεκοσμημένον, φυλάττειν, ὥστε ὑπουργεῖν τῷ βασιλεῖ μετά γε τὴν συνουσίαν, ᾗ ἐνετέλλετο αὐτῇ ὁ πατήρ. Ἐπεὶ δὲ ἄγοντες τὴν γυναῖκα ἐνεχείρισαν τῷ βασιλεῖ, θεασάμενος ἐκπλαγῆναι τῷ κάλλει αὐτῆς καὶ ἐρασθέντα συγγενέσθαι, πειθομένην τὴν παῖδα τῷ πατρὶ κατὰ τὰ ἐντεταλμένα, τῷ τε λεντίῳ αὐτίκα φιλοφρονουμένην ἐκμάσσειν τὸ αἰδοῖον. Καὶ ὡς ἥψατο ἐν ὑγρότητι γενομένου, αὐτίκα πυρέξαι τὸν βασιλέα καὶ μετ' οὐ πολὺ ἀποθανεῖν. Τελευτῆσαι δὲ καὶ τὴν γυναῖκα αὐτοῦ, ὡς ἐπ' αὐτὴν ἐπελήλυθε [2.46] τὸ κόνειον (διανεμηθὲν ἐγένετο δι'

This city has the most surpassingly beautiful women in Italy, and among them are virgins too. So, learning about her beauty—this king was, in any case, an insatiable womanizer—he demanded that she be given over to him. The Tuscans consented, based on their agreement, and urged her father to adorn his daughter with the most splendid ornaments, and give her to the king. Now, it happened that this girl's father was a doctor and he was a master practitioner of his art and had extensive experience. He was unable to evade this request, but so as not to hand over his daughter, he mixed the most powerful hemlock that he could—in this city, more than in any other of Italy, they make a stronger potion of hemlock than in the other cities—and soaked a towel in it. He gave it to his daughter so that, after the king had had intercourse with her, she was to wipe his genitals with the towel, as was only seemly. She took the towel, which was impressive to behold and adorned with gold thread, and kept it close so that she could use it on the king after intercourse, as her father had instructed her. When they brought the woman and delivered her to the king, he was struck by her beauty and, becoming aroused, had sex with her. The girl then followed her father's instructions and, with a kindly gesture, wiped the king's genitals with the towel. Upon contact it became moist, and the king immediately grew feverish and died soon afterward.[122] The woman also died, as the hemlock came into contact with her too (for through 66

ὑγροῦ τὸ κόνειον ἁψαμένους[8] τοῦ λεντίου). Τελευτήσαντος μὲν οὖν οὕτω τοῦ βασιλέως τόν τε στρατὸν διαλυθῆναι, ἀποχωρήσαντα ἐπ' οἴκου, καὶ τὴν πόλιν ἐλευθέραν γενέσθαι τῆς πολιορκίας. Λέγουσι δὲ Ἰταλῶν τινες, ὡς οὐχ ὁ πατὴρ εἴη ὁ τὸ λέντιον δεδωκὼς τῇ γυναικὶ καὶ ἐγκερασάμενος, ἀλλ' ἡ βουλὴ τῆς πόλεως αὐτὴν συσκευάσασα τῷ καλλίστῳ κόσμῳ, ὡς εὐπρεπεστέραν φανῆναι τῷ βασιλεῖ, καὶ τὸ λέντιον ἐπιδοῦναι, τούτῳ δὴ φιλοφρονεῖσθαι βασιλέα ἐς τὴν συνουσίαν. Ἀλλὰ ταῦτα μὲν ἐς τοσοῦτον λεγόμενα παρίεμεν, οὐκ εὐπρεπῆ ὄντα.

67 Μετὰ δὲ τὴν τελευτὴν τοῦ βασιλέως Λαντισλάου τὴν γυναῖκα αὐτοῦ ἐνοχλουμένην εἰς τὴν βασιλείαν ὑπό τε τῶν Ἰταλῶν καὶ ὑπὸ τῶν τῆς χώρας ἀρχόντων, πράγματα παρεχόντων αὐτῇ γημαμένῃ Ῥαινερίῳ τῷ Προβεντίας βασιλεῖ, ἀνεψιῷ δ' ὄντι τοῦ Κελτῶν βασιλέως, παραδοῦναί τε τὴν βασιλείαν τῆς Παρθενόπης. Ταύτην δ' εἶναι θυγατέρα ἐπυθόμεθα τοῦ Ταράντου τε καὶ τῆς Ἰαπυγίας ἡγεμόνος, τοῦ Οὐρσίνων οἴκου ἤτοι Ἀρκίων, ὡς ἂν ταύτῃ Ἑλληνιστὶ λέγοιτο, ἀνδρὸς τὰ μέγιστα δυναμένου ἐν τῇ χώρᾳ ταύτῃ τῆς Νεαπόλεως. Τὸν μὲν οὖν Ῥαινέριον παραλαβόντα τὴν βασιλείαν διαγενέσθαι βασιλεύοντα ἔτη δυοκαίδεκα· ἐν τούτῳ δὲ Ἀλφόνσον τὸν Ταρακόνων βασιλέα καὶ Σαρδόνος καὶ Βαλεντίας, οἴκου ὄντα τῶν Μεδίνων, στόλον [2.47] ναυπηγησάμενον μέγιστον, ἐπαγομένων αὐτὸν τῶν ἐν Σικελίᾳ Πανορμέων, ἀφικέσθαι τε ἐς Σικελίαν καὶ ὑφ' αὐτῷ σύμπασαν ποιησάμενον ἔχειν, μετὰ δὲ ταῦτα ἀπὸ ταύτης τῆς νήσου ὁρμώμενον κατασχεῖν τὴν ἐν τῇ Παρθενόπῃ ἀκρόπολιν τὴν μεσόγαιον· εἰσὶ γὰρ τῇ

the liquid, the hemlock spread to whomever touched the towel).[123] When the king died, the army was disbanded and returned home, and the city was freed from the siege. Some Italians say that it was not the father who gave the towel to the woman and mixed the potion but, rather, the city council outfitted her with the most beautiful adornments, so that she might appear as decorous as possible to the king, and gave her the towel to use, as an act of kindness, on the king during intercourse. But let us leave the matter there, for it is not decorous to speak more of it.

After the death of King Ladislao, his wife was harassed in 67
the management of royal affairs by the Italians and the lords of the land, who caused her trouble after she married René, the king of Provence, who was a nephew of the king of the French, and she handed over to him the kingdom of Parthenope.[124] We have ascertained that she was the daughter of the ruler of Taranto and Apulia, from the house of Orsini, or "the Bears," as it would be called in Greek.[125] He was a very powerful man in the kingdom of Naples. René took over the kingship and survived as king for twelve years. It was during his reign that Alfonso, the king of the Aragonese, Sardinia, and Valencia, from the house of Medina,[126] built a huge fleet at the instigation of the people of Palermo, in Sicily, and he went to Sicily and subjected it all to his authority.[127] After that, he set out from this island and took over the citadel of Parthenope {Naples}, the inland one. For this city has two

πόλει ταύτῃ δύο παράλιοι ἀκροπόλεις καὶ μία μεσόγαιος. Στρατὸν δ' ἐπαγόμενος ἐπολιόρκει τε τὴν πόλιν, καὶ μηχανὰς προσφέρων ἐπειρᾶτο ἑλεῖν· ἔνθα καὶ ὁ ἀδελφὸς αὐτοῦ βληθεὶς τηλεβόλῳ ἐτελεύτησε. Μετ' οὐ πολὺ δὲ παραστησάμενος εἷλέ τε καὶ κατέσχε τὴν πόλιν. Μετὰ ταῦτα τήν τε ἀκρόπολιν ἐπολιόρκει, τήν τε παράλιον καὶ τὴν μεσόγαιον. Τὴν μέντοι μεσόγαιον παραστησάμενος λιμῷ ἐξεπολιόρκησε, τὴν δὲ παράλιον παραδόντων αὐτῷ τῶν φυλάκων κατέσχε καὶ φρουρὰν ἐγκαθίστησιν.

68 Ἡ δὲ τοῦ βασιλέως γυνὴ ἐπολιορκεῖτο μὲν ἐν τῇ πρὸς τῷ τῆς πόλεως λιμένι ἀκροπόλει· καὶ ὅ τε ἀνὴρ αὐτῆς ὑπεξῆλθεν ἀπελαυνόμενος, καὶ ἀπέπλει ἐπὶ Προβεντίας ὡς στρατόν τε ἐπάξων ὅτι τάχιστα καὶ τιμωρήσων τῇ γυναικί. Ἔνθα ἡ βασίλεια Φορτίαν τὸν τῆς Μάρκης ἡγεμόνα μεταπεμψαμένη, καὶ τότε δὴ ἐν Ἰταλίᾳ μέγα δυνάμενον τὰ ἐς στρατηγίαν, τόν τε Ἀλφόνσον ἐξήλασε τῆς πόλεως. Ἐκβαλοῦσα ἐκεῖνον ἴσχει τὴν πόλιν, συνεπιλαβομένου τοῦ Φορτία αὐτῇ. Ὡς δὲ ἐπ' αὐτῇ τὰ πράγματα ἐγένετο, τήν τε ἀκρόπολιν ἐπολιόρκει τὴν πρὸς τῷ ὄρει μεσόγαιον καὶ ὡς οὐκ ἠδύνατο ἑλεῖν προκαθεζομένη, λιμῷ ἐπολιόρκει. Μετὰ δὲ ταῦτα χρόνου οὐ πολλοῦ διελθόντος, τοῦ [2.48] Φορτίου διατρίβοντος ἐν Ἰταλίᾳ καὶ ἔχοντος ἀμφὶ τοὺς οἰκείους πολέμους, ὡρμημένος ἀπὸ Σικελίας ὁ Ταρακῶνος βασιλεὺς Ἀλφόνσος τήν τε Καλαβρίαν ὑπηγάγετο μὲν πρῶτα, μετὰ δὲ ταῦτα στράτευμα συλλέξας ἐπήλασέ τε δεύτερον καὶ κατέσχε τὴν πόλιν.

69 Καὶ ἥ τε βασίλεια Ῥαινερίου ὑπεξέσχεν ἐκ τῆς ἀκροπόλεως ἐπὶ τὸν παῖδα αὐτῆς, ἡγεμόνα Ταράντου καὶ

citadels on the coast and one inland.[128] He brought up an army, besieged the city, and attempted to take it by bringing up engines. His brother was wounded there by a cannon and died.[129] But shortly after he invested the city, he captured it and took it over. After that he besieged the citadel, both the inland one and the coastal one. He captured the inland citadel after starving it out in a siege, and the coastal one when its garrison surrendered it to him. He installed his own garrison there.

Meanwhile, the wife of the king [Ladislao] was being besieged in the citadel that is by the harbor of the city.[130] Her husband had secretly withdrawn and departed, sailing for Provence in order to lead back an army as quickly as he could and avenge his wife.[131] Thereupon the queen summoned Sforza, the lord of the Marche, who then had great military power in Italy, and drove Alfonso away from the city.[132] Having thrown him out, she strengthened her hold over the city, with Sforza's assistance. Control of affairs returned to her hands and she besieged the citadel, the inland one by the mountain, but as she was unable to take it by siege, she tried to starve it out. A short time later, when Sforza was away in Italy as he had his own wars to fight, King Alfonso of Aragon set out from Sicily and first subjected Calabria; after that he assembled an army, embarked on a second campaign, and occupied the city.[133] 68

René's queen escaped from the citadel and went to her son, the ruler of Taranto and Apulia. For after the death of 69

Ἰαπυγίας· τὸν γὰρ δὴ ἡγεμόνα τῆς Ἰαπυγίας ἐγήματο μετὰ τὴν τελευτὴν Λαντισλάου, ἀφ' ἧς ἔσχε παῖδα τοῦτον τὸν Ἰαπυγίας ἡγεμόνα. Ὡς μέντοι Ἀλφόνσος κατέσχε τὴν πόλιν καὶ χώραν τὴν Γήπονον καλουμένην, ἐπολέμει πρὸς τὸν Ἰαπυγίας ἡγεμόνα παῖδά τε τῆς Μαρίας βασιλίδος, καὶ ἐπιὼν κατεστρέφετο τὴν χώραν. Χρόνου δὲ ἐπιγινομένου πρέσβεις τε πέμπων παρ' αὐτὸν ὁ τῆς Ἰαπυγίας ἡγεμὼν ἠξίου τε αὐτῷ σπένδεσθαι, ἐφ' ᾧ καὶ ἐπιγαμίαν ποιησάμενος· ἡρμόσατο γὰρ δὴ ὁ βασιλεὺς ἐπὶ τῷ παιδὶ αὐτοῦ νόθῳ Ἰνφεράνδῳ τὴν ἀδελφιδοῦν τοῦ Ἰαπυγίας ἡγεμόνος, θυγατέρα δὲ τοῦ Βενόζης ἄρχοντος. Καὶ σπονδὰς ποιησάμενοι, ἐφ' ᾧ ξένους τε καὶ ὑπηκόους εἶναι τῷ βασιλεῖ Ἀλφόνσῳ, μετεπέμπετο ἐπὶ τὴν Νεάπολιν, ἔνθα δὴ ἀφικόμενος ἐς δέος καθίστατο, μὴ ἁλῷ ὑπὸ τοῦ βασιλέως. Καὶ διὰ τόδε τὸ δέος ἔδοξε παθεῖν τὰ ἐς φρένας. Οὕτω μὲν ἐς Ἰταλίαν ἐπὶ τὴν βασιλείαν τῆς τε Σικελίας καὶ Παρθενόπης ἀφίκετο Ἀλφόνσος ἀπὸ Ταρακῶνος· ἐλθὼν δὲ ἐς Ἰταλίαν διέτριβεν αὐτοῦ τὰ μὲν πρὸς τοὺς Τυρρηνοὺς τὰ δὲ [2.49] πρὸς τοὺς Οὐενετοὺς πολεμῶν, τὰ δὲ καὶ σπενδόμενος διετέλει. Ἰανυΐους μὲν ἐπῆγε στόλῳ μεγάλῳ Ῥαινέριος βασιλεὺς ἐπὶ τὴν πόλιν, καὶ ἐπειρῶντο ἀποβῆναι· καὶ ὡς οὐχ οἷοί τε ἐγένοντο, ἀπέπλεον ἐπ' οἴκου.

70 Ἀλφόνσος μὲν οὖν τὴν Λιγύων χώραν καὶ Ταρακῶνος ἐπέτρεψε τῷ ἀδελφῷ, βασιλεῖ γενομένῳ Ναβάρης· τοῦτον γὰρ ἀπὸ Ταρακῶνος ἐπαγόμενοι οἱ τῆς Ναβάρης χώραν ἐνοικοῦντες, ὅτι γυναῖκα ἐγεγαμήκει τοῦ βασιλέως θυγατέρα, καὶ σφίσιν ἐστήσαντο βασιλέα κατὰ τὰ σφῶν αὐτῶν ἔθιμα. Οἱ γὰρ πρὸς ἑσπέραν οἱ πλείους σχεδόν τι

Ladislao she had married the ruler of Apulia, and he had a son with her, namely this current ruler of Apulia. When Alfonso occupied the city and the so-called Terra di Lavoro, he fought a war against the ruler of Apulia, the son of queen Marie, and conquered his land in the attack.[134] Some time later the ruler of Apulia sent envoys to him asking to make a treaty with him, on condition that they make a marriage alliance. The king [Alfonso] married his illegitimate son Don Ferrante to the niece of the ruler of Apulia, the daughter of the lord of Venosa.[135] They made a treaty by which they would be allies and subjects of King Alfonso, and he [presumably Don Ferrante] was sent to Naples, where he lived in terror that he might be captured by the king. Because of this fear, his mind seems to have become unhinged. Thus did Alfonso come to Italy from Aragon and claim the kingdom of Sicily and Parthenope. When he came to Italy, he spent his time fighting against the Tuscans on the one hand and the Venetians on the other, and he also made some treaties. King René led a large Genoese fleet against the city and attempted to make a landing. But they were not able to do this and so they sailed back home.[136]

Alfonso, meanwhile, entrusted the land of the Ligyans[137] 70
and Aragon to his brother, who had become king of Navarre. He had been brought in from Aragon by the inhabitants of the land of Navarre because he had married the daughter of their king, and so they appointed him king according to their custom.[138] Now, most of the rulers in the

ἀποφέρονται μὲν καὶ τὰς τῶν πόλεων προσόδους, ἀρχὰς δὲ οὐ πάνυ τι αὐτοῖς ἔξεστιν ἐγκαθιστάναι ἐς τὰς πόλεις ἢ φυλακάς, ἀλλ' αὐτοί τε οἱ ἐπιχώριοι τάς τε ἀρχὰς μετίασι καὶ φυλακὰς καταστησάμενοι τὴν χώραν ἐπιτροπεύουσι, καὶ τὰ πάτρια σφίσι βιάζεσθαι οὐκ ἔξεστι τοὺς ἐπιχωρίους τὸν βασιλέα παρὰ τὰ σφῶν αὐτῶν ἔθιμα. Τότε μὲν οὖν, ὡς ἐπαγομένων σφίσι βασιλέα τῶν Ναβάρης ἀστῶν ἐπὶ τὴν χώραν τὸν Ἀλφόνσου ἀδελφὸν ἐγένετο αὐτῷ ἀπὸ τῆς γυναικὸς αὐτοῦ παῖς καὶ ἐτράφη ἀμφὶ τὰ δώδεκα ἔτη γεγονώς, τὸν μὲν παῖδα κατέσχον αὐτοῦ, τὸν δὲ βασιλέα ἀπεπέμψαντο, φάμενοι ὡς ἐπεί τε ἐγένετο παῖς, οὐ μετεῖναι αὐτῷ τῆς βασιλείας ἔτι τοῦ λοιποῦ, ἀλλ' εἰς τὸν παῖδα ἀνήκειν. Ταῦτα μὲν ὕστερον οὐ πολλῷ ἐγένετο. Ὅτε δὲ ἐπὶ Ἰταλίαν ἀφίκετο Ἀλφόνσος, τόν τε ἀδελφὸν κατέλιπεν ἐπιτροπεύειν τὴν χώραν αὐτοῦ.

71 Ἄρχεται δὲ αὕτη ἀπὸ Βαλεντίας τῆς χώρας. Καὶ ἡ Βαλεντία [2.50] πόλις ἐστὶ μεγάλη τε καὶ εὐδαίμων, καὶ βασίλειά ἐστιν ἐν αὐτῇ βασιλέως Βαλεντίας. Ὤικηται δὲ αὕτη ἡ πόλις ἀπὸ τοῦ πορθμοῦ τῶν Ἡρακλείων στηλῶν διέχουσα σταδίους ἀμφὶ τοὺς ἑπτακοσίους, ἀντικρὺ Σαρδόνος τῆς νήσου. Μετὰ δὲ ἡ Ταρακῶν καλουμένη χώρα διήκει ἔστε ἐπὶ Βαρκενώνην. Ταύτῃ διαδέχεται τῆς Ταρακῶνος χώρα ἐπὶ Προβεντίαν τὴν Γαλατίαν. Ὥστε δεῖ λέγειν τοὺς ὅρους τῆσδε τῆς βασιλέως χώρας· τὸ μὲν πρὸς ἕω ὁρίζοιτο ἂν τῇ Γαλατίᾳ τῆς Προβεντίας, τὸ δὲ πρὸς ἑσπέραν τῇ Ἰβηρίᾳ, τὸ δὲ πρὸς ἄρκτον τῇ Ναβάρῃ. Βαρκενὼν δέ ἐστι πόλις τῶν πρὸς ἑσπέραν πλούτῳ τε καὶ δυνάμει ὑπερφέρουσα, διοικεῖται δὲ ἐς ἀριστοκρατίαν

west are barely able to take for themselves something from the cities' revenues, but they are not really allowed to install magistrates in the cities or garrisons; rather the locals themselves appoint their magistrates and supervise their lands by placing their own garrisons. Nor is it allowed for the king to violate tradition and make the locals do something contrary to ancestral custom. So at that time, when the citizens of Navarre brought into their land the brother of Alfonso to be their king, his wife bore him a son. When he was raised to about the age of twelve, they took his son but expelled the king, saying that now that he had a son he himself could no longer be king, as the throne belonged to the son.[139] These things happened shortly afterward. When Alfonso went to Italy, he left his brother to supervise his territory.

This realm begins in the land of Valencia. The city of Va- 71
lencia is large and prosperous, and holds the royal court of the king of Valencia. This city is located at a distance of about seven hundred stades from the straits by the Pillars of Herakles, and faces the island of Sardinia. After it is the land called Aragon, and it extends to Barcelona. The land of Aragon follows upon this and extends to Provence, in France. I should specify the borders of the king's land: to the east it is bounded by France, that is Provence; to the west by Castile; and to the north by Navarre. Among all the cities in the west, Barcelona is exceptional in wealth and power. It is governed for the most part by an aristocracy, and it has a

τετραμμένη τὸ πλέον, καὶ ὑπὸ βασιλεῖ Ταρακῶνος ἀξιοῖ πολιτεύεσθαι ἐς τὰ πάτρια. Ἀντικρὺ δὲ ταύτης Κύρνος ἐστὶ νῆσος εὐδαίμων τε καὶ πολυάνθρωπος, καὶ ἡ περίοδος τῆς νήσου λέγεται ἀμφὶ τοὺς δισχιλίους σταδίους. Ἔστι δὲ παρ' αὐτῇ καὶ νῆσος ἑτέρα, ἡ μείων καλουμένη. Αὕτη καὶ ἐν τῇ ὑπὸ τῷ Ταρακώνων βασιλεῖ ταττομένη ἄρχοντα λαμβάνει. Σαρδὼ μέντοι ἡ νῆσος, μεγίστη τε οὖσα καὶ ἀμφὶ τοὺς πεντακισχιλίους σταδίους ἔχουσα τὴν περίοδον, ὑπὸ τῷ βασιλεῖ τούτῳ διατελεῖ. Δύο δὲ πόλεις εἰσὶν ἐν αὐτῇ εὐδαίμονες, Ὀρστάγιά τε καὶ Καγέρη. Ἡ μὲν πρὸς ἕω τῆς νήσου, ἡ δὲ πρὸς μεσημβρίαν ἔχουσα ᾤκηται. Κουρέλιον δ' ἐν ταύτῃ τῇ νήσῳ οἱ ἁλιεῖς δρέπονται ἀπὸ θαλάσσης τῆς νήσου, καὶ ἐντεῦθεν εἰς [2.51] τὴν ἄλλην ἀφικνεῖται οἰκουμένην.

72 Ἰβηρία δὲ ὡς ἔχει, ἀρξαμένη ἀπὸ Γαλατίας, ἀφ' ἧς χώρας Κελτίβηρες διαδέχονται καὶ Γασκώνη χώρα, ὑπὸ τῷ Κελτῶν βασιλεῖ διατελοῦσα. Μετὰ δὲ τὸ πρὸς ἕω Πεσκαΐων χώρα διαδέχεται, ἐπὶ Ἰβηρίαν διατείνουσα. Ἰβηρία δὲ μεγίστη οὖσα τῶν πρὸς ἑσπέραν χώρα, μετά γε τὴν Κελτικήν, διήκει ἐπ' ὠκεανὸν τὸ πρὸς ἑσπέραν, τὸ δὲ πρὸς ἕω Ναβάρῃ τε καὶ Γαλατίᾳ, καὶ τὸ πρὸς μεσημβρίαν τῇ Πορτουγαλλίᾳ, ἥτις παράλιος οὖσα χώρα ἐπὶ τοῦ ὠκεανοῦ ἐπὶ πολὺ διήκει, καὶ τῇ τῶν Λιβύων τῆς Γρανάτης χώρᾳ· ἐντὸς δ' ἐστὶ τὸ τοῦ Ἰακώβου ἱερόν.[9] Πορτουγαλλία δ' ἐχομένη τῆς Ἰβηρίας διήκει ἐπὶ τὴν ἐντὸς θάλασσαν τοῦ πορθμοῦ, ἐπὶ τὴν τῆς Γρανάτης χώραν. Τῆς δὲ Ἰβηρίας χώρας, μεγίστης τε οὔσης καὶ εὐδαίμονος, πόλεις εἰσίν, ἐν αἷς τὰ βασίλεια, ἥ τε Σιβίληνα καλουμένη, μεγάλη τε καὶ

claim on the king of Aragon to be governed in accordance with its own traditions. Facing it is Corsica, a prosperous and populous island, and the circumference of the island is said to be about two thousand stades. There is another island next to it, called the "Lesser."[140] It too is subject to the king of the Aragonese and receives its lord from him. The island of Sardinia is very large and has a circumference of about five thousand stades; it too is subject to this king. There are two prosperous cities on it, Oristano and Cagliari. The former is in the eastern part of the island, the latter is located in the south. The fishermen on this island harvest coral from the sea around it, and from there it comes to the rest of the world.

As for Castile, it begins at France, which land is next to 72
the Celtiberians and the land of Gascony, which is subject to the king of the French. Next toward the east is the land of the Biscayans, which extends to Castile. Castile is the largest of the western lands, after France. In the west it extends to the Ocean, to the east to Navarre and France, and to the south to Portugal, which is a coastal land that extends for quite a distance along the Ocean, and to Granada, the land of the North Africans. It holds the shrine of Santiago. Portugal is adjacent to Castile; it extends to the sea that is inside[141] the straits, to the land of Granada. The land of Castile is very large and prosperous and has cities with palaces, such as the one called Seville, which is very large and populous;

πολυάνθρωπος, καὶ Κορδύβη, Μορσίκη καὶ τὸ λεγόμενον Τολέδον καὶ Σαλαμάγκη. Καὶ ἱερὸν δὲ τοῦ Ἰακώβου ἐν ταύτῃ τῇ χώρᾳ ἐστὶ παρὰ τὸν ὠκεανὸν καὶ τὴν ἐκτὸς θάλασσαν. Διήκει δὲ καὶ πρὸς τὴν ἐντὸς θάλασσαν ἡ τοῦ Ἰβήρων βασιλέως χώρα. Πορτουγαλλία δὲ ᾤκηται πρὸς τῷ πορθμῷ, ἀπὸ Γρανάτης ἀρξαμένη, ἐπί τε τὸν πορθμὸν καὶ τὴν ἐκτὸς θάλασσαν ἄχρις Ἰβηρίας. Γρανάτη δὲ ἡ χώρα, μεσόγαιος οὖσα, ἐπὶ τὴν Ἰβηρίαν καὶ Γαλατίαν διατείνουσα, οὐ [2.52] πάνυ τι οὔτε τῇ ἐντὸς θαλάσσῃ οὔτε τῷ ὠκεανῷ προσχρῆται.

73 Ὁ μέντοι Ἰβηρίας βασιλεὺς μέγιστον δύναται τῶν εἰς τόνδε τὸν χῶρον, καὶ οἴκου ὢν τοῦ βασιλείου τῆς Γαλατίας, τῶν Λιβύων τὴν τῆς Γρανάτης χώραν ἄγων καὶ φέρων, οὐ παύεται διαπολεμῶν. Καὶ φόρον μὲν ἀπάγει ὁ τῆς Γρανάτης Λιβύων βασιλεὺς τῷ Ἰβήρων βασιλεῖ, ὁπότε σπένδοιτο· πολλάκις δὲ ἐπελαύνων πολιορκεῖ τε τὴν πόλιν καὶ τὴν χώραν αὐτοῦ ληΐζεται. Ὀρεινὴ δέ ἐστιν ἐπ' ὄρους, ὃ ἀπὸ τῆς ἐντὸς θαλάσσης ἀρξάμενον κατατείνει ἐπὶ τὸν ὠκεανόν, ἐπὶ τὴν Πορτουγαλλίαν χώραν. Οὗτοι μὲν οὖν οἱ βασιλεῖς πρός τε ἀλλήλους διενεχθέντες τε ἐπολέμησαν πολλαχῇ, καὶ κοινῇ πρὸς τὸν βάρβαρον.

74 Τά τε ἄλλα καὶ πρὸς τὸν Ἰβηρίας τοῦτον βασιλέα Ἀλφόνσος ὁ Ταρακῶνος βασιλεύς, πρὶν ἢ ἐς Ἰταλίαν ἀφικέσθαι, διεπολέμησεν ἀπὸ αἰτίας τοιᾶσδε, καὶ αὐτός τε ἑάλω ὑπὸ στρατηγοῦ τοῦ Ἰβήρων βασιλέως, Ἀλβάρου τοὔνομα, ἔχειν δὲ καὶ τραύματα ξυνέβη ἀμφοῖν. Ὡς δὴ συλλέξας στράτευμα, καὶ τὸν ἀδελφὸν αὐτοῦ Ναβάρης βασιλέα παραλαβών, ἐστρατεύετο ἐπὶ τὸν Ἰβηρίας

Cordoba; Murcia; the one called Toledo; and Salamanca. And the shrine of Santiago is in this land, beside the Ocean and the outer sea. The land of the king of Castile extends also to the inner sea. Portugal is located by the straits, beginning from Granada and extending toward the straits and the outer sea as far as Castile. The land of Granada is inland and extends toward Castile and France; it is adjacent to neither the inner sea nor the Ocean.[142]

The king of Castile is the most powerful of all in this 73
region, and is of the royal house of France.[143] He does not cease to wage war against the North Africans, harassing the land of Granada. The king of the North Africans in Granada pays tribute to the king of Castile, whenever he makes a treaty. The latter king has often marched out, besieged that city, and plundered its land. It is mountainous because of a mountain that begins at the inner sea and extends to the Ocean, to the land of Portugal. These kings have fallen out with each other and gone to war many times, but they have also fought in common against the barbarian.

Before he went to Italy, Alfonso, the king of Aragon, 74
fought against the king of Castile for many reasons, including the following.[144] He himself was captured by the general of the king of the Castilians, a man by the name of Álvaro,[145] and both men were wounded. When he assembled his army and took with him his brother, the king of Navarre, he marched against the king of Castile and invaded Castile,

βασιλέα, ἐσέβαλεν ἐς τὴν Ἰβηρίαν, ἐπαγομένων αὐτὸν ἐπὶ τὴν χώραν τῶν ἐν τῇ χώρᾳ εὐδοκιμούντων ἐνίων διὰ τὸ πρὸς τὸν Ἄλβαρον μῖσός τε καὶ ἔχθος αὐτῶν· τοῦτον γὰρ ἰδιώτην ὄντα ἀπὸ Ταρακῶνος καὶ ἀπὸ μικροῦ πάνυ ὡρμημένον καὶ ἐπὶ ἀρετῇ ἐπίσημον γενόμενον, ὡς παραχρῆμα ἐπεδίδου μέγα, ὑπὸ [2.53] πάντων δὲ δι' ἀρετὴν τιμώμενον στρατηγόν τε ἀπέδειξε κατὰ τὴν χώραν αὐτοῦ, καὶ ἐπὶ στρατηγίας καθιστάμενος μέγα ἁπανταχοῦ εὐδοκίμει. Τότε δή, ὡς παρὰ τῷ Ἰβήρων βασιλεῖ ἐπὶ Ἀλφόνσον πεμφθεὶς σὺν τῷ στρατεύματι, ὑπήντα αὐτῷ κατὰ τὴν χώραν ὡς ἐναντιωσόμενος. Ἐπεὶ δὲ ἐπιὼν ὁ Ἀλφόνσος, συμπαραλαβὼν καὶ τὸν ἀδελφόν, ἐν τῇ Ἰβηρίᾳ ἐγένετο καὶ ἐπήλαυνεν, ἐνταῦθα αὐτῷ ὑπαντιάσας ὁ Ἄλβαρος ἐστρατοπεδεύετο, καὶ κήρυκα ἐπιπέμπων προηγόρευεν ἀπαλλάττεσθαι, ἢν σωφρονῇ, ὡς ἔχει τάχιστα ἐκ τῆς χώρας· καὶ ἀποκριναμένου, ὡς οὐκ ἐπὶ τοὺς ὄνους τοῦ πατρὸς αὐτοῦ ἄπεισιν ἐς νομὴν αὐτοὺς ἄξων, ἀλλὰ στρατηγήσων αὐτῷ πάρεστιν, ἐς μάχην ἐτάσσετο, καὶ συμβαλὼν ἐμάχετο ἀμφοῖν τοῖν ἀδελφοῖν. Μάχης δὲ καρτερᾶς γενομένης, ὡς οἱ περὶ Ἄλβαρον ἐτρέψαντο τοὺς Ταρακῶνας, ἐπεδίωκον ἀνὰ κράτος, καὶ ἄμφω τὼ ἀδελφὼ συλλαμβάνουσι, καὶ πολλοὺς τῶν Ταρακώνων κατέβαλλον ἐν τῇ διώξει. Ὡς δὲ ἀπηχθήτην παρὰ τὸν Ἰβήρων βασιλέα ἄμφω τὼ βασιλέε, κακὸν μὲν οὐδὲν εἰργάσατο αὐτούς, ὅρκοις δὲ καὶ πίστεσι καταλαβὼν τοῦ λοιποῦ μηδὲν πλέον νεωτερίζειν περὶ τὴν ἑαυτοῦ χώραν, ἀφῆκεν ἀσινεῖς ἀπιέναι.

75 Μετὰ δὲ ταῦτα Ἀλφόνσος ἀφίκετό τε ἐς Ἰταλίαν, ὡς

instigated to come against it by some of its leading men who hated and detested Álvaro. For the latter had been an ordinary man from Aragon who had risen from humble origins and had attained distinction through his merit. He advanced quickly and was honored by everyone for his valor, so the king appointed him general over his land and, established in that position, he was esteemed greatly everywhere. At that time, when he was sent by the king of the Castilians with an army against Alfonso, he marched through the land to oppose him. When Alfonso set out, taking his brother with him, entered Castile, and advanced, Álvaro went out to meet him and made camp. He sent a herald to proclaim that Alfonso should depart as quickly as he could from the land, if he had any sense left in him. Alfonso replied that he had not come at the head of his father's donkeys, to lead them to pasture, but to be a general, and so he deployed for battle. So Álvaro attacked too and fought against both brothers. The battle was fierce until Álvaro's men routed the Aragonese and pursued them with all their might. They captured both brothers and cut down many of the Aragonese in the pursuit. When the two kings were brought before the king of the Castilians, he did no harm to them, but bound them with oaths and pledges not to ever again attempt anything against his land, and then released them to return, unharmed.[146]

After that Alfonso went to Italy, as I recounted earlier, 75

πρότερόν μοι δεδήλωται, καὶ ἐπὶ τὴν Σικελίαν, καὶ κατασχὼν τὴν Νεαπόλεως βασιλείαν πρός τε τοὺς Ἰανυΐους ἐπολέμει, ἔνθα δὴ καὶ ἑάλω ὑπὸ τούτων, ὡς ἐν τῷ ἔμπροσθεν ἐπεξῆλθον λόγῳ, καὶ ἀχθεὶς παρὰ τὸν Μεδιολάνου ἡγεμόνα αὖθις ἀπελύθη. Τὴν μέντοι γυναῖκα αὐτοῦ καταλιπὼν ἐν Ταρακῶνι οὐκέτι πάλιν ἀφίκετο ὀψόμενος πολλῶν ἐτῶν, αὐτοῦ [2.54] δὲ ἐς ἔρωτας τὰ πολλὰ διατρίβων διεγένετο, χρηματίζων τε ἔρωτι καὶ τοῖς ὅπλοις. Ἧι μὲν αὐτῷ τὰ κατὰ τὴν Ἰταλίαν ἀπέβαινεν, ὕστερόν μοι δηλοῦται προϊόντι τῷ λόγῳ ἐς ἀφήγησιν.

76 Τῷ δὲ βασιλεῖ Ἰβηρίας περὶ οὗ μοι ἐλέγετο, συνῆπται πόλεμος πρὸς τὸν βασιλέα Λιβύων τῶν ἐν Γρανάτῃ, οἳ δὴ ἀπὸ Λιβύης τὸ παλαιὸν διαβάντες καὶ Ἀλμερίαν πόλιν παράλιον τῆς Εὐρώπης κατασχόντες, διέχουσαν ἀπὸ Λιβύης ὡσεὶ σταδίους πεντήκοντα καὶ διακοσίους, καὶ ἐντεῦθεν ὁρμώμενοι τήν τε Ἰβηρίαν σφίσιν ὑπηγάγοντο, καὶ ἔργα λαμπρὰ ἀποδεικνύμενοι ἐπὶ Κελτικήν, τὴν χώραν αὐτῶν ἐπὶ μέγα αὔξοντες, προηγάγοντο καὶ ἐπὶ Ταρακῶνα καὶ Βαλεντίαν. Πρὸς τούτοις δὴ ἀπὸ τῶν Κελτῶν κατιόντες οἱ τῶν Ἰβήρων βασιλεῖς διεδέξαντο τὸν πρὸς τοὺς Λίβυας τούτους πόλεμον, ἐς πόλιν ἐχυρὰν συνελάσαντες, μετὰ δὲ ταῦτα ἐπολιόρκουν, καὶ ἐς δεῦρο ἔτι τελοῦσι τῇ πόλει τε ἐπελαύνοντες αἰεί τε καὶ στρατὸν ἐπάγοντες.

77 Καὶ δὴ ὁ τῶν Ἰβήρων βασιλεὺς δόμνος Ἰωάννης, ὃς πρότερόν μοι ἐλέγετο, ἐπελαύνων, προάγοντός τε τοῦ Ἀλβάρου καὶ ἐποτρύνοντος βασιλέα ἐξελεῖν τοὺς Λίβυας, ὡς δὴ καταστρεψόμενος ἐπῆγε τὸν στρατὸν ἐπὶ τὴν πόλιν. Ἐνταῦθα ὡς οἱ Λίβυες ἐπολιορκοῦντο δεινῶς καὶ ἐς τὸ

and against Sicily. Conquering the kingdom of Naples, he fought against the Genoese and was captured by them, as was narrated in the previous account; conveyed to the ruler of Milan, he was again released.[147] He left his wife in Aragon and would not see her again for many years,[148] but while there he spent much time in love affairs, dealing in love and arms. How things turned out for him in Italy, I will explain later, as my narrative advances.[149]

The king of Castile, whom I just mentioned, was involved 76
in a war with the king of the North Africans in Granada.[150] The latter long ago crossed over from North Africa and occupied the city of Almería on the coast of Europe, which is at a distance of about two hundred and fifty stades from North Africa. Setting out from there they subjected Castile to themselves, performed glorious deeds against France, increasing their territory greatly, and then advanced against Aragon and Valencia. The kings of the Castilians, descended from the French, inherited the war against these North Africans and drove them together into a fortified city, where they then besieged them. And to this day they continue to press hard against that city and always lead armies against it.[151]

The king of the Castilians, Don Juan, whom I mentioned 77
above, marched also, induced and stirred up by Álvaro to get rid of the North Africans, and he led the army to the city with the intention of conquering it. The North Africans were then fiercely besieged and were starved to the very

ἔσχατον λιμοῦ ἀφικόμενοι, ἐς ἀπορίαν ἀπελαθέντες μηχανῶνται τοιόνδε. Ἡμιόνοις δυοκαίδεκα ἰσχάδων φορτία συσκευασάμενοι ἤλαυνον ἐπὶ τὸ στρατόπεδον· τὰς δὲ ἰσχάδας ὡς κατὰ [2.55] μίαν ἑκάστην διασχίζοντες ἐνέβαλον ἐντὸς χρύσινον ἕνα, καὶ συνετέθειντο αὖθις. Τὸ δὲ νόμισμα τῆς Ἰβηρίας χρυσοῦν δύναται χρυσίνους Οὐενετῶν δύο ἕκαστον. Ταύτας δὲ τὰς ἰσχάδας ὡς ἐσκευάσαντο οὕτω καὶ ἐπὶ τοὺς ἡμιόνους ἀνετίθεσαν, ὥστε δύνασθαι φέρειν ἕνα ἕκαστον, ἤλαυνον ἐπὶ τὴν τοῦ Ἀλβάρου σκηνήν. Τὸν δέ, ὡς ἐπέγνω τὸ ἐν ταῖς ἰσχάσι χρυσίον, ἐρέσθαι τὸν φέροντα, ὅ τι βούλοιτο αὐτοῖς τὸ χρυσίον ἐν ταῖς ἰσχάσιν. Ὁ δὲ τοὺς ἡμιόνους ἐλαύνων ἀπεκρίνατο, ὡς τὸ χρυσίον τῆς πόλεως συναγαγὼν ὁ βασιλεὺς ἐπιπέμπει, λέγων, ὡς "ἤν τε ἕλῃς τὴν πόλιν, ἤν τε μὴ ἕλῃς, πλέων τούτου χρυσὸς οὐκ ἄν ποτε γένοιτό σοι ἀπὸ τῆς πόλεως. Καὶ ἢν ἐξέλῃς τὴν πόλιν, ἀποβαλεῖς ἐσαῦθις ἀπὸ Λιβύης πολλαπλάσιον ἐσόμενον σοί τε καὶ ἡμῖν· ἢν δὲ μὴ ἐξέλῃς τὴν πόλιν, ἕξεις καὶ τοῦ λοιποῦ, ὅσα ἂν ἀπὸ Λιβύης ἐς ἡμᾶς κομίζεται, ταμιεύεσθαι." Ταῦτα πυθόμενον λέγεται καὶ Ἄλβαρον, φέροντα τὰς ἰσχάδας, ἀφικέσθαι ἐς ὄψιν τῷ βασιλεῖ, καὶ διαχύσαντα τὰς ἰσχάδας εἰπεῖν, "ὦ βασιλεῦ, τὸ δένδρον ἐκεῖνο, ὃ φέρει τοιοῦτον ἡμῖν καρπόν, οὐ καλῶς ἔχει ἡμῖν ἐκκοπῆναι· τοιούτῳ γάρ τοι καρπῷ οὐκ ἔχοιμεν ἂν ἔτι τοῦ λοιποῦ χρῆσθαι, καὶ ἡμεῖς οὐκέτ' ἂν ἐν δέοντι χρησαίμεθα τῇ εὐδαιμονίᾳ, κατακόρως αὐτῇ ἐμφορούμενοι ἐν τῷ παρόντι. Ὁρᾷς, ὡς τὰς ἀμπέλους ἀφαιροῦνται, ὅσον ἱκανῶς ἔχει αὖθις ἀποδιδόναι καρπόν. Ἢν δὲ βιάσηταί τις αὐτήν,

limit of their endurance. Not knowing what else to do, they contrived the following. They placed twelve loads of dried figs on mules and sent them to the camp. They had slit each fig open individually, placed a gold coin inside, and then sealed it up again. Each Castilian gold coin is worth two Venetian gold pieces. When they prepared the figs in this way and placed them upon the mules, so that each could bear one load, they drove them to Álvaro's tent. When he realized that the figs were full of gold, he asked the bearer about the meaning of the gold in the figs. The mule driver replied that the king had gathered all the gold in the city and had sent it along, saying that "whether you take the city or don't take it, you will never get more gold from it than this. And if you take the city, you will immediately lose all that will come in the future to you and to us from North Africa, many times what you see here. But if you do not take the city, you will have more to store up in the future, as much as comes to us from North Africa." It is said that when Álvaro learned this, he took the figs, went into his own king's presence, and poured out the figs, saying, "O king, it would not be a good idea for us to cut down that tree which bears such fruit for us; for we would then never again be able to make use of said fruit, and we would no longer be able to tap this abundance when we need to, that is if we glut ourselves on it right now. You see how the vine is pruned just enough so that it again yields fruit. If you force it too much, it is of no use to you

οὐκ ἔχει χρῆσθαι αὐτῇ [2.56] ἐς τὸ δέον." Ταῦτα ἀκούσαντα τὸν βασιλέα, ὡς ἔδοξέν οἱ προσφυῆ λέγειν, ἀπαγαγεῖν τὸν στρατόν.

78 Τούτῳ μὲν οὖν ἀγαγόντι τὴν βασιλέως Πορτουγαλλίας θυγατέρα ἐγένετο παῖς Ἔρρικος τοὔνομα, ἀνὴρ τὰ πολέμια ἀγαθός, ὃς ἐπεί τε ἠγάγετο τοῦ Ναβάρης βασιλέως θυγατέρα καὶ οὐκ ἐγένετο αὐτῷ συγγενέσθαι, ἀπεπέμψατο, καὶ δευτέραν ἐσηγάγετο γυναῖκα ἀνεψιὰν αὐτοῦ, θυγατέρα τοῦ Πορτουγάλλων βασιλέως, εἶδος λεγομένην πασῶν τῶν εἰς ἐκεῖνα τὰ χωρία εἶναι καλλίστην, ὑποτιθεμένων αὐτῷ τῶν ἀρίστων, ὡς ἢν ἄλλην ἐσαγάγοιτο γυναῖκα, οἷός τε ἔσοιτο συγγενέσθαι. Τὴν μέντοι θυγατέρα τοῦ Ναβάρης βασιλέως ἠνάγκασε ἐς τὸ τῶνΝαζηραίων σχῆμα ἰέναι, καὶ ἀπέδωκεν αὐτῇ χρήματα.

79 Ὁ δὲ Πορτουγαλλίας βασιλεὺς οἰκίας ἐστὶ τῶν Γαλατίας βασιλέων. Συμβάλλομαι δὲ τήνδε τὴν χώραν ἀπὸ παλαιοῦ πρὸς τοὺς Λίβυας διενεχθέντας τοὺς Κελτῶν βασιλεῖς καταστρεψαμένους ὑφ' αὑτοῖς ποιήσασθαι καὶ παραδοῦναι τοῖς ἐξ αὑτῶν γινομένοις. Ὡς δὲ καὶ τὴν Ναβάρης βασιλείαν ἀνήκειν ἐς τὴν οἰκίαν τῶν Γαλατίας βασιλέων νομίζεται, καὶ μηδενὶ ἑτέρῳ ἐξεῖναι παρελθεῖν ἐς τήνδε τὴν βασιλείαν· καὶ γὰρ καὶ τήνδε Κάρουλος ὁ αὐτοκράτωρ καὶ οἱ μετ' ἐκεῖνον βασιλεῖς φαίνονται τήνδε αὑτοῖς καταστρεψάμενοι τὴν χώραν ἀπολιπεῖν τοῖς ἀπὸ τῆς οἰκίας αὐτῶν ἐσομένοις. Τὸν μέντοι ἀδελφὸν Ἀλφόνσου ἐπηγάγοντο ἐπὶ τῷδε τῷ λόγῳ, ὡς ἐπεὶ ἔγημε γυναῖκα τοῦ οἴκου τῆς Γαλατίας, ἢν μὲν γένηται αὐτῷ παῖς, τόνδε μηκέτι τοῦ λοιποῦ διατρίβειν ἐν τῇ χώρᾳ, ἀλλὰ τὸν παῖδα

when you need it." When the king heard this, it seemed reasonable to him and he led the army away.[152]

This man [Juan II] married the daughter of the king of 78
Portugal and had a son named Enrique [IV], who became good at warfare and later married the daughter of the king of Navarre.[153] But he was not able to consummate his marriage and so he sent her away and married a second time, his cousin this time, a daughter of the king of Portugal, who was said to be the most beautiful of all women in that region.[154] His leading men had suggested to him that, if he were to marry another woman, he would be able to have intercourse with her. So he forced the daughter of the king of Navarre to assume the monastic habit and gave her money.

The king of Portugal is of the house of the kings of 79
France.[155] I conclude that long ago the kings of the French conquered this land in their struggle against the North Africans, subjected it to themselves, and then passed it on to their descendants.[156] Even the kingdom of Navarre is believed to belong to the house of the kings of France,[157] and no one else is allowed to ascend its throne. For it seems that the emperor Charlemagne and the kings after him conquered this land and left it to the future members of their house. They brought in the brother of Alfonso on those terms, namely that when he married a woman of the house of France and had a son by her, he would no longer reside in the country, but would leave the son behind as their king

καταλιπόντα σφίσι βασιλέα αὐτὸν οἴχεσθαι ἀπαλλαττόμενον, ἢν δὲ μὴ γένηται αὐτῷ παῖς, μετὰ τὴν τελευτὴν αὐτοῦ ἀποδοῦναι [2.57] τὴν ἀρχὴν ἐπὶ τὸν Γαλατίας βασιλέα. Καὶ τόνδε δεξάμενον τοὺς λόγους ἐπὶ τούτῳ παρελθεῖν ἐς τὴν Ναβάρης βασιλείαν. Καὶ γεννηθέντος αὐτῷ παιδὸς αὐτόν τε ἀπεπέμψαντο, καὶ τὸν παῖδα σφίσιν ἀπέδειξαν βασιλέα, τὰ πρὸς μητρόθεν ὄντα οἴκου τῶν Γαλατίας βασιλέων. Ταῦτα μὲν οὖν ἐς τοσοῦτον ἐχομένῳ τῆς τοῦ λόγου συμπάσης ὑποθέσεως ἀναγέγραπται ἐς ἀπόδειξιν· ἐπάνειμι δέ, ὅθεν τὴν ἐκβολὴν τοῦ λόγου ἐποιησάμην, ἄχρι τοσοῦτον διενεχθείς.

and would take himself elsewhere; but if he did not have a son, after his death his throne would revert to the king of France. Having agreed to these terms, he received the throne of Navarre, and when his son was born they sent him away and appointed his son as their king, for, through his mother, the latter belonged to the house of the kings of France.[158] These things, then, have been here recorded at such a length as a presentation of research that contributes to the overall theme of the work. I now return to the point where I began this digression, having been led so far away.

Note on the Text

It is now certain that Laonikos stopped working on the *Histories* between 1464 and 1468, and probably closer to the beginning of that period.[1] The earliest extant manuscript of the work is the fifteenth-century Par. gr. 1780, copied by Demetrios Angelos, an intellectual in Constantinople with wide-ranging interests, including medical, historical, and philosophical.[2] Angelos is not (yet) attested after the late 1470s, and a watermark in that manuscript dates it closer to the middle of the century.[3] Therefore, that copy was made soon after Laonikos finished the work and almost certainly in Constantinople, and it was made by an able scholar who is probably not responsible for the many errors in grammar that the text contains.[4] It is likely that the errors were already in the original that Laonikos produced and left unrevised.

That earliest manuscript also contains a number of interpolated passages on the history of the empire of Trebizond, the fate of its imperial family, and the geography and religious history of its neighbor Georgia; these passages were not written by Laonikos and were introduced into Book 9 and possibly Book 10 as well. They must have been added soon after Laonikos finished working on the text. I have proposed that the interpolator, and possibly the author, of those passages was none other than Georgios Amiroutzes,

an intellectual from Trebizond who had been close to the royal family, implicated in some of the events recounted in the interpolations, and connected to Demetrios Angelos and Kritoboulos, the historian of Mehmed, at the Ottoman court in Constantinople.[5] These were the circles among which the work first circulated. The work would eventually be exported to the West and recopied many times.[6] The Greek view of the rise of the Ottoman Turks and the fall of Byzantium would therefore be represented by Laonikos's *Histories* and not by the histories of Doukas and Kritoboulos, which survived in one manuscript apiece and long remained unknown in the West.

The Greek text produced here is that of Jenö (Eugenius) Darkó, published in 1922–1923 in Budapest (see Bibliography). That edition is rare and its surviving copies tend to crumble at the touch. An unexpected stroke of luck from a different direction facilitated the making of this translation. In 2006 the Department of Cultural Technology and Communication of the University of the Aegean completed a project to digitize and upload texts in the public domain relating to the Orthodox tradition, including Laonikos's *Histories;* 25 percent of the funding for this came from the Greek government, and the remainder from the European Regional Development Fund. This digitization project, part of the ongoing effort to develop Optical Character Recognition software for Greek polytonic texts, produced, as far as I can tell, a perfect scan of the Darkó edition (only some spaces were lost, which I restored). As for the text itself, its poor state has long invited aggressive emendation by editors. I have mostly refrained from adding my conjectures to the existing heap that future editors will have to sort

through. In a few places, however, I have restored the reading of the manuscripts when it seems to me that it makes better sense than the emendations Darkó proposed or accepted (or any sense at all). These are listed in the Notes to the Text. The page numbers of the Darkó edition are indicated by square brackets.

A new edition by Herbert Wurm and Michael Grünbart is set to appear in the series *Corpus Fontium Historiae Byzantinae,* but it is unlikely to appear soon. The editors will face serious challenges. They are unlikely to want to print the text with the many grammatical errors it contains, but how far should their corrections go? As for the punctuation in particular, knowing well that this has recently become a controversial subject, I would support a highly structured, interventionist system that would guide the reader through each sentence as if it were modern German, like Jakob Haury's Teubner edition of Prokopios. The text is hard enough on its own, and the punctuation can be of assistance.

Sigla

< > = addition by editor

[ ] = seclusion by editor

[[ ]] = interpolated passage

[. . .] = lacuna

Notes

1 Kaldellis, "The Date." It was previously believed, on the basis of a mistaken understanding of his coverage of Bohemian history, that he was writing as late as the 1490s.

2 Mondrain, "Jean Argyropoulos" and "Démétrios Angelos."
3 Wurm and Gamillscheg, "Bemerkungen."
4 See the Note on the Translation in the Introduction, above.
5 Kaldellis, "The Interpolations."
6 Wurm, "Die handschriftliche Überlieferung."

Notes to the Text

Book 1

1 *I prefer Bekker's* συμφερομένους *over the MSS (and Darkó's)* συμφερομένοις.

2 τὸν *add. Tafel.*

3 *I have restored the MSS reading here over the correction* Ποτίδαιαν.

4 *I prefer the alternate MSS reading here over* γενομένους.

5 *I have corrected* καθισταμένων.

6 *I have restored the MSS lacuna here, which Darkó filled with* ἕν τε καὶ τριάκοντα.

7 *While this might be what LC wrote, he probably meant* ἐξ ἑσπέρας.

8 *I have restored the MSS reading over Darkó's correction* Τζερνομιανὸν.

9 *I have restored the MSS reading* ἔχει *and accepted Hamaker's emendation of* γενόμενος ἐφ' ὑμῖν. *No solution is satisfactory; Darkó's text makes little sense.*

10 *I have restored the MSS reading over Darkó's correction* Νήσιον.

Book 2

1 *I have restored the MSS reading over Darkó's correction* Βαζιλείης.

2 *Darkó does not mark this lacuna.*

3 *I have restored the MSS reading over Darkó's correction* Βωκερίνην.

4 *This phrase, which breaks up the syntax and sense, and is repeated from above, is possibly an intrusion.*

5 *There may be a lacuna here.*

6 *In place of* ἔχειν τὴν, *the MSS all have* ἔχοντι.

7 *Darkó and the MSS have* ἀκίζεις.

Book 3

1 *I have throughout restored the MSS reading over Darkó's correction* Χεσίην.

2 *I have restored the MSS reading over Darkó's correction* Χαρκόβιον *(which was founded in the seventeenth century).*

3 *I have corrected the MSS* Τεμήρη.

Book 4

1 *I have corrected the MSS* Χασάνη.

2 *I have restored the MSS reading over Tafel's correction* Εὐγανέων.

3 *I have restored the MSS reading over Tafel's correction* Βαρβαρόσσης.

4 *I have throughout restored the MSS reading over Darkó's correction* Κιόζην.

5 *I prefer this variant MSS reading over* τούτου *(which creates genealogical problems).*

6 *I have throughout restored the MSS reading over Darkó's correction* Φωκίδα.

Book 5

1 *I have accepted Bekker's emendation of* αὐτῷ.

2 *I have corrected the MSS* Ἀμουράτεω.

3 *This is an emendation of* Ἀμυθάονι.

4 *John Duffy proposes changing this to* ἄλλως *(when he entered the land from a different route), but nothing is said about routes, either before or after.*

5 *John Duffy proposes changing this to* ἐς τοῦτο τῶν πρὸ αὐτοῦ *(the most excellent victory of those before him up to that point). Compare 1.58 above:* πλεῖστα δὲ ἐς τοῦτο τῶν πρὸ αὐτοῦ βασιλέων δόξαντος αὐτοῦ ἐνευδοκιμεῖν.

6 *I would supply a* γενόμενος *at this point.*

7 *I have accepted John Duffy's emendation of* λεγομένων, *which he supports by the parallel expressions at 4.49, 5.78, 10.13.*

8 *John Duffy would support Fabrot's emendation to* ἁψαμένου. *See the note to the translation for the sense that would yield.*

9 *I have throughout restored the MSS reading over Darkó's correction* Ἱερόν.

Notes to the Translation

Books 6, 7, 8, 9, and 10, referenced below, appear in volume 2 (DOML 34).

Book 1

1 That is, the Hindu Kush; compare Arrian, *Anabasis* 5.3–5.

2 That is, Alexander the Great; see 1.4 below.

3 The name is normally written Arsakes, but Laonikos is here following the tradition of Ktesias, who links Arbakes to Sardanapalos: in Diodoros of Sicily, *Bibliotheke* 2.24–25.

4 Sardanapalos is generally thought to be based on the Assyrian king Aššur-bani-apli (668–627 BCE), but is possibly a composite character reflecting legends about multiple kings.

5 That is, Constantine the Great. Laonikos is reflecting traditions here similar to those in the *Donation of Constantine.*

6 Laonikos designates an "emperor" (as opposed to just a "king") by using the late Byzantine title *basileus kai autokrator,* which does not mean "king and emperor."

7 This was the Fourth Crusade (1202–1204); see also 4.49 below and 4.24 for the Venetian role.

8 On July 25, 1261, under Michael VIII Palaiologos.

9 This refers to Ioannes VIII Palaiologos (1425–1448) and the Council of Ferrara-Florence (1438–1439), not to his grandfather Ioannes V Palaiologos (1341–1391), who traveled to Hungary (1366) and Rome (1369) seeking aid from the West at the cost of Union. The Council of Ferrara-Florence is discussed also at 6.7–16.

10 Presumably the Greeks.

11 That is, the Bulgarians and the Serbs.

12 That is, the Ottoman Turks.

13 This describes the territory of the empire around 1430.

14 That is, the Mongols.

15 This clause is unclear. It could conceivably refer to the seventh climatic zone.

16 Here probably the Seljuk Turks.

17 It is otherwise unknown.

18 That is, after Muhammad. 'Umar I (634–644) was in fact the second caliph of Islam, following Abu Bakr (632–634).

19 That is, the Golden Horde. Laonikos translates "Horde" as *agora,* not entirely inaccurately.

20 In the fifteenth century, the Ottoman dynasty began to claim descent from the Oğuz, a Turkic confederation that had ruled parts of Central Asia.

21 The story of Gündüz-Alp has been modeled on that of Deiokes in Herodotos, *Histories* 1.96–100.

22 Ertoğrul is attested as Osman's father on the latter's coins.

23 Laonikos has projected onto Ertoğrul the feats attributed to Umur Beg, emir of the coastal beylik of Aydın (1334–1348), which we know from Enveri's exactly contemporary *Düsturname.* He raided the islands, the Peloponnese, and Euboia, and sailed his ships up the same river.

24 'Ala' al-Din Kay-Qubad III, one of the last Seljuk sultans of Rum (1284, 1293–1294, and 1301–1303).

25 That is, Willow Tree.

26 Osman, eponymous emir of the Ottoman (Osmanlı) Turks (ca. 1281–1326).

27 In 1303.

28 Karaman was the eponymous ancestor of the Turkish rulers of southern and central Anatolia. Philadelpheia was not within his dominion, being in western Asia Minor. Laonikos seems to have confused Gregoras's definition of the territories of Germiyan (Καρμάνος in Gregoras, *Roman History,* 1:214), which touched upon Philadelpheia, with those of Karaman (Καραμάνος in

Laonikos). In later passages, Laonikos mistakenly ascribes the eponym of Germiyan, Alishur, to Karaman. He calls Germiyan Κερμιανός (see 5.34 below).

29 The emir Saruhan (ca. 1313–ca. 1350) was the first Turkish ruler and eponym of western Anatolia (Manisa). His territories were mostly in Lydia.

30 The emir Karası (ca. 1313–ca. 1335), son of Kalamshah, was the first Turkish ruler and eponym of northwestern Anatolia (Balıkesir and Bergama), in northern Lydia.

31 Teke was the name of the Turkish emirate in southwestern Anatolia, around Attaleia, founded ca. 1321 by Yunus b. İlyas b. Hamid (1321–1324). Laonikos is quite inexact about its location.

32 This is how Laonikos refers to the Jandarid rulers of Kastamonu, who acquired Sinope in 1322, but the identity of "Umur" is unknown.

33 Germiyan was the dominant Turkish emirate in western Anatolia, centered on Kütahya. Its first known emir was Yakub (d. 1320), a descendant of Alishur. Ikonion is not in Karia, but in Karaman.

34 On April 6, 1326. Actually, it may have surrendered to his son, Orhan.

35 In 1326.

36 Laonikos is here describing the origin of a mobile administrative center that formed around the early sultans' military retinues (for a detailed description of it at a later stage, see 5.11–14 below). He calls it literally "the gates" *(thyrai),* probably because this was how ancient writers referred to royal courts, especially the Persian court (e.g., in Herodotos and Xenophon). The Ottoman court was later called the Porte (French for "gate," used to refer to the government as a whole), so that is an appropriate translation for Laonikos's *thyrai,* though possibly only a coincidence.

37 That is, Ottomans.

38 It is difficult to identify these events, and we cannot rely on their placement in Laonikos's narrative to determine relative chronology. According to Gregoras, *Roman History,* 1:535, Mon-

gols crossed the Danube and defeated some Turkish bandits in 1337. The raid against Thrace by the eight thousand Turks, however, who returned to Asia unharmed and with much loot, is placed by Gregoras in 1340 (*Roman History,* 1:548).

39 Andronikos II Palaiologos (1282–1328) and his grandson Andronikos III (1328–1341), son of Michael IX (who had died on October 12, 1320), fought a civil war, on and off, between 1321 and 1328.

40 Actually the Bulgarians; see 1.25 below. The Serbs joined Andronikos III just before the end of the civil war.

41 See 1.15 above.

42 In 1310, Andronikos II and Halil agreed that the latter would return to Asia, but Halil ended up bringing more Turks from there and ravaging Thrace for two years. For Halil's origins, see the notes to 1.19 below.

43 In 1312, Stefan Milutin of Serbia (1282–1321) lent infantry, and the Genoese blockaded the peninsula from the sea.

44 In fact, Halil and most of his men were massacred.

45 'Izz al-Din Kaykawus II, Seljuk sultan of Konya (1246–1261), fled to Michael VIII Palaiologos in 1261 when he could not cope with Mongol pressure. He converted but was detained to be used as a pawn. In 1264 he fled to the Mongols of the Crimea. Those of his followers who remained behind converted (Gregoras, *Roman History,* 1:101) and became known as the Tourkopouloi, but in 1305, when Michael IX used them in battle near Raidestos against the Catalans (see below), they went over to the enemy (Gregoras, *Roman History,* 1:229–32).

46 The Catalan Grand Company, previously active in Sicily and including many Calabrians and Sicilians, arrived in the east in September 1303.

47 Laonikos's chronology is confused: the Catalans were sent against Osman (d. 1326), not his son and successor Orhan (1326–ca. 1360), and against the other Turks in Asia Minor.

48 The Catalans relieved Philadelpheia from a siege in April 1304, but the Turks were Germiyan, not Ottoman.

49 In 1308, but this is a highly selective and simplified presentation of complicated events.

50 The ancient name of Kassandra was Potidaia; Laonikos's mistake was corrected by previous editors, but I have restored it.

51 The Turks split from the Catalans in early 1309 (or 1311) after their victory over Gautier de Brienne; see 1.20 below. The Tourkopouloi, who were Christians, went over to the Serbian king Milutin, because they were conscious of having betrayed the Byzantines. They were eventually destroyed by him. The other group was under Halil, and their story is told in 1.18 above; see Gregoras, *Roman History,* 1:254–55, for their split from the Catalans.

52 This actually refers back to the beginning of 1.18, although Laonikos is probably not aware of it.

53 On March 15, 1311, the Catalan Grand Company defeated Gautier de Brienne, duke of Athens, at the battle of the Kephissos near Thebes, and took his duchy. Some historians believe that the battle should be relocated to Halmyros in Thessaly.

54 By "later," Laonikos must mean many decades later; they ruled his native city of Athens, and he should not be accused of ignorance here, only imprecision.

55 Osman did not attack Philadelpheia, but Laonikos may be thinking of the Turkish siege of the city he referred to at 1.18 above. Philadelpheia seems to have been attacked in 1324 by Germiyan and Aydın. Nikaia fell to Osman's son Orhan in 1331; see 1.24–26 below.

56 This is Laonikos's way of referring to the Jandarid rulers of Kastamonu, who acquired Sinope in 1322; see 1.14 above.

57 Osman died in 1326. This picks up from 1.15 above.

58 *Iliad* 22.60; *Odyssey* 15.348.

59 This sentence is obscure.

60 Laonikos is the only source to mention strife among the sons of Osman. Orhan had a number of brothers, but the succession seems to have gone smoothly. Orhan ruled from 1326 to ca. 1360.

61 It is unclear whom Laonikos means here by "the rulers of the

Oğuz." If he means the Ottomans, then he is correctly disputing that there was dynastic conflict in 1326.

62 The emirate of Karası was absorbed in 1346.

63 In 1328.

64 This clause is obscure. Laonikos is returning to the circumstances of the rise of Andronikos III against his grandfather Andronikos II, previously discussed at 1.17 above.

65 Mihail Asen III, somewhat inaccurately called Mihail Šišman, was Bulgarian emperor (1323–1330). He married Andronikos III's sister Theodora upon divorcing his first wife, Anna, sister of Stefan Uroš III of Serbia, in 1324, and aided Andronikos III against his grandfather.

66 These events happened after the fight for Nikaia, recounted below, and so did not set the stage for them. After Mihail Asen III was killed in battle against the Serbs (at Velbăžd, in 1330), Stefan Uroš III secured the Bulgarian throne for his sister's son, that is, Mihail Asen III's son Ivan Stefan (1330–1331). Ivan Aleksandăr, Bulgarian emperor (1331–1371), a sister's son of Mihail Asen III, seized the throne by expelling his cousin, the Serbian protégé Ivan Stefan, in 1331. He defeated Andronikos III and recovered Bulgarian losses in Thrace in 1332, concluding a treaty whereby his eldest son (Mihail Asen IV) and Andronikos III's daughter (Eirene) were to wed.

67 In 1329.

68 On June 10–11, 1329.

69 On March 2, 1331.

70 Orhan never reached as far as Philadelpheia.

71 Ioannes VI Kantakouzenos (1347–1354, proclaimed in 1341: see below) married his daughter Theodora to Orhan in 1346, in Selymbria.

72 Orhan captured Ankara in 1354, although it had to be retaken by Murad I in 1362.

73 Andronikos III's son by Anna of Savoy was Ioannes V Palaiologos, emperor from 1341 to 1391 (though often sidelined by members of his family); he was nine at the time, not twelve. Andronikos III died on June 14, 1341.

74 Andronikos III had not in fact left Kantakouzenos as regent.

75 Kantakouzenos, excluded from the regency by the empress Anna, the *megas doux* Alexios Apokaukos, and the patriarch, declared himself emperor in late 1341 and obtained entry into Constantinople as coruler of the underage Ioannes V in 1347. He married his daughter Helene to Ioannes V in 1347. Kantakouzenos reigned until 1354, when he was forced to abdicate; see 1.41 below.

76 Orhan died in ca. 1360.

77 In fact, it was Murad who succeeded Orhan in ca. 1360. Süleyman, who had fought in Thrace extensively (see below), had died already, in ca. 1357, in a hunting accident.

78 See 1.18 above: Halil and most of his followers had been killed over fifty years before.

79 See 1.18 above. This was possibly Tzympe (location uncertain), in 1352.

80 This sentence is obscure.

81 Süleyman was sent by his father, Orhan, to assist Ioannes VI Kantakouzenos against the Serbs and Thessalonike in 1348, but Orhan recalled him at the last minute, in 1350; in 1352 Süleyman defeated the Serbian allies of Kantakouzenos's rival Ioannes V. In 1354, he captured Gallipoli after an earthquake (see 1.37 below) and raided Thrace.

82 Stefan Uroš IV Dušan, king of Serbia (1331–1345), then emperor of Serbs and Greeks (1345–1355).

83 Skopje had been in Serbian hands since 1282.

84 That is, the Balkans.

85 This must be a mistake on Laonikos's part for "east."

86 Stefan Dušan acquired Kastoria in 1342–43.

87 There is no evidence that Serbian armies operated close to Constantinople.

88 Laonikos means Andronikos II Palaiologos (1282–1328), although Stefan Dušan did not come to the throne until 1331, and his attacks on Byzantium followed in the 1340s.

89 In ca. 1348.

90 Laonikos throughout confuses Žarko (d. before 1371), who ruled

the coasts of Zeta, with his father-in-law, Dejan Dragaš, who governed eastern Macedonia and the Struma valley around Kumanovo, Štip, and Velbăžd (see also 1.42, 1.52, and 2.25–26 below for Dejan's sons).

91 Kantakouzenos (*History,* 2:260) claims that Bogdan was a brother of the despot Jovan Oliver (d. 1356), whose lands in western Macedonia were eventually taken by the sons of Dejan Dragaš.

92 "Kral" is the Serbian word for king *(kralj),* here designating Vukašin Mrnjavčević, who in 1365 was promoted to king as coruler of Dušan's son and successor Stefan Uroš V. Jovan Uglješa was Vukašin's brother and lord of Serres and western Thrace after Dušan's death. Both were killed at Černomen (in 1371) fighting against the Turks (see 1.34 below).

93 Vuk Branković (d. 1397) was the son of the *sebastokrator* Branko Mladenović and governed regions in northern Macedonia (Skopje) and Kosovo after Dušan's death. He married Mara, daughter of the Serbian prince Lazar I Hrebljanović, whom he supposedly betrayed on the battlefield of Kosovo in 1389 (the tradition is not unanimous; see below 1.56). Lazar ruled northern Serbia by the Danube, but Vuk's son Đurađ did succeed Lazar's son Stefan as ruler of northern Serbia in 1427. There is some confusion between Vuk and Lazar in this passage. Vuk's genealogy is given correctly at 1.56 below.

94 The *župan* Nikola Altomanović (d. 1373) governed Hum and western Serbia, not Kastoria. Kastoria was ruled by Nikola Bagaš Baldovin, whom Laonikos probably means here.

95 Stefan Dušan's *kaisar* Grgur Preljub (d. 1356) governed in Thessaly, while Dušan's brother Simeon Uroš (d. 1370) was given Epeiros and then took Thessaly (in 1359).

96 The territory of Prilep was given by Dušan to Vukašin Mrnjavčević (see note above). It passed from him to his son Marko Mrnjavčević (d. 1395). Ohrid was held by the *kaisar* Mladen and then by his son, the *sebastokrator* Branko Mladenović. It later came to Vukašin's vassal, the Albanian Andrea Gropa, and then passed to Marko.

97 Stefan Dušan died on December 20, 1355.

98 Stefan Dušan's men actually fought against each other after his death.

99 Mihail Asen III, somewhat inaccurately called Mihail Šišman, was Bulgarian emperor (1323–1330). It is unclear why he is being mentioned here.

100 This was in 1371, although Süleyman was long dead at that point. See 1.28 for the context.

101 See 1.28 above.

102 While it is not elsewhere attested, a victory by the Serbs over some Turkish forces before the battle of Černomen (see below) cannot be ruled out.

103 The battle of Černomen (or Marica) took place on September 26, 1371. The commander of the Turkish forces was not Süleyman, who had already died, but probably Lala Shahin.

104 The precise date of the capture of Adrianople (in the late 1360s) is unknown. It was not, as Laonikos states above, after the battle of Černomen.

105 It fell to the Turks either in 1363 or 1371 (after the battle of Černomen).

106 Laonikos has condensed his information too much, so the reference is unclear. He may be referring to Evrenos, Lala Shahin Pasha, or Hajji İlbeği.

107 At Bolayır, on the Gallipoli peninsula.

108 We know at least two sons of Süleyman: Ishak and İsmail.

109 In fact, Murad I (ca. 1360–1389) assumed power directly upon the death of his father Orhan.

110 The final clause is obscure. The earthquake occurred on March 2, 1354, and enabled the Turks, under Süleyman, to seize Gallipoli. It was Kantakouzenos in peacetime who had offered to pay the Turks to vacate the peninsula; Süleyman was not faced with Serb and Bulgarian aggression.

111 This might be a reference to "White Croatia," vaguely located south of Poland.

112 See below for a list of the peoples to which he is referring.

113 This phrase is obscure.

114 The logic is confusing.

115 This clause is obscure.

116 For these events, see 1.25 above. The narrative is about to pick up from the start of 1.38.

117 Ivan Šišman, Bulgarian emperor (1371–1395).

118 On September 19, 1383, but the city was actually under Byzantine control: see 1.49 below (referring back to 1371, when the Byzantines took Serres). Laonikos has here bypassed most of Murad I's reign.

119 Lala Shahin Pasha was a Turkish raider active in Thrace under Murad I and the first *beylerbeyi* of Rumelia. It is possible that he commanded at the battle of Černomen in 1371; see 1.34 above.

120 Referring probably to the events of 1388, when Ivan Šišman was forced to accept vassal status.

121 Ivan Aleksandăr's daughter Tamara (Thamar), previously married to the *despotes* Konstantin, was given in marriage to Murad I by her brother Ivan Šišman in or after 1371; it is not clear, however, that Tamara was a daughter of Ivan Aleksandăr's second marriage. He had divorced his first wife, Teodora of Wallachia, and married a Jewish convert to Orthodoxy, who also assumed the name Teodora, in the late 1340s. At any rate, this marriage occurred well before the fall of Serres in 1383.

122 Ivan Aleksandăr's daughter Maria (Kyratza) married Andronikos IV, the son of Ioannes V, in 1355, one year after the removal of Ioannes VI Kantakouzenos; their son was Ioannes VII. See the following section. But Andronikos IV was not ruling at this time.

123 In October 1349.

124 Matthaios Kantakouzenos was made coemperor in 1353.

125 In 1354.

126 Actually he made his move from the island of Tenedos.

127 Ioannes VI Kantakouzenos abdicated and, on December 10, 1354, became a monk with the name Ioasaph. Laonikos seems to have confused his monastic name with that of his son (see below).

128 This refers to the Grand Master of the Hospitallers, the Knights of Rhodes, at this time Roger de Pins (1355–1365).

129 Matthaios was forced by Ioannes V to abdicate his title in 1357. He and his father, the former Ioannes VI, joined Manuel in the Peloponnese in 1361, although Manuel retained power until his death in 1380. It appears that Matthaios gave up his imperial pretensions when he abdicated; he did not seek to regain the throne. Before his abdication, however, he was held in various islands, including Lesbos and Tenedos. A visit to Rhodes is otherwise unattested.

130 Maria (Kyratza) was the daughter of Ivan Aleksandăr. The marriage was arranged in 1355, when both were children, and the wedding occurred before 1366; see also 1.40 above. Laonikos is the only source to mention a treaty between Ioannes V and Murad at this point, and its historicity has been questioned.

131 This is confused: Andronikos IV, Manuel II, Michael (not Demetrios), and Theodoros I (ruler of the Peloponnese, 1382–1407) were the sons of Ioannes V and Helene Kantakouzene, not of Andronikos IV and Maria (Kyratza) of Bulgaria.

132 Jovan Dragaš was the son of Dejan Dragaš, not Žarko (a confusion throughout Laonikos's narrative); Žarko was married to Jovan's sister. See 1.31 above and the notes there.

133 Jovan Dragaš and his brother Konstantin effectively became vassals of Murad following the battle of Černomen in 1371; see 1.34 above.

134 For Bogdan, see 1.31 above.

135 This episode seems to reflect the second of three phases of conflict between Murad and the emirs of Anatolia, dating to 1376/77. The others were in 1362 and 1387.

136 The so-called Rebellion of the Princes is supposed to have taken place in 1373. But Ottoman sources place the rebellion of Savcı against his father, Murad, in Asia Minor, in 1385, and do not mention Andronikos (who died in that year). It is possible that two events have been conflated and moved to Europe. In 1373 Andronikos IV and Ioannes V clashed (the former may have had

Turkish help, but not from a son of Murad). Andronikos and his son Ioannes VII were arrested and blinded by Ioannes V, enabling the latter to make Manuel his heir, and this was perhaps a purely internal Byzantine matter. See now P. Katsoni, *Μία επταετία κρίσιμων γεγονότων: Το Βυζάντιο στα έτη 1366–1373* (Thessalonike, 2002).

137 Across the Golden Horn, opposite from Blachernai.

138 This phrase is obscure.

139 The sense is obscure.

140 This sentence is likely corrupt. The "supervisor" (or administrator) may have been "captured" rather than "taken on." Manuel Palaiologos, son of Ioannes V, had been governing Thessalonike since 1369, and he took Serres in November 1371, in the aftermath of the Serb defeat at the battle of Černomen (see 1.34 above). But the events described below (Hayreddin's siege of Thessalonike and Manuel's visit to Murad) belong to a later period: in 1382 Manuel had proclaimed himself independent emperor in Thessalonike (1382–1387), which led to a long siege of the city by the Turks. Laonikos has telescoped events between 1371 and 1382; for the intervening years, see 2.4–6 below.

141 Çandarlı Kara Halil Hayreddin Pasha was later recognized as the first powerful Grand Vizier of the Ottoman Empire (1364–1387) and credited with the institution of the janissaries. His two sons Ali and İbrahim succeeded him (they appear in later books below).

142 The Turks had attacked Serres and Thessalonike briefly in 1372 but accomplished nothing. This passage refers to the events of 1383.

143 The siege actually lasted for four years.

144 Manuel attended upon Murad at Prousa, in the summer of 1387, after spending some time on Lesbos (see 1.55 below).

145 Murad's speech is obscure throughout.

146 Manuel was exiled to Lemnos by his father for two years, from 1387 to 1389.

147 This was in 1387, after a four-year siege. The city was treated leniently.

148 Dragaš was the son of Dejan Dragaš, not Žarko (a confusion throughout Laonikos's narrative); Žarko was married to Dejan's daughter. See 1.31 above and the notes there.

149 For Bogdan, see 1.31 above.

150 Ioannes VI Kantakouzenos took the monastic name Ioasaph; see 1.41 above.

151 Laonikos seems to have embellished Ioannes V's trip to Italy with details from the later trip of his son Manuel II to western Europe (from 1399 to 1402, on which see 2.29 below). In 1369 Ioannes traveled to Rome to submit personally to the pope (on October 18) and in the spring of 1370 to Venice, to resolve outstanding disputes, where he was detained until 1371. He did not go first to Venice or at all to France.

152 Andronikos IV governed during his father's absence, from 1369 to 1371.

153 This refers back to the first period during which Manuel was in charge of Thessalonike, starting in 1369; see 1.49 above.

154 In 1371.

155 There is a ten-year gap between this sentence and the previous one. Laonikos is now discussing the settlement of territories that took place in 1381 and 1382.

156 Theodoros I Palaiologos, son of Ioannes V, ruled the Peloponnese from 1382 to 1407.

157 Manuel Kantakouzenos had died in 1380; his brother Matthaios retired and then died in 1383. See 1.41 above.

158 This is now referring to the same rebellion mentioned at 1.49 above.

159 The Rebellion of the Princes allegedly occurred in 1373; see 1.44–48 above. Laonikos has dated the settlement of 1382 over ten years too early.

160 In April 1387; see 1.51 above.

161 Francesco II Gattilusio, ruler of Lesbos (1384–1404).

162 In the summer of 1387; this supplements the narrative in 1.49–50 above.

163 Lazar I Hrebljanović, prince of Serbia (1371–1389). This was the campaign of 1389, resulting in the battle of Kosovo.

164 Lazar gave one daughter to Ivan Šišman, Bulgarian emperor (1371–1395), in 1386, and another, named Mara, to Vuk Branković in ca. 1371. For Vuk, see also 1.31 above. His genealogy is given correctly here.

165 The territories of the *župan* Nikola Altomanović in western Serbia were taken by a coalition of his enemies, including Lazar, in 1373. By 1372, in the aftermath of the battle of Černomen, Lazar had also taken Priština, from Marko Mrnjavčević, the son of the fallen Vukašin, but seems to have soon ceded it to his ally Vuk Branković. As for Nestea, a proposed emendation is Nesion. If this refers to Niš, that city had been part of Lazar's realm. It was taken by the Turks in 1386. For Laonikos's confusions over this Nikola, see 1.31 above.

166 The battle of Kosovo was fought on June 15, 1389.

167 In fact, Turkish traditions stressed the role of Miloš.

168 For Süleyman's burial near Gallipoli, see 1.36 above.

169 Actually, Murad I reigned from ca. 1360 to 1389.

170 This discussion refers forward to the battle of Ankara, in 1402; see 3.55–57 below.

171 Bayezid I, Ottoman sultan (1389–1402).

Book 2

1 Actually, Lazar was executed after the battle.

2 For the conflicting versions of the battle of Kosovo, see also 1.56–57 above.

3 Bayezid attacked the kingdom of Bosnia (Illyria) and the Albanian lands in 1392. By this time all Serbian lands except Hum had become Ottoman vassals.

4 See 1.48 above; that is, on the eyes of Andronikos IV and his son Ioannes VII.

5 They escaped from confinement in 1376, although it is not clear from where. Laonikos now picks up the story from 1.48 above, when it began during the reign of Murad I.

6 Actually, Murad I, for we are now back in 1376.

7 Ioannes V and his sons Manuel II and Theodoros I (later the

ruler of the Peloponnese, 1382–1407) surrendered on August 12, 1376, and were imprisoned in the tower of Anemas. Andronikos IV immediately rewarded his allies, giving Tenedos to the Genoese and Gallipoli back to the Turks.

8 His reign lasted from 1376 to 1379.

9 They escaped in June 1379, possibly with Venetian help.

10 Again, this was still Murad I.

11 In reality, in 1381 Ioannes V was forced to recognize Andronikos IV and Ioannes VII as heirs to the throne. Manuel went off and declared himself independent emperor in Thessalonike (see 1.49–51 and 1.55 above). Andronikos died on June 28, 1385 (so before Bayezid came to the throne), and Ioannes took the throne briefly in 1390 but was expelled by Manuel, who then became sole emperor after the death of his father, Ioannes V, in 1391.

12 In 1390.

13 Kara Iskender, son of Kara Yusuf, was the ruler of the Kara Koyunlu (Black Sheep), a Turkic confederacy in eastern Armenia. He ruled from 1420 to 1438, long after Bayezid's death. The latter's contemporary was his father, Kara Yusuf (1391–1400 and 1406–1420); see also 3.71–72 below and 7.69. But no hostilities between Bayezid and the Black Sheep are recorded; to the contrary, in 1400 Kara Yusuf sought refuge with Bayezid, which was one of Timur's pretexts for attacking Bayezid. For Shemakha and Erzinjan, see below.

14 It is not clear who these "Assyrians" are.

15 Besieged by his rival brother Jihanshah in 1438, Iskender was murdered by his concubine, Khan Sultan (Layla), and her lover, his son Shah Kubad (Khwandamir, *Habibu's-siyar,* p. 345); see 3.71–72 below.

16 Bayezid took Erzinjan in 1400, but from Mutahhartan, the city's governor, who had rebelled against the eastern Anatolian principality of Eretna in 1379. Bayezid sent his family captive to Prousa. Erzinjan was not, however, in the territory of the Black Sheep; they were to its east. The Ak Koyunlu (White Sheep), a rival confederacy, under Kara Yülük captured Erzinjan in 1410.

17 In 1398 Bayezid annexed the lands of Janik in Niksar, Samsun,

and Çarşamba (on the northern coast of Asia Minor), as part of the same campaign that brought him Sivas (Sebasteia); see the following note. Amastris, however, is not near Kolchis. Perhaps it is an error for Amisos.

18 Kara Yülük Osman, often translated as "Black Eel" Osman, was the ruler of the Ak Koyunlu (White Sheep) Turkic federation, from 1403 to 1435 (de facto in charge since 1396); see also 3.71–72 and 5.33 below. Shemakha was not in the territory of the White Sheep, and Bayezid never went near it. Perhaps Laonikos has confused it with Sivas (Sebasteia), which Bayezid, sending his son Süleyman, relieved from a White Sheep attack (in fact, under the command of Kara Yülük) in 1398, and then took it over himself. Doukas, *History* 15.5, links Bayezid's campaigns against Sebasteia and Erzinjan.

19 Bayezid annexed these emirates, including Germiyan, in 1390–91, so before the campaigns mentioned above. By "Metin" Laonikos probably means the emirate of Hamid.

20 See 2.50 below.

21 In fact, Bayezid campaigned against Karaman twice, in 1391 and 1397–98. Its ruler then, 'Ala' al-Din (1361–1398), was Bayezid's brother-in-law and was executed by him in 1398. As for the name Alishur, it belonged to the founder of the emirate of Germiyan, Yakub b. Alishur (d. after 1320), but Laonikos refers to the ruler of Karaman as "Karaman Alisourios" (see note on 1.14 above). Turgut was the name of a clan in central Anatolia associated with Karaman, whom it supported against the Ottomans; see 5.33 below.

22 See 1.14 above for corrections. Laonikos does not mention Menteşe there and has Karası as the son of Kalamshah.

23 This is how Laonikos refers to the Jandarid rulers of Kastamonu and Sinope (see 1.14 above), whose territory Bayezid annexed in 1393.

24 For these events, see the notes on 2.8 above.

25 This probably refers to raids in 1398 after the battle of Nikopolis (which took place in 1396; see 2.20 below). Illyria here is again the kingdom of Bosnia.

26 In 1394. Bayezid's attempt to move into the Peloponnese fol-

lowed a series of complaints that had been put to him by his vassals during the winter of 1393–94; those meetings are described at 2.25–27 below. Laonikos has broken the narrative into two parts and reversed their order.

27 According to other versions of this tale, the bishop's name was Serapheim.

28 Epikernaioi is transparently related to the term *epikernes/pinkernes,* designating a high court official (the wine bearer), attested several times among the leading magnates in Byzantine and Serbian Thessaly. It is possible that it became a family name and that on the eve of the Ottoman conquest Domokos was governed by a member of that family on behalf of Thessaly's *kaisar* Manuel Angelos Philanthropenos, or even that the Philanthropenoi had carried that title at some earlier point.

29 Salona (Amphissa; or La Sola; De Sula; Laonikos's "Delphi") was ruled by the widow of Luis Fadrique of Aragon, count of Salona, Zetounion, and Siderokastron (Arachova), who died in 1382. His widow was Helene, the daughter of Matthaios Kantakouzenos, briefly coemperor with his father (on him, see 1.41 above). Her story is told more fully below.

30 Her daughter was named Maria, one of the most sought-after heiresses in Latin Greece.

31 Possibly a certain Murad Beg.

32 In 1382.

33 That is, Neopatras (Hypate), by Lamia. Laonikos is here referring generally to the Catalans in Greece. Luis Fadrique was the vicar-general of the duchies of Athens and Neopatras (1375–1382). He was the grandson of Don Alfonso Fadrique, the illegitimate son of Federico II of Sicily.

34 Sigismund of Luxembourg was king of Hungary (1387–1437) and was later to become German king (1410–1437), king of Bohemia (1419–1437), and Holy Roman emperor (1433–1437), among other titles.

35 Vienna was actually the capital of the Habsburg dukes of Austria. But Sigismund's daughter and heiress did marry a Habsburg (Duke Albrecht V of Austria/King Albrecht II of Germany), and later in the fifteenth century the unrelated king of

Hungary (Mátyás I, 1458–1490) did control Vienna, making it his residence during the period from 1485 to 1490.

36 At the time of these events (1394–1396), Sigismund had not yet acquired all these titles.

37 The mistake that Germany begins at the Pyrenees seems to be unprecedented, but the notion that the Tartesos River originated in the Pyrenees had precedent, especially in pseudo-Aristotle, *Meteorology* 1.13 (350b), who seems to be quoted directly here, and in the philosophical tradition thereafter (Olympiodoros, Psellos, etc.). Laonikos is probably referring to the Guadalquivir. In general, see Herodotos, *Histories* 2.33.

38 Laonikos calls it Argentia, from ancient Roman Argentoratum.

39 That is, for someone looking south. The manuscripts spell what we call Denmark in many ways (*Dakia, Datia, Dastia, Dasteia;* Plethon, *Corrections to Some of the Mistakes in Strabo,* has *Dateia*), and the term may refer to all of Scandinavia.

40 It has been proposed that Laonikos has confused Vienna with Bremen here.

41 This has implausibly been conjectured to be Basileia, that is, Basel; or else Cilli or Aquileia.

42 *Breme* here is an emendation of *Blene,* but this is uncertain.

43 From 1308 to 1395 the Hungarian monarchs were Capetian Angevins from Naples (Károly I, Lajos I, Mária, and Károly II), from 1387 to 1437 Luxembourgs from Bohemia (Sigismund), from 1438 to 1440 Habsburgs from Austria (Albert and László V), from 1440 to 1444 Jagiellonians from Poland-Lithuania (Ulászló I), from 1444 to 1457 Habsburgs from Austria again (László V), and from 1458 to 1490 a "national" Hungarian king, Mátyás I "Corvinus."

44 Laonikos is here referring to the position of Regent-Governor held by Hunyadi; see 7.14.

45 It is odd that Laonikos pretends not to know the ethnonym *Oungroi,* because it was well established in Byzantine and international usage. It is also not clear which name he means by "this name" (presumably what he calls them, Paionians, but they did not call themselves that).

46 Sigismund never ruled Vienna.

47 In 1387, through marriage.

48 Laonikos misdates Sigismund's appointment as German king (1410) and coronation as emperor of the Romans by the pope (1433) by placing them before the Nikopolis campaign (1396). He was crowned by Eugenius IV, but we cannot be sure this is whom Laonikos means here. The pope at the time of the crusade was Boniface IX, but the expedition was also supported by Benedict XIII in Avignon.

49 See 1.6 above for appointing the Holy Roman emperors. For the French (Charlemagne) in Iberia, see also 2.32–34 and 5.79 below.

50 Sigismund and Venice were at war on and off during the 1410s.

51 That is, Milan under Filippo Maria Visconti. Sigismund received the Iron Crown there on November 25, 1431.

52 Philippe II of Burgundy sent his son Jean the Fearless (count of Nevers and later Jean II of Burgundy) in nominal command.

53 The battle of Nikopolis was fought on September 25, 1396.

54 The Burgundian general was Jean the Fearless (see 2.19 above). Another captive was the French commander Jean le Meingre, called Boucicaut, marshal of France, son of his like-named father, both of them involved in the Hundred Years' War. The high-ranking captives were later ransomed, but many of the rank-and-file were executed.

55 Mircea I the Old, prince of Wallachia (1386–1394 and 1397–1418). Ottoman armies raided Wallachia frequently after Nikopolis, but the campaign that Laonikos is introducing here occurred the previous year, in 1395.

56 Moldavia was called this after the rule of Bogdan I (ca. 1363–ca. 1367).

57 "Prasovos" is obviously a reference to the Carpathians, but whether it reflects the city of Brassó (Hungarian; now Romanian Braşov) or the Prahova River is unclear. There is no mountain with that name.

58 Kazimierz IV of Poland (1446–1492) and Lithuania (1440–1492). For his Mongols, see 3.25 below.

59 Dan I, prince of Wallachia (1383–1386); elsewhere he is said to have been killed by the Bulgarian emperor Ivan Šišman.

60 Actually, the campaign about to be recounted took place one year before Nikopolis, in 1395 (though later the Ottomans did accuse Mircea of aiding Sigismund).

61 The origins of Evrenos, son of İsa Beg, are uncertain. He was the most important raider of the fourteenth century and died in 1417. He was powerful already during the reign of Murad I.

62 This is a whitewashed account of the campaign, which led to the battle of Rovine (May 17, 1395), an Ottoman defeat.

63 This was in the winter of 1393–94. The meeting is described in detail by Manuel II in his *Funeral Oration* for his brother Theodoros (pp. 134–43). Laonikos seems not to realize that he is here recounting the preliminaries of the invasion of Thessaly and the Peloponnese that he already described at 2.10–13 above.

64 The Dragaš brothers, Konstantin (ruler of Kumanovo until 1395) and Jovan, were the sons of Dejan Dragaš, not Žarko (a confusion throughout Laonikos's narrative). Their mother was Stefan Dušan's sister; Žarko was married to Dejan's daughter. Konstantin's daughter was the mother of Konstantinos XI, the last emperor of Byzantium.

65 Stefan I, prince of Serbia (1389–1427), son of Lazar I, prince of Serbia (1371–1389).

66 Theodoros took over Monemvasia in 1391/92.

67 Ioannes VII Palaiologos had held the throne briefly in 1390 and was Manuel's rival and "alternate" at this time.

68 For Hayreddin, see 1.49 and 1.51–52 above. Çandarlı Ali Pasha succeeded his father as grand vizier (1387–1406).

69 Around 1378.

70 Manuel II Palaiologos had married Konstantin Dragaš's daughter Helene on February 10, 1392, but the conspiracy to rebel, recounted here, took place in the winter of 1393–94.

71 Actually, Eudokia of Trebizond, daughter of the emperor Alexios III and widow of Taj al-Din, emir of Janik (ca. 1348–1387), had married Konstantin Dragaš, Manuel's future father-

in-law, in 1387. "Kolchis" is how Laonikos normally designates the empire of Trebizond.

72 Konstantin Dragaš seems not to have joined the other rulers in this rebellion and died in 1395 fighting on the Ottoman side at the battle of Rovine (for which see 2.24 above).

73 Actually, Theodoros remained with Bayezid until it became clear that the sultan intended to invade the Peloponnese, at which point Theodoros escaped to defend his dominions; see 2.10–13 above (Laonikos does not realize that the events he is describing here took place earlier in the same year as those in 2.10–13 above).

74 The siege, or blockade, of Constantinople lasted from 1394 to 1402. Many of the other wars described above (Rovine, Nikopolis) took place while it was going on.

75 Actually eight years.

76 This sentence is obscure.

77 While Ioannes VII seems to have traveled to Italy (in 1389 or 1390, and 1392), this episode is not reported in other sources and is unlikely, because the Genoese were his allies in his struggle against Manuel.

78 On December 4, 1399. Bayezid was actually in Asia Minor at the time, and Ioannes VII at his base in Selymbria.

79 Manuel departed on December 10, 1399.

80 Manuel reached Venice in early 1400 and traveled from there to Milan, where he was received by Gian Galeazzo Visconti, duke of Milan (d. 1402).

81 Charles VI the Mad, king of France (1380–1422), suffered from a recurring mental illness. Manuel reached Paris in June 1400 and stayed there until December, when he went to England (Laonikos does not mention the journey to England, although he does below offer a description of Britain). Manuel resided in Paris again, from February 1401 to November 1402, after his return from England.

82 Laonikos has shifted all of France's neighbors counterclockwise.

83 On Denmark see note to 2.14 above.

84 For the Hundred Years' War, see 2.35–37 below. The dukes of Burgundy supported different sides in different phases of the war. But the sense of this sentence is obscure.

85 Laonikos uses Genoa's Latin name *Ianua* (door). He knows that it was sometimes under French control: see 5.58 below.

86 René the Good was duke of Anjou and Provence (1417–1480) and king of Naples (1435–1442).

87 The Pont Saint-Bénezet, built in the late twelfth century.

88 In what follows, Laonikos relies on Charlemagne romances like the *Song of Roland*. For the appointment of the French as emperors of the Romans, see 1.6 and 2.18 above.

89 During the Hundred Years' War, the English and their allies took Paris in 1420.

90 The English under King Edward III (1327–1377) took Calais after a siege in 1347.

91 Actually, Philippe VI (1328–1350) tried to bring a relief force during the English siege but withdrew.

92 The following is probably the battle of Poitiers, September 19, 1356.

93 That is, Agincourt, October 25, 1415 (from the false derivation "Chagrincourt").

94 This phrase, which breaks up the syntax and sense, and is repeated from above, is possibly an intrusion.

95 The preceding narrative can refer to any number of engagements in which Joan of Arc was involved. She died in 1431.

96 This refers mainly to the 1440s.

97 The English held Calais until 1558.

98 Laonikos is either thinking of the islands of Frisia or following Diodoros of Sicily, *Bibliotheke* 5.22.2–3, on promontories of Britain that become islands with the tides.

99 The syntax of this sentence is unclear.

100 This passage is probably corrupt and seems also to have a lacuna. The Soul of the Universe (or World Soul) was a Neoplatonic notion accepted by Laonikos's neopagan teacher Plethon and rejected by most Orthodox theologians.

101 The narrative picks up from 2.29 above.

102 Actually, Manuel returned via Genoa and Venice.

103 This double invasion of the Peloponnese took place in 1397, before Manuel had even left for the West.

104 This sentence is obscure.

105 Persuaded by his ally and father-in-law, Nerio, the ruler of Athens, Theodoros I Palaiologos had given Argos to the Venetians in 1394 to secure their help against the Turks.

106 Theodoros negotiated with the Hospitallers to sell the Despotate to them in 1399–1400. The deal was being implemented when it was botched by the inhabitants of Mistra. He had already sold Corinth to them in 1397, when the Venetians turned down his initial offer (the alternative was to lose it to the Turks). Theodoros had bought Corinth from Carlo I Tocco the previous year, after besieging it for a number of years.

107 The bishop of Lakedaimon may have been Neophytos, who is attested earlier, ca. 1394.

108 According to his brother Manuel II, Theodoros had planned all this in advance (*Funeral Oration,* pp. 204–5), but this is unlikely. These events at Mistra took place in the autumn of 1400, but the retrocession of the Peloponnese took years to arrange, as the Hospitallers had paid an advance and occupied cities.

109 Yakub took Argos on June 3, 1397.

110 This is what Laonikos calls the *akıncı* raiders, Ottoman irregulars, whom some scholars, following some Turkish sources, have dignified with the term *gazi,* holy warriors.

111 These were Mongols moving westward after Timur's defeat of the Golden Horde (recounted in Book 3); see also 3.25 below for this group. They arrived probably in 1398.

112 See 2.8 above and the notes there.

113 Bayezid took Melitene (Malatya) from the Mamluks in the summer of 1399, by sending his son Süleyman.

114 Possibly this is a switch of reference to Timur.

115 This picks up their story from 2.9 above.

116 Bayezid's nickname Yıldırım translates to "Thunderbolt," but Laonikos calls him a "Hurricane."

117 For Timur's attack on the Mamluks of Egypt, see 3.38–43 below.

118 This sentence is obscure.

119 "Hero" is how Laonikos and many Muslim speakers in the work refer to Muhammad.

120 This story is picked up again at 3.48 below.

121 This passage is unclear, but it seems to correspond to Muslim divorce. *Quran* 2.230: "So if he divorces her she shall not be lawful to him afterward until she marries another husband; then if he [i.e., the second husband] divorces her there is no blame on them both [the original couple] if they return to each other (by marriage)" (trans. M. H. Shakir). It is not clear where the spleens come from, but they almost certainly refer to the rule of triple *talaq* (the divorce is final if the husband says "I divorce you" three times to his wife). These rules and passages were, of course, subject to interpretation and variation. The interpretation of the second marriage as "adultery" may be Laonikos's own, although it may have been understood that way by Muslims, given how the practice was used as an insult here. See also 3.16 below.

122 Timur's chief wife is often identified as Saray Mulk-khanum, previously married to one of his allies and rivals, Husayn of Balkh.

123 This sentence is obscure.

124 Timur did not approach Sebasteia from Malatya (the south) but from Erzerum and Erzinjan (the east).

125 Timur generally did not displace established dynasties but required them to accept him as their overlord, including by mentioning him in the *khutbah* (Islamic public sermons). For this list of his demands, see also 3.48 below.

126 The first campaign, against Sebasteia, took place in 1400; see 3.1 below.

Book 3

1 In 1400; for the campaign against Sivas (Sebasteia), see 3.44–47 below.

2 Nothing definite is known about Timur's parents or ancestors.

His father is normally called Taraghai, of the Barlas clan. Timur was born on April 8, 1336.

3 Timur's wound was probably received in one of the battles that accompanied his rise to power, in ca. 1364. The Persian appellation Timur-i Lang (Lame Timur) gives us our "Tamerlane."

4 The passage is unclear.

5 Mirza is a title attached to the name of many sons of emirs, and Haydar was a common name, so it is impossible to link them to specific individuals known from other sources.

6 It is possible that by this classical ethnonym Laonikos means the Chaghadai; see 3.24 below, and the end of this chapter (3.3).

7 Probably Kesh (Shahr-i Sabz in modern Uzbekistan), some seventy kilometers south of Samarkand, although Laonikos's narrative is unspecific.

8 One should probably not try to identify this vague and confused account with events known from sources closer to the events. In 1360 Tughluq Timur, khan of the eastern division of the Ulus Chaghadai, or Moghulistan (see 3.24 below and note there), invaded Transoxiana and invested Timur with leadership of his tribe, the Barlas, as a rival to its previous chief, Hajji Beg. But Timur had to step down. In 1361 Tughluq Timur invaded again, gave Timur command again, but soon had to go into exile. When the emirs of the Ulus Chaghadai, under Husayn, drove out the Moghuls, Timur had regained control of his tribe (certainly by 1364). Timur spent from 1366 to 1368 in exile again, outside the Ulus Chaghadai, seeking support against Husayn, now his rival. By 1370 he had eliminated Husayn and maneuvered himself to lead the Ulus Chaghadai.

9 It is not clear what "master and king" Laonikos means. The emirs ruling the Ulus Chaghadai tended to appoint puppet khans from the Mongol dynastic line to give them legitimacy, and Timur had done the same. Moreover, in 1370 he married Saray Malik Khanım, daughter of Qazan (khan of the Ulus Chaghadai, 1343–1346), and thus married into Chaghadai's line. Laonikos may have heard how Timur displaced Husayn in 1369–70 and took his wives for himself and his men. The narrative of

conquests is also confused here. Timur gained control of Samarkand in 1370 without a siege (when he took over the Ulus Chaghadai), while Baghdad surrendered to him in 1393 and was captured by him in 1401.

10 This passage is unclear. It is possible that it refers to Timur's self-doubts.

11 It is difficult to know what contemporary states or people lie behind the labels "Hyrkanians" and "Kadousioi" (on the latter, see below and 3.12). Classical Hyrkania was to the south and southeast of the Caspian Sea; Kadousia was to its southwest (Media Atropatene). In the 1370s and early 1380s, Timur campaigned extensively against Moghulistan (to the northeast of the Ulus Chaghadai), Khorezm (south of the Aral Sea), Khorasan (the kingdom of Herat), and Sistan (to the south). It was in 1384–85 that he began to move against Mazandaran and Gilan (as far as Tabriz), which would correspond to Hyrkania and Kadousia. The latter would then appear to have been ruled by the Jalayirids of Iraq and northwestern Iran (with centers at Sultaniyyah and Tabriz), whose ruler Sultan Ahmad (1385–1410) was repeatedly driven out by Timur between 1385 and 1405.

12 By Massagetai here Laonikos probably means the Mongols generally (in this region the Chaghadai, on whom see 3.24 below and the note there).

13 It is risky to identify these rivers given the fluidity of these names in and after antiquity.

14 Timur never campaigned against Arabia, certainly not Arabia Felix (described below).

15 There was no Arabian state in ca. 1400.

16 Timur's wars never reached Arabia; it is not clear what events Laonikos is referring to here.

17 'Umar I (634–644) was in fact the second caliph of Islam, following Abu Bakr (632–634).

18 Actually, his father's name was 'Abd-Allah. Ali was Muhammad's first cousin, son-in-law, and later successor as the fourth caliph (656–661).

19 Actually, five times a day.

20 This *may* be channeling the slander that Muslims worshipped Aphrodite, but more likely Laonikos is simply using the classical Roman names for the days of the week, as there was not a convenient Greek one.

21 For these divorce laws, see 2.54 above and the note there.

22 It is not clear what this refers to; possibly *jinn*.

23 For a description of these ceremonies, see 8.69–70.

24 Many Muslim states enslaved Armenians. This may be a garbled reference to the tradition that Muhammad was led astray by a heretic (usually an Arian) named Bahira; this story shows up in early Armenian sources too.

25 That is, 622–632.

26 Muhammad actually died and is buried at Medina.

27 ʿUmar I (634–644) was in fact the second caliph of Islam, following Abu Bakr (632–634).

28 This is garbled, as Muhammad had no surviving son.

29 This is a reference to the *hajj*, but Muhammad was buried in Medina, not Mecca, and visiting his tomb was not part of the *hajj*.

30 The (polemical) notion of Muhammad's floating tomb was promoted by many Western medieval sources.

31 Or "displayed."

32 These Skythians were the Mongols of the Golden Horde, ruled by khan Toqtamish (1379–1395), who had actually been one of Timur's protégés. In the winter of 1385–86, Toqtamish attacked Tabriz, now under Timur's authority. Timur responded with a three-year invasion of the Caucasus and northern Iraq and Iran. In 1387 Toqtamish invaded Transoxiana. This brought Timur back to his base, and for the next four years he fought in the north against the Sufi dynasty in Khorezm and the Moghuls, who had aided Toqtamish (for Timur's clashes with the Horde, see 3.34–37 below and the notes there). In 1394 Toqtamish again raided the Caucasus, which resulted in Timur's devastating incursion of 1394/95. Laonikos is probably referring to the second of Toqtamish's attacks (of 1387), and so his "Khataians" must be one of Timur's northern neighbors (being, as he says below, to

the east of Hyrkania), probably the Moghuls. It is possible that Laonikos's term is related to *Cathay,* which had gained currency for (northern) China (Mongol-controlled at this time). Timur did not campaign there at this time, although he did set out to do so at the very end of his life. Still, Laonikos's usage is imprecise.

33 One of the methods by which Timur diluted the power of the tribes was to bring in many foreign soldiers loyal only to himself and his structures of government. When Laonikos says that the Persians had experience of war with the Skythians, he means campaigns of Darius recounted in Herodotos (see below).

34 Neither do we.

35 See 3.38 below.

36 The Ulus Chaghadai was a Turko-Mongol khanate, one of the four main divisions of the Mongol Empire, and included a significant portion of Central Asia, including Transoxiana and parts of modern Afghanistan. The eponym of the khanate was Chinggis Khan's son Chaghadai. By Timur's time, the Ulus Chaghadai had shifted to the west and south and had lost its eastern portion, or Moghulistan. This western Ulus was the base for his rise and conquests. When the sources refer to the Chaghadai, they mean the ruling nomadic element of this tribal federation. For Timur and India, see 3.64–69 below. He ransacked much of northwestern India in 1398, sacking Delhi.

37 That is, the family of Chinggis Khan; as far as the Golden Horde was concerned, the house of Chinggis Khan's eldest son, Jöchi.

38 Hajji Giray was the first khan of the Crimea (1427–1466).

39 See 2.48 above.

40 Kazimierz IV of Poland (1446–1492) and Lithuania (1440–1492). For his Skythians, see also 2.22 above.

41 The Mongol raids started in the 1220s.

42 Belgorod Dnestrovskij, also known as Akkerman.

43 Tafel emended this to Kharkov, which, however, was not founded until 1654. Ditten proposed changing it to Rostov or Pskov.

44 A Polish term for Livonia.

45 That is, the Teutonic Order.

46 The Knights of Santiago in Spain, although there were actually multiple Spanish orders; and the Hospitallers, the Knights of Saint John on Rhodes.

47 A people in Lithuania: see the following section.

48 The Samogitians did not convert to Christianity until 1413.

49 Bohemia was Christian since the ninth century. This may be a confused or polemical reference to the Hussite movement. For the alleged conversion of the Bohemians, see also 8.49 and 8.58.

50 See 3.67 below.

51 Belgorod (Akkerman) was the capital of Moldavia between 1448 and 1455.

52 That is, between Wallachia and Moldavia.

53 That is, Vilna.

54 For the debate over the origin of the Slavs, see also 1.29 and 1.38–39 above and 10.16–17.

55 These are the Mongols of Hajji Giray, north of the Black Sea; see 3.25 above.

56 Both are people of the Caucasus; for the Mingrelians, see also 9.35.

57 This passage is unclear.

58 The next few sections recount Timur's attacks on Toqtamish's Golden Horde, but Laonikos's account has only a vague relation to reality. In 1391 Timur defeated Toqtamish and pursued his army as far as the Volga. In 1395 Timur advanced deep into the Horde's territory, reaching Moscow and sacking the Horde's capital, Saray.

59 This is a factual aspect of the 1395 campaign (see previous note), but it also replays aspects of King Darius's expedition against the Skythians in Herodotos (Laonikos makes the comparison himself at 3.22 above).

60 Shahrukh was one of Timur's sons and his successor as padishah of the Timurids (1405–1447); see 3.70 below. As he was born in 1377, he would have been fourteen and seventeen at the time of

his father's two expeditions against the Horde. His involvement in them is not otherwise attested.

61 That is, Georgia.

62 Timur had first campaigned in the Caucasus (taking Tiflis in Georgia) in 1386 and in Armenia in 1387. But he did so again in 1399–1400, after his great campaign against the Golden Horde, so Laonikos is probably referring to this instance here. But the Mongols had ceased to be any threat after 1395.

63 Actually, Toqtamish had done this in 1385–86 and again in 1394, before Timur's punishing expedition of 1394–95, after which the Mongols could not bother him; see 3.21 above and the note there.

64 This was the Syrian campaign of 1400–1401. Damascus fell in March 1401; Timur had captured Aleppo and Emesa (Homs) the previous fall.

65 The Mamluk sultan at this time was al-Nasir Faraj (1399–1412), whose reign was disastrous.

66 See 3.43 below.

67 The figure is, of course, unrealistic. Cairo (and Egypt) had suffered population decline since a high point in 1340, due to plague, famine, and political instability. The population in ca. 1400 was perhaps 150,000.

68 Pseudo-Aristotle, *Meteorology* 1.13 (350b12).

69 The latter is probably a reference to dualists generally. There were no actual Manicheans in Mamluk Egypt.

70 Laonikos is confused here. After the sack of Baghdad by the Mongols of Hülegü in 1258, the Abbasid caliphs came to reside at Cairo as protégés of the Mamluk sultans. The arrangement continued until the Ottoman conquest of the Mamluk sultanate in 1517.

71 The manuscripts say "from Tyre *(Tyros)* of Alexandria," but this has been emended to *Pharos.*

72 The Ituraeans were an Arab people who lived in Lebanon in antiquity.

73 Laonikos is probably referring to the city walls, which had been pulled down many times in recent centuries.

74 For Laonikos's confused notions about the *hajj,* see 3.20 above.

75 "Samos" cannot refer to the Greek island here; possibly it is *Sham,* the Semitic name for Syria-Palestine, or else the text is corrupted.

76 The Mamluk sultan al-Ashraf Barsbay (1422–1438) raided Cyprus annually between 1424 and 1426, capturing its king, Janus of Lusignan (1398–1432), on July 7, 1426, and ransacking its cities. The king was restored as a Mamluk vassal in 1427.

77 Cyprus was conquered by King Richard I of England (1189–1199) from its Byzantine ruler Isaakios Komnenos in 1191, during the course of the Third Crusade. Richard sold the island to the Templars, but they decided against holding it, and it was given to Guy of Lusignan, former king of Jerusalem (1186–1192), in part as compensation for abdicating that throne.

78 Aleppo fell to Timur in October 1400, Damascus in March 1401.

79 This king is a bundle of confusions. For the problematic term Khatai, see 3.21 above and the note there. The "Nine" seems to be a reference to the Toquz Oğuz (the Nine Oghuz), an ancient Turkic confederacy that is first found around the Altai and later as far west as Transoxiana. As for India, it was Timur who invaded it (1398–1399), not the reverse. The eastern opponents who gave Timur difficulty were the eastern Chaghadai, but they did not rule India (and Timur was the ruler of the Ulus Chaghadai). See also 3.64 and 3.66 below: in the latter passage, Laonikos identifies this king of the nine/of India with the Chaghadai.

80 See 2.49–50 above.

81 Sebasteia (Turkish Sivas) had been a part-time capital of the Seljuk sultans of Rum, then the capital of the Mongol emirate of Eretna (fourteenth century).

82 Bayezid's son Ertoğrul, formerly a governor of western Anatolia, had died in 1396, in a different war; see 3.47 below.

83 The siege of Sebasteia lasted for two weeks in August 1400.

84 For Ertoğrul, see 3.44 above. A relief operation for Sebasteia seems to have been organized by another son, Süleyman.

85 For this list of demands, see also 2.57 above. When Timur de-

feated Bayezid, he did issue coins in his own name in Asia Minor: C. Foss, *Survey of Medieval Castles of Anatolia,* v. 1: *Kütahya* (BAR v. 261, 1985), 15. But Laonikos is jumping ahead two years in this section, from Sebasteia (1400) to the Asia Minor campaign (1402); in the middle was the Syrian campaign, on which see 3.43 above.

86 See 2.54 above.

87 This clause is obscure.

88 For Ali, see 2.25 above.

89 Çandarlı İbrahim Pasha was more likely Ali's brother, another son of Hayreddin. He would be grand vizier from 1421 to 1429 under Murad II.

90 Herodotos, *Histories* 8.97–107.

91 This sentence is obscure.

92 The battle of Ankara was fought on July 28, 1402.

93 The European army, commanded by Bayezid's son Süleyman, may have been on the left.

94 Musa was one of Bayezid's sons, a protagonist in the Turkish civil wars, recounted in Book 4.

95 Olivera, daughter of Prince Lazar I of Serbia, married Bayezid in 1390. Bayezid had other wives, but it is unclear which other wife Laonikos refers to here (if not, confusingly, the same one twice).

96 Compare Homer, *Iliad* 7.127.

97 The point of the question is unclear.

98 See 2.58 above.

99 The siege began on December 2, 1402, and lasted for two weeks.

100 That is, by a coalition of Western powers, including the Hospitaller Knights of Rhodes.

101 For the confusing identity of this king, see 3.43 above and the note there. The narrative picks up from 3.61.

102 At 3.69 below, Laonikos says that Musa was let go, which is more likely.

103 Actually, Bayezid reigned from 1389 to 1402.

104 Bayezid died on March 9, 1403, at Philomelion/Akşehir, which is not in Ionia (see the end of the previous section).

105 The MSS *Syênê* has been emended to *Sinê* here. Syene was a city in Egypt.

106 India did (almost) come under the control of the sultanate of Delhi in the early 1300s, but by 1400 it was in disarray, not least because of Timur's invasion in 1398. Otherwise, the political geography of this section is garbled beyond redemption.

107 It is not clear whether this refers to India or to China; possibly the latter, as only China is named at 3.66 above.

108 A *medimnos* was a unit of dry volume roughly equal to fifty liters (thirteen gallons).

109 For the war of Semiramis against the Indians, see Diodoros of Sicily, *Bibliotheke* 2.16–19; for Cyrus's war against the Massagetai, see Herodotos, *Histories* 1.201–14.

110 At 3.64 above, Laonikos had said that he escaped.

111 Actually, Timur had invaded India in 1398. It was China that he set out to attack in 1405, and he died on the way.

112 Shahrukh was Timur's successor until his death in 1447. Baysunqur was Shahrukh's son and coruler until his death in 1433 (so Timur's grandson). 'Abd-al-Latif (a great-grandson of Timur) was a son of Uluğ-Beg (the son and successor of Shahrukh); he died in 1450.

113 Timur's arrangements for the succession were more complicated, but Shahrukh did eventually establish himself as the supreme ruler, padishah (1405–1447).

114 Timur died on February 17 or 18, 1405, at Otrar, having begun a campaign to conquer China.

115 Shahrukh actually outlived his father by four decades, until 1447. Baysunqur was a son of Shahrukh, on whose behalf he governed parts of Khurasan until predeceasing him in 1433. But in the immediate aftermath of Timur's death, there was fighting among his sons and grandsons. Timur's designated successor, Pir Muhammad, did in fact die soon (in 1407).

116 Uluğ-Beg was the son and successor of Shahrukh, under whom he had already served as governor of Samarkand; he reigned as padishah of the Timurids for only two years (1447–1449). 'Abd-al-Latif was the eldest son of Uluğ-Beg, who rebelled against his

father and killed him, ruling briefly as padishah of the Timurids (1449–1450).

117 Muhammad Juki was son of Shahrukh; he governed Balkh (1443–1444).

118 Babur was the son of Baysunqur. He had been Uluğ-Beg's governor of Samarkand since 1447 and later became padishah (1452–1457).

119 Neither Baysunqur nor Juki held Samarkand, and both predeceased their father, Shahrukh. Moreover, in just two sentences Laonikos has called Baysunqur both Juki's father and brother. It is possible that he has projected onto Juki aspects of the career of Abu Sa'id (a great-grandson of Timur from another line), who captured Samarkand in 1451 with the assistance of Uzbek tribes (Skythians), taking it from 'Abdullah, another great-grandson of Timur, and fought against Babur.

120 The Ak Koyunlu (White Sheep) Turkic confederacy controlled northern Mesopotamia, western Armenia, and Kurdistan. Kara Yülük (often translated as the "Black Eel"), or 'Uthman (Tk. Osman), ruled them from Amida (Diyarbakir), between 1403 and 1435. But the Timurids did not attack the White Sheep, who were their allies against the Black Sheep, the Kara Koyunlu, a rival confederacy in eastern Armenia. Juki's father, Shahrukh, made three incursions against them (1420–1421, 1429, and 1434–1436); Tabriz changed hands each time. In 1435 Shahrukh arrived in Tabriz and sent his son Juki against Iskender, the ruler of the Black Sheep (1420–1436; see 3.8 above), replacing him with his brother Jahanshah, who was expected to be more subservient to the Timurids (see 3.72 below). Laonikos seems to have confused the two federations at this point. It is also not clear where Laonikos thinks Shemakha is.

121 'Ajam is the Arabic word for Persian or Iranian.

122 Jahanshah was indeed the son of Kara Yusuf and his second successor as ruler of the Black Sheep (1438–1467), after his brother Iskender (on whom see below); he began as a Timurid protégé (placed in power by Juki, Shahrukh's son) but later turned on the Timurids and took over much of Iraq and western Iran. He was

born in 1397, so he cannot have been the grandson of Juki (who was born in 1402).

123 Kara Yusuf was the ruler of the Black Sheep confederacy (1389–1400 and 1405–1420), an enemy of the Timurids, who fled to Mamluk Egypt under Timur and recovered control of Azerbaijan after his death in 1405. He certainly did not marry a daughter of Juki (see following note). Juki married Khanum, the daughter of Kara Yülük of the White Sheep (see note above), which may have caused the confusion here.

124 Jahanshah was installed in power in Tabriz by Shahrukh, via his son Juki, in 1435. He later broke from the Timurids and took Iraq, much of western Iran, Hyrkania, and western Khurasan with Herat. Jahanshah took Baghdad in 1446 and Erzinjan in 1450. Babur's son Shah Mahmud was eleven when he succeeded to the throne, in 1457, and was quickly expelled by other Timurids, so this cannot be who is meant.

125 See 7.69 for the same information (that later passage also clarifies the convoluted syntax of this one). Juki's sons Muhammad Qasim and Abu Bakr governed briefly in the area of Balkh, on the opposite end of the Timurid Empire, between 1444 and 1447. They cannot be meant here.

126 Uzun Hasan was the grandson of Kara Yülük, ruler of the White Sheep (Ak Koyunlu), and he ruled between 1453 and 1478. He was not descended from Iskender, ruler of the Black Sheep, who was his main enemy (before Jahanshah). In fact, Kara Yülük was killed in battle with Iskender in 1435, when Shahrukh intervened against the Black Sheep and set up Jahanshah against Iskender. Uzun Hasan fought a war against Jahanshah and would destroy him in 1467, although Laonikos seems unaware of this development. Hasan was also the main Eastern rival of Mehmed II; see 9.40 and 9.70–73.

127 Laonikos again cannot mean by this name the place we know as Shemakha.

128 In 1450/51 Babur fought against and killed his rival Sultan Muhammad (a grandson of Shahrukh) precisely in Media, but he was then forced back east by Jahanshah and the Black Sheep,

who took most of Iran from the Timurids at this point. Laonikos has presented those events from the standpoint of the war between the Black and the White Sheep, as if Babur was called in by the former to help them against the latter. At 7.69 he presents the same events, only it seems there that Juki takes the place of Babur.

129 This sentence refers to events fifty years before those of the surrounding narrative.

130 Janik was on the northern Anatolian coast, to the west of the empire of Trebizond (Kolchis). Hasan is not known to have attacked it. He did marry Theodora Komnene, the daughter of the emperor Ioannes IV of Trebizond (1429–1460), in 1458.

Book 4

1 Actually, Süleyman seems to have been the eldest; only Laonikos makes this claim.

2 This İsa the Younger was in reality called Yusuf; see 4.12 below.

3 İsa established himself as ruler at Bursa (Prousa) between August and November 1402.

4 The clause is likely corrupt. In fleeing from Timur, İsa had accompanied his brother Süleyman across the straits, by August 1402. He sought refuge in Constantinople late in spring 1403, after being defeated by Mehmed at the battle of Ulubad. By May 18, 1403, he had returned to Bursa with Süleyman's support to resume the war against Mehmed.

5 Actually, İsa was defeated, captured, and executed by Mehmed in Asia Minor (by September 1403). In this war, İsa was allied to İsfendiyar, the Jandarid emir (1385–1393 and 1402–1440) of Kastamonu (Laonikos's Sinope), but also possibly to Süleyman. Between late 1403 and early 1404, Süleyman moved against Mehmed and took Bursa, pushing him back to east-central Asia Minor. Laonikos has fused the two wars. İsa did not hold power for four years.

6 Musa, a minor, had been placed under the custody of Mehmed. He was probably used by Mehmed now to distract Süleyman. For his release by Timur, see 3.59 and 3.69 above.

7 The Jandarid ruler of Kastamonu at that time was İsfendiyar (1385–1393 and 1402–1440).

8 Probably in 1409. This is Mircea I the Old (1386–1394 and 1397–1418).

9 For Mircea's many sons, see 2.23 above.

10 Mircea had a nephew, Dan II, who would later rule Wallachia on five occasions between 1420 and 1431, but he was not yet prince of Wallachia, so perhaps his status here is an anachronism.

11 In late 1409 or early 1410.

12 Some sources identify her as the daughter of Theodoros I Palaiologos, Manuel's deceased brother. Ilario Doria seems to have married an illegitimate daughter of Manuel named Zampia (Isabella). A daughter of that Doria was later married to Mustafa in 1422, which might explain the confusion here.

13 Süleyman and his army were ferried over by the Byzantines on June 14, 1410, and fought the battle of Kosmidion with Musa on the next day.

14 Stefan I, son of Lazar I, and prince of Serbia (1389–1427).

15 Dan II was Mircea's nephew, not son; see 4.4 above and the note there.

16 Referring here back to the treaties he had made in 1403, in the immediate aftermath of his father's defeat by Timur. The Byzantines gained Thessalonike and much territory around it, as well as coastal lands by the Sea of Marmara and Black Sea.

17 In February 1411.

18 Vuk and Stefan were not the same person, but rival brothers, sons of Lazar I (killed after the battle of Kosovo, in 1389). Their sister Olivera had indeed married Bayezid I in 1390 (see 3.59 above). Vuk had betrayed Musa at the battle of Kosmidion (see 4.5 above) and was executed by him in 1410, before the fall and death of Süleyman. Stefan was loosely allied with Süleyman at that time, after Kosmidion, and Laonikos seems to be referring to Musa's hostility against him (rather than Vuk), as Smederevo was in his territories and was besieged in 1411.

19 In August 1411.

20 This Manuel is unknown apart from his involvement in this event. He was presumably the son of Ioannes V.

21 This is a questionable narrative.

22 This Bogdan is mentioned by Konstantin the Philosopher, *Life of Stefan Lazarević,* p. 53, in the final battle between Musa and Mehmed.

23 Orhan's bid for power took place in the winter of 1411–12.

24 This refers to Bayezid's son Yusuf who moved to Constantinople and converted to Christianity, taking the name Demetrios.

25 Mehmed had been ensconced in central Anatolia ever since his father's death, when he was fifteen. He was Süleyman's main rival and it was he who had released Musa against him. During his Anatolian years, Mehmed was indeed allied with the emirate of Karaman. Between 1402 and 1419, the emir of Karaman was Mehmed II.

26 This is clearly an abbreviated legendary tale; Doukas, *History* 22.10, tells a similar tale about the young Mehmed and his later Grand Vizier Bayezid. The *hapax* χορδοποιὸς might also mean "sausage maker."

27 The name Alishur actually belonged to the founder of the emirate of Germiyan, Yakub b. Alishur (d. after 1320), but Laonikos often refers to the ruler of Karaman as "Karaman Alisourios" (see note on 1.14 above).

28 A number of battles were fought between the supporters of Musa and Mehmed before the issue was settled. Their locations and sequence in the different sources are difficult to reconcile. The first battle, at any rate, in early 1412, was a defeat for Mehmed.

29 This may be a reference to a son of Bayezid Pasha, grand vizier between 1413 and 1421.

30 Propontis often means Bosporos.

31 Possibly an error for (or manuscript corruption of) Paristrion.

32 Actually, Mehmed returned to Anatolia, although he was allied to Stefan. He returned to Serbia in 1413, before defeating Musa at Çamurlu (see 4.16–17 below).

33 I have been unable to identify this Murad.

34 What follows is an account of the battle of Çamurlu, south of Sofia, on July 5, 1413.

35 Niš and Znepolje, so Stefan's territory now reached almost to Sofia.

36 By 1417 Mehmed had recovered most of the Dobrudja, taken by the Wallachians after the battle of Ankara.

37 Manuel arrived in March 1415, and the wall was built in twenty-five days, in April and May.

38 Herodotos, *Histories* 8.71.

39 Compare Prokopios, *Buildings* 4.2.27. A Justinianic inscription was actually found when the 1415 wall was built (Sphrantzes, *Chronicle* 4.2). It may have been seen there by Laonikos later.

40 Actually, Manuel's brother and ruler of the Peloponnese, Theodoros I, had died in 1407; at that time (and not in 1415), Manuel established his own son, Theodoros II, as despot; see 4.48 and 4.60 below.

41 There was a minor rebellion in the Peloponnese after the completion of the wall, which Manuel suppressed.

42 It is not clear which one is meant here.

43 Actually, the Jandarid ruler of Sinope at this time was İsfendiyar (1385–1393 and 1402–1440); his grandson İsmail was emir when Mehmed II took over the principality (see 9.63–69). In 1417 İsfendiyar had to cede some towns to Mehmed I and later the copper mines to Murad II (see 5.35 below).

44 The war between the Ottomans and Venice was waged primarily in the Aegean, especially around Euboia (Negroponte), in 1416 and 1417, and was occasioned by Venetian support for Mustafa, whose first bid for power is recounted in 4.44–46 below (with no connection to the Venetian war).

45 This clause is obscure.

46 It is not clear what place Laonikos has in mind here; certainly not the ancient city of Kyrene (in eastern modern Libya).

47 The Venetians deposed Ostasio III da Polenta and annexed Ravenna in 1440; he died in 1447.

48 For Laonikos's view of the Fourth Crusade (1202–1204), see also 1.6 above.

49 Pope Alexander III (1159–1181) was expelled from Rome by the emperor Friedrich I Barbarossa (1152–1190) from 1162 to 1165

and 1167 to 1178. Pope and emperor met in 1177 in Venice and negotiated the Peace of Venice, which put an end to the conflict. The battle of Legnano (May 29, 1176), in which Barbarossa was defeated, was not, however, a naval engagement.

50 The War of Chioggia (1378–1381) was fought between Venice and Genoa over possession of the Aegean island of Tenedos.

51 In a surprise attack, on August 16, 1379.

52 The Genoese were enclosed on December 22, 1379.

53 The ruler of Padua was Francesco I da Carrara, called "the Old" (1350–1388), an ally of the Genoese.

54 The meaning of this clause is obscure, possibly a blockade of Genoese waters.

55 Presumably Genoa.

56 Venice conquered Padua from Francesco II da Carrara, called "Novello" (1388 and 1390–1405) in 1405.

57 The city gave itself to Venice in 1339, although it was subsequently lost for brief periods.

58 Venice conquered Verona in 1405 from Francesco II da Carrara of Padua (who had taken it from the Scaligeri in 1404).

59 Vicenza was ceded to Venice by the Visconti of Milan in 1404; Brescia surrendered itself to Venice in 1426, deserting the Visconti.

60 In some Italian versions, the founder of the house of Visconti was called Angelo. Perhaps Laonikos calls them Mariangeli because of the names of the Visconti dukes, Gian Maria (1402–1412) and Filippo Maria (1412–1447). It was under them, and their father, Gian Galeazzo (1378–1402, lord, then duke after 1395), that Milan became the dominant city in northern Italy. The wars between Milan and Venice lasted from 1425 until 1454.

61 See 4.25 above.

62 This is perhaps a confusion of his name, Angelo, with the Greek word for the English people (Anglos).

63 The Visconti crest depicts a serpent that has swallowed a man up to the waist. Many fabulous origin tales were told about the family.

64 Filippo Maria Visconti (1412–1447).

65 Francesco Bussone, called Count of Carmagnola, was a condottiere in the service of Milan who offered his services to the Venetians in 1425 and was appointed captain general in 1426. Although he won the battle of Maclodio (1427), he dragged out military operations to secure more pay for his soldiers and himself; he was arrested in Venice and tried and executed in 1432.

66 Francesco Sforza, marquis of Tricarico in the kingdom of Naples, was successively in the service of Naples, the papacy, and the Visconti of Milan.

67 See 6.20–24.

68 Actually, it was Francesco Sforza, not Francesco Bussone di Carmagnola, who was related by marriage to the Visconti dukes of Milan. Laonikos gets it right at 6.21.

69 That is, the doge.

70 This was the Minor Council, instituted in the late twelfth century.

71 This was the *Avogadoria de Comùn* (Municipal Attorneys), charged with investigating allegations and violations and defending the interests of the commonwealth.

72 The Council of Ten, instituted in 1310, focused on activities that threatened the state.

73 The Council of Forty *(Quarantia),* instituted in the later twelfth century, functioned as the highest court in Venice.

74 The Signoria consisted of the doge, the Minor Council, and the three leaders of the Quarantia.

75 Bajamonte Tiepolo, son of Giacomo Tiepolo, son of the doge Lorenzo Tiepolo (1268–1275), organized a conspiracy with other Venetian nobles against doge Pietro Gradenigo (1289–1311) in 1310. It was Bajamonte's standard-bearer who was struck and killed by the rock; he himself was sent into exile to Istria and died in or after 1329. His attempted coup led to the creation of the Council of Ten, for which see 4.35 above.

76 This passage is corrupt, and has been restored even as it is.

77 Jacopo Foscari, son of the doge Francesco Foscari (1423–1457), was tried for bribery and corruption in 1445 and exiled. After he returned, on November 5, 1450, he mortally wounded the coun-

cil member Ermolao Donà, who had been among those who had condemned him. Arrested in January 1451, Jacopo was tortured and exiled to Candia. Accused of a further conspiracy in 1456 and tried again at Venice, he was condemned to life imprisonment in Chania, where he died shortly afterward.

78 This war was fought from 1416 to 1417. Pietro Loredan would later defeat the Genoese at Rapallo in 1431.

79 The battle was fought on May 29, 1416.

80 Actually, Loredan was greeted triumphantly upon his return. I have been unable to find any evidence for a trial in the Venetian records.

81 The treaty was not finalized until November 6, 1419.

82 Mustafa had been lost on the battlefield at Ankara in 1402 but was not found among the dead. The Jandarid emir of Sinope and Kastamonu was still İsfendiyar (1385–1393 and 1402–1440).

83 Still Mircea I the Old, prince of Wallachia (1386–1394 and 1397–1418).

84 Mehmed's version ultimately prevailed, and Mustafa was known as "false Mustafa."

85 This was in May 1416. Mustafa had actually raised a rebellion but fled from Mehmed's armies to Thessalonike. Its governor was Demetrios Laskaris Leontaris, acting for the prince Andronikos (on whom see 4.47 below).

86 Junayd (Cüneyd), former emir of Aydın, had been dispossessed by Mehmed I in 1414.

87 Mehmed I died on May 21 or 26, 1421. For Mustafa's release, see 5.1 below.

88 Ioannes was born in 1392, Andronikos in 1400, Theodoros between 1394 and 1399, Konstantinos in 1405, Demetrios in 1407/8, and Thomas in 1409/10, so Laonikos almost gets the order right. Two other sons died young.

89 Ioannes VIII Palaiologos was associated as emperor between 1403 and 1407 and was formally crowned as fully fledged coruler in 1421. Sophia of Montferrat, daughter of Marquis Teodoro II Paleologo of Montferrat (a descendant of Andronikos II Palaiologos), married Ioannes in January 1421 as his second wife,

but they were divorced in 1426. It is entirely unclear what Laonikos means when he says that Manuel made Ioannes "archpriest" (bishop) of the Greeks.

90 Anna of Moscow, daughter of the grand prince Vasilij I of Moscow, had actually married Ioannes earlier, ca. 1411, and died in August 1417. His third wife, married in 1427, was Maria Komnene, daughter of Emperor Alexios IV of Trebizond; she died in 1439. Apparently Laonikos has confused her with his first, Russian, wife.

91 For the period 1408 to 1423.

92 In 1423.

93 In 1428 or 1429. Actually, he died as a monk in the Pantokrator monastery in Constantinople.

94 Theodoros II, son of Manuel II, succeeded Theodoros I, Manuel's brother, when he died in 1407 (for Manuel's brother see 1.55, 2.27, and 2.45 above). Theodoros II ruled there until 1443, when he resigned and became governor of Selymbria.

95 Theodoros II Palaiologos married Cleope Malatesta in 1421, who died in 1433. She was the daughter of Malatesta II, lord of Pesaro (1385–1429).

96 See 5.27 below.

97 Nerio I Acciaiuoli had become lord of Corinth by 1366/67, conquered Athens in 1386 and its acropolis on May 2, 1388, and became ruler of Athens-Thebes and Neopatras; he was formally promoted to duke of Athens by King Ladislao of Naples in January 1394 but died in November of that year. Theodoros I married Nerio's eldest daughter, Bartolomea, in the spring of 1384.

98 That is, the Fourth Crusade (1202–1204); see also 1.6 above.

99 The Genoese Zaccaria were actually latecomers to Achaïa. Martino Zaccaria of Chios became baron of Chalandritsa, Veligosti, and Damala in 1324 by marriage; his grandson Andronico Zaccaria became baron of Arkadia (in Messenia) in 1386 by marriage to its heiress; his son Centurione Zaccaria dispossessed his aunt's sons and became the last prince of Achaïa, in 1404. By 1430 he was reduced to being a dependent of his new son-in-law, Thomas Palaiologos, and died in 1432.

100 A reference to the Catalan and/or Navarrese companies: the former held Athens, Thebes, and Neopatras from 1311 to 1386/88 (and Salona until 1394), while the latter held Achaïa from 1386/96 to 1404.

101 Nerio came to Greece probably in 1366/67 as lord of the Castellany of Corinth, taking over from his brother Donato in serving Angevin interests.

102 Euboia (Negroponte) was subdivided among triarchs *(terzerii)* from the Veronese family dalle Carceri (who are the "Lombards" here). After a long period of Venetian influence, it became fully dependent on Venice in 1390.

103 Around 1370 Nerio married Annesa Saraceni, the daughter of Saraceno de Saraceni, one of the lords of Euboia, with whom he had two daughters, Bartolomea (whom he married to Theodoros I Palaiologos in 1384) and Francesca (whom he married to Carlo I Tocco, for whom see 4.51 below). As for "Prothymos," Nerio I's illegitimate son, Antonio I (for whom see 4.56–57 below), had two adopted daughters, Benvenuta Protimo and Anonyma Protimo.

104 Nerio I died on September 25, 1394. In fact, he left Corinth to his daughter Francesca, the wife of Carlo I Tocco, who sold it to Theodoros I Palaiologos in 1396, after the latter besieged it for a number of years.

105 Nerio's daughter Francesca was married to Carlo I Tocco, count of Kephallenia, duke of Leukas (1375/77–1429), despot in Ioannina (1411–1429) and Arta (1416–1429).

106 A group of small islands in the Ionian Sea, off the coast of Akarnania.

107 In fact, Carlo I Tocco succeeded to his father, Leonardo I Tocco, who had ruled Kephallenia and Zakynthos/Zante (1357–1375/77) and Leukas (from 1362). Leonardo I was the son of Giovanni Tocco by Margherita, daughter of Giovanni I Orsini, who had been count of the islands between 1304 and 1317. The Orsini had been dispossessed by the kings of Naples in 1325, but in 1357 the islands were granted to Leonardo Tocco, as an heir of the Orsini.

108 Possibly to be identified with Jacopo de' Rossi, Andrea de' Guidi

de Strione, and Marino or Mano Meliaresi, governors of the Tocco realm in 1449, after the death of Carlo II.

109 The last Orsini counts of Kephallenia and Zakynthos had taken Epeiros in 1317 as maternal descendants of the Angelos despots of Epeiros; their Tocchi successors renewed this claim and took advantage of the chaotic state of affairs in Epeiros after the Serb and Albanian takeover; see below.

110 The Albanian settlement of parts of northern Greece seems to have commenced in the 1320s. They never acquired mastery over Thessaly. Argyrokastron was held by Gjon Zenebishi, ruler of the Principality of Gjirokastër (in southern Albania) on and off between 1386 and 1418, whereupon it passed to the Turks. Kastoria was taken by Andrea Muzaka (Musachi), the lord of Berat, from Marko, the son of Vukašin, soon after the latter's death at Černomen in 1371 (see 1.34 above), and he held it until the mid-1380s, when it was taken by the Turks.

111 The Albanian infiltration into Epeiros seems to have begun in the 1340s but intensified in the 1350s.

112 He is otherwise unknown.

113 In fact, the first Albanian rulers in Arta came from the Losha clan and held the city from 1359 to 1375, after the death of Nikephoros II of Epeiros. The Shpata clan took Arta in 1375, but its leader had already ruled at Angelokastron since 1359.

114 The Angevins of Naples had held Kerkyra (Corfu) since 1267.

115 This may refer to the expedition of Juan Fernández de Heredia, grand master of the Hospitallers (1377–1396) and ruler of Achaïa (1377–1381) by concession from the queen of Naples, Giovanna I (1343–1381). He attempted to take Arta in 1378 but was defeated by Gjin Bua Shpata (d. 1399, lord of Arta since 1375), captured, and sold to the Ottomans (though soon ransomed).

116 Tomo Preljubović (or Thomas Komnenos Palaiologos) was the Serbian despot at Ioannina (1366–1384). His daughter Eirene was betrothed (and later married) to Gjin Losha, the son of the despot Pjetër Losha of Arta in 1370. In 1375, after he took Arta, Gjin Bua Shpata was promised Preljubović's half-sister Helene, but the two men were enemies and she died before she could be

married to Shpata. Preljubović did not participate in the defeat of Heredia.

117 Carlo I Tocco was the son of Maddalena Buondelmonti, the sister of Esau Buondelmonti, who was despot at Ioannina (1385–1399 and 1400–1411). Since 1399 Carlo had been expanding at the expense of the Shpatas of Arta, who made an alliance with Esau against his nephew Carlo in 1410. But Carlo never came into conflict with his uncle, who died in 1411. By "Aitolia" Laonikos often means Epeiros.

118 Maria Angelina Doukaina Palaiologina.

119 Preljubović was murdered on December 23, 1384, by his bodyguard. Esau Buondelmonti became despot at Ioannina by marrying Preljubović's widow (she died in 1394, and he married twice again). Esau's participation in Heredia's expedition and his eventual marriage to Preljubović's widow are confirmed by other sources.

120 The referent is unclear here.

121 This action is otherwise unattested. Carlo I Tocco visited Musa and gave an illegitimate daughter to him, probably in 1412. For Esau's son, see the following note.

122 Esau died on February 6, 1411. Within a month, a revolution in Ioannina expelled his Serbian widow, Jevdokija Balšić, and their young son, Giorgio (Giourges), and the citizens invited Carlo to be their new ruler. The grammar of this passage overall is confusing.

123 That is, Swamp. The manuscripts actually have *Aietos,* which has been emended.

124 Angelokastron was held by Carlo I Tocco since at least 1408. As a last resort, Pal Shpata had given it to the Turks in 1406 (and it was held by Evrenos's son Barak, on whom see 4.16 above and 4.63 below). Pal gave Naupaktos to the Venetians; Carlo claimed it and held territory around it, but he never controlled it.

125 That is, of Nerio I Acciaiuoli, duke of Athens; see 4.51 above.

126 Nerio I of Athens died in September 1394. In fact, he left Corinth to his daughter Francesca, the wife of Carlo I Tocco,

who sold it to Theodoros I Palaiologos in 1396, after the latter attacked it (1394–1396), arguing that his own wife, Bartolomea, Nerio's eldest daughter, had been effectively disinherited. See also 4.50 above. Nerio's mistress (and mother of Antonio) was Maria Rendi.

127 Actually, Nerio I Acciaiuoli took Athens (1385–1388) from the Catalans, not the Navarrese. The former had conquered Athens, Thebes, and Neopatras in 1311 (see 1.20 above). Laonikos seems to confuse or fuse the two companies. Moreover, the Venetians were designated by Nerio as the executors of his will, not its beneficiaries, and they took the opportunity to seize Athens (1394–1402) in order to protect it from a Turkish attack. In his will, Nerio left the city of Athens to the Latin Church of Athens and its metropolis, the Parthenon.

128 See 2.10–13 above.

129 Antonio I Acciaiuoli ruled Thebes (1394–1435), adding Athens (1402) and its acropolis (1403), which he took from the Venetians.

130 In the summer of 1402.

131 In early 1403.

132 This is our only source for this marriage. When Antonio died in 1435, his wife was Maria, possibly surnamed Melissene, who was not the daughter of a priest. For Maria, see 6.50.

133 Antonio married one of his adopted daughters to Antonello II Caopena, the son of Alioto Caopena, ruler of Aigina. Antonello ruled Aigina from 1440 to 1451, whereupon he died without heirs and left the island to Venice.

134 This daughter was given in 1402 to Niccolò II Giorgio (Zorzi), the last marquis of Bodonitsa (1411–1414) and (first) lord of Karystos (1406–1436).

135 It is possible that Manuel II pronounced a funeral oration over his brother's tomb when he was at Mistra in 1407/8, but the long text of the *Funeral Oration* that we have, and that was written for delivery two years later, was not delivered in person by the emperor, but by Isidoros (possibly the later metropolitan of Kiev and All Rus') and Theodoros Gazes.

136 See 4.19 above. This was in 1415.

137 Murad II, Ottoman sultan (1421–1444 and 1446–1451), was born in 1404. Mehmed I had at least three sons: see below.

138 This Mustafa is known as Küçük Mustafa (Little Mustafa) and was born in 1411.

139 This sentence is somewhat obscure. That Mehmed considered dividing his kingdom is unlikely. Doukas, *History* 22.10, reports that Mehmed planned to entrust his *other* two sons to Manuel, to protect them from Murad, but they were not turned over by the new regime (23.4).

140 Or, "the son of Hajji Therizes." Evrenos's father was İsa Beg "Prangi" (a name variously interpreted). "Therizes" is how Laonikos elsewhere renders Firuz (also 6.54, 7.10, 7.15, and 8.46). A Hajji was one who had gone on pilgrimage to Mecca, which is prominently recorded in Evrenos's epitaph *(Haci Awranuz bin İsa)*. This may lie behind Laonikos's composite name-form.

141 This is probably Mehmed Beg Mihaloğlu (d. 1423), descendant of a Byzantine deserter to the Ottomans, who played a key role in Mehmed's victory over Musa.

142 For some of Evrenos's many campaigns, see 2.24, 2.44, and 2.47 above.

143 See 4.8 and 4.15 above.

144 Evrenos's tomb in Giannitsa was discovered in 1974.

145 Turahan, son of Yiğit Beg, is actually first mentioned after Mehmed I's death, in 1422/23. He appears often below, during the reign of Murad II, as the governor of Thessaly.

Book 5

1 Mehmed I died on May 21 or 26, 1421, at Edirne (Adrianople); his death was concealed for many days. In theory he was sultan since 1413.

2 For Mustafa, see 4.44–45 above.

3 Ioannes VIII Palaiologos was still coruler with his father, the aging Manuel II (until 1425).

4 This phrase is unclear.

5 This was in the autumn of 1421.

6 For Junayd, see 4.45 above.

7 On January 20, 1422.

8 Mihaliğ, now Karajabey, just west of Lopadion.

9 Junayd was lured away from his alliance with Mustafa by the machinations of Murad II, who sent his brother Hamza to offer him back his patrimony, Aydın (which Laonikos calls Smyrna).

10 Giovanni Adorno of New Phokaia.

11 Actually, closer to three months.

12 That is, Mehmed Beg.

13 By June 1422 Murad besieged Constantinople and built earthen ramparts along the entire length of the walls; simultaneously his forces besieged Thessalonike.

14 "Grand master of the horse."

15 "Lords of the standard."

16 That is, "weapon masters," "arms bearers," elite cavalry.

17 That is, "poor ones."

18 That is, "salaried ones."

19 That is, bronze.

20 The assault was made on August 24, 1422.

21 On September 6, 1422.

22 Karaman here is Mehmed II (1402–1419 and 1421–1423), married to the sister of Murad II and Mustafa, named İncu. This Mustafa was called Küçük Mustafa (Little Mustafa), to distinguish him from his (supposed) uncle. He was the twelve-year-old son of Mehmed I, born in 1411.

23 That is, the winter of 1422–23.

24 That is, wine pourer; see 5.12 above.

25 In late February 1423.

26 A member of the ruling house of Janik in Neokaisareia (Niksar), and kingmaker of Mustafa.

27 That is, Mihaloğlu, Mehmed Beg.

28 See 4.47 above.

29 Thessalonike fell on March 29, 1430.

30 That is, Sinan Beg, the general of Europe. This was in 1430.

31 On July 4, 1429. For Carlo I, see 4.51 and 4.56 above.

32 Carlo I's heir in Arta and Ioannina was Carlo II (1429–1448), son of his brother Leonardo II, who had died in 1418/19. Ercole had been given Angelokastron and the Acheloös as far south as Naupaktos; Memnon was lord of Aetos in Akarnania.

33 Ioannina surrendered on October 9, 1430.

34 The narrative goes back now, to Turahan's 1423 campaign in the Peloponnese (he crossed the Isthmos on May 21–22). A later campaign took place in the spring of 1431: see 6.1.

35 On June 5, 1423.

36 Both Evrenos (d. 1417) and Turahan (d. 1456) served as *uçbey* (marcher lord) in Thessaly.

37 This campaign cannot be securely identified.

38 Loukas Notaras had concluded the treaty in February 1424.

39 See 4.48 above.

40 Ioannes VIII and Konstantinos arrived in the Peloponnese in December 1427.

41 In March 1428 Konstantinos married Maddalena (renamed Theodora), daughter of Leonardo and niece of Carlo I Tocco; she died two years later.

42 Patras surrendered on June 5, 1429. For its bishop, see below.

43 Centurione II Zaccaria was the last prince of Achaïa (1404–1432); his brother Stefano Zaccaria was the archbishop of Patras (1404–1424; d. 1442).

44 Patras had been bought by the pope in 1270, and he appointed its archbishop.

45 Pandolfo Malatesta, brother of Theodoros II Palaiologos's wife (Cleope), was archbishop of Patras from 1424; he died in 1441.

46 Glarentsa was captured by a Catalan force on July 17, 1430, and sold back to the Byzantines a few days later.

47 Centurione Zaccaria's mercenary captain Franco Oliverio seized Glarentsa in 1418; to save appearances he was married to a daughter of Centurione and "received" it as her dowry. Oliverio sold it to Carlo I Tocco in 1421.

48 Presumably Thomas Palaiologos; see above for its capture by the Catalans.

49 Centurione Zaccaria was besieged by Thomas Palaiologos in Chalandritsa in the summer of 1429. Peace was arranged by Thomas's brothers in September 1429, and in January 1430 Thomas married Caterina, Centurione's daughter and heiress. This left Centurione with the title of prince of Achaïa and his own barony of Arkadia (Kyparissia in Messenia), until his death in 1432, when that too passed to Thomas.

50 This attack took place in 1433. Serbia had previously been invaded immediately after the succession of its new prince Đurađ Branković (1427–1456), in 1427 /28.

51 Mara, daughter of Đurađ Branković, married Murad II in 1435.

52 Saruja (or Saruca) Pasha was *beylerbeyi* of Rumeli until 1436; Halil Pasha, son of İbrahim Pasha Çandarlı (grand vizier until 1429), became grand vizier in 1443.

53 The name Alishur belonged to the founder of the emirate of Germiyan, Yakub b. Alishur (d. after 1320), but Laonikos often refers to the ruler of Karaman as "Karaman Alisourios" (see note on 1.14 above). The ruler of Karaman at this time was İbrahim II (1424–1464). The war described here is probably that of 1426 to 1427.

54 For the episode of Mustafa, see 5.18–19 above.

55 This sentence seems out of place.

56 The Turgut were a clan in central Anatolia associated with Karaman, which they supported against the Ottomans.

57 Pisidia does not border on Syria, so it is hard to identify this group, whose name may be based on that of the Arsakids.

58 Murad *(Amourates)* is here an emendation of *Amythaon.* It may mean something else entirely.

59 This sentence is unclear. The Turgut were actually allies of Karaman against the Ottomans.

60 For the White Sheep and Kara Yülük, see 3.72 above and the notes there.

61 Kandyloron is attested only in Laonikos and cannot be identified.

62 Yakub II of Germiyan bequeathed his lands to Murad II in

1429; the emirate of Aydın was abolished upon the death of Junayd in 1426. Saruhan had long since been annexed, in 1410.

63 İlyas Beg of Menteşe, who had been restored by Timur, had been forced to accept Ottoman sovereignty in 1414. His sons Layth and Ahmed succeeded him in 1421, but Menteşe was definitively annexed in 1424. Aşıkpaşazade, *History of the House of Osman,* pp. 153–154, reports that Ahmed was confined for two years, then fled to Kara Yülük (of the White Sheep), Egypt, his home (Menteşe?), and finally Persia.

64 The grammar actually has Karaman take Ikonion and occupy the land (etc.), but this is probably a poorly written sentence by Laonikos, with a subject switch in the middle.

65 Actually, the Jandarid ruler of Sinope at this time was İsfendiyar (1385–1393 and 1402–1440); his grandson İsmail was emir when Mehmed II took over the principality (see 9.63–69), but Laonikos confuses İsfendiyar with İsmail (see also 4.20 above). Murad II took over his copper mines before 1440.

66 "Son of Turgut" reflects the term Turgutoğlu, here probably Hasan Beg.

67 Đurađ Branković (1427–1456), prince of Serbia and father of Murad II's wife, Mara (see 5.31 above).

68 Actually, prince Stefan I of Serbia (1389–1427), Lazar's son, had been granted Belgrade and the banate of Mačva by King Sigismund of Hungary in 1403 as a Hungarian vassal and settled there with his court; to this were added further fiefs in Hungary in 1411. When Đurađ Branković became prince of Serbia in 1427, he had to surrender Belgrade to Sigismund in exchange for being granted his predecessor's other fiefs in Hungary.

69 Smederevo surrendered to Murad II in August 1439.

70 Grgur and Stefan were blinded in May 1441; Laonikos has inserted the event between the sieges of Smederevo (1439) and Belgrade (1440), on which see below.

71 Murad II marched on Belgrade in 1440 but failed to take it after a six-month siege (April to October).

72 This was İsa Beg; he invaded Bosnia in 1439.

73 The Bosnian king was Tvrtko II (1404–1409 and 1421–1443).

74 This was in 1439.

75 Stjepan Vukčić of Hercegovina (1435–1466) was the nephew of Sandalj Hranjić (1392–1435); see 10.29–30.

76 Kotromanići was the name of the Bosnian royal house, but not of Hercegovina. Otherwise, it is not clear what Laonikos is referring to here.

77 Gjon Kastrioti of Mat, Tiranë, and Krujë in northern Albania, became an Ottoman vassal and converted to Islam in 1431.

78 That is, the land of the Arianiti family; see below.

79 This is Gjergj Arianiti.

80 Gjon Kastrioti died in 1437; his son was Gjergj Kastrioti, better known as Skanderbeg (Skënderbeu); see 7.29.

81 Gjerg Arianiti's revolt began in 1433.

82 The Albanian victory took place at Bërzeshtë, north of Berat in central Albania, in 1433.

83 Depas was also known as Bua Thopia, a son of Gjon Zenebishi, who had ruled Argyrokastron until its conquest by the Ottomans in 1416 (by Mehmed I, not Bayezid I) and died in exile on Kerkyra in 1418. Bua Thopia returned to reclaim Argyrokastron in 1434. Mrkša Žarković, son of Žarko by the Dragaš brothers' sister, had ruled Valona and Kanina until his death in 1414; his widow, Ruđina Balšić, held Valona until the Ottoman conquest in 1417.

84 For Murad's campaign against Karaman in 1434, see 6.1; at 5.32–34 above, Laonikos is probably referring to the earlier campaign (1426–1427).

85 This was in the winter of 1434–35.

86 The battle took place on March 22, 1442.

87 This was still in 1442.

88 This was the battle of the Ialomiţa River, a series of clashes culminating on September 6, 1442.

89 See the notes to the Greek text for a proposed emendation at this point.

90 Modern Hunedoara.

91 Stefan Lazarević (1389–1427). Hunyadi was born in ca. 1400.

92 This story is certainly untrue.

93 For the conflict that Laonikos seems to have in mind, see 5.52 below.

94 Hunyadi was appointed Ban of Severin in 1438 by the Hungarian king Albert (Albrecht II of Germany/V of Austria); Transylvania was not entrusted to him until 1445.

95 Referring to the battle of Nikopolis in 1396; see 2.20 above.

96 No reason is given.

97 This seems to be a confused reference to the succession struggle and civil war of 1439 to 1440. Hunyadi successfully supported the candidacy of the young Polish king Władysław III (1434–1444) = King Ulászló I of Hungary (1440–1444), against claims by Sigismund's daughter Erzsébet, widow of the Hungarian and Bohemian king Albert (Albrecht II of Germany/V of Austria); she defended the rights of her newborn son Ladislaus V to the Hungarian and Bohemian throne; see 8.59.

98 This Dan was possibly the son of Dan II (prince of Wallachia on and off between 1420 and 1431). He was put forth as a Hungarian protégé (1435–1436) but achieved limited success against Alexandru I Aldea (1431–1436) and his brother Vlad II Dracul (1436–1442 and 1443–1447), the father of Vlad III Ţepeş ("Dracula"). It is likely that Laonikos has confused Dan here with his brother Basarab II (1442–1443), because it was he who interrupted Vlad II's reign (with Hunyadi's armed support).

99 Alexandru I Aldea and Vlad II Dracul were indeed the bastard sons of Mircea I (1386–1394 and 1397–1418); Dan's father, Dan II, was their first cousin.

100 In fact, it was Vlad II Dracul who recovered his throne with Ottoman support and agreed to an annual tribute in 1443.

101 Considering the confusion of Dan with his brother Basarab II, the contemporary ruler of Moldavia was probably Ştefan II (1442–1447).

102 Gotthia is the principality of Theodoro (Mangup) in the Crimea, loosely dependent on the empire of Trebizond (Kolchis). S. Karpov, *Istorija trapezundskoj imperii* (St. Petersburg,

2007), p. 398, dates this raid to 1427/28 rather than the 1440s implied by its placement in Laonikos's narrative.

103 Filippo Maria Visconti, duke of Milan (1412–1447), ruled Genoa from 1421 to 1435.

104 Laonikos uses Genoa's Latin name *Ianua* ("door"); see also 2.31 above.

105 Genoa was a republic governed by a merchant oligarchy. From 1339 to 1528 it was ruled intermittently by lifetime doges but suffered from instability. The Doria and Spinola dominated the dual captainship of the people before the institution of the doges. Unlike them, the Adorno and Campofregoso families frequently filled the office of doge.

106 Genoa was under the rulers of Milan from 1353 to 1356 and 1421 to 1435 and under the king of France from 1396 to 1409 and 1458 to 1461.

107 Genoa and Aragon began to clash over Sardinia in the mid-fourteenth century.

108 Genoa and Milan fought together against Alfonso V the Magnanimous of Aragon in Italy starting in 1421, when Filippo took over Genoa. Venice went to war against Milan in 1425; Genoa and Venice had fought many wars in the past.

109 Kerkyra had been under Venetian rule since 1386 and was formally annexed in 1401. This is a reference to the attack of 1432, which was repelled by the local Greeks. The Genoese had attacked Kerkyra also in 1403.

110 Alfonso V the Magnanimous, king of Aragon (1416–1458) and Naples (1442–1458).

111 The Genoese took Gaeta in 1424; the battle of Ponza, in which Alfonso V was captured by the Genoese, took place on August 5, 1435 (he had been trying to take Gaeta back). Ponza is an island a few kilometers from Gaeta, not its harbor; Alfonso was with his fleet during the whole battle.

112 The Genoese admiral was Biagio Assereto.

113 Alfonso V left Milan on December 1, and Filippo Maria Visconti lost control of Genoa on December 27, 1435.

114 Filippo Maria Visconti died in 1447.

115 The Crown of Aragon included the kingdoms of Aragon, Valencia, Majorca, "Sardinia and Corsica" (consisting of Sardinia alone), Sicily (since 1409), and the principality of Catalonia.

116 The kingdom of Naples/Parthenope was conquered by Alfonso V in 1442; see below.

117 The house of Anjou, a branch of the Capetian dynasty, had governed Naples since 1266.

118 That is, southern Latium and northern Campania.

119 That is, Magna Graecia.

120 Ladislao (1386–1414) was the last king of Naples in the male line of the house of Anjou.

121 Ladislao began his conquests in central Italy in 1407, took Rome in 1408 (and again in 1413), and invaded Tuscany in 1409, but was driven out. He made peace with Florence in 1410 and again in 1414, shortly before his death.

122 Ladislao died on August 6, 1414.

123 If the emendation is accepted (see the corresponding notes to the text), the sense would be "the hemlock spread through the liquid when the towel came into contact with it [the liquid]," that is, the bodily fluids of sex.

124 Actually, Ladislao's widow was Marie d'Enghien, countess of Lecce, but she had no part in the succession. It was his sister Giovanna II who succeeded as queen regnant (1414–1435). She adopted Alfonso V of Aragon, then Duke Louis III of Anjou as her heirs. Louis died in 1434 and was succeeded as duke of Anjou and as Giovanna's heir by his younger brother René the Good (on whom see 2.31 above). René succeeded Giovanna as king of Naples (1435–1442), until he was expelled by Alfonso V of Aragon. René was a cousin, not a nephew, of the Valois king of France.

125 Before her marriage to Ladislao, Marie d'Enghien had been the wife of Raimondo Orsini del Balzo, prince of Taranto (1398–1406).

126 The royal house was called Trastámara, but Alfonso was born at Medina del Campo.

127 Alfonso did not conquer Sicily, which he inherited from his father Fernando I in 1416. But he did arrive with his fleet at Palermo on February 10, 1421, and made Sicily his base for the conquest of the mainland.

128 The citadels of Naples were the seaside Castel dell'Ovo and Castel Nuovo and the inland Castel Capuano. Alfonso took Naples at the invitation of Giovanna, who had adopted him, in July 1421, but in 1423 she revoked the adoption in favor of Louis III of Anjou. After months of fighting around the city, Alfonso left for Spain on October 15, 1423. Alfonso besieged Naples again in September 1438, when it was being held by René, but failed and lost his brother (see below); the Aragonese garrison in the Castel Nuovo resisted until August 1439. The final siege was between 1441 and 1443 and was a success for Alfonso. Laonikos has conflated aspects of these sieges.

129 Pedro, duke of Noto, was killed in a campaign against Naples, in 1438.

130 During the fighting of 1422–23, Giovanna had shut herself in the Castel Nuovo.

131 René had fled for Provence in 1441, so this refers to a later siege.

132 Muzio Attendolo Sforza, the father of Francesco I Sforza (future lord of Ancona in the Marche and duke of Milan, 1450–1466), had fought for Giovanna in 1423; he died on January 3, 1424. His son Francesco also opposed Alfonso starting in 1438, when Alfonso made further attacks on Naples. This reference has nothing to do with René's wife, Isabelle, duchess of Lorraine (1431–1453).

133 Alfonso entered Naples as its king in February 1443, having taken it the previous autumn.

134 Laonikos seems to have confused three women here: (1) Marie d'Enghien (the widow of Ladislao but not the wife of René), who had in fact retired to her family's lands at Lecce and Taranto, and died in 1446; (2) Ladislao's sister and heiress Giovanna II of Naples, who died in 1435; and (3) René's wife, Isabelle, duchess of Lorraine (1431–1453), who had no part in this

story. As for Marie, her marriage to Raimondo Orsini of Taranto preceded that to Ladislao; their son was Giovanni Antonio Orsini, prince of Taranto (1420–1463).

135 In 1444 Alfonso V married his illegitimate son, the future Neapolitan king Ferdinando I (1458–1494), to Isabella of Chiaramonte, daughter of Tristan de Clermont by Caterina; Caterina was the sister of Giovanni Antonio Orsini (prince of Taranto) and the daughter of Marie d'Enghien.

136 Genoese fleets, upholding French interests, harassed and attacked Naples in 1453, when René was active in Italy, and in 1454. René's son Jean II of Lorraine attempted to reconquer Naples from 1458 to 1461 but failed.

137 This is what ancient Greek sources called the Ligurians (as far west sometimes as the Gulf of Lyon); it is unclear what part of the kingdom of Aragon Laonikos means here.

138 Alfonso's younger brother, the future Juan II of Aragon (1458–1479), had become king of Navarre by his marriage in 1425 to its heiress Blanca (1425–1441), daughter of King Carlos III of Navarre (1387–1425).

139 The son was Carlos of Viana, who, at the age of twenty, claimed the throne of Navarre as his mother's heir in 1441, but his father refused to yield it. Juan II never lost Navarre. His son predeceased him in 1461.

140 That is, Minorca. Laonikos omits Majorca; also, the Aragonese kingdom of Sardinia was called "Sardinia and Corsica" but did not actually include Corsica.

141 One manuscript correctly has "outside."

142 But at 2.33 above, Laonikos correctly claims that (the territory of) Granada is by the sea. The city, at any rate, is inland. At this time, Granada was ruled by the Arab Nasrid dynasty, the last Muslim dynasty to rule it.

143 The kings of Castile were descended, in the male line, from the counts of Burgundy in the Holy Roman Empire, not from the kings of France.

144 From 1420 King Juan II of Castile (1406–1454) and his constable Álvaro de Luna clashed with a noble faction headed by the

king's Aragonese cousins, Alfonso V's brothers Juan and Enrique; the civil war in Castile led to Alfonso's intervention, but he was defeated (1430).

145 Álvaro de Luna, duke of Trujillo (d. 1453), was long the power behind the throne of Juan II of Castile.

146 Alfonso toyed with the idea of attacking Castile in the 1420s, especially 1429, and armies did march around, but there was no decisive battle such as Laonikos describes, nor was Alfonso taken prisoner. The dispute with Castile was settled on July 25, 1430.

147 See 5.62–64 above. Alfonso never moved against Sicily; he owned it.

148 Alfonso's wife was his cousin Maria, sister of Juan II of Castile.

149 See 8.63 and 8.66–67.

150 Juan II of Castile (1406–1454) and his constable Álvaro declared war on Granada in 1431.

151 See also 2.32–33 above. The city meant here is Granada.

152 In fact, the Castilians imposed a protégé, Yusuf IV (1431–1432), on the throne of Granada.

153 In 1418 Juan II of Castile married his cousin Maria of Aragon (d. 1445), sister of Alfonso V, and in 1447 Isabel of Portugal. Enrique IV of Castile (1454–1474) was actually Juan's son by Maria. He, in turn, married his cousin Blanca of Navarre, daughter of Juan II of Navarre, in 1440, but had no offspring from this union, and divorced her in 1453.

154 Enrique married Joana of Portugal in 1455; she produced a daughter, Juana, in 1462.

155 They were descended from the French kings via the Capetian dukes of Burgundy.

156 See also 2.32–33 and 5.76 above.

157 The kings of Navarre at that time were indeed descended from the French Capetians through a daughter of Louis X of France and Navarre, and through a younger son of Philippe III of France.

158 See 5.70 above for these events.